Business:
Its Nature and
Environment

An Introduction　　　　　**7th Edition**

Raymond E. Glos, Ph.D., C.P.A.
Dean Emeritus
School of Business Administration
Miami University
Oxford, Ohio

Harold A. Baker, Ph.D.
Formerly Professor of Marketing
School of Business
John Carroll University
Cleveland, Ohio

Consulting Editor: **Arthur J. Noetzel**
Academic Vice President
John Carroll University

Published by

G71 **SOUTH-WESTERN PUBLISHING CO.**

Cincinnati Chicago Dallas New Rochelle, N.Y.
Burlingame, Calif. Brighton, England

ISBN: 0-538-07710-7

Library of Congress Catalog Card Number: 75-158512

2 3 4 5 6 7 8 K 9 8 7 6 5 4 3 2

Printed in the United States of America

Preface

Five years have elapsed since the previous edition of this text was published. During this relatively short period of time, changes in the business world have been numerous, startling, and far-reaching. Attitudes of people toward business and attitudes of business toward people have undergone dramatic alterations. The interaction of forces within and without the economic community has suddenly required business managers to reassess values formerly taken for granted.

These recent revolutionary upheavals in what used to be an evolutionary capitalistic system have caused the authors to select a new title for this text. *Business: Its Nature and Environment—An Introduction* reflects not only a culmination of previous revisions of chapters and subject matter emphasis but also an acceleration of changes that normally would have been spread out over several years. We have now concluded that it is no longer possible to explain what business is all about and how it operates without extensive reference to its economic, social, and legal environment.

As a part of the change in emphasis as reflected by a new title, a chapter on Ethics and Social Responsibilities has been added to Part 1. It stresses the current belief of enlightened businessmen that their firms should engage in such nonprofitable activities as employing the disadvantaged, promoting civic and educational projects, and fighting pollution. This stress on environmental factors is also reflected in practically all other chapters of the text, for none has escaped being revised to a greater or lesser extent.

Another major change has been the enlargement and division of the chapter that in the sixth edition was titled Organization and Management. The second of the two chapters now assigned to these topics devotes considerable attention to current thinking on the subject of management. It describes how managers have come to recognize that contributions from the social and behavioral sciences may be just as important to decision making as the cold facts on which they formerly relied.

In order to allow for these new chapters as well as changes in emphasis without adding an undue amount of copy to the text, some topics have been condensed and others omitted. The chapter on location and layout has been deleted although some of its coverage appears elsewhere. The two chapters formerly devoted to the control of competitive and noncompetitive businesses by all levels of government have been combined. The chapter that was titled Opportunities in Business now appears in Appendix A. For those instructors who wish to give additional emphasis to career selection, we believe the material in this appendix will prove satisfactory, adequate, and helpful. These modifications have resulted in the number of chapters in the text being reduced from 30 to 29. Another change has been the substitution of a new comprehensive case for one that had appeared in both the fifth and sixth editions.

Although increased attention has been devoted to the environment in which business operates, it should be noted that we have retained the word "introduction" as a part of our new title. The authors believe that the basic objectives of an introduction to business course that have been stressed in previous editions are still valid and, once again, are worthy of itemization as follows:

1. The student should obtain an understanding of the whole area of activity known as business. For the student who continues in a business curriculum, this complete view will provide him with a framework into which he can fit the segments as he subsequently studies in greater detail such subjects as accounting, marketing, finance, and management.
2. The student will acquire a vocabulary of business terms. This acquisition will prove invaluable in later courses as well as in reading newspapers and magazines or listening to the radio or television on topics related to business.
3. The student will learn what capitalism is and how it functions, which seems to be misunderstood by large segments of our population. As a result, he should be a better citizen of this country.
4. Both by direction and indirection, the student will have his attention focused on the many and varied careers available in the business world. His ability to make an intelligent vocational choice will be enhanced.

5. The student will acquire some understanding and gain some experience in the methods and procedures used by businessmen to arrive at decisions.

Striving to write a text that achieves these objectives in an environmental framework involves a selection of topics and a judgment as to the extent of providing details about each of the numerous facets of business. We believe we have provided an in-depth treatment of the major areas of business that is consistent with the wide coverage necessary for a survey type text.

Once more the authors are happy to express their appreciation to the many users of previous editions of this text who have made numerous constructive criticisms for changes. Our special thanks go to our consulting editor, Dr. Arthur J. Noetzel, Academic Vice President, John Carroll University. We are also indebted to Dr. James M. A. Robinson, Dean, Faculty of Business, University of Calgary, and Dr. Richard D. Steade, Associate Professor of Management, Colorado State University, who made a number of suggestions designed to improve this edition and have also contributed copy for the text and student supplement. Finally, we express our appreciation to Dr. Peter J. Watry, Instructor in Economics and Business, Southwestern College, who provided the manuscript for the transparency masters, a new supplementary item for this edition.

R. E. G.
H. A. B.

Contents

Part 1

Business and Society

Prologue to Part 1

Business and Society

The three introductory chapters of this text are designed to acquaint students with the basic principles of our economic system, the environment in which it operates, and the ethical considerations applicable to it. The social responsibilities that are increasingly coming to be expected of the business community are examined in some detail.

Chapter 1 recognizes that business may properly be regarded as economics in action. A broad view is presented of the economics and major characteristics of capitalism. A brief discussion of other economic systems enables students to identify the major points of difference between those systems and capitalism.

Chapter 2 directs attention to the many influences, both favorable and otherwise, to which business in this country is subject. The increasing public interest in the physical aspects of the environment indicates quite clearly that business does not operate in a vacuum but must continually cope with new problems in this field. The emergence of the phenomenon called "consumerism," with its broad implications for business, suggests some of the current forces that are appearing on the economic horizon.

Chapter 3 traces the growing importance of ethical conduct on the part of business. Attention is also directed to the emerging concept that business does not operate solely for the benefit of businessmen, but that theirs is a social responsibility to the public at large.

Chapter 1

Nature of Business

Business may be considered as the sum total of the organized efforts and procedures by which the people of a nation endeavor to provide the goods and services that are requisite to the maintenance and improvement of the standard of living to which they aspire. The history of man is that of a fairly continuous striving toward the betterment of his living conditions, although admittedly with wide differences in methods employed and objectives achieved. In some areas of the earth, there appears to be scant evidence of progress in this direction, due, perhaps, to isolation from the rest of the world, meager resources available, lack of educational facilities, and apparent satisfaction with conditions as they are. Among the more enlightened nations of the world, however, steady progress toward ever higher standards of living is evidenced through the constant efforts of their people to enrich their lives through better and higher education and through the production of more and better commodities and services and their widespread distribution throughout society.

The purpose of this book is to consider in a systematic manner the methods by which businesses in the United States are organized and managed so as to earn a profit by satisfying the wants of the people. This study will begin with an examination of capitalism, which is the term customarily applied to the economic system under which American business operates. This system is in contrast to alternative economic systems, such as socialism or communism, which will be described briefly at the end of this chapter.

Before proceeding to an examination of the salient features of capitalism, it should be pointed out that capitalism in the United States, as well as in many other countries, is market-oriented—that is, its fundamental purpose and reason for being is to produce goods and services for the benefit of consumers. And a company's success or failure is dependent on its providing something that the market (the public) needs, wants, and is able and willing to pay for. This is in contrast to the product-oriented policies that have been characteristic of other economic systems, notably socialism and communism. No small part of the faltering economic progress of those countries that have embraced these two latter systems has been due to their dedication to the philosophy of producing goods as such without much, if any, regard as to whether consumers needed or wanted them.

WHAT IS CAPITALISM?

Capitalism is an economic system in which individuals, with comparative freedom from external restraint, produce goods and services for public consumption under conditions of competition and with private profit or gain as the principal motivating force. These goods and services move from producers to consumers by means of an exchange (or sales) procedure in which the common medium of payment is usually money or some acceptable substitute for it, such as credit.

At the outset, it should be understood that capitalism is an economic, not a political, system. Capitalism flourishes best, however, in a country with a democratic form of government. The importance of understanding our kind of capitalism cannot be overemphasized in view of the attacks that have been leveled against this institution, both at home and abroad, within recent years. Not only have the proponents of communism, consisting of the spokesmen of Russia, Red China, and countries behind the "Iron Curtain," decried capitalism as an economic system and a way of life, but in this country voices other than those of American communists have been raised to call into question many of the fundamental tenets of our economic order. To evaluate these criticisms properly, our economic system must be thoroughly understood.

Capitalism, in its purest form, is what emerges in a situation where the outstanding circumstance is freedom. This type of capitalism is often called *laissez faire*, a French term that signifies noninterference by government in the conduct of business by individual businessmen and firms. American business, in the earlier years of its existence, probably typified laissez faire capitalism to a considerable extent. In recent years, however, the increase in restraints by government upon business has been such that our economy is frequently referred to as a "modified capitalism." In fact, since the early 1930's, the trend toward the abridgement of freedom in many phases of business has been a notable aspect of the twentieth century. There is reason for believing that the future will witness a continuance of this trend, particularly with regard to the federal government. Vigorous enforcement of the antitrust laws, the Civil Rights Act of 1964, minimum-wage laws, and the growing power of governmental agencies, such as the Federal Trade Commission, are in line with this trend.

In order to facilitate an examination of the characteristics of capitalism, the fundamental factors in the system will be considered in three groups—the basic freedoms of capitalism, the role of individuals in capitalism, and other aspects of capitalism.

THE BASIC FREEDOMS OF CAPITALISM

The following factors comprise the basic freedoms of capitalism: (1) private property, (2) private enterprise, and (3) freedom of choice.

Private Property

Capitalism can operate only where the institution of *private property* prevails. This means that individuals and business firms have the right to purchase, own, and sell property of all kinds, including land, buildings, machinery, and equipment. It also implies that businessmen have the right to ownership of the goods which they produce and to any profits which may come about through the sale of these goods.

Private Enterprise

The second important freedom of capitalism is *private enterprise*, which means that most business ventures in this country are owned by individuals who have invested their own funds in businesses of their own choosing, from the operation of which they hope to realize gains (or profits) for themselves. This is true regardless of the size of the companies. Large enterprises such as General Motors Corporation, Standard Oil Company of New Jersey, and National Cash Register Company, as well as such small businesses as a hardware store or a barbershop, are all private enterprises. In no sense are they public or government projects, such as the United States Postal Service, police and fire departments, county homes, and the Tennessee Valley Authority.

Even though a corporation must go through certain routine formalities to secure a charter to conduct its business, it is still a private enterprise. The state, in granting a charter, does not enter into partnership with the corporation, does not supply any of the capital, nor does it agree to share in any of the losses that may be suffered. Nor may the state ordinarily require that the concern applying for a charter show that there is any need for its being brought into existence, or refuse a charter if such proof is not forthcoming.

Thus this characteristic of capitalism, private enterprise, pertains to ownership and indicates that business is owned by private individuals rather than by public bodies, such as federal, state, or local governments. Private sources of capital are used to secure the needed funds to start and operate a business. The dealings between businesses are private transactions and, if not illegal in nature, they are customarily not of public concern. The efforts put into the management of business are those of private individuals whose judgments and decisions determine the paths that the business follows.

Freedom of Choice

An outstanding characteristic of capitalism, especially in a country with a democratic form of government, and one which differentiates it from all other economic systems, is the extent to which everyone affected by it has, to a considerable degree, freedom of choice in his economic actions. The businessman is free to choose the field of business in which he will engage and to manipulate the factors of land, labor, capital, and management as he sees fit in order to achieve the highest measure of profit. He may also choose his customers with almost complete freedom.[1] Workers are at liberty to choose the jobs that they wish, in the trades or callings that they prefer, and in the companies that offer them the best returns for their efforts. Consumers are singularly free in their choices of the goods and services that they wish to buy because there is no compulsion for them either to purchase or to refrain from so doing. This freedom of choice is found at all economic levels; the chief limiting factor, as a general rule, is that of the financial resources of the individuals themselves.

A variant on the concept of freedom of choice is that of *freedom of contract*. This means that individuals or firms are free to enter into

---

[1] The Civil Rights Act of 1964, as well as several state laws, prohibits places of public accommodation from refusing to serve their customers on the basis of race, religion, color, or national origin. This prohibition includes hotels, motels, restaurants, cafeterias, and theaters.

contracts that call for the performance of services or the delivery of goods, provided that there is no violation of law involved, in accordance with the dictates of their own best judgments. Likewise, they may decline to enter such contracts on the same basis.

THE ROLE OF INDIVIDUALS IN CAPITALISM

Four groups of individuals play essential roles in capitalism: (1) entrepreneurs, (2) management, (3) workers, and (4) consumers.

Entrepreneurs

The term applied to the individual, or group, who engages in business under the capitalistic system is entrepreneur. This is a French word for which no completely accurate or satisfactory counterpart exists in the English language. The word "enterpriser," a fairly literal translation, is not at all in common usage.

An *entrepreneur* may be regarded as the one who, having the necessary capital or being able to secure it, enters business in some form in which he believes that there is an opportunity for profit to himself. Subject to certain outside influences, such as competition, laws, government action, and chance, he manages the business as he wishes.

The entrepreneur brings his business into being and operates it because he believes that he can secure a profit by so doing and he is willing, at least tacitly, to accept the risk of loss. He knows that the more efficiently he can operate his business, the larger will be his profits and the better his chances of surviving competitively. Therefore, he keeps a close watch on his costs of doing business and is ever alert to new and cheaper ways of operating. Lower costs frequently result in lower prices and enhanced quality of the goods and services available to consumers. The entrepreneur thus is seen as the prime initiator of all economic activity in a capitalistic system.

The entrepreneurial functions may be performed by a single individual in the form of a sole proprietorship, or by several individuals, either as a partnership, corporation, or some other form of business ownership.

Among the critics of our economic system are those who would substitute some measure of governmental ownership and operation of certain types of business enterprise for private entrepreneurship. This is particularly true in the field of public utilities, notably the generation and distribution of electric power. It should be pointed out, however, that the government is neither equipped nor intended to assume the risks of enterprise, nor are the incentives to more efficient operation present when the government runs a business.

Management

The individuals charged with the responsibility of operating business enterprises and of endeavoring to do so profitably are commonly referred to as *management*. In the earlier days of business in this country, the owners were also the management, a circumstance that is still to be found in small-scale firms. In most of the larger companies, however, particularly those with great numbers of stockholders (or owners), the managements have come to consist of individuals who may not own any stock in the companies that they operate. Management, in these instances, comprises groups of salaried persons, whose incentives for the efficient direction of the enterprises with which they are connected come from the expectation of higher salaries and possibly job security, rather than from profits.

The separation of management and ownership in large businesses has become an important aspect of American capitalism. This does not mean, necessarily, that the owners of business enterprises in this category are powerless to control the actions of management, particularly if the profit return is not up to their expectations. There are ways, to be discussed in a later chapter, whereby situations such as these can be rectified. But the fact remains that the day-to-day operation of many businesses is in the hands of salaried managers and that the control function of ownership has been largely delegated to management.

The importance of management in the setting of American capitalism can scarcely be overemphasized. The decisions made by management, acting either as owners or as top-ranking employees, are vital to the successful functioning of our economic system. This has become increasingly apparent in recent years as many business firms have grown markedly in sales, number of employees, variety of products, physical plants, and financial requirements. Indeed, some students of American business believe that the further growth of many of these companies will be limited by their ability to discover or develop managerial personnel capable of successfully directing these enterprises.

Workers

Capitalism is dependent upon a large group of individual workers who must perform the actual physical and mental labor that is necessary to bring into being all of the many and varied types of goods and services that the system produces. Included among the worker group are those that are skilled, semiskilled, and unskilled. One definition of workers might be that they are those who have no authority over other workers, for as soon as an individual achieves control over other workers, he ceases to be a worker and becomes a part of management.

It should be noted, however, that workers are not helpless pawns in the capitalistic system. They are free to move from one company to another if in so doing they believe that they may better themselves. Their right to form unions to protect their interests and improve their economic status is established by law. In many states there is legislation limiting the hours of work for women and minors.

Consumers

The role of the consumer in a capitalistic economy is a dual one. In the first place, every individual is a consumer. Each one of us must consume a minimum amount of food and drink in order to sustain life. Upward from this lowest point of consumption are various gradations of consumptive levels. Any modern economic system, such as capitalism, exists for the primary purpose of providing the goods and services required by the consumers who are a part of it. Consumer demand for the products of the system, however, determines the success or the failure of the individual firms that comprise the economic organization of the country, and, to a considerable degree, the level of business activity in the nation. *Consumer demand* may be defined as the desire for goods and services coupled with the requisite purchasing power.

In order that a person may consume goods in our economic system, he must possess purchasing power so that he may buy those things which he needs and wants. In most instances this purchasing power comes into being when its possessor is paid for doing (producing, in the broad sense of the term) something, whether the payment is in the form of wages, rent, profits, or other types of income. The consumer thus emerges in a second role, that of a producer. For various reasons, some historic and some psychological, consumers have generally thought of themselves as producers first, and consumers second. In their attempts (either singly or in groups, such as labor unions) to better their economic status, consumers have customarily sought greater rewards in their roles as producers, such as higher wages, rather than by endeavoring to achieve the same objectives through the improvement of their positions as consumers, by way of more prudent purchasing. Business and government are also end purchasers of goods and services, absorbing about one third of the total, but are customarily placed in a separate category from consumers. A further reference to consumers will be found on pages 33 and 48 of Chapter 2.

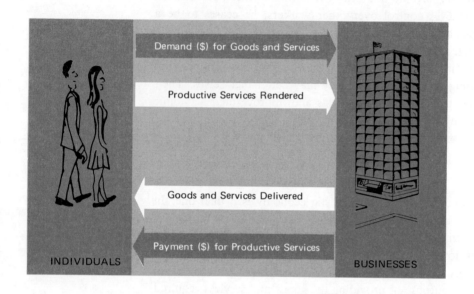

Figure 1-1

The Circular Flow of Economic Activity

OTHER ASPECTS OF CAPITALISM

A number of additional items are essential to an understanding of the operation of capitalism: (1) capital, (2) production, (3) distribution of goods, (4) price, (5) competition, (6) risk, and (7) profit.

Capital

Capital can best be understood in terms of its two forms—capital goods and capital funds. *Capital goods* consist of such things as tools, equipment, buildings, fixtures, patents, and land, as well as raw materials in the process of manufacture, and merchandise for sale. *Capital funds* refer to money that is available from individual savers or from groups through savings institutions for investment in business enterprises. The capital needed by a business may be obtained through the investment of the entrepreneur, by borrowing from others, and by using the funds resulting from business profits and retained in the business.

The owners of capital, known as capitalists, contribute their resources to a business either as owners or creditors. If they assume the risks of entrepreneurship, they are interested in profits; if as creditors, in interest on their investment. In either event, capital funds or goods will not be forthcoming unless the capitalists see an opportunity for a satisfactory return on their investment or loan. If such a return does not appear to be in prospect, the investment or loan will not be made and the business project in question will not be initiated or continued. It is probable that the term "capitalism" owes its origin and meaning to its dependence upon the decisions and actions of the owners of capital.

Production

Production, as used in its broadest economic sense, means the furnishing by the entrepreneur of some economically valuable goods or services that are to be sold to others. Economists commonly speak of production as the creation of utilities. Production, in this sense, includes not only the manufacture of such products as automobiles, food, radios, and so on, but also their transportation and their distribution at wholesale and retail.

In its narrower and more common business usage, production refers to the physical manufacture of goods, whether this be a simple extractive process, such as lumbering or mining, or the highly complex types necessary to produce rubber tires, washing machines, and electrical appliances. It is in this latter sense that production will be used in this text.

Distribution of Goods

Distribution may be regarded as the ways by which the output of production is made available to its users, the consumers. From the standpoint of the capitalistic system, the entrepreneur in distribution is one who seeks profit by providing the facilities whereby products may reach their destination. He, like the entrepreneur in production, will use the factors of land, labor, capital, and management in those combinations that appear to him best from the standpoint of profits.

The production entrepreneur usually must undertake some of the duties of the distribution entrepreneur in order to dispose of his product; whereas the latter only occasionally enters the field of production. Chain stores and others who have undertaken the manufacture of some of their own branded goods both produce and distribute. This latter development is the result of the seeking of greater profits by distribution entrepreneurs.

Price

Under capitalism the movement of goods from the producer to the consumer takes place on an exchange basis; or, to use the customary phrase, a sale takes place. The buyer gives something of value to the seller in exchange for the goods that the seller has available for sale. In our economy this "something of value" is money, our medium of exchange; and the amount of money for which a good or service is exchanged is the *price*.

The price at which a commodity is bought and sold is partly determined by supply and demand. As the price of a commodity increases, the amount of that commodity offered for sale tends to increase and the amount purchased tends to decrease. Contrariwise, as the price of a commodity decreases, the amount purchased tends to increase and the amount offered for sale tends to decrease.

Presumably over a period of time the prices that sellers receive will be high enough to cover their costs of doing business and yield them their desired profits. If prices are too low, the sellers will supposedly withdraw from their present business and enter more profitable fields. On the other hand, it is presumed that the prices that the buyers will pay over a period of time must at least equal the satisfaction or usefulness that they will receive from the purchase of the goods. If prices are too high, buyers will withhold their purchases or transfer them to other, lower-priced goods.

While the abovementioned supply-and-demand situation unquestionably has a certain amount of validity, it would be an oversimplification to presume that it is the only explanation of this phenomenon of capitalism. The factors that enter into the determination of prices are exceedingly complex, involving a large number of elements, psychological as well as economic. A more extensive discussion of this phase of capitalism will be presented in Chapter 10.

Competition

Under capitalism the entrepreneurs in each line of business compete with each other in the sale of their products or services.[2] Thus *competition* is basic to the capitalistic system. The institution of free, private enterprise implies freedom on the part of any entrepreneur to enter any field of

[2] There are certain exceptions to this rule, as in the case of such public utilities as electric power, gas, water, telephone, and transportation companies, which enjoy a more or less monopolistic situation, subject to regulation by some governmental agency.

business and to compete with those already established therein for the favor of the buyers in the market.

Early economists propounded the concept of *pure competition*. Four criteria were assumed under this concept: (a) a large number of sellers are in the market, all selling an identical product; (b) all buyers and sellers are completely informed about all markets and prices; (c) there is free movement in and out of the market by buyers and sellers; and (d) no individual buyer or seller is able to influence the price, which is determined by supply and demand, or the total of the actions of all of the buyers and sellers. Under these assumptions competition was solely on the basis of price. Over time it became evident that, except for a few farm products, such as wheat, corn, and soybeans, pure competition simply did not exist. Eventually supplanting it was the theory of *imperfect competition*, which can be classified into oligopoly and monopolistic competition.

Oligopoly assumes a market situation in which comparatively few firms produce identical or similar products, and where individual firms have the ability to influence price. *Monopolistic competition* assumes that there are many makers of goods with identical end usage who brand their products to differentiate them from those of their competitors. This practice is known as *product differentiation*. In this manner the producers of these branded goods hope to convince consumers that their products are different from, and presumably better than, those of their competitors in some important aspect so that they may escape having their goods compared with those of other manufacturers of similar wares. Through this practice producers endeavor to create a "brand loyalty" among consumers, so that they may avoid the rigors of strictly price competition. The large number of different brands to be found among consumer goods lends credence to this theory.

Other concepts of competition. Born of the depression of the 1930's, there came into being what is known as *handicap competition*, the purpose of which was to lessen the impact of price competition on identical goods between large and small retailers—those who sell directly to consumers. Laws were passed in many states [3] that, in effect, prevented the large retailers from offering these goods at lower prices than the small ones. Thus the small retailers were given assistance in their competition with the large operators. Many of these laws are still in effect.

A phenomenon that first appeared in the middle 1940's has given rise to a still further classification of competition. The growth of supermarkets,

---

[3] A further discussion of these laws will be found in Chapter 10.

discount houses, suburban shopping centers, self-service, and a host of new products (or older ones redesigned) has been given the name of *innovistic competition*. This type of competition subordinates, to some extent, the role of price and stresses instead customer convenience and novelty, both in goods and the places where they may be purchased. It is a dynamic type of competition that threatens the status quo of many of the historic competitive practices in the area of consumer goods. Many observers believe that innovistic competition will be the rule for the foreseeable future.

Importance of price. There is, however, a strong conviction that price will continue to retain its preeminence as a base for competition, despite the inroads of innovation, service, convenience, prestige, and reputation. An entrepreneur endeavors to gain a competitive advantage by lowering his prices. This action causes his competitors to try to meet the new lowered prices and, in some instances, to go below them. The extent to which this price-cutting action will go is determined largely by two factors, the amount sold and the operating costs of the entrepreneurs concerned. If the sales are great enough to take all of the products of the producers in a given field, the competitive price will tend to be that at which all producers are making at least a satisfactory profit. If the amount purchased is not great enough to achieve this end and if it can be increased by lowering the price, then the operating costs of the entrepreneurs enter the picture. Obviously the producers with the lowest costs can go farther in the direction of lowering prices than can their less efficient competitors. It should be equally apparent that, when the price goes below the production and distribution costs of any producer, he cannot long remain in business unless he can reduce his costs and thereby become more efficient in his operations.

This situation provides the clue to the presumably beneficent social character of competition. Through its operation, people are supposed to secure their goods and services at the lowest possible prices based on the highest attainable efficiency of the producers. Those entrepreneurs who are unable to achieve this standard of efficiency are assumed to retire from business; thus the public is rid of the high cost of inefficient producers. There is also, according to this presumption, a never-ending effort on the part of all producers to lower their costs, both to increase their profits and to give them a possible competitive advantage thereby.

This is obviously a simplification of this part of our economic system, as there are many factors operating to offset and supplement this more or less purifying competitive movement. But it is still basically true in a large segment of our economic life, and the student's attention is directed to it at this point in order that he may understand something of the stronger trends that characterize capitalistic economies.

In spite of the lip service that is paid to competition by businessmen, the fact of the matter is that many of them do not like it so far as their being exposed to it is concerned. They want the sellers from whom they buy to compete in order that the prices which they have to pay may be as low as possible; and they likewise desire competition among their buyers in order that they may sell at the highest possible prices. But they do not care for a competitive situation into which they themselves must fit.

Risk

Risk is always present in private enterprise. Of greatest importance is the risk of complete failure—of bankruptcy—in which case the entrepreneur stands to lose all of his investment. In the case of the sole proprietorship or partnership he may possibly also lose his personal property and savings. This risk is apt to be greater when a new business is being launched than after it is well established. A similar danger exists, however, when an old concern fails to keep abreast of the times and loses out to newer, more wide-awake competitors.

At all times a firm must be aware of the risks that are inherent in competition—chances of loss through shifts in the price level, changes in style and fashion, and the appearance of substitutes on the market that sometimes render present models obsolete. The switch from steam to diesel power in railroad locomotives is a good example of the risk involved in the use of substitutes for materials formerly used. The market for coal has been substantially reduced by this changeover. When the development of atomic power reaches the stage where it can be adapted generally to industrial operations, it is likely that all other forms of energy will be adversely affected.

The appearance of innovistic competition in the past couple of decades has markedly enhanced the risk aspects of entrepreneurship in all economic areas. Especially is this true in the field of small business where the effect of mergers of large firms, the increase in number and types of goods, and the speed with which these phenomena have come into being, have added to the risk burdens of small entrepreneurs. Two other factors are noteworthy as contributors to risk. These are automation, which involves the substitution of mechanical for human effort with a frequently resulting reduction in cost; and electronic data processing through the use of computers, which permits of the assembling and use of large amounts of vital information by management.[4] For those firms unable or unwilling to utilize either or both of these factors, the risk of falling behind competitively may be serious.

Other sources of potential loss are to be found in changes in the desirability of business locations, in distribution methods, and in public demand. All of these risks must be accepted by entrepreneurs as integral parts of capitalism. On their ability to meet the situations surrounding these hazards will depend their success or failure in their respective enterprises.

Certain other risks can be met to a considerable degree through insurance. These include losses from such items as fire, theft, flood, wind, death of important executives, and accidents for which the business must assume responsibility. Any risk that can be shifted to others by insurance or other devices, however, is not of the type regarded as implicit to entrepreneurship.

Profit

For all practical purposes, business *profit* may be considered to be the excess of the income of an enterprise over the costs of its operation. Profits or the anticipation of profits constitute the inducement to capitalists to invest in private enterprise in an ownership capacity. It is not necessary at this point to enter into an analysis of what may be properly considered as the costs of operating a business. The significance of profits in the present discussion lies in their role as determinants of action by the owners of capital.

The question may well be raised as to the amount of profit, in any given instance, that is required to induce capitalists to invest in the enterprise in question. No absolute quantitative answer can be given, and there are wide variations among different lines of business. The question, however, is not unanswerable if attention is directed to the term that signifies the opposite of profits, namely, losses.

Losses arise when the income of a business is insufficient to cover its costs; they are an ever-present possibility of risk in any private enterprise under capitalism. The entrepreneur accepts the risk of loss when he enters business in the quest for profits. Some writers in the field of economics have claimed that profits are justified as inducements to the entrepreneur to assume the risks of loss in any private enterprise. Whether or not there is any justification, moral or social, for profits is not of any moment in

---

[4] Automation is treated in Chapters 2 and 17 and data processing in Chapters 2 and 24.

this discussion, but it is here that the clue may be found to the answer to the question presented above. Speaking broadly, it may be said that in order to induce entrepreneurs to enter any given business, they must be convinced that the prospective profits are potentially greater than the possible losses. The expectation of profits and the fear of losses provide incentives for effective management, risk-taking, and innovation.

THE ECONOMIST'S CONCEPT OF CAPITALISM

For many years economists, who study the operation of economic systems, have propounded various theories designed to explain the operation of capitalism. These theories have ranged all the way from explanations of the functioning of capitalism as an organic whole (*macro-economics*) to a consideration of the decisions to be made by individual firms with regard to prices and profits (*microeconomics*). Not infrequently some of these theories have been at variance with others put forth at earlier times. This has been particularly true of those theories which have undertaken to explain the reasons for the varying levels of business activity, the more or less cyclical periods of prosperity and recession that have occurred throughout the history of our economy.

It is not within the province of this text to undertake a minute scrutiny of these theories but rather to set forth briefly the basic elements of the two that economists have most recently had under discussion. The older, or *classical theory of capitalism*, makes the following assumptions: (a) normally there is full employment of labor and, if this condition does not exist, it is only a temporary deviation; (b) all income from the production of goods and services will be spent immediately to buy the current goods and services required, or invested in capital goods such as materials, machinery, and buildings, and consumer goods that are destined to be put into inventories of sellers; and (c) the production of goods creates an equivalent amount of demand, and therefore aggregate supply and demand will always be equal. A conclusion which the classical theory propounds, then, is that the forces of supply and demand, together with investment, are adequate to keep the economy operating at its highest level and in a state of equilibrium.

The more recent theory, called the *income-expenditure analysis*,[5] differs from the classical theory in several respects. It holds that the economy can be in equilibrium without full employment. This theory states that the

---

[5] This theory is also known as the national income theory or the Neo-Keynesian theory.

level of business activity, and also of employment, at any one point in time, is based on the volume of demand for goods and services by both consumers and businessmen, and the volume of investment by businessmen in economic goods of all kinds. Inasmuch as the level of consumption is presumed to be fairly steady for any level of income, the rate of business activity and the level of employment depend upon the amount of investment. Consumers, however, may not spend all of their incomes for goods and services but save some for various reasons. This will tend not only to reduce consumption but, unless the savings are invested in economic goods, will also tend to lower the investment rate. Therefore, it is held that if the rate of consumption, and particularly the rate of investment, are not great enough to insure relatively full employment, government spending must provide the additional expenditures necessary to raise the level of employment.

The federal government has for many years embraced the concept of the income-expenditure theory with respect to its responsibility for achieving and maintaining full employment in the country. As a means of attaining this objective, a long series of annual deficits have been incurred, which may or may not have produced the desired result. One of the results of this course of action has been a steady increase in the national debt and interest on that debt. There are sharp differences of opinion among economists and businessmen regarding the desirability of the continuance of this situation and of its eventual effect on the economy of the country.

The foregoing brief explanation of the classical and income-expenditure theories should help to explain some of the fiscal policies of the federal government and the recommendations in this area that have been made by economists who embrace the income-expenditure analysis.

THE ROLE OF ECONOMISTS

Until the depression of the 1930's, economists were generally thought of as cloistered savants, whose theories and attitudes appeared to have little visible influence on business practices and governmental policies. There had been a number of depressions in the history of the country from which the economy had always emerged; and, while certain economists had occasionally suggested that these recoveries were needlessly delayed, it appears that neither businessmen nor governmental officials paid much attention to their proposed remedies for business slumps. The depression of the 1930's was different, apparently, and by 1933 not only had many businessmen despaired of a quick recovery, but also they turned to the federal government in the hope of some sort of a solution to the continuing low level of business activity.

At about this time, an English economist, John Maynard Keynes, proposed that the federal government should embark on a program of spending, the purpose of which was to stimulate the recovery of the economy. The federal government followed Keynes' suggestions to some extent, and there was a visible improvement in the level of business activity. Whether this was due in any considerable measure to the Keynesian theory has been a matter of dispute among economists, businessmen, and government officials. The onset of World War II in 1939 and the involvement of this country after Pearl Harbor in December, 1941, provided a stimulus to business that overshadowed any prior government spending for recovery. But during the late 1930's, and to a large extent thereafter, economists became active in government and their theories and viewpoints came to exert an increasing measure of influence on federal economic and fiscal policy.

Since the end of World War II, the theories of Lord Keynes have achieved even greater attention. The persistently high level of business activity, with a few minor deviations, is largely credited to the fact that the federal government, guided to a considerable extent by economists, has adopted policies that have permitted business and consumers to take those steps deemed most likely to keep the economy in high gear.

The Employment Act of 1946, a federal law sometimes referred to as the *full employment act*, placed upon the federal government the responsibility for taking such measures as seem advisable to maintain the economic health of the nation. A federal Council of Economic Advisers was established to "develop and recommend to the President national economic policies to foster and promote free competitive enterprise, to avoid economic fluctuations or to diminish the effects thereof, and to maintain maximum employment, production, and purchasing power." It prepares an Annual Economic Review for the President, who transmits an Economic Report to the Congress. Thus the current discussion regarding unemployment is not over the role of government, as such, but over the solution to the problem of unemployment in an era of prosperity. The question seems to be whether this is due to *structural unemployment*, which refers to the difficulties involved in matching available people and jobs, or to an inadequate growth of aggregate demand in the country.

It appears that there is a substantial measure of agreement among economists that the Keynesian doctrines point the way toward continued prosperity in the country; and many businessmen have come to accept, if not embrace, the role of economists and their theories in the mosaic of

business environment. It appears that these theories can operate successfully to brake a downward economic trend, but only the future will reveal
if it is economically and politically possible to reverse the upward trend
and still maintain an acceptably robust level of business activity.

CHARACTERISTICS OF PRESENT-DAY BUSINESS

Business in this country has developed several special characteristics
that illustrate its dynamic nature. These are: (1) specialization, (2) mass
production, (3) large-scale business, and (4) the growing importance of
research.

SPECIALIZATION

The trend toward specialization in industry has been noteworthy at
all levels. Workers have tended to specialize and the jack-of-all-trades,
so common years ago, has been largely replaced by the specialist, the
worker who is trained to excel at one, relatively small, task. Thus the
all-round machinist, who could operate all types of machine tools, has
given way to the individual who is equipped to run only a lathe or a drill
press. The machines are adjusted and made ready for operation, not by
the general machinist, but by a set-up man, a specialist in grinding and
setting the cutting tools by which the work is shaped into the finished
product. The advent and growth of automation and of computers have
required the commensurate development of highly trained and skilled
specialists who are capable of performing the intricate tasks involved in
preparing, operating, adjusting and, where necessary, repairing these complicated devices.

Companies have also developed along specialized lines. There are
many firms that produce items which have no separate utility in themselves,
but which must be combined with other goods to form some sort of a
whole that is useful to man. For example, an automobile is made up of a
great many parts which, apart from the car, have little usefulness. Spark
plugs, tubeless tires, upholstery fabric, cotter pins, and piston rings are
a few parts that are the products of specialized industries. While it is true
that the great motor car manufacturers, such as Ford and General Motors,
have tended to produce more of the items that go into their cars, a large
number of parts are still made by firms that produce nothing else. This
tendency is an outstanding characteristic of business in this country.

MASS PRODUCTION

This phenomenon of our industry is responsible, to no small degree, for the availability, at low cost and in large numbers, of such goods as airplanes, telephones, radios and television sets, and many other commodities that help to give us the highest standard of living known to man.

Mass production does not merely mean the producing of a large number of any given item. It involves a manufacturing technique that not only results in the creation of a great quantity of goods but also brings about a reduction in unit costs, which, in turn, permits lower prices and greater sales. This technique consists mainly of a standardization and interchangeability of parts; the use of the assembly line, whereby the item to be produced moves slowly along a belt or chain and undergoes a series of additions of component parts until it emerges at the end completely assembled; and the subdivision of the labor element into a series of simple, repetitive operations. This process probably originated in the automobile industry but has spread to many other fields. The production technique known as automation is particularly applicable to mass-production industries.

LARGE-SCALE BUSINESS

Most businesses start on a relatively small scale and many never experience more than a moderate growth. Some, however, have grown to great size. Among the large-scale businesses in manufacturing are General Motors Corporation, International Business Machines, and the United States Steel Corporation. In the field of merchandising are the Great Atlantic and Pacific Tea Company, J. C. Penney, and Federated Department Stores. Large public utilities include American Telephone and Telegraph Company, Pacific Gas and Electric Company, and Consolidated Edison Company of New York. Financial institutions in this size grouping include First National City Bank of New York, Bank of America, Prudential Insurance Company, Metropolitan Life Insurance Company, and Manufacturers Hanover Trust Company. Their capital, sales, properties, and number of employees are all on a vast scale. Some are mass production companies; while others, the nonmanufacturing group, are not. Their size, which is one of their outstanding characteristics, is a development of the last 50 years or more. A significant development of the past decade or so is the growth of mergers where two or more firms come under a common ownership and management, thereby creating large and strong competitors in the areas affected.

GROWING IMPORTANCE OF RESEARCH

A characteristic of present-day business that has increasingly manifested itself in recent years is that of research. *Research* may be defined as the systematic investigation of the facts surrounding any given situation with the hope that more effective methods may be found. Research in business is carried on in production methods, materials, personnel, marketing, products, packaging, and advertising. The ever-growing pressure of competition is the major force behind this increased emphasis on research. In order for producers to remain competitive, it becomes imperative for them continuously to engage in research, both to discover better and cheaper methods of manufacture and distribution and to search for new products and improvements in their present product lines.

The term *research and development*, often shortened to R and D, has become quite common as descriptive not only of the research aspect of this activity but also of the application of the results of the research to cost-saving methods, to the adding of new products, or to the enhancing of the sales value of old ones. Large sums of money are committed annually to R and D projects and, to an ever-increasing extent, the judgments and decisions of top management are being influenced by the findings of research in business.

SIZE OF BUSINESS FIRMS

American business is carried on by firms that range in size from the small enterprise in which a single person conducts his business, such as a shoe repair or an upholstering shop, through medium-sized firms, such as grocery wholesalers or paper box manufacturers, to such industrial and commercial giants as the General Motors Corporation and the Great Atlantic and Pacific Tea Company, whose sales volumes amount to billions of dollars annually and who employ many thousands of workers. In the chapters that follow attention will be given to companies of all sizes.

Over 98 percent of all enterprises in the United States can be classified as small businesses according to Congressional definition. A retail store or a dealer in services whose annual sales do not exceed $1 million is classified as a small business. A wholesaler whose annual sales do not exceed $5 million is a small businessman. A manufacturing company that does not have more than 250 employees is ordinarily classified as a small business; and under some circumstances, it retains that classification even though it employs up to 1,000 workers. Small businesses, therefore, are very important in our economy.

Table 1-1 below presents certain pertinent data for the 20 largest industrial corporations in the United States for 1970. Of particular note are the wide variations between different firms in assets, employees, and specifically in net income as a percent of sales.

Table 1-1

THE 20 LARGEST INDUSTRIAL CORPORATIONS RANKED BY SALES, 1970

| Rank | Company | Sales | Assets | Em- | Net Income as % |
		(Thousands of Dollars)		ployees	of Sales
1	General Motors	18,752,354	14,174,360	695,796	3.2
2	Standard Oil (N. J.)	16,554,227	19,241,784	143,000	7.9
3	Ford Motor	14,979,900	9,904,100	431,727	3.4
4	General Electric	8,726,738	6,309,945	396,583	3.8
5	International Business Machines	7,503,960	8,539,047	269,291	13.6
6	Mobil Oil	7,260,522	7,921,049	75,600	6.6
7	Chrysler	6,999,676	4,815,772	228,332	—
8	International Tel. & Tel.	6,364,494	6,697,011	392,000	5.6
9	Texaco	6,349,759	9,923,786	73,734	12.9
10	Western Electric	5,856,160	3,743,623	215,380	4.3
11	Gulf Oil	5,396,182	8,672,298	61,300	10.2
12	U. S. Steel	4,814,368	6,311,038	200,734	3.1
13	Westinghouse Electric	4,313,410	3,358,167	145,000	2.9
14	Standard Oil of California	4,187,762	6,593,551	44,610	10.9
15	Ling-Temco-Vought	3,771,724	2,582,004	99,447	—
16	Standard Oil (Ind.)	3,732,827	5,397,471	47,551	8.4
17	Boeing	3,677,073	2,621,819	79,100	0.6
18	E. I. du Pont de Nemours	3,618,400	3,566,600	110,685	9.1
19	Shell Oil	3,589,546	4,609,763	36,754	6.6
20	General Tel. & Electronics	3,439,219	7,739,272	172,000	6.1

Reprinted from the May, 1971, *Fortune Directory* by special permission: © 1971, Time, Inc.

CLASSIFICATION OF BUSINESS

Two basic classes of business firms are industrial and commercial. *Industrial businesses* include all businesses that are engaged in producing things—by extraction from the earth, by fabrication in the factory, or by construction on a building site. In the classification of *commercial businesses* are to be found firms engaged in marketing, such as wholesalers and retailers; in finance, such as banks and investment concerns; and in the service field, which includes advertising, repair services, laundries, hotels, and theaters. Table 1-2 presents selected data on manufacturing, selected services, retail trade, and wholesale trade for a recent year.

NUMBER OF UNITS, DOLLAR VOLUME OF SALES, AND NUMBER OF EMPLOYEES FOR SELECTED TYPES OF BUSINESS

Type of Business	Number of Units	Sales (Billions of Dollars)	Number of Employees	
Manufacturing	311,125	557,767	19,339,000	**Table 1-2**
Selected Services	1,187,814	60,542	3,841,200	
Retail Trade	1,763,324	310,214	9,380,616	
Wholesale Trade	311,464	459,476	3,518,969	

Source: U.S. Bureau of the Census, *Statistical Abstract of the United States: 1970.* (91st edition.) Washington, D.C. 1970.

OTHER ECONOMIC SYSTEMS

Every society follows a certain system of ideas, called an *ideology*, that serves to set forth and embody its concepts of the fundamental values and meanings of human life. There is a large measure of difference between the ideology of capitalism and those of socialism and communism, which are the two major other economic systems that exist. The ideology of capitalism embraces the concept that the greatest good of the largest number of people should be the goal of society. To implement this ideology, the individual citizen should enjoy the greatest amount of freedom, hence the acceptance of laissez faire as an underlying principle in capitalism. Over the years the tendency has developed for the government to impose an ever-increasing number of restraints on the freedom of our citizens, but with the fundamental idea that their well-being would be advanced through this trend. However, we have not moved too far away from the basic concept of the primacy of humans in our society.

Socialism, while adhering to the notion of the desirability of human welfare, is that form of economic system that subscribes to the belief that the major instruments of production—factories, mines, banks, stores, transportation facilities, and farms—should be owned and controlled by the government for the benefit of society as a whole. Both capitalism and socialism are market-oriented but differ in their beliefs as to where ownership and direction of their economies should be located.

Communism is a radical doctrine based on the writings of Karl Marx in which the concept of a classless society and the absence of the state as an instrument of social control were advocated. Soviet Russia (the Union of Soviet Socialist Republics) is the leading exponent of communism. As yet there is little evidence of the disappearance of government. Rather, the state is the ruling power over the entire economic system. Production takes place for its own sake, with only slight regard for the needs and wants of the people. Only recently has there been any evidence that the idea of market orientation has gained credence among the rulers of Russia and that the desires of the people are being given consideration in the planning of the production of goods and services.

It should be noted, however, that true communism, as proclaimed by Marx and Engels, his collaborator, has not yet been achieved in Russia nor is there any evidence that it will be in the foreseeable future. A more correct term for the Russian economy might be that of *state capitalism* with all of the instruments of production and distribution owned and controlled by the government.

Perhaps one of the most outstanding points of difference is that of incentives. In our capitalistic economy, a number of built-in incentives play a significant role in inducing workers at all levels to exert their best efforts at their jobs and in persuading those who have saved funds to invest in business enterprise. These inducements are both monetary and social. They include not only profits for entrepreneurs, wage incentives and opportunities for promotion for employees, but also the prestige that attaches to success in almost all lines of economic endeavor. Under socialism and communism, workers are supposed to do their best for the state without personal incentives. If extra effort is required, it is presumed to be forthcoming because the government has ordered it and not because of any personal gain that may be achieved by the workers.

In this connection it should be noted that profit, as an economic incentive, has reappeared on a small scale in Russia, with a few firms being given the freedom to set prices in accord with the requirements of consumers. This resulted from the failure of government to produce goods which consumers would buy with the consequent pile-ups of unsold merchandise in the state stores and warehouses. Between 1964 and the present, several thousand factories producing both industrial and consumer goods have been placed under a profit system with beneficial results both to consumers and to producers. Whether this trend will be continued is problematical at the moment in view of the state of political uncertainty among the present rulers of Russia.

BUSINESS TERMS

Check the following list to make certain that you can define or explain each term. The numbers following the terms are page references.

business	3	handicap competition	13
capitalism	4	innovistic competition	14
laissez-faire	4	risk	15
private property	5	profit	16
private enterprise	5	macroeconomics	17
freedom of contract	6	microeconomics	17
entrepreneur	7	classical theory of capitalism	17
management	8	income-expenditure analysis	17
consumer demand	9	full employment act	19
capital goods	10	structural unemployment	19
capital funds	10	mass production	21
production	11	research	22
distribution	11	research and development	22
price	12	industrial businesses	23
competition	12	commercial businesses	23
pure competition	13	ideology	24
imperfect competition	13	socialism	24
oligopoly	13	communism	25
monopolistic competition	13	state capitalism	25
product differentiation	13		

QUESTIONS FOR DISCUSSION AND ANALYSIS

1. Do you believe that market orientation is a preferable policy to product orientation? Explain.
2. Would a return to laissez faire be a desirable policy in this country? Justify your opinion.
3. Why is private property vital to capitalism?
4. Do you think that the United States Postal Service, now operating like a private enterprise, will be any more efficient than it was formerly? Explain.
5. Do you regard the tendency toward the separation of ownership and management in many large companies as a favorable or unfavorable trend from the standpoint of the public good? Explain.
6. Why have consumers thought of themselves as producers first and consumers second?
7. Some critics of business regard product differentiation as a wasteful practice. Do you agree? Give reasons.

8. Do you think that handicap competition is fair to consumers, inasmuch as it results in their having to pay higher prices than if it did not exist? Why?

9. A basic tenet of socialism is "to each according to his need, from each according to his ability." Do you think that this would be workable in a capitalistic economy? Why or why not?

10. Some critics of capitalism say that it tends to put "profits before people." Do you agree? Explain.

PROBLEMS AND SHORT CASES

1. Critics of American capitalism claim that there is a steady trend away from price as the basic element of competition in this country. On the basis of such retail pricing as you may have observed, particularly as evidenced by prices of competing commodities, would you think that such criticism is justified? In your opinion how would a greater emphasis on price competition be achieved? Do you think that this would be desirable from the standpoint of (a) producers and (b) consumers?

2. Refer to Table 1-1 on page 23, which presents the 20 largest industrial corporations, and compute (a) the ratio of sales to employees and (b) the ratio of assets to employees for (1) Standard Oil of California, Shell Oil, and Standard Oil (Ind.) and for (2) International Business Machines, U. S. Steel, and Westinghouse Electric. What do you infer from your figures?

3. With the increasing growth of large-scale industry in many lines of business, there has developed a growing concern for the small business, whose survival may be threatened by the strength of large companies. What suggestions do you have for measures that might be taken to help small business, and how would you go about making them effective?

SUGGESTED READINGS

Bach, George Leland. *Economics: An Introduction to Analysis and Policy*, 7th Edition. Englewood Cliffs, New Jersey: Prentice-Hall, Inc., 1971.

Bjork, Gordon C. *Private Enterprise and Public Interest: The Development of American Capitalism*. Englewood Cliffs, New Jersey: Prentice-Hall, Inc., 1969.

Brandis, Royall. *Principles of Economics*. Homewood, Illinois: Richard D. Irwin, Inc., 1968.

Eells, Richard S. *Conceptual Foundations of Business*, Revised Edition. Homewood, Illinois: Richard D. Irwin, Inc., 1969.

Gill, Richard T. *Economics and the Private Interest*. Englewood Cliffs, New Jersey: Prentice-Hall, Inc., 1970.

————————. *Economics and the Public Interest*. Englewood Cliffs, New Jersey: Prentice-Hall, Inc., 1968.

Gruchy, Allan G. *Comparative Economic Systems: Competing Ways to Stability and Growth*. Boston: Houghton Mifflin Company, 1966.

Hailstones, Thomas J., and Michael J. Brennan. *Economics: An Analysis of Principles and Policies*. Cincinnati: South-Western Publishing Co., 1970.

Hartman, Richard I., Terrence P. Hogan, and John T. Wholihan, eds. *Modern Business Administration: Introductory Readings*. Glenview, Illinois: Scott, Foresman and Company, 1969. Part 1.

Howard, William W., and Edwin L. Dale, Jr. *Contemporary Economics: Problems and Policies*. Lexington, Mass.: D. C. Heath and Company, 1971.

Kirkland, Edward C. *A History of American Economic Life*, Fourth Edition. New York: Appleton-Century-Crofts, 1969.

Lynn, Robert A. *Basic Economic Principles*, Second Edition. New York: McGraw-Hill Book Company, 1970.

McConnell, Campbell R. *Economics*, Fourth Edition. New York: McGraw-Hill Book Company, 1969.

Monsen, R. Joseph, Jr., and Borje O. Saxberg, eds. *The Business World: Introduction to Business Readings*. Boston: Houghton Mifflin Company, 1967. Part One.

Poe, Jerry B. *The American Business Enterprise: Introductory Text and Cases*. Homewood, Illinois: Richard D. Irwin, Inc., 1969.

Russel, Robert R. *A History of the American Economic System*. New York: Appleton-Century-Crofts, 1964.

Samuelson, Paul A. *Economics, An Introductory Analysis*, Eighth Edition. New York: McGraw-Hill Book Company, 1970.

Wykstra, Ronald A. *Introductory Economics*. New York: Harper & Row, 1971.

Chapter 2

Economic Business Environment

Business does not operate in an economic vacuum. In this country, as in all other capitalistic countries, business operates in a multifaceted environment which is of itself subject to a large measure of change. The relationship between business and its environment is one of mutuality; that is, business influences the various factors of its environment, and these forces, in turn, exert pressures on the business community. This interaction constantly affects the public and is reflected in the public's attitude towards the actions of businessmen as they endeavor to provide at a profit the goods and services which the country requires.

Before undertaking the more detailed study of the various facets of business, it is desirable to look into this business-environment relationship from a historical standpoint in order to comprehend better its complexity.

HISTORICAL SETTING

An understanding of the factors that make up the environment in which business functions will be aided by a brief consideration of the following historical aspects of the situation: (1) the land and the people and (2) the industrial revolution.

THE LAND AND THE PEOPLE

The United States comprises a very large territory, with a widely varied climate and vast natural resources of timber, metal ores, waterways, water power sources, and fertile farmland. At the time that the first settlers began arriving, these resources were almost completely undeveloped. This was virgin land, admirably adapted to support an agricultural and industrial population.

With few exceptions, the people who migrated to this country in the early days of its history were strong, courageous, adventurous, and self-reliant. In many instances they came here to be free from oppression—political, economic, or religious. Deeply ingrained in many of them was an intense suspicion of and dislike for a strong central government, coupled with a belief in the dignity of hard work. While they naturally brought with them from England and Europe many of the customs and habits of thought of their native lands, they were confronted with new problems, in strange surroundings, that demanded of them new and different approaches to the solution of questions of survival and of making a satisfactory living. The attitude taken by the ruling groups in England and elsewhere that the settlements in America were to have the status of colonies, contributing needed materials to the mother countries and at the same time remaining always dependent upon and subservient to them, aroused a deep sense of resentment among the colonists and served as a stimulus to them to become more completely self-sustaining and politically independent of the countries from which they and their parents had come.

Thus was the attitude of self-reliance and independence developed here. It manifested itself in the belief that a man's success in life was, in a large measure, due to his own energy, courage, and resourcefulness. It spawned the concept of "going into business for one's self" that was a dominant characteristic of our economic thinking for many years, and which survives even to the present.

An important by-product of this type of thinking was the general attitude that private business enterprise was important. Success in business was regarded highly, and successful businessmen were honored and respected as leaders in their communities. Even though the doctrine of *caveat emptor*, let the buyer beware, was generally accepted by the people, they accorded honor and prestige to the leading entrepreneurs of the times.

THE INDUSTRIAL REVOLUTION

The middle of the 18th century has been commonly, if possibly somewhat inaccurately, accepted as the time of the onset of what is called the *industrial revolution*. Stated briefly, this revolution consisted of the application of mechanical power to productive processes hitherto derived from human or animal sources; the extensive development of machinery to which the new power sources could be applied, and the establishment of the *factory system*, under which production workers were assembled in a central location as opposed to the precedent *domestic system*, under which the workers performed their productive tasks in their own homes. The effect of the industrial revolution was to bring about a far-reaching change in business organization. Whereas formerly production was carried on in small, family groups, with minimal capital requirements, now the advent of mechanical power, complicated machinery, and extensive factory buildings called for large amounts of capital and, to an increasing extent, for more competent managerial personnel.

The industrial revolution developed principally in England but moved, within a relatively short time, to America where it had a profound impact on the industrial development of the country. Prior to this time, business had been conducted to a large extent on a local basis, with most firms being of relatively small size. Furthermore, the philosophy of laissez faire was predominant here, as it was abroad. The industrial revolution brought about a gradual increase in the size and scope of manufacturing establishments that was accelerated by the demands for war matériel generated by the Civil War. After the war, with the progressive opening up of the western parts of the country to a growing population, with a consequent broadening of markets and of business activity, large companies began to appear and the dominance of the corporation began to emerge. Along with this trend there came a gradual weakening of the laissez faire idea, brought about by the competitive practices of some of the large concerns, which were believed to be inimical to the best interests of the country. This development was the source of many of the business environmental factors of the present time.

THE MULTIFACETED ENVIRONMENT OF BUSINESS

There can be little doubt but that business is the dominant institution in our capitalistic economic system. Among the critics of business are many who believe that business holds the power to manipulate the country in any way that it sees fit. Consider the awesome resources of the top firms in this country, the vital statistics of a few of which appear on page 23. If by some weird selective catastrophe the 150 largest companies were to disappear, the effect upon the country would be absolutely devastating. Imagine having no railroads, no gasoline or oil, no trucks to transport food, and no automobiles. Try to visualize a situation where there would be neither lights, power, nor telephone communication, especially in the largest concentrations of population. The food processing industry would stop, the distribution of goods would be hindered, and a national credit debacle would occur.

But none of these great enterprises has the power to bring about such a disaster, even if its managers should wish to do so. Power in this country is distributed among other groups, such as government agencies, labor unions, farm blocs, civil rights groups, antipollution advocates, and individual citizens—all of whom are cognizant of their rights to oppose and restrain the power of the giant corporations. Business managers are acutely aware of this countervailing power which they take into consideration in their decision-making activities. So, while the dynamism of business and its contribution to our national standard of living cannot be denied, it should be apparent that its power is not absolute but, rather, is curbed and balanced along with the other vital constituents of the country.

Basic to an understanding of business is a recognition of its integral relationships with the following facets of its environment: (1) public opinion, (2) governmental action, (3) influence of labor, (4) business cycles, (5) big and little business, (6) foreign competition, (7) social problems, (8) pollution, and (9) growth of consumer credit.

PUBLIC OPINION

In a democracy the influence of public opinion makes itself felt in many ways, among which are letters to the editors of newspapers and periodicals; editorials that reflect the impact of these letters on the editors and publishers of a free press; the writings of observers and commentators on public affairs; demands upon government made by interest groups for action to protect them from some actual or imagined dangers; the election or defeat of candidates for political office on the basis of the positions that they have taken regarding current issues of public interest; and, occasionally, through more or less spontaneous uprisings of members of the public in support of or against certain issues that affect them.

All of these methods have been employed at one time or another as a means of bringing the power of public opinion to bear on the actions and policies of the business community. In many, if not most instances, public opinion has been instrumental in bringing about changes in business practices of which the public disapproved.

There is a strong reason to believe that there exists a rather broad misconception of the role of profits in our economy, coupled with a suspicion that while profits are possibly necessary, they are too high for the public good in some instances. The belief persists that many business firms, particularly the larger ones, could reduce their prices substantially without endangering their continued existence. The statements of dollar profit volume before taxes, which are issued periodically by many large companies, publicize amounts that are frequently beyond the comprehension of many people and serve to confirm the suspicion that profits are too large. It would doubtless be helpful, from the standpoint of a better understanding of profits, for the public to realize that the net earnings of many companies are used by them for reinvestment, which provides for additional productive capacity and jobs. Also, that many corporations use their earnings (profits) to make dividend payments to their stockholders, who frequently number in the thousands.

It is quite probable that large segments of the general public, particularly those who do not own or manage business enterprises, are quite ignorant of the economics of business operation, know little about accounting and finance, and hence are unable to understand the relationships between capital investment and the need for an adequate return to investors. Many educators and businessmen are aware of this situation and have been trying to do something about correcting it, but with little apparent success. Doubtless the disparity between the income of the average citizen and those of business executives, which are published from time to time, tends to accentuate this attitude.

The Consumer as Final Arbiter

Another important aspect of public opinion is the summation of the actions of individual consumers in accepting or rejecting products and services that business offers to them. Without legislation or regulatory bodies, consumers show their approval or disapproval of goods and services by the simple process of buying or not buying them. This is one of the most potent methods of making certain that the products and the services provided by business are those which are needed and desired by the public. Although the determination by producers of the acceptability of their products prior to their being offered for sale presents a most difficult problem, the decision of the public will come, quickly and definitely, once the products are available for purchase. While there is no complete agreement on the exact percentages involved, it has been frequently said that 8 out of every 10 new products that appear on the market fail to win public approval and are relegated to the scrap heap. This aspect of the business environment is one of which all makers and sellers of goods and services are constantly aware.

The Corporate Image

A factor in the environment of both large and small business, but particularly in the case of the former, is what has come to be known as the *corporate image concept*. This refers to the impression of a corporation that is held by the public, which may be either good or bad. A firm may be regarded as beneficent, ruthless, public spirited, progressive, conservative, reliable, or any one of a number of favorable or unfavorable characterizations. No small part of the activities of public relations firms consists of endeavoring to create and preserve favorable corporate images for their clients. The image that the public has of small businesses is important, but somewhat less so than with big business, possibly because of the personal contacts that small businessmen have with their customers.

GOVERNMENTAL ACTION

When the people of this country believe that something should be done which they are unable to do for themselves, they usually turn to some branch of government to secure the desired action. At the federal level nearly all types of business that engage in interstate commerce have been affected by government action to some extent, frequently through some form of regulation. In many instances the pattern has been for the Congress to pass certain laws designed to regulate some field of business or phase of business activity, and then to establish federal agencies to administer these laws. For example, the Interstate Commerce Commission was established in 1887 to regulate the railroads under the Interstate Commerce Act. The Federal Trade Commission was authorized in 1914 and established in 1915 to administer the Federal Trade Commission Act and the Clayton Act. In the same manner, the Federal Communications Commission, the Federal Power Commission, the Food and Drug Administration, and many others were created by Congress to handle problems in their respective fields.

An interesting aspect of this form of governmental action is that the decisions reached by these agencies, in dealing with matters which properly come within their authority, have the force of law and are, in fact, commonly referred to as *administrative law*. Thus, it becomes clear that a part of the environment of business consists of edicts of administrative agencies issued under the authority of laws passed by the Congress. These rulings may be just as important as the original law and may require an equal degree of compliance. Many of these administrative agencies will be discussed in some detail in certain chapters that follow.

Another contact that government has with business is the administration of the Sherman Antitrust Act of 1890 by the Department of Justice. Also, the area of taxation at all governmental levels is a significant factor in this phase of the business environment. The monetary and fiscal policies of the federal government, bearing on such matters as interest rates, foreign aid, and the federal budget, affect business in many different ways. The trend toward governmental ownership and operation of power generating and transmission facilities is one of concern to private business in this area, as well as to the users of electric power.

The powers of the federal government to levy and adjust the duties on goods from other countries has a profound effect upon the impact of foreign competition on domestic manufacturers. The farm price-support program, whereby the prices of certain agricultural products have been supported at levels above those which would be obtained in a free market, affects those whose business requires them to deal with these commodities.

Since the days of the so-called New Deal of the early 1930's, there has been a growing belief in government circles that the maintenance of a prosperous economy and of high-level employment is the concern and, to a considerable extent, the responsibility of the federal government. Successive administrations and Congresses have followed this concept with increasing intensity. The underlying philosophy of government action in this area has been that of endeavoring to provide a favorable governmental and economic climate, rather than to undertake the actual manipulation of the business system itself.

The civil rights legislation has had a dual impact on business firms. They are required to avoid discrimination, on a racial basis, in the hiring and promoting of employees. It is probable that most companies have complied with this requirement. However, a new element has entered the scene which has the potential of causing serious trouble. Militant black unionists are claiming that both the employers and the unions are guilty of discrimination and have threatened reprisals unless they are given a greater voice in union affairs and in dealing with their employers.

The federal Consumer Credit Protection Act, also known as The Truth-in-Lending Act, became effective on July 1, 1969. This act requires that all creditors must disclose certain basic information so that the consumer will know what credit and/or late payment charges cost.

INFLUENCE OF LABOR

With the passage of the National Labor Relations Act of 1935, organized labor, which had hitherto played a somewhat minor role in the business environment, grew in size and importance. Employers were required to bargain with the unions that represented their employees, and such vast industrial areas as the steel and automobile fields were thoroughly unionized. Union membership rose rapidly from a low of around 3 million members in 1934 to approximately 19 million in 1968. The New Deal of the 1930's and the so-called Fair Deal of the immediate post-World War II period encouraged the growth of organized labor's economic and political power, with the result that the traditional freedom of action and decision in the area of labor relations, which businessmen had long enjoyed, was greatly curtailed, and the owners and managers of business firms discovered in the new-found strength of labor a formidable opponent in bargaining and in politics.

The exemption of labor from the antitrust laws, under the Clayton Act of 1914, has given the unions an advantage in their dealings with business that many businessmen regard as unfair but about which they have been able to do nothing to date. Some of the more liberal labor leaders have suggested that the profits of certain companies are too large and have called into question the methods by which their costs are allocated and their prices computed. A small group of labor leaders have even suggested that labor should have a voice in the management of business enterprises. The growth in the influence of labor is a significant item in the environment of business.

BUSINESS CYCLES

The history of business activity in this country has been one of alternate prosperity and depression. This movement has been termed the *business cycle*. During periods of prosperity, the volume of production, employment, profits, and prices rise. In times of depression, they decrease. For many years the belief prevailed in business and governmental circles that these cyclical movements were inevitable and there was little that anyone could do about them. When the downward movement of the business cycle was slight and of short duration, the term *recession* was applied. After each depression (or recession) the recovery usually reached a higher level than in the past.

The depression of the 1930's, which was one of great severity and which followed the post-World War I era of prosperity, brought a change in the thinking of governmental officials and many businessmen. Instead of merely waiting for the downward trend of the cycle to run its course, attempts were made through a number of legislative enactments to induce a recovery. As noted in Chapter 1, whether or not these had any effect on the depression is uncertain, as the approach of World War II brought with it a substantial measure of recovery and the entrance of this country into the conflict late in 1941 raised the level of production to a new high and dispelled all thoughts of depression for several years.

In 1949, 1953-54, 1957-58, and 1960-61, recessions of relatively brief duration occurred, each followed by a recovery period. One notable aspect of these times, however, was that unemployment, which had historically increased during depressions and decreased during prosperity, failed to improve during the recovery periods of these years but, in the opinion of many officials in the government, remained abnormally high. This situation led to a widespread discussion of the emerging effect of business cycles on employment and of the part that government might be able to play in decreasing unemployment.

BIG AND LITTLE BUSINESS

The presence of very large firms with huge resources, well-trained managerial and operative personnel, and extensive research facilities has brought about an intensification of competition that has been apparent at all levels of business. Small firms in many lines of business must follow the lead of the large firms in order to compete successfully, a factor in the environmental picture that has been emphasized by the relatively high rate of failures among small companies.

For big business, the problem of competing with alert small firms is always present, but the pressure involved is much less than it is for small companies. However, there is an aspect of this situation that many large firms, particularly in retailing, have had to meet and learn to live with. This concerns certain types of legislation, passed at the behest of small businesses, that have been designed to equalize the competitive advantages that the large firms would otherwise enjoy. Examples include laws to prevent price cutting by retailers, to prevent price discrimination by sellers, and to establish price floors for certain commodities; and chain-store tax laws. Whether or not these laws are in the best interest of the public is an open question. The legislative bodies involved apparently thought so at the time that they were enacted. Thus the environment of big business is affected by the presence of a large number of small firms.

Numerous projects, either government sponsored or under private auspices, utilize the facilities of both large and small companies. For example, in the fabricating of Telstar, our first communications satellite, 1,249 companies participated either as subcontractors or suppliers under the leadership of the American Telephone and Telegraph Company.

For big business, competition is rugged; for small business, it has become a life-or-death matter. In an attempt to help the small businessman meet the rigors of competition, the Small Business Administration was established by Congress in 1953. Many of the laws mentioned earlier were adopted to relieve the pressure of competition on small businesses. In some instances, a few large firms have sought relief from the severity of competition through collusion with their competitors, mainly in the area of prices. This is illegal and has resulted in fines for the companies and, in one case, imprisonment of the officials involved.

There is an area, however, in which small businessmen have been able to achieve a remarkable measure of success. This is called *franchising*, a procedure by which companies with well-known names grant franchises or licenses to small businessmen with some capital to invest, which permits the latter group not only to be in business for themselves but also to benefit from the reputations, guidance, and know-how of the franchising companies. Actually franchising is quite an old practice, for automobile and tire manufacturers have franchised their dealers for many years. The great growth of franchising, however, dates from shortly after the end of World War II when many servicemen wanted to go into business for themselves and found this method a most attractive one. The important features for success in this field are (a) adequate capital, which may range from a few thousand dollars upward to $500,000 (the latter figure is normally required in the motel business); (b) favorable sites; (c) strict adherence to sound business practices; (d) a willingness to work long hours; and (e) practical and helpful direction from the franchisers.

Among the types of business where franchising is prevalent are restaurants, grocery stores (e.g., IGA), gas stations, soft drink bottlers, car washes, carpet-cleaning services, beauty salons, coin operated laundries, dry cleaning establishments, income tax services, and automobile parts and accessories. Some of the well-known franchisers are Avis, Hertz, McDonald's, Midas Mufflers, Coca Cola, Rayco, Burger King, the Ben Franklin Variety Stores, Howard Johnson's, Holiday Inns, and Ramada Inns. At present there are around 600,000 franchised outlets in the United States, with more being added each year. The International Franchise Association has been organized to establish and maintain a strict code of ethics for the industry.

FOREIGN COMPETITION

A sizable volume of foreign trade, both in exports and imports, has long been regarded as a favorable item in the nation's business complex.

Certain products of foreign lands have always found a market in this country, some encountering competition from domestic producers and others catering to a demand not being adequately supplied here. An example of the latter is the Volkswagen, which has had a phenomenal sale, in a size class that our car manufacturers had previously generally ignored. English bone china dinnerware, French perfumes, and Swedish glassware fall into the same category. When producers in this country have been affected by foreign competition, in some instances tariff walls have been erected to equalize the competition between our manufacturers and those in other countries with lower costs.

The Marshall Plan of 1948 was designed to help the war-ravaged countries of Europe to reestablish their economies. Under its operation, these nations were given modern tools and instruction in how to use them. The consequence of this action over the years has been to create strong competitors in Europe, who are capable of delivering goods in this country, even allowing for tariffs, at prices equal to, and in many cases below, those of our own manufacturers. The range of goods involved has been broadened with the result that a considerable number of American producers have been forced to add foreign competition to an already tough domestic competitive situation. With the possible extension, both in numbers and power, of the European Common Market, this competition could become even more rigorous, although attempts are being made by the Administration in Washington to reach agreements with the Common Market countries that will counterbalance this to some extent through a growth in our exports. From 1964 to 1967, under the auspices of the General Agreement on Tariffs and Trade (GATT),[1] the Kennedy Round of tariff negotiation was conducted covering a wide range of commodities. The average reduction of tariff duties was on the order of 35 percent.

SOCIAL PROBLEMS

Under the philosophy of laissez faire, the assumption was implicit that the well-being of individuals was achieved through their own efforts and accomplishments and that the status of each person was more or less a reflection of his energy and ability. Over the years from the start of the industrial revolution until the depression of the 1930's, there had been a gradual shift in public opinion away from this reliance on the individual toward the belief that there are some circumstances where action by government would bring about more certain relief from troublesome situations.

[1] Further reference to GATT will be found on page 292, Chapter 12.

The 1930's, with the crushing weight of high unemployment and failure of many businesses, appear to have accelerated this trend and to have brought about a fairly widespread belief that it was the function of government to assume responsibility for the welfare of its citizens and to take such steps as seemed necessary to implement this obligation. Such items as aid to the unemployed, social security, racial desegregation, aid to education, public housing, slum clearance, urban renewal, and many other projects came into being under the philosophy of this new belief.

To an increasing extent businessmen have become involved in bringing about the concept of responsibility in the solution of many of these social problems. Furthermore, numerous students, mainly at the college level, have spoken out for the implementation of such remedial action on the social problems of the country as seems desirable to them at this time. Among other things, they have pressed business to take active steps in correcting these problems. This has created a deep concern among businessmen, particularly corporation executives whose prominence as leaders in their fields has placed them in a singularly vulnerable position with regard to the development of methods to aid in solving these problems. A factor that may be an indication of a growing tolerance, if not complete approval, of this development is found in the increasing number of prominent business executives who have accepted important posts in the federal government, many of cabinet rank. Further reference to this emerging involvement will be found in Chapter 3.

POLLUTION

An environmental factor, which has been present for some time but which has only recently attracted public attention, is the matter of pollution of the air, water, and land in this country as well as in other parts of the world. From the evidence presently at hand, no small part of this situation can be laid at the door of business, both directly and indirectly. The discharge of industrial waste into the rivers and lakes of this country has polluted its waters, thus destroying not only fish but also other organic matter and elements which would normally serve to purify water over time. Cities, however, have also added to water pollution through the discharge of raw or partially treated garbage and sewage into rivers and lakes. Air pollution is brought about by the emission of smoke from industrial stacks and of carbon monoxide from motor vehicles. Many fertile farm lands have been destroyed as a result of the development of interstate and other highways. The indiscriminate use of pesticides has resulted in the transmission of dangerous drug compounds both to humans and animals. While many people have for some time been more or less dimly aware of these ecological problems, it has been only in the last few years that the realities of the situation have become painfully evident.

A great deal of thought and effort is now being given in attempting to curb pollution, and a large part of this will result in action—voluntary or otherwise—by the business community. An outstanding example is the endeavor on the part of automobile manufacturers to engineer their motors so as to diminish, if not entirely eliminate, carbon monoxide from the exhausts of their cars. The federal government, under the provisions of the Water Quality Act of 1965 and the Clean Water Restoration Act of 1966, is establishing water-quality standards and making plans for their adoption on a nationwide scale. Other measures for controlling, if not eliminating, the causes of pollution are under consideration by all levels of government. It may be expected that those industries whose manufacturing processes bring about the emission of noxious fumes and organic wastes will be under great pressure to modify their procedures so as to eliminate these pollutants. And although industry is by no means the source of all pollutants, it may expect increasing pressures from government and public opinion to lead the way in solving this problem since it possesses the research facilities and the techniques for the development of pollution controls.

The cost of reducing air, land, and water pollution has been estimated to run from $10 to $20 billion annually.[2] Most likely, however, any expenditures will eventually be shared between government, i.e., the taxpayers, and industry—in what proportion, it is still unknown. But it seems certain that both higher prices and higher taxes will be required to pay for the necessary cleanup.

GROWTH OF CONSUMER CREDIT

The practice of paying bills for goods and services some time after the goods are received or the services rendered has been a standard business procedure for many years. In an effort to accelerate the payment process in transactions between business firms, discounts for prompt payment are quite commonly granted. Consumers have usually been given similar time concessions for paying their bills, but without the advantage of discounts.

Within the past few years a new element has entered the consumer credit field in the form of *credit cards*, which are credit instruments issued by a wide variety of sellers of goods and services. One of the pioneers in

[2] *The Cincinnati Enquirer*, August 16, 1970.

this movement was the American Express Company, which was soon joined by the Diners Club and Carte Blanche, now owned by the Avco Corporation. Today practically all department and specialty stores either use the charge-a-plate system or issue their own credit cards. The major producers of gasoline and oil for automobiles have long provided credit cards for their customers, which cover accessories and, in many cases, motel accommodations as well. Many airlines offer travel-now-pay-later plans, and not too long ago even the banks joined the credit-card movement with the issuance of two bank credit cards: BankAmericard and Master Charge. The banks associated with the use of each of these cards collect from card-holding consumers and remit to the sellers less a commission.

One of the major results of the credit card movement has been a notable increase in the amount of consumer credit, both granted and outstanding. Another has been a sizeable increase in the cash reserves required of the sellers involved in order to pay their own bills and meet their payrolls. With more and more consumers taking advantage of the credit card privilege, many sellers have found the adoption of data processing equipment a necessity in order to cope with the volume of paper work that this credit system entails.

One other aspect of the growth of consumer credit is the increase in installment credit, with or without the use of credit cards, which recently was placed at $104 billion, a level twice that of mid-1962.

CHANGE AS AN ENVIRONMENTAL INGREDIENT

The element of change is inescapable, and it is most unwise for any businessman to ignore it. The pervasive nature of change affecting so many aspects of the business scene has suggested the observation that the only permanent element in the environment of business is change. Of particular importance are the changes related to the following factors: (1) automation, (2) science, (3) electronic data processing, (4) simulation and models, (5) the shift in emphasis from production to distribution, (6) defense contracts and space technology, (7) population growth and suburbanization, (8) the shift from an industrial to a service economy, and (9) consumerism.

AUTOMATION

Since the beginning of the industrial revolution, there has been a continuous search by entrepreneurs, both individual and corporate, for ways in which to cut costs and thereby to achieve either competitive price advantages or larger profits. This has brought about the progressive substitution of machines for human labor, permitting a greater measure of production with the same labor force, or maintaining the same productive output with fewer workers. The past twenty or more years has witnessed a notable acceleration of these efforts, and the term *automation* has come to be applied to it. This phenomenon has made itself felt in the environment of business in a number of ways. Competition among companies that have been able to automate and those that have not has become more severe. The accelerated obsolescence of machinery has presented many firms with serious financial problems since they have been compelled to replace their present machinery with the newer tools of automation. The personnel aspects of the automation problem have been singularly difficult. The introduction of automated machinery has frequently brought about the abolition of the jobs of many skilled and semi-skilled workers for whom the problem of finding new jobs has been quite difficult. In unionized industries the resistance of the labor leaders to the dismissal of their members has placed additional burdens on the managements of the companies involved whose competitive survival hinged on their ability to achieve the cost savings that automation offered. At the same time there appeared, in many instances, a shortage of the highly skilled workers whose abilities were required to set up, adjust, and repair the new machines.

SCIENCE

In the past two decades, there has been a remarkable advance in the area of science, particularly in the productive techniques of business. Stimulated both by the uncertainties of the international situation, such as the so-called cold war, and the growing competition from those nations that were more or less devastated by World War II, research in the physical and technological sciences has been extended under both governmental and private auspices.

Items of consequence involve the discovery and growth of atomic fission as a source of power; the development of artificial substances called plastics; new techniques in manufacture, such as the use of oxygen in the production of steel; and the promise of greater advances in metallurgy and allied fields resulting from the space program.

The environmental aspects of this advance in science are that manufacturers are and will be in ever greater danger of some scientific breakthrough that may place upon them the burden of scrapping some of their current productive equipment in order to remain competitive, or of falling behind if they are financially unable to keep abreast of competition. New products will doubtless arise, which will render obsolete some well-established ones. Progress in the fields of electronics and miniaturization will offer attractive opportunities for alert manufacturers. From the standpoint of personnel, technically trained manpower is in ever-increasing demand; and at the executive and managerial levels, the problems to be met will require administrative abilities of a high order.

Many economists believe that *innovation*, in the form of new processes, products, machinery, or techniques, is essential to the continued growth of our national economy. It brings about an increase in production, employment, and income, all of which serve to spur the economy to greater heights of activity. While some decline in volume of business may follow eventually, it is believed that this decline will be of less intensity than the expansion and that further innovation will result in an ever-higher rate of production.

A further development in this area is the result of inquiry into the contributions that the *behavioral sciences* might be able to make to business. Leaders in the fields of economics, sociology, psychology, and cultural anthropology have joined with forward-looking executives in exploring the areas of business in which the principles of their professions might be helpful.

ELECTRONIC DATA PROCESSING

With the development of electronic data processing equipment, called computers, great stress is being placed on the assembling and analysis of the quantitative aspects of business operations. While close attention has long been paid to this area of business information, the tremendous increase in the amount of quantitative data that can be assimilated by these machines, plus the speed with which they operate, has provided management with noteworthy assistance in decision making.

Computers have come into constructive usage in an ever-increasing number of business areas. Users of computers have found the following advantages in their installation: saving of clerical labor costs, saving of time in preparing reports, greater accuracy, and the development of new information. Computers had, at first, been utilized to perform routine recording operations, such as billing, preparing payrolls, cost compilations, and maintaining inventory data. More advanced applications are the costing and scheduling of complex technical projects; the revealing of the fastest and most economical routes for incoming and outgoing goods; the

analysis of the effectiveness with which salesmen are covering their territories; the scheduling of machines in a factory so as to achieve the optimum production; a recording and analysis of sales; the most advantageous
location for branch plants and sales offices, considering the sources of raw
materials, transportation costs, and customer locations; and the practically
instant retrieval of reports previously stored in the so-called memory
of the computer. The attempt has even been made, but without too great
a measure of success, to use computers to discover the best advertising
media for certain products.

SIMULATION AND MODELS

A comparatively new development, and one that has been made possible by the introduction of computers, is the use of *simulation* or *business
games* and the development of *models* or mathematical equations designed
to represent desired business situations. These devices have been used in
management training courses in which the participants are given certain
data concerning the company and are asked to make decisions regarding
future actions. These decisions are then referred to the computer, which
has been previously programmed as to the consequences of these various
moves, and the trainees can then determine whether their choices are wise
or not.

THE SHIFT IN EMPHASIS FROM PRODUCTION TO DISTRIBUTION

The advances in productive techniques, partly the result of the
advance in science, has made it possible to produce more goods than can
be sold profitably. While it is recognized that substantial segments of our
people have substandard incomes and that the rate of unemployment is
doubtless too high, there is probably sufficient idle productive capacity to
take care of the needs and wants of these unfortunates were their incomes
to rise to an acceptable level. This situation points up one of the emerging
aspects of the business environment—the shift in emphasis from production to distribution. Ways must be found, within the attainable limits of
average incomes, to dispose profitably of the goods that our productive
capacity is capable of producing.

DEFENSE CONTRACTS AND SPACE TECHNOLOGY

One of the key items in the changing environment of business is the
presence of an increasing volume of contracts for research, development,

and manufacture of defense hardware, awarded by the federal government. During the different wars in which this country has participated, the weapons required for their prosecution have been furnished, in the main, by private business. At the conclusion of these conflicts, until the end of World War II, it was customary for the companies concerned to return to the manufacture of their former lines of peacetime products. Since 1945, however, with the onset of the cold war, the development of nuclear energy for weaponry and propulsion, and the growth of interest in the exploration of space, an ever-increasing number of federal defense and space research, development, and production contracts were awarded to qualified business concerns. In many instances, very large companies are devoting all or most of their productive facilities to the handling of these contracts, which amount to many billions of dollars annually. In 1968 the country's expenditures for defense were on the order of $80 billion or between 8 and 9 percent of the gross national product.[3] With the winding down of the Vietnam conflict, it would appear that the volume of federal defense contracts will drop rather substantially in the years ahead.

POPULATION GROWTH AND SUBURBANIZATION

The years immediately following World War II witnessed a marked upturn in the birthrate in this country, which reached its peak in 1957. Since that time there has been a steady decline with demographers wondering if the present trend will continue or whether it will reverse itself again as it has done from time to time in the past. Regardless of the direction of the birthrate in the future, the growth in population has resulted in a sizable increase in the demand for goods and services of all kinds, as well as the ever-growing necessity of creating jobs for those who reach working age. Now, with the birthrate falling, the shift in the types of goods and services required will reflect the decreasing demand for the classifications of goods needed by children, and this will move in a sort of ebbing tide as the years pass and the young people grow up.

The so-called population explosion of the post-World War II years is apparently slowing down, but the overall effect of the population increase will mean that there will be somewhere between 225 and 237 million people in this country by 1980, according to the estimates of the Census Bureau of the United States. And with the continued growth in personal income, indicated in the chart on page 47, it appears that business will benefit through the combination of these two factors.

[3] An explanation of the gross national product will be found on page 633, **Chapter 26.**

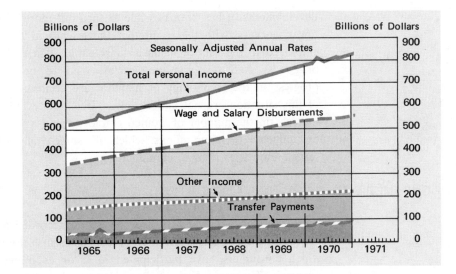

Figure 2-1

Sources of Personal Income

Source: *Economic Indicators*, February, 1971. Prepared for the Joint Economic Committee by the Council of Economic Advisers.

There has also been a marked migration of families from the cities to the suburbs. This trend has affected the construction industry, both in the building of homes and in the requisite facilities, such as shopping centers, service stations, medical buildings, schools, and hospitals. Those industries which manufacture the articles that go into the furnishing and equipping of these structures have shared in the increase of business in their areas. Many firms have moved their offices from the cities to the suburbs in order to be nearer to where their employees live and, in cases of expansion, to provide greater parking facilities for them and for the firms' customers. There has been a noteworthy growth of industrial parks in the suburban areas, apart from the residential sections, that has markedly affected many of the operational phases of industries.

THE SHIFT FROM AN INDUSTRIAL TO A SERVICE ECONOMY

Historically the economy of the United States has been regarded as devoted principally to the production of goods rather than of services. This concept has been based on the impact of the industrial revolution on the manufacture of and demand for goods of all kinds. It has also been affected by the historic preponderance of employment in industry as contrasted to the workers in the services. Dating from around 1953, and brought about by the growth of automation and other technological developments, it has been possible to turn out more and more goods with fewer workers, with the result that the growth in the number of people employed in the service fields is more rapid than that in the production of goods. And this condition is expected to become accentuated as progress in the technology of manufacture continues. The consequences of this situation are not entirely clear, but among them appear to be an increase in the number of women employed and a possible weakening of the influence of labor unions, which are somewhat less important in the service industries than in manufacturing.

CONSUMERISM

A phenomenon which has recently been accorded a growing measure of publicity has been referred to as *consumerism*, although the extent to which consumers have participated in it or even been aware of it is uncertain. Perhaps a better term to describe it is the *consumer protection movement*, as its basic motive seems to be that of safeguarding consumers from inferior or dangerous products. There have been two phases of this movement. One which has received the greater measure of publicity has been the activity of a private citizen, along with a group of associates, who has undertaken with considerable success to direct Congressional and public attention to the need for safety devices on automobiles, among other things. The other aspect of this phenomenon has been the appointment by the President of the United States of a Consumer Representative as a part of the executive branch of the government.

The main source of trouble appears to be a belief, possibly quite widespread, that many consumer products are poorly constructed, do not give satisfactory service, and are overpriced. Where repair service is required, the servicemen are poorly trained, their work is apt to be shoddy, and their charges are exorbitant. There is also a pervasive belief that manufacturers of consumer goods exert little, if any, effort to discover the needs and wants of consumers; instead they produce what they think consumers will accept, and they employ sales and advertising gimmicks to convince consumers to purchase their offerings.

Consumers generally are more or less inarticulate, and their complaints rarely gain much public attention. However, the message appears to have reached the ears of the Administration and members of Congress, resulting in the introduction of a large number of bills several of which have become law, such as the Fair Packaging and Labeling Act and the Child Protection and Toy Safety Act. Others will doubtless be enacted in the months and years to come.

There are four areas upon which consumerism bears: (a) safety and the recall of defective goods; (b) the development of some procedure for the handling of consumer grievances; (c) the improvement and standardization of product warranties; and (d) the provision of more information to consumers concerning the goods that they are asked to buy and how well these will perform in their possession and use. Only time will reveal the extent to which these areas are implemented by the producers and how successful their efforts will be in bringing safer and more satisfactory products to the consumer market. However, consumerism has provided the Administration and the members of Congress with an apparently potent political issue which may be expected to persist over time and which will doubtless bring about a general improvement in consumer products and possibly a greater degree of confidence in business in the minds of consumers.

ENVIRONMENTAL TRENDS FOR THE SEVENTH DECADE

The onset of the seventh decade of the twentieth century has raised a certain measure of speculation concerning some of the possible environmental changes that may affect business during the ten years that it will encompass. There are certain currently discernible factors that suggest some of the developments that might take place in the area of business environment. A few of these factors are presented here for the purpose of stimulating student thinking about their possible impact on the business community in this country. The sequence in which these are listed does not necessarily indicate their relative importance: (1) intensified consumerism, (2) expanded demand for goods and services, (3) increased foreign competition, (4) moderated profit motive, (5) modified attitude towards labor unions, and (6) increased pressure from minority groups.

INTENSIFIED CONSUMERISM

The growth of consumerism in the 1970's would appear to depend on several factors which are presently apparent. Among these are: (a) the extent to which the basic opinions and desires of consumers can be discovered, both through research by producers and by the success or failure of goods they offer for sale; (b) the development of greater numbers of trained and reliable appliance and automobile repair personnel, coupled with the production of more durable consumer goods; and (c) the degree of sustained interest in consumer protection that develops in Congress.

EXPANDED DEMAND FOR GOODS AND SERVICES

The combination of a substantial population growth with the growing affluence of many segments of our society should bring about expanded markets for goods and services. As this personal prosperity extends further down the social scale, it may be expected that the already expanding market for goods will continue to grow. The trend toward a greater degree of individualistic preferences should also bring about an increasing measure of product differentiation.

INCREASED FOREIGN COMPETITION

A notable feature of the economic scene in Europe is the enhanced growth of productive techniques and capacity. This may serve to intensify competition not only against American goods sold in European markets but also for European products sold in this country. The rising spirit of economic nationalism throughout the world may also unfavorably affect American producers who seek world markets for their goods.

MODERATED PROFIT MOTIVE

Already some slight evidence exists that the dominant role of profit, so vital an aspect of capitalism, may be weakening in favor of a greater degree of social consciousness on the part of business. As will be pointed out in Chapter 3, a number of prominent businessmen have begun to engage in activities designed to help alleviate some of the more pressing social problems in this country and have committed some of their company resources to the achievement of these objectives. In many instances this has involved the expenditure of company funds that might otherwise have contributed to the firm's profits. There is reason to expect that this phenomenon will not only continue but also heighten over time.

MODIFIED ATTITUDE TOWARD LABOR UNIONS

As the population grows, so will the labor force, and with it a probable expansion of union membership. Also, the average age of union members will doubtless become lower, following a trend already evident. This should produce a greater militancy with increased pressure for higher wage settlements and thus affect the attitude of government towards labor organizations. Whether this may provoke more or less stringent labor laws will depend upon the attitude of legislators toward union actions.

INCREASED PRESSURE FROM MINORITY GROUPS

The latter years of the 1960's have witnessed a growing pressure among minority groups for a greater and more rewarding measure of participation in the economic and social life of the nation. Business has been called upon to provide more and better job opportunities. It may be expected that both the demands of minority groups and the response by business will continue to expand in the years ahead, hopefully with a minimum of friction.

BUSINESS TERMS

QUESTIONS FOR DISCUSSION AND ANALYSIS

1. Do you think that business exerts a greater degree of influence on its environment than the environment does on business? Explain.
2. Is success in business as highly regarded at the present as it was in the early years of this nation? Why or why not?
3. To what extent do you believe that public opinion is actually effective in determining the policies of business?
4. Are consumers generally aware of the provisions of the federal Consumer Credit Protection Act? Explain.
5. Do you believe that labor unions should be exempted from the antitrust laws? Defend your position.
6. Do you think that the public is aware of the fact that many small business firms are part of a franchising operation?
7. Is it your opinion that big business should assume the burden of clearing up the pollution in this country? Why or why not?
8. Do you think that the expansion of the use of credit cards results in people buying more than they can afford? Explain.
9. Do you agree with the economists who believe that innovation is essential to the continued growth of our national economy? Why or why not?

10. Do you believe that consumers are really interested in consumerism or is this merely the result of the activities of a few zealots? Explain.

PROBLEMS AND SHORT CASES

1. With the emergence of the pollution problem in this country, opinions have been voiced by various sources to the effect that there should be a slowing down of the industrial growth of the country in order to permit government and industry to take steps in eliminating the sources of air, water, and land pollution and restoring those elements which have been harmed. Prepare a short paper setting forth your opinion regarding the desirability of such slowing down, how it could be done, and its effects on the economy of the country and on the labor force in particular. Consult the *Readers' Guide to Periodical Literature* and the *Business Periodical Index* in your school library as well as newspapers and magazines.

2. The service industries consist of all activities that do not produce something tangible, according to a recent definition. This source includes retailers, wholesalers, and government, along with the more commonly accepted service groups. The Bureau of the Census excludes the first three in its listing of Selected Services. Prepare a short paper defending either the inclusion of the controversial three categories or supporting the Census determination.

3. To become more thoroughly acquainted with consumerism, prepare an essay setting forth in some detail the activities of the consumer advocates and the resulting action taken by industry and government to implement their suggestions. Conclude your essay with a brief evaluation of the economic and social value of consumerism. Refer to the sources named in Problem 1 for information in this field.

SUGGESTED READINGS

Bearden, James, ed. *The Environment of Business: Perspectives and Viewpoints.* New York: Holt, Rinehart and Winston, 1969. Part I.

Carson, Robert B., ed. *The American Economy in Conflict.* Lexington, Mass.: D. C. Heath and Company, 1971.

Davis, Keith, and Robert L. Blomstrom. *Business and Its Environment.* New York: McGraw-Hill Book Company, 1966.

Hailstones, Thomas J., Bernard L. Martin, and Frank W. Mastrianna. *Contemporary Economic Problems and Issues*, Second Edition. Cincinnati: South-Western Publishing Co., 1970.

Chapter 3

Ethics and Social Responsibilities

This chapter will discuss two important aspects of American business—namely, business ethics and the social responsibilities of the business community. *Business ethics* consists of those principles and practices that are concerned with morals and good conduct as they are applicable to business situations. For example, a customer chooses a model of a portable television set in a department store, charges it to his account, and later receives an unopened carton which is delivered to his home from the store's warehouse. The customer expects the carton to contain a set in perfect working order identical to the one he selected in the store, and the store expects him to pay what he owes when his account becomes due. This mutual trust which is so necessary for the operation of our economic system is based, in large part, on business ethics.

Referring to the transaction above, in the event that later experience with the set indicates that it is one of the few from which harmful rays emanate, the manufacturer should recall it and all others which exhibit the same characteristic and replace them with sets in which the injurious factor has been removed. This should be done even though many of the users may have been unaware of the presence of this factor prior to the producer's recall of the sets. Thus the concept of social responsibilities on the part of business implies that there is something more to be expected of a firm than the obtaining of a profitable return to the owners, which has been the rationale of laissez faire capitalism.

BUSINESS ETHICS

Throughout recorded history the concept of business ethics has meant different standards of conduct to different people at different times. As an example, the ownership and use of slaves was rarely considered a moral issue in this country until a few years before the Civil War. Even today there is no common denominator that applies to business throughout the world. In this country we have a heritage from the religious traditions of Western Europe, based on the Bible. The Ten Commandments and the Golden Rule established standards of conduct for business as well as personal behavior.

Prior to the onset of the Industrial Revolution, business had been largely dominated for several centuries by rulers of kingdoms, city states, and countries. Business ethics was largely subordinated to the needs and decrees of kings who ruled by so-called divine right. Piracy on the high seas, slave trading, and oppression of colonies were commonplace. *Mercantilism,* an economic system consisting of government domination of business to the end that the wealth of the country would be increased, held full sway. The ethical ingredient of personal choice was largely missing.

There was much dissatisfaction with mercantilism, particularly in England in the eighteenth century, and a growing support for what was called natural law. This concept, which held that man had certain rights that could not be invalidated by laws, was written into the Constitution of the United States. The economic doctrines stemming from this concept were first expounded by Adam Smith when, in 1776, his famous book *The Wealth of Nations* was published. This work had a profound influence in England and, somewhat later, in the United States.

ETHICS IN THE NINETEENTH CENTURY

The latter part of the eighteenth century, when Adam Smith's treatise was gaining favor, saw the advent of the factory system, the invention of machinery, the application of mechanical power in industry, and, in brief, the beginnings of the Industrial Revolution. By the early 1800's it also brought forth a capitalistic economic system of the laissez-faire type. The new theory was that business and economic progress would be advanced more rapidly and effectively if each individual was free to pursue his profit-making activities without governmental restraint. What was good for the individual would, in the long run, prove to be best for the nation.

The acceptance of this doctrine, which placed responsibility for business decisions on individuals, might have produced business ethics on a high plane. Actually, in the United States, particularly after the Civil War, the inherited concept of a golden rule in business transactions was eagerly replaced by a belief that any action a businessman could take to increase his profits was moral because it would prove to be good for the public and for the country. The doctrine of caveat emptor held full sway and individuals who reaped huge profits, regardless of the methods used, were held in high esteem. The so-called robber barons were deeply religious on Sunday but during the week were ruthless competitors.

Toward the close of the nineteenth century a wave of public indignation against unethical practices in business gave rise to legislation that gradually had an effect on the whole moral tone of business. One of the offenders had been the railroads whose rate structure had harmed farmers and given favored business units exorbitant profits. In 1887 Congress passed the Interstate Commerce Commission Act to bring the railroads under government control. Another direction taken by business had been the creation of monopolies in certain areas of business. The Sherman Antitrust Act, passed in 1890, made combinations and conspiracies in restraint of trade illegal. These laws will be discussed in later chapters, but at this point it will suffice to note that laissez faire, with its resulting lack of acceptable business ethics, had not worked to the benefit of the public.

MODERN TRENDS IN BUSINESS ETHICS

It is probably fair to say that most businessmen today recognize that the maintenance of high ethical standards in their dealings with each other is also good for their firms. Considerable evidence supports the contention that "honesty is the best policy," which is, perhaps, another way of saying that good ethics makes for good business. A firm with a reputation for using questionable practices in its dealings is likely to find itself without customers and, in some instances, on the receiving end of a legal action.

Both industries and individual companies have taken positive steps to indicate their belief in and support of ethical practices. Many trade associations have adopted a *code of ethics* that is expected to serve as a guide to their members. (See Figure 3-1 on page 56 for the American Marketing Association Code of Ethics.) These codes are printed, and framed copies are frequently found hanging in the offices of the individuals or firms who comprise the association. A large number of business firms have drawn up codes that are binding on their employees. Some of these are stated in general terms, but others deal with specific problems, such as accepting bribes or expensive gifts and conniving with competitors.

The importance of business ethics received national recognition in 1961 when the Department of Commerce of the federal government organized

AMA Code of Ethics

As a member of the American Marketing Association, I recognize the significance of my professional conduct and my responsibilities to society and to the other members of my profession:

1. By acknowledging my accountability to society as a whole as well as to the organization for which I work.

2. By pledging my efforts to assure that all presentations of goods, services and concepts be made honestly and clearly.

3. By striving to improve marketing knowledge and practice in order to better serve society.

4. By supporting free consumer choice in circumstances that are legal and are consistent with generally accepted community standards.

5. By pledging to use the highest professional standards in my work and in competitive activity.

6. By acknowledging the right of the American Marketing Association, through established procedure, to withdraw my membership if I am found to be in violation of ethical standards of professional conduct.

Figure 3-1

AMA Code of Ethics

a Business Ethics Advisory Council consisting of a group of outstanding American businessmen, educators, clergymen, and journalists. This Council made its first report in 1962 in a publication titled *A Statement on Business Ethics and a Call for Action*. Following is an excerpt from this pamphlet:

Business enterprises, large and small, have relationships in many directions—with stockholders and other owners, employees, customers, suppliers, government, and the public in general. The traditional emphasis on freedom, competition, and progress in our economic system often brings the varying interests of these groups into conflict, so that many difficult and complex ethical problems can arise in any enterprise. While all relationships of an enterprise to these groups are regulated in some degree by law, compliance with law can only provide a minimum standard of conduct. Beyond legal obligations, the policies and actions of businessmen must be based upon a regard for the proper claims of all affected groups.

APPLICATION OF ETHICS TO BUSINESS DECISIONS

A basic concept in a capitalistic economic system is that the major function of the management of business units is to maximize profits for the benefit of the owners. As long as actions are legal and not immoral, any decision that might enhance the return on the investment would appear to be a proper course of action. At this point, however, a question can be raised that has ethical overtones. Is a business run for the benefit of its owners or should it be operated as well for the benefit of its employees, its customers, its suppliers, the government, and the public in general?

As an example, in recent years some firms have closed down inefficient plants and moved to new locations. This is legal and certainly not immoral. But what about the effect on the employees who live in the community and on the community itself? In some instances, ethical rather than profit motives have resulted in a decision to modernize the old plant rather than to move. Or, what should management do with an old and valued employee who has lost his executive ability but who still lacks a year of reaching retirement age? The profit motive would certainly dictate that he be fired.

In contemporary America the focus of ethical behavior in business can rest neither on the honesty or personal foibles of the people involved with business nor on the assumption that a firm has a being of its own. Ethical behavior must focus on the relationships among business firms, managers, employees, consumers, and society. Although a business firm has a high degree of independence in its operation, it must execute its affairs in such a way as not only to attain its objectives but also to further social values and serve the national purpose. It is frequently quite difficult to differentiate between the concepts of ethics and of social responsibility. Actions taken in the interest of ethics are often the end result of an awareness by businessmen of their social responsibilities in the communities where they live. Probably as widespread a definition of ethical behavior as any is that given by a number of executives in a research undertaken a few years ago which indicated that "what my feelings tell me is right" is the concept by which they endeavor to conduct their business operations.

The truth is that many management decisions are based on more than the data so painstakingly prepared by accountants, statisticians, budget officers, and others. This fact introduces an element in decision making that is not susceptible of measurement and that cannot be fed into a computer. It raises a question about the validity of the concept of maximizing profits when ethical considerations come into conflict with an otherwise profitable course of action. From the public viewpoint, it is comforting to discover that many business units have consciences which dictate that they try to make profits honestly and honorably.

THE SOCIAL RESPONSIBILITIES OF BUSINESS

While there is a growing belief that certain social responsibilities devolve upon business (the Business-Consumer Relations Code shown in Figure 3-2 on page 59 is a striking evidence of this development), no general agreement exists among those interested as to the specific nature and extent of such responsibilities. In the sections which follow, some of these obligations will be examined together with a presentation of the conflicting viewpoints on these topics.

THE TRADITIONAL VIEWPOINT

The position taken by many entrepreneurs of the 19th century was that their exclusive obligation was to make profits for themselves and their stockholders. This conviction was validated to a great extent by the economic theory of the time which taught that profit seeking was the only acceptable way of life for businessmen. The primary obligation of management was believed to be that of earning profits which could be distributed to the owners. This credo of managerial responsibility to the stockholders has, in many companies, carried over into the present. A corollary belief was that the seeking and securing of profits would automatically be beneficial to the country as a whole. If this point of view should prevail, business would feel no sense of responsibility for the welfare of society. The presumption is that the social needs of the country would be cared for through private philanthropy on the part of the dividend-receiving stockholders or through the agencies of government. And a substantial portion of the business community still holds this belief.

EARLY EVIDENCES OF CORPORATE SOCIAL RESPONSIBILITIES

As the country grew in population, a number of institutions emerged for which financial support from outside sources became necessary to their survival. Among these were colleges and universities, libraries, hospitals, and art museums. Wealthy owners of successful businesses felt the need to make large contributions to these various institutions. Amos Lawrence, in 1847, gave a grant of $50,000 to Harvard University. Andrew Carnegie established a number of libraries bearing his name.

Business-Consumer Relations Code

We reaffirm the responsibility of American business to:

1. Protect the health and safety of consumers in the design and manufacture of products and the provision of consumer services. This includes action against harmful side effects on the quality of life and the environment arising from technological progress.

2. Utilize advancing technology to produce goods that meet high standards of quality at the lowest reasonable price.

3. Seek out the informed views of consumers and other groups to help assure customer satisfaction from the earliest stages of product planning.

4. Simplify, clarify, and honor product warranties and guarantees.

Figure 3-2

5. Maximize the quality of product servicing and repairs and encourage their fair pricing.

6. Eliminate frauds and deceptions from the marketplace, setting as our goal not strict legality but honesty in all transactions.

7. Ensure that sales personnel are familiar with product capabilities and limitations and that they fully respond to consumer needs for such information.

8. Provide consumers with objective information about products, services, and the workings of the marketplace by utilizing appropriate channels of communication, including programs of consumer education.

9. Facilitate sound value comparisons across the widest possible range and choice of products.

10. Provide effective channels for receiving and acting on consumer complaints and suggestions, utilizing the resources of associations, chambers of commerce, better business bureaus, recognized consumer groups, individual companies, and other appropriate bodies.

Adopted by the Chamber of Commerce of the United States February 26, 1970

Leland Stanford created a university, also bearing his name, in California. John D. Rockefeller founded the University of Chicago in 1896 and later endowed the General Education Board with $53 million to help in the education of Southern Negroes. In 1914 Henry Ford created a sensation in the industrial world by raising his workers' wages from $2.34 a day to $5.00 a day; two years later he established the Henry Ford Trade School where boys were taught a trade. He also changed his hiring policies to encourage the employment of various types of disadvantaged persons as well as blacks and instituted a profit-sharing system for the benefit of his employees. It is perhaps notable that all these men either made these benefactions from their own funds or owned the companies whose profits provided them.

In 1951 the A. P. Smith Manufacturing Company gave $1,500 to Princeton University for such educational use as the school wished. Here was an instance of a corporation using its funds, legally the property of the stockholders, for a purpose not connected with its own business. Nevertheless, in 1953 the New Jersey court ruled that this action was not illegal, for prior to this case the revision of the Federal Revenue Act in 1935 had included a section which permitted corporations to deduct up to five percent of their net income for contributions made to eleemosynary institutions. Since then the contributions made by business corporations have grown to somewhere near the five percent limitation.

THE INCREASING INVOLVEMENT WITH SOCIAL NEEDS

The preceding section indicated some of the early activities of businesses and businessmen in the area of assuming social responsibilities. In this section more detailed attention is given to the involvement of business with social needs. Some of these needs have received the attention of business for a very long time and others have received attention only recently.

The Labor Factor

Traditional economic theory, as well as actual practice, regarded the elements of production—land, labor, and capital—as more or less impersonal factors to be manipulated in such a way as to bring about the largest measure of profit. However, business today is far from regarding labor impersonally as the result of grappling with questions such as these:

1. Should business be concerned with the well-being of its employees as well as their productivity?

2. Should business pay a wage level that would permit its employees to lead healthful and contented lives?

3. Should workers be permitted to band together for the purpose of bargaining with their employers on matters of wages, hours, and other conditions of employment?

4. Should business take care of its superannuated employees?

5. Should a small firm be required to pay its employees a legally established minimum wage even though to do so may endanger its solvency?

6. Are there any business decisions in which representatives of labor or the local communities are entitled to a voice?

7. Does business have any responsibility to assist disadvantaged persons, such as ghetto dwellers, minority racial groups, ex-convicts, former servicemen, and school dropouts, to become self-supporting members of their communities?

The Civic Factor

Some questions relating to the social responsibilities of business which might be categorized as civic factors are:

1. Should business assume some share in revitalizing many of our larger cities where the presence of ghettos and slum areas present problems of sociological significance?

2. Should business encourage and make major contributions to civic drives to alleviate poverty?

3. Does business have an obligation to help support public and private educational institutions?

4. Is it the province of the business community to lend its assistance to the efforts that are being made to eradicate social injustice in this country?

The Economic Factor

In this area there is a single question the answer to which has been debated in board rooms, classrooms, and in the public press: Does business discharge its social responsibilities when it makes a good product or service, pays good wages, and yields a good profit to its owners, or is something further required of the business community?

The Ecological Factor

Should business be held responsible for and contribute to the elimination of the *ecological problems* which are receiving so much attention at the present? Among these are air and water pollution, solid wastes disposal, noise pollution, traffic congestion, and the despoiling of the open spaces that is found in so many parts of the country today.

The Product Safety Factor

Does the responsibility of business include the determination of the safety of its consumer products *before* they are placed on the market for sale? Already the following products are covered, to a greater or lesser degree, by law: foods, drugs, cosmetics, motor vehicles, insecticides, firearms, cigarettes, products with radiological hazards, toys, and certain flammable fabrics. However, there are a large number of products not covered by law which have been found to be hazardous to consumers. Among these are color television sets, fireworks, floor furnaces, hot-water vaporizers, infant furniture, ladders, power tools, rotary lawnmowers, and wringer washers. Spokesmen for consumer groups have repeatedly called the attention of the public to the need for the development of safety standards in the manufacture of these and other products which are sold to consumers.

THE RIGHTS OF STOCKHOLDERS

As stated earlier, traditionally and legally managements of corporations have had a single, overriding responsibility, namely, that of operating their companies in such a manner as to yield the greatest possible profits for the owners. This and only this has been their duty, for the rationale behind the investing in corporations by stockholders has been the expectation of dividends. It has long been the history of firms whose profits were not satisfactory for their stockholders to replace current managements by those who could produce (or promise to) profits that would be acceptable to the owners. The concept was held that management was the custodian of the owners' invested funds, and that a return on these is the only raison d'etre for the company's existence. The diversion of profits by management for socially worthwhile objectives has occasionally been referred to as involuntary taxation of the affected stockholders. Articles have appeared in the newspapers telling of the protests of stockholders at the annual meetings against the actions of the companies' executives in using the corporations' funds for socially responsible causes rather than distributing them as dividends.

It has to be recognized that, at least at the start, business firms came into being because people with funds were willing to invest them in new enterprises. As some of these firms prospered and grew, in many instances to great size, personnelwise there came about a separation between the owners and the management. Many of the latter had a minimal, if any, cash investment in the enterprises which they directed. At the same time new owners came into the picture through the purchase of shares of stock in these companies. These new owners had had no part in the founding of the companies; and their principal, if not sole, motive for investing was that of securing a satisfactory return for their money. To many of them the use of the companies' earnings for the exercise of social responsibility was a contingency which they had not previously contemplated and of which they disapproved, in some cases quite vehemently. And from a purely legalistic standpoint they were correct.

This is not to imply that all stockholders of companies with socially conscious managements disapproved of this diversion of the firms' profits, as there is abundant evidence that many of their owners were quite sympathetic to the idea of business assuming part of the burden of endeavoring to relieve some of the social ills of the country. And it seems probable that there will be a continuing increase in the number of these socially-minded investors. Nevertheless, it must be recognized that these contributions by the companies concerned do involve a corresponding diminution of the return to their stockholders.

CURRENT STATUS OF BUSINESS' SOCIAL RESPONSIBILITIES

The federal government, together with many of the state and local governing bodies, has provided the means by which some of the questions in the preceding sections of this chapter have been solved, in whole or in part. Without going into a recital of all the legislative acts involved, many of which will be discussed later in the chapters to which they are pertinent, here a brief summary should be adequate to indicate the areas affected.

1. Laws which place a floor under wages and a ceiling over the hours worked per week.
2. The Social Security Act and Medicare.
3. Laws that require management to bargain with its employees on wages and hours.
4. The Civil Rights Act.
5. The Manpower Development and Training Act.
6. Workmen's compensation.
7. Safety device requirements.

As for the action taken by business, several steps have been taken by firms and executives who have endeavored to recognize and to take part in what they conceive to be their duty in the realm of business' social responsibilities. Although the examples cited below are grouped according to certain areas of social needs that need to be alleviated, actually some of these organizations are engaged in more than one area of social responsibility.

Employment, Training, and Retraining

In a recent report to its stockholders, the General Motors Corporation included the following statements:

Employment Policy and Social Responsibilities

General Motors' nondiscrimination in employment policy, which has been in effect for many years, provides job opportunities in our plants and offices to all qualified applicants regardless of age, race, color, sex, creed or national origin. More than 80,000 nonwhites, many with responsible positions, are employed in GM offices and plants all over the U.S., representing 13% of the total employment of GM in this country. All employee training and educational opportunities are available to white and nonwhite employees on an equal basis, and many have improved their skills and moved to higher job classifications as a result of these opportunities.

General Motors and GM people are active in programs aimed at aiding the disadvantaged. In April, 1968, GM set a national goal of job opportunities for over 12,500 hard-core unemployed by July, 1969. In the first nine months of the program more than 23,300 hard-core unemployed have been hired, or 183% of the original goal. In addition, GM provided summer employment for over 2,500 disadvantaged youths.

GM also assists servicemen through Project Transition, a program to prepare men awaiting separation from the armed forces for re-entry into civilian life. Some younger servicemen have no skills except those acquired in the service, which often are unsuitable for civilian occupations. To help servicemen take productive places as civilians, GM offers courses in automotive service and appliance repair at training centers near Armed Forces locations. About 1,000 men have taken advantage of the program.

At an annual meeting of the American Can Company, William F. May, Chairman of the Board and President, made the following statements:

People and Activities

The final subject I would like to discuss with you this morning is the same one which received so much attention, and quite deservedly, in our annual report—people.

I would like to tell you about three activities in this area: Our involvement in the "hard core" program, our commitment to increased minority representation, and about a motion picture which the company produced that has, as its theme, the chances for minority representatives to enter the mainstream of the nation's economic life.

As pointed out in our annual report, we have developed a plan for improving opportunities for minority representatives within the company in the next two years. Part of this plan, you may recall, provided for increasing minority group representation throughout the corporation in all job categories by a total of 1,000 persons by the end of this year.

In addition, we are committed to a program of promoting, upgrading or hiring 500 members of minority groups into job categories of officials, managers, technicians, sales workers and draftsmen by the end of 1970.

Hard Core Program

Since the inception of the corporate hard core program, the company has hired 452 hard core out of the 4,681 employed at the participating plants. Our hiring experience is almost double our 5 percent commitment to the national program. Even though our turnover rate has been higher than we would like to see, we feel the program has been worthwhile.

I would like to stress that the objectives I've just cited are not quotas. We intend to pursue affirmatively our dedication as an "equal employment opportunity employer," regardless of numbers.

As indicated in our annual report, one of our special concerns during 1968 was in resolving an unusual situation involving our facility and the community of Bellamy, Ala. Details were given in the report, so that I shall say here only that progress is continuing in seeking to assist the community to become self-governing.

After we have proceeded with the business of this meeting, I would like to introduce a film that represents another element in the discussion of human values as they are found in today's business community.

It is called "Making It" and runs 27 minutes in length. "Making It" is an odd film in a way—odd in the manner in which it came about and a good deal different in its approach to a current problem.

The film resulted from some basic research we were doing in connection with a teaching-machine concept. The teaching-machine program was eventually sold to Westinghouse Corporation with a provision for royalties to our company. We retained the film. Those of us who had a chance to see the film were touched by its message of hope and encouragement. We also felt that some of the young men in the film, who haven't made it yet, had some enlightening things to say about how Negroes feel.

We showed the film to some outsiders, including leaders in the Urban League and in the NAACP. They encouraged us to give it a wider audience, for the good it might do.

We have done that, and through schools, civic clubs, hard core training programs, TV stations and in many other ways the candid message of the film is beginning to reach millions of people—both black and white.

I hope you will find the film interesting. Let me just emphasize that everyone who speaks is a Negro. None of the speakers are actors. No script was used—the men who speak are speaking for themselves, in their own words.

I hope you may share our feeling that it speaks pretty much for itself.

Procter and Gamble has concentrated its efforts in the area of employment by taking a dual approach to this problem. Within the company organization attention has been focused on upgrading underprivileged members of all races, particularly Negroes. The other phase consists in a comprehensive program to seek out and employ Negro men and women for a wide variety of job opportunities within the company. Programs to train underqualified applicants for clerical positions so that they can meet the company's entry-level requirements have also been undertaken.

A black Baptist minister formed the National Advisory Council to support his organization, Opportunities Industrialization Centers, Inc., which motivates and then trains the unemployed and the underemployed. Led by prominent business executives, the Council is seeking immediate government support for its 80 OIC centers.

The National Alliance of Businessmen, founded in 1968 with Henry Ford II as one of its leaders, is promoting changes in *JOBS* (Job Opportunities in the Business Sector) to make it more effective in its mission to upgrade employees who are already in low-wage, dead-end jobs. (See Figure 3-3 on pages 68-69.) JOBS' main effort is to hire and train the hard-core unemployed for entry-level jobs, and it receives grants of $2,900 per trainee from the Department of Labor.

In Rochester, New York, several business firms led by Eastman Kodak Company and Xerox Corporation have entered into a broad program behind an organization known as *FIGHT* (Freedom, Independence, God, Honor, Today). The purpose of FIGHT is basically to secure more jobs for Negroes, but one aspect of its program also calls for the locating of black-owned businesses in black neighborhoods. Another organization called Rochester Jobs, Incorporated operates as a clearinghouse for jobs for the hard-core unemployed. Many other companies throughout the country are establishing training courses for the hard-core unemployed as well as ex-convicts, in many instances teaching them to read and write and do problems in arithmetic in addition to actual job training (See Figure 3-4 on page 71).

Construction and Housing

The Citizens and Southern National Bank, the largest bank in Georgia, has undertaken the task of slum cleanup in Atlanta and several other Georgia communities with the aid of civic-minded citizens in these areas. The bank is also embarked on a program of low-interest loans to citizens for home purchase or renovation, or to low-income businessmen who want to start their own businesses.

Construction for Progress, Inc., is a joint venture of the Celanese Corporation and American-Standard, Inc. These firms collaborated in the construction of a new building project for the New York City Housing Authority which it sold to the Authority for about 15 percent less than the bids which the city has been receiving on public housing.

Health and Old Age Programs

Health plans, such as Blue Cross and Blue Shield, have been widely established throughout the business community, with contributions being made by either both employers and employees or employers only. Many companies have also established retirement plans for their older employees which are designed to augment the amounts that are available through Social Security. In some cases both the employees and the companies make contributions; in others, the companies alone carry this burden.

Environmental Quality Control

David Rockefeller, Chairman and Chief Executive Officer of The Chase Manhattan Bank, recently said, "In the past, American businessmen have done immense good for mankind by making our economy efficient and productive. Now the businessmen, as citizens, must take into account a wider range of objectives including the preservation of the environment in which we live."

E. I. du Pont de Nemours and Company has invested large sums in air and water pollution control facilities. In addition, over 900 of the company's employees have been working full time in its environmental control program. The company has also made grants to many colleges and universities for capital improvements during the past 50 years, and it is now turning its attention to programs in secondary schools and special projects aimed at improving educational opportunities for disadvantaged young people. In Wilmington, Delaware, where the headquarters of the company is located, a three-year grant of $50,000 per year has been made to the public schools to assist an experimental "community school" program to keep schools open day and evening all year with special educational programs. The company has also given support to a low-rent apartment housing project in the center of the city of Wilmington.

Several other firms have taken an active interest in improving the quality of the environment in this country. The Chemical Bank of New York has initiated a program of granting special low-interest loans for upgrading apartment house incinerators and oil burners to reduce the soot and dirt in the air. American Cyanamid and New Jersey's Middlesex County Sewer Authority have teamed up for a municipal waste treatment

JOBS is

Because 15,000 American companies knew a

Because 100,000 hard-core unemployed

Last March, the National Alliance of Businessmen was formed to work with the Government on a problem of critical national importance. The Program: J O B S (Job Opportunities in the Business Sector). The Task: to hire, train and retain the nation's hard-core unemployed. To find and fill 100,000 jobs by July 1969; 500,000 by 1971.

They are being hired.

The first year's goal has been reached seven months ahead of schedule! In the nation's fifty largest cities J O B S is progressing at the rate of 20,000 placements per month— *over double the anticipated rate.* At the end of December, 100,000 hard-core workers were on the job...earning an average of $2.25/hour.

They are being trained.

Companies are bringing the hard-core into the mainstream of American business by providing the new workers with special training both educational and vocational. And by conducting imaginative "sensitivity" programs to help foremen and supervisors understand the unique problems of the hard-core.

Extra training costs are being shared by Industry and Government. In two-thirds of the cases these costs have been voluntarily absorbed by the individual employers. One-third of participating companies have signed

Figure 3-3 (page 1)

working

sound business proposition when they saw it.

are now on payrolls instead of relief rolls.

contracts with the Department of Labor.

They are being retained.

Two out of every three hard-core workers have remained on the job...better than the normal rate for all entry-level jobs.

Based on this high job retention level and upon the success of the training programs, *97% of employers surveyed said they will continue hiring the hard-core.* They maintain that the J O B S Program is "the most practical way to solve the problem of the hard-core unemployed."

J O B S is still urgent business!

Success to-date has been extremely encouraging. But thousands of the hard-core are still waiting...waiting for the chance to develop their abilities; waiting to fill industry's growing need for skilled workers.

Special training funds continue to be available through MA-4 contracts with the Department of Labor. Call the National Alliance of Businessmen office in your city for complete details.

The J O B S Program is more than an obligation to the country and to the economy. It's a prime business opportunity for your company.

National Alliance of Businessmen

Figure 3-3 (page 2)

program. In Middletown, Ohio, the Armco Steel Corporation has made a drastic change in its steel-making operation in order to eliminate the smoke which had long flowed from its smokestacks, thereby taking a great step toward the purifying of the air in that community. Some firms with plants on or near the Great Lakes have been taking steps to overcome the pollution that their industrial discharges have helped to bring about. There is an active interest among oil refiners, electric power plants, and the producers of aluminum to devise and put into operation apparatus that will reduce, if not completely eliminate, pollution of air and water which has been, heretofore, a concomitant of their productive processes.

The Sierra Club, composed of some 110,000 nature lovers, is an all-volunteer national conservation group dedicated to stopping environmental spoilage through the bringing of suits against those offenders who decline to take the necessary steps to reform their pollution-causing processes. There are more than 120 Sierra Club chapters throughout the country and, among other things, they have fought to protect California redwood trees and the Grand Canyon of the Colorado River.

The Council on Economic Priorities was established in 1970 by a group of young people many of whom are employed in the financial district of New York City. In the words of one of its organizers: "We aren't out just to attack the big companies, we are starting a campaign for corporate responsibility." The Council plans to draw up detailed studies on how big business "meets human needs" in the areas of race relations, pollution and damage to the environment, and how its overseas investments operate in a social sense. Not only will the Council publish its findings which will reveal delinquencies on the parts of firms in the areas affected, but it also expects to report positive results where it finds that companies are doing a good job in upgrading minority employees or protecting the ecology.

Other Endeavors by Business

To ease the tensions between the black and the white communities following the disastrous riots in Detroit in 1967, a group of businessmen, educators, lawmakers, and ghetto residents established the New Detroit Committee.

Other worthwhile endeavors include the substantial contributions made by business firms to local civic fund drives, such as those of the YMCA and YWCA. It is not uncommon to see the executives of many of these companies take time off from their duties to assist in these projects. They are also active as members of the Boards of Trustees of a large number

Figure 3-4

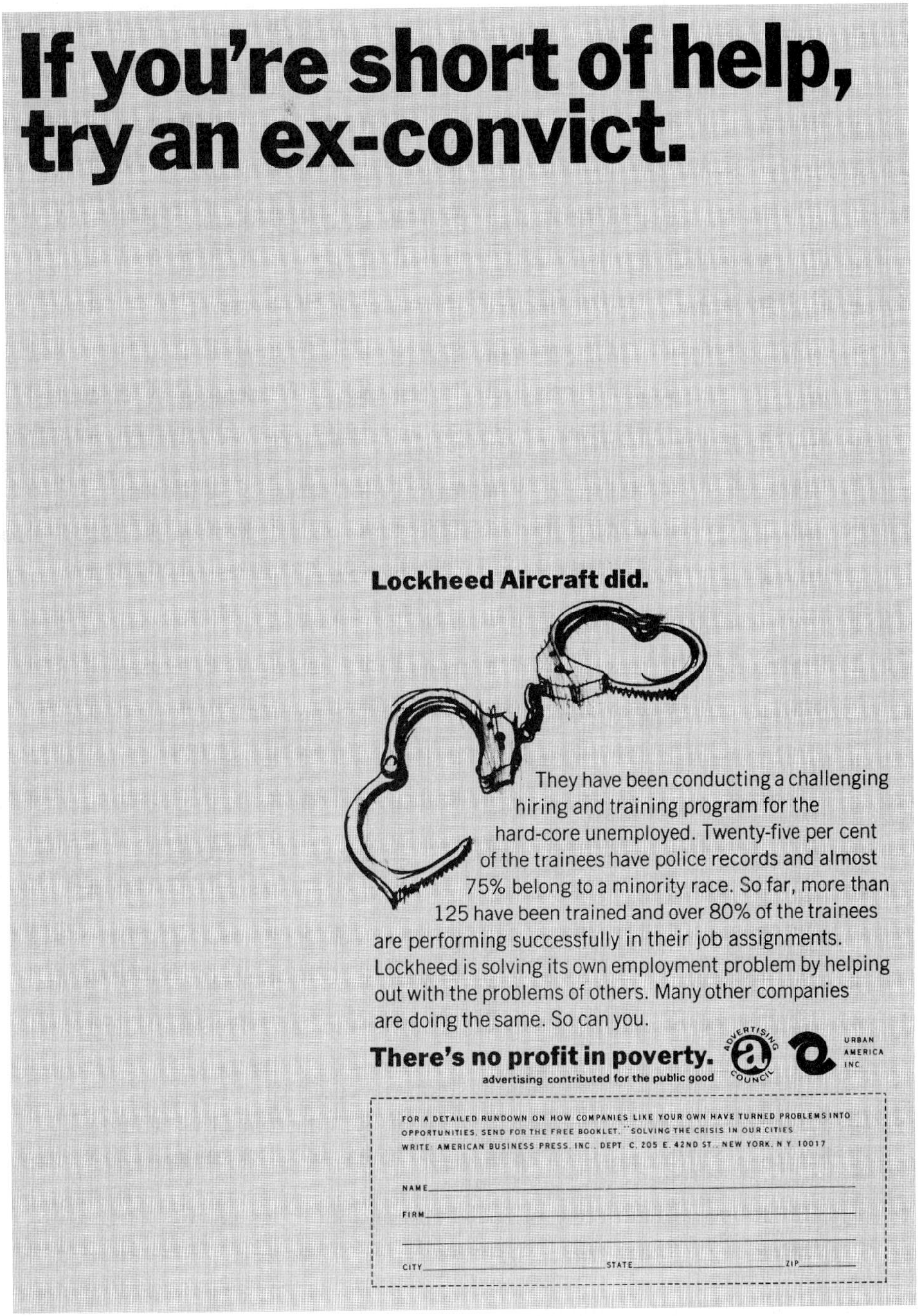

If you're short of help, try an ex-convict.

Lockheed Aircraft did.

They have been conducting a challenging hiring and training program for the hard-core unemployed. Twenty-five per cent of the trainees have police records and almost 75% belong to a minority race. So far, more than 125 have been trained and over 80% of the trainees are performing successfully in their job assignments. Lockheed is solving its own employment problem by helping out with the problems of others. Many other companies are doing the same. So can you.

There's no profit in poverty.
advertising contributed for the public good

ADVERTISING COUNCIL

URBAN AMERICA INC.

FOR A DETAILED RUNDOWN ON HOW COMPANIES LIKE YOUR OWN HAVE TURNED PROBLEMS INTO OPPORTUNITIES, SEND FOR THE FREE BOOKLET. "SOLVING THE CRISIS IN OUR CITIES." WRITE: AMERICAN BUSINESS PRESS, INC., DEPT. C. 205 E. 42ND ST., NEW YORK, N.Y. 10017

NAME_____

FIRM_____

_____

CITY_____ STATE_____ ZIP_____

of colleges and universities, and not infrequently they contribute to the support of educational institutions, both personally and by persuading their firms to make periodic donations. And there are those who give of their time and energy in backing the work of Little League Baseball teams and the Boy and Girl Scout Troops.

Finally, there are the foundations, usually created by wealthy individuals and bearing their names, which have made significant contributions in the field of education, medicine, welfare, and research. Among these are the Carnegie, Ford, Rockefeller, Sloan, and Mott foundations.

FUTURE STATUS OF BUSINESS' SOCIAL RESPONSIBILITIES

In the socially uncertain times of the present, events not presently discernible can alter trends that now seem quite evident. However, unless some unsuspected circumstances arise to shift the direction in which the social responsibility of business seems to be moving, it appears reasonable to assume that there will continue to be an ever-increasing participation by successful firms in the task of recognizing the social problems of the country and of trying to do something about them.

BUSINESS TERMS

business ethics	53	ecological problems	61
mercantilism	54	JOBS	66
code of ethics	55	FIGHT	66

QUESTIONS FOR DISCUSSION AND ANALYSIS

1. In your contacts with businessmen where a question of business ethics was involved, in your opinion did they act ethically or not? Give some examples to support your conclusions.
2. Should all good ethical practices be enacted into law? Explain your answer.
3. What is your opinion of the value of industry codes of ethics?
4. Do you think that codes of ethics developed by industrial firms would be more or less effective than those promulgated by associations such as the Business Ethics Advisory Council? Explain.
5. If a firm adopts a philosophy of social responsibility, would this have a favorable effect on its sales? Why or why not?
6. Do you believe that the primary obligation of management is to earn profits for its owners? Explain.

7. Should the standard of living of its employees be a primary concern to the management of a company? Why?

8. Would you expect such organizations as the National Alliance of Businessmen to continue to hold the interest and support of its member firms over time? Explain.

9. Do you believe that business, as a whole, subscribes to the actions being taken by a few firms to promote environmental quality control? Why or why not?

10. How effective over the long run would you expect such organizations as the Council on Economic Priorities to be?

PROBLEMS AND SHORT CASES

1. Many firms are faced with the necessity of deciding whether or not to relocate their plants. Present a comprehensive discussion of this question, giving reasons for and against such a decision from the standpoint of the social responsibility of the company to its employees and to the inner city when they move from the city to the suburbs.

2. In the past few years several instances have been reported where attempts have been made by socially conscious individuals to penetrate the annual meetings of large corporations for the purpose of persuading the officers and directors of these firms to take a more socially responsible attitude in the conduct of their business. Present a report on at least one of these incidents and indicate what action, if any, should be taken in response to these requests. Consult recent back files of *Business Week, Fortune, The Wall Street Journal,* and other periodicals which may be found in your school library.

3. The ecological problems which are facing the country have aroused the interest and action of a number of the nation's large companies. There is need for the enlistment of many more firms in this endeavor, more or less on a continuing basis. Assemble a portfolio of the names and activities of as many of the participating companies as you can discover through research in your school library. Give your opinion as to the probable effectiveness of these actions in remedying the situations that are affecting the ecology of the country at this time.

SUGGESTED READINGS

Baumhart, Raymond C., S.J. *Ethics in Business.* New York: Holt, Rinehart and Winston, 1968.

Doeringer, Peter B., ed. *Programs to Employ the Disadvantaged.* Englewood Cliffs, New Jersey: Prentice-Hall, Inc., 1969.

Garrett, Thomas M. *Business Ethics.* New York: Appleton-Century-Crofts, 1966.

Garrett, Thomas M., *et al. Cases in Business Ethics.* New York: Appleton-Century-Crofts, 1968.

Gilliland, C. E., Jr., ed. *Readings in Business Responsibility.* Braintree, Mass.: D. H. Mark Publishing Company, 1969.

Goldman, Marshall I. *Controlling Pollution: The Economics of a Cleaner America.* Englewood Cliffs, New Jersey: Prentice-Hall, Inc., 1967.

Greenwood, William T., ed. *Issues in Business and Society.* Boston: Houghton Mifflin Company, 1964.

Haddad, W. F., and G. D. Pugh, eds. *Black Economic Development.* Englewood Cliffs, New Jersey: Prentice-Hall, Inc., 1969.

Heyne, Paul T. *Private Keepers of Public Interest.* New York: McGraw-Hill Book Company, 1968.

Larson, John A., ed. *The Responsible Businessman: Business and Society: Readings from "Fortune."* New York: Holt, Rinehart and Winston, 1966.

Towle, Joseph W., *et al.*, eds. *Ethics and Standards in American Business.* Boston: Houghton Mifflin Company, 1964.

Part 2

Ownership, Organization, and Management

Prologue to Part 2

Ownership, Organization, and Management

Business enterprises in a capitalistic society are, with few exceptions, privately owned by one, two, or even millions of individuals. In addition to a suitable type of ownership, these businesses must have an effective internal organization and they must be managed efficiently in order to survive in a competitive environment. The ramifications of these three basic characteristics of the vast majority of business units are explained in Part 2.

As to ownership, a major distinction among the various nongovernmental forms available is whether or not the firm is incorporated. Chapter 4 discusses the unincorporated types with particular emphasis on sole proprietorships and partnerships since these classifications numerically dominate the entire business scene. Chapter 5 describes the corporation as well as a few other incorporated forms of business ownership. The overpowering impact of corporations on the economic life of our country is stressed.

The internal organization of a business firm is the primary topic of Chapter 6. Regardless of the form of ownership, all enterprises that have more than a handful of employees should fit each person on its payroll into a planned organizational pattern. Then, to provide direction to the firm's operations by way of planning ahead and to control activities to make sure that goals are being achieved, every enterprise has to be managed. Management techniques and theories, including methods of arriving at decisions, comprise the subject matter of Chapter 7.

Chapter 4

Unincorporated Businesses

In the United States and other countries with a capitalistic economic system, the vast majority of business units are owned by one person or by two or more individuals joined together for ownership purposes. This situation is inherent in an economic system with the characteristics of private property and private enterprise. By contrast, under socialism basic industries are owned by the government; and in countries embracing the current version of communism, almost all business activity is conducted by state-owned units.

The foregoing remarks should not be construed as completely eliminating government ownership of business in a capitalistic economy. For example, municipalities frequently sell water and operate passenger buses; some states have a monopoly of liquor sales and own recreation facilities such as parks; and everyone is familiar with the fact that the federal government owns the United States Postal Service and runs our space program. But in this country these illustrations are the exception rather than the rule, and they are relatively insignificant in the total business picture.

Another characteristic of business ownership in the United States is that the all-important private sector can be divided into two major categories. One includes all forms of unincorporated business ownership; the other, all types that have been incorporated. The distinction between the two is simply whether the business was organized by one or more individuals who neither applied to nor received permission from any governmental body to operate, or whether it was chartered by a state or, rarely, the federal government.

A further breakdown of the two major types discloses that sole proprietorships and partnerships dominate the unincorporated category and that a high percentage of incorporated businesses are corporations. The extensive use of these three forms of business ownership comprises a part of the environment in which business operates in the United States. Despite the availability of optional unincorporated and incorporated forms, which will be described in this and the next chapter, an individual or group of persons starting a business almost universally decides to organize either a sole proprietorship, a partnership, or a corporation.

The type of ownership used can be and frequently is vital to the success of a business enterprise. A sole proprietorship, for example, may fail for want of capital that could have been provided by a partnership or corporation. Or partners may disagree so violently that the success of the firm is jeopardized by internal strife, which could have been avoided had there been a single owner. Since an understanding of ownership is basic to an understanding of business, two chapters will be devoted to an explanation of the various forms of business ownership and their uses. This chapter will dwell at some length on sole proprietorships, partnerships, and other forms of unincorporated business ownership. Chapter 5 will be devoted primarily to the corporation, although other forms of incorporated businesses will also be discussed.

SOLE PROPRIETORSHIPS

A *sole proprietorship* is a business owned by one person and operated for his profit. Such an individual who goes into business for himself is, for certain purposes, classified as self-employed. The term "sole proprietorship" is interchangeable with single proprietorship, individual enterprise, sole ownership, and individual proprietorship.

CHARACTERISTICS OF A SOLE PROPRIETORSHIP

Although a few large proprietorships do exist, typically the sole proprietorship is the ownership form for the small-town restaurant, the neighborhood grocery store, the local TV and radio repair shop, and the bakery. The owner, aided by a few employees, conducts a small business that usually caters to the consuming public. Although the owner may employ someone to manage his business, more commonly he is the active manager of his firm.

The capital necessary for operating the business is normally provided by the sole proprietor from his own wealth, frequently augmented by borrowing. Responsibility for all decisions is his, and he usually makes them personally rather than by delegating them to employees. The business may well be his sole source of livelihood and, if it is, his ability to operate it at a profit is vitally important to him and his family.

A sole proprietorship can be identified by the named used, such as Bob's Garden Center, Robert Gordon, Proprietor; but in most instances the public does not know the form of business ownership used by the small businesses they patronize. Sole proprietorships can take names such as The University Men's Shop or even Maplegrove Wallpaper Company. In the latter case, since there is an implication that the firm is a corporation, registration of the name may be required by the state.

In the United States over six million individuals engage in business on their own account either on a part-time or full-time basis. To this total could be added approximately three million persons, primarily farmers, who are also working for themselves. Table 4-1 below shows the number of sole proprietorships by industrial divisions and also the annual volume of business and profit in each category. An analysis of these figures shows that the total receipts for the average sole proprietorship are slightly more than $30,000 and that the average net profit is approximately $4,700.

Table 4-1

SOLE PROPRIETORSHIP INCOME TAX RETURNS
NUMBER, BUSINESS RECEIPTS, AND NET PROFITS BY INDUSTRIAL DIVISIONS

Industrial Divisions	Number of Returns	Business Receipts	Net Profit (Loss)
		(Millions of Dollars)	
ALL INDUSTRIAL DIVISIONS	6,005,930	$184,743	$28,325
Mining	43,488	1,220	(74)
Contract construction	663,301	19,334	2,887
Manufacturing	172,333	6,673	757
Transportation, communication, electric, gas, and sanitary services	285,910	6,175	925
Wholesale and retail trade	1,909,640	106,886	7,644
Finance, insurance, and real estate	515,872	7,760	2,501
Services	2,390,247	36,548	13,645
Nature of business not allocable	25,139	148	39

Source: U.S. Department of the Treasury, Internal Revenue Service, *Statistics of Income, 1968.* Agriculture, forestry, and fisheries omitted. Due to rounding, items may not add to totals.

A comparison of these figures with similar data shown in Table 4-2 on page 85 and Table 5-3 on page 117 for partnerships and corporations will reveal another important characteristic of the sole proprietorship form of business ownership. Although constituting approximately 72 percent (almost three out of four) of all forms of ownership, the volume of business done by sole proprietorships is less than 12 percent (about one ninth) of the total of all these types.

ADVANTAGES OF THE SOLE PROPRIETORSHIP

Why is the sole proprietorship the most common form of business ownership? Aside from the innate urge many people have to go into business for themselves, some with the hope of high profits and others merely because they enjoy being the "boss," sole proprietorships have several advantages: (1) ownership of all profits, (2) ease and low cost of organization, (3) freedom and promptness of action, (4) tax savings, (5) personal incentive and satisfaction, (6) high credit standing, (7) secrecy, and (8) ease of dissolution.

Ownership of All Profits

No other form of organization permits one person to own 100 percent of the profits earned by the business. In a partnership or a corporation the amount shared with others may be limited if one person has a substantial ownership percentage, but some portion of the profits will be distributed to other individuals. A man going into business may debate whether to borrow funds needed beyond his own wealth or to find a partner with sufficient cash to provide the necessary amount. If he adopts the first course of action, all of the profits will be his. If he enters into a partnership agreement, however, some of the profits will be divided as long as the business continues in that form.

Ease and Low Cost of Organization

Anyone can usually go into business without "red tape" or special legal procedures. For example, a farm hand who finishes painting a barn in the evening decides that he likes painting better than other farm chores, and the next morning he quits the farm to become a house painter. He can work by himself or, if his services are much in demand, he may hire others to work for him. In the latter case he may dignify his occupation by calling himself a painting contractor.

Restrictions on becoming a businessman are not numerous or serious. Of course, the type of business chosen must be legal. In some instances a license is required by the state, city, or county. For example, in most localities a restaurant cannot operate without being approved by a county board of health and, if alcoholic beverages are served, it must secure a license from the appropriate state. An interesting exception to the no-restriction rule is that banks may not be organized by a single proprietor.

A sole proprietorship also costs less, if indeed anything at all, to be organized. The form is so simple and the amount of capital involved frequently is so little that no formal statement of ownership is required. By contrast, partnerships usually incur legal fees in drawing up a partnership agreement, and a corporation must pay an incorporation fee to the state from which it receives its charter.

Freedom and Promptness of Action

A sole proprietor has the maximum of freedom in his actions. He is the "boss"; his decisions are final. He may expand his business at will; he may add new products or discontinue old ones at his discretion; he may sell or close his business as he wishes; and he may change from one kind of business to another as he pleases. Furthermore, these decisions can be made promptly because he need not consult others nor secure approval from any other individual or group. For the individual who does not work well with or for others, the sole proprietorship is the ideal form of business ownership.

A sole proprietor is also free from government control to a greater extent than is any other form of business ownership. He is usually allowed to do business in states other than the one in which he resides without special permission; he can work as many hours a day or week as he chooses; and he may pay himself a large or a small salary. This freedom, however, is not complete. He must abide by state and federal labor laws as they apply to his employees; he must file reports if they are requested by authorized government agencies; and he cannot ship certain merchandise into states that prohibit such shipments. Such government restrictions affect some sole proprietorships more than others, but for the vast majority they have little effect on the owner's freedom of action.

Tax Savings

As contrasted with corporations, special taxes are not levied against an individual in his role as a sole proprietor. He must pay regular individual and business taxes, such as those on his income, his property, and his payroll, but these are not levied as special taxes against the form of business ownership. A possible but unlikely exception to tax savings for sole proprietorships could occur if the owner received such a large income from his business, or from his business and other sources, that the applicable federal income tax rates exceeded those on corporations.

Personal Incentive and Satisfaction

A man in business for himself has everything to lose if his efforts are not successful; this makes him willing to devote a maximum amount of time, thought, and energy to the successful prosecution of the activity for which his firm was organized. Since there is no penalty for overtime, he may find himself working 12 hours a day and 7 days each week. Nevertheless, if his business is successful, the owner enjoys a sense of accomplishment that cannot be matched when the glory must be shared with others.

High Credit Standing

Anyone who extends credit to a business owned by one person may look beyond the value of the firm to the nonbusiness wealth of the owner. In contrast, an extension of credit to a corporation must be based entirely on the ability of the business to repay the debt. Assuming that a sole proprietorship and a corporation are identical in size and in the nature of the wealth owned, the credit standing of the sole proprietor usually will be better than that of the corporation unless the individual involved owns no assets beyond those invested in his business.

Secrecy

In some businesses the success of the enterprise is based on a secret process or formula. In others, general knowledge of profit margins, lease agreements, or other operative information might injure the competitive position of the firm. The sole proprietorship offers the best possibility that such information will not become known to others, particularly when the one person who knows these secrets is also the owner of the business.

Ease of Dissolution

Although it may not be as easy to dissolve a sole proprietorship as it is to form one, there are no legal complications and the procedure may be very simple. For example, a building contractor who has completed a construction project decides that it would be better for him to accept a job offer as a carpenter. Assuming that he has paid for the materials and labor used as a contractor, this decision is all that is needed to wind up his business as a sole proprietor.

DISADVANTAGES OF THE SOLE PROPRIETORSHIP

Although the advantages of a sole proprietorship are more numerous than are the disadvantages, any one of the objections to this type of business ownership may outweigh all of the favorable factors. Before deciding that the sole proprietorship is the best form of business ownership, consideration should be given to the following possible disadvantages: (1) unlimited liability, (2) limitation on size, (3) difficulties of management, (4) lack of opportunities for employees, and (5) lack of continuity.

Unlimited Liability

Unlimited liability refers to the availability of a person's wealth beyond the amount invested in a business to satisfy the claims of creditors of the business. For a sole proprietorship it means that practically everything an individual owns is subject to liquidation for the purpose of paying business debts. Every year thousands of sole proprietorships discontinue operations either voluntarily or because of failure. In each case creditors expect to collect the amounts owed them either from the business itself or from the nonbusiness assets of the owner of the firm.

Limitation on Size

The investment in a sole proprietorship is limited to the amount one person can raise by investing his own estate, by borrowing, or by a combination of the two. If the business to be organized or expanded requires a substantial amount of capital, it may well be that the individual will find it necessary to choose another form of ownership.

Many of today's partnerships and corporations started out as sole proprietorships and changed because of capital requirements. For example, a sole proprietor operating a print shop determined that he could double his volume of business and profits by purchasing certain equipment that involved an immediate cash outlay of $36,000. Not having this amount of money on hand or being able to raise it, his only recourse was to change his form of business ownership.

Difficulties of Management

Since a sole proprietorship is ordinarily a small business, the owner often assumes the responsibility for managing such diverse tasks as purchasing, merchandising, extending credit, financing, and employing personnel. He may be unusually capable of handling some of these functions but unable to perform others. For example, a retail store with a large volume of business went into bankruptcy because the owner was so generous with extension of credit and was so poorly qualified to collect accounts that finally there was not sufficient money left to pay current bills.

Lack of Opportunity for Employees

If an employee of a sole proprietorship proves to be an unusually able man, he may not be content to work indefinitely for the owner. Even though he is well paid, including a generous bonus based on profits, he may not be satisfied with a continuing status of being merely an employee. If the owner wishes to retain his services, it may be necessary to form a partnership or a corporation in order to extend to this individual an opportunity to become a part owner of the business. Otherwise the employee may quit and, as frequently happens, start a competitive business in the same locality.

Lack of Continuity

The death of the proprietor terminates the life of his firm, as does his insanity, imprisonment, or bankruptcy. Furthermore, the physical inability of the owner to continue work often forces the enterprise to close its doors. One man may build up a fine business, but it is profitable only so long as he is able to run it. At his death his widow or other heirs may try to continue the business, but they frequently lack the knowledge or the ability to operate it successfully.

PARTNERSHIPS

The Uniform Partnership Act [1] defines a *partnership* as "an association of two or more persons to carry on as co-owners a business for profit." Such a relationship is based on an agreement, written or oral, that is

---

[1] The following ten states have not adopted the Uniform Partnership Act: Alabama, Florida, Georgia, Hawaii, Iowa, Kansas, Louisiana, Maine, Mississippi, and New Hampshire.

both voluntary and legal. A partnership is also referred to as a "copartnership."

CHARACTERISTICS OF PARTNERSHIPS

Although the typical partnership is larger than the typical sole proprietorship, most partnerships are relatively small businesses. Even though the average annual total receipts for partnerships amount to approximately $94,000, more than 92 percent gross less than $200,000 a year. Table 4-2 below shows that the classification "Finance, insurance, and real estate" holds first place among partnerships in contrast with sole proprietorships where this industrial division ranked fourth out of seven categories. The main reason for this number one ranking is that partnerships are a common form of business ownership for brokerage firms that sell real estate, insurance, and securities.

Table 4-2

PARTNERSHIP INCOME TAX RETURNS
NUMBER, BUSINESS RECEIPTS, AND NET PROFITS BY INDUSTRIAL DIVISIONS

Industrial Divisions	Number of Returns	Business Receipts (Millions of Dollars)	Net Profit (Loss) (Millions of Dollars)
ALL INDUSTRIAL DIVISIONS	796,754	$75,205	$10,751
Mining	13,227	970	73
Contract construction	49,691	7,411	802
Manufacturing	32,666	5,547	545
Transportation, communication, electric, gas, and sanitary services	15,207	1,230	151
Wholesale and retail trade	209,326	34,416	2,279
Finance, insurance, and real estate	298,536	9,375	1,067
Services	176,277	16,220	5,824
Nature of business not allocable	1,824	35	10

Source: U.S. Department of the Treasury, Internal Revenue Service, *Statistics of Income, 1968.* Agriculture, forestry, and fisheries omitted. Due to rounding, items may not add to totals.

Some of the partnerships that do business in every city, town, and village can be identified by the firm name; others cannot. Names such as Stone & Wilson or McDonald & Son usually denote a partnership, whereas the London Furniture Mart might or might not be owned and operated as a partnership. If a fictitious partnership firm name is used, such as Wright and Wrong, some states require that a record showing the names of all partners be filed in the county office.

Of the three common forms of business ownership, partnerships are the least popular despite the sizable total of 796,754 not counting approximately 120,000 additional partnerships engaged in agriculture, forestry, and fisheries. There are more than seven times as many sole proprietorships and almost twice as many corporations. Despite a growing economy, the number of business firms using the partnership form of business ownership has shown a steady decline in numbers for the past several years. The classification now ranks a poor third among the three widely used forms of business ownership, whereas it occupied second place ahead of corporations as late as the 1950's.

The Partnership Contract

It is most desirable, although usually not necessary, that the agreement between the parties be written and signed. Such a contract, known as *articles of partnership* or "articles of copartnership," may prevent misunderstanding and ill will among the partners at a future date. An oral contract is especially unsatisfactory if profits and losses are to be divided on any basis other than equal shares because positive proof is required to overcome the presumption of equality among partners.

The common provisions of a partnership contract cover the following:

1. The name of the firm.
2. The location and the type of business.
3. The length of life of the partnership agreement.
4. The names of the partners and the investment made by each.
5. The distribution of profits and losses.
6. A provision for salaries of partners.
7. An agreement on the amount of interest to be allowed on capital and drawing account balances.
8. A limitation on withdrawals of funds.
9. A provision for an accounting system and a fiscal year.
10. The method that will be followed in case of the withdrawal of a partner from the firm and other causes of dissolution.

Figure 4-1 on pages 88 and 89 shows how these items of information are included in formal articles of partnership.

Number of Partners in Partnerships

Data provided by the Internal Revenue Service indicate that the vast majority—almost three fourths—of partnerships in this country consist of

two partners. When the number of partnerships with three and four partners is included, the coverage increases to more than 92 percent. Most of
the larger partnerships, in terms of members, are in the professions such
as law and public accounting. For example, some firms of certified public
accountants have over 500 partners. Retail stores, restaurants, and bowling alleys, if operated under the partnership form of business ownership,
usually have two partners with the possibility of a third or fourth member.
Exact percentages for each of five groupings are shown in Table 4-3.

PERCENTAGE DISTRIBUTION OF NUMBER OF PARTNERS

Table 4-3

Two partners	73.1%
Three partners	13.8
Four partners	5.5
Five to nine partners	4.6
Ten or more partners	3.0
	100.0%

Source: United States Department of the Treasury, Internal Revenue Service.

Variations of the General Partnership

Whenever the word partnership appears by itself, the reference is
always to what might more correctly be termed a *general partnership*,
that is, one in which all partners have unlimited liability. However, other
variations of the general partnership have been developed that are useful
for certain purposes.

Limited partnership. In a *limited partnership* one or more partners
can have limited liability as long as at least one partner has unlimited
liability. A limited partnership cannot be formed unless enabling legislation has been enacted, but most states have passed the Uniform Limited
Partnership Act so that this restriction is not usually a problem. Under this
act a detailed statement concerning the limited partnership must be filed
with the appropriate official at the county courthouse. The limited partner
cannot be active nor appear to be active in the management of the firm,
and his name cannot be used in the name of the firm. The purpose of a
limited partnership is to allow an individual to provide capital, on which
he expects a return, without assuming liability for debts beyond the amount
of his investment.

Articles of Partnership

THIS CONTRACT, made and entered into on the second day of January, 1973, by and between George C. Good and Arthur W. Hills, each of Columbus, Ohio.

WITNESSETH: That the said parties have this day formed a partnership for the purpose of engaging in and conducting a laundry, pressing, and dry cleaning business, and the doing of all things necessary and incident thereto, under the following stipulations which are made a part of this contract:

1. The said partnership shall commence on the second day of January, 1973, and continue from and after said date for a period of ten years at the pleasure of said partners; and shall be otherwise terminated by the death, bankruptcy, insolvency, or disability of either of the said parties thereto, or under the provisions for such act hereinafter set forth.

2. The business shall be conducted under the firm name of The Good Hills Laundromat at 987 N. High, Columbus, Ohio 43201.

3. The investments are as follows: George C. Good agrees to contribute to the capital of said partnership the sum of $30,000.00 and Arthur W. Hills the sum of $20,000.00, which shall be paid on the date of the execution of this agreement, and by the execution thereof by said partners the receipt of same is hereby acknowledged.

4. All profits and losses arising from said business are to be shared as follows: George C. Good, 60 percent; and Arthur W. Hills, 40 percent.

5. Each of said partners shall devote his entire time, skill, labor, and experience to advancing and rendering profitable the interests and business of said partnership, and neither partner shall engage in any other business or occupation whatever on his individual account during the existence of said partnership without the written consent of the other partner.

6. A systematic record of all transactions is to be kept in a double-entry set of books in which shall be promptly and properly entered an account and record of all the transactions and business of the partnership. All books of account and all contracts, letters, papers, documents, and memoranda belonging to the partnership shall be open, at all times, to the examination of either of the partners. On December 31 hereafter a statement of the business is to be made, the books closed, and each partner credited with the amount of the gain or charged with his share of the loss. A statement may be made at such other times as the partners agree upon.

7. Each partner shall furnish to the other, on request, full information and account of any and all transactions and matters relating to the business of the partnership, within his knowledge.

8. All moneys received by, or paid to, said partnership shall be daily deposited in the Ohio National Bank, Columbus, Ohio, except a small change account used in the operations of said business not to exceed $30.00, or in such other bank as said partners may mutually agree upon. All disbursements of partnership moneys in excess of $10.00 shall be made by check on said partnership bank account. Checks for amounts drawn on partnership accounts may be drawn by either of said partners.

9. No partner shall at any time sign the firm name, or his own name, or pledge the firm's credit, or his own individual credit, in any manner as surety or guarantor on any paper, bill, bond, note, or draft or other obligation whatsoever. Neither shall he assign, pledge, or mortgage any of the partnership property, or his interest therein, or do anything or permit any act whereby the firm's money, interest, or property, or his interest therein, may be liable to seizure, attachment, or execution.

10. Each partner shall promptly pay his individual debts and liabilities and shall at all times indemnify and save harmless the partnership property therefrom.

11. Each partner is to have a salary of $650.00 per month, the same to be withdrawn at such time or times as he may elect. Neither partner is to withdraw from the business an amount in excess of his salary without the written consent of the other. Interest at the rate of 6 percent per annum shall be allowed on the amount of investment each partner shall have in the business in excess of his original contribution as determined at the close of each month. Salaries and interest shall be considered expenses of doing business before arriving at net profit or net loss.

Figure 4-1 (page 1)

12. The duties of each partner are defined as follows: George C. Good is to have general supervision of the business and have charge of the accounting records, correspondence, and credits and collections. Arthur W. Hills is to have supervision of all machinery used within and without the business and the purchase of supplies and equipment. Each partner is to attend to such other duties as are deemed necessary for the successful operation of the business.

13. One partner may, at any time, dissolve said partnership by written notice of his intention to do so, delivered or mailed to the other partner, and said partnership shall be dissolved at the expiration of sixty days after the giving of such notice.

14. At the time of giving notice of dissolution of said partnership, or any other termination thereof as set out in the first stipulation above, an inventory and appraisement of all assets and property of said partnership shall be made by three disinterested parties engaged in the same or similar business in this vicinity, to be chosen by the partners to this agreement or their legal representative, at the true value to the business thereof; and an account shall be taken of all assets and liabilities. After payment of all debts and liabilities of said partnership, the assets and property so remaining shall be divided between the partners, their heirs and assigns, in the proportion in which the capital of said partnership has been contributed by each. Provided, however, that if either of the original partners to this agreement desires to carry on the said business he shall have the first option to take over said business at the net value as calculated from the account so made and assume all operations thereunder in his own right and relieve the other partner, his heirs and assigns from all liabilities. Said option to be enforceable shall be exercised within ten days after the accounting of the partnership has been made. Each partner for himself, his heirs and assigns hereby agrees to execute all instruments necessary or proper to invest the other with the property, real, personal or mixed, so taken over by him.

15. No changes, alterations, additions, modifications, or qualifications shall be made or had in the terms of this contract unless made in writing and signed by each of the partners.

IN WITNESS WHEREOF, the parties have hereunto set their hands to duplicate copies hereof, the day and year first above written.

Signed in the presence of:

STATE OF OHIO, COUNTY OF FRANKLIN, SS:

Personally appeared before me, a Notary Public within and for said State and County, the above named George C. Good and Arthur W. Hills, the parties to the foregoing contract, who each acknowledged the signing thereof to be his voluntary act and deed, for the uses and purposes therein mentioned.

IN WITNESS WHEREOF, I have hereunto set my hand and seal this second day of January, 1973.

Notary Public, Franklin County, Ohio

Figure 4-1 (page 2)

Joint ventures. When two or more persons join together for the purpose of a single undertaking, such an association is called a *joint venture* or "joint adventure." Usually, although not necessarily, the undertaking is of short duration. For example, 20 investors may join together to buy 80 acres of farmland adjacent to a city. The land is then developed into a subdivision, the lots are sold, and the joint venture is ended.

During the relatively short life of the joint venture, each participant is in the same legal position as a general partner in a partnership. Despite this hazard of unlimited liability, the management of the undertaking is frequently delegated to one individual. This difference is in line with the basic distinction between a joint venture and a general partnership, namely, that a joint venture is not a continuing business.

Syndicates. A *syndicate* is an association of two or more individuals or companies for a particular purpose, which almost always involves a financial transaction. It differs from a joint venture in that the activity is financial, and syndicates need not be terminated after the purpose is completed. In contrast with a general partnership, a member can sell his interest in the syndicate to a buyer of his choice who then assumes the rights and risks of the former owner.

The most common type of syndicate in use today is the *underwriting syndicate*. This is an association of investment banking companies formed for the purpose of selling a large issue of corporation bonds or stocks. Management is in the hands of the company that forms the underwriting syndicate. Because of the commodity handled by an underwriting syndicate, each member's liability is effectively, even if not legally, restricted to the agreed-upon portion of the total issue.

Mining partnerships. Another special type of partnership that has been legalized in some states is the *mining partnership*, which is an association of two or more individuals for the specific purpose of conducting mining operations. It differs from a general partnership in that, when there are numerous members, management is delegated to one or a few partners, shares of ownership are issued and can be sold without the consent of other partners, and profits are distributed on the basis of the number of shares owned. Unlimited liability for debts of the mining partnership is effective against the owners only for necessary costs of operating the mine, and the death or incapacity of a partner does not dissolve it.

Kinds of Partners

The individuals who comprise a partnership are known as *partners* or *copartners*. They are classified in several different ways, depending upon their extent of liability, participation in management, share of profits, and other factors.

General and limited partners. A member of a general or limited partnership who has unlimited liability for the debts of the firm is a *general partner*. Usually such a partner is active in the management.

A member of a limited partnership who does not assume responsibility for the debts beyond the amount of his investment is a *limited or special partner*. This type of partner is not permitted to take an active part in the management.

Secret, silent, dormant, and nominal partners. An individual who is active in the affairs of a partnership but who is not known to the public as a partner is a *secret partner*. A person who is known to the public as a partner but does not take an active part in the management is a *silent partner*. A partner who does not take an active part in the management and who is not known to the public as a partner is a *dormant or sleeping partner*.

A man who is not actually a partner but who publicly announces himself as a partner or allows others to hold him out as a partner is a *nominal partner* even though he does not share in the profits or does not have an investment in the business. Under certain circumstances courts have held that a nominal partner may obligate firm members by his acts or become liable for the debts of a partnership.

Senior and junior partners. A general partner who has a substantial investment in the firm, who receives a relatively larger percentage of the profits, and who, by virtue of age and years of association with the firm, assumes a major role in the management, is a *senior partner*. A *junior partner* is the opposite of a senior partner. Normally he is a young man only recently admitted to a partner's status. He does not have very much money invested, receives only a minor share of the profits, and is not expected to assume responsibility for major decisions even though he has equal voting rights with other partners.

ADVANTAGES OF THE PARTNERSHIP

Partnerships, as well as other forms of unincorporated businesses including sole proprietorships, share some advantages when contrasted with corporations and other forms of incorporated business ownership. A partnership can be organized as easily as a sole proprietorship although it is highly desirable that a lawyer be engaged to assist in drawing up written articles of partnership. The tax situation is comparable to that described under the advantages of a sole proprietorship although the Internal Revenue Service does require an annual partnership information return. Freedom from governmental regulation approximates that of sole proprietorships, but it is not quite as extensive due to a variety of state laws covering partnerships. There are also several distinctive advantages of the partnership, namely: (1) larger amount of capital, (2) credit standing, (3) combined judgment and managerial skills, (4) retention of valuable employees, (5) personal interest in business, and (6) definite legal status.

Larger Amount of Capital

In a sole proprietorship the amount of capital is limited to the personal fortune and credit of one individual. In a partnership the capital can easily be doubled, trebled, or otherwise increased by bringing in additional owners. An inventor with little capital, for example, may locate a rich man who is willing to become a partner by contributing a major portion of the total capital needed to produce and market the inventor's product.

Credit Standing

Assuming three firms exactly equal in size, one a sole proprietorship, another a corporation, and the third a general partnership, the partnership would usually enjoy the highest credit standing. As in the case of the sole proprietorship, the personal wealth of the owners is available to satisfy business debts; and two or more owners should be an improvement favorable to creditors. In the case of the corporation, the owners do not risk their personal fortunes to satisfy business debts.

Combined Judgment and Managerial Skills

The old adage that two heads are better than one is true in the case of many partnerships. Partners can consult each other about proposed actions, and a wiser course of procedure may result. Sometimes two or three men complement each other in securing maximum operating efficiency. Adams is a genius at producing precision tools, but he loses all interest in them as soon as they pass final inspection. Brown, on the other hand, is an outstanding salesman but has no interest in the problems of manufacturing. As partners, the two men are very effective, but neither would be a success as a sole proprietor.

Retention of Valuable Employees

Changing to a partnership offers an opportunity for a sole proprietorship to retain the services of a valuable employee by making him a partner. It also provides the same opportunity to existing partnerships, although new articles of partnership are necessary. Legal and professional accounting firms make extensive use of the practice of admitting new partners.

Personal Interest in Business

Since each general partner is liable for the actions of the other partners as well as his own, he is vitally concerned in every move made by the business. A sense of responsibility to those with whom he is closely associated enhances the personal interest factor. Compared to the average corporation, this advantage may be very important in the ultimate success of the firm. Only in the sole proprietorship, where little or no opportunity exists to share or delegate responsibility, does the personal interest factor have greater weight.

Definite Legal Status

Partnerships are one of the oldest forms of business ownership. Over centuries a series of court decisions have established clear-cut answers to the questions of rights, powers, liabilities, and duties of partners. A partner should have no difficulty in securing a concise answer from a lawyer on any legal question that he might care to raise concerning the partnership.

DISADVANTAGES OF THE PARTNERSHIP

After noting the many excellent advantages of partnerships when contrasted with sole proprietorships and corporations, the question might well be raised as to the reason or reasons for the relative lack of popularity for this form of business ownership. It appears obvious that one or more of the following disadvantages must frequently weigh heavily against selecting the partnership as the preferred type of business ownership: (1) unlimited liability of the partners, (2) lack of continuity, (3) managerial difficulties, (4) frozen investment, and (5) limitation on size.

Unlimited Liability of the Partners

The greatest disadvantage is that of unlimited liability of the partners. Each general partner is liable personally for the partnership debts. If one partner makes an unwise commitment, even against the wishes of his partners, all the partners may be liable for the loss that results. If partnership *A*, *B*, and *C* fails with net losses totaling $100,000, and if neither *A* nor *B* has any private resources except what he had invested in the business, the entire loss would fall on *C*, assuming that he owns assets that, when liquidated, are adequate to cover the debts.

Lack of Continuity

If a partner dies or withdraws from the business, the partnership is dissolved. Also, if a partner becomes insane or takes out bankruptcy papers, the business is terminated. The more persons there are in a partnership, the greater are the chances that this will occur. Frequently the remaining partners find it possible to buy out the interest of the individual who withdraws or dies, and they can reorganize the business with little outward change. If it is necessary to admit a new partner to assume the interest of the old one, however, it may not always be easy to find an individual who is satisfactory to all of the old partners and who will work in reasonable harmony with them in the operation of the business.

Managerial Difficulties

Although better decisions usually result from the combined judgments of two or more partners, such divided control can also cause trouble. If some partners are not active in the business, time can be lost in making contact with them. Although any partner can take an action that is legally binding on the partnership, he might be reluctant to do so on important matters. Furthermore, the friendly spirit among partners that drew them together in the first place can give way in time to distrust and enmity. If the number of partners is odd, such as three or five, the minority will be outvoted by the majority. If the number of partners is even, some written agreements provide for referral to a disinterested party in case the partners are equally divided on a proposed course of action.

Frozen Investment

For an individual who wishes to invest some money in a business, the partnership form may prove to be a poor choice from the viewpoint of liquidity and transferability. It is almost axiomatic that it is easy to invest in a partnership and difficult to withdraw these funds. If a partner withdraws or dies, the existing firm is dissolved. Even if the remaining partners or outsiders are willing to purchase the vacated interest, it is often extremely difficult to arrive at a fair price.

Limitation on Size

The advantage held by a partnership over a sole proprietorship as to availability of capital can easily become a disadvantage when contrasted with a corporation. Some businesses, such as those producing steel or making automobiles, require the investment of millions of dollars by the owners. A partnership, even if composed of several wealthy individuals, would have great difficulty in raising adequate capital for organizing a successful firm in many lines of business.

OTHER UNINCORPORATED FORMS OF BUSINESS OWNERSHIP

In addition to special types of partnerships, a few other legal forms of business ownership are available that do not require incorporation. These include joint-stock companies, business trusts, and unincorporated associations.

JOINT-STOCK COMPANIES

Joint-stock companies were important in the early development of our nation but have now been almost universally replaced by the corporation. They were formed by drawing up *articles of association*, not unlike articles of partnership, with the addition of stating the number of shares of stock to be issued and providing for an annual meeting at which the stockholders would elect a board of directors. Joint-stock companies resemble general partnerships in that all have unlimited liability. They differ in that management is delegated to a board of directors, ownership is represented by shares of stock that can be sold or transferred to others, profits are distributed on the basis of the number of shares owned, and the firm is not affected by the death of one or more stockholders.

BUSINESS TRUSTS

A *business trust* is a form of ownership in which investors, under a trust agreement, transfer cash or other property to a small number of trustees who manage the firm for the benefit of the owners. This is an entirely different approach to organizing and operating a business when contrasted with other types of unincorporated ownership described in this chapter. The trustees issue certificates of beneficial interest, called *trust certificates* or *trust shares*, to those who organized the trust, and these shares provide the basis for the distribution of profits.

If the trust agreement gives the investors any control over the management, such as the right to elect trustees, courts have held that each owner has unlimited liability. Since one of the reasons for using the trustee device is to secure the advantage of limited liability without incorporating, the customary procedure is to deny the owners any right to elect the trustees or to have any voice in management. The holders of trust certificates do have the right to sell them to a buyer of their choice, and the death of an owner does not affect the continuation of the trust. Business trusts are also known as *common-law trusts* or *Massachusetts trusts*.

UNINCORPORATED ASSOCIATIONS

An *unincorporated association* can be formed by any number of persons or companies by drawing up and signing an agreement. It differs from other special forms of business ownership in that its purpose is always nonprofit and it exists to render a service to its members. National fraternal organizations, trade associations, and the like are frequently unincorporated associations as are most security exchanges, bank clearinghouses located in large cities, and retail credit associations. In the business world there is usually a fee to join the association, and its expenses of operation are divided among its members based on their use of the services rendered. The members elect a board of governors, or directors, or trustees, who employ personnel to run the organization. Although the members probably have unlimited liability, the nonprofit and service nature of an unincorporated association are such that this risk is negligible.

BUSINESS TERMS

QUESTIONS FOR DISCUSSION AND ANALYSIS

1. Is governmental ownership and operation of some activities clearly identified as belonging in the area of business inconsistent with the environment in which a capitalistic economic system operates?

2. Do sole proprietorships receive a sentimental support from the general public that is lacking for other types of business enterprises?

3. Why do so many people go into business for themselves despite the statistics that show a low level of annual profits for sole proprietorships?

4. Why should creditors of a sole proprietorship or partnership have access to the nonbusiness wealth of the owner or owners to satisfy their legitimate claims?

5. Despite an expanding economy the number of businesses using the partnership form of ownership is less today than ten years ago. What reasons can you give for the decline in popularity of partnerships?

6. Two men in a rowboat fishing by themselves agree to form a partnership with *A* contributing $20,000 and *B*, $10,000. The new business proves very successful and at the close of the first year $18,000 in profits are available for distribution. *A* claims that he is entitled to $12,000 while *B* says he always understood that profits were to be divided equally. Who is correct and why?

7. Would a valuable employee have a better chance of becoming a partner if the firm he works for is currently a partnership rather than a sole proprietorship?

8. Isn't a limited partner more likely to become dissatisfied with his status in a partnership than the general partner or partners?

9. Is there any difference between a general partnership and a joint venture if the business is expected to continue for a number of years such as five or more?

10. Why is more extensive use not made of business trusts and unincorporated associations as forms of business ownership?

PROBLEMS AND SHORT CASES

1. Capt. Marion McDonnell of the United States Army, who had been commissioned at the time he was graduated from college, was nearing the end of the R.O.T.C. military service requirement. His current and probable terminal assignment was at a base in Florida, a state that he considered ideal for the year-round outdoor living that he and his

family enjoyed. In anticipation of returning to civilian life, he had purchased a home in the city adjacent to the military base and his wife and two young children already considered themselves as members of the community.

McDonnell was an avid and excellent golf player and had noted that the nearest driving range was 22 miles away. Consequently, he decided that following separation from service he would like to own and operate a combination driving range and putt-putt golf course. An investigation of available sites produced only one tract of land within the city limits large enough for both activities although farm land approximately a mile from the center of town could be purchased. The owner of the city property was anxious to sell but, because his land was zoned commercial, he felt that it was worth $32,000. In contrast, an adequate amount of farm land could be purchased for $4,000. A local savings and loan association expressed the willingness to loan a maximum of 75 percent of the purchase price of either location.

In addition, despite the availability of credit from suppliers, McDonnell calculated that equipment for a driving range would require cash in the amount of $2,000 and that a putt-putt course would involve an additional cash outlay of at least $7,000. By stretching his personal resources, including a savings account, Capt. McDonnell believed that he could scrape together an amount close to $10,000. In talking over his financial problem with his favorite golfing companion, a local insurance agent by the name of John Park, he was surprised when Park suggested that he would be willing to become a partner and contribute $15,000 for a one-half interest in the business if McDonnell would invest $5,000. Furthermore, he was willing to establish an hourly pay rate of $4.00 for the owners with the expectation that McDonnell would devote long hours each week to the business whereas he would not be available except on weekends. Such wages paid to either or both of them would be a charge against earnings, reducing the amount of profits to be divided equally.

On the basis of these facts, should Capt. McDonnell go into business for himself or should he form a partnership with John Park? Support your recommendation with a list of the advantages and disadvantages of each course of action and give the reasons for your decision.

2. For five years Dorothy Green and Vera Walker were employed in Denver, Colorado, at the same beauty parlor, where they became fast friends. About a year ago Dorothy Green was married to a Robert Alden and moved into the old Alden home located at 101 Front Street, near the downtown business area. Vera Walker continued at her old job but, after careful investigation and with the consent of Alden, she and Dorothy have decided to open a beauty parlor in the Alden house to be called the Dover Beauty Salon.

Each partner agrees to invest $7,500 in cash. Dorothy Alden is to receive $150 a month as rent for the portion of her home devoted to the business, a salary of $500 a month, and 40 percent of the profits. Vera Walker is to receive a salary of $600 a month in addition to 60 percent of the profits. She is to be in charge of buying equipment and supplies, handling receipts and disbursements, paying bills, and keeping the books of account. Dorothy is to be in charge of appointments, advertising, promotional activities, and is to serve as receptionist.

Vera agrees to devote 40 hours each week to the business and Dorothy, 30 hours. Overtime, if necessary, is to be paid for at the rate of $5 an hour. The books are to be closed on June 30 and December 31 of each year; the agreement is to run for ten years; and in case the firm is dissolved, the net assets are to be divided in the ratio of their capital accounts at that date. Neither partner is to withdraw cash from the firm other than salaries, rent, overtime payments, and net profits without the written consent of the other.

Using the above information plus any additional assumptions you care to make that are not inconsistent with the stated facts, draw up articles of partnership for Dorothy Alden and Vera Walker.

3. For the past eight years George Ringling and Albert Loring have operated a job print business under the name of the R. & L. Print Shop. The partnership has been profitable, clearing about $12,000 a year for each man, and it has been the sole source of support for both families. Consequently, net income has been withdrawn regularly and the $15,000 originally contributed by each partner, which is invested in machinery, paper, inks, and supplies, has remained relatively stationary.

The firm has been renting an old building that is barely adequate for their needs. Paper has to be purchased in small quantities because of the lack of storage space, and there is no room for a larger press. They do not have a lease, but the owner seems content with receiving $250 each month and has not raised the rent over the past eight years. Ringling and Loring have been aware of the possibility of a long over-due rent increase and also that no other location is now available in their community.

They discussed this situation with Ronald Morgan, their banker and personal friend, who expressed a willingness to build a structure designed to fit their present and anticipated needs on property that he owns. He estimated the cost at $60,000 and indicated that he would be willing to lease the completed building for $400 a month for a period of ten years. As an alternative to a lease, he proposed that Ringling and Loring take him into the firm as a limited partner. In return for his investment, which would be the completed building, he wished to receive one third of the net profits of the business after an allowance of $500 a month as a salary to each of the two general partners. It is estimated that taxes and insurance on the new building will average $100 a month and that the building will last 40 years.

Should Ringling and Loring admit Morgan to the R. & L. Print Shop as a limited partner? Give reasons for your decision.

SUGGESTED READINGS

Anderson, R. A., and W. A. Kumpf. *Business Law*, Eighth Edition. Cincinnati: South-Western Publishing Co., 1968. Part VIII.

Bandy, W. R., *et al. Business Law: Text and Cases*, Second Edition. Boston: Allyn and Bacon, Inc., 1968. Chapter XXXII.

Broom, H. N., and J. G. Longenecker. *Small Business Management*, Third Edition. Cincinnati: South-Western Publishing Co., 1971. Part B.

Corley, R. N., and R. L. Black, Jr. *The Legal Environment of Business*, Second Edition. New York: McGraw-Hill Book Company, 1968. Chapter Seven.

Robert, W., and R. Corley. *Dillavou & Howard's Principles of Business Law*, Eighth Edition. Englewood Cliffs, New Jersey: Prentice-Hall, Inc., 1967. Book Five.

Donaldson, E. F., and J. K. Pfahl. *Corporate Finance—Policy and Management*, Third Edition. New York: The Ronald Press Company, 1969. Part I.

Litka, M. P. *Business Law*. New York: Harcourt Brace Jovanovich, Inc., 1970. Part 4.

Lusk, H. F., *et al. Business Law—Principles and Cases*, Second Uniform Commercial Code Edition. Homewood, Illinois: Richard D. Irwin, Inc., 1970. Part V.

Niswonger, C. R., and P. E. Fess. *Accounting Principles*, Tenth Edition. Cincinnati: South-Western Publishing Co., 1969. Chapter 15.

Wyatt, J. W., and M. B. Wyatt. *Business Law*, Third Edition. New York: McGraw-Hill Book Company, 1966. Part Eight.

Chapter 5

Incorporated Businesses

Prior to the middle of the nineteenth century a substantial portion of business activity was carried on in the United States by sole proprietorships and partnerships. Difficulties of transportation, lack of manufacturing facilities, and a sparse population were some of the reasons that small business enterprises dominated the business scene. Although a few importing and exporting companies, railroads, canals, and financial institutions showed signs of growth prior to our Civil War, it was not until after 1865 that large business units emerged in such areas as manufacturing and retailing. In order to assemble the amount of capital required for these large organizations, entrepreneurs turned to incorporated forms of business ownership.

This chapter will describe some of these types of ownership and their uses with a considerable amount of emphasis given to the corporation. The importance of incorporated business units can hardly be overemphasized as one form or another is used by all of the private industrial, commercial, and financial giants. These large enterprises are responsible, to a great extent, for the high standard of living we enjoy. Only big businesses can mass produce and mass merchandise goods and services at prices consumers can afford to pay. At the same time it would be a mistake to assume that all incorporated business units are necessarily large when, in fact, many are as small as the typical sole proprietorship or partnership.

CORPORATIONS

Among the types of incorporated businesses, the importance of the corporation warrants the attention that will be given to it in this chapter. Even though there are approximately four times as many sole proprietorships and half as many partnerships, corporations account for more than four fifths of all business receipts and more than two thirds of all net profits. They employ millions of workers, are owned by millions of investors, and their activities and actions have a profound effect on today's economic life.

Corporations have an impact on the lives of every person in the United States. Despite their reputed impersonality, most of our population can identify such abbreviations as A & P, Goodyear, A. T. & T., Sears Roebuck, GM, and a host of others. This familiarity is evidence of the widespread influence corporations have achieved and of consumer dependence on these giants for goods and services.

NATURE OF THE CORPORATION

What is this form of business ownership that is so important in our economy? Probably the most famous definition of a corporation was written by Chief Justice John Marshall of the United States Supreme Court in 1819 in the case of *Dartmouth College* v. *Woodward*:

> A *corporation* is an artificial being, invisible, intangible, and existing only in contemplation of law. Being the mere creature of law, it possesses only those properties which the charter of its creation confers upon it, either expressly or as incidental to its very existence. These are such as are supposed best calculated to effect the object for which it was created. Among the most important are immortality, and, if the expression may be allowed, individuality; properties, by which a perpetual succession of many persons are considered as the same, and may act as a single individual. They enable a corporation to manage its own affairs, and to hold property without the perplexing intricacies, the hazardous and endless necessity, of perpetual conveyances for the purpose of transmitting it from hand to hand. It is chiefly for the purpose of clothing bodies of men in succession with these qualities and capacities that corporations were invented and are in use.

This definition emphasizes the fact that the corporation is a *legal entity*, which is another way of saying that the law has created an artificial being endowed with the rights, duties, and powers of a person. The definition also includes the concept of many people united into one body that does not change its identity with changes in ownership, and one that may have perpetual life.

THE CORPORATE STRUCTURE

The structure of a corporation sheds further light on this form of business ownership. Its status as a legal entity stems from a *charter*, which is a document issued by a state authorizing the formation of a corporation. The owners are called *stockholders*, or *shareholders*. Except in a few instances when voting rights may have been restricted on certain classes of stock, they vote the shares they own (one share = one vote) at an annual meeting called primarily to elect a *board of directors*. These individuals represent the stockholders, and they elect the high-ranking *corporate officers*, such as president, vice president or vice presidents, secretary, and treasurer. These officers are responsible for the day-by-day operation of the corporation and report periodically to the board of directors. Although some boards of directors may meet as seldom as once a year, monthly meetings lasting a few hours or even a full day are more common. In large corporations the board divides itself into committees that meet separately and in addition to full board meetings.

Figure 5-1 below pictures in a simple manner the organization of the corporate form. The stockholders may number in the thousands or even millions. Boards of directors usually have between 9 and 17 members although there are numerous exceptions at both ends of the scale. It is customary to include among the members of the board at least the president of the corporation and, frequently, other top ranking officers.

Figure 5-1

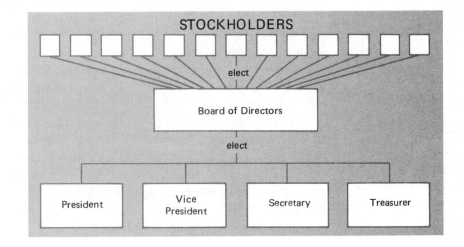

Chart of Corporate Structure

Stockholders

The stockholders of a corporation have purchased shares of stock in the company; hence, they are also called shareholders. In small firms these individuals, or at least some of them, run the corporation as well as own all or most of it. In large corporations the vast majority of the stockholders own shares purchased either as an investment or speculation and have absolutely no direct connection with the management of the corporation.

Once each year stockholders have an opportunity to vote for a slate of board members and, frequently, a few other items such as the appointment of a firm of certified public accountants to audit the books. If a stockholder can be present at the meeting, he may cast his votes in person. If, as is more likely, he cannot attend the meeting, he may send his *proxy*, which is a written authorization for someone else to cast his votes for him. Usually a majority of the voting stock outstanding must be represented at each annual meeting.

Since a corporation is required to have an annual meeting at which a quorum of over one half of the voting stock must be represented, the solicitation of proxies is a legitimate corporation expense. In corporations with a large number of stockholders, this procedure usually results in board members perpetuating themselves in office or selecting their own successors. Occasionally a group of dissatisfied stockholders may attempt to solicit proxies for a rival slate of board members. Because they must do this at their own expense, proxy battles are relatively rare when the corporation has thousands of stockholders although, if the dissidents win the election, the new board will probably vote to reimburse those who financed the opposition.

A method of electing members of the board of directors that may allow a minority group of stockholders to secure representation is *cumulative voting*. Under this plan, if there are 15 directors to be elected, the owner of a single share of voting stock can cast 15 votes in any manner he chooses. For example, he can cast one vote for each of 15 men or 15 votes for one man. By concentrating their voting, the owners of a modest fraction of the entire stock issue can elect at least one individual to the board. Cumulative voting is required by law in approximately half of the states; in most other states it is permitted if a corporation wishes to include such a provision in its bylaws.

In addition to voting for members of the board of directors, the stockholder votes on any amendments to the charter, on bylaws (unless this authority is delegated to the board of directors), on such broad policies as retirement or pension plans for officers and employees, on dissolution of the corporation, and, as stated, on the choice of the firm of certified public accountants to make the annual audit of the books and records.

Other stockholder rights include the following:

1. To receive dividends in proportion to his holdings of stock, provided, however, that such dividends have been legally declared by the board of directors, which has sole authority to do so.
2. To hold or to sell stock certificates registered in his name.
3. To share pro rata in the assets that remain after the debts have been paid when a corporation is dissolved.
4. To subscribe to additional stock offerings before such stock is made available to the general public, unless this right is waived.
5. To inspect the books and records when good cause is shown.

Board of Directors

As soon as stockholders have elected a board of directors, responsibility for directing the affairs of the business rests with this body. The usual term of office is one year although some corporations have longer terms, such as three years with only one third of the board members up for election at any annual meeting. The members of the board of directors of most small corporations are usually the stockholders who own all or most of the shares of stock. The stockholders of many large corporations elect to their boards outstanding businessmen who have no other connection with the firm, as well as some officers of the company. Of 19 directors of the General Electric Co., 15 are "outsiders" and only 4 are company executives. On the other hand, only 3 of the 17 directors of the American Brands, Inc. provide the broader perspective associated with noncompany directors, frequently called public members, and the other 14 are "insiders."

Within the framework of the charter that authorized the creation of the corporation, the board of directors is usually delegated the authority by the stockholders to adopt a set of *bylaws*. These specify the rules and regulations under which the board operates. Some of the important provisions in a set of bylaws cover the time and place of the stockholders' regular meetings, methods of calling special meetings of stockholders, the number of directors and their organization and remuneration, the names of the officers to be chosen by the board of directors, the duties of these officers, provisions for filling vacancies on the board, rules for the issuance and transfer of stock, provisions for publishing an annual statement and other accounting matters, and the method by which the bylaws can be amended.

Final authority for the actions of a corporation rests with the board of directors; but it customarily votes on, and usually approves, recommendations coming to it from the chief executive officer or other officials of the company. In large corporations the board rarely initiates changes in policies although it may make a choice among alternate courses of action. The individual members are not liable for actions of the board except when it does something illegal, such as declaring a dividend out of nonexistent profits.

Corporate Officers

The bylaws usually specify the officers of the corporation to be elected by the board of directors. The president is normally the chief executive of the company, but some corporations delegate more power to the chairman of the board. The vice president or vice presidents are usually vested with specific powers. It is not uncommon to have a vice president in charge of sales, a vice president in charge of production, and so on.

The secretary, who is in possession of the corporate seal, signs or countersigns many corporation documents. He also attends all meetings of the stockholders and directors and keeps the minutes of these meetings. The finances of a corporation are under the supervision of a treasurer; in recent years, however, much of the responsibility for this detail has been transferred, in some corporations, to an elected officer called the controller.

Name

All corporations must obviously have a name. The only restriction in choosing a name is that the one under consideration cannot be the same, or so nearly the same as to cause confusion, as that of another corporation already doing business in the state. Some states specify that the last word of the name be Corporation, Company, Incorporated, or Limited. In the United States the abbreviations Corp., Co., or Inc. are commonly used. Corporations chartered in Canada and England usually end the firm name with the abbreviation Ltd.

SEPARATION OF OWNERSHIP AND MANAGEMENT

Another feature of corporations, particularly the industrial, commercial, and financial giants, is the distinction between ownership and management. In the small corporation one stockholder may own 99 percent of the shares outstanding or three or four individuals may each own a substantial number of shares. When the outstanding shares are closely held, the chances are good that all owners are on the board of directors, each is an officer, and they all manage the business. Except for the ownership form, the situation is not unlike that of sole proprietors and partners working for themselves. In large corporations that have thousands of stockholders (see Table 5-1 below), however, the executives, as a rule, do not own very many shares; and even the total holdings of all management personnel are an insignificant percentage of total shares outstanding. When this condition exists, the result is a separation between ownership and management.

CORPORATIONS IN THE UNITED STATES WITH 300,000 OR MORE STOCKHOLDERS

	Name of Corporation	Number of Stockholders
	American Telephone & Telegraph Co.	3,083,000
	General Motors Corp.	1,339,000
	Standard Oil Co. (New Jersey)	782,000
Table 5-1	International Business Machines Corp.	549,000
	General Electric Co.	508,000
	General Telephone & Electronics Corp.	451,000
	Ford Motor Co.	382,000
	United States Steel Corp.	345,000
	Radio Corporation of America	317,000

Source: New York Stock Exchange, 1970.

The effect of divorcing ownership from management is that the executives regard the stockholders as just one group who must be kept satisfied rather than as their "bosses" to whom, by way of the board of directors, they should be solely responsible. Decisions rendered take the stockholders into consideration, but only on an equal and separate basis with the rank-and-file company employees, the firm's customers, the government, and the general public. The concept of maximizing profits for the benefit of the stockholders is not as potent a factor in decision making as it is when there is no separation between management and ownership.

ADVANTAGES OF A CORPORATION

The corporate form of business ownership, when compared with other types, has several important advantages. If this were not the case, corporations would not dominate our capitalistic system. Although there is some logic to the order in which these advantages are listed in the following paragraphs, it should be remembered that under a given set of circumstances any one of the factors might prove to be of maximum importance.

The principal advantages of a corporation are: (1) limited liability of stockholders, (2) larger size, (3) transfer of ownership, (4) length of life, (5) efficiency of management, (6) ease of expansion, and (7) legal entity.

Limited Liability of Stockholders

The corporate form of business organization offers the owners the advantage of *limited liability*, which means that each stockholder risks only the amount he invests in the corporation. If the company proves unprofitable and fails, creditors cannot look beyond the assets of the corporation for funds to settle their just claims. Since a corporation is a separate entity, it rather than its owners owes the debts. There is little question but that this advantage is one of the major reasons why over 30 million individuals own stock of corporations. If Robert Tyler, a successful lawyer, invests $10,000 in the Stone Manufacturing Company, his total risk on this investment is exactly $10,000 even though his remaining personal wealth may be sizable.

Larger Size

The original size of a sole proprietorship or a partnership is limited to the amount of capital that one man or several men can provide by recourse to their own fortunes or by borrowing. The corporation, by dividing its ownership into shares of small denomination, can attract capital from thousands of individuals. If it is necessary to secure capital amounting to millions of dollars in order to organize a firm, a corporation is the only feasible form of ownership that can be used.

Transfer of Ownership

Ownership evidenced by stock certificates gives maximum ease of transfer. If Andrews sells his interest in a corporation to Bennett, he merely endorses his stock certificate and this change of ownership is recorded in the books of the corporation. As a general rule, corporations allow their stockholders to transfer ownership to anyone at any time;

some corporations that have only a few stockholders attempt to control the ownership group by restricting transfers to the corporation itself or other remaining stockholders. Through the medium of stockbrokers and organized stock exchanges, millions of shares of stock change hands daily.

Although a corporation usually has no voice in the matter of who buys its shares of stock, it is responsible for keeping an accurate record of the stockholders. Because large corporations are subject to numerous changes in owners, some find it advantageous to hire a separate organization, usually a bank, to handle this task.

Length of Life

The corporation has potentialities of a permanent existence. The death or incapacity of stockholders, officers, and employees usually has little bearing on the continued existence of the business. If the business can thrive and prosper, it can remain in business indefinitely. Corporations with over one hundred years of continuous life are not uncommon. Many well-known firms, such as the Procter and Gamble Company, are included in this group.

Efficiency of Management

Unlike proprietorships and partnerships, the owners of a corporation do not manage it except to the extent that directors and officers are also stockholders. In the small corporation this dual role may be quite extensive on the part of management, but it is not true for medium- and large-size corporations. The corporate structure permits delegation of authority by the stockholders to the board of directors and by it to the administrative officials. Corporations frequently seek and secure the services of outstanding individuals on their boards of directors. These men give a continuity to management that is valuable. The board hires the top executives and, if these individuals do not perform efficiently, they can be replaced.

Another reason for the more efficient management of corporations stems from the attribute of size. In large corporations it is possible to delegate duties to specialists in various lines and to pay salaries high enough to attract the most competent individuals. On the payroll of such a firm may be found a purchasing agent, a sales manager, an advertising manager, a production superintendent, accountants, lawyers, and other specialists. In small firms, notably sole proprietorships and partnerships, one individual may have to perform many functions and it is unlikely that he will be equally efficient in the many diverse duties he must perform.

Ease of Expansion

A sole proprietor, assuming that he has tapped his resources to the limit, cannot expand without changing his form of business ownership, except to the extent that he allows profits to remain in the business. The partnership offers limited additional possibilities to the extent that one or more partners may be added to the firm. In contrast, the corporation has an almost unlimited opportunity for expansion just as long as investors are willing to purchase additional shares of stock. Furthermore, large corporations find it much easier to borrow substantial sums of money because the amounts needed are large enough to interest appropriate financial agencies in marketing the securities. In general, large corporations have attained a high degree of confidence among the members of the investing public, who are willing to purchase securities that are issued for expansion purposes.

Legal Entity

A corporation can sue and be sued, make contracts, and secure title to property in its own name. In this respect, the corporation is in sharp contrast to the sole proprietorship and partnership, which must use individual names in legal matters even though operating under firm names not unlike those of corporations.

DISADVANTAGES OF CORPORATE OWNERSHIP

The corporate form of business ownership has its disadvantages as well as its advantages. Some of the more important disadvantages follow: (1) taxation, (2) organization expenses, (3) government restrictions and reports, (4) lack of personal interest, (5) lack of secrecy, (6) relative lack of credit, and (7) charter restrictions.

Taxation

In addition to an annual franchise tax in the state of incorporation, an annual payment is required by every state from corporations for the right to do business in that state. Similar fees are not exacted from sole proprietorships and partnerships. Furthermore, some states levy taxes on the net income of corporations to the extent it was earned within the state and, not infrequently, they levy special taxes on certain types of corporations such as public utilities, railroads, and insurance companies.

Of even more importance, and a major disadvantage of the corporate form of business ownership, is the federal tax on income. The minimum rate on the first $25,000 of income has varied in recent years from 30 percent down to 22 percent, and the applicable rates on income in excess of $25,000 has varied from 52.8 percent down to 48 percent. Then, when the corporation distributes all or a part of its earnings after taxes to its stockholders, these individuals must pay personal income taxes on dividends received in excess of $100. The only exception to this double taxation occurs when a corporation has 10 or fewer stockholders and elects to be taxed in the same manner as a partnership.

Organization Expenses

Of all the various forms of business enterprise, corporations are the most expensive to organize. An incorporation fee must be paid to the state in order to receive a charter. Furthermore, stock certificates and record books must be purchased. Because of the legal nature of a corporation, it is usually advisable to engage a lawyer to assist in the organization procedures. For both large and small businesses, these costs may prove to be a real drawback.

If, for example, the United Resources Co. wishes to secure a charter from Delaware, a popular state for this purpose, it will be subject to the incorporation fees charged in this state as shown below:

For each share of authorized capital stock up to 20,000 shares without par value .... ½ cent

For each share in excess of 20,000 shares and up to 2,000,000 shares without par value .... ¼ cent

For each share in excess of 2,000,000 shares without par value .... ⅕ cent

For each share up to 20,000 shares having par value ...... 1 cent

For each share in excess of 20,000 shares and up to and including 200,000 shares having par value .... ½ cent

For each share in excess of 200,000 shares having par value ⅕ cent

In no case less than $10. Each one-hundred-dollar unit of par-value stock shall be counted as one taxable share.

Assume that this new corporation wishes to issue 3,000,000 shares of a $50 par preferred stock and 5,000,000 shares of no-par common stock.[1] The cost of its charter is shown in Table 5-2.

COST OF A CHARTER—AN EXAMPLE

Preferred Stock—3,000,000 Shares $50 Par

(Tax rates on par stock are based on $100 of par value. Since it takes two of the above shares of $50 par to equal one taxable share, the computation below is on the 1,500,000 taxable shares involved.)

20,000 taxable shares at 1 cent each	$ 200	
180,000 taxable shares at 1/2 cent each	900	
1,300,000 taxable shares at 1/5 cent each	2,600	
1,500,000 taxable shares	$ 3,700	**Table 5-2**

Common Stock—5,000,000 shares no par

20,000 shares at 1/2 cent each	$ 100
1,980,000 shares at 1/4 cent each	4,950
3,000,000 shares at 1/5 cent each	6,000
5,000,000 shares	11,050
Total cost of preferred and common stocks	$14,750

Government Restrictions and Reports

Because the corporation is a creature of the government, various departments of the state and federal governments have the right to exercise certain restrictions and to require certain reports. For example, a corporation cannot conduct business in a state in which it is not registered. This registration involves the payment of a special tax.

All types of annual and special reports, which frequently become burdensome and costly to the corporation, must be prepared. Some corporations, particularly public utilities, find it necessary to maintain report departments for the sole purpose of providing governmental bureaus and agencies with figures that must be furnished.

Lack of Personal Interest

A corporation has an identity of its own. All who work for a corporation, therefore, assume the role of employees. This relationship sometimes

[1] See Chapter 19 for a discussion of par and no-par stock.

results in a lack of personal interest in the success or failure of the organization unless the employee is also a stockholder. It is probable that the efforts of many firms to sell stock to their employees have been motivated by a desire to mitigate the effects of this disadvantage. It is assumed that these employees will work harder in order to increase profits that will then flow to their pocketbooks in the form of dividends.

Managers draw a salary paid by the corporation; and they take it for granted that, as long as they produce reasonable profits, they will continue to be paid. Mistakes resulting in a loss of potential profits are detrimental to the corporation, but ordinarily a reduction in profits that might have been earned does not affect executives individually as it would if their role were that of a sole proprietor or a partner. It should be noted, however, that lawsuits filed against executives which seek to hold them personally liable for corporate losses suffered because of their incompetence or dishonesty have been increasing in recent years.

Lack of Secrecy

A corporation is duty bound to make an annual report to each stockholder. If it has only a few stockholders, these reports ordinarily do not become available to outsiders. When a considerable number of stockholders are involved, however, the annual reports become public property. Generally, such figures as sales volume, gross profit, net profit, total assets, and other financial matters are furnished in some detail. Furthermore, payments to each director and to each of the three highest paid officers of the corporation whose aggregate remuneration during the year exceeded $30,000 are detailed in the proxy statement. Other corporations, sometimes keen rivals, have an opportunity to examine the financial details of all companies that find it necessary to disclose this information.

Relative Lack of Credit

It may seem strange that corporations do not enjoy higher credit ratings than proprietorships and partnerships, but size for size this is true. Creditors of a $25,000 corporation can look only to the assets of the organization for any debts incurred whereas a $25,000 proprietorship or partnership offers the additional security of the owners' private fortunes.

Charter Restrictions

A sole proprietor can change his business almost at will. A corporation, on the other hand, must state the business it intends to pursue at the time of applying for a charter. Unless the charter of a corporation is amended, the company may not engage in any type of business not covered by the original permit.

Some states grant charters with a wide latitude in permissible corporate activities. Nevertheless, an unanticipated opportunity may suddenly present itself that cannot be seized because the type of business involved is not within the scope of the charter.

ORGANIZING A CORPORATION

After weighing the advantages and the disadvantages, if the decision is to form a corporation, it will be necessary to secure a charter from one of the 50 states. The federal government charters national banks, federal credit unions and savings and loan associations, a few government corporations, and some scientific and educational organizations; but all industrial and commercial corporations are organized under state laws.

Although incorporation laws in the several states vary in detail, they follow a general pattern. The first step necessary is to secure an application form, usually from the secretary of state of the state in which the corporation is to be formed. This form provides spaces for the name of the corporation, the names of the principal stockholders, the number and the types of shares of capital stock, the place of business, the type of business, and so forth.

When the application form is available, it is filled out, with special care given to fulfilling all specific requirements. Most states require at least three stockholders. Also, the minimum amount of capital for a business corporation is at least $500; frequently, the smallest permitted amount is $1,000.

After the requirements have been met, the completed papers with the requisite *incorporation fee* are forwarded to the state capitol. This charge varies with the number of shares of stock that the proposed corporation wishes to be permitted to issue, but a minimum fee of from $10 to $25 is customary.

The selection of the state in which to file incorporation papers depends on a number of factors. Usually, if a corporation plans to concentrate its activities within one state, it will be advantageous to secure its charter from that state. If its operations will be conducted in all 50 states, the choice may hinge on the cost of the incorporation fee, the lack of charter restrictions, and the amount of the continuing franchise tax. A *franchise tax* is an annual levy by a state on corporations it has chartered granting permission to continue in business for another year.

CLASSIFICATION OF CORPORATIONS

Corporations may be classified as follows: (1) private and governmental corporations; (2) profit and nonprofit corporations; (3) stock and nonstock corporations; (4) domestic, foreign, and alien corporations; (5) close and open corporations; and (6) industrial classifications.

Private and Governmental Corporations

A *private corporation* is one chartered, owned, and operated by individuals either for the profit of its owners or for social, charitable, or educational purposes. The vast majority of corporations are private in nature, and by far the larger number are organized with the intent of making a profit. A *governmental corporation* is one organized by the federal government, a state, a city, or some other political subdivision. Examples of governmental corporations are incorporated cities, municipally owned water companies, state universities, and the Commodity Credit Corporation. Governmental corporations are sometimes referred to as public corporations but, unless this meaning is made clear, there may be confusion with private corporations owned by the general public.

The Communications Satellite Corporation is an interesting mixture of a private and governmental corporation. The ownership is private, but the Corporation was authorized by the Congress and three members of the board of directors are appointed by the President. Of the remaining twelve board members, six are elected by the companies owning stock and six by the individual stockholders.

Profit and Nonprofit Corporations

A *profit corporation* is a privately owned business, using the corporate form, that operates to make profits for its stockholders. The vast majority of all corporations in the United States are of this type. A *nonprofit corporation* is somewhat of a misnomer in that its receipts may exceed its disbursements but a distribution is never made to its owners, and any income that may result from its operations is used to further the purposes for which it was organized. Governmental as well as social, charitable, religious, and educational corporations are examples of this classification.

Stock and Nonstock Corporations

Business corporations issue *stock certificates*, representing shares of ownership, which provide a basis for distributing the profits to the stockholders. In general, governmental corporations, as well as private corporations not organized to make profits for their members, do not issue stock. Examples of such private corporations are churches, hospitals, and schools.

Domestic, Foreign, and Alien Corporations

A corporation is usually organized under the laws of one state. In that state the business is regarded as a *domestic corporation*; but in every other state in which it may operate, it is considered a *foreign corporation*. For example, the United States Steel Corporation, which is organized under the laws of New Jersey, is considered a domestic corporation in that state; but in Pennsylvania, where it has numerous offices and factories, it is a foreign corporation.

A company doing business within the United States that has been organized in another country, such as Canada, Mexico, England, or The Netherlands, is known in the United States as an *alien corporation*.

Close and Open Corporations

If the stock of a corporation is not available for purchase by outsiders, it is a *close corporation*. Usually it is owned by only a few stockholders, most of whom are probably active in the management. Family corporations and corporations that have been formed by converting sole proprietorships or partnerships into the corporate form are typical of the close classification.

If the stock of a corporation is available for purchase by anyone having sufficient funds, it is an *open corporation*. Most of the large corporations are open, and shares can be purchased through the agency of a stockbroker. Within recent years many close corporations, needing funds for expansion or for other reasons, have "gone public," that is, have made shares available to investors. As previously mentioned, this has given rise to the use of the term "public corporation" for what is, more accurately, an open corporation.

Industrial Classifications

Private, profit-making, business corporations may be classified in several ways. Moody's Manuals, which include a description of almost every corporation in the United States, as well as those in foreign countries, are issued in four volumes. These are headed Industrials, Banks & Finance,

Public Utilities, and Transportation. Within the manuals there is a further breakdown; for example, the Industrial volume is subdivided into aviation, chemical, petroleum, tobacco, and many other categories.

The Department of the Treasury, Internal Revenue Service, classifies corporations into the same major industrial divisions used for sole proprietorships and partnerships. Table 5-3 below shows these groups, the number of income tax returns filed by each, the total receipts, and the net profits. Since all business corporations must file returns regardless of whether or not any profits have been realized, the figures in this table reflect an accurate picture of the number and financial success of corporations operating in each classification.

Table 5-3

CORPORATION INCOME TAX RETURNS
NUMBER, BUSINESS RECEIPTS, AND NET PROFITS BY INDUSTRIAL DIVISIONS

Industrial Divisions	Number of Returns	Business Receipts (Millions of Dollars)	Net Income (Deficit) (Millions of Dollars)
ALL INDUSTRIAL DIVISIONS	1,515,678	$1,382,519	$85,057
Mining	12,929	13,657	1,502
Contract construction	126,908	70,797	1,686
Manufacturing	191,908	624,400	44,034
Transportation, communication, electric, gas, and sanitary services	65,958	108,501	10,462
Wholesale and retail trade	473,515	440,180	10,243
Finance, insurance, and real estate	408,170	77,325	15,175
Services	230,242	47,549	1,956
Nature of business not allocable	6,048	110	(2)

Source: U.S. Department of the Treasury, Internal Revenue Service, *Statistics of Income, 1968*. Agriculture, forestry, and fisheries omitted. Due to rounding, items may not add to totals.

OTHER INCORPORATED BUSINESSES

Although the corporation is the dominant form of incorporated business ownership, there are a few other types that, in specific areas, are more widely used. Since in each case the business conducted is of a corporate nature, it seems obvious that there are unique advantages attached to the firms which use these different forms of incorporated business ownership. Such advantages will be pointed out in the following description and explanation of (1) cooperatives, (2) credit unions, (3) mutual companies, and (4) savings and loan associations.

COOPERATIVES

Cooperatives, or *co-ops* as they are commonly called, are incorporated under the laws of a state. They are to be distinguished from corporations in the following respects:

1. Each cooperative unit is owned by the user-members of the group.
2. Each member has only one vote regardless of the number of shares of stock that he owns.
3. There is a limitation on the amount of stock that each member may own.
4. The capital for the enterprise is subscribed only by the members.
5. Interest is paid on the investment of each member-stockholder.
6. Dividends are paid on a patronage basis, in proportion to the amount of goods that each member has bought or sold through the co-op. These are referred to as *patronage dividends*.

Cooperatives have all of the advantages of corporations although the requirement of ownership by user-members limits the size and ease of expansion. They also have a tax advantage in that patronage dividends are considered a refund of overpayments rather than a distribution of profits, and the federal government provides financial assistance not available to profit-seeking corporations. In agricultural co-ops, members are frequently intensely loyal to their firm and support the business with zeal and enthusiasm.

On the other hand, cooperatives lack the profit-making incentive common to other forms of ownership, which appears to be a serious handicap. Also, there is an unfortunate tendency to rely on volunteers, e. g., members of the board of directors customarily are not paid for their services, and the salary scales for employees are frequently on the low side.

The most extensive use of co-ops is in the field of agriculture. Farm products that are marketed through farmer cooperatives include citrus fruits, butter, potatoes, milk, prunes, apricots, wool, grains of all kinds, livestock, eggs, poultry, and rice. Such well-known brands as Sunkist oranges and Sun Maid raisins are the property of *producer cooperative associations* engaged in the marketing of these products grown by their many members. There are more than 7,000 producer cooperative associations in the United States with annual sales in excess of $8 billion. In addition to producer co-ops, there are approximately the same number of farmer-owned *buying cooperatives* whose purchases of seeds, gasoline, farm machinery, etc., total about $3 billion annually.

Although *consumer co-ops*, which are user-owned retail outlets of goods and services, have long been a dominant factor in such countries as Denmark and Sweden, their influence in the United States has been relatively minor, particularly in the retailing of consumer goods. Aided by the Rural Electrification Administration, a federal agency, the sales of electricity by consumer cooperatives has grown, and rural telephone co-ops have also increased, again with federal financial aid. In other retail areas the cooperative movement has failed to generate any enthusiasm among our general public.

CREDIT UNIONS

A *credit union* is a type of financial institution designed to assist a homogeneous group to save money and loan it to one another. For example, the group may be the employees of a firm, members of a church, or residents of a community. A credit union is an incorporated entity that can secure a charter from a state or, unlike cooperatives and corporations, from the federal government.

Each member of a credit union purchases at least one share, which usually costs $5; in some instances members pay a membership fee of 25 cents. All members elect a board of directors from among themselves who serve without pay. The board elects officers who are likewise not paid, except that some larger credit unions may employ an office manager and the necessary clerical help. If the credit union is organized among the employees of a factory or business establishment, it is customary for the company to provide them free office space.

By using funds available from shares sold to members, on which there is no limit, loans are made to other members. Most of these loans are for amounts ranging from $100 to $500 although some credit unions make larger loans. Interest is usually charged at the rate of one percent a month on the unpaid balance. Net earnings provide funds to pay dividends on shares outstanding and, in some instances, to reduce the interest charge on loans to less than 12 percent a year.

There are approximately 22,000 credit unions with 17,000,000 members in the United States. Total assets owned are in excess of $10 billion. Most credit unions are relatively small with memberships ranging from 100 to 1,000. This type of incorporated business ownership is currently operating in 70 countries although approximately one half of all credit unions are located in the United States.

MUTUAL COMPANIES

Mutual companies receive a charter from a state, but the owners are the users of the service rendered rather than being stockholders. There are two primary uses of mutual companies: life insurance companies and savings banks. The purchaser of a policy from a mutual life insurance company is automatically a member as is the individual who deposits money in a mutual savings bank. These owners theoretically elect a board of directors to manage the business. Actually, since it is unusual to solicit proxies from policyholders or depositors, the owners rarely bother to vote and boards of directors tend to be self-perpetuating.

Mutual companies have most of the advantages of corporations including limited liability. They also enjoy special federal income tax treatment. For example, dividends on life insurance policies are considered a partial refund of premiums paid by the policyholder. Mutual savings banks can insure their accounts with an agency of the federal government and can borrow funds from the federal home loan bank system.

Over one half of all life insurance companies are organized as mutuals, and these mutual companies own assets of $130 billion. For legal reasons most mutual savings banks are located in the Middle Atlantic and New England states but, despite this restriction, their total assets amount to $71 billion. These figures seem to indicate that, despite the lack of pressure from stockholders for dividends, mutual companies have been aggressive and efficiently managed.

SAVINGS AND LOAN ASSOCIATIONS

Savings and loan associations are financial institutions that accept deposits from savers and loan these funds to borrowers to build homes. In those that are mutually owned, which are the ones of concern here, both savers and borrowers are members; and they elect a board of directors who manage the association. The major difference between savings and loan associations and mutual companies is that, in the former, charters are available from the federal government as well as from a state. Usually there is also a difference in voting in that a saver has a vote for each $100 invested up to a limit of 50 votes. A borrower is normally required to become a member by buying one share which entitles him to one vote.

There are about 6,000 savings and loan associations operating in the United States and, of these, approximately 90 percent are mutual type companies. Total assets of these associations amount to $120 billion contributed, in large measure, by some 40 million buyers of shares. The advantages of this type of incorporated business ownership are similar to those applying to mutual companies, and the desire of management to pay dividends to depositors has led to efficiency of operation for most savings and loan associations.

BUSINESS TERMS

QUESTIONS FOR DISCUSSION AND ANALYSIS

1. Voters are accustomed to making a selection when public officials are elected. Stockholders only rarely have a comparable privilege when electing the members of the board of directors of their corporation. Do you think this situation needs correcting? Why or why not?

2. When given a choice, most corporate managements oppose cumulative voting for members of the board of directors of their companies. Why?

3. Should the board of directors of a corporation include more public members than insiders? Why or why not?

4. Are corporate managers more likely to be willing to incur expenditures to reduce pollution attributable to their firms than sole proprietors or partners? Give reasons for your choice.

5. Why should stockholders of a corporation have the advantage of limited liability?

6. Assume a comparison among three firms exactly the same size and in the same business. One is organized as a sole proprietorship, another as a partnership, and the third as a corporation. Is the management of the corporation likely to be the most efficient?

7. Why should corporations be subject to more and heavier taxes than sole proprietorships and partnerships?

8. Does an open corporation have any control over the composition of its stockholder group? Could it refuse to transfer a large block of stock to a convicted murderer serving a life sentence?

9. Why has the somewhat limited success of cooperatives in this country been more or less restricted to businesses closely related to agriculture?

10. How can a savings and loan association organized as a corporation compete with a savings and loan association organized as a mutual company since the latter has no stockholders clamoring for dividends?

PROBLEMS AND SHORT CASES

1. A group of promoters decide to incorporate the Farm Machinery Leasing Corporation with an authorized capital stock of 5,000,000 shares of preferred stock with a par value of $10 a share, and 10,000,000 shares of no-par common stock. Ohio and Delaware have been suggested as logical states in which to file incorporation papers. The cost of obtaining a charter may prove to be a vital factor in the choice between the two states.

Compute (a) the amount of the incorporation fee in Ohio, (b) the amount of the incorporation fee in Delaware (see page 111), and (c) the amount of savings one state offers over the other.

Incorporation fees for Ohio make no distinction between par and no-par stock and are as follows:

First 1,000 shares .... 10 cents a share
1,001 to 10,000 shares .... 5 cents a share
10,001 to 50,000 shares .... 2 cents a share
50,001 to 100,000 shares .... 1 cent a share
100,001 to 500,000 shares .... ½ cent a share
Over 500,000 shares .... ¼ cent a share

2. Using the information in Table 5-3 on page 117, compute (a) the percent of total number of returns for each division to the number of returns for all industrial divisions, and (b) the percent of business receipts for each division to the total business receipts for all industrial divisions. List each set of percentages in descending order.

What conclusions can be drawn from these computations?

3. In 1962, Andrew Bonwit's father died and, as the sole heir, he became the owner of the family candy business. Actually he had been managing Bonbons by Bonwit, the firm name, since shortly after his graduation from college in 1956 on a salary and bonus arrangement. His father had been unwilling to admit Andrew as a partner, so the business had continued as a sole proprietorship.

In the next ten years young Bonwit opened retail outlets, established dealerships, leased a factory building, and increased sales from a previous average of $78,000 a year to $842,000 in 1972. Employees grew in number from 10 men and women to 118. Instead of a one-man show he now had a sales manager, advertising manager, controller, and factory manager reporting to him.

Bonwit and his wife have four children, two boys and two girls, whose ages range from 6 to 16. His firm has been very profitable and, in addition to his ownership of the business, he has outside investments totaling $625,000. Currently, the firm has adequate cash resources and no long-term debt, but the lease on the factory building expires in three months and Bonwit faces the choice of a 50 percent increase in rent or purchasing the building for $475,000.

Bonwit's lawyer has suggested to him that it might be wise for him to incorporate the business. There would appear to be no difficulty in selling stock to employees and friends for $500,000 and payment by the proposed corporation to Bonwit for the existing business would approximate $1,000,000, which would guarantee Bonwit voting control of the corporation.

On the basis of this information, answer these questions: (a) What are the arguments in favor of and against incorporation of this business? (b) Would you advise Mr. Bonwit to incorporate his business?

SUGGESTED READINGS

Anderson, R. A., and W. A. Kumpf. *Business Law*, Eighth Edition. Cincinnati: South-Western Publishing Co., 1968. Part IX.

Bandy, W. R., *et al. Business Law: Text and Cases*, Second Edition. Boston: Allyn and Bacon, Inc., 1968. Chapters XXXII and XXXIV.

Broom, H. N., and J. G. Longenecker. *Small Business Management*, Third Edition. Cincinnati: South-Western Publishing Co., 1971. Part B.

Corley, R. N., and R. L. Black, Jr. *The Legal Environment of Business*, Second Edition. New York: McGraw-Hill Book Company, 1968. Chapter Seven.

Curran, W. S. *Principles of Financial Management*. New York: McGraw-Hill Book Company, 1970. Chapter 2.

Dawson, T. L., and E. W. Mounce. *Business Law Text and Cases*, Second Edition. Lexington, Massachusetts: D. C. Heath and Company, 1968. Part VIII.

Robert, W., and R. Corley. *Dillavou & Howard's Principles of Business Law*, Eighth Edition. Englewood Cliffs, New Jersey: Prentice-Hall, Inc., 1967. Book Five.

Donaldson, E. F., and J. K. Pfahl. *Corporate Finance—Policy and Management*, Third Edition. New York: The Ronald Press Company, 1969. Part I.

Litka, M. P. *Business Law*. New York: Harcourt Brace Jovanovich, Inc., 1970. Part 5.

Lusk, H. F., *et al. Business Law—Principles and Cases*, Second Uniform Commercial Code Edition. Homewood, Illinois: Richard D. Irwin, Inc., 1970. Part VI.

Niswonger, C. R., and P. E. Fess. *Accounting Principles*, Tenth Edition. Cincinnati: South-Western Publishing Co., 1969. Chapter 16.

Wyatt, J. W., and M. B. Wyatt. *Business Law*, Third Edition. New York: McGraw-Hill Book Company, 1966. Part Eight.

Chapter 6

Organization for Management

Most of the world's work is done by people working together in groups. By cooperating with others man is able to amplify human capacities and thereby enhance human welfare. For example, in one of Aesop's fables, a blind man who could walk carried a man who could see but could not walk. Thus, because these men organized and coordinated their efforts, they found that they could do more than either one of them could without the other.

The idea of organization, however, is more complex than coordination and cooperation. It means more than simply "working together." The word "organization" has two basic meanings. The first is a static concept and refers to the structure or pattern of relationships among people working together. In this sense schools, clubs, community groups, companies and business firms, governmental agencies, hospitals, political parties, and churches are called organizations. The second meaning of organization is dynamic and refers to the process by which groups attain their goals and by which group structures change and grow. The differences between these two meanings may be likened to the differences between a snapshot and a moving picture.

This chapter will explain the key features of organization as a process, then describe organizational structures used by business, and finally return to the process view in a discussion of the modern theory of organizational behavior.

ORGANIZATIONAL PROCESS

One basic element in organization is coordination of effort; but for coordination to be meaningful and helpful, there must be cooperation among the parties concerned. Cooperation assumes some kind of work division among the participating individuals. Work division causes people to specialize in particular tasks. Within a cooperating group certain individuals assume, or are assigned, responsibility for the accomplishment of the subgoals of an organization. The very idea of responsibility implies that each work unit submit to some kind of authority for the sake of achieving a common goal. *Authority* may be defined as the right to make decisions that guide the actions of others. The authority needed for coordination may range from self-discipline to complete authoritarian domination, but some type of authority is required in any organization.

The elements of the organizational process may be put together with varying degrees of formality. In a social club, coordination, goals, work division, specialization of effort, and authority may be very loosely defined. In most business concerns the organization tends to be much more formal. This formality arises because the goals and the means of achieving them are set forth by those in positions of responsibility and authority. In a *formal organization* there is a plan that describes how work activities are to be divided and coordinated to achieve an overall goal. The term *informal organization* refers to those patterns of cooperation and coordination that arise among members of a formal organization but which are not covered by the organizational plan. As an example, employees from several departments may regularly have lunch together and talk about the firm for which they all work. Even though completely unorganized, informal groups are a very real and important part of any complex organization. The manager can scarcely afford to ignore their existence despite the fact that they do not appear on the formal organization chart.

An *organizational plan* is a blueprint or description of the process of coordinating the efforts of a number of people for the achievement of some explicit goal through the division of work and through the assignment of different levels of authority and responsibility. Because organizations may change goals, find new ways of dividing and coordinating work activities, and modify the scope of authority and responsibility, the process of organizational planning is a continuing challenge to management.

MANAGEMENT AND ORGANIZATION

Management, which is discussed at some length in Chapter 7, may be said to include all the personnel of a business whose duties include the making of decisions affecting their firm's affairs and assuming the responsibility both for the implementation of these decisions and for the results that flow from them. Theirs is the responsibility of making certain, or trying to, that their firm's objectives are attained, whether these be profits, market share, growth, quality of product or service, community prestige, or any combination of these.

Organization is the process by which management endeavors to achieve its objectives by combining the efforts of the people under its supervision. This process is a necessity in both small and large companies regardless of whether the firm is a sole proprietorship, a partnership, or a corporation. While the success of a company may be attributed to many causes, the skill with which management determines and implements its organizational plan is one of the major factors in the end result.

For small businesses, such as an independently owned hardware store, the details of organization for purposes of management are comparatively simple. The owner, who is usually the manager, employs a few persons to sell, to keep the stock in order, to make such deliveries as are necessary, and to keep the store clean. The owner usually buys the merchandise, handles the office work, assigns duties to his employees, establishes the policies of the company, and directs the operation of the entire business. There is little need for a complex organization in a firm of this size and the owner-manager has few problems in this area.

If the organization is somewhat larger or if it has expanded over the years, the problem of a satisfactory organization arises. If the business is a sole proprietorship, the owner must delegate some authority and responsibility. In a partnership the segregation of functions, a factor in creating an internal structure, is often recognized in the articles of partnership by stating the duties of each partner. This delineation of authority and responsibility works out even more naturally in a corporation if the board of directors elects such officers as a vice president in charge of sales, a vice president in charge of manufacturing, and a treasurer. These positions are merely the beginnings of a plan for the organization of a firm, however, and need to be expanded to include all employees.

IMPORTANCE OF ORGANIZATIONAL STRUCTURE

An *organizational structure* is a framework within which management can adequately control, supervise, delegate, and fix responsibilities, and synchronize the work done by divisions, departments, and individuals. It is a plan by which a large business can attain the same efficiency as, or greater efficiency than, a small business run effectively by one person. It should not be created or allowed to grow in a haphazard manner. Only by building a planned organizational structure, taking into account all pertinent factors applicable, can a business achieve maximum operating efficiency. In highly competitive areas, proper organization may prove to be the necessary advantage one firm has over another.

An organizational structure also plays an important part in improving and maintaining employee morale. Just as a college football team cannot measure up to its capabilities unless eleven men are playing as a unit, no firm can operate smoothly unless employees "pull together." The familiar phrase *esprit de corps*, as applied to industry, means that loyal employees are working harmoniously alongside of, and in cooperation with, each other. They are eager to promote the welfare of the firm, and its continuing success is a matter of personal pride to each individual.

Although it is true that the payment of good wages is an important part of employee morale, loyalty and the urge to do a good job cannot be bought by money alone. An organizational structure that allows each worker to know what he is supposed to do, to whom he is responsible, and the part he plays in the overall picture may prove to be more important than the size of the pay check that he receives.

FACTORS IN ORGANIZATIONAL PLANNING

The structure of an organization, in its broadest sense, deals with the overall organizational arrangements that provide the means to accomplish the goals of the enterprise. Once its objectives have been established, the mass of work necessary to achieve these objectives must be divided into manageable units; and the authority relationships must be established among those who will be manning these units. In formalizing the organizational structure, then, the following factors should be considered: (1) classification of business activities, (2) departmentalization, (3) decentralization of authority, (4) levels of authority, (5) delegation of authority, (6) span of management, (7) clearly defined duties, (8) flexibility, and (9) communication.

Classification of Business Activities

The major activities of a manufacturing concern are production, marketing, finance, and accounting and statistical controls. Nonmanufacturing enterprises omit production from their scope of operations. These classifications may well provide the starting point for the construction of an organization plan, although two or more functions may be combined under one executive or in a department. An illustration of such a grouping is found in the common practice of designating a financial officer who is also in charge of accounting and statistical controls.

Departmentalization

Departmentalization is the practice of subdividing the work necessary to achieve the objectives into units within an organization. It affects the horizontal dimension of an organization's structure. In one sense it is an extension of the classification of business activities into additional subdivisions.

Several levels of departmentalization may result from these additional units such as departments, divisions, branches, or sections. The basis for the subdivision usually takes one or more of five main forms: by function, by process, by geographical area, by product, and by customer. These subdivisions may exist in any business simultaneously. The people reporting to a vice president for production may be grouped functionally according to the major tasks they perform as follows: production engineering, research and development, purchasing, manufacturing, quality control, and shipping. In the manufacturing department of a job shop operation, the departments may be subdivided by process, based upon techniques or equipment, into: the lathe department, the grinding department, the polishing department, the paint department, and the assembly department. Railroads, airlines, chain stores, gas and oil distributors, and public utilities frequently departmentalize along the lines of geographic regions. Companies that manufacture a wide range of different products may group activities in terms of products. For example, the groups reporting to top management of American Machine & Foundry Company are: electrical products group, tobacco machinery group, bowling products group, recreational products group, general products group, governmental products group, and an international products group. A hardware firm may group its activities into a wholesale and a retail division in order to serve different types of customers.

Decentralization of Authority

The act of delegating the authority for making managerial decisions to those at lower levels in the organization is called *decentralization*. The degree of decentralization in an organization is not measured by the quantity of decisions that are passed down the line, however, but rather by the importance and scope of these decisions and their general impact on the organization.

The position is sometimes taken that a firm is decentralized when its management is physically dispersed, e.g., when central management is geographically separated from its divisional or branch manager. This viewpoint is not entirely correct as authority to make managerial decisions may be delegated by a boss to a subordinate sitting at the desk next to him. Likewise, a central manager may be heavily involved in the decisions that are made in distant divisions. Although decentralization of decision-making authority usually goes hand in glove with physical dispersion, one is not necessary to the other. Care should be taken, therefore, to distinguish between the concept of decentralization of decision-making authority and that of physical decentralization or, as it is more clearly termed, physical dispersion.

In many very large companies, frequently with diversified product lines, the concept of decentralization has been extended to the point where each product line becomes the basis of a more or less semiautonomous division. In such a situation the responsibility for designing, producing, and selling its product line and of making a profit is given to the division management. This situation is known as *divisionalization.* The General Motors Corporation and the E. I. du Pont de Nemours and Company have been pioneers in this philosophy of decentralization. Among other companies that follow this practice are the General Electric Company, IBM, and Continental Can Company. The rationale behind this practice is that these firms have become too large and their product lines too varied for a centralized management to supervise satisfactorily, so that each division acts almost as though it were an independent company. This is particularly true in the case of General Motors, where genuine competition exists between the top-priced lines of Chevrolet and the lower priced lines of Pontiac. The same situation prevails between the corporation's higher priced cars. Where divisionalization exists, each division has its own producing and selling departments, as well as its ancillary services such as personnel and accounting.

All large companies, however, do not look with favor on divisionalization. Probably the most recent example of this attitude is the United States Steel Corporation which has done away with seven of its steel-making divisions and established in their stead two large manufacturing and sales departments that took over the activities of the former divisions. The term applied to this procedure is known as *functionalization* or the adopting of a functional type of control structure. With this sort of arrangement, a firm's physical operations may be dispersed, but the managerial control for all of its different operations is centralized; that is, a single sales force sells all of its different products and the manufacturing plants are directed from the home office. When the firm is not physically decentralized but is organized according to its basic activities, such as production, marketing, finance, purchasing, and personnel, each of these departments is regarded as a functional area, but it reports to and is supervised by higher levels of authority and responsibility.

Such an arrangement is also known as a *functional organization*, with the focus of responsibility centering on the president. In a large company this concentration of responsibility may overburden the chief executive with supervisory duties, leaving him too little time for creative thinking and acting. It also tends to create a shortage of potential managers because of the centralizing of authority at the top. This latter situation has been recognized by the managements of many firms who have sought to discover and implement various procedures to overcome it.

The use of the term "functional" may be somewhat confusing to beginning students of business because the same term is used with quite a different meaning, as will be explained on page 136.

Levels of Authority

The existence of levels of authority is characteristic of most coordinated group effort. Even in informal groups leaders emerge. The resulting separation between leaders and followers produces a two-level group. In a large, complex business organization the number of levels of authority may be quite extensive. Regardless of the stratification, at each successively lower level in the organization there is a decreasing amount of authority, a narrowing of the scope of authority, and frequently a shift in the nature of authority. Also, with each lower level of authority there is the tendency to grant fewer symbols of status or prestige to the position holder. The levels of authority within an organization are also called the *hierarchy of authority*.

Delegation of Authority

While it is true that the final responsibility for all decisions rests with the top man or men in any organization, it is not logical to allow every decision to be referred to the owner or to the president. Every employee who is placed in charge of the work of others expects to be held responsible for the performance of this work and to be allowed to exercise some measure of authority over his subordinates. Thus, authority and responsibility naturally go together and should be clearly understood by managers and subordinates alike.

Delegation is the process that ties together task responsibilities and the authority needed to achieve the tasks. As such, it is a key management concept and must be incorporated in any organizational structure. Basically, delegation is the managerial technique that allows the manager to assign duties and commensurate authority to others and, at the same time, gain from these others the recognition of their responsibility to either perform the assigned work or to bring to the manager's attention the reasons why the job cannot be accomplished. This recognizes that there should be a distribution of authority so that no man has so many decisions to make that he cannot discharge his duties effectively. The boss should carefully develop two-way communication channels that will encourage the subordinate to discuss delegated tasks with him.

Span of Management

In preparing an organization plan it is necessary to decide the extent to which duties are to be subdivided and the proper sequence of authority. In a small firm the treasurer may be the chief accountant, auditor, controller, and credit manager, whereas a larger organization would have department heads for each of these divisions. Even in a large firm, however, the type of work and the skill of the workers would play an important part. If a machine shop employed only highly skilled workers, the chances would be that each would know his job so well that very little supervision would be needed. In this case a single foreman might have a large number of employees under him without the need for any intermediate supervision. The same situation would be true if a large number of unskilled workers were hired to do a simple task requiring very little direction. On the other hand, if it was necessary to hire untrained help to perform tasks requiring a fair amount of skill, no single supervisor could direct the work of more than a few people.

The problem of the optimum number of persons that can be efficiently supervised has been receiving increased attention in many firms. It has been divided into two parts: (a) the number of subordinate executives that a top executive can effectively control, called the *span of executive control* or *span of management*, and (b) the number of operatives, such as salesmen, clerks, or production workers, that a subordinate executive can effectively handle, which has been termed the *unit of supervision*. Studies in these two areas indicate that the proper number in each type is dependent upon the complexity of the situations involved as well as upon the skill and experience of the personnel concerned. These two latter factors apply to supervisors as well as workers.

Clearly Defined Duties

The job every employee is expected to do should be clearly defined to the point that it is different from that expected of others and does not overlap duties assigned to other workers. Unless this is done, there is bound to be friction among employees at all levels. If it is the job of the repair department to keep all machines in good operating order, the foreman in the production department should not be blamed for a slowdown in production based on mechanical breakdowns. On the other hand, if it is the duty of the foreman to see that his machines are kept in operating condition, there should be no doubt as to where this responsibility lies.

Flexibility

Any organization plan that unduly hampers the ability of the employee to express his individuality and initiative robs the organization of one of the most valuable assets of our type of economic society. A certain amount of regimentation is desirable but, when it stifles the worker to the place where he is just a cog in a machine, the firm loses rather than gains. There will always be exceptions to every plan, and some executives spend much of their time handling variations from the routine that has been established. Even though a foreman may have the right to dismiss an employee from his department, that man might be a valuable employee under a different boss or in another line of work.

Communication

Business executives have become increasingly aware of the importance of adequate channels of communications in internal organization. The term "communication," as used in this sense, means that there should be facilities for an uninterrupted flow of orders, instructions, questions, responses, explanations, ideas, and suggestions between top management and the rest of the organization. This flow should be a two-way facility, from management to employees and from employees to management. Aside from the customary orders and instructions concerning the normal routine of operations, management frequently wishes to explain some of its policy decisions, or to give information about the company's products, finances, plans for expansion, and personnel changes. By so doing, management hopes to bring about a better understanding among its workers of the salient facts concerning the company. Employees, on the other hand, often have ideas for saving time, labor, and materials. They may have grievances of one kind or another that should reach the ears of the management. In planning the details of an organization, therefore, provision should be made for the creation and maintenance of a good two-way communication system. The communication from the lower to the higher echelons of an organization, especially with respect to information concerning the results of orders previously issued by top management, is known as a *feedback*. Further reference to this practice occurs in Chapter 13.

The Organization Chart

A common practice in companies of any considerable size is the construction of a formal *organization chart*, an example of which appears in Figure 6-1. While this chart does not customarily spell out the duties and responsibilities of each position, it serves to indicate the areas of authority within a company. If, as is occasionally found, the names of the executives and department heads are included, this implies the need for revision when promotions, transfers, resignations, or other changes occur. The failure of some firms to make the necessary changes in order to keep the information up to date has occasioned criticism of the organization chart practice.

FORMS OF ORGANIZATIONAL STRUCTURE

After a consideration of the principles involved in forming an organization structure, the next step is to decide upon the type that is best suited to a particular situation. Only two basic organization forms are in common use today, the line and the line-and-staff. The line organization is found mainly in small firms, while large concerns customarily follow the line-and-staff pattern. A third form, called the functional organization by its originator, F. W. Taylor, served as a theoretical transition between the line and the line-and-staff. The committee organization, a fourth form, is never found alone but always as a suborganizational grouping in either line or line-and-staff types. These four types of organization structures are known as: (1) line organization, (2) Taylor's functional organization, (3) line-and-staff organization, and (4) committee organization.

LINE ORGANIZATION

A *line organization* is one in which there is a direct flow of authority from the top executive to the rank-and-file employee, usually through several lesser executives at various managerial levels. It is sometimes called

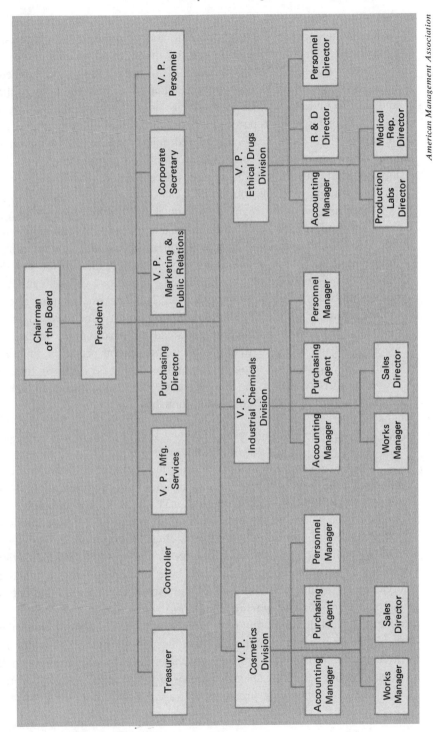

American Management Association

Figure 6-1

A Formal Organization Chart

the military type because each person has someone immediately over him. Although modern armies have become too complex to rely exclusively on a line organization, they still use the direct chain of command.

Figure 6-2 shows an illustration of a line organization applied to business. There are many advantages inherent in this form. It is simple and easy to understand. Responsibility is clearly defined and each worker, regardless of his rank, reports to but one individual. This simplifies discipline. Decisions can usually be rendered quickly, and executives must produce or be replaced. As long as each employee carries out the orders of his immediate superior, he is relatively free from criticism, which makes for harmonious working conditions.

There are, however, many disadvantages to the line type of organization. Each supervisor needs to be a master of many diverse angles to his job. He should be able to handle his men, keep the machines running, invent new processes, recommend pay increases, and train new employees. Frequently he may be outstanding at one or two of his numerous responsibilities and very poor at others. The line organization also has the disadvantage of placing so much final authority and direction at the top that the individual concerned, instead of devoting his attention to working out important matters of policy and general practices, finds most of his time devoted to reading reports and rendering decisions on operating problems. Coordination of the different "lines" is difficult to achieve, particularly in a complex, large-scale industry.

TAYLOR'S FUNCTIONAL ORGANIZATION

Taylor's functional organization is a transitional form between the line and the line-and-staff types. It is so designated here to differentiate it from the functional type described on page 131. It was originated by F. W. Taylor in the 1880's to remedy the great weakness of the line form—the concentration of too many duties in a single supervisor. Taylor divided each foreman's job into its basic components and established a functional foreman with authority over each of these divisions. Taylor's functional organization in its pure form carries the use of specialists to the extreme in that there is no single line of authority but rather multiple lines of authority affecting each employee. Every worker is responsible to someone of higher rank for each important specific part of his job. The foreman in charge of setting up a job on a machine supervises all workers to this extent. Another foreman may be in charge of personnel, and all workers report to him concerning problems of wages, hours, and shifts. The man

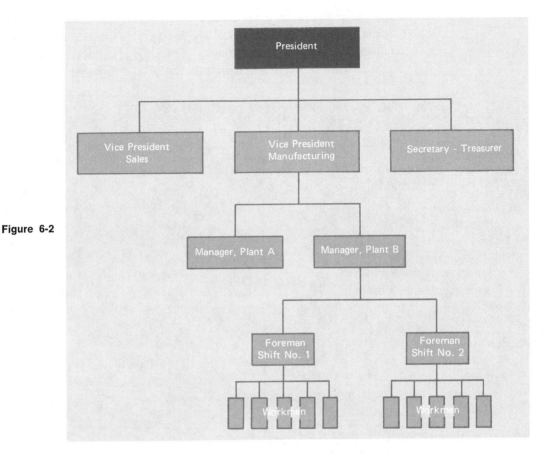

Figure 6-2

Line Organization for Plant B of a Manufacturing Corporation

Note: The details of the organizational structure for the sales department, the secretary-treasurer's office, and Plant A have been omitted.

in charge of accounting tells each worker what he shall do regarding filling out timecards and other job cost records. Likewise, the repair foreman handles the problems of damage to machinery and tools for an entire factory. (See Figure 6-3 for an example.)

The principal objection to Taylor's functional type of organization is that workers have more than one boss at the same level. Even though each boss directs only a specific part of the employee's work, friction and overlapping are bound to develop. Disciplinary problems are difficult to handle. Divided control is more likely to retard production than to speed it up. In actual practice firms have found that a line-and-staff organization can secure the advantages claimed for Taylor's functional type without acquiring its inherent disadvantages. Consequently, this functional form is rarely, if ever, found in intelligently managed companies.

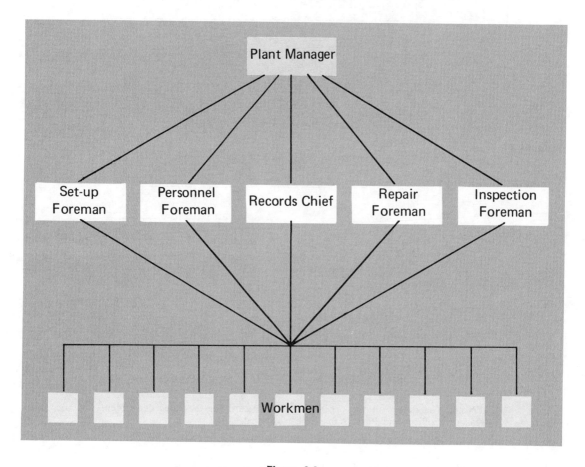

Figure 6-3

Functional Organization for a Manufacturing Operation

Note: Each workman is responsible to five foremen.

LINE-AND-STAFF ORGANIZATION

The *line-and-staff organization* is the next logical step beyond the functional concept. It eliminates the problem of requiring each supervisor to be highly competent in each phase of his job while preserving the advantage of giving each worker, at any level, a single boss. This is accomplished by using specialists, but by giving them staff or advisory status instead of actual line authority, as in Taylor's functional form. For example, a personnel department will study all salary and wage problems throughout a factory. This does not mean that the foreman is not consulted regarding personnel problems nor that he loses any authority, but advice is available from experts in that particular field. An engineering department will work on new processes and new designs and methods of handling the raw materials. Again, the foreman will probably be consulted and may contribute ideas, but he is not primarily responsible for this important function of the business.

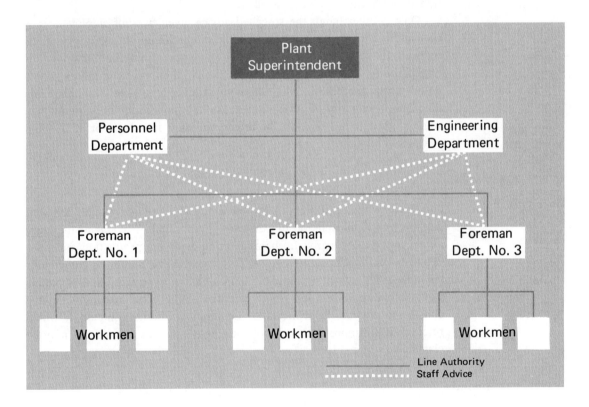

Figure 6-4

Line-and-Staff Organization for the Manufacturing Operation of a Small Business

Note: Staff functions in this business are performed by the personnel and engineering departments.

Figure 6-4 shows a line-and-staff organization plan. Note that foremen are not responsible to more than one supervisor but that specialists are available for specific problems. There is no overlapping of control. Today's military services are essentially line-and-staff organizations in that extensive use is made of specialists in all lines who are attached to the various branches—for example, psychologists with every branch of the service.

The many advantages of the line-and-staff plan have made it the most popular form of business organization. It introduces a note of flexibility into the rigid form of the line organization. The use of specialists can be incorporated without departing far enough from the line plan of organization to lose the important advantages already enumerated. It incorporates the principles of division of labor without losing the important combination of authority and responsibility.

On the other hand, the so-called advice given by staff employees may be construed as demands, which can lead to divided authority or serious friction. In some cases the foremen and supervisors may try to shift responsibility to staff employees for actions taken on their advice which do not prove successful. Also, department managers, superintendents, and others in managerial positions may cease to give thought and attention to some of their duties that can be referred to staff members for advice and a recommendation.

Line Departments

The key to the determination of which are line and which are staff departments is the relationship that any given department has to the basic objectives of a company. In manufacturing firms the production and sales departments are customarily regarded as having line status, as the goal of the companies is to make and sell things at a profit. In retail and wholesale firms both buying and selling are essential to the firms' purposes and are considered as line departments or functions. In some companies, where research is an important aspect of their activities, this department may be classified as line.

Staff Departments

While there is a measure of difference of opinion among authorities as to the designation of certain departments as line or staff, the consensus of opinion would probably classify those departments that exist mainly for advisory and service purposes as staff functions. Among these would be personnel, public relations, and finance.

It should be understood that the foregoing classification is based on the relationship of these departments to the company as a whole. Within all departments, whether basically line or staff, certain positions are regarded as line if there is any authority vested in them. Thus, the head of the personnel department is a line executive within that department. He is the superior of the other employees in the department, but he has a staff job in relation to the firm itself.

COMMITTEE ORGANIZATION

The *committee organization* type is one in which a formally constituted group drawn from those associated with a firm replaces an individual at any or all supervisory levels. Although here itemized as a separate type of organizational structure, it is rarely used except as a modification of one of the types already described. Most frequently this plan is incorporated into a line-and-staff organization with a committee that replaces a staff officer or that provides additional advisory functions.

Much is to be said for incorporating committees into an organization structure. If nothing else, the committee form allows several people to have an influence in making a decision that will probably affect their work, and the understanding of the background makes for a more enthusiastic acceptance of the new policy. The old adage that two heads are better than one is probably true; and the ultimate report of a committee, combining the judgment of several individuals, is likely to be better than one man's opinion. Furthermore, decisions reached by committees are frequently less personal.

Committee organization has its drawbacks, too. It is usually a slow method of arriving at a decision, and sometimes important matters are held up by committees. Time is spent on argument rather than action. Frequently committee decisions are compromises when the only hope of success would be vigorous prosecution of one viewpoint or the other. Also, the chances of securing action on a committee report are less than when one executive is interested in seeing his own ideas placed into operation. A somewhat different criticism of committees is that this organization form may usurp the decision-making functions of executives.

THEORIES OF ORGANIZATION

Historically three theories of organization have had some influence on management thought and practice: (a) the classical doctrine, which is concerned with the makeup of formal organization; (b) the neo-classical theory, which has been interested principally in the human relations aspect of organizations; and (c) modern organization theory, which conceives of organization as a system and centers around the idea of systems analysis.

Systems analysis, basically, is the recognition of the effect of a change in any one part of the system on all of the other ingredients of the system. It recognizes the interrelation of all component elements of a system. In this instance a firm is regarded as a system. According to this approach, there are six segments to an organization as a social system: (a) the individual, (b) the formal organization, (c) the informal organization, (d) status and role patterns, (e) the physical environment, and (f) communication.

People are selected for work in a firm primarily for their skills. These skills may be similar for a large number of people but, nevertheless, skills differ individually from person to person. Moreover, people not only differ in the character and level of skills, but each differs uniquely in personality, experience, expectations, values, education, and training. It is the purpose of organization to give unity to these individual variables.

As noted earlier in this chapter, the formal organization is the interrelated pattern of jobs in the system or firm. It is the result of giving serious consideration to the factors involved in organizational planning. Its structure is portrayed in the organizational chart.

The informal organization consists of groups of people in firms whose grouping does not appear as such in the formal organization. These are people who may or may not be in the same departments but, due to their being located near each other in a plant or office and performing similar tasks even though they have dissimilar occupational interests, tend to form small groups, who communicate with each other and exert a subtle influence on the organization of the firms for whom they work. For example, executives in the sales and production departments might belong to the same golf clubs and discuss the firm's problems on the course.

Modern theories of organization draw heavily from sociology and psychology. From sociology the modern organizational theories have borrowed the concepts of status and role. *Status* is usually defined as the rank or position of an individual in a group or of a group in relation to other groups. *Role* refers to the behavior or activities of a person who occupies a certain status. A status is a set of privileges and duties; a role is the acting out of this set of duties and privileges.

Thus far, an organization is seen as a process of moving related parts: people working within the structure of a formal organization, forming informal social interrelations, and developing certain status and role patterns. All of this action takes place within a specific physical environment that may, in turn, influence the employee in the daily execution of his work.

Essential to the operation of an organizational system is communication. Through communication the actual operation of an organization brings out the fusing of "personalization" and "socialization"—the balancing of personal, individual goals with those of the firm.

ORGANIZATIONAL EFFECTIVENESS

One of the major contributions of systems analysis to the study of the organization process is the recognition that every system has multiple functions and multiple goals, some of which may be in conflict with each other. For this reason it is a narrow view to attempt to judge the effectiveness of a business organization in terms of a single standard, such as profit maximization, high productivity, efficient service, or good employee morale. Modern theorists insist that a broad view must be taken. They define *organizational effectiveness* as the capacity of an organization to survive, adapt, maintain itself, and grow in the face of changing conditions. An effective business organization is one that meets the following criteria:

1. It has the managerial ability to solve problems and to react with flexibility to changes in the social, political, and economic environment. The current emphasis on environment places an increasing burden on management's ability and willingness to assume an active role in this vital area.

2. It has a sense of identity; it knows what its goals are and what must be done to achieve them; and this knowledge is widely shared by all members of the organization.

3. It is realistic in its planning in that it can judge correctly the impact of relevant changes in markets and technology on the company's future.

4. It provides for integration or fusing of personal, individual goals and enterprise objectives.

BUSINESS TERMS

QUESTIONS FOR DISCUSSION AND ANALYSIS

1. Do you think the concept of informal organization is a valid one? Explain.

2. Many small companies do not have organization charts. Do you think this is a desirable policy? Explain.

3. Can a firm expect to have a favorable esprit de corps among its employees if it does not have an organization chart? What reasons can be given either in favor of or against a chart?

4. How is it possible for competing companies to operate successfully when some follow the practice of decentralization of authority while others adhere to the centralization of authority practice?

5. Which of the philosophies of organization would you regard as preferable, divisionalization or functionalization? Explain.

6. If a subordinate manager questions the wisdom of an order given him by his superior, what should his reaction be to this situation?

7. Would the average factory worker be concerned with whether he was working in a line or a line-and-staff organization? Explain.

8. Would you regard a board of directors of a corporation as an example of the committee type of organization? Explain.

9. Do you believe that there should be a greater awareness of the individual in business organizations as is maintained by some students of business? Explain.

10. Do you believe that status and role are gaining in importance in the business world? Justify your answer.

PROBLEMS AND SHORT CASES

1. Using the current catalog of your school as a source of information, construct an organization chart of the institution.

2. The Bellvue Corporation is a well-known firm that produces a large line of small electrical appliances for consumer use in several plants that are located in different parts of the country and sells them through a number of sales offices that are located in the larger cities. Its sales are made to department stores, discount stores, and hardware and appliance wholesalers. Assume that the company has decided, after many years of centralized management, to adopt a policy of decentralization in as many managerial areas as possible. State the areas of action that should be delegated to the plant managers and field sales managers and what areas should be retained by the home office of the company.

3. The Marsh Corporation which manufactures building materials and supplies has long been regarded as one of the leaders in the industry. Albert Marsh, the son of the founder of the company, is the current president and chief executive officer. The stock of the company is held by the Marsh family. For several years Marsh has been in poor health and has permitted the managers of the branch sales offices gradually to assume such a degree of authority that they are practically independent organizations selling the Marsh products with a minimum of direction and control from the home office. Over the past few years the sales and profits of the company have been failing to keep pace with those of the industry generally. The efforts of Marsh to elicit the reasons for this trend have met with an indifferent response from the branch managers who, in some instances, appeared to resent the intrusion of the head office into what they seemed to regard as their own private realms. Finally, in desperation, Marsh employed a management engineering firm to analyze the situation and present a solution to the sales and organizational problems of the company.

   Write a report embodying your suggestions for remedying the organizational problems, bearing in mind that there are 25 sales branches, each with a sales manager and from 10 to 15 salesmen. The managers are all men over 50 who have been with the Marsh Corporation for an average of 25 years. It is important that the sales organization morale be sustained so that sales will not suffer. You may make whatever other assumptions you desire in preparing your report.

SUGGESTED READINGS

Albers, H. H. *Principles of Management: A Modern Approach*, Third Edition. New York: John Wiley & Sons, Inc., 1969. Part II.

Dale, E. *Management: Theory and Practice*, Second Edition. New York: McGraw-Hill Book Company, 1969. Chapters 10-15.

Flippo, E. B. *Management: A Behavioral Approach*, Second Edition. Boston: Allyn and Bacon, Inc., 1970. Part III.

Haimann, T., and W. G. Scott. *Management in the Modern Organization.* Boston: Houghton Mifflin Company, 1970. Part Four.

Hodge, B. J., and H. J. Johnson. *Management and Organizational Behavior*. New York: John Wiley & Sons, Inc., 1970. Chapters 6, 7, and 18.

Hodges, H. G., and R. J. Ziegler. *Management in the Modern Organization*. Boston: Houghton Mifflin Company, 1970. Part IV.

Koontz, H., and C. J. O'Donnell. *Principles of Management: An Analysis of Managerial Functions*, Fourth Edition. New York: McGraw-Hill Book Company, 1968. Part Three.

Litterer, J. A. *Organizations*, Second Edition. New York: John Wiley & Sons, Inc., 1969. Volume I.

McFarland, D. E. *Management Principles and Practices*, Third Edition. New York: The Macmillan Company, 1970. Part Three.

Sisk, H. L. *Principles of Management*. Cincinnati: South-Western Publishing Co., 1969. Part III.

Terry, G. R. *Principles of Management*, Fifth Edition. Homewood, Illinois: Richard D. Irwin, Inc., 1968. Part III.

Vorch, D., Jr., and D. A. Wren. *Principles of Management—Resources and Systems*. New York: The Ronald Press Company, 1968. Chapters 7 and 8.

Chapter 7

Management Activities

Management involves people and their activities. In the business world and in a small firm, one or a very few persons, usually the owner or owners, constitute the management. In larger companies a greater number of individuals are involved and, as previously noted, there has been a trend toward the separation of ownership and management in medium-size to large corporations.

With the exception of the small firm, businesses usually have three levels of management: (a) top management, (b) middle management, and (c) operating (or operative) management. *Top management* includes the president; the general manager; vice presidents in charge of production, sales, purchasing, personnel, and finance; and the treasurer. The term *administrative management* is sometimes used in referring to top management. *Middle management* is composed of department managers, branch office and plant managers, and production superintendents. *Operating management* is made up of plant supervisors and foremen and the heads of subdivisions of the larger departments. These are the members of the management team whose major task is the immediate supervision of the workers themselves.

If one were to observe a manager (regardless of his level) going about his daily work, he would see him performing a great variety of commonplace activities. Managers make and receive telephone calls; read, write, and sign letters; go on trips; attend meetings; speak and listen to individuals and groups; and monitor the movement of people, materials, and machines.

After observing several managers at work, one may arrive at two conflicting conclusions. He may conclude that the various managerial jobs differ so widely in content and scope that no generalization about managerial activities is possible. On the other hand, he may conclude that there is not much difference between the work of managers and nonmanagers.

It is true that sometimes managers engage in activities that are not managerial in nature. An example is the sales manager who actually sells and perhaps has a set of customers of his own, in addition to managing the sales force. Again, the director of a research department may actually carry out some research himself. The "working foreman" or lead man works right along with the group he is supervising. In each of these cases, the managers are actually spending only part of their time on management. When a man is engaged in guiding subordinates, deciding how to achieve a particular goal, or checking to see that events conform to plans, he is acting as a manager.

A worker who is promoted to a supervisory position soon realizes that there is a gap that separates management functions from other work activities. He no longer can "do" his accustomed work directly. He must get others to do it. He no longer operates a machine with a built-in degree of predictability. He finds himself engaged in complex human relationships. Success on the job cannot be determined in terms of his own output, waste, scrap, or hourly earnings. His superiors are judging his success by how well he gets others to work for him. The special character of management functions often poses serious problems of adjustment for most new supervisors.

The basic difference between managers and nonmanagers may not be readily visible to the observer, but it can be simply stated—decision making. That which basically distinguishes a manager from a nonmanager is the capacity and willingness to make decisions, and the survival of a manager in a company depends to a large extent upon the wisdom of his decisions.

DECISION MAKING

Possibly the foremost responsibility of management at all levels, but especially top management, is the making of decisions. It permeates all functions of management. In accord with the broad operational policies set forth by the board of directors, top managements are daily confronted with the necessity of deciding on courses of action that will best achieve the goals to which their companies are dedicated. In many, if not most, instances, the decisions involve the making of choices between two or more alternative courses of action. And at the top echelon of management, from which the basic procedural orders for the companies' operations emanate, correct decisions may be vital to the continued success of the firms or even their survival. Farther down the managerial ladder, there is usually a decrease in the number and quality of alternatives available to the managers involved; but the importance of correct decisions at these levels is, nevertheless, essential to the well-being of the companies.

The ability to make correct decisions in business has long been recognized as a prime attribute of successful management, but until comparatively recently there has been little apparent need for inquiry into the decision-making process. However, with the growth of large corporations, with their vast resources in the areas of finance, productive capacity, and manpower, and the increased tempo of competition, the possible consequences of unwise decisions, both on the companies involved and on the economy generally, have served to focus the attention of students of business on the methods by which decisions are made, insofar as these can be discovered.

The steps included in decision making have been known for quite some time. They are: (a) the recognition of the problem involved, (b) its definition and analysis into its essential parts, (c) the attempt to establish two or more alternative solutions and to evaluate them comparatively, (d) the selection of the solution believed the most favorable, and (e) the adoption of this solution and the implementation of it through the issuing of the necessary orders. These steps may be taken in a few moments by an executive, or they may require a much longer time, depending on the complexity and importance of the problems at hand.

In the past few years a number of things have come into being that have brought the decision-making process into a sharper focus. From the purely mechanical side, the rapid and extensive development of high-speed computers and data processing procedures have added immeasurably to the quantity of information available to the executive, thereby enabling him to base his decisions on far greater amounts of relevant data than previously. In addition to this, social and behavioral scientists have become aware that decision making by management is not only an economic activity dependent on accurate data, but it reaches also into the fields of sociology, psychology, anthropology, mathematics, philosophy, and political science. From each of these fields of knowledge have come theories and concepts which, it is hoped, will aid management in making its decisions and bring about results that will be beneficial not only to the firms involved but also to the society of which they are a part. Those who have been active in this area are hoping to develop a general theory of decision making that will synthesize the contributions from the various disciplines into a valid and useful whole. At present this appears to be a development of some future time. It is believed, however, that the results of both correct and incorrect decisions are of sufficient consequence to warrant continued research in this area.

The question may well be raised regarding the extent to which these new theories and concepts are being communicated to and used by management. A definitive answer to this question is not presently possible, but there is some evidence that management is aware of the growing importance of correct decision making and is receptive to some degree to any suggestion from whatever source that may be of assistance in fulfilling the rigorous responsibilities of this area.

MANAGEMENT FUNCTIONS

In the process of decision making and, to some extent, aside from it are functions that managers perform as parts of their jobs. The functions of a manager that are truly characteristic of his work as a manager may be broken down into categories in which managerial decisions are made. These are (1) planning and policy making, (2) organizing, (3) directing, (4) controlling, (5) staffing, (6) representing, and (7) innovating. It is in these functions that a manager must be skilled if he is to accomplish his work through the efforts of other people.

PLANNING AND POLICY MAKING

Planning and particularly policy making concern top management more than they do management at lower levels of authority. Any organizational structure that does not free these individuals from routine tasks, leaving ample time for these important functions, is not accomplishing its purpose.

Planning, which occurs more frequently than policy making, may be defined as the process of setting objectives, formulating strategy, and deciding among alternate courses of action. The need for planning in any organization becomes more obvious as various levels of management from the president on down develop an awareness of the precise nature of desired objectives. The first step in any type of planning is an explicit statement of goals. It is the answer to the question: What must be accomplished in the next month and what should be achieved in five years?

A plan is, therefore, a predetermined but flexible course of action to reach a particular objective or set of objectives. A plan is an outline of the specific steps required to reach the objectives. It is the answer to the question: How shall the goals be achieved?

To reach a goal depends on strategy. Strategy is a consideration of (a) the order in which each step of the plan is to be undertaken, (b) the timing of each step, (c) its cost, and (d) the communication and coordination needed so that each step is understood, accepted, and carried out. It takes time to prepare plans, to communicate them, and to implement them. Between the date of preparing plans and the beginning of implementation—the stage in which plans are actually put into operation—there must be *lead time*. For example, in the automobile industry the lead time for designing a new model is determined by the need for completed designs by other departments before starting to plan for the acquisition of new tools, for the purchase of raw materials, and so on.

Three kinds of information are needed for planning: environmental information, competitive information, and internal information. *Environmental information* describes the social, political, and economic aspects of the climate in which a business operates or may operate in the future. *Competitive information* explains the past performance, programs, and plans of competitors. *Internal information* indicates the company's own strengths and weaknesses. Examples of environmental information are population trends, price level movements, transportation costs, labor force supply, and foreign trade forecasts. Competitive information includes organized data on the present and prospective profitability, return on investment, share of the market, and sales trends of competing companies. Internal information for planning should stress the elements of strength that give a company an edge over its competitors. Most frequently these are seen in cost variations relative to changes in sales volume, share of the market, delivery performance, community standing, reputation in the industry, and labor relations.

A few illustrations of policy making that also involve planning may indicate the type of decisions that require a solution, usually by top management.

1. Assuming that the demand for a product is beyond the capacity of a manufacturing plant, the problem arises as to whether to meet the demand and, if the decision is in the affirmative, how to produce more. Perhaps a new plant can be purchased or built, or the problem may be solved by installing a two- or three-shift operation.

2. What should be done in case a union makes demands that management is unwilling to grant? Should a compromise be reached or will

it be more satisfactory to maintain a firm stand even if doing so results in a strike?

3. Within a few years a bond issue is going to mature. Will the company have enough cash on hand to pay this debt, or should steps be taken to secure funds from other sources to repay the original obligation?

ORGANIZING

Once plans have been made and policies determined, the job of carrying these out becomes one of organization and operation. If a firm is running smoothly, it may seem to an outsider that the whole process is relatively simple. Goods are shipped on time because they have been made and stored in advance of receiving an order and because packaging and transportation facilities of the right type and kind are available when needed. Actually, all of this smooth flow could not have been accomplished without an efficient organization operating under competent managerial supervision.

DIRECTING

The *directing* function of management involves the ability to guide and motivate subordinates in such a manner as to achieve the objectives of the enterprise and, at the same time, to build an enduring, satisfying relationship between the subordinates and the enterprise. This important and basic function will be discussed more fully in a later section on managerial leadership.

CONTROLLING

At all levels of management there must be control, all the way from knowing how much money the firm is making or losing to knowing the number of parts of a particular size and shape that are on hand. A proper organizational structure allows for the delegation of authority for control to individuals at various levels of management, depending upon the importance or type of the factor involved. Top management should not be concerned with the problem of whether a minimum of 100 or 200 one-horsepower motors should be kept on hand but it is concerned with the total dollars tied up in the parts inventory.

Controlling may be defined as the managerial process that measures current performance against expected results and taking the necessary action, if needed, to reach the goal in the future. The control process consists of a cycle of four steps:

1. Deciding in advance what should be accomplished or what will constitute good performance.
2. Measuring current, actual performance in quantitative terms, if possible.
3. Comparing current activity with the standards or norms of expected performance.
4. Taking corrective action, if needed, so as to achieve the desired results in the future.

There are many ways to check actual performance against standards. A few of the most common are: direct observation by the supervisor, consultation through informal contacts with subordinates, periodic audits or review of operations, special investigations, and formal management control reports.

Since the first step in the control cycle, as noted above, is the result of planning activities, there must be feedback between control and planning. Feedback, in this instance, is the process of adjusting future actions based upon data gathered about past performance. Efforts at controlling will indicate whether past planning has been effective; these will indicate whether expected standards of performance are too easily achieved, reasonable, or unobtainable and will raise the question whether new plans should be formulated.

Two control problems frequently arise in large businesses that are not present in smaller organizations. One of these is that of *absentee management*, a condition that exists when executives of a large corporation have their offices in one city whereas their operating divisions are scattered throughout the country. Absentee management frequently requires the delegation of substantial authority to the men in the field, and considerable reliance must be placed on reports and occasional plant visits.

Another problem of a large firm is whether to operate on the basis of a centralized management or a decentralized management. This issue arises when a firm's operations are physically dispersed, such as the large chain-store organizations and many others that have plants and offices located in different parts of the country. Here the question refers to the measure of authority that is to be delegated to the field executives and how much is to be retained by the home office management. For example, in a firm embracing the philosophy of *decentralized management* the branch offices might be permitted to handle their own personnel problems, to set quotas for their salesmen, to make local adjustments, and to conduct dealer relations. In a company that follows the practice of *centralized management*, these matters would be reserved for the home office. Examples have been known of two competing firms, each apparently successful, which have followed different, conflicting policies.

STAFFING

Organizing establishes the positions within an organization and assigns the duties to each. By *staffing*, the manager attempts to find the right person for each job. This is an ongoing managerial activity since people will quit, be promoted, be transferred, be discharged, or retire; and in the case of a growing company, new positions are created that must be filled. Staffing implies that the manager will regularly observe his subordinates' performance to judge where they are weak and will seek to strengthen them by training.

REPRESENTING

At various times the manager must represent his company to the outside world. These outside groups include the general public, the local community, banks, labor unions, trade associations, and numerous different governmental agencies. Sometimes this function is merely to be accessible and pleasant to visitors. At other times it is a matter of subtle negotiations. *Representing* is the function that brings the manager in contact with the people outside his company.

INNOVATING

If the job of the manager is to be creative, he must innovate. *Innovating* is finding new or better ways for his people to achieve goals or discarding old procedures that are no longer needed. The manager can exercise this function in several ways: he may develop new ideas himself; he may combine old ideas in a new way; he may adapt the ideas of others for his own use; or he may stimulate others to develop and carry out new ideas. The alert manager realizes that his department cannot stand still— it must go forward or fall back.

This outline of management functions has some hidden difficulties when one attempts to apply them to a specific managerial job. First, the list does not tell which functions are most important. It does not help the manager allocate his time on the job. All are important parts of the manager's job, but the significance attached to each one may vary at different times and in different organizations. Secondly, the terms used to name the function are vague and somewhat overlapping. It can be argued, for example, that planning is incomplete without innovating and controlling and that organizing encompasses staffing.

The list of management functions, however, does help in distinguishing managerial work from nonmanagerial efforts. It reveals to some degree the complexity of managerial tasks. It emphasizes that the manager's work is concerned with ideas and people, rather than with impersonal operations and things. It helps the manager give specific focus to his decision making. Figure 7-1 presents the management functions in graphic form.

Figure 7-1

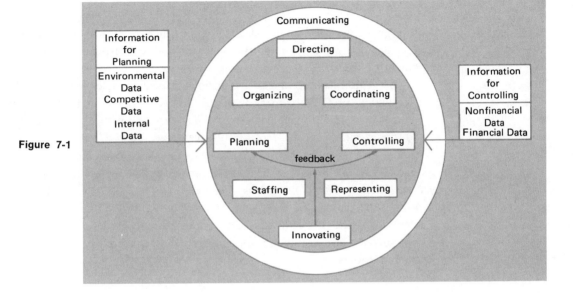

Management Functions

MANAGERIAL LEADERSHIP

When a person thinks of management in general, he may think almost instinctively of the three basic activities that are formally regarded as elements of the directing function: (1) leadership, (2) motivation, and (3) communication. This is quite understandable since the directing function of management, as previously defined, involves the ability to guide and motivate subordinates in such a manner as to achieve the objectives of the enterprise and, at the same time, to build an enduring, satisfactory relationship between the subordinates and the enterprise. A relationship of this sort is based upon the recognition that the subordinates have differing goals of their own that must be satisfied to some degree if they are to contribute effectively to the activity over time. These three elements which a manager must use in directing in order to breathe life into the organization—to put into action the plans and organization that have already been discussed—will be considered.

LEADERSHIP

The formal manager may rely basically on the authority that has been delegated to him in order to mobilize the resources under his command toward achieving the necessary tasks. Beyond this formal delegation, however, he may also employ leadership in order to motivate subordinates to contribute willingly, and over and beyond a marginally acceptable amount, to the goals.

The skillful leader realizes that various leadership styles may affect the performance of the organization or group with which he is dealing in different ways. The three basic *leadership styles* are autocratic, democratic, and laissez-faire. The *autocratic* (boss-centered) *leader* makes decisions on his own without consulting others; the *democratic* (subordinate-centered) *leader* invites participation of subordinates in the decisions that affect them; and the *laissez-faire leader* leaves many of the decisions up to his subordinates to make—he gives them a "free rein" over their activities. Figure 7-2 indicates seven representative gradations of leadership behavior in a continuum moving from boss-centered to subordinate-centered leadership.

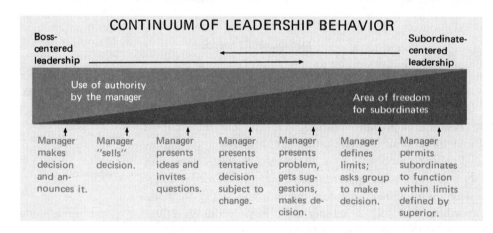

Figure 7-2

Continuum of Leadership Behavior

Source: R. Tannenbaum and W. H. Schmidt, "How to Choose a Leadership Pattern," *Harvard Business Review*, Vol. 36, No. 2 (March-April, 1958), p. 96. Reproduced with permission.

In their classic article referred to in connection with Figure 7-2, Tannenbaum and Schmidt suggest that no one of these styles is always the more
effective but that the effectiveness of the leader will depend upon his ability
to select correctly and employ a leadership style based upon an accurate
assessment of three basic forces at any particular time: (1) forces in himself; (2) forces in his subordinates; and (3) forces in the situation.

Forces in the Manager

Perhaps the major force within a manager that moves him toward
either a boss-centered leadership or a subordinate-centered leadership
pattern is his value system. How strongly does he feel that subordinates
should have a share in making the decisions of the department? Douglas
McGregor, in his book *The Human Side of Enterprise*,[1] outlined two
opposing theories of management that he called *Theory X* and *Theory Y*.
If a manager accepts the assumptions of Theory X, he will tend toward
a work-centered, authoritarian pattern of leadership. If the values of a
manager closely follow Theory Y, he will emphasize a participative, group-
centered style of leadership. The basic assumptions of each of these
theories are shown in Figure 7-3.

Theory X	Theory Y
1. Work is distasteful; it is an onerous chore to be performed in order to survive.	1. Work is as normal as play.
2. The average person has an inherent dislike of work and will avoid it if he can.	2. External control and the threat of punishment are not the only means for directing effort toward company objectives. People will exercise self-direction and self-control in working toward objectives to which they are committed.
3. Most people must be coerced, controlled, directed, or threatened with punishment to get them to put forth adequate effort toward the achievement of company objectives.	3. Commitment to objectives depends upon the rewards associated with their achievement.
4. The average person prefers to be directed, wishes to avoid responsibility, has relatively little ambition, and wants security above all.	4. The average person learns under proper conditions not only to accept but to seek responsibility.
	5. The capacity to exercise a relatively high degree of imagination, ingenuity, and creativity in the solution of organizational problems is widely, not narrowly, distributed in the population.
	6. Under the conditions of modern industrial life, the intellectual potentialities of the average human being are only partially utilized.

Figure 7-3

Opposing Theories of Management

[1] Douglas McGregor, *The Human Side of Enterprise* (New York: McGraw-Hill
Book Company), 1960.

Forces in the Subordinates

The second factor that influences the pattern of leadership exercised by a manager is the set of forces operating within his subordinates as a group. If a manager obtains affirmative answers to most or all of the following questions, he will probably be inclined to stress subordinate-centered approaches to decision making. The questions are: (a) Do the members of my department have a high desire for independence? (b) Are they ready to assume responsibility? (c) Can they tolerate uncertainty? (d) Are they deeply interested in the problem to be solved? (e) Do they understand and accept the company's objectives? (f) Do they have the knowledge and experience to deal with the problem? (g) Do they expect to share in the decision making? Negative answers to these questions move the manager toward a boss-centered pattern of leadership.

Forces in the Situation

A manager's pattern of leadership depends greatly upon the situation he is facing. The situation, in turn, depends on the type of organization, the effectiveness of the subordinates working together as a group, the nature of the problem to be solved or the decision to be made, and the pressure of time. Each company has its own concept of the "good manager," and this concept will push the manager in the direction of tradition. The subordinates as a group may lack unity and have little ability to work together. In this situation the manager is forced toward a dominating role. Problems differ in scope—some can best be handled by one person while others require the collaboration of a group for solution. If a problem calls for immediate solution, then it is difficult to involve other people. When time pressure is less intense, the subordinate-centered pattern of leadership becomes more feasible.

Leadership cannot be conferred on a man by promoting him to a management position. It is earned by the active understanding of (a) the factors that influence individuals and groups to act the way they do; (b) the dynamics of organizational life; and (c) his own needs, goals, motivations, and prejudices as a manager.

Each manager sees his leadership problem in his own way, depending on his particular background, knowledge, and experience. Four factors within the manager influence his pattern of leadership. These are: the confidence he places in his subordinates; his own leadership inclinations; his feelings of security in an uncertain situation; and his value system. In determining the degree of confidence he places in his work group, the manager is likely to consider the knowledge, competence, and adaptability of each of his subordinates. There are managers who seem to act more comfortably and naturally when they can decide and direct their subordinates' activity; others operate more comfortably in a team role. If a manager feels a great need for stability and predictability in his situation, he is reluctant to delegate work to others or to permit others to make decisions because releasing the control of decision making to others reduces the predictability of the results.

MOTIVATION

In the practice of management, the word "motivation" has a history that falls roughly into three phases. Up to the time around World War I, the typical manager gave little thought to motivation. The pattern of leadership was strongly boss-centered. A subordinate either did as he was told or he was fired or transferred. In the years between World War I and II, motivation was based on various rewards. The typical view seems to have been, "Treat employees well and they will work harder out of loyalty and gratitude." Money was considered to be the chief means of spurring workers on toward superior performance. Changed social conditions and a deeper understanding of the attitudes of people at work have indicated that earlier ideas of work motivation were misleading. Behavioral scientists and effective managers now recognize that motivation depends more on internal or psychological incentives than on fear or rewards. *Motivation* is not coercing, coaxing, or persuading people to do what is wanted, but rather a process of creating organizational conditions that will cause employees to strive for superior performance.

Current management thinking about motivation has been strongly influenced by the findings of behavioral scientists. Neither the managers nor the scientists, however, believe that they have found the key to the complex problem of work motivation. At this time a considerable amount of practice and theory center around two concepts: (1) the relationship between morale and productivity, and (2) the hierarchy of needs.

Morale and Productivity

For a long time the connection between morale and productivity was thought to be direct and simple. It was believed that if morale were high productivity would be high. Studies by the Survey Research Center of the University of Michigan indicate that employees may be happy and morale may be high, but productivity may be low. People may enjoy high morale and still fail to produce. This conclusion does not mean that morale can be ignored because it does not assure high levels of production. Employee morale does play a part in motivating people. It is the starting point, a springboard. Good morale, however, does not mean that by itself it will cause employees to jump to higher levels of performance.

Hierarchy of Needs

A. H. Maslow [2] proposed the theory that basic human needs may be arranged in an ascending order—in a hierarchy. Before his theory was developed, puzzling facts were noted. For example, it was generally assumed that people work to satisfy material needs. Money was thus assumed to be the great incentive. When, however, attitude surveys were taken and working people were asked what was most important to them in their jobs, good wages frequently took third or fourth place behind "challenging work," "chance for advancement," and even, in some cases, "a good boss."

Maslow's theory explains the seeming contradiction. He suggested that there is a *hierarchy of needs.* People give precedence to the first of these needs until it is relatively well satisfied. When the first need is almost satisfied, the second level of needs becomes dominant. Relative satisfaction of the second level leads to a third level, and so on through the series. Once a level is relatively satisfied, it ceases to operate as a primary motivator and is replaced by motivational forces created by needs of a higher order. Maslow's hierarchy of needs is as follows:

1. Physiological needs—for food, drink, and shelter.
2. Safety needs—for protection against danger and threat from the environment or from other people.
3. Social needs—for belonging, affection, and love.
4. Esteem needs—for self-respect, recognition, and the good opinion of others.
5. Self-fulfillment needs—to believe in the value of one's work and to find satisfaction in it, to realize one's potential, and to be what one can be.

The failure to understand this last level of needs may cause a manager to complain, "I have given my people everything—good pay, pleasant working conditions, and the opportunity to have comfortable contact with one another—and yet they still are dissatisfied." Maslow's theory helps explain the situation. It is because the employees have the first four levels of needs at least partially satisfied that the fifth level—the need for self-fulfillment—arises. The emergence of this last level of needs will cause

---

[2] Abraham H. Maslow, *Motivation and Personality* (New York: Harper & Brothers), 1954.

discontent unless the manager can find the ways and means of contributing to its satisfaction.

COMMUNICATIONS

In recent years behavioral scientists have studied the process of communication systematically. They have found, for example, that the typical manager spends about 70 percent of his working day in writing, reading, speaking, and listening. Moreover, the greatest portion of this time is usually spent in face-to-face, oral communication. These studies also have pointed up the great complexity of *interpersonal communications*. By tracing step by step how an idea of one person is transmitted to another, they have identified many barriers that distort messages.

Studies of interpersonal communications have shown that each oral exchange of ideas involves six different messages:

1. What the speaker means to say.
2. What the speaker actually says.
3. What the listener hears.
4. What the listener thinks he hears.
5. What the listener replies to the speaker.
6. What the speaker thinks the listener has replied.

The first four messages are direct messages and the last two are feedback messages. Without feedback messages there is only one-way communication from speaker to listener. A two-way communication is usually slower but is more accurate than a one-way communication. In two-way communication there is feedback not only of information but also of feelings, and for this reason two-way communication can produce both positive and negative results. For example, if the listener consistently feeds back that he does not understand, the speaker may begin to feel irritated, uncertain, or frustrated. Two-way communication usually permits more listener control. The listener knows what he understands and comprehends and can request repetition, clarification, examples, or a slower pace.

When the effect of two-way communication is positive, barriers to communication may be reduced. Barriers to interpersonal communications are factors that impede, distort, or cause a breakdown in the exchange of ideas and feelings. Barriers may be created in many ways. Some of the more common barriers are those generated by different meanings of words, by the lack of skill in listening, by the self-interest of the speaker, and by use of influence or authority to stop feedback. A speaker stressing how a communication effort will benefit himself soon loses the attention of the listener who is interested largely in how the effort will benefit himself or others in the organization.

Managers occupy positions of influence and authority over their subordinates. This position can be easily abused so as to "shut up" opposition or to block adverse questioning. Communication fails when a manager obtains compliance with his direction by authority rather than by understanding.

MANAGERIAL PERFORMANCE

The findings of much of the research in managerial behavior point to the conclusion that the effective performance of management functions does not come about by chance or by some mysterious process. Sound decision making, competent leadership, the development of motivation, and good communications are not matters of birth or accident. Effective managerial performance depends directly on the skills of the manager, the level of his own motivation, and the environment of the organization in which he works. It is the combined effect of these three factors, and not any one by itself, that determines a manager's performance.

SKILLS OF THE MANAGER

Since a manager directs the work of others and takes responsibility for achieving results through these efforts, it can be seen that his effectiveness rests on three skills: technical, human relations, and administrative.

Technical skill implies a competence in a particular activity. It involves an understanding and proficiency in methods, processes, procedures, and techniques. Technical skill involves specialized knowledge and is readily recognized as important to the work of the tool and die maker, the computer programmer, the accountant, the tax lawyer, the engineer, and many others when they carry out their specialized work.

Human relations skill, or proficiency in human relations, is primarily concerned with working with people. It is this skill that enables a manager to work effectively as a group member and to build teamwork among the subordinates he leads. It is based on an acute understanding of the differences and similarities among people. Human relations skill depends, on one hand, on an understanding of what subordinates mean by their words and actions and, on the other hand, on the manager's ability to communicate clearly with them. Human relations skill must be practiced continuously since it involves sensitivity not only when decisions are made and problems solved but also in day-to-day contacts with others.

Administrative skill, sometimes called conceptual skill, involves the ability to see the company as a whole and to understand the total situation relevant to it. This skill is exercised by recognizing how the various departments or divisions of a company are interrelated to one another and by perceiving how the company fits in the total fabric of society. A manager with administrative skill sees how various parts of the company work interdependently among themselves and are affected by outside changes in the social and economic environment. For example, when a major change is made in marketing policy, the change may have serious impact on the production, finance, research, and personnel of the organization. In turn, the change in marketing policy may result from, or even create, changes in governmental policy, labor relations, the location of plants, and consumer behavior. Administrative skill is concerned with integrating all the activities and interests of a company toward a common set of objectives.

All of these skills have relatively different importance at different levels of management. Human relations skill is essential at every level. Technical skill has its greatest importance at the lower levels of management, while administrative skill becomes increasingly critical in top management positions.

LEVEL OF MANAGER'S MOTIVATION

Skills must be used, knowledge must be put into action, and this transformation depends on motivation. The motives of managers also follow Maslow's hierarchy of needs. Since managers generally have greater opportunity to satisfy the lower levels of needs, we can expect them to be more concerned with satisfying their esteem and self-fulfillment needs. It is for this reason that many managers are concerned with the impact and scope of their decision making.

WORK ENVIRONMENT OF THE MANAGER

A carefully developed organizational structure makes effective managerial performance more likely. The dynamics of the organizational process, however, creates pressures upon managers. The effective manager learns to absorb or resolve these pressures.

Managerial pressures are those forces within a company that push for change, conformity, uncertainty, or goal conflict. The pressures of change are those that cause a manager to be concerned over job transfers, reorganization, and geographic moves. While in every organization there are forces at work that will upset or change conditions, there are at the same time forces seeking stability and uniformity. Each manager faces the expectations of others in the organization that he should "fit the mold." There are pressures upon him to conform to the usual ways of operating and behaving. The third type of pressure on the manager tests his tolerance of uncertainty. Many decisions must be made when information is unavoidably incomplete. The manager must risk his reputation and decide in the face of unknown future events. Finally, decisions to work toward one goal may have to be made at the expense of some other goal. A department head may wish to give raises to all of his subordinates at a time when budget information indicates that he should reduce costs. A president may have to choose between maintaining good community relations by continuing production in an inefficient, high labor-cost plant or relocating the plant in a different city.

One might say that managerial activities are defined by a position description that states the manager's duties and authority and by a title that locates his position in the organizational structure. In a formal sense this is true, but it is an oversimplification. This chapter has shown that the manager's activities are numerous and complexly interrelated. The way he goes about his work results from the interplay of the organization, his subordinates, and his own personality. His work abounds in both strains and possibilities. Finding a way to cope with the tensions and to grow in effectiveness is a genuine challenge to him.

BUSINESS TERMS

QUESTIONS FOR DISCUSSION AND ANALYSIS

1. Some writers in the field of organization and management maintain that the board of directors of a corporation is a part of top management, while others do not. What is your opinion in this matter?

2. Name several areas of decision making that might naturally be delegated to middle management. Can you justify your choices?

3. Does planning involve all three levels of management? Give some examples to support your conclusion.

4. Some managers adopt the so-called open door policy for dealing with their subordinates. Others do not. Which policy would you regard as conducive to better employee morale? Explain.

5. Should management consult with its employees before making any important decisions? Justify your answer.

6. Under which of the three basic leadership styles mentioned in the text would you prefer to work? Explain.

7. Which of McGregor's theories, Theory X or Theory Y, do you regard as being more correctly representative of the attitudes of most workers toward their jobs? What factors influenced your choice?

8. Does a successful manager necessarily have to be a leader of the men in his department? Why?

9. Do you think that self-fulfillment plays a significant part in the average worker's attitude toward his job? Why or why not?

10. Do you think that managerial ability is an innate human trait or can it be learned by anyone who is ambitious to advance in business? Explain.

PROBLEMS AND SHORT CASES

1. The A. B. Corporation is an old, well-established firm that has been one of the leaders in the field of specialized machine tool manufacture. The management of the company, which is strictly family owned, has always relied on the sons of the founders as a source of managerial personnel. However, a considerable number of the management group are either approaching retirement age or have reached the stage of personal affluence where they have been thinking of devoting their energies to some other fields, such as sports, travel, and the pursuit of hobbies of one kind or another. The company is, therefore, faced with the problem of replacing the retirees and the others whose interest in the firm is lessening. Among the younger members of management there are very few who are connected with the family.

   In recent years the competition in this field has become increasingly severe from firms whose managements have not only developed new machinery but have been able to reduce their costs and prices to the extent that the A. B. Corporation's prices are getting more and more out of line with those of their competitors. The problem that faces the board of directors of the A. B. Corporation is the replacement of those managers whose age or diminished interest in the company presents them with the necessity of finding a new and more aggressive managerial group within a relatively short period of time. The level of managers below the top management consists of a group who have been with the firm for many years and have become accustomed to the more or less relaxed philosophy of the present owner-management personnel. The operative employees of the firm have embraced the same pattern of thought and action.

Your problem is that of deciding whether the board of directors should endeavor to instill in the present managers a greater degree of recognition of the competition that the company is facing, or to look to outside sources for people who can improve its competitive position and inspire those at the lower managerial and operative levels to put forth greater efforts to aid in this endeavor. Present a short paper stating your decision in this situation, giving your reasons and how you think a new management group could inspire the workers so as to achieve the requisite improvement in the company's competitive status.

2. There are some companies who follow the practice of requiring its management personnel, at all levels, to be active participants in civic affairs in the communities where they have plants or branch offices. In some instances the continuance of the managers' connection with these companies is in no small measure dependent upon their identification with local civic activities.

Opposed to this viewpoint are those firms who are more or less indifferent regarding their managers' participation in the affairs of their communities. In some instances such firms prefer that their managers devote all of their energies to company business and disapprove of their being identified with local civic movements in any way. Prepare a short paper setting forth the advantages and disadvantages, from the companies' standpoint, of each of these contrasting points of view and indicate which you feel is preferable, giving reasons for your decision.

SUGGESTED READINGS

Hicks, H. G. *The Management of Organizations.* New York: McGraw-Hill Book Company, 1967.

Hodges, H. G., and R. J. Ziegler. *Management in the Modern Organization.* Boston: Houghton Mifflin Company, 1970.

Johnson, R. A., *et al. Operations Management.* Boston: Houghton Mifflin Company, 1970.

McFarland, D. E. *Management Principles and Practices*, Third Edition. New York: The Macmillan Company, 1970.

Sisk, H. L. *Principles of Management.* Cincinnati: South-Western Publishing Co., 1969.

Starr, M. K. *Management: A Modern Approach.* New York: Harcourt Brace Jovanovich, Inc., 1971.

Part 3

Marketing

Prologue to Part 3

Marketing

This part is concerned with the segment of our economic system that provides the method by which the goods and services available to consumers are distributed to them. The emerging change in emphasis from production to distribution is highlighted at several points.

Chapter 8 presents a broad view of the distribution process and identifies the different classes of goods. It spells out the functions that are performed at all levels in making goods and services available to consumers. Chapter 9 deals with the institutions whose function is to distribute these goods and services. Particular attention is given to the wide variety of retail stores and the continuing evolution of the old into newer types of institutions. The question is raised regarding the environmental aspects of consumerism on retailers. Chapter 10 is concerned with prices and pricing. Factors which determine price are examined, as are the laws on pricing.

Chapter 11 treats the dynamic field of advertising, with an analysis of the types of advertising and the media by which it reaches the consuming public. Methods of evaluating advertising effectiveness are discussed along with some of the current criticisms of advertising.

Chapter 12 takes up the subject of international trade. Certain economic theories in this field are explained, as are the use of foreign exchange and the role of tariffs. The concept of international business and the rise of multi-national firms are given careful consideration.

Chapter 8

Marketing — Nature and Scope

In the comparison that was made in Chapter 1 between capitalism and other economic systems, emphasis was placed on the market orientation of business in the United States. The goods and services which are produced in this country come into being because the producers believe that they are wanted and can be sold profitably. It is through the mechanisms of marketing that the task of making these goods and services available to potential users is accomplished.

THE ROLE OF MARKETING

Marketing involves a twofold task: (a) discovering what goods and services consumers need and want, and (b) providing these items for them in the places where they are, at the times that they want them, and at prices that they are able and willing to pay. And as with every other part of economic activity, this mission must be accomplished at a profit to the entrepreneurs who are engaged in it. Freedom of choice is one of the basic ingredients of capitalism, and the organization and operation of marketing are such that consumers are able to avail themselves of this privilege of choice from among the many types of goods and services that are offered to them.

CHANGED EMPHASIS IN MARKETING

In recent years there has been a shift in emphasis, among firms producing goods intended for use by consumers, from the manufacturing to the marketing phases of their operations. With the onset of the industrial revolution in the mid-18th century, there came into being productive facilities that permitted the manufacture of greater quantities of goods and at lower prices than had previously been possible. This condition focused the attention of businessmen on the technological aspects of manufacturing and relegated marketing to a comparatively minor role. This situation remained about the same until the depression of the 1930's, when the problem of disposing of the goods that the productive facilities of the country were capable of making brought about a basic change in the thinking of many forward-looking manufacturers. From being absorbed with the problem of how to make more and more goods, they turned to the question of whether the goods that they had been producing were what consumers really wanted. Attempts were made to discover consumers' desires, and, where possible, to redesign their products in greater conformity to their findings.

After the interruption to this movement by World War II, the quest was resumed by many producers of consumer goods; and in the early 1950's, this trend became known as *consumer-oriented management* or the *total marketing concept*. This involved reversal of the marketing philosophies of many manufacturers. Whereas formerly it had been considered as the job of marketing to sell those things that production decided to make, now it became the duty of marketing to discover what consumers wanted and to inform production of its findings so that these goods could be made. It was then the province of marketing, through advertising, sales promotion, and personal selling to inform consumers of the availability of the goods and to urge them to purchase. Marketing thus assumed the vital burden of finding out what consumers wanted, a formidable task in many instances, and one which many companies have found quite difficult to accomplish. However, an increasing number of manufacturers of consumer goods have adopted this method of operation with its enhanced scope and responsibility for their marketing divisions.

Some commentators on marketing have cited the rise of consumerism as evidence of the failure of the total marketing concept—that business has been looking at marketing from the seller's, rather than the buyer's, point of view. Doubtless this has been true in many companies. A somewhat more sympathetic attitude toward the total marketing concept would see consumerism more as evidence of the difficulties involved in the endeavor to penetrate consumer thinking about the types of goods desired and the reaction to goods offered for purchase. There is little doubt but that the attempts to discover consumer preferences and reactions will be prosecuted with greater vigor as a result of the growth of consumerism. The manufacturers of industrial and commercial goods have required no such shift in marketing philosophy because their close contacts with customers have long provided them with accurate and dependable information concerning needed goods.

COST OF MARKETING

In a country as large and as populous as the United States, with the highest standard of living that the world has ever known, a marketing system broad enough to provide for the distribution of the goods and the services desired by its people must necessarily be vast and intricate. Over 1.7 million retail stores have approximately 8.4 million employees, and some 300,000 wholesale businesses employ over 3 million people. In addition, manufacturers of goods of all sorts utilize an unknown, but very large, number of salesmen to promote their products to industrial and commercial users as well as to wholesale and retail establishments.

As might be expected, a marketing system of this magnitude is quite costly. Approximately 50 percent of the dollar value of the retail prices that consumers pay for goods represents the marketing cost. Opinions differ as to whether or not this cost is too high. Under competitive conditions, it is reasonable to assume that sellers at all levels are striving to lower all of their costs, including those incurred in marketing. It is conceivable that under some authoritarian economic (and probably political) system goods could be distributed more cheaply; but it is doubtful if the same opportunity for buyer choice and real satisfaction could be realized under such a plan as is generally true with our present marketing arrangement. The validity of this latter assumption has been borne out by reports on the dissatisfaction of consumers in many so-called Iron-Curtain countries where the needs and preferences of consumers have been traditionally subverted to the planning decisions of the State managers.

APPROACHES TO THE STUDY OF MARKETING

There are four basic approaches to the study of marketing: (a) the commodity approach, which identifies and defines the goods concerned; (b) the functional approach, which considers the tasks that are performed in this field; (c) the managerial approach, which deals with the steps taken by marketing management to achieve its objectives; and (d) the institutional approach, which examines the different types of firms that are found in the field of marketing. In this chapter the commodity, functional, and managerial approaches will be discussed. In the following chapter, the institutional approach will be presented. In order that all references to them in this chapter may be clear, however, it should be understood that wholesalers and retailers are called *marketing institutions* or *middlemen*.

BASIC TYPES OF ECONOMIC GOODS

The commodity approach to the field of marketing involves a study of the basic types of economic goods. To facilitate the study of this aspect of marketing, goods are divided into the following three classes: (1) industrial goods, (2) commercial goods, and (3) consumer goods.

INDUSTRIAL GOODS

Industrial goods are destined for use by industry in the production of commercial goods, consumer goods, or other industrial goods. Examples of industrial goods are machinery, tools, raw materials, fabricated materials, and supplies. The important point in this connection is the immediate destination of the goods at the time that the characterization is made. In most instances this is relatively simple; iron ore, for example, could hardly be other than in the industrial goods category, as its customary destination is the blast furnace where it is made into pig iron. In some cases, however, this destination is not so obvious. An automobile tire, for instance, as it emerges from the last productive operation in a tire factory, may be either an industrial or a consumer good. If it is slated for shipment to an automobile factory, there to become a part of the assembly of an automobile, it is an industrial good. On the other hand, if it is to be sent to a tire dealer, eventually to be sold to some car owner to replace one of his worn tires, it is a consumer good.

COMMERCIAL GOODS

Commercial goods, which are included by some writers in the class of industrial goods, consist of many items that are not intended for use in the fabrication of other goods but which are destined for use in business in the form in which they are purchased. In this category are cash registers, office machines and equipment, store fixtures, stationery and supplies, filing cabinets, and office furniture. Computer hardware, described in

Chapter 24, is new to the field of commercial goods. A few of these goods may be classified also as consumer goods, depending upon their immediate destination. Typewriters bought for home use are an example.

CONSUMER GOODS

Consumer goods are destined for use by the individual ultimate consumer in such form that they can be used by him without further commercial processing. From the standpoint of the typical consumer, consumer goods may be further classified as (1) convenience goods, (2) shopping goods, and (3) specialty goods.

Convenience Goods

These are goods that consumers like to be able to purchase conveniently, immediately, and with a minimum of effort. They are not bought until needed and, when needed, their purchase is not long deferred. They include such items as cigarettes, popular-priced candies, newspapers, chewing gum, and many grocery products. *Convenience goods* are relatively low in price and are usually branded; they are purchased by both men and women; they are found in most types of stores. When purchased on the spur of the moment, they are called *impulse merchandise.*

Shopping Goods

These are goods in the purchase of which the consumer desires to compare the offerings of competing stores on various bases, such as price, quality, and style. In this classification are included many goods of the type usually found in the downtown department stores, such as women's clothing, furniture, dress goods, and millinery. *Shopping goods* are frequently unbranded; but if they do bear brands, consumers are not interested in them. For example, most curtains and draperies are branded, but consumers appear to pay little attention to this fact when shopping for them. They are concerned with materials, style, and design. Shopping goods are bought more frequently by women than by men and are found customarily in the medium-price range.

Specialty Goods

The consumer is willing to go to considerable effort to secure *specialty goods*, for which a brand preference usually exists. Examples of goods of this class are automobiles, men's clothing and shoes, high-priced watches, and electrical appliances. Specialty goods are always branded. They are bought more frequently by men than by women. There are, of course, individual differences of opinion between consumers concerning the same article, one regarding it as a specialty good and another as a shopping good. The classification given above, however, is made on the basis of the purchasing habits of the average consumer.

MARKETING FUNCTIONS

In the marketing of industrial, commercial, and consumer goods, certain inescapable tasks must be performed. These tasks are called *marketing functions*. It is through their performance by the marketing institutions involved that the costs of marketing arise and competitive advantage is gained by those firms who are able to achieve greater efficiency and lower expenses in the execution of these tasks. Although there are some differences of opinion among marketing authorities as to which activities to include in this group of functions, the following are generally accepted: (1) buying, (2) selling, (3) transportation, (4) storage, (5) standardization and grading, (6) financing, (7) risk bearing, and (8) marketing information.

BUYING

Buying involves the selection of the kind of goods to be bought and the determination of the quality desired as well as the proper quantity needed for the specified purpose as defined by the user. The buyer also must select the sources of the goods that he wants. In many business houses buying procedures are established to take care of the details of routine purchasing and to make certain that all purchase orders are executed in a uniform fashion.

SELLING

An important characteristic of a capitalistic economy is *speculative production*, the manufacture of goods before orders for them are received. Manufacturers produce the things that they think consumers will want and then try to sell them. For example, toy manufacturers produce their entire line of Christmas products months before the holiday selling season opens. They hope that consumers will like and buy the things they have made. Although speculative production does not apply to all types of goods, since some goods are made to order, it is characteristic of a great many lines; and it involves the necessity of finding a market for the speculatively produced goods if the manufacturers are to continue to be in business.

Wholesalers and retailers customarily maintain stocks of goods from which their customers may make their purchases. They, likewise, usually engage in selling to assure the steady outgo of their wares.

A widely used term sometimes considered synonymous with selling but one that has various meanings for different circumstances is *merchandising*, defined by the American Marketing Association as follows: [1]

> The planning and supervision involved in marketing the particular merchandise or service at the places, times, and prices and in the quantities which will best serve to realize the marketing objectives of the business.

Another somewhat simpler definition of merchandising which has had rather wide acceptance is that it is having the right merchandise, in the right place, at the right time, at the right price, and in the right quantity. This is, of course, a counsel of perfection, but it is at least a goal toward which sellers should continuously strive.

Selling can be conveniently divided into three parts: (1) personal selling; (2) advertising, which has been called impersonal selling; and (3) sales promotion, which includes those activities that supplement personal selling and advertising.

Personal Selling

Selling involves a wide variety of tasks, which vary in importance with the nature of the business concerned. These include discovering potential customers, acquainting them with available goods, and endeavoring to persuade them to purchase the goods. Some selling is educational in its character, having as its principal objective the dissemination of facts concerning certain products, particularly new ones, while other types of sales effort are purely competitive, aiming to accomplish the sale of goods in competition with other similar products.

The personal selling process is a rather complicated procedure, combining in varying proportions the personality and persuasiveness of the salesman, the urgency of the needs of the prospective buyer, the impact of competitive offerings, and the financial condition of the customer.

---

[1] From *Marketing Definitions: A Glossary of Marketing Terms,* compiled by the Committee of Definitions of the American Marketing Association.

It is important to distinguish between the several kinds of personal selling as each involves different techniques and approaches by salesmen.

House-to-house selling. An unknown number of salesmen call at the homes of consumers for the purpose of inducing them to buy a wide variety of goods. Personal solicitation of consumers in their homes is mainly confined to a few products such as Fuller Brushes, Avon, and Beauty Counselor cosmetics. The reasons for the slack in house-to-house selling to consumers are the increasing reluctance of housewives to admit strangers into their homes and the fact that most men are at work during the day and their wives do not wish to assume the responsibility for the purchase of expensive items, such as appliances, aluminum storm doors and screens, porch enclosures, and central air conditioning. To manufacturers of such merchandise, the problem of contacting potential buyers is probably met with advertising in most instances.

There are other types of house-to-house selling in the areas of insurance, investment securities, automobiles, real estate, and many others. In most instances prospective customers are sought by way of advertising. There is also a considerable measure of telephone solicitation, the effectiveness of which is unknown.

Retail selling. Retail selling is noteworthy in that it induces customers to come to the stores, not infrequently as the result of advertising. In this circumstance it is assumed that the customers are more or less presold on the goods before they come to the stores. The selling involved consists of a knowledge of the merchandise, of prices, and of a pleasant personality. In many stores, where salespeople are employed, no attempt is made to "sell" the customers or the goods, but rather the emphasis is placed on helping them to find the items that will best satisfy their needs.

Self-service stores—in the areas of food, drugs, and variety-store merchandise, where consumers make their selections without the assistance of salespeople—have experienced a notable growth in recent years. Here, however, the selling is merely transferred from personal selling to mass display. In the absence of salespeople, the task of acquainting consumers with the availability of goods and of their appealing characteristics has had to be assumed, in a large part, by advertising.

Selling to business. Salesmen who sell to other than consumers can be divided into those who sell to wholesalers and retailers and those who sell to manufacturers. The former group visit the offices or stores of their customers for the purpose of selling merchandise for resale. Their sales approach may emphasize the newness of their offerings, price, proposed or actual advertising campaigns, and the probable acceptance of their goods by consumers. They meet trained, professional buyers whose own livelihood and job tenure depend on their accurate knowledge of consumers' needs and wants. In the case of department and specialty stores, the buyers also regularly visit the market cities for the purpose of selecting merchandise, as well as receiving the salesmen in their stores. Further comment on this practice will be found in Chapter 9.

Those who call on manufacturers require an expert comprehension of their customers' needs and an understanding of how the products or services which they have for sale will benefit the users. Personality traits enter the picture also, but only when accompanied by product knowledge.

Advertising

Advertising employs many media, such as newspapers, magazines, direct mail, billboards, radio, television, and catalogs. For the preparation of certain types of advertising, notably that of manufacturers of nationally known products, specialized groups, known as *advertising agencies*, are employed. They prepare much of the advertising to be found in magazines, such as *Look* and *Life*, and on radio and television. Most other advertising, particularly that of a local character, is created by the staffs of the companies concerned.

Sales Promotion

Sales promotion consists of those selling activities which supplement the personal selling and advertising of goods. It is most highly developed among firms who market widely advertised consumer goods. When it exists as a separate department, its responsibilities are to supplement the sales and the advertising departments, to coordinate their efforts, and to maintain liaison with dealers and consumers. Among these promotional procedures are (a) the preparation of catalogs, sales manuals, point-of-purchase advertising and displays and (b) the enlisting of dealer cooperation for the display and sale of goods, dealer merchandising aids, contests, premiums, coupons, sampling campaigns, and demonstrations. In large firms separate sales-promotion departments have been established to supervise these operations, while in others they are divided between the sales and the advertising departments.

TRANSPORTATION

Goods must be transported, in most instances, from the places where they are produced to the places where they will be consumed. Transportation has a dual duty to perform—goods must be taken to the places where they are wanted when they are wanted. In the language of the economists, the former involves the creation of *place utility*, whereas the latter is spoken of as providing *time utility*.

The transportation function involves the use of railroads, waterways, motor trucks, pipelines, and airplanes. The needs of the market, plus the competition among these various agencies, have resulted in the development of many specialized services, such as fast-freight and motor-truck schedules known to the trade as "hot shot" runs, refrigerated cars and trucks, and *store-door delivery*. By means of this last service, trucks owned by a railroad pick up goods at the factory and transport them to the railroad terminals, where the goods are loaded into freight cars; then, after the arrival of the goods in the destination city, they are taken by truck to the place of business of the company that purchased the goods.

STORAGE

Storage is another essential marketing function. In many lines of business, goods are produced considerably in advance of the time of sale and, consequently, they must be stored for varying periods of time. The manufacturer, the wholesaler, and the retailer all store goods to some extent; hence all of them perform the storage function.

An important post-World War II development that has had a profound effect on certain aspects of the storage function is the availability of frozen foods of many kinds. This process requires that all marketing institutions handling these goods provide adequate facilities for keeping them in a frozen state until they are purchased by consumers. Manufacturers, wholesalers, and retailers have had to install special containers where the requisite cold temperatures can be maintained. The freight cars and trucks used to transport these foods must likewise keep similarly low temperatures. At the consumer level, there has been a notably large sale of home freezers and of refrigerators with special compartments for storing frozen foods. One result of this development has been that many foods, such as strawberries, peaches, and raspberries, that could formerly be obtained only during the relatively short growing and ripening season because of their extreme perishability, are now available the year round in frozen form.

Goods may be stored in warehouses with or without any special equipment for air conditioning. The most common type of air conditioning is temperature control; in this type the temperature may range from that in rooms that are merely "cool" to that in rooms where subfreezing temperatures are maintained.

Although many business firms have the facilities for storing their own goods, others use the facilities of public storage warehouse companies. Many of these issue warehouse receipts to the storers as evidence of their receipt of and custody over the stored goods. These receipts may be taken to a bank, and a loan may be obtained by the storer, for which the warehouse receipts are deposited as collateral. Then, before the storer or any customer of his can withdraw the goods from storage, the loan must be repaid to the bank in order to obtain the warehouse receipt, for the warehouse company will not release the goods until the receipt is surrendered.

A variant of this procedure, which is called *field warehousing*, consists of the storing of the goods on the premises of the manufacturer or the distributor, with the warehouse company assuming custody. A space is fenced off for storing the goods, and a custodian is employed to look after the goods and to tend to their proper receipt and release. In this instance the warehouse goes to the goods, so to speak, instead of the goods going to the warehouse. Substantial savings in handling, transportation, and storage charges may result from field warehousing.

STANDARDIZATION AND GRADING

The development and maintenance of standards is of value in helping buyers and sellers to transact business in an intelligent and helpful manner. There may be standards of quantity, such as weights and measures and container and can sizes, or standards of quality, which are concerned with such differences in goods as grade, substance, wearability, and serviceability.

In the realm of canned and frozen fruits and vegetables, the development of intelligible standards of quality as guides to consumers in their purchasing has taken two forms. The first of these forms involves the determination of specific grades of canned goods and the utilization of such symbols as *A*, *B*, or *C*, which are placed on the labels. This practice is known as *grade labeling*. A canner who wishes to designate his goods as *U. S. Grade A, B,* or *C* may do so by utilizing the Continuous Inspection Service of the United States Department of Agriculture. Figure 8-1 on page 180 illustrates the use of this service by a canner. The second system, which describes the contents on the labels, is called *descriptive* or *informative labeling*. Most of the large canners and many of the smaller ones use this procedure. Since the sale of frozen fruits and vegetables has increased markedly in recent years, many packers of these foods have adopted a combination of grade and descriptive labeling for their products. The Great Atlantic and Pacific Tea Company has long followed this latter practice.

Figure 8-1

A Grade and Descriptive Label

FINANCING

Handling of any economic good calls for a method of financing. If the goods are paid for immediately, the buyer must provide the necessary funds, which may be either his own or those that he has borrowed. If payment is postponed, the seller extends credit to the buyer for a period of time and thus temporarily assumes the burden of financing the transaction. Since a great many sales are made on credit, this phase of the financing function is of considerable importance. Manufacturers extend credit to wholesalers, wholesalers to retailers, and retailers to consumers.

In many instances the selling institutions are able to perform this function without recourse to outside financing agencies. It frequently happens, however, that such assistance is required because of the limited financial resources of the sellers. Banks and finance companies are employed for the purpose of providing the funds. Their methods of operation are explained in Chapter 18.

RISK BEARING

The mere act of owning goods carries with it the inescapable burden of assuming certain risks in connection with them. These risks arise from the following possibilities:

1. The goods may be damaged or destroyed in some manner.
2. They may deteriorate and become unsalable or useless, or their usefulness or salability may be impaired to some extent.
3. They may be stolen.
4. The price may move unfavorably.
5. The goods may be rendered obsolete by new inventions or by style influences.

When goods are sold on credit, the seller assumes a risk even though he no longer owns the goods because the buyer may not pay what he owes.

MARKETING INFORMATION

If the businessman hopes to achieve success in the face of the rugged competition that is characteristic of many fields, he must have market information upon which to base his decisions. This information covers such topics as prices, the extent of the market, location of the market, consumer preferences, the character of the demand, and conditions of supply.

The many sources of market information include reports of government agencies, trade papers, commodity exchanges, bureaus of business research, private research organizations, and the firm's own records. Every marketing institution is a source of market information, and every marketing executive or entrepreneur must provide himself with a certain amount of market news in order to operate his business intelligently.

Marketing Research

Marketing research is the scientific study of problems that arise in the field of marketing. It is not regarded as a marketing function, although the findings of some marketing research projects may be utilized as segments of the marketing information function. It involves inquiry into selling and buying methods, advertising, the location of markets, consumer buying habits and motives, and many other topics. Since marketing research is a comparatively recent development, many questions of techniques, methods, and objectives remain to be answered fully. Specialists in marketing research are either independent operators or are in the employ of advertising agencies and/or firms with large marketing problems. Much marketing research is also carried on in collegiate schools of business.

Marketing research involves four steps: (a) the formulation of pertinent questions about the subject of the research, (b) the collection of facts about the subject, (c) the analysis of these facts, and (d) the presentation of conclusions or a proposed plan of action based upon the analysis. This is the so-called scientific method that aims to secure the truth concerning the questions brought before it.

Some of the more pressing questions to which marketing research endeavors to find the answers are: What is the market for a new product? What do users think about the products that they now use? Why do they buy certain merchandise and refuse to buy certain other goods? Where are the users of a given product situated? What is their income status, age, education, and so on? Do they buy goods because they hear them advertised on the radio or television? Which of two or more proposed advertising campaigns will have the greatest appeal to consumers? At what prices will consumers buy the largest number of any given item?

The list is practically endless, and the answers that are obtained may not be valid a few weeks or months later. Techniques of investigation to meet these widely differing problems are equally varied. It is through the operation of marketing research that the manufacturers of consumer goods who have embraced the concept of consumer-oriented management, mentioned earlier in this chapter, try to discover the wants of consumers, and, obviously, their success or failure in this endeavor will measure the extent to which this idea can contribute to their profitable operation.

Marketing and Computers

While the impact of computers on marketing has been somewhat less than on some other areas of business, there is increasing evidence that electronic data processing is making appreciable progress in this field. Some of the applications of this new tool are daily reports of inventories and sales of chain and department stores; the handling of incoming orders in many different industries and their dispatch to branch plants or warehouses for filling, thereby shortening the time between the receipt of the order and its shipment; the managing of production, warehousing, and shipping by major food manufacturers; and the building of mathematical models to simulate the results of proposed marketing programs.

A TYPICAL MANUFACTURER'S SALES ORGANIZATION

Rather wide differences exist in the organizational details of manufacturers' sales organizations. These differences depend principally on the geographic extent of their sales operations, and on the character and complexity of their lines of goods. Many producers sell only in the areas surrounding their factories, while others operate on a region- or country-wide basis. Some produce rather simple lines, consisting of one or a few items; others have much wider offerings, sometimes dozens of articles that may or may not be closely related. Obviously there will be differences in the sales organizational details of each of these various types of producers. The organization chart shown in Figure 8-2, however, is typical of producers who make a varied line of goods and sell them over a broad area.

Figure 8-2

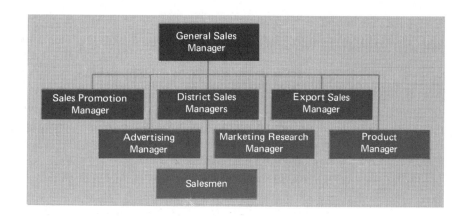

Organization Chart for a Manufacturer's Sales Organization

THE SALES MANAGER

The key man in any sales organization is the sales manager. Sometimes he is known as Director of Sales or as Vice President in Charge of Sales. When a firm has a number of subsidiary sales offices, the title

General Sales Manager is frequently employed to designate the top sales executive in the company. The heads of the smaller sales offices are known as branch, regional, zone, state, or city sales managers in accordance with the designation of the sales territories of which they are in charge. In instances where subsidiary sales groups are based on products rather than on territories, the subordinate sales executives may be known as sales managers for product *A*, *B*, or *C*.

The sales manager of a company is responsible for all aspects of the firm's sales activities. Either he or those under his direction must hire, train, control, and, where necessary, discharge salesmen. His responsibilities also include the establishment of sales territories, salesmen's routes, quotas, methods of salesmen's stimulation and compensation, and the control of sales expenses. Marketing research and the determination of the products to be sold come under his authority. This is particularly true with regard to the addition of new products to a line or the elimination of old ones. It is becoming increasingly common for the sales manager to have general supervision over the advertising and sales promotion departments.

THE PRODUCT MANAGER

In the marketing organizations of some large producers of consumer goods with extensive product lines, usually bearing different brand names, a number of junior executives are known as *product managers*. The Procter and Gamble Company was one of the first to establish these positions, but many other companies have followed suit. The function of a product manager is to concentrate on all aspects of the promotion of a single brand of his employer's product line, including its selling, advertising, display, sales promotion, and profit. And, according to a recent survey, in many companies his authority is quite limited, being confined to attempts to secure for his brand, through persuasion, the active cooperation of the different sections of the marketing division. It would be wise in a company with a large number of different products, however, to give the product managers the responsibility of securing the maximum marketing effort for each brand, rather than concentrating in the sales or marketing manager the sole responsibility for the promotion of all of them. What needs to be worked out is an effective balance of authority and responsibility in those companies where the performance of the product managers has been something less than satisfactory.

THE MARKETING MANAGER

An interesting development of recent years is the emergence of a number of new titles—Marketing Manager, Director of Marketing, and Vice President of Marketing being the most common. These new titles imply the recognition of the philosophy of the total marketing concept and its implementation through the enlarging of the scope and responsibility of the marketing department. The eventual extent of the authority of the marketing manager is not clear; but in one of the largest companies in the country it involves not only a supervision of the marketing program but also authority in such fields as product research and development and production scheduling, areas traditionally the responsibility of the engineering and production departments.

Whether or not this departure from established practices marks the beginning of a trend cannot be foretold at this time. It appears, however, to be a recognition of one of the basic truths in marketing, namely, that the most successful companies are those whose goods come the closest to being what consumers want; and, furthermore, that the marketing division, being nearest to consumers, is the one to determine what items should be made and to estimate the quantity that can be sold.

MARKETING STRATEGY

The intensified competition of today, so characteristic of nearly all lines of business, has presented marketing managers with the necessity of developing effective marketing strategies with which to maintain their present shares of the market and, hopefully, to increase them. Along with this responsibility has gone that of preserving or improving their profit positions. They must endeavor to secure the greatest amount of revenue for the least amount of expenditure. The actions taken by marketing managers consist of various manipulations of the *marketing mix,* which includes the following elements in the marketing area that are subject to control: (a) the product mix; (b) the distribution mix; (c) the communications mix; (d) the service mix; and (e) the logistics mix.[2]

The *product mix* is the adjustment of the product line so that the market is best served. The *distribution mix* is that choice of channels of

[2] For a further treatment of this concept, see Thomas A. Staudt and D. A. Taylor, *A Managerial Introduction to Marketing* (2d ed.; Englewood Cliffs, New Jersey: Prentice-Hall, Inc., 1970).

distribution which is most economical and best attuned to the market. Another aspect is the determination of the nature of the distributive pattern: (a) intensive—the use of all possible retail outlets; (b) selective—the restriction to a few retail outlets in each sales area; (c) exclusive—the use of only one retail outlet in each sales district. The *communications mix* involves the employment of the elements of personal selling, advertising, and sales promotion in such proportions as to achieve the optimum return to the company. The *service mix* means the determination of service and guaranty policies so as to produce the desired customer satisfaction. The *logistics mix* is concerned with the physical distribution of goods; it involves the selection of storage and transportation facilities in such a combination that the merchandise is moved from producer to purchaser at the lowest cost consistent with the purchaser's demand for service.

THE CONSUMER

Marketing authorities classify consumers according to three types: (1) the industrial consumer, (2) the commercial consumer, and (3) the individual or ultimate consumer who, in the absence of qualifying terms, is the individual to whom the word consumer applies.

INDUSTRIAL AND COMMERCIAL CONSUMERS

Industrial consumers are identified as business institutions that purchase goods, usually industrial goods, for use in their business operations. Manufacturing industries, mines, and the construction industry are among the kinds of businesses that are customarily included in the industrial consumer classification. *Commercial consumers* include hotels, offices, banks, schools, hospitals, and theaters.

THE ULTIMATE CONSUMER

Broadly speaking, an economic system exists primarily for the purpose of satisfying the needs and wants of the ultimate consumer. This is particularly true of capitalism, under which consumers have practically complete freedom of choice in their selection of goods. They can accept or reject the offerings of producers in accordance with their judgments as to whether the goods will or will not satisfy their desires. It would appear, therefore, that those producers whose goods most nearly conform to the wants of the consumers will meet with the greatest measure of success in the competition for the consumers' favor. With this in mind, it would seem as if one certain way of a producer's assuring his success would be to ascertain what consumers want and then to make his goods in accord with his findings.

At this point the first important problem comes into the picture; namely, that it has proved difficult for sellers to find out what consumers want. This is not to imply that consumers do not have very decided preferences about the details of the goods that they want. The power of discrimination, however, operates only in the presence of competitive offerings of goods. This means that the seller who asks consumers what they would like, in regard to the details of the commodities that they will buy at some future date, will receive unsatisfactory answers because the element of competition is missing. If he produces his goods and offers them for sale to consumers in competition with those of other makers, however, he will discover quite quickly and definitely whether or not he has made something that they will buy.

The consumers' inability to decide what they want in advance of its being offered to them for purchase has been recognized by producers for many years. As a result, three broad policies have emerged that have governed manufacturers in their determination of the essential details of the goods that they make. The first of these policies has been that of endeavoring to discover, by research or experimentation, some indication of the basic preferences of consumers; then fabricating the goods as nearly as possible in consonance with these imputed wishes; and, by advertising or personal selling, informing the customers of what has been done. The General Motors Corporation has long followed this procedure, trying to discover consumers' automotive preferences through their Customers' Research Staff.

The second policy, probably followed by a majority of manufacturers, involves the making of the goods that the producers believe the public will desire. Not much, if any, research is done. The producer then endeavors to sell the public on the idea that the goods are exactly what consumers want. Adherents of this policy have tried to justify it on the basis of the acknowledged difficulty of securing trustworthy information regarding their preferences from consumers. On the whole, this procedure has probably operated to benefit consumers, and the goods produced under it have generally been satisfactory.

A third policy that has been coming into increasing use involves the *test market.* Under this procedure producers of consumer goods select certain geographic areas—frequently single cities—and introduce their new products, with or without advertising or sales promotion, for the purpose of gauging potential consumer demand. This may go on for weeks or months before the producers decide either to expand their distribution to cover a much wider area or to discontinue the goods being tested if consumer response is not deemed to be satisfactory.

AIDS TO CONSUMER BUYING

Buyers of industrial and commercial goods and those who purchase consumer goods for wholesalers and retailers have long been recognized as a quasi-professional procurement group with a thorough knowledge of the goods that they require and the sources from which they may be bought. By way of contrast, there is considerable evidence that many consumers lack the buying skill and discriminative judgment that should be theirs if they are to receive the greatest value for the money that they pay for goods and services.

Some businessmen and many of the more economically minded consumers who have recognized this lack of buying skill have endeavored to make available to consumers certain aids that are helpful in remedying this situation. Consumers' Research and Consumers Union were established some years ago by consumer groups for the purpose of testing consumer goods and of publishing their findings for the benefit of subscribers to their services.

A number of prominent retail organizations have undertaken to make merchandise information more readily available for consumers. Among these are Macy's; Sears, Roebuck and Company; and Marshall Field and Company. Many stores provide their salespeople with information about the goods that they handle, which they, in turn, can pass on to consumers. This is called *specification selling.*

So-called *seals of approval,* emanating from such organizations as *Good Housekeeping* magazine, the Underwriters' Laboratories, the American Medical Association, and the American Dental Association, are intended to identify goods that are outstanding.

The question naturally arises, to what extent do consumers take advantage of these aids to better buying? A definite answer is not possible because of the paucity of available data on the subject. The combined circulation of the publications of Consumers' Research and Consumers Union is placed at around 1,300,000 annually, with a readership estimated at better than three persons a copy. The extent to which these readers are influenced in their actual buying is unknown. Department store executives, in commenting on the attitude of consumers toward specification selling, have indicated that they appear to evince little interest in such information. The effect of the various seals of approval on consumer buying habits is likewise unknown, but there is little evidence to suggest that it is of much consequence. There is a pervasive belief among manufacturers and distributors of consumer goods that consumers would benefit the entire economic system were they to become better informed about the goods which they buy.

BUSINESS TERMS

QUESTIONS FOR DISCUSSION AND ANALYSIS

1. Despite the adoption of the total marketing concept by many producers of consumer goods, every year large numbers of products appear but are not accepted by the public. Why is this so?

2. Attempts by producers of shopping goods to build consumer acceptance through branding their products have been generally unsuccessful. Why?

3. Name some convenience goods other than those mentioned in the text.

4. Specialty goods are usually distributed on a restricted or exclusive basis. Why?

5. Do consumers ever perform any of the marketing functions? If so, which ones?

6. Does the growth of self-service stores imply that retail salespeople are a vanishing type of employee? Explain.

7. Why are not more consumer goods grade labeled?

8. The results obtained by marketing research in the fields of industrial and commercial goods are generally considered to be more accurate and reliable than those secured for consumer goods. Why should this be so?

9. Do you believe that the securing of information from consumers concerning the goods that they will buy is as difficult as many producers appear to think? Explain.

10. Are consumers becoming more interested in being better informed about the goods that they buy? Explain your yes or no answer.

PROBLEMS AND SHORT CASES

1. Design a questionnaire that you think would be helpful in answering one of the following questions in marketing research:

   a. Will the sales of the Volkswagen be adversely affected by the reintroduction of small cars by automobile producers in this country?

   b. What are the opinions of adults toward supersonic airplane transportation?

   c. What are the attitudes of adults with regard to the effectiveness of the United Nations?

2. The Dalton Company is an old-line, well established manufacturer of medium priced bedroom furniture. The company is well known in the furniture trade and to the department and furniture stores through whom it has traditionally sold its merchandise. Recently the sales manager of Dalton received an inquiry from a buyer of furniture representing Montgomery Ward, who asked if he would be interested in making furniture for their retail stores and mail order trade. The Montgomery Ward man agreed to a scale of prices that would yield a satisfactory margin of profit to the Dalton Company, but the sales manager was concerned about the effect on the firm's present customers if it should sell to Montgomery Ward also, with whom many of them are competitive. You are asked to analyze this situation and to advise the Dalton sales manager as to the proper course of action that he should take. Give your reasons.

SUGGESTED READINGS

Buskirk, Richard H. *Principles of Marketing*, Third Edition. New York: Holt, Rinehart and Winston, 1970.

Kerby, Joe Kent. *Essentials of Marketing Management*. Cincinnati: South-Western Publishing Co., 1970.

Taylor, Weldon J., and Roy T. Shaw, Jr. *Marketing: An Integrated, Analytical Approach*, Second Edition. Cincinnati: South-Western Publishing Co., 1969.

Wentz, Walter B., and Gerald I. Eyrich. *Marketing, Theory and Application*. New York: Harcourt Brace Jovanovich, Inc., 1970.

Chapter 9

Wholesaling and Retailing

The pattern for the marketing of goods in the United States consists of a large number of wholesalers and retailers whose responsibility is that of making available to consumers the products of the manufacturers of this and many other countries. Before presenting a description of the different types of middlemen who operate within the marketing structure of the country, attention is directed to the paths which the goods follow on their way to the ultimate consumer.

CHANNELS OF DISTRIBUTION

The routes that goods take in their progress from producers to consumers are known as *channels of distribution*. These channels vary according to the nature of the goods, the market, the character of the demand, and the competition among sellers. The channels of distribution for consumer goods differ somewhat from those for industrial and commercial goods, mainly in that, with rare exceptions, the latter two types of goods are not sold through retailers. The pattern for consumer goods is presented first.

CHANNELS FOR CONSUMER GOODS

The most direct channel of distribution for consumer goods is found where the producer sells directly to the consumer. This channel is used by many house-to-house selling firms, such as Fuller Brush and Avon Products, and by some producers who distribute by mail order, such as the New Process Company.

Producer⸺⸺⸺➤Consumer

In another channel producers sell to retailers, who in turn sell to consumers. This channel represents the path taken by goods handled by department stores and chain stores.

Producer⸺⸺⸺➤ Retailer⸺⸺⸺➤Consumer

A third channel is utilized where the wholesaler enters the picture between the producer and the retailer. This is the traditionally characteristic method whereby goods have been distributed in this country. It is still the prevalent system for goods that reach the consumer through the small independent retailer, such as a grocer, a druggist, a hardware dealer, or a clothing specialty shop.

Producer ⸺⸺⸺➤ Wholesaler⸺⸺⸺➤ Retailer⸺⸺⸺➤ Consumer

A producer may adopt any one or more of these channels in his endeavors to have his goods reach the final consumers in as large quantities as possible. Many producers sell direct to the chains and larger independent stores, and at the same time utilize wholesalers to reach the smaller independent retailers. The channel of distribution pattern then would be like the following:

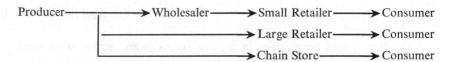

A variant on this type of distribution channel is found where producers sell directly to city retailers, regardless of their size, but utilize wholesalers to reach small town and country retail stores. The channel pattern is as follows:

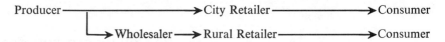

CHANNELS FOR INDUSTRIAL AND COMMERCIAL GOODS

The major difference between the channels of distribution for industrial and commercial goods and those for consumer goods lies in the fact that, as a general rule, there are no retailers in the former scheme. The two channels found in the industrial and commercial field are:

Producer ————————————————→ Industrial or Commercial Consumer

Producer ———→ Wholesaler ———→ Industrial or Commercial Consumer

The first of these two channel patterns may include producers' branch offices with or without stocks of goods for delivery to customers.

With all types of goods, there are instances where a class of wholesalers known as agents and brokers is utilized. This occurs where the characteristics of either the sellers or the buyers are such that the former find it more profitable to employ agents and brokers than to use their own salesmen. Under these circumstances, in the case of consumer goods, sales are made to wholesalers or to retailers, but not to individual consumers.

The problems that arise in connection with the choosing of channels of distribution and of examining them for possible changes as occasions arise are among the most important that producers are called upon to solve.

WHOLESALING

Wholesaling includes all of the marketing functions and activities that involve the sale of goods where the purpose for making the purchase is a business or profit motive. This obviously does not include sales to individual consumers. This broad segment of marketing embraces all of the following types of transactions.

1. Sales to retailers.
2. Sales to wholesalers.
3. Sales to manufacturers, railroads, mines, and other producers.
4. Sales to hotels and restaurants.
5. Sales of building supplies and equipment to building contractors.
6. All of the operations of functional middlemen, such as brokers, selling agents, and others, who facilitate the movement of goods from sellers to buyers, without taking title to them in the process.
7. Sales of supplies and equipment to beauty salons and barbershops.
8. All sales of farm products to other than the final consumers.

The discussion of wholesaling in this chapter will be concerned primarily with sales to retailers and to other wholesalers.

Table 9-1 presents a summary of the number and sales volume of the major types of wholesalers as classified by the United States Census of Business for 1967.

Table 9-1

NUMBER AND SALES VOLUME OF SELECTED TYPES OF WHOLESALERS IN THE UNITED STATES, 1967

	Number of Establishments	Sales Volume (Thousands of Dollars)
Merchant Wholesalers	212,993	$206,055,065
Wholesale merchants	204,783	181,775,733
Importers	5,171	10,353,989
Exporters	2,272	9,507,734
Terminal grain elevators	767	4,417,609
Merchandise Agents, Brokers	26,462	61,347,036
Auction companies	1,594	4,792,386
Merchandise brokers	4,373	14,030,462
Commission merchants	5,425	14,068,048
Import agents	270	1,790,666
Export agents	548	3,372,043
Manufacturers' agents	12,106	15,256,996
Selling agents	1,891	6,889,890
Purchasing agents, resident buyers	255	1,146,545

Source: Bureau of the Census, *1967 Census of Business*.

MERCHANT WHOLESALERS

Merchant wholesalers are wholesale establishments that buy and sell merchandise on their own account; that is, they take title to the goods which they handle. The more important wholesalers in this group are: (1) wholesale merchants, (2) importers and exporters, (3) wagon, truck distributors, and (4) rack merchandisers.

In addition to these four groups, there are wholesalers in the industrial goods field who are known as *industrial distributors*; they operate in the fields of industrial equipment, machinery, and parts. *Specialty wholesalers* carry limited or short lines in the areas in which they operate. Thus in the grocery field, this type would confine itself to coffee or canned goods, or to a few other lines.

Wholesale Merchants

Wholesale merchants are the regular or full-service wholesalers who exist in many lines of business. They sell goods principally to retailers. They buy and sell merchandise on their own account; carry stocks in their places of business; assemble in large lots and redistribute in smaller quantities, usually through salesmen; extend credit to customers; make deliveries; and render advice to the trade. Among the types of merchandise handled by wholesale merchants are groceries, drugs, hardware, and dry goods. The term *jobber*, which still persists in a few lines of business and which had at one time a special significance, is now regarded as being synonymous with wholesale merchant.

Importers and Exporters

Importers and *exporters*, as the names imply, are wholesale merchants who buy and sell, respectively, in the foreign market.

Wagon, Truck Distributors

Wagon, truck distributors make sales and deliveries to retailers from stocks that they carry in their trucks. They are found principally in the grocery field. They carry a limited assortment of merchandise, consisting of nationally advertised goods and fast-moving perishable items. Their practice is to sell for cash and in original packages. Examples of wagon distributors are those wholesalers who deliver tobacco products, soft drinks, milk, and bread to grocery stores and supermarkets. This type of merchant wholesaler is included under "Wholesale merchants" in Table 9-1.

Rack Merchandisers

The tendency on the part of supermarkets to add nonfood lines to their stocks of groceries has brought into being the first new type of operator that has appeared in the field of wholesaling in a long time. This is known as a *rack merchandiser*, *rack jobber*, or *service merchandiser*. The term "rack" stems from the type of fixture used to display these nonfood items. Among these goods are toiletries, drug products, housewares, records, hosiery, magazines, stationery, greeting cards, kitchen gadgets, etc.

The operating practices of rack merchandisers follow a fairly common pattern in many of their activities, while showing a considerable degree of variance in other phases of their services. Almost without exception they warehouse the merchandise, build the displays, replenish stocks in the stores as needed, and price the goods. In some cases they also retain title to the merchandise and pay the stores a certain percentage of the retail price of the goods sold to consumers; in others they sell outright to the retailers. Some rack merchandisers take back items that have remained unsold after a period of time; others assume no such responsibility. Although combined by the Bureau of the Census with wholesale merchants, rack merchandisers are of sufficient importance in the supermarket field to warrant their inclusion at this point.

MERCHANDISE AGENTS AND BROKERS

The outstanding characteristic of this group of wholesalers is that they do not take title to (become the legal owners of) the goods with which they deal. They are in business for themselves and negotiate purchases and sales in domestic and international trade in behalf of principals who do take title to the goods. They may or may not take possession of the goods involved. An additional important function that many of them perform is the furnishing of marketing information. Such wholesalers commonly receive their remuneration in the form of commissions or fees. The term *functional middlemen* has been frequently used as a group designation for this type of wholesaler. The more important wholesalers in this classification are: (1) manufacturers' agents, (2) merchandise brokers, (3) commission merchants, (4) selling agents, and (5) auction companies.

Manufacturers' Agents

Manufacturers' agents are middlemen who sell part of the output of certain manufacturers on an extended contractual basis. They are limited in respect to territory and to prices and terms of sale. Their principal duty is to sell goods in accordance with the desires of their clients, although they may also warehouse some of the merchandise. They usually represent two or more producers whose goods are noncompetitive in nature. Manufacturers' agents are prominent in the fields of machinery, industrial equipment and supplies, dry goods, men's and women's clothing, furniture and house furnishings, and groceries. In some lines of business the term "manufacturers' representative" is coming into common usage in the place of manufacturers' agent.

Merchandise Brokers

Merchandise brokers are wholesale agent middlemen whose task is to negotiate transactions between sellers and buyers without having direct physical control of the goods. They may represent either a seller or a buyer in any given transaction, but not both. They conclude purchases or sales in the name of their principals. Their powers of determining prices or terms of sale are usually limited by their principals.

The term "broker" is also commonly applied to those individuals and institutions that are active in the investment field. The term is also found in real estate and personnel placement. The merchandise broker, however, is the only one who is regarded as a marketing institution.

Commission Merchants

Commission merchants are agent middlemen who transact business in their own names on a commission basis and who have direct physical control over the goods assigned to them. They operate in the fields of groceries, livestock, cotton, and grain.

Selling Agents

Selling agents are independent business enterprises operating on a commission basis, whose principal function is to sell the entire output of a given line of goods for one or more manufacturers with whom they maintain continuous contractual relationships. They are found in such fields as textiles, coal, metals, and food. They have full authority with regard to prices and terms of sale.

Auction Companies

Auction companies sell at wholesale by the auction method. Sales are conducted under definite rules and are usually made to the highest bidder. They operate in the tobacco, livestock, and fresh fruit and vegetable fields. Auction companies represent sellers of goods.

WHOLESALE SERVICES

Wholesaling performs a necessary marketing service in our competitive, profit-motivated economy, the cost of which is broadly equated to the economic values that it creates. A large number of producers, located in many different areas, must move their products to industrial and commercial consumers and to numerous retailers, who are also widely scattered. In the years immediately following the close of World War I, there was a fairly widespread belief that wholesalers were an unnecessary part of the marketing structure, whose elimination would result in lower prices to consumers. The fact that wholesaling has continued as a vital part of our distributive system is a strong indication of its value.

Services Rendered to Manufacturers

The services rendered to manufacturers by wholesalers are: (a) contact retailers, (b) store for manufacturers, (c) assume credit burdens, and (d) other services.

Because the operational scope of most wholesalers is strictly local in character, they are able to establish an intensive contact with retailers and, frequently, at a lower cost to the manufacturers than the latter would incur if their own salesmen called on the retailers.

Wholesalers in many lines maintain large stocks of goods from which they make deliveries to their retail customers. By this practice they perform a storage function that the manufacturers would otherwise have to undertake. This permits the manufacturers to routinize their productive processes and usually to lower their production and storage costs.

If a manufacturer sells direct to retailers on any basis other than a purely local one, he must establish a system of credit administration that may be very extensive and costly. When wholesalers are used, they invariably assume this burden, which enables the producers to reduce the task of extending credit to that of a few, usually well-rated wholesale houses.

Wholesalers render to manufacturers still other services. Among these may be the granting of financial assistance to producers who happen to be in temporary need of funds, as well as interpreting local needs to manufacturers and thereby assisting them to fabricate their goods so as to make them more salable than would otherwise be the case.

Services Rendered to Retailers

The following services are rendered to retailers by wholesalers: (a) simplify buying problems, (b) prompt delivery, (c) storage service, (d) credit facilities, and (e) merchandising aids.

A retail store usually stocks goods that are manufactured in many different parts of the country, if not of the world. If these goods were not assembled locally by wholesalers, retailers would need to devote much of their time either to traveling extensively to contact producers or to interviewing manufacturers' salesmen who would be calling on them. In either instance, they would have to take much time out from their normal storekeeping duties. Wholesalers assume most of these tasks and thereby simplify the retailers' buying problems.

Wholesalers are able to give retailers prompt delivery service. Because of their nearness to their customers, wholesalers are able to give them much more rapid delivery service than retailers could normally expect from manufacturers. This service enables retailers to maintain balanced stocks and not run short of needed merchandise.

By maintaining large stocks of goods from which retailers may draw when needed, wholesalers absorb a part of the retailers' storage burdens. If retailers bought direct from manufacturers, they would need to store the goods themselves, which would require larger storage facilities and tie up greater amounts of capital in inventory.

Wholesalers grant credit to retailers. The fact that many wholesalers operate solely in a fairly small market area permits them to offer credit to their customers on a basis that would be difficult, if not impossible, for the retailers to secure from the producers. This service may be exceedingly valuable to retailers who find themselves temporarily short of funds.

Wholesalers offer merchandising aids to their customers. Salesmen for wholesalers are frequently able to help their retailer customers by making suggestions to improve their displays, selling techniques, accounting procedures, and so on. Some go so far as to prepare and distribute sample advertising insertions, store layouts, and accounting books. Not many manufacturers could duplicate these services.

BYPASSING WHOLESALERS

Despite the services that wholesalers render to both manufacturers and retailers, many manufacturers and retailers have undertaken to bypass the wholesalers by dealing directly with each other. Instances of this are to be found in the buying practices of department stores, chain stores, and mail-order houses, and in the selling policies of many producers who deal with these types of retailers, as well as those who maintain sales offices, with or without stocks, in various parts of the country. This means that these institutions must perform the storage, financing, market risk, buying, and selling functions that would otherwise be done by wholesalers.

A variant on this practice by manufacturers is where the producers sell direct to retailers located in large urban areas, while using wholesalers in all other cases, as is shown in the last diagram on page 192.

Why Manufacturers Bypass Wholesalers

Manufacturers sometimes bypass wholesalers in distributing their goods for three reasons. (a) They believe that by calling directly on the retailers who handle their products they are able to secure better control of the retail market and thus prevent their competitors from obtaining too large a share of the available business. (b) They feel the need for stronger promotional effort than wholesalers, who may be carrying many other manufacturers' goods, are able to give them. (c) In many instances they are forced to sell direct in order to meet competition.

Why Retailers Bypass Wholesalers

Likewise, there are three main reasons why retailers sometimes take the initiative in buying direct from manufacturers. (a) The principal reason is that they can frequently secure lower prices by taking over some of the wholesalers' functions and dealing directly with the producers. (b) In the handling of women's apparel, the sudden style changes, to which this type of merchandise is subject, make the time element of great importance and impel retailers to deal directly with the producers, particularly if they feature "style firsts" in their communities. (c) Retailers may buy direct from manufacturers because their competitors follow this practice and are able to undersell them unless they follow suit.

DOES DIRECT SELLING LOWER COSTS?

In order to answer this question accurately, it would be necessary to make rather detailed studies of the distribution costs of a large number of different lines of merchandise, a procedure that is not in order in a book such as this. It is possible, however, to observe what happens when goods are sold direct and to draw certain rather general conclusions from this examination (see Figure 9-1).

The movement of goods in the marketing channels involves the performance of some or all of the marketing functions by the institutions handling the merchandise; and it is in the performance of these functions that marketing costs arise. When the wholesaler in any line of merchandise is bypassed, the marketing functions incidental to the movement of the merchandise, which would usually be taken care of by the wholesaler, are taken over by the manufacturer and/or the retailer. If these two are able to perform the functions only as cheaply as the wholesaler, then the saving will be largely in the elimination of the wholesaler's profit. If they are more efficient than the wholesaler, there may be additional savings;

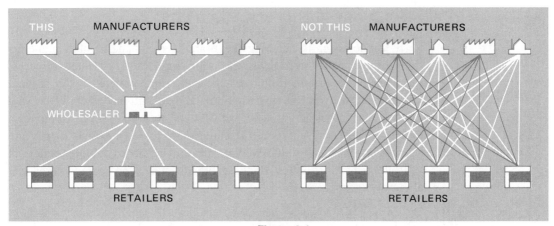

Figure 9-1

Direct vs. Indirect Selling

likewise, if they are less competent than the wholesaler, the savings may be reduced, even to the point where they may vanish and extra costs may arise. Comparative cost data are not available for alternate distribution channels, but the fact that direct selling has persisted in many areas appears to indicate that it is cheaper for both sellers and buyers than the utilization of wholesalers.

HOW WHOLESALERS HAVE REACTED

The wholesalers have not been unaware of the tendency for retailers to bypass them, nor have they sat idly by while it has progressed. They have endeavored to combat this trend, with varying degrees of success, in a number of ways: (1) increased efficiency, (2) development of private brands, and (3) formation of voluntary chains.

Increased Efficiency

By a careful examination of their costs, through better selection and training of their employees, and particularly through a revision of their methods of storage and handling orders, many wholesalers have succeeded in reducing their own distributive expenses. A form of automation in the food and drug wholesale business involves the use of forklift trucks, continuous chain conveyors, mechanical driverless tow trucks, and gravity conveyors, all of which are guided by electrical computers that preprint invoices and assist in selecting the goods ordered.

Development of Private Brands

If a wholesaler is handling the branded merchandise of a manufacturer, he has no protection against the manufacturer's selling direct to the retailers, because the latter still have the same brands to offer to their customers. To overcome this situation and to entrench themselves with their retailer customers, many wholesalers have developed their own brands. If they are successful in selling these to retailers and if they are accepted by consumers, the wholesalers are in the enviable situation of controlling the distribution of these brands, which no manufacturer can take away from them.

Formation of Voluntary Chains

By associating several retailers on a voluntary chain basis, many wholesalers have been able to become firmly established in their communities and to be virtually immune from the possibility of being eliminated through the actions of either the manufacturers or the retailers, or both.

RETAILING

Retailing is that segment of marketing where the products of the consumer goods industry are purchased by the ultimate consumers for their own personal use or that of their families. It is the point in the channel of distribution where the offerings of manufacturers of consumer goods are accepted or rejected. It is where the validity of the total marketing concept is either proved or disproved.

The marketing institutions that operate in this field are retailers. Their contribution to the economic life of the nation arises through their creation of place, time, and possession utilities; that is, they bring the goods to places that are convenient for consumers to purchase, at the times that they want them, and they provide the facilities by which consumers may secure possession of the goods of their choice. Through the creation of these utilities, retailers, as is true of wholesalers, add value to the goods they sell.

Retailing is a dynamic field—a scene of intense competition, of daring innovations, and of rapid change. It features dramatic sales promotion and advertising in which only those store types whose goods, locations, service, and operational methods are in line with changing trends can hope to survive the rigors of competition. Stores that have followed long-established, previously successful policies of location, layout, customer service, and merchandise selections are finding that their very existence is being threatened by competitors whose new methods of operation appear to hold an almost irresistible attraction for many consumers. The dynamism portrayed by this situation has given rise to the term *scrambled retailing,* which is illustrative of the unsettled conditions in this economic area.

One of the major causes of this acute competitive situation is the dramatic rise in the population of the country and the concomitant growth of the suburban areas of most of our large cities. Accompanying this factor has been the increase in the number of automobiles in use, with the resulting need for more parking facilities, both in the downtown sections and in the suburbs, and the ensuing traffic congestion that is a feature of all metropolitan areas to an increasing degree.

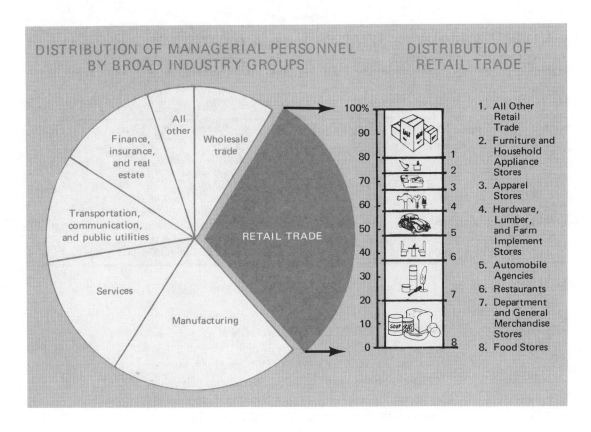

Figure 9-2

Retailing and Management

As shown in Figure 9-2, retailing is the largest area of employment for managers. The requirements for managerial success in retailing include considerable retail experience, keen merchandise judgment, an intuitive understanding of customer preferences, a sense of showmanship, bargaining ability for trading with suppliers, a knowledge of the latest developments in retail accounting, and, of course, the ability to direct the personnel of the store. Coupled with this should be a good measure of physical stamina and a recognition that retailing is practically a way of life, at least to the successful retail manager.

Table 9-2 below shows the ten largest retailing firms in the United States in 1970, with their invested capital and net profit as a percentage of sales. The notable differences between the invested capital of food and nonfood stores is of interest.

Table 9-2

THE TEN LARGEST RETAILING COMPANIES RANKED BY SALES, 1970

Rank	Company	Sales ($000)	Invested Capital ($000)	Net Income as % of Sales
1	Sears, Roebuck & Company	9,262,162	7,623,096	5.0
2	Great Atlantic & Pacific Tea Co.	5,650,000	957,073	0.9
3	Safeway Stores	4,860,167	875,705	1.4
4	J. C. Penney	4,150,886	1,627,055	2.7
5	Kroger	3,735,774	767,777	1.1
6	Marcor	2,804,856	2,459,730	2.1
7	S. S. Kresge	2,595,155	926,227	2.6
8	F. W. Woolworth	2,527,965	1,436,297	3.0
9	Federated Department Stores	2,096,935	1,165,770	3.9
10	Food Fair Stores	1,762,005	363,472	0.6

Reprinted from the May, 1971, *Fortune Directory* by special permission: © 1971, Time, Inc.

RETAILERS CLASSIFIED BY TYPES OF OPERATION

Retailers are classified by their locations, such as downtown or neighborhood; by the types of goods handled, such as food, drugs, shoes, and hardware; by the types of operation; and on the basis of ownership. This chapter will deal with the last two categories.

When the operation of retailers forms the basis for classification, the various types are: (1) general stores, (2) department stores, (3) specialty stores, (4) single-line stores, (5) specialty shops, (6) supermarkets,

(7) discount houses, (8) limited-price variety stores, and (9) other types of retailers.

General Stores

The earliest type of retail outlet in this country was probably the *general store.* In the early years of our history, it was found in villages or at country crossroads as the only retailing institution in the community. It carried a broad range of goods, from food and clothing to farm implements, feed, and seeds; and it frequently housed the post office. A few of this type are still to be found in the more sparsely settled areas.

A novel development in the general store field is exemplified by the National Farm Stores, Inc., which with some 30 or more stores has produced a modern version of the old country general store. These stores carry a wide variety of goods for farmers and are located in a few of the agricultural producing areas of the country.

Department Stores

Department stores are large establishments located in downtown shopping areas of cities. They handle a wide range of goods, including clothing, furniture, housewares, floor coverings, toys, millinery, lamps, draperies, yard goods, and small wares such as notions, cosmetics, and handkerchiefs.

Department stores stress the service side of their business. Free delivery, liberal credit, the acceptance of telephone and mail orders, gift wrapping, the privilege of almost unlimited return of purchased merchandise, rest rooms, nurseries for infants and children, and restaurants are among the inducements held out to their customers.

These stores may be independently owned, or they may be units of chains. At this level of retailing there is practically no difference in the operating practices and merchandising policies of chains and independents.

Most department stores buy direct from the manufacturers. They, as well as the specialty stores, utilize *resident buying offices,* most of which are located in New York City, with a few in Chicago, St. Louis, and Los Angeles. These facilities may be either independent or owned by one or more stores. Department store chains not infrequently have their own resident buying offices, as do such groups as the Associated Merchandising Corporation which is an association of noncompeting department stores. Some of the services of resident buying offices are shown in Figure 9-3 on page 206. In addition, they provide office space for visiting buyers when they are in the market cities and assist them in contacting suppliers, even furnishing display rooms where the salesmen for manufacturers may show their wares to buyers.

Figure 9-3

Services of a Resident Buying Office

Department stores rely on newspaper and direct-mail advertising, together with elaborate window and floor displays, to inform their customers of the availability of their merchandise and to attract them into their stores. Highly skilled advertising and display personnel direct these activities. Among the more prominent department stores in the country are Macy's and Lord & Taylor in New York, Hudson's in Detroit, Marshall Field in Chicago, Jordan Marsh in Boston and Florida, and Bullock's in Los Angeles.

A rather remarkable development of the late 1960's is known as a *boutique*, a small shop, featuring many different kinds of merchandise, with a wide range of prices. Located mainly in large department stores, they are so arranged as to give customers the impression of being exclusive and more or less separated from the large stores of which they are actually a part. Some of the names that these shops bear are quite unusual and, presumably, attractive to the type of customer to whom they appeal. Among these are Zoo's Who (for fun furs), the Espresso Shop, the S'fari Room, S'il Vous Plait, and L'Arcade Elegante.

Branch department stores. The trend for downtown department stores to establish branch stores in the suburbs of our large cities, which began in the early 1930's, has accelerated greatly in recent years. Examples of this development are to be found in the suburbs of many cities, such as New York, Boston, Philadelphia, Cleveland, Chicago, and Los Angeles. Frequently these branch stores are located in or near suburban shopping centers; and in some instances the sponsoring stores have established controlled shopping centers, incorporating their branches as the focal points in these enterprises.

Since the onset of this branch-store movement, there has been considerable speculation as to whether it might eventually replace the downtown shopping center. The migration of city population to the suburbs, the increase in the volume of automobile traffic, and the parking difficulties that confront consumers who wish to patronize the downtown stores have all been factors that have tended to contribute to this speculation. In many cities, however, countermeasures have been undertaken, such as the erection of parking garages or the provision of large parking lots, together with free bus transportation to and from these facilities.

Sears' and Ward's stores. The department stores operated by Sears, Roebuck and Co., and the Montgomery Ward and Co., division of Marcor, Inc., the country's two largest mail-order houses, constitute an important segment of retailing. In most instances, the Sears stores have been located in the larger cities, usually some distance from the downtown shopping centers, and have featured large parking lots for their customers. By contrast, the Ward stores have usually been located in the smaller cities and, where possible, in the main shopping districts of these towns. Unlike the department stores with which they compete, these stores carry very few nationally advertised manufacturers' brands of merchandise but confine their offerings mainly to goods bearing their own brands.

Specialty Stores

A *specialty store* might be defined as a department store minus the merchandise customarily known as home furnishings, such as housewares, furniture, floor coverings, electrical appliances, toys, china, and glassware. It is directly competitive with department stores. Specialty stores tend to confine their apparel offerings to women's wear and accessories, but some of them specialize in men's apparel and accessories, such as sporting goods and luggage. The buying, advertising, and service policies of these stores are identical with those of department stores. Several large specialty stores have formed a buying group, known as the Specialty Stores Association, which maintains a buying office in New York City. Specialty stores are both independent and chain owned.

Single-Line Stores

The *single-line store* is the small store, independently owned, that carries a single line of merchandise, such as food, hardware, drugs, millinery, or men's furnishings. In the interest of consistency, gasoline filling stations, automobile dealers, flower shops, tire and accessory stores, furniture stores, appliance stores, jewelry stores, antique and gift shops, and restaurants should be included in this category; but many of their operating procedures and problems are different. Chain stores handling the same kinds of goods are excluded because many of their merchandising methods are different from those of the independents.

The typical single-line stores are to be found everywhere, in the downtown and the neighborhood areas and in the newly developed suburban shopping centers. The more or less isolated stores, located at or near street intersections in residential areas, are frequently of this type. They offer free delivery, extend credit to their customers, and accept telephone orders. A trend in the grocery field among these stores in recent years is the growth of the cash-and-carry system as well as that of self-service.

Single-line stores range in size from those that are literally holes in the wall to fairly large establishments with modern fixtures, adequate lighting, and general attractiveness. These stores customarily buy the bulk of their goods through wholesalers, although some of the larger ones deal directly with the manufacturers. Their advertising is usually limited, except in small towns, as they customarily cannot afford to use the metropolitan daily newspapers. In villages and suburban communities where weekly newspapers are published, many single-line stores have been able to utilize these advertising media advantageously.

Specialty Shops

A *specialty shop* is a store, often a member of a chain, that confines itself to a small segment of the merchandise in any single category, usually in the apparel field. Stores of this type handle dresses, or millinery, or shoes, and sometimes a combination of apparel items, such as hosiery, handbags, and shoes, or millinery and neckwear. Specialty shops are to be found in all retail areas, in the downtown as well as the neighborhood business communities and suburban shopping centers.

The buying practices of specialty shops vary according to sales volume. Those with larger sales tend to buy direct, while the smaller stores buy through wholesalers. They rely heavily on window displays to attract customers, as only the largest shops can afford to use newspaper advertising. Some of the independently owned boutiques belong in this category.

Supermarkets

Despite the fact that supermarkets have become predominant in the grocery field, there is no generally accepted definition for this type of retail outlet. A composite of the definitions of several trade periodicals in this field would describe a *supermarket* as a departmentized food store, with most departments on a self-service basis, having a minimum sales volume ranging from $375,000 to $1,000,000 a year.

Although supermarkets originated in the 1930's, their period of greatest growth dates from around the end of World War II, and they have come to be preeminent in the food field. They are both chain and independently owned. In the case of the chains, large numbers of their smaller, counter-service grocery units have been closed. An interesting aspect of supermarket development has been the progressive addition of a large number of nonfood items. Among these are toilet goods, proprietary drugs, hosiery, magazines, records, kitchen utensils, small tools, glassware, hardware, and dinnerware.

In some parts of the country, small, self-service grocery stores are called *superettes*, a term that is intended to indicate their relationship to supermarkets. In many instances these superettes are former service stores that have been converted to self-service.

The success of the supermarkets has caused many students of retailing to speculate regarding the extent to which self-service will be adopted in nonfood fields. Already over 600 drugstores in this country, as well as a considerable number of variety and small department stores, are on a more or less total self-service basis.

A post-World War II development that has attained considerable stature in supermarket purchasing is the *buying committee*. This group, which is composed of the top marketing and purchasing personnel in the company concerned, is charged with the duty of determining the acceptability of new items that are offered to their stores for sale. The great increase in the number and variety of goods, both food and nonfood, which have come on the market in the postwar period and the impossibility of a supermarket buying them all is the cause of the rise of the buying committee. Where such a group operates, the individual buyers do not have the authority to approve new items, but merely to purchase those which have been previously passed by the committee. Over 90 percent of supermarkets are reported to utilize this method of appraising new products offered to them. As an additional duty, the buying committees of many chain supermarkets review the proposed promotional campaigns of manufacturers and decide whether or not their stores will cooperate with these endeavors through advertising and display.

Discount Houses

An important post-World War II development has been the growth of discount houses. Owned by both chains and independent operators, the *discount houses* have offered merchandise at substantially lower prices than their competitors, many of whom are department and appliance stores. They have based their low prices on a curtailment of service and, in recent years, by securing a growing volume of sales on a relatively constant expense, thereby permitting them to operate on a smaller markup than their older competitors. These stores have often specialized in electrical appliances, television and radio receivers, furniture, floor coverings, power mowers, sporting goods, and air conditioners.

Discount houses buy their goods through wholesalers in some instances and directly from the manufacturers in others. They usually sell strictly for cash and offer delivery service only on major appliances, such as stoves or refrigerators. A recent development in this field has been the appearance of discount drugstores. Customarily operating on a self-service basis, these stores feature fast-selling drug and cosmetic items at prices markedly below those of the independent drugstores and some of the chains.

In recent years there has been a pronounced trend in the discount-house field toward the broadening of their merchandise offerings. Many have been adding apparel lines to their traditional hard lines of merchandise and are thus moving in the direction of becoming full-fledged department stores.

A number of discount houses sell only to consumers who have purchased memberships. These are called *closed-door discount houses*. Members are frequently selected from more or less cohesive groups, such as government employees or labor unions, and only they are permitted to buy in those stores. Merchandise offerings parallel those of department stores. These stores are frequently known by abbreviations such as FAME, GEM, or GEX, which indicates the nature of their membership. For example, GEX stands for Government Employees Exchange. Since the prices of these stores approximate those of department stores and regular discount houses, the reason why consumers will pay membership fees to secure their goods is not entirely clear.

A relatively recent development in the discount field has been the addition of food departments by discounters in many parts of the country. In retaliation for this move, several of the large food chain operators have opened *discount supermarkets*, stores with lower prices based on curtailed advertising, elimination of trading stamps, elaborate inventories, and check-cashing services. Frequently these new stores bear different names from those of the parent companies, for example, the A & P has opened a number of A Mart stores.

Limited-Price Variety Stores

In 1879 F. W. Woolworth established the first store of this type, which became known as 5-and-10-cent stores because of the original limitation on the prices of goods carried. More recently the price lines of these stores have been advanced, with some goods priced as high as $25 or more. As a result, the original designation is no longer applicable, and in its place the term *limited-price variety stores* is a more accurate description and is in accord with the usage of the trade, if not of the public. Examples of this type, in addition to the F. W. Woolworth Company, are the S. S. Kresge & Company and the J. J. Newberry Company. The chains do about 90 percent of the business in this field, and a rather large group of independents obtain the rest. It is anticipated, however, that the independent group will increase its share of the business in the future.

Variety stores handle a wide array of merchandise from small wares, toys, housewares, candy, toiletries, stationery, electric appliances and bulbs, and light hardware, mostly in the low-price ranges, to table and floor lamps, furniture, and apparel items in the medium-price fields. Historically these stores have been on a cash-and-carry basis, but during the past few years, several of them have made charge accounts available to qualified customers.

The buying practices of the independent variety stores customarily involve the use of wholesalers, whereas all of the chains buy direct from the manufacturers. The Ben Franklin Stores, a franchise operation in the variety store field, buys from City Products Corporation, a wholesaler which is owned by Household Finance Corporation. These stores function as a voluntary chain.

Other Types of Retailers

A number of other, somewhat less important, types of retailers deserve brief mention.

House-to-house selling. One of the principal deterrents to the success of house-to-house selling, aside from the prejudice against it on the part of many housewives, is the so-called *Green River Ordinance*, so named because it originated in Green River, Wyoming. Such a local law has been enacted in many small communities to hamper or restrict the activities of itinerant house-to-house peddlers. Ordinances of this type ordinarily involve the payment of a fee to secure a permit to call at the local homes. These ordinances were originated by local merchants and enacted at their request in order to prevent competition between them and the house-to-house salesmen. The United States Supreme Court has upheld the constitutionality of the Green River Ordinance of Alexandria, Louisiana. A *huckster* is a house-to-house salesman who differs from other house-to-house salesmen in that (a) he carries his stock of goods with him and makes deliveries on the spot and (b) he calls repeatedly on the same customers, frequently every working day of the week, and comes to be well known to them. Hucksters are customarily residents in the cities where they operate. Huckstering includes the fields of bread and fresh fruits and vegetables.

Mail-order houses. *Mail-order houses* sell and deliver goods by mail, making use of catalogs, newspaper advertising, and direct mail to attract customers. They offer a very wide variety of goods such as food, electrical appliances, plumbing supplies, tools, and clothing. There are a large number of mail-order houses but most of them are comparatively small businesses. Only a few are of outstanding size, principally Sears, Roebuck; Montgomery Ward; and Spiegel, Inc.

Service retailers. *Service retailers* sell services rather than goods, in most instances. Many service retailers possess professional skills that comprise their stock in trade, while others maintain facilities for processing their customers' belongings. Included in this category of retailers are dry cleaning shops, barbershops, beauty salons, reducing salons, bowling alleys, shoe repair and shoe shining places, automobile and bicycle repair shops, and radio and television repair centers.

Vending machines. Although *vending machines* date back to the 1880's, their recent growth has been phenomenal. In a recent year the National Automatic Merchandising Association released the following statistics regarding their operations: Sales of over $3.2 billion were achieved in such commodities as cigarettes, bottled drinks, candy, coffee and hot beverages, soft drinks in cups, milk, ice cream, cigars, and gum. Some four million machines are involved in this volume of business.

A few department stores have been experimenting with vending machines to promote the sales of small items, such as packaged hosiery, cosmetics, handkerchiefs, and costume jewelry. Among the latest developments to aid vending-machine customers are change-making machines, some of which are capable of providing change for a dollar bill.

RETAILERS CLASSIFIED ON THE BASIS OF OWNERSHIP

On the basis of ownership, retailers are classified as independents or as members of a chain.

Independents

Independents include most stores that are individually, and usually locally, owned—principally small stores, such as grocery, drug, shoe, and variety stores. Although the members of voluntary chains are technically independents, they are excluded from this discussion because of their merchandising practices, which will be described later.

The typical independent retail store is a small operation, usually managed by the owner or owners. It is rarely incorporated;[1] sole proprietorships and partnerships predominate. These stores are usually rather inadequately financed, and many of them are never very far from insolvency. As a general rule they buy through wholesalers and do little advertising. Their selling efforts could hardly be called aggressive. Their accounting methods are often most rudimentary. Their profits are low if,

[1] For several years one of the authors taught classes made up of independent retailers. Of the 150 or more members of these classes, less than half a dozen had incorporated their businesses.

indeed, many of them ever realize any profits at all. Many of them are conducted inefficiently and at a high cost. In every community, however, there are capable independents, whose methods are up-to-date and whose profits reflect their ability. Many small store operators employ accountants who visit their stores once or twice a month and assume complete responsibility for the store's accounting, even to the point of making out the monthly bills for the customers and of paying the store's invoices from their suppliers. The term "Mom and Pop stores" is occasionally used to designate those small, family-owned-and-operated grocery stores that are to be found in many communities.

Chain Stores

There is a notable lack of agreement among governmental and retailing authorities as to the minimum number of stores that should constitute a *chain*. The Census of Business avoids the term "chain," using instead *multiunit organization*, and applies this designation to "two or more stores in the same general kind of business operated by the same firm." *Food Topics*, a grocery trade journal, defines food chains as organizations operating "four or more" stores, while the *Progressive Grocer* establishes eleven stores as the minimum number. These variations have existed for a number of years and complicate, to some extent, the determination of the number of stores, their total sales, and their share of the market.

The term *corporate chain* is commonly used to distinguish this type of operation from the voluntary chain. This group also includes manufacturer-controlled retail stores and leased departments, which are found mainly in department and specialty stores. Chain stores operate in the fields of groceries and drugs; in variety, apparel, automobile accessories, shoes, tobacco, and department stores; and in filling stations.

The chain method of operation is of importance as it furnishes the key to the truth of the claim that chain store prices are lower than those of independents. In this discussion department store chains are excluded, as they do not follow the customary pattern of chain operation.

CHAIN STORE POLICIES

The distinctive nature of chain stores is indicated by the policies that are generally followed in connection with: (1) buying, (2) warehousing, (3) merchandising policies, (4) chain advertising, (5) merchandise specials, and (6) operational policies.

Buying

Chain systems customarily practice central buying; that is, all of the merchandise for the stores is purchased at some central office rather than by the individual store managers. This policy results in the purchase of large quantities of merchandise and, as a result, the chains obtain quantity discounts and carload freight rates, both of which effect savings in merchandise costs.

Chains also buy direct from the manufacturers, instead of through wholesalers, thereby saving at least the wholesaler's profit. They may do some manufacturing of the goods they sell. Buying committees, which were discussed earlier in this chapter, are of importance in chain groups that operate supermarkets.

Warehousing

The grocery and drug chains maintain warehouses to which nearly all of their merchandise is shipped and from which it is distributed to the stores as needed. Because of their control over the stores, the chains are in a position to plan their buying, warehousing, and delivering so as to incur the lowest possible costs in this overall procurement operation.

Merchandising Policies

Chain retail merchandising policies are designed to bring about reduced store operating costs, which can be reflected in competitively lower prices. Among the principal merchandising policies are the following:

1. Sales for cash only.[2]
2. No delivery service.
3. Telephone orders not accepted.
4. Only fast-moving items carried.
5. Vigorous exploitation of private-branded merchandise.
6. Ruthless marking down of old or slow-moving merchandise.

Chain Advertising

Chain store groups that are located in cities of any size have a distinct advantage over their independent competitors, with the exception of voluntary chains, in that they are able to utilize the daily papers as effective and inexpensive advertising media. A single insertion, identified with the chain,

---

[2] As previously noted, certain variety chains are now extending credit to their customers.

serves as an advertisement for each store in the chain, and the cost per store is relatively low. The copy for the newspapers—as well as for store posters, signs, and other forms of advertising—is customarily prepared at the central office. This results in uniformity and low cost.

Merchandise Specials

It has long been the practice of chain stores to select certain items from their stock, reduce their prices somewhat, and feature them in their advertising for the purpose not only of selling these items, but also of attracting customers who will buy other full-priced goods. In certain instances the depth of the price reduction and the prominence of the goods affected have brought into being the term *loss leaders*, which are those specials where the prices are so low as to give rise to the suspicion that they are being offered at or near their cost to the stores. These are almost always goods that are nationally known, both as to their quality and their customary prices. The fair and unfair trade laws, noted on pages 217-218, have discouraged this practice somewhat.

Operational Policies

The careful selection and training of personnel are outstanding characteristics of chain store operation. Many firms have formal training courses for their employees, particularly those that are designated for promotion to executive positions within the stores or the central offices.

Retail accounting has been brought to a high state of development in the chain systems. With all stores subject to the same accounting procedures, the chain management has a very effective tool to detect weaknesses and remedy them.

Many chains maintain real estate departments, staffed by experts in this field who endeavor to secure the best leasehold terms for their stores, check on the adequacy of present or prospective sites, assume responsibility for the remodeling or moving of stores, and generally seek to operate this phase of the business as efficiently as possible.

VOLUNTARY CHAINS

There are two types of *voluntary chains*—those sponsored by independent wholesalers, and those promoted by groups of cooperating retailers, who customarily establish and own the wholesale houses that serve them. The former group is more important than the latter as far as numbers are concerned. Their merchandising policies and practices, which are practically identical, are as follows:

1. Through the wholesale houses, they buy collectively and thereby secure quantity discounts and carload freight rates. This is perhaps the greatest advantage that voluntary chains have over the unaffiliated independents.
2. They develop and push group private brands, which they control and on which they sometimes make larger unit profits than on nationally advertised manufacturers' branded goods.
3. They advertise collectively, employing a common layout identified with their group. Because of the number of stores involved, they are able to use the daily papers at a very low cost per store. This is a second important advantage that voluntary chains have over the independents not thus associated.
4. They feature weekly specials in direct imitation of the corporate chains.
5. They adopt standard store fronts and, as far as possible, standard interior layouts.
6. They adopt standard accounting methods and record keeping.
7. The latest developments in retailing are noted by the members or the wholesalers, and information concerning them is disseminated to all of the stores.

The strength of the voluntary chains has been in the cooperative spirit of the members and, by the same token, their principal weakness has been the lack of positive control within the group. Nevertheless the voluntary chain system has permitted thousands of retailers to achieve many of the savings of chain operation while still maintaining a large measure of their independence. It has likewise made better storekeepers of many of them. Voluntary chains are found mainly in the fields of groceries, variety goods, and automobile accessories.

ANTICHAIN LAWS

In the years during which the chain stores were experiencing their greatest growth, there was a concerted movement among wholesalers and independent retailers to prevent this growth from reaching a point where the chains would endanger the existence of the independents. This movement took the form of a number of laws, both federal and state, that were sponsored by the independent group. In the main, these laws were designed to prevent the chains from selling at lower prices than independent stores.

The chain-store tax laws, in effect in 12 states, impose special tax burdens on the chains in order to increase their expenses. The so-called fair-trade laws, presently in effect in 27 states, together with the McGuire

Act, a federal statute, are designed to prevent the chains from cutting prices on certain branded items. Unfair-trade laws, which are operative in 26 states and which specify minimum markups for retailers, are also intended to curb chain price-cutting. The Robinson-Patman Act, a federal law, forbids many of the practices whereby the chains formerly secured price concessions from their vendors.

TRADING STAMPS

The trading stamp idea is quite old, having originated in 1891; but during the past few years it has grown to a most astonishing volume, with somewhere between $25 and $30 billion of retail sales being covered by stamps in a recent year. It is estimated that over 80 percent of American families save *trading stamps*, which are issued by some 370 stamp companies—on the usual basis of one stamp for each 10 cents of purchase value—and that redemptions of around $540 million at retail prices occur annually.

THE RETAILING REVOLUTION

The kaleidoscopic changes that have been taking place in the field of retailing during the past few years have caused some observers to call it the *retailing revolution*. Underlying this phenomenon is a basic change in the distribution of consumer goods. The traditional merchandise lines of many stores have been altered and augmented, sometimes by competition and often by the innovations of the retailers. One phase in this change has been the great increase in nonfood items carried by the supermarkets and, because of competition, by many smaller food stores. The discount house has brought about changes that extend throughout the general merchandise field. Not only are the discount houses in many instances approaching the status of department stores, but also many department stores have endeavored to copy to some extent the price and merchandising policies of the discounters. E. J. Korvette, Inc., one of the pioneer discount houses, has taken over the former building of Saks, a department store on 34th Street in New York City for many years. The F. W. Woolworth Company has a chain of 16 department stores known as Woolco. J. C. Penney, for years a leading merchandiser of clothing and other soft goods and a limited line of home furnishings, has greatly broadened its lines by adding appliances, sporting goods, tires, and auto accessories. The S. S. Kresge Company, an old-line variety store chain, has moved into the large variety-department store field, as well as into discounting through some 122 K-Mart discount centers.

The discount houses, in turn, are broadening the area of their merchandise offerings, adding larger assortments of men's and women's apparel and, in several instances, operating full-scale supermarkets as adjuncts to their own lines. The Walgreen Company, one of the country's largest drug chains, has acquired several small department stores that it plans to operate as discount houses. The list grows, and the lines of demarcation between department stores and discount houses appear to be becoming more indistinct as each invades the other's merchandise offerings and policies.

The question naturally arises as to how this change affects consumers. Apparently they like it, since it permits them to make more of their purchases under one roof and at competitive prices. Some observers have wondered about the effect on the *carriage trade* of the department stores, whose merchandising policies have been keyed to such customers, venturing into the discount field and losing thereby, presumably, much of the "store image" that had been carefully cultivated for nearly one hundred years in some cases. This poses a sociological problem the answer to which is not completely clear; but there is a suggestion that the carriage trade has been gradually disappearing over the years, and that its place has been taken by well-to-do groups of consumers to whom merchandise values and lower prices are of greater import than the prestige gained by trading at a store with an old-established name. There is certainly abundant evidence that the managers of the stores think so. This is not to imply that prestige is a lost merchandise asset. There are still many people of means who patronize men's and women's specialty stores and shops, such as Bonwit Teller, Milgrim, Franklin Simon, and Best & Company, and many locally owned prestige stores in our large cities. There does still exist a measure of label-conscious vanity among both men and women. The question that concerns retailers in this merchandise area is whether the number of these consumers is on the increase or on the decline.

CONSUMERISM AS A RETAILING ENVIRONMENTAL FACTOR

A number of the food chains have initiated a practice that is known as *open dating*. This consists of passing on to their customers information concerning the age of certain perishable products such as eggs. These dates have long been furnished, usually in code, by producers to wholesalers and retailers to indicate the times when such products should be removed from the retailers' shelves since they would no longer be fit for human consumption. Now, both as a sales promotional device and in recognition of the apparent growth of consumerism, several chains have devised methods of marking the packages that will reveal this information to consumers. At the moment it is not possible to judge the extent of the eventual spread of this practice throughout the grocery trade, but the stores that have adopted it feel that it has increased consumer confidence in their methods of doing business.

While the recent growth of consumerism has affected practically all elements in the production and distribution of consumer goods, it has probably borne more heavily on retailers than on any other segment of the economic community. This is mainly because retailers have the most contact with consumers and would be the first to hear their comments on unsatisfactory goods or services. It is the retailers, not the producers, to whom the consumers have directly expressed their complaints and from whom they have expected satisfaction. Whether this situation has assumed any greater proportions in recent years than formerly is difficult to determine; but if consumerism is as widespread as its spokesmen claim, the retailers have doubtless been experiencing a worsened environmental situation because of this new factor in the national scene.

BUSINESS TERMS

QUESTIONS FOR DISCUSSION AND ANALYSIS

1. As shown in the diagram on page 192, some producers of consumer goods use wholesalers to reach the small retailers, but sell direct to large retailers and chains. Do you think that this practice discriminates against the small retailers? Explain.

2. Why does not the Census Bureau list the rack merchandiser, when his presence and activities are well known in the grocery trade?

3. In many, if not most, communities there are a few retailers in the food field who extend credit to their customers and make deliveries to their homes. Their prices are generally somewhat higher than those of the cash-and-carry type stores. In an era of severe price competition in the food business, how can the stores survive who offer more service but at higher prices?

4. How do you account for the survival of general stores in the present era of mass merchandising?

5. Would you expect the independent boutique which is not connected with a large store, such as a department or specialty store, to be able to survive the severe competition of the larger stores? Why?

6. Why have the supermarkets added a large variety of nonfood items to their stocks of goods for sale?

7. Why are the Sears and Ward stores able to confine a large portion of their merchandise offerings to goods bearing their own brand names?

8. In many communities some supermarkets offer trading stamps, while others do not. How can this conflicting practice survive?

9. Do you believe that Green River Ordinances are of benefit to consumers? Explain.

10. Do you expect the growth in numbers of such stores as Kresge's K Mart and Woolworth's Woolco to cause a substantial drop in the number of old-line variety stores? Explain.

PROBLEMS AND SHORT CASES

1. The continuing movement of population from the central cities to the suburbs has raised a number of questions, some sociological in nature and others having to do with the survival of the downtown shopping areas as viable retail locales. While many department stores originally met the problem of suburban growth by establishing branches in these areas, which seemed to be a satisfactory solution at the time, the present condition of downtown traffic, inadequate parking facilities, and the increasing reluctance of suburban residents to come to the central city for their shopping and entertainment needs has renewed the anxiety of the downtown store owners with regard to the wisdom of continuing to maintain their downtown operations.

Assume the role of an adviser who has been called in by a group of department and specialty store operators to suggest ways by which suburban residents can be induced to return to the downtown stores for their shopping needs. Select a city with which you are familiar and devise a plan to submit to the group which you think will help to solve their problem in this area.

2. S. W. Butler is a mechanically inclined individual who has developed and patented a machine that could be of considerable assistance to suburban homeowners or renters in the watering of their lawns. It combines a hose reel with a water driven propelling mechanism on wheels which, when connected to a sill cock, will cause the whole machine to move slowly across the grass while sprinkling a wide stretch of the lawn. The speed of the sprinkler and the width of the spray can be regulated by means of a control which can be pre-set by the owner.

Butler has several thousand dollars in savings which he wishes to invest in the introduction and promotion of his invention, although not enough to support any advertising other than descriptive folders or pamphlets. He and a friend who has the facilities for manufacturing the machine have formed a partnership. Butler will undertake the sale of the product.

Prepare a distributive plan for this product that will indicate the distribution channels that should be used and the types of wholesalers and retailers who should handle it.

3. The Newsom Company, a long-established, high-prestige department store in one of the large cities, is concerned over the competition that it has been receiving from the discount houses in the area. In addition to its downtown store, this firm maintains four branch stores in the outlying suburban shopping centers. It has always stressed the quality of its merchandise and the reputation and reliability of its organization. The discount-house competition has become of such severity that the store management is seriously considering establishing its own discount operation as a means of preserving its sales and profit position. Among the questions that confront the management is whether they should enter the discount field; if so, whether the discount operation should be conducted in their present stores or in different locations; and whether the name of the Newsom Company should or should not be identified with the projected discount stores.

Advise the company on these points, giving your reasons.

SUGGESTED READINGS

Beckman, Theodore N., N. H. Engle, and R. D. Buzzell. *Wholesaling,* Third Edition. New York: The Ronald Press Company, 1959.

McGregor, C. H. *Retail Management Problems,* Fourth Edition. Homewood, Illinois: Richard D. Irwin, Inc., 1970.

Rachman, David J. *Retail Strategy and Structure: A Management Approach.* Englewood Cliffs, New Jersey: Prentice-Hall, Inc., 1969.

Chapter 10

Prices and Pricing

The concept of prices and the procedures of pricing practices are the end results of centuries-long evolutionary processes. Primitive man subsisted on the fruits of his own labor, a situation which can still be observed in some of the more remote areas of the world. A step above this situation came about when man ceased to raise or make all of the things that he needed but relied on his neighbors for some of them. This condition brought about the concept of value in which a unit of one man's product was considered to be worth the same, more, or less than that of his neighbor. The equating of values gave rise to the practice of *barter,* in which a bargaining procedure was usually the basis for establishing the value of one product in terms of another. Aside from this, there was the necessity for a man with a product to offer to find someone who not only wanted it but had, in turn, something that the former required. Both of these situations were cumbersome and time-consuming. As time passed, money came into being and provided a common and acceptable medium of exchange for expressing the values of goods and services. Along with this came *prices* in which these values were expressed which greatly facilitated their purchase and sale. It is with prices and pricing practices that this chapter is concerned.

APPROACHES TO PRICE DETERMINATION

As noted in Chapter 1, there are several bases for competition, with price probably being the most important. At the retail level of distribution, particularly, sellers often stress some factors other than that of price in their appeals for consumer purchase of their products. Substituted for price are style, satisfaction, durability, prestige, taste, service, reliability, and many others. This is known as *nonprice competition*. Where fair trade or unfair trade laws are in force (see pages 231-232), the establishing of floors below which prices may not go more or less automatically de-emphasizes prices as a competitive weapon and turns the consumer's attention to some other aspect of competition. Some critics of nonprice competition believe that it results in a watered-down competitive situation, while advocates of the practice feel that it places competition on a higher plane than price and directs the consumer's attention to all of the satisfaction-producing aspects of competing goods. In the majority of instances, nevertheless, prices are established in business by sellers, who take into account a number of factors. Three basic methods are followed by sellers in setting their prices. These methods are as follows:

1. With known unit costs of production, distribution, and overhead, the seller adds a desired profit and compares the resultant figure with the prices of competition. Depending upon the nature of the product and the rigor of its competition, he then determines whether he must meet competition, price his product below it, or, in a fortunate circumstance, above his competitors' prices.

   When a seller, usually a producer, establishes his prices at a predetermined level, he is following a policy of *administered prices*. This predetermined level is usually that used by competitors so that price competition will be de-emphasized in his appeal for sales. Some marketing authorities refer to administered pricing as "judgment pricing."

2. In a situation where competition sets the price above which the product may not be sold, the seller works backward from that price to the permissible unit cost and then determines whether or not the available margin is sufficient to enable him to operate profitably. This procedure could result in a decision not to make the product in question, if the apparently available profit is unsatisfactory. As a possible alternative course, the seller may endeavor to secure lower prices from his suppliers or increase his efficiency in order to bring his costs down to a level that will permit him to compete in the market.

3. When a firm has two or more products with a common source and with individual unit costs difficult to determine, the pricing procedure involves the attempt to secure a satisfactory profit from the pricing of the separate products, which may or may not involve a close relationship between the prices and the presumed costs of each item. This is what is known as a *joint cost* situation and is found in the petroleum, lumber, and livestock industries. For example, a butcher buys a side of beef at so many cents per pound; but in pricing the different cuts, such as porterhouse, sirloin, and round, he takes into account their relative appeal to consumers and prices them accordingly. He endeavors to set his

price per cut so as to realize a satisfactory profit on each side of beef that he handles.

At the consumer level, with such exceptions as auctions, sales of antiques, objets d'art, or casual sales, the prices are initially set by the sellers. If the good or service is not purchased at that price, the seller must change his price to the value set upon it by the customer. A *casual sale* is one that is outside the province of organized business, such as the sale of an old lawn mower by one person to his neighbor. At other than the consumer level, it is not uncommon for would-be buyers to specify the prices above which they are unable or unwilling to go. Professional buyers, such as purchasing agents and chain and department store buyers, customarily endeavor to secure the lowest available prices through a bargaining process with their suppliers.

PRICE DETERMINING FACTORS

Those individuals in sellers' organizations who have the authority to set the prices that are asked for the products to be sold may take one or more of the following factors into account: (1) markup percentage, (2) price lines, (3) suggested prices, (4) price leadership, (5) what the traffic will bear, (6) demand elasticity, (7) monopoly price, (8) monopolistic competition, (9) price legislation, and (10) price policies.

MARKUP PERCENTAGE

At all levels of business, but particularly at wholesale and retail, it is customary for sellers to arrive at their prices through the use of markup percentages. These markups are expressed as percentages either of cost or of selling prices.[1]

There are two methods of using markup as a means of setting prices. One involves the use of a markup table as shown in Table 10-1 on page 226. The other requires the use of one or more of the basic formulas shown in Table 10-2 on page 227.

---

[1] In the retail field there is a sharp divergence of practice in this regard. Some stores use the markup on cost, while others figure it on the retail price. Most large stores and the chains follow the retail method, whereas smaller stores adhere to the cost, and older, method. Leading retail authorities are in agreement that the retail method is the more advanced and useful of the two, although it is a trifle more difficult to apply. The advantages of the retail method lie in obviating the need for placing two sets of figures on the price tag, the selling price in dollars and cents and the cost in code; in facilitating the operating of the retail method of inventory; and in placing the markup percentage in the same terms or base as the gross margin and expense percentages, which are always expressed in terms of retail.

RETAIL PRICE MARKUP TABLE

How to Use This Table. Find the desired markup percentage based on selling price in the column at the left. Multiply the cost of the article by the corresponding percentage in the column at the right. Add this amount to the cost in order to determine the selling price.

Desired Markup Percentage (Based on Sales Price)	Equivalent Percentage of Cost	Desired Markup Percentage (Based on Sales Price)	Equivalent Percentage of Cost
5.0%	5.3%	20.0%	25.0%
6.0	6.4	25.0	33.3
7.0	7.5	30.0	42.9
8.0	8.7	33.3	50.0
9.0	10.0	35.0	53.9
10.0	11.1	37.5	60.0
12.5	14.3	40.0	66.7
15.0	17.7	42.8	75.0
16.7	20.0	50.0	100.0

Table 10-1

A markup is supposed to cover the cost of handling the article to be priced, a portion of the firm's expenses, and a certain amount of profit. Because of the difficulty of establishing these costs accurately for individual articles, like items are grouped into classes for which costs can be discovered, and the average or group markup to establish the retail price for a single item is used. Thus, in a store using the retail price markup method and having established an average markup of 50 percent for a given merchandise group, the person setting the price for an article in the group that costs $5 per unit would arrive at $10 as the selling price of a unit, through reference to the appropriate columns in the table.

Or, if he were using the formula method:

$$
\begin{aligned}
\text{Cost} + \text{markup} &= \text{Retail} \\
\$5 + 50\% &= 100\% \\
\$5 &= 100\% - 50\% \\
\$5 &= 50\% \\
\$5 + 50\% &= \$10 = \text{Retail}
\end{aligned}
$$

If this store were using the cost markup method, however, and wished to secure a retail price that would involve a markup of 50% on cost, the resulting price would be $7.50.

$$
\begin{aligned}
\text{Cost } (100\%) + \text{markup } (50\%) &= \text{Retail} \\
\$5 + \$2.50 &= \$7.50
\end{aligned}
$$

FORMULAS FOR MARKUP CALCULATIONS

Cost + markup	= Retail
Cost	= Retail — markup
Markup	= Retail — cost
$\dfrac{\text{Markup}}{\text{Retail}}$	= Markup expressed as a percent of retail
$\dfrac{\text{Markup}}{\text{Cost}}$	= Markup expressed as a percent of cost

Table 10-2

If a seller wishes to translate markup as a percent of retail into a percent of cost, or vice versa, the two formulas shown below are useful:

$$\frac{\text{Markup as a percent of retail}}{100\% - \text{markup as a percent of retail}} = \text{Markup as a percent of cost}$$

$$\frac{\text{Markup as a percent of cost}}{100\% + \text{markup as a percent of cost}} = \text{Markup as a percent of retail}$$

PRICE LINES

Price lines consist of a series of predetermined prices that are the only ones at which merchandise is offered for sale. For example, goods in a certain department might be offered only at $1.95, $3.95, and $5.95. No intermediate prices, such as $2.50, $3.25, or $5, would be used.

When a retailer wishes to establish price lines where they have not been used before, it is customary for him to list all of the prices that he has been using and to note the sales at each price for a period of time, say six months. He then selects those prices at which the largest number of merchandise units have been sold and discards the others, marking the goods at these rejected prices up or down to the new price lines, as the case may be.

SUGGESTED PRICES

Manufacturers sometimes print suggested retail prices on the containers of their products. Retailers may or may not adhere to these prices when they determine their own resale prices. Cut-rate stores frequently make a practice of pricing these goods below the prices suggested by the producers with a view to effecting a favorable price comparison. In some instances these prices are established by manufacturers who wish to maintain them under the fair trade laws.

PRICE LEADERSHIP

In any business field there may be certain acknowledged leaders who apparently set their prices without too much regard for the other members of the trade but whose price moves are rather quickly followed by their competitors. To a considerable extent the United States Steel Corporation in the steel business and the various Standard Oil companies in the field of gasoline and oil have been price leaders. The reasons for this price leadership are usually prestige, size, aggressiveness, and prominence.

Some writers have expressed the opinion that price leadership is effective only when prices are being raised, and that the action of nonprice leaders in cutting their prices will necessitate similar price reductions by the supposed leader.

WHAT THE TRAFFIC WILL BEAR

Although this phrase has a rather unpleasant sound since it implies excessively high profits, it is nevertheless a rather widely used indicator of the upper limits to the prices that may be set by sellers. A seller who knows his market is aware of the price limits above which he cannot go and retain his customers. These limits cut across many of the other factors that enter into his price-determining procedures. "What the traffic will bear" reflects the attitude of the user of the product toward its value to him. Thus a special instrument that will aid a surgeon in performing a difficult operation might be worth $100 to him, even though it might cost only $15 to produce. The value may be in greater safety or comfort for the patient, more effective performance by the surgeon, or improved operating techniques.

DEMAND ELASTICITY

This term refers to the effect that a change in the price for an item has on the quantity demanded. If changing the price of an article produces a significant alteration in the quantity demanded, it has *demand elasticity* or *an elastic demand*. Likewise, if a price change does not bring about a significant difference in the quantity demanded, the article has *inelasticity of demand*. The assumption is, of course, that the quantity demanded will move in the opposite direction from price. Examples of goods with demand elasticity are the items advertised as week-end specials by grocery stores, such as breakfast foods. The classic example of demand inelasticity is salt; regardless of the price of salt, people use a fixed amount.

As used by many economists, the demand elasticity concept embraces the idea of an actual change in the total demand for a product. There is, however, another aspect of this subject that is reflected in the action of consumers who switch from brand *A* of a product to brand *B* when the price of the latter is lowered. In such a circumstance the total demand for the basic product remains unchanged, but the sales of brand *B* have increased at the expense of brand *A*. This is known as *cross elasticity of demand*. Although it is probable that most retailers have never heard of these terms, they are usually quite aware of the items whose sales can be increased through price cutting and act accordingly. The weekly specials of supermarkets embody this type of selective price cutting and are illustrative of price competition at the retail level.

MONOPOLY PRICE

The presence of a monopoly implies the complete control of the price by the monopolist and the absence of competition. In the business world at large, there are very few pure monopolies. Those that do exist, such as the public utilities in most localities, are subject to governmental regulation to the extent that their freedom to set their prices is greatly, if not completely, curtailed. With this type of monopoly this discussion is concerned only to the extent of pointing out that prices are established or changed only with the consent of some governmental regulatory commission.

MONOPOLISTIC COMPETITION

When two or more sellers of goods that satisfy the same needs or wants strive to persuade the same groups of buyers to purchase their wares, competition is said to exist. This applies to all levels of economic activity, manufacturers, wholesalers, and retailers. In the case of certain agricultural products, and possibly a few others, the fact that there is little, if any, difference between the products of different producers places competition very largely on a strictly price basis. This situation is probably as close to the economists' concept of pure competition as is to be found in our economic system. With most other products, however, the producers are able to differentiate their products to a greater or less extent and escape the rigors of pure price competition.

The term monopolistic competition [2] describes competition between firms that have differentiated their products and have secured thereby certain aspects of monopoly, but which must still compete with each other for the favor of the buyers. These monopolistic characteristics may be those of location, of ingredients, of processes protected by patents, or even of trade names. For example, Ford, Chevrolet, and Plymouth engage in a spirited competitive battle in the low-priced car field. The Ford Motor Company, however, has a monopoly on the name Ford as applied to motor cars as, in turn, do the other two firms in the case of the names of their automobiles. Each maker also has a monopoly on certain features of design and construction. Thus the development of brand names and of minor differences between products are regarded as evidences of monopolistic competition in practice. Examples of this practice are to be found also in such commodity areas as cigarettes, liquid refreshments, soaps, men's clothing, and television receiving sets.

The seller who enjoys some aspects of monopoly must always remember, however, that there are very few commodities for which there are no substitutes; and if he raises his prices too high, he may cause his customers to turn to other products 'that may serve the same purpose.

PRICE LEGISLATION

In a number of instances both federal and state legislation affect prices, directly or indirectly. The federal price-control plans that were in effect during the period of World War II and the Korean War were intended to prevent prices from rising under the stress of the unbalanced supply-demand situation brought about by these conflicts. Currently the federal government, aside from persuasion and threats, has restricted its activities in this area to legislation providing support prices for agricultural commodities and, through the United States Postal Service, to rates charged for various classes of mail. To the extent that goods and services to be priced come within the influence of these enactments, the seller must be governed by them when establishing his prices.

The actions of the various states in regard to price legislation fall into two categories: (1) *fair trade laws*, which legalize resale price maintenance, and (2) *unfair trade laws* (with some variations on this title), which endeavor to establish minimum price levels below which goods cannot be sold.

[2] This discussion is an amplification of the topic "imperfect competition" mentioned on page 13 in Chapter 1.

The manufacturer of a branded product may wish to prevent whole-salers and/or retailers from establishing a price on it that is lower than the price at which the manufacturer wishes it sold. For example, a pro-ducer of a branded toothpaste might wish retailers to sell it at 50 cents, whereas the retailers might prefer to price it at 39 cents.

Until the mid-1930's, there were only two methods by which a producer could control the prices at which his products were offered to the public. One of these methods was for the manufacturer to sell on consignment, whereby the producer retained title to the goods even though they were actually on the retailers' shelves. General Electric light bulbs have long been handled on this basis. This method was far too costly for most manufacturers, as it involved a very large capital investment in stock in the dealers' stores.

The second method was through the execution of contracts with dealers in which the retailers agreed to maintain the prices stipulated by the manufacturer. There was, however, no compulsion in this method, as dealers were free to refuse to sign the contracts and the producer's only recourse consisted of refusal to sell to uncooperative dealers.

Acting under the authority of the various state fair trade laws, passed in most states in the 1930's, producers can execute contracts with retailers specifying the prices below which their branded products may not be sold. Through the *nonsigner clause* each contract becomes binding on all other retailers in the state, including those who may not have signed the con-tract, when due notice of its existence was given to them. The McGuire Act, a federal statute enacted in 1952, legalizes these contracts where the producers are located in different states from the retailers. The legality of the nonsigner clause in interstate commerce is uncertain, but several state courts have recently declared it to be a violation of their respec-tive constitutions.

In Virginia in 1958 and in Ohio in 1959 a new type of fair trade law appeared that was designed to avoid the possible illegality of the nonsigner clause. Under these laws, signed contracts are unnecessary for the pro-ducers to maintain their prices. All that is required is that the manu-facturers formally notify wholesalers and/or retailers of the prices that they wish maintained, and acceptance of the goods by the middlemen carries with it agreement to maintain the prices. The highest courts in both states have declared these laws constitutional. In 1965 North Dakota amended its Fair Trade Act to bring it into line with those of Virginia and Ohio.

Fair trade contracts have been executed for drugs, cosmetics, jewelry, silverware, tobacco, electrical appliances, some foods, and other items.

In the opinion of the proponents of so-called fair trade, the purpose of the laws is to prevent price cutters from putting their competitors out of business by their tactics. Opponents, however, assert that its purpose is to put an end to competition on the items affected and to raise prices to consumers needlessly. These two points of view, which have been argued at length, appear completely irreconcilable.

Unfair Trade Laws

Unfair trade laws, operative in 26 states under such diverse titles as unfair trade practices act, unfair sales act, unfair practices act, unfair sales practices act, and fair sales act, have a common theme. Under them, sellers—producers, wholesalers, and retailers—are forbidden to sell goods at less than their cost plus, in many states, certain specified percentage markups. These laws, like the fair trade laws, are designed to prevent price cutting and have sometimes been called "anti-loss-leader" laws, since the form of price cutting against which they were ostensibly enacted has been the loss leader. Unlike the fair trade laws, however, which affect only goods bearing a producer's brand and then only if the manufacturer wishes the price maintained, the unfair trade laws apply to all products branded or not.

Several states have similar laws applicable to specific commodities, such as cigarettes, dairy products, gasoline, bakery products, and alcoholic beverages.

PRICE POLICIES

Another group of items affect the setting of prices by sellers. These items, called price policies, might be regarded as the basic, underlying philosophies that sellers follow. They determine the general framework around which each seller fits his pricing structure. The more common price policies are: (1) low prices, (2) high prices, (3) stable prices, (4) odd prices, (5) delivered prices, (6) one price versus varying price, (7) discount policy, and (8) markdowns.

Low Prices

Some sellers follow the plan of having low prices for their goods. A well-known Eastern grocery chain uses the slogan "We sell for less," and the price setters in this organization are instructed to price their wares at the lowest prices consistent with the company's operating expenses and profit philosophy. From the time of their first appearance, low prices have been the principal sales appeal of the discount houses.

High Prices

This policy is embraced by numerous department and specialty stores, dealers in fancy groceries, and manufacturers of quality goods. In most shopping centers one or more stores carry merchandise much the same as that of their neighbors, but whose prices are noticeably higher than those of the others. In some instances these prices represent better merchandise; in others they reflect a desire to secure a higher profit per unit. In either event, when the products are bought, the prices paid reflect real or imaginary values perceived by the buyer.

Stable Prices

Many sellers follow their merchandising and operating costs rather closely in pricing their goods. When these costs go up or down, prices likewise go up or down. Opposed to this policy is that of stable prices, whereby a price, once established, tends to remain constant for long periods of time regardless of the fluctuations of the costs of the goods or of the expenses of the sellers involved. Examples of this policy are to be found in products where the retail prices are printed on the packages.

Odd Prices

One school of merchandising thought holds with the idea that $2.95 is a more appealing price than $3, that 19 cents will sell more goods than 20 cents, and $99.95 is more effective than $100. The underlying theory of this policy is that $1.98 makes the prospective buyer think of $1 plus some cents, rather than of a price slightly less than $2. That this concept is widely held is apparent from an inspection of the price lines of many stores of all types.

Delivered Prices

Some manufacturers adopt the policy of establishing their prices on what is called a "delivered basis." This means that the price quoted to the buyer is *f.o.b.* (free on board) *destination*. It includes all transportation costs and is the price that he must pay to take delivery of the goods at his receiving dock or the freight terminal in his city.

Opposed to this plan is the practice of quoting *f.o.b. shipping point* (or factory), that is, the seller will place the goods on a common carrier at the factory loading dock and all further transportation charges are to be paid by the buyer over and above the quoted price. The pricing of automobiles is an example of this latter policy. Some sellers located in the eastern part of the country take account of transportation costs by advertising "prices slightly higher west of the Mississippi River."

One Price Versus Varying Price

Most retail pricing is of the "one price" variety, that is, the established price applies to all comers and is not subject to "higgling" by individual customers. At other sales levels, however, this policy does not always hold true. Although some manufacturers and wholesalers follow it rather rigidly, many others may lower their prices from time to time in favor of particular purchasers. This flexibility of price may come about because of the superior bargaining skill of certain buyers or because of the size of their purchases.

A varying price policy has the effect of enabling large buyers to secure lower prices than their smaller competitors. To prevent this practice from placing small buyers at too great a disadvantage, the Robinson-Patman Act of 1936 was passed by the Congress. This act, which was in the form of an amendment to Section 2 of the Clayton Act, prohibited sellers engaged in interstate commerce from discriminating in price or terms of sale between purchasers of goods of like grade and quality; it prohibited the payment of brokerage or commissions where the recipient of the fee is subject to the control of the party to a transaction other than the one making the payment—so-called *false brokerage*; and it forbade sellers to grant advertising allowances or other services unless these concessions were available to all purchasers on "proportionately equal terms."

Although it is doubtful if this act has forced many companies to adopt a strictly one-price policy, it has definitely limited the bases on which a varying price policy can be practiced and has served to place large and small buyers more nearly on an equal footing in the price phases of their purchasing.

Discount Policy

Sellers who elect to pursue a varying price policy have two principal methods by which they may put this plan into effect: (a) through simple price concessions and (b) by means of a discount policy. An example of the first method is the lowering of a price of $1.50 per unit to $1.35.

A *discount* may be defined as a reduction in price made by a seller to a buyer on one or more of the following bases:

Trade discounts. A *trade discount*, which is based on the list price of the product, recognizes the different functions performed by wholesalers and retailers. For example, if the list price, which is frequently the price charged the retail customer, is $45 and the trade discount is 33⅓ percent, the wholesaler's price to the retailer is $30. Trade discounts are also known as *functional discounts*, a term which takes cognizance of the different levels at which the marketing functions are performed by the marketing institutions involved.

When a *chain of discounts* is granted by the seller to the buyer, the list price is followed by several trade discounts, which are customarily applied in turn to an ever-lessening figure. For example, an invoice for $100 less 40%, 10%, and 5%, would be figured as follows:

$100 — $40 (40% of $100) = $60
$60 — $6 (10% of $60) = $54
$54 — $2.70 (5% of $54) = $51.30 = net amount paid by the buyer.

This method is used by sellers who desire to discriminate legitimately between their customers by granting or withholding one or more of the discounts in the chain. It also permits them to change their prices by adding or subtracting a discount, without the necessity of reprinting their price lists each time such a price change becomes necessary.

Quantity discounts. A *quantity discount* is offered by some sellers as a reward to buyers who order in large quantities. Presumably the large sales under this policy save the vendors storage, packing, and perhaps transportation charges. Quantity discounts may either be cumulative or noncumulative in character. Cumulative quantity discounts permit buyers to utilize two or more separate purchases in the computation of the quantities to which discounts may apply, whereas the noncumulative type is applicable only to single purchases. Thus, if a seller offered a 10 percent quantity discount for orders of 100 units or more, with the cumulative type the buyer would qualify with purchases of 25, 35, 25, and 15 units each, whereas with the noncumulative he would be obliged to purchase at least 100 units in a single order. Both cumulative and noncumulative quantity discounts are permissible under the Robinson-Patman Act provided the vendor bases the discounts on some demonstrable savings that result from selling larger quantities or a large total volume of business to the customers to whom they were accorded.

Cash discounts. A *cash discount* differs somewhat from the foregoing group in that it is given neither as a reward for large purchases nor in recognition of differences in functions performed. It is simply an inducement offered by the seller to encourage the buyer to pay his bill within a short time after the goods have been delivered. The cash discount takes many forms, the most common of which is 2/10, net/30; that is, if the invoice is paid within 10 days after its date, the buyer may deduct 2 percent of the amount of the invoice in making his remittance; and if the buyer elects not to pay the bill within the 10 days, he has 20 additional days in which to pay the full amount before the invoice becomes overdue. In some lines of business, notably apparel, cash discount rates run up as high as 6 percent and 8 percent. Unlike some of the other discount types, cash discounts are usually available to all the customers of a seller.

None of the above discounts is usually available to ultimate consumers, except in those instances where public utilities permit cash discounts if their bills are paid by a specified due date.

Markdowns

A type of formal price reduction that differs somewhat from a discount is the *markdown*. In this instance, for any one of several reasons, sellers, usually retailers, reduce the price of an item either on a temporary or permanent basis. The most common types of markdowns and the reasons for them follow: (a) promotional, which are designed to attract customers for a brief period of time, after which the price is marked up to its original level; (b) competitive, which are made to meet the lower price of a competitor and which may or may not be permanent; (c) clearance, the objective of which is to rid the stock of the merchandise affected; (d) employee discounts, which customarily involve the giving of lower prices to the store's employees; (e) breakage, which reduces the value of damaged merchandise, often to zero; and (f) pilferage, where goods are stolen and not recovered, with a markdown to zero. In the interest of accurate accounting for a store's operations, intelligent managerial operating methods require that all markdowns including, when necessary, the full sales price of articles broken or stolen, be recorded.

UNIT PRICING

An environmental factor which is one segment of the consumerism movement has appeared in recent months. This is known as *unit pricing* which consists of marking the price per ounce on all products in a super-market or grocery store where the producer has printed the total ounces on the container or label. It has long been the practice of many manufac-turers of canned or packaged products, who package them in more than one size, to offer promotional "specials" which specify so many cents off for certain size packages. The producers of detergents and soap powders, among others, commonly use several different size boxes or bottles, with the presumption that the larger sizes sell for less per ounce. As a sales promotion gesture, they regularly offer what appear to be meaningful price reductions on selected sizes of their products. The promoters of unit pricing claim that frequently the price per ounce for the "specials" is either no less than the regular price or even greater. For this reason the backers of unit pricing maintain that the price per ounce, if displayed, would reveal whether or not the "specials" actually represent a saving to the buyers. The manufacturers of the specially priced goods have vigorously opposed the practice of unit pricing, with considerable success thus far, but it appears probable that the backers of consumerism will eventually succeed in getting their idea across and that over time unit pricing will become standard practice (at least in the more prominent grocery stores and supermarkets). This will obviously involve increased effort on the part of the producers of the affected goods in the area of pricing.

COUPON OFFERS

It is not uncommon for producers of consumer products, either for the purpose of promoting the introduction of new items or to accelerate the sale of current ones, to distribute *coupons* by mail, through inclusion in the packages, or by displays in the stores. The presumption is that by using the coupons consumers may effect worthwhile savings. It is not possible to judge the extent of the savings involved other than by a study of the price per ounce for the product without the coupon as compared with the price with the coupon. Also, especially when introducing a new product in an old established line of merchandise, the producer often offers a "cash" bonus—obtainable by sending in one or more box tops or some part of the package label or carton.

PRICE IN RELATION TO SUPPLY AND DEMAND

For a competitive situation, economists have advanced several theories to explain how the price of any given commodity is set, the movement of prices, and why the price level is where it is at any one time. The *equilibrium theory of prices,* which probably has the largest number of adherents among economists, assumes that two forces operate in the field of price—supply and demand. These forces bring about a price at which the quantity demanded by buyers equals the quantity that sellers are willing to supply. Some of the units of the commodity that are necessary to make up this quantity are produced by those whose costs of production are so high that they make little or no profit, but who decide, nevertheless, to remain in business.

The theory further assumes that if the current price for a commodity is found to be above the theoretical equilibrium point, two things will happen, both of which will force the price downward: (a) the higher price will discourage would-be buyers, thereby reducing the quantity demanded; and (b) the opportunity for profits afforded by the higher price will attract new producers into the field, whose added products will increase the quantity supplied. The effect of this reduced demand and increased supply will be to reduce the price, probably below the equilibrium point. When this takes place, the results are the reverse of the condition just described: (a) the lowered price attracts buyers, increasing the quantity demanded; and (b) the diminished profits, which then occur, force some high-cost producers to leave the field, thereby reducing the quantity supplied. This brings about an upward movement of price toward the equilibrium point.

Figure 10-1 portrays a graphic representation of the operation of the equilibrium theory. Curve *D-D'* represents the quantities of the product that could be sold at the various price levels. Curve *S-S'* represents the quantities that sellers would be willing to supply at the different price levels. Point *P*, where 500 units would be demanded at $5 each, portrays the point of equilibrium where demand and supply are equal.

ASSUMPTIONS IN THE EQUILIBRIUM THEORY

The equilibrium theory is probably the explanation most widely accepted by economists of what takes place in a competitive price situation and is based on the following assumptions:

1. No difference exists between one producer's product of any given commodity and another producer's product of that same commodity (e.g., corn, wheat, soybeans, etc.).
2. Buyers do not purchase because of whim, caprice, or prejudice, but solely on the basis of the lowest price offered.
3. Both buyers and sellers have a complete knowledge of market conditions including a knowledge of supply, demand, and price.
4. Pure competition assumes the presence of the above three preceding conditions.

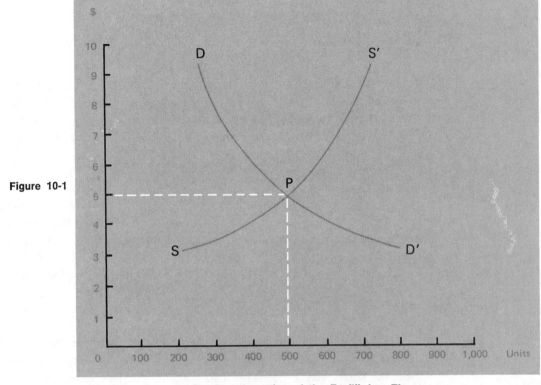

Graphic Illustration of the Equilibrium Theory

FACTORS NOT INCLUDED IN THE EQUILIBRIUM THEORY

Certain circumstances that are to be found in business today are excluded by the equilibrium theory. Some of the more important of these are: (1) other factors influencing purchases, (2) monopolies and quasi monopolies, (3) price-fixing by private agreements, (4) brand influences, (5) the one-price system, and (6) consumer indifference.

Other Factors Influencing Purchases

Factors other than price that influence purchases include quality, service, vendors' prestige, and chance.

Monopolies and Quasi Monopolies

Although there are comparatively few pure monopolies in our economic system, many firms enjoy certain aspects of monopoly because of location, control of sources of raw material, and rights protected by patent, copyright, and trade-mark laws.

Price-Fixing by Private Agreements

Private agreements may be illegal, but they sometimes remain in force for long periods of time before they are detected. Although the existence of price-fixing cannot be denied, it must be recognized that the responsible businessman knows it to be illegal and considers it to be unethical.

Brand Influences

These cause many consumers to demand the products of certain manufacturers merely because they have come to prefer these brands without much regard to the value of competing brands. Thus, a housewife may insist on a certain soap or hair shampoo because advertising has convinced her that they are the only satisfactory products on the market.

The One-Price System

The *one-price system* prevails in most retail stores where the price of an article is determined by the storekeeper, is customarily displayed on or near the goods, and is not subject to bargaining by the customers. Customers must either pay the established price or go without the article. However, if a sufficient number of customers refuse to pay the price, the seller will have to choose between realizing a loss on the unsold goods or reducing the price.

Consumer Indifference

This indifference is manifested by the failure of consumers to give heed to informative labeling or advertising, to employ rational buying motives when making purchases, or to bother to inform themselves about the prices of competing stores on certain identical items. It is a fairly common practice for two or more competing stores to offer eggs of the same grade at different prices, and for some consumers to buy the higher-priced ones.

CONCEPTS OF SUPPLY AND DEMAND

Despite the factors that are excluded from the equilibrium price theory, this theory sets forth the basic elements in competitive pricing.

In the absence of restraining factors, such as wartime price controls or governmentally supported prices for certain agricultural products, prices tend to rise when demand exceeds supply, and to fall when the reverse is true. In the industrial goods field, and in consumer goods at other than the retail level, considerable bargaining takes place before sales are consummated.

At the retail level, however, the long-established one-price system in this country probably has tended to prevent the demand side of the demand-supply equation from being as effective as it is at other sales levels. It is true, as a general rule, that raising the prices of many articles at retail will result in fewer units of the goods being sold. There are many exceptions to this situation, however, and so many other factors than price that influence consumers in their buying that the weight of demand in the price-determining process at the retail sales level is considerably less than in wholesale transactions. For example, the influence that advertising exerts on consumers in endeavoring to convince them of the advantages of one brand of goods over competing brands is undoubtedly a factor in inducing them to pay more for certain products than they might if advertising were not present in the picture. Brand loyalty on the part of consumers also appears to blind them to the possibility that lower-priced items of approximately the same value are available in the market.

The term *cost-price relationship* has appeared with increasing frequency in the trade and public press and occasionally in the halls of Congress. While often used by sellers in a rebuttal to the charge that their prices are too high, it has served to emphasize a well-known economic axiom, namely, that if overall costs are increased without a corresponding increase in productivity, the result will be an increase in unit costs. This, in turn, will bring about either an increase in the unit price or a decrease in the unit profit. In endeavoring to justify their increased prices, many sellers have claimed that their costs, especially their labor costs, have increased more rapidly than has their productivity. The labor unions have sought to combat these statements in various ways, which have included a criticism of the sellers' methods of determining productivity.

Elements Affecting Seller's Prices

When a seller undertakes to establish the price at which he hopes to sell his wares, he takes the following elements into account.

Cost of the goods. If the seller is a manufacturer, his costs will include not only the costs of manufacture, both direct and overhead, but also his cost of selling. If the seller is a wholesaler or a retailer, he will consider how much he paid for the goods originally, together with his costs of doing business.

Profit philosophy. Sellers tend to embrace one of two profit philosophies. Either they seek a high profit per unit of goods sold, with relatively higher prices and with a presumed restricted sales volume, or they accept a lower unit profit, with comparatively low prices and an implied high volume of sales. There are, of course, a large number of possible gradations of position between these two extremes.

Seller's attitude toward competition. At all levels of trade, but particularly at retail, some sellers pay little attention to the prices of their competitors and rely on other appeals to sell their goods. Certain department and specialty stores are adherents of this pricing philosophy. On the other hand, some sellers will not be undersold by their competitors on identical or similar merchandise. A third type follows the practice of always being below the prices of its competitors.

General or local business conditions. A factor that must always influence a seller in determining his price is the state of general or local business conditions, whether good or bad. This is a complicated matter that cannot be expounded here; but the effect, as far as price-setting is concerned, is that during bad times a seller will set his prices with greater regard for competition and, perhaps, at figures that include lower unit profits than during good times.

Elements Affecting Prices Buyers Will Pay

Buyers approach their prospective purchase transactions with rather definite ideas as to how much they are willing to pay and often with sharply defined upper limits beyond which they will refuse to go. The factors that influence the buyers in arriving at these conclusions with regard to the prices that they will pay are discussed below.

Consumer's personal economic status. Constantly underlying the attitude of every consumer toward prices is his personal economic status. In other words, the poor man's outlook toward a purchase transaction is different from that of a well-to-do or a rich man.

A variant on this concept is the consumer's appraisal of his future economic status, his beliefs regarding the probable permanence of his job and, for an older person, whether or not he expects to receive a pension upon retirement. Thus the consumer's attitude is conditioned not only by present but also by possible future conditions.

Consumer's subjective value reactions. In every consumer's mind, when he decides to make a purchase, is the idea that any given item of merchandise is worth just so much to him. The value thus approximated may or may not bear a close relationship to the price being asked for that item. If it is close, the purchase will probably be made; if it is not, the consumer may refrain from buying at the time.

Effect of advertising or sales efforts of sellers. Advertising and the sales efforts of sellers tend to create in the mind of the consumer an uncritical attitude toward prices. Consumer preference is created for certain brand names on a wide variety of bases, such as service, prestige, and pride of ownership. The result is that the consumer approaches the purchase of these goods with price as a secondary consideration.

Buyer's knowledge of his resale market. This factor and the one following (condition of the supply market) apply principally to the buyer who purchases goods for resale, either in their present state or altered in some way. Examples of such buyers include the wholesale or retail buyers who buy apparel for resale to their respective customers, and the industrial purchasing agents who buy steel sheets, for example, to be formed and fabricated into automobile bodies.

In instances such as these, the buyers usually have rather clear ideas concerning the prices that their customers will pay for the goods that they are about to purchase or make. Hence their attitudes toward the prices that they are willing to pay are customarily well formulated and frequently committed to writing in advance of the buying situation. Industrial purchasing agents are often not permitted to pay more than certain prices for the items that they buy.

Condition of the supply market. This factor applies to the prices that buyers will offer with the same force that it applies to prices that sellers seek. When supplies are short, prices tend to rise and, when the market is oversupplied, they tend to fall. This is also true of the consumer market.

WHAT CAUSES PRICES TO MOVE?

Prices are said to rise or fall, as though a price—which is basically a value symbol—possessed some innate power of movement. Actually prices are determined by human beings, usually those who have something to sell or who are in position to establish the sales prices for their companies' goods or services. The exceptions to this are to be found at auctions, where would-be buyers indicate the prices that they are willing to pay for the items offered for sale; in casual sales; and in the sales of new automobiles where the trade-in value of a used car is involved.

Figure 10-2 illustrates the trend of consumer prices since 1964. With the price level of 1957-1959 taken as 100, the changes since then indicate the gradual upward movement of consumer prices of all items. Note in particular the accelerated movement since 1968 and the preponderant influence of services on this trend. Note further that wholesale prices during this period maintained a somewhat greater degree of stability.

At this point it seems fitting to look into the reasons for price changes. Some economists have come forth with two explanations for rising prices: the *cost-push concept* and the *demand-pull concept*. Under the cost-push concept the rising cost of labor and materials forces sellers either to raise their prices or narrow their profit margins; naturally, they are reluctant to take the latter course. With labor unions constantly striving, usually successfully, for wage increases and other costly benefits, producers are forced to raise their prices accordingly. All these factors tend to bring about a general price increase which may occur repeatedly. Obviously the cost-push theory has a high degree of validity.

The demand-pull concept assumes a shortage of certain goods for which buyers bid against each other in order to secure their needed amounts. At levels other than that of consumers, this is not an infrequent circumstance. While this situation, under the equilibrium theory of prices, would attract more suppliers and eventually cause prices to drop, the experience of the past few years does not appear to bear out this presumption. Goods in many lines are in plentiful supply, yet their prices remain high and seem to be going higher. And there is scant evidence that consumers are bidding against each other for goods to satisfy their needs. Rather, it may be said that consumers are apparently willing to pay these constantly rising prices and are thereby permitting sellers all along the line to pass along to them the cost increases which have been at the root of the rising prices.

The one inflexible component in the whole situation of rising prices has been the rigidity of the demands of organized labor. Unions have been able to negotiate two- or three-year agreements which contain provisions for periodic raises over the life of the agreement. As yet there is very little evidence that labor will agree to accept a reduction in wages

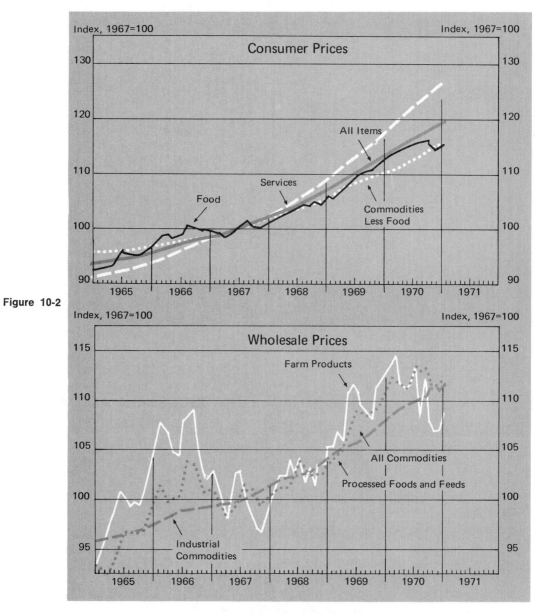

Figure 10-2

Price Developments

Source: *Economic Indicators*, February, 1971. Prepared for the Joint Economic Committee by the Council of Economic Advisers.

or even a continuance of the current rates when the agreements expire. This, plus the fact that consumers continue to pay the higher prices, explains to a considerable degree the reason why the price level has long maintained its upward trend.

BUSINESS TERMS

QUESTIONS FOR DISCUSSION AND ANALYSIS

1. Do you think that nonprice competition at the retail level would bring about better or poorer grades of goods for consumers? Explain.

2. Is a price system an inevitable requirement for the successful operation of capitalism? Why?

3. Is a joint cost pricing procedure a fair one for consumers? Why or why not?

4. Should the federal government have the power to fix prices for goods and services in this country? Why or why not?

5. Do you think that the fair trade laws penalize the retailer who is able to reduce his operating expenses? Why or why not?

6. Should chain stores be prevented by law from pricing their goods at lower levels than independent stores? Why or why not?

7. Is the one-price system employed by most retail stores a fair procedure for consumers? Explain.

8. How can two stores in the same competitive area sell identical products at different prices?

9. In a period of rapidly rising prices, would you recommend the imposition of price controls by the federal government as some labor leaders have suggested? Why or why not?

10. Do you think that there is any validity to the demand-pull concept as an explanation for rising prices? Explain.

PROBLEMS AND SHORT CASES

1. a. A specialty store buys $1,150 worth of merchandise; the terms are 6/10, net 30. The invoice is dated January 15 and is paid on January 24. How much is remitted to the seller?

   b. A retailer buys a lot of merchandise for $1,150 with trade discounts of 30%, 10%, and 5%. How much do the goods cost him?

2. Using the Retail Price Markup table on page 226 or the formulas on page 227 that are applicable, calculate the answers to the following problems:

   a. Markup on cost is 20%, cost is $12. Find the retail selling price.
   b. Markup on cost is 37.5%, retail price is $6.40. Find the cost.
   c. Markup on retail price is 25%, cost is $13.60. Find the retail price.
   d. Markup on retail price is 30%, retail price is $40. Find the cost.

3. Frank Pudney, a retired businessman with adequate financial resources, has been growing bored at his enforced idleness. He has recently been given the opportunity to purchase a remodeled gas station in an excellent location. The former owner had allowed the original station to run down rather badly and the sales of gasoline, oil, tires, and accessories had fallen to a very low level. As a means of reestablishing the sales volume, the refining company had purchased the station and completely rebuilt it. The gasoline was a well-known name brand and, when the company had learned of Pudney's dissatisfaction with retirement, it offered to sell him the station on very attractive terms. After considerable negotiations, both parties were in agreement except for the retail price of the gasoline. Pudney wanted to price it two or three cents below the prices of competing gas stations, believing that in this way he could win back the trade that the old station had lost and, when this had been accomplished, he would raise the price one cent at a time over a few weeks until it was on a par with competition. The refiner was reluctant to agree to this proposal but recognized that something would have to be done to recover the lost patronage. Pudney was favorably known in the community, and the refiner realized that his ownership of the station and identification with the producer could be a strong sales stimulant. However, as a matter of company policy it had never sanctioned a price cut of this sort. Yet it knew of no other possible buyer at this time.

Consider all sides of this question and then make a decision for the company either to accept Pudney's proposal or to reject it and attempt to find another buyer who would be willing to maintain the going price of gasoline in the community.

SUGGESTED READINGS

Brennan, Michael J. *Theory of Economic Statics*, 2nd Ed. Englewood Cliffs, New Jersey: Prentice-Hall, Inc., 1970.

Dooley, Peter C. *Elementary Price Theory*. New York: Appleton-Century-Crofts, 1967.

Hibdon, James E. *Price and Welfare Theory*. New York: McGraw-Hill Book Company, 1969.

Lipsey, Richard G., and Peter O. Steiner. *Economics*, Second Edition. New York: Harper & Row, 1969. Parts II and V.

Lynn, Robert A. *Basic Economic Principles,* Second Edition. New York: McGraw-Hill Book Company, 1970. Part 4.

Maxwell, W. David. *Price Theory and Applications in Business Administration.* Englewood Cliffs, New Jersey: Prentice-Hall, Inc., 1970.

Samuelson, Paul A. *Economics: An Introductory Analysis,* Eighth Edition. New York: McGraw-Hill Book Company, 1970. Part 3.

Silk, Leonard S. *Contemporary Economics, Principles and Issues.* New York: McGraw-Hill Book Company, 1970. Part II.

Trescott, Paul B. *The Logic of the Price System.* New York: McGraw-Hill Book Company, 1970.

Watson, Donald S. *Price Theory and Its Uses.* Boston: Houghton Mifflin Company, 1968.

Chapter 11

Advertising

Advertising has frequently been referred to as "the voice of business" the purpose of which is to inform consumers of the goods and services which the business community makes available and to urge upon them the desirability, if not the necessity, of purchasing the preferred items for their own personal advantage, as well as at a profit to the advertisers, in accord with the basic tenets of capitalism.

The Definitions Committee of the American Marketing Association defines *advertising* as "any paid form of nonpersonal presentation and promotion of ideas, goods, or services by an identified sponsor." Another definition, which reflects some of the latest thinking in this area, is "advertising is constructive communication with consumers." This latter definition embraces the concept that advertisers should endeavor to make a purposeful contact with consumers. This circumstance is mutually beneficial in that consumers are informed of the availability of goods for which they have a need and the advertisers secure a profit through providing these goods. It also assumes that the advertising appears in the right media, with the right appeals, at the right times, at the right prices, for the consumers whose needs will be best satisfied by the goods involved.

Advertising is a one-dimensional means of communication. It involves one-way communication that appeals to the sense of sight and/or hearing. Understanding the unidimensional basis of advertising is essential to recognizing the role of advertising in our economic system. Communication theory indicates that the meaning of any communication is defined by the receiver of the communication, not by the giver. According to this theory, it is how an advertisement is perceived that gives meaning to that advertisement. One's perception of a given advertisement may or may not coincide with either the perception of others or the intent of the advertiser. Consequently, an advertisement to be successful and stimulate action must be perceived by a large segment of society and by the advertiser in the same way. Furthermore, the consumer's perception must be such that he expects to obtain some satisfaction by initiating the action suggested by the advertisement; otherwise, the consumer pays no attention to the message of the advertisement.

It is within this framework of communication theory that advertising must be assessed so that man can begin to recognize that advertising per se does not create change. Change comes from man. Advertising is not primarily responsible for the present state of our society or for the future of our society. Man is responsible for that. But advertising does reflect change. It is within this context that the nature of advertising as a marketing function will be investigated.

TYPES OF ADVERTISING

The two basic types of advertising are commodity and institutional. *Commodity advertising* is designed to sell one or more definite, identified commodities, and usually it describes and extols their good qualities or satisfaction-giving features, or their prices.

Within the general category of commodity advertising are several subtypes. (a) *Primary advertising* is intended to stimulate an interest in and a desire for a certain class of goods, particularly some new type of product that has just come on the market, or in which the public has yet to manifest any appreciable interest. (b) *Selective advertising* is supposed to impel consumers toward the purchase of a particular brand of goods, such as a Ford Pinto or a pair of Nettleton shoes. It is quite common to find primary and selective advertising in the same advertisement. (c) *Mass advertising* is advertising that appeals to a cross section of the populace. (d) *Class advertising*, on the other hand, is directed at special groups of people, such as newly married couples, golfers, or college students. (e) *Publicity* is information about a product that is supplied to the advertising media, usually newspapers or magazines, by the producer, which the publisher may or may not use. It usually appears in editorial or news form and frequently does not include the name of the maker. Publicity is not paid for by the manufacturer of the goods.

A type of commodity advertising that cuts across the first four types just mentioned is known as *name advertising*. This type occurs where the nature of the product, its ingredients, the manner in which it is used, the product benefits to be expected, or the fact that it is very well known to the public suggests the desirability of advertising its name, with non-technical copy, often in an attractive setting. Name advertising is commonly employed for cigarettes, soft drinks, aspirin, alcoholic beverages, and cosmetics.

Institutional advertising is created for the purpose of getting some message across to the public, which may or may not be closely related to the sale of any particular merchandise. By means of institutional advertising a firm may announce a change in location, the adoption of a new policy, the acquirement of a new line of goods, or anything else that might be of general interest to their customers. Institutional advertising is sometimes referred to as nonproduct advertising.

Another form of institutional advertising exists when several advertisers issue a joint advertisement for the benefit of all of them. Advertisements of this sort may be devoted to trying to sell goods or merely to promoting ideas. The advertisements of the Association of American Railroads, the American Gas Association, and the American Institute of Laundering are examples of group institutional advertising.

ADVERTISING MEDIA

Of paramount importance to advertisers is the selection of the media that will carry their advertising. The term *media*, which is commonly used in the advertising world, refers to the different types of vehicles or devices by which advertising reaches its audience. These include the following: (1) newspapers, (2) magazines, (3) radio, (4) television, (5) direct mail, (6) outdoor, (7) transportation, (8) business papers, and (9) other media.

In the discussion of media types that follows, four of the bases of comparison that will be utilized require some preliminary explanation. They are: (a) *geographic selectivity,* which refers to the ability of a medium to deliver the advertiser's message to a particular geographic area, such as a designated city or metropolitan community; (b) *interest selectivity*, which means the capacity of a medium to deliver the advertiser's message more or less exclusively to groups of consumers who would presumably be interested in the product being advertised, such as homeowners for room air conditioners or farmers for tractors; (c) *flexibility*, which refers to the ability of the advertiser to change his message, if need be, a relatively short time before the advertisement is to appear; and (d) the *identity of the audience,* which means the extent to which the names, addresses, and pertinent characteristics are known to the media.

Table 11-1 below presents a list of the 10 leading national advertisers in major media for 1970. On page 253 Table 11-2 presents an authoritative estimate of the advertising volume by medium for 1970. A completely accurate statement of the dollar volume of advertising in this country cannot be secured, however, because of the lack of reliable data concerning such advertising types as circulars, small newspapers, and some kinds of direct mail. The table is adequate, however, for the purpose of observing the relative standing of the various media that are used.

NEWSPAPERS

The daily and, in smaller communities, weekly newspapers are exceedingly useful media for certain kinds of advertising. They have a high circulation, relative to the number of people who might see them, and their readers are usually concentrated in a comparatively small area.

Newspapers are especially effective in carrying the advertisements of local merchants who wish to reach all parts of the cities concerned. Department stores, specialty stores, and food and drug chains commonly use newspapers to good advantage. In large cities, however, small stores

THE TOP TEN NATIONAL ADVERTISERS OF 1970 IN MAJOR MEDIA

Rank	Company	Total Expenditures
1	Procter & Gamble Co.	$186,746,100
2	General Foods Corp.	109,299,600
3	Bristol-Myers Co.	102,229,800
4	Colgate-Palmolive Co.	90,267,300
5	R. J. Reynolds Industries	77,843,900
6	American Home Products Corp.	76,542,400
7	General Motors Corp.	74,231,300
8	Sterling Drug Co.	67,807,100
9	Warner-Lambert Co.	67,487,600
10	Lever Bros. Co.	64,207,600

Table 11-1

DOLLAR VOLUME OF ADVERTISING IN THE UNITED STATES BY MEDIUM, 1970

	Medium	Volume (Millions of Dollars)	Percent of Total
	Newspapers	$ 5,850	29.6
	Magazines	1,321	6.7
	Television	3,660	18.6
Table 11-2	Radio	1,278	6.5
	Farm Publications (Regional)	32	0.2
	Direct Mail	2,736	13.9
	Business Papers	714	3.6
	Outdoor	237	1.2
	Miscellaneous	3,887	19.7
	TOTAL	$19,715	100.0

Reprinted by permission from *Marketing Communications*, February, 1971. Copyright 1971 by Decker Communications, Incorporated.

whose patronage is limited to customers from surrounding residential areas usually find the cost of metropolitan newspaper advertising too great and the coverage too extensive. Community newspapers, usually published weekly, are used quite frequently by these small stores.

National advertisers find newspapers an excellent way to secure local coverage and to tie in their messages with the sales efforts of their dealers in the community.

Newspapers are quite selective from a geographical standpoint because through them it is possible for an advertiser to pinpoint his advertising to the metropolitan areas that he wishes to reach. From the standpoint of interest selectivity or ability to reach special groups, newspapers reach all economic and social levels of the people and have a general, rather than a special, appeal. Most papers, however, contain specially edited sections, such as sports, the women's page, school news, and church notices, which may help the advertiser with a message for consumers interested in such topics.

A favorable characteristic of newspaper advertising is its flexibility or timeliness. In most cases, changes in advertising copy can be made up to within a few hours of the time the paper goes to press. This permits advertisers to follow national or local events, the weather, or changes in their own internal situations with great speed. It is even possible in times of great urgency to alter advertising insertions between editions.

With the daily newspapers, a substantial portion of their readers are known through their home-delivery lists. Somewhat less is known about those who purchase their papers at newsstands or vending machines. Many daily papers maintain research departments that endeavor to classify their known readers on the bases of income, education, religion, age, and many other characteristics that are useful for advertisers to know.

MAGAZINES

Since America has a large number of magazine readers, magazines constitute a very important advertising medium for many classes of advertisers. For the advertisers with nationwide distribution, the fact that most magazines have countrywide coverage makes these media singularly advantageous. For advertisers with a more limited geographic distribution of their goods, regional editions of many magazines provide access to these smaller markets without requiring them to pay for circulation in the areas where their products are not sold. Among the magazines of general editorial interest, *Life, Time,* and *Reader's Digest* offer regional editions; *Esquire* offers advertisers' space in issues that go exclusively to 500,000 identified homeowners. This type of service is rapidly spreading among the magazine publishers.

As regards interest selectivity, the general editorial group, including those just mentioned, reach groups of rather divergent interests and are, therefore, effective media for products with a wide appeal. Most others, however, are consciously directed toward readers who are included in rather specifically defined interest groups. In this class of magazines are those appealing to farmers, women, young people, homemakers, and the various trade journals. Magazines in the last group circulate only within the trades affected, such as groceries, drugs, and metals.

Magazine advertising is not flexible, in that the lapse of time between the deadlines for advertising copy and the public appearance of the issues is so great as to incur the risk that the themes of the insertions may be out of date by the time they reach the readers. Many magazine publishers require that the completed copy for advertisements be submitted from four to six weeks before the time that they will reach the newsstands or the homes of subscribers. This situation makes it rather difficult for national advertisers to tie up their advertising with unscheduled but important events, such as international crises, unseasonal weather, or sudden changes in the economic life of the nation.

As with newspapers, magazines have their subscription lists, which are classified according to the pertinent factors involved and which reveal important information for advertisers.

Established as a major medium for advertising in the late 1920's, radio maintained a very satisfactory position among competing media until the advent of television in the immediate post-World War II years. Since then, it has suffered to some extent. This has been particularly true of network radio. Local or *spot radio*, on the other hand, has held up remarkably well and appears to be capable of continuing as a profitable advertising medium both for station owners and advertisers. Its effectiveness, however, appears to be greater during the daylight hours than at night when television commands the larger audience.

Radio is an excellent medium for territorial selectivity because an advertiser can select just those stations that broadcast into the areas that he wishes to reach. For any radio station, the outer limits of its listening audience can be determined quite accurately. This may differ somewhat at night from the daytime, but research has defined the territorial coverage for most stations in a rather convincing fashion.

Interest selectivity, on the other hand, is somewhat less certain because the make-up of the listener group for any one program cannot be ascertained with any great degree of accuracy. Advertisers customarily assume that listeners of various types will be attracted to programs that offer entertainment of the sort that will appeal to them—for example, sports broadcasts for men. There is always the possibility, however, that the people to whom their programs are directed may be listening to other radio stations or may not even have their radios turned on. This makes for considerable uncertainty in determining the character and extent of the audience for any one program. In recent years, the adoption of FM (frequency modulation) radio transmission by an increasing number of stations that feature principally music has apparently resulted in attracting a large number of music-loving listeners.

Radio advertising is exceedingly flexible because it is possible to effect changes in the copy, if necessary, even while a program is in progress. This permits advertisers to capitalize to the fullest possible extent on sudden events to which they may wish to tie in their messages.

Except for such information as might be secured through research into radio listening and letters to the stations, relatively little is known about the identity of the listening audience. This is especially true with regard to those who listen to their car radios, since no satisfactory method has been devised to contact them.

Radio is a form of advertising that relies on sound to deliver its story. Unlike many of the other media, where the printed message may be accessible for varying lengths of time with the chance that it will be seen more than once and thus acquire the advantage of repetition, the *radio commercial*, as it is called in the trade, must be heard when it is spoken or sung, or it is forever lost. Furthermore, if a listener is tuned in to one program, he can hear none of the others that are broadcast at the same time, and they are lost to him forever unless he learns of them from others. In an attempt to overcome this situation, the so-called *spot announcement* has come into being, whereby short, frequently recorded commercials are given on many different stations in the time between programs. These announcements also occur during *station breaks*, which are for the purpose of permitting the stations to identify themselves. These same conditions and practices apply to television.

TELEVISION

This medium, the newest one in advertising, has assumed a most important place. While still behind newspapers in percentage of total advertising, it has passed direct mail, magazines, and radio. The combination of the spoken word and the visual presentation of products and their benefits, which television offers, has been most intriguing and alluring to many advertisers. The extension of color TV and the further usage of ultra-high frequency program transmission and reception should add to the stature of television as an advertising medium.

Two factors have arisen, however, that could conceivably affect the willingness of advertisers to use television. The first is the very high cost of television programs, such as $200,000 for a one-minute commercial during the playing of the Super Bowl, which tends to discourage advertisers with limited budgets. The second is the uncertainty of a reliable pattern of consumer use of television receiving sets. Unlike radio, which requires only part of the listeners' attention, television demands that viewers concentrate solely upon it; they must cease all or most other activities at the time. The weight of accumulated evidence appears to indicate that viewers will scan the program announcements quite carefully and select only those programs that appeal to them, leaving their sets turned off the rest of the time. There is some doubt, however, in the minds of many advertisers regarding the exposure of viewers to the commercial announcements. There is evidence that many viewers do not remain in their chairs during these intervals, but take advantage of these breaks to perform various household chores, such as preparing snacks and liquid refreshments, returning to their viewing at the conclusion of the commercials.

The matters of geographic and interest selectivity, flexibility, and identity of the audience are essentially the same for television as for radio.

DIRECT MAIL

This widely used advertising medium takes on a number of different forms. Postcards, letters, catalogs, folders, and booklets are commonly used. Direct mail can be used by any advertiser, large or small, because of the wide variability of its coverage. Mail may be sent to a few prospects in a single neighborhood or to millions of persons located in all parts of the country.

The basis of all direct-mail advertising is the mailing list. Lists may be compiled from a variety of sources and may be classified almost endlessly. It is most important that the lists be assembled with the utmost care and that they be kept up to date. Through the manipulation of the list, direct-mail advertising can be made extremely selective, regarding both geographical location and consumer interests. Depending somewhat upon the elaborateness of the copy, this medium can be changed rather quickly in accordance with important events; and of course any copy can be changed or discarded entirely up to the time that the mailing is effected. Audience identity is a function of the care and accuracy with which the mailing lists are compiled and kept current. There are many companies who compile and classify lists of businesses and consumers which are available on a fee basis to sellers who wish to use direct mail solicitation.

OUTDOOR ADVERTISING

This medium—utilizing either paper posters, painted bulletins, or electrically illuminated displays—is one of the older forms of advertising. It is available to almost any type of business, from the largest to the smallest, through the utilization of a large number of posters down to a single one. Outdoor advertising is directed at people who are outside of their homes or offices and are presumably bound on some sort of errand, business or social. Many, if not most of these people, will be riding in automobiles; therefore, the time that each reader is exposed to the advertising is necessarily brief. For this reason, the amount of subject matter that can be placed on a poster is limited. The most satisfactory results are achieved with trade names, slogans, and pictures of the products in use. Certain very elaborate and costly displays, known as *spectaculars*, may command sufficient attention to permit the use of relatively long advertising messages. The size of spectaculars and their intricacy, brilliant illumination, and location enable them to attract large audiences of passers-by. Examples of spectaculars are to be found in most large cities; Times Square in New York City is specially notable in this regard.

Outdoor advertising is quite selective, particularly in terms of geographic coverage. The ability of an advertiser to reach any locality that he wishes is limited largely by the availability of sites. As far as interest selectivity is concerned, outdoor advertising is effective only insofar as particular groups are located near, or pass by, the places where the advertising is displayed. The Traffic Audit Bureau, a research organization, conducts traffic counts at selected billboard sites to evaluate the passing auto traffic both qualitatively and quantitatively.

The flexibility of outdoor advertising is determined by the time required to reprint or repaint those displays that are out of date. Since this may take several days or weeks, there is always the chance that some event may take place which will make the selling theme obsolete. Because of the nature of this medium, name advertising is predominant.

The Highway Beautification Act of 1965 provides for control of outdoor advertising in areas adjacent to the Interstate Highway System and the primary system, which includes state roads and streets that receive federal aid for their construction and maintenance. The basic purpose of this legislation is to limit the number, lighting, and spacing of advertising within 660 feet of the nearest edge adjacent to the highway systems.

TRANSPORTATION ADVERTISING

In street cars, buses, subways, and commuters' railroad cars, *car cards* are used where they may be seen by people on their way to and from work and on shopping trips. Transportation advertising is used for all types of advertisers—national, regional, or local. By a judicious selection of the routes to be employed, even small merchants who draw their trade from single communities in the large cities have been able to utilize this medium advantageously. Transportation advertising is selective only to the extent that it reaches the riders in a given locality or with similar interests. Its flexibility approximates that of outdoor advertising.

BUSINESS PAPERS

The term *business papers* is applied to a considerable number of trade, industrial, and professional magazines and newspapers that circulate only among businessmen and that are useful in advertising industrial or business goods and services. Prominent among business papers are *American Machinist, Metalworking Production, Aviation Week & Space Technology, Chemical Engineering, Coal Age, Modern Manufacturing, Industrial Distribution, National Petroleum News*, and *Textile World*.

OTHER MEDIA

Other advertising media include store displays, packages, sampling, catalogs, and advertising specialties.

All stores feature merchandise displays to some extent, ranging from the artistically appealing show windows and interior displays of department and specialty stores to the crudely assembled piles of unassorted goods to be seen in some of the smaller neighborhood shops. Many manufacturers provide store displays for their dealers, often requiring their salesmen to set them up to assure their being used.

Most manufacturers utilize the exterior of the packages in which their goods are enclosed for brief advertising messages. They may use inserts, describing and praising their wares. Labels are also used to carry short selling messages. The use of packages and store displays is called *point-of-purchase advertising*.

Another form of advertising that has been used with some effectiveness is merchandise sampling. Crews of distributors go from house to house, leaving either small samples of the products being advertised or coupons that can be redeemed at the local stores. Sometimes a combination of these two methods is used. In most instances, sampling is confined to food, candy, and detergents.

Catalogs are rather widely used in advertising industrial or business goods. In fact, many producers of these items confine their advertising efforts to this type of medium. Two outstanding examples of catalog advertisers are the mail-order catalogs of Sears, Roebuck and Company and the Montgomery Ward and Company division of Marcor, Inc., which have long been published on a semiannual basis by these two firms. As a general rule, however, sellers of consumer goods use catalogs to a lesser extent than do those of industrial goods.

Advertising specialties consist of a large number of different items that are useful in carrying an advertiser's name or a brief sales message. Among these are calendars, match folders, ash trays, bottle openers, pencils, ballpoint pens, key tags, blotters, coin purses, emery boards, and rulers.

THE ADVERTISING AGENCY

The advertising agency is a specialized institution that assists businessmen in all phases of their advertising effort. Advertising agencies were originally space sellers for the media, but they now help to create advertising for business firms that seek their services.

An advertising agency is equipped to undertake all phases of the preparation and execution of advertising for its clients. It handles the complete advertising campaign, which includes writing copy, creating art work, and selecting and making contracts with the media. Formerly the agencies were active in the production of network television shows, but recently the networks have taken over most of this area. Such secondary activities as product and market research, designing of packages and labels, and consultation on marketing matters generally are among the services of the larger agencies.

Figure 11-1 shows the organization of a typical advertising agency, on the basis of the functions performed.

Practically all national magazine and newspaper advertising is produced by agencies, whose specialized talents enable them to perform these functions better than the advertisers could themselves. Agencies are used by almost all firms that advertise on a large scale with the exception of department stores, most of whom maintain their own advertising staffs.

Oddly enough, the principal method by which the agencies are compensated dates back to the period when they operated as space brokers for the publishers. Under this system they are paid a 15% commission by the media on the basis of the space or time cost of the advertising placed by them in behalf of their clients, the advertisers. For example, assume that an agency, acting for a client, buys space in a magazine that costs $30,000. The magazine bills the agency for $30,000, less the 15% commission of $4,500, or a net of $25,500. The agency, in turn, bills the client for the full $30,000, and when this is paid by the client, deducts the $4,500 and remits the $25,500 to the magazine. Agencies regularly report their *billings* to the trade press for statistical purposes.

Other, less important, forms of advertising agency compensation are service charges and fees. Service charges include the cost of materials and services, which are purchased by the agencies from outside sources. These include art work, photography, engravings, and related services. Fees are used frequently to cover agency services, such as research and sales promotion, where there are no advertisements created and inserted from which commissions could be received from the media.

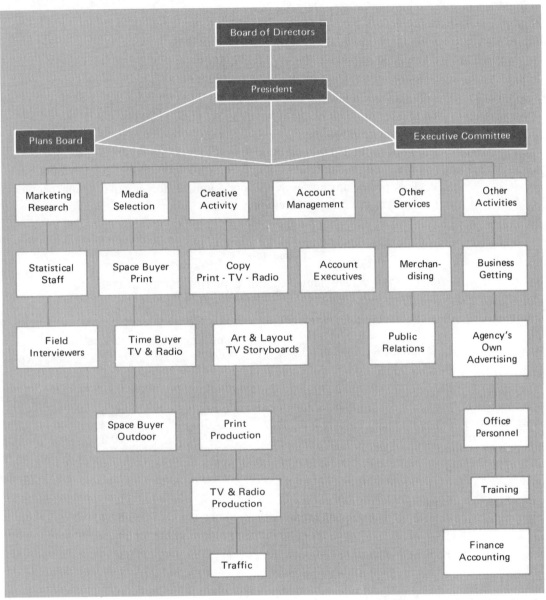

American Association of Advertising Agencies

Figure 11-1

A Typical Advertising Agency Organization Chart by Functions

An interesting aspect of the advertising agency is the rapid turnover of personnel in this field of employment. This is not to imply that employment in an advertising agency is of uncertain duration but, rather, that recently there has been an almost amoeba-like phenomenon in the formation of new agencies by the personnel of other pre-existing agencies. For the most part this has affected agencies with relatively low billings, compared to the leaders who are represented in Table 11-3 below. And there has been some question in the trade press regarding the salability of the productions of the new agencies; but the fact remains that many of the younger members of the advertising fraternity, apparently becoming impatient with their progress in the older, more established agencies, have struck out on their own with rather widely varying degrees of success. This points up, however, the opportunities for creative young people in the dynamic field of advertising.

Table 11-3

THE TOP TEN ADVERTISING AGENCIES IN THE UNITED STATES RANKED BY WORLD BILLINGS, 1970

Rank	Agency	Domestic Billings	International Billings (Millions of Dollars)	Total World Billings
1	J. Walter Thompson Co.	$436.0	$328.0	$764.0
2	McCann-Erickson	246.5	300.4	546.9
3	Young & Rubicam	356.4	163.8	520.2
4	Ted Bates & Co.	254.0	160.2	414.2
5	Leo Burnett Co.	283.0	106.0	389.0
6	Batten, Barton, Durstine & Osborn	324.4	26.0	350.4
7	Doyle Dane Bernbach	249.7	41.7	291.4
8	Grey Advertising	201.0	50.4	251.4
9	Ogilvy & Mather	159.0	91.2	250.2
10	Foote, Cone & Belding Communications	179.0	61.6	240.6

Reprinted with permission from the February 22, 1971, issue of *Advertising Age.* Copyright 1971 by Crain Communications, Inc.

From the foregoing discussion of agency charges and fees, one may gather that the services of an advertising agency are generally utilized by large business firms rather than by small businesses for budgetary reasons. Selecting a particular advertising agency is customarily the prerogative of the *advertising manager* of a large company. It is he who acts as the point of contact between the advertising agency and his employer. He interprets his firm's objectives to the agency, accepts or rejects the copy that is prepared by it, and handles the budgetary details. Of course, if the company does not use an agency, the advertising manager has charge of the preparation and insertion of the company's advertising.

ADVERTISING IN THE SMALL BUSINESS

There are thousands of small businesses, manufacturers, wholesalers, and particularly retailers with restricted markets and even more restricted advertising budgets. For most of these businessmen, an advertising agency is out of the question; consequently, they must prepare their own copy and find a medium to carry it.

For the small manufacturer, there are trade journals in which can be placed a modest advertisement that will reach the eyes of prospective customers. He may also use direct mail. Dealer display pieces are often helpful in promoting his sales, too, if he can afford them.

The small wholesaler faces a different type of problem. His customers are probably confined to the city where he is located, and very few trade journals have so small a circulation. He must rely on direct mail and augment this with broadsides, which can be enclosed with the merchandise when it is delivered to customers. *Broadsides, dodgers,* or *throw-aways* are sheets containing advertising matter that can be distributed to prospective customers. They are frequently printed on colored paper of a cheap grade and are thrown away immediately after being read.

Small retailers usually confine their advertising activities to window and interior displays. For those who wish to go beyond this, there is direct mail if they can secure good lists and the facilities for duplicating their copy. Broadsides are often circulated in this manner. They may also find the local community newspaper, if one is published, of value. Many small retailers have found the use of spot radio an effective and relatively inexpensive method of broadcasting their advertisements.

IS ADVERTISING EFFECTIVE?

Without doubt, advertising is effective, that is, it helps to sell goods. The answer to the question, however, is not so simple as that. It resolves itself into weighing the effectiveness of one medium against another, of one type of television program compared with another, of one advertising theme against another, and many other equally pertinent questions.

To discover the answers to some of these problems, the practice of testing advertising effectiveness has developed. Many methods of testing are in common usage, each peculiarly suited to the medium employed or the appeal to be weighed. The following will be discussed here: (1) the consumer pretest, (2) the inquiry test, (3) the sales test, (4) readership reports, and (5) testing radio and TV advertising.

THE CONSUMER PRETEST

The customary procedure of the *consumer pretest* consists of selecting a group of consumers to whom are submitted samples of advertising copy that have not been released for publication, for the purpose of selecting the one that appeals to them the most. They may be asked to rank the advertisements in terms of attractiveness, attention getting, or persuasion. The consumers may be contacted through personal interviews or by mail. This method is useful for prejudging the effectiveness of different advertisements but not that of competing media. This procedure is also identified by the terms "consumer jury" or "consumer panel."

THE INQUIRY TEST

The *inquiry test* consists of devising a procedure whereby those who are exposed to the advertisements to be tested are induced to make inquiry concerning the advertised merchandise. Then the inquiries are counted, and the advertisement with the greatest number of responses is regarded as the most effective. Readers of such advertisements in newspapers or magazines, for example, may be encouraged to reply by the use of coupons, keyed to reveal the media from whence they came or the advertisements of which they were a part; or they may be offered some sort of a reward, such as a sample of the advertised merchandise or a souvenir.

A follow-up on the effectiveness of the inquiry test is to relate the number of inquiries to the number of sales resulting from each advertisement. This is sometimes rather difficult to do; but where it is possible, it provides a good check on the test itself. For a test to be satisfactory, there should be a close correlation between the number of inquiries received and the sales that followed as the result of each advertisement.

THE SALES TEST

The procedure in the *sales test* is to select two cities, as nearly alike as possible, and run new advertising in one while not advertising in the other. The sales that occur in both areas during the test period can then be compared for the purpose of judging the effectiveness of the advertising. There are a number of variations on the sales test, such as running one set of advertisements in one area and a different set in the other. Care must be taken to choose cities that are similar, and an examination should be made of the chosen areas during the test to make certain that no external factors enter the picture to destroy the validity of the comparison.

READERSHIP REPORTS

A form of testing that has attained considerable prominence is the *Readership Reports* published by Daniel Starch and Staff, an organization of consultants in marketing research. The procedure is to seek out readers of certain magazines and newspapers and endeavor to discover the extent to which they paid attention to the advertisements in these media. The results are in the form of "noted," which means that the reader recalled seeing the advertisement; "seen-associated," which shows that the reader associated the advertisement with the advertiser; and "read most," which indicates that the interviewee read over 50 percent of the advertisement.

TESTING RADIO AND TELEVISION ADVERTISING

One of the major problems in connection with testing the effectiveness of radio and television advertising is to discover who is listening to the programs. The presence of a radio or television receiving set in a home does not tell whether or not the instrument is turned on or, if it is, to what station it is tuned.

Various methods have been devised to attempt to answer these questions, one of which involves the use of the telephone. Batteries of telephone operators are employed to call homes at random during the broadcasting time, and to endeavor to discover if the radio or television sets are turned on and, if so, the stations to which they are tuned. This test is known as the *coincidental method.*

Probably the best known testing method, and certainly the most controversial, is the Nielsen *Audimeter.* This is a mechanical device that is installed in the home near the radio or television set to which it is attached and which records on a tape the times when the set is turned on and to what station or channel. Each tape must be replaced every two weeks and returned to the A. C. Nielsen Company for analysis. The fate of many prominent television programs hangs on the evidence revealed by the Audimeter. The controversial aspect of this method arises through criticism of the quality and quantity of the homes where the Audimeter is installed. Some 1,100 households, where Audimeters are placed, are regarded by Nielsen as an adequate and accurate sample of the television viewing public of the country. In addition, Nielsen uses weekly diaries of television viewing which are filled out by family members in 2,200 homes. Many people in the television broadcasting business have questioned both the quantity and accuracy of these samples.

CRITICISMS OF ADVERTISING

Advertising in general and individual advertisements have long been the targets of adverse criticism. Some of the expressions of disapproval have been actually criticisms of business itself and many of its practices. Among these have been claims that much advertising is merely competitive; that it stresses minor differences in products which serve the same purpose and are essentially the same; that it causes consumers to want—and presumably to purchase—goods that they would not desire if they were not exposed to the advertising; and that it is designed to create demand for products. In answer to these criticisms it should be noted that competition is a fundamental principle of capitalism; that product differentiation [1] is a method by which producers of homogeneous products endeavor to make their goods appear slightly different from those of their competitors; and that, in many instances, consumers would not know of the existence and availability of many products if they were not advertised.

In the criticism that advertising creates demand, it must be admitted that many, if not most, advertisers believe that demand creation is one of the main functions of advertising. A demand for a commodity cannot exist without a knowledge of the availability of the commodity on the part of potential users. But demand must be more than mere knowledge of the existence of a commodity; it must involve the desire for it on the part of prospective purchasers.

It is very difficult for consumers to make their wishes known to the producers in such manner as to serve as a guide for production schedules. In order to avoid the stalemate that might otherwise theoretically follow this situation, it is only natural that manufacturers should make what they think the public wants and then try to convince consumers that they should buy the advertised goods. There is obviously the possibility that the goods produced and promoted may be of little value

[1] See Chapter 1, page 13.

to consumers, but this seems to be a risk inherent in a situation where the buyers are practically inarticulate. It seems, therefore, that the demand-creation concept is a perfectly defensible philosophy, considering the inability of buyers to make known their wants in advance.

Other criticisms are: (1) that advertising makes the goods advertised cost more than would be the case if they were not advertised; (2) that others are in poor taste or offensive to the public; (3) that many advertisements are false or misleading; and (4) that many advertisements are fatuous, pointless, and only casually related to the products involved. (This last criticism has come from many advertising people as well as from the public.) All these criticisms will be examined in turn.

DOES ADVERTISING MAKE GOODS COST MORE?

Advertising is a selling cost and, like all other costs, must be covered by the selling price of the advertised article. One might say, then, that anything that increases the cost of an item increases its price. This is, however, an oversimplification of the cost-price relationship, which needs to be examined more closely.

There are two types of costs—direct and indirect. *Direct costs* are those that can be directly allocated to the production of a commodity, such as materials and labor. *Indirect costs* are those that cannot be directly allocated, such as occupancy expenses, superintendence, power, and administrative costs. Roughly speaking, the total direct and indirect costs divided by the number of items produced will give the cost per item.

A peculiarity of indirect costs is that they tend to remain fixed over wide ranges of output. It is conceivable that the total indirect cost of producing an item would be the same whether the production were 100 or 1,000. It is obvious, then, that the indirect cost per unit would be much less for 1,000 units than for 100 or even 500.

Advertising is generally regarded as an indirect cost and, if the result of advertising a commodity is to increase its sales greatly, it is entirely possible that this sales increase may be of sufficient magnitude to bring about a decrease in unit costs that more than offsets the increase in total cost due to the advertising expense. If this is true, then the lowered unit cost would permit the producer to lower his price, which might give him a competitive advantage in selling his product.

It may be stated, then, that (a) when advertising results in increased sales, (b) when these increased sales result in lowered unit costs, and (c) when the lowered unit costs result in lowered prices, advertising not only does not increase the price of goods but actually decreases it. There are probably many instances where all of these conditions are not present, in which cases it may be said that advertising either increases the prices of goods or at least does not decrease them.

IS ADVERTISING IN POOR TASTE?

The only possible answer to this criticism must necessarily be equivocal. That there have been occasional advertisements which have violated the accepted standards of good taste is undeniable, although there is reason to believe that these have been few and far between. That the majority of advertisements conform to these standards is likewise certain. There have been those advertisements that are offensive to some people, while perfectly acceptable to others. Under the pressure of competition, it is entirely possible that some creators of advertising have exceeded the bounds of good taste for some segments of the public. Advertising agency executives, however, are aware of this possibility and generally endeavor to prevent the appearance of any advertisements that might provoke displeasure. Some instances of name advertising, particularly on radio and television, may appear to be inane but not necessarily in poor taste.

ARE MANY ADVERTISEMENTS FALSE OR MISLEADING?

Among the criticisms of advertising, none has been more cogent than those that have flayed the prevalence of untruth in its messages. This does not mean all advertising is untrue, for such is not the case; but it does mean that too many advertisements have contained statements or claims that were not strictly true.

It is practically impossible to define untruthfulness to the satisfaction of all concerned. The advertiser who proclaims that his product is the best in the world may believe that it is, but what of his competitor who makes the same statement about his product? Obviously they both cannot be right. In fact both products may be inferior to any number of others. This sort of thing, which is quite common, is called harmless *trade puffery*. It merely amounts to a certain amount of public breast-beating.

Untruthfulness in advertising assumes many forms, among which are false testimonials, exaggerations, false claims, misrepresentation, false or near-false labeling, and the use of confusing terminology. It is a sad commentary on the gullibility of many consumers that they can be misled by such frauds. It is scandalous that some businessmen would resort to such unethical and irresponsible tactics. Unfortunately, such behavior by a relatively few tends to undermine public confidence in all advertising, to the detriment of those advertisers who follow the policy of checking their copy carefully to make certain that it contains nothing but the truth. There are many such firms, and they are keenly aware of the transgressions of their less ethical competitors.

ARE MANY ADVERTISEMENTS FATUOUS AND POINTLESS?

A casual reading of advertisements for cigarettes, alcoholic beverages, and cosmetics, among others, can hardly avoid creating the impression that the derogatory adjectives that come with this criticism are applicable to a large percentage of them. In many cases this is true with name advertising, as previously noted. In others—and this thought comes from the advertising fraternity itself—it would seem to indicate that the creators of this type of copy are more interested in the originality of their advertising copy than in the selling power of their advertisements. It is doubtful that any harm results from advertisements of this sort, but the extent to which they induce customers to purchase is certainly subject to question. Unfortunately, the sponsors of some of the more "far out" advertisements appear to be satisfied with the results of their advertising.

ENSURING TRUTH IN ADVERTISING

There is no single method of ensuring that a certain amount of untruth will not appear in the advertising of the country as long as a system of free private enterprise continues. It is furthermore probable that we will never be able to purify our advertising copy to the complete satisfaction of everyone.

A number of steps designed to protect the public and ethical business leaders from some of the more flagrant and harmful types of false advertising have been taken: (1) industry self-regulation, (2) action by media, (3) Better Business Bureaus, (4) action by federal agencies, and (5) *Printers' Ink* statutes. These and other methods have accomplished much in cleaning up the advertising picture, which is unquestionably on a far higher plane than it was some years ago.

INDUSTRY SELF-REGULATION

A great many business houses enforce rigid codes of ethics upon themselves in order to make certain that their advertising is as strictly in accord with the truth as human watchfulness can assure.

Recognizing that false or misleading advertising reflects unfavorably on all members of the trade, some industries have endeavored to establish the machinery for self-regulation. The Proprietary Association, made up of manufacturers of pharmaceutical preparations and patent medicines, is a good example. By means of argument and moral suasion, they have endeavored to prevent some of the members of the trade from continuing advertising that was manifestly false.

A number of industries have cooperated with the Federal Trade Commission in setting up Trade Practice Rules which, among other things, may prohibit false advertising, misbranding, and deception on the part of its members. Among the groups whose Trade Practice Rules include strong condemnation of false or deceptive advertising are the Tobacco Smoking Pipe and Cigar and Cigarette Holder Industry, the Cosmetic and Toilet Preparations Industry, and the Fountain Pen and Mechanical Pencil Industry. The television networks undertake to censor certain types of medical advertising that refer to bodily functions not normally a part of polite conversation.

The major difficulty with self-regulation is that it is entirely a voluntary matter. There is no method of compelling recalcitrant members of the trade to hew to the straight and narrow path if they wish to break away from it. This method, therefore, democratic and desirable as it is, can be only partly successful.

ACTION BY MEDIA

Nearly all media have certain minimum ethical standards to which all advertising must conform in order to be acceptable for publication. They recognize that false advertisements reflect not only on the advertisers but also on the media in which they appear. Many publishers also feel a moral obligation toward those advertisers whose copy is on the level and with whom unethical advertising would be unfair competition.

BETTER BUSINESS BUREAUS

Better Business Bureaus, which are well known for their activities to protect consumers, were originally established by businessmen for the purpose of protecting themselves from the unfair competition of the less ethical members of the community and were only incidentally protectors of consumers. The critical examination of all local advertising, particularly that of retailers, has long been foremost among the duties of these bureaus. Their weapons have been twofold—publicity for the offending firms and recourse to the federal courts when false advertising was sent through the mails. Many Better Business Bureau offices maintain service departments that will advise consumers on complaints made against specific advertisers. The extent to which this service is utilized has not been disclosed.

ACTION BY FEDERAL AGENCIES

The two principal agencies for the combating of fraudulent advertising are the Federal Trade Commission and the Food and Drug Administration. The Federal Trade Commission Act of 1914 established the Commission and gave it authority to prevent the use of unfair methods of competition in interstate commerce. In 1938 the Wheeler-Lea Act (an amendment to the Federal Trade Commission Act) added to the duties of the Commission by giving it authority to prevent "unfair or deceptive acts or practices in commerce."

Following the passage of the Wheeler-Lea Amendment (which prohibited the false advertising of food, drugs, cosmetics, and therapeutic devices), the Federal Trade Commission maintains a Bureau of Deceptive Practices which scrutinizes the advertising of newspapers, magazines, catalogs, and radio and television broadcasts to detect false or misleading advertising in these fields. The Commission is thus enabled to investigate instances of alleged or suspected false advertising and to issue cease and desist orders when the advertising is found to be in violation of the Federal Trade Commission Act.

The Federal Food, Drug, and Cosmetic Act of 1938 strengthened the hands of the Food and Drug Administration in its dealing with false labeling of "foods, drugs, devices, and cosmetics." Both this agency and the Federal Trade Commission have been diligent in their efforts to suppress false advertising.

PRINTERS' INK STATUTES

In 1911, *Printers' Ink*, now *Marketing Communications*, a leading marketing trade periodical, set forth a model statute that was designed to aid in eliminating dishonest advertising. Persons interested in truthful advertising undertook the task of inducing state legislatures to adopt laws embracing its principles. As a result, 43 states have passed laws based on the *Printers' Ink* pattern. These laws, of course, are confined in their application solely to intrastate advertising, and their value has been lessened in some instances by poor enforcement. They do indicate, however, an awareness of the need for corrective action in this area.

THE ADVERTISING COUNCIL

In 1941 a group of individuals representing national advertisers, advertising agencies, and the major media founded *The Advertising Council*, dedicated to the idea that advertising could and should be used in the public interest as it had been in the private interest. During World War II this organization undertook the task of publicizing the many activities that the country required for the successful prosecution of the war effort. After the war the Council promoted such things as the need for better schools, accident prevention, ownership of U. S. savings bonds, prevention of forest fires, and many other worthwhile causes. In this way the leaders of the advertising field are endeavoring to implement the concept that advertising is a potent force for social good in this country.

BUSINESS TERMS

QUESTIONS FOR DISCUSSION AND ANALYSIS

1. Do you believe that our present economic system could operate successfully without advertising? Why or why not?

2. With the rapid growth of suburban shopping centers near large cities, would you expect that community newspapers would become more valuable as advertising media for small suburban stores? Why or why not?

3. Do you think that direct mail advertisements which are addressed to the individuals to whom they are sent are more or less effective than when addressed simply to "Occupant"? Why or why not?

4. What is your opinion of the advertising effectiveness of large search-lights whose beams sweep the sky at night near the advertiser's place of business?

5. Why do most department and chain stores create their own advertising rather than use agencies?

6. Why has the controversy concerning false advertising centered mainly around consumer goods and only rarely around industrial goods?

7. Some observers have said that if the volume of all consumer goods advertising were to be cut in half, there would not be a measurable decrease in the volume of consumer goods sold. Do you agree? Explain.

8. What is your attitude toward the long television commercials that are commonplace in the television movies?

9. Some critics of advertising have stated that advertising should be limited to statements of the availability of goods and to descriptions of them and should make no attempt to influence or "sell" consumers. Do you agree? Why or why not?

10. Is there a need for censorship of advertising, as has been claimed in recent years? Explain.

PROBLEMS AND SHORT CASES

1. The term "institutional advertising" has sometimes been referred to as "nonproduct advertising." Many people are not aware of the frequency with which this type of advertising appears in the different advertising media. Collect a portfolio of institutional advertising, prepare a written report of the objective of each advertisement, and indicate your own opinion as to the probable effectiveness of each.

2. Among the different advertising media there are wide differences in the accuracy with which their audiences or readers can be identified. Identify the probable audiences for newspapers, magazines, radio, television, outdoor, direct mail, and transportation advertising. Justify your reasons for each medium.

3. The efforts of the Advertising Council are very worthy of student attention. Collect a portfolio of Advertising Council insertions and present a written commentary giving your opinion of the worthwhileness of their productions. In other words, do their insertions impress you favorably or unfavorably?

SUGGESTED READINGS

Dunn, S. Watson. *Advertising: Its Role in Modern Marketing*, Second Edition. New York: Holt, Rinehart and Winston, 1969.

Frey, Albert Wesley, and Jean C. Halterman. *Advertising.* New York: The Ronald Press Company, 1970.

Kleppner, Otto, and Irving Settel, Eds. *Exploring Advertising.* Englewood Cliffs, New Jersey: Prentice-Hall, Inc., 1969.

Littlefield, James E., and C. A. Kirkpatrick. *Advertising: Mass Communication in Marketing,* Third Edition. Boston: Houghton Mifflin Company, 1970.

Longman, Kenneth A. *Advertising.* New York: Harcourt Brace Jovanovich, Inc., 1970.

Mandell, Maurice I. *Advertising.* Englewood Cliffs, New Jersey: Prentice-Hall, Inc., 1968.

Wheatley, John J. *Measuring Advertising Effectiveness: Selected Readings.* Homewood, Illinois: Richard D. Irwin, Inc., 1969.

Chapter 12

International Trade

The term *international trade* is applicable to the buying and selling of goods and services among business firms of different countries and to the payments that are made for them. The origin of international trade goes back to the period when businessmen who had more goods to sell than could be absorbed in their own countries undertook to find markets for them in other lands. From these small beginnings developed a practice that has grown to the impressive proportions of today's trade between the nations of the world. Strictly speaking, international transactions between private citizens of the countries concerned should be included in this category also, but because of their relative size and infrequency they are usually disregarded. It is through the functioning of international trade that the products of any one country are made available to the other nations of the world. The discussion through much of this chapter will center on the role of the United States in this economic area.

WHY NATIONS TRADE

The reasons for international trade may be classified as: (1) business reasons, (2) economic reasons, and (3) political reasons.

BUSINESS REASONS

Businesses in this country import goods from abroad because: (a) the goods either are not available in this country or, if available, are not in sufficient supply for our purposes; (b) the prices are lower than for similar goods produced domestically; and (c) by so doing, the importing firms are more certain of a foreign market for their products—the firms from whom they buy abroad may be willing, in turn, to purchase their goods.

American firms endeavor to sell their products in foreign countries: (a) to increase the total volume of their sales, possibly to the point where their production rate may approach the optimum volume; (b) because of less competition, either from United States or foreign sellers; (c) to level off seasonal sales fluctuations, particularly through sales to those countries located south of the equator whose seasons are the direct opposite of ours; and (d) because of a demand for their goods in other countries.

ECONOMIC REASONS

The two economic reasons for the development of international trade are called (1) the theory of absolute advantage and (2) the theory of comparative advantage. They are useful as a means of indicating the underlying economic bases for the development of international trade and its persistence in the face of formidable obstacles.

Theory of Absolute Advantage

There are two aspects to the *theory of absolute advantage*. A few countries possess through pure chance certain goods that cannot be obtained in significant quantities elsewhere. Natural diamonds in South Africa, emeralds in Colombia, and helium in the United States are some examples. Under these circumstances trade will take place between these countries and any others who need or desire these goods.

Trade will also occur in instances where, although several nations are capable of producing the same goods, certain countries are able to produce them more cheaply. As a result, they become the sources of supply for these items and sell them to other countries because of their cost advantage. The areas in which countries may have this aspect of absolute advantage might be skilled or unskilled labor, patented processes, managerial know-how, climate, or abundance of raw materials. Here the theory holds that countries will concentrate their productive efforts on the goods in the manufacture of which they have an absolute cost advantage and abstain from the production of goods in which they are at an absolute disadvantage. The surpluses of some goods thus produced and the need for other goods thus created bring about the movement of goods in the channels of international trade as each nation tries to sell the goods that it makes and to buy the goods that other nations make, both on the presumed basis of absolute advantage. Two examples of this aspect of the theory of absolute advantage are the manufacture of linen cloth in Ireland and the growing of bananas in Costa Rica.

Theory of Comparative Advantage

The *theory of comparative advantage* assumes that trade will take place between nations that are capable of producing the same products, but where certain nations have a comparative advantage in the production of certain products in comparison with other products. For example, even though Country *A* may have lower costs than Country *B* in the production of, say, twelve different products, it will tend to concentrate on the production of those items, perhaps four, in which its comparative cost advantages are the greatest, leaving the production of the remaining eight to Country *B*. Under these circumstances Country *A* might import the remaining eight products from Country *B*.

In the more highly developed industrial nations of the world the trend has been definitely away from following the theory of comparative advantage, at least regarding the products of a mechanized economy. The trend has been toward the manufacture of everything that would come into this general category and to employ trade barriers, usually tariffs, to equalize the cost differences on goods coming from countries that are able to produce them at less cost. It is, of course, obvious that the extension of this trend would have the effect of lessening the volume of trade between countries. Later in this chapter we shall note some of the more recent steps that have been taken by various nations to reverse this trend and to increase the volume of international trade in some parts of the world.

POLITICAL REASONS

Many people feel that the greatest possible volume of world trade between nations is desirable as an important step in the direction of world peace. Countries that have extensive business dealings with each other are presumed to be on a more friendly basis than those whose contacts are few in number or virtually nonexistent. Except for the nations in the communist bloc, the volume of trade betwen the United States and most of the other countries of the world has been growing since the end of World War II. No small part of the trade with the nations of Western Europe has been motivated by the attempt to strengthen their economies as a bulwark against the encroachment of communism.

CHARACTERISTICS OF INTERNATIONAL TRADE

International trade has several characteristics in common with domestic trade. The goods and services offered must have the power to satisfy human wants; there must be people somewhere who want them and are able and willing to pay for them; there must be a commonly accepted and trusted medium of exchange in which values may be expressed or quoted; and the goods and services offered must be quoted at prices that will both find ready buyers for the entire amounts that are for sale and yield reasonable profits to the sellers. Sales effort is likewise required, both to bring the goods to the attention of prospective buyers and to effect their sale.

It is with the following characteristics of international trade that are unlike those of domestic trade, however, that this discussion is principally concerned: (1) language differences, (2) use of foreign exchange, (3) trade barriers, and (4) increased transportation costs. Other differences, such as customs, habits, legal systems, governmental attitudes toward business, and political systems in the various countries, also serve to differentiate international from domestic trade.

LANGUAGE DIFFERENCES

Except for trade between countries speaking a common tongue, language differences must be overcome. These affect the necessary correspondence, the creation of advertising, and the labeling and marking of the goods. To take care of this situation, some firms employ foreign-language speaking correspondents and interpreters. Translation services are available from a number of sources, such as the larger chambers of commerce, the Pan-American Union, and international trade clubs.

The post-World War II years have witnessed the gradual spread of English as an acceptable common business language in many areas of the world, notably in parts of Western Europe and Latin America.

USE OF FOREIGN EXCHANGE

Every nation has its own peculiar currency—the dollar in this country, the yen in Japan, the drachma in Greece, the peso in Mexico, the guilder in The Netherlands, and the lira in Italy. This situation requires not only a mechanism whereby the seller may be paid in his own currency while the buyer makes payment in his, but also a method whereby each of these national currencies may be expressed or valued in terms of every other one. At one time gold served as a common denominator for all currencies; but for several years the so-called gold standard has been nonexistent, and this fact has greatly complicated the problem. The possible fluctuation in these relative values does not help to simplify this situation.

Bills of Exchange

Because different monetary standards exist, the system of *foreign exchange* has evolved which makes it possible for buyers and sellers in international trade to pay and receive payment for goods and services. Money is seldom shipped abroad in the settlement of international trade transactions. The typical method of settlement is by means of *bills of exchange*, which are nothing more nor less than the drafts [1] used in domestic trade, except that they may be written in terms of francs or marks instead of dollars.

When an exporter sells goods or renders service to a foreign importer, he draws a bill of exchange ordering the importer to pay him a stated amount of money either on sight or a specified number of days in the future. Since he ordinarily will not want to wait until it matures to cash it, he takes it to his bank and discounts it. This means that the bank gives him cash for it, less certain interest and accommodation charges. This transaction may be effected before the bill of exchange is presented to the importer if his credit standing is good; otherwise, time must be spent to send it to him for acceptance and for its return before the exporter can present it for discount.

The discounting bank, or its larger city correspondent, simply credits the bill of exchange to its account in the country where it was drawn; and when the bill becomes due, it is presented to the importer by a bank in his own country, and payment is effected and the transaction completed without any money being sent from the importer to the exporter. This same discounting bank is then in a position to sell drafts on its foreign balances to American importers who thus reimburse the bank for the money it paid to the American exporter when it discounted his original bill of exchange. Likewise, the importer has funds available abroad to pay the amount he owes to the exporter in that country without sending actual cash.

Rates of Exchange

Bills of exchange are bought and sold in a so-called foreign exchange market, which is located in the large financial centers of the United States

[1] See Chapter 18, page 432.

and of the world. The prices of these bills are known as the *rates of exchange.* Before World I, when gold could be shipped between countries, these exchange rates were kept within narrow limits because of the possible alternative of actually shipping gold in or out of the country if the price of the bills of exchange exceeded the cost of shipping the gold. At present, gold cannot be shipped, except in rare instances, hence the demand for and the supply of the bills of exchange determine their price (rate of exchange). Thus, if American exporters sell a lot more to importers in India than our importers buy from India exporters, the supply of bills will exceed the demand, the rate of exchange will go down, and the exporters will be harmed as their bills will bring less in the market. Likewise, importers in all countries will be encouraged to buy more in India by virtue of the lower price of the instruments used to pay for their purchases. In time, a balance will be reached that will bring the rate up again.

TRADE BARRIERS

All countries, for one reason or another, interpose barriers that tend to restrict the free flow of goods across their borders. Some barriers apply to exports, such as the prohibition of the shipment of military strategic items from the United States to countries behind the Iron Curtain; for the most part, however, barriers apply to imports. The chief barriers are quotas, exchange controls, and tariffs. *Quotas* are quantitative restrictions that may be expressed in terms of physical amounts or value. When the use and availability of foreign exchange is officially restricted in order to make it possible for a government to achieve a certain degree of favorable trade balance, *exchange controls* are said to be in effect. Since it is through the manipulation of tariff schedules that foreign-made goods are encouraged or discouraged from entering a country, the subject of levying and of administering tariffs on imports is of sufficient importance to warrant a rather thorough discussion of this particular trade barrier at this point.

A *tariff* is a system of customs duties levied against goods being imported into the country. According to the purpose for which it is designed, it may be a revenue tariff or a protective tariff. A *tariff for revenue only* is designed principally to raise revenue for the government and is not designed primarily to discourage imports. Revenue rates are usually relatively low, since the lower they are, the greater the quantity of imports and hence the larger the amount of revenue. The purpose of a *protective tariff* is to keep out of the country goods that would otherwise undersell domestic goods of the same or similar kind—goods in the production of which other nations have a comparative advantage.

Reasons for the Protective Tariff

To understand the meaning and implications of the protective tariff, it is necessary to inquire into the arguments that have been advanced in its behalf and to examine their validity to some extent.

The military argument. This argument holds that all industries vital to the national defense should be kept alive through tariff protection if necessary. It has been proposed that, when this needs to be done, subsidies be employed, perhaps even from the outset, and that the costs be properly labeled as those of national defense.

The home-industry argument. This argument holds that, if foreign goods are kept out of the country, domestic manufacturers will enjoy a larger home market than would otherwise be the case. The argument has been used by business interests that have been interested more in protecting their own existence from foreign competition than in promoting American industry generally. With high tariffs to keep out foreign competition, individual firms thus protected are able to get higher prices for their products than if tariffs were lower. High-cost producers, who might be forced out of business if subjected to the competition of efficient foreign producers, are enabled to continue to operate while thus protected.

The infant-industry argument. The tenor of this argument is that young, struggling industries in this country should be protected from competition from foreign producers until they have had a chance to get well established. There is a certain amount of merit to this thesis, provided that the protection is continued only until the infant has attained competitive maturity. The difficulty arises in determining how long this protection is needed and when it should be discarded. Furthermore, each industry might require a different period of time to mature. Administratively, this part of the problem is extremely difficult.

The wages argument. The theme of this argument is that, by excluding foreign goods made by lower-paid labor, goods made by higher-paid domestic labor can be sold in this country, thereby serving to maintain or raise domestic wages. There are several aspects to the consideration of the wages argument. First, by keeping out goods made by lower-paid labor of other countries, the prices of competing American goods may be raised to American buyers, thus leaving them less money with which to buy other goods. Second, in the years since World War II, there has been remarkable economic growth in many parts of the free world. In many instances this has been the result of financial assistance rendered by the United States, coupled with instruction in modern managerial techniques given by representatives of American industrial companies. This industrial growth has resulted in higher standards of living for the people of these countries. And while it is true that their wage scales are still substantially below those of this country, their productivity is growing and, in addition to their being able to offer goods to our buyers, in some cases for less than they can be purchased here, these nations offer a challenging market for the producers in this country.

The favorable-balance-of-trade argument. The term *favorable balance of trade* refers to a situation where a country's exports exceed its imports. On the other hand, when a country's imports exceed its exports, it is said to have an *unfavorable balance of trade.* The measure of the prosperity of a country, as far as its international trade is concerned, however, is not to be found in its export or import position, but rather in the effect that its international trade has on the standard of living of its people. If a people can import certain goods at prices lower than the cost of making those goods themselves, they should do so and concentrate their productive efforts on making other goods that they can produce more cheaply than other countries can and sell these goods abroad. However, the problem of convincing business and labor leaders of this truism is a difficult one.

Types of Tariff Duties

There are three types of tariff duties: specific, ad valorem, and compound. The rates affecting all commodities are set forth in the tariff acts.

Specific duties are amounts levied at so much per unit, or pound, or ton, of the commodities affected. For example, the specific duty on butter is 7 cents per pound and that on champagne and all other sparkling wines is $1.36 per gallon.

Ad valorem duties consist of levies based on some aspect of the value of the goods in question. For example, the ad valorem duty on hides is 3 percent of their value.

Compound duties involve both specific and ad valorem levies. For example, ethylene glycol (antifreeze) has a duty of 2.4 cents per pound plus 12 percent ad valorem, and men's suits, 37½ cents per pound and 21 percent ad valorem.

INCREASED TRANSPORTATION COSTS

A factor in which international trade differs from domestic trade, mainly in degree, is that of transportation costs. Although it may cost less to ship goods from Boston to Quebec than from Seattle to Miami, in general the transportation costs incident to international trade are considerably higher than those incurred in moving goods within this country.

ROLE OF THE UNITED STATES IN WORLD TRADE

Our federal government has always felt compelled, for one reason or another, to exercise its influence in the field of international trade. Generally this has been done in a genuine and sincere effort to safeguard and promote the interests of the citizens in their international transactions, on the ground that individually they were not strong enough, or could not afford, to do this for themselves.

These activities of the government have manifested themselves in a myriad of ways. Merchant fleets have been subsidized or built with public funds. The diplomatic, and particularly the consular, services of the government seek to assist international traders in establishing and extending their commercial activities by advising them concerning international governmental regulations. Commercial treaties with general and specific agreements concerning the rights and the obligations of the signatory countries have been concluded.

Introduced in 1922 and continued up to the present, federal legislation has empowered the President of the United States to change tariff rates without reference to Congress, subject to certain restrictions or limitations. The purpose was to speed up the adjustment of rates in accord with changing conditions, as compared with the cumbersome and log-rolling methods of legislative changes in the tariff laws.

EFFECT OF NATIONALISM

International trade is or should be a two-way arrangement, that is, a country should buy as well as sell goods and services. Although it is to be expected that exports and imports will not balance out evenly in every instance and that the differences will be settled in some acceptable fashion, it is an economic fallacy to assume that a country can always sell more than it buys. Yet this is exactly what the growth of economic nationalism has tended to bring about. Great emphasis has been placed on the export of goods to other countries, but the notion that imports should play a prominent part in the economy of the nation has been decried and barriers have been erected in the path of the free inflow of goods.

The concept of a nation's relationship to world trade as being purely that of a seller is one that dates back to the mercantilists in England. The mercantilists believed that the country's prosperity, as far as international trade was concerned, depended on exporting merchandise and importing only gold as payment for the exports.

This philosophy has been further emphasized by the phraseology employed to describe our country's position in terms of a favorable or an unfavorable balance of trade. Furthermore, the balance of trade idea embraced purely "visible" or merchandise items, such as machinery, shoes, and typewriters, and ignored the "invisible" items, such as loans to foreign countries, payments for insurance abroad, or money spent by tourists. The use of these terms has been most unfortunate in that it has appeared to portray a situation of advantage or disadvantage that was not necessarily or even usually true.

The idea that a nation should be economically self-sufficient, as far as the United States is concerned, received considerable impetus during World War II because the early enemy conquests cut off our supply of many essential raw materials, such as rubber and quinine, necessitating our searching for substitutes or doing without until the enemy was defeated. Many business and political leaders hold to the belief that, as far as possible, we should never permit ourselves to be caught in this position again. The implementation of this conclusion would result in our endeavoring to produce a number of commodities that can be grown or produced much more cheaply abroad. This may be regarded as a purely defensive measure, but it is bound to have an adverse effect on the extension of our international trade, particularly our imports. The increasing world tensions of the past few years, however, will doubtless place the matter of national safety well ahead of the notion of the general desirability of extended world trade, at least in the thinking of many people in this country.

EXTENT OF OUR INTERNATIONAL TRADE

Our international trade varies quite measurably from year to year, depending upon a number of factors, including trade barriers, price levels, the state of the economy in various nations, international trade agreements, and the presence or absence of war anywhere in the world. The basic trend of both exports and imports of merchandise, however, has been upward as is indicated by Figure 12-1 below.

Figure 12-1

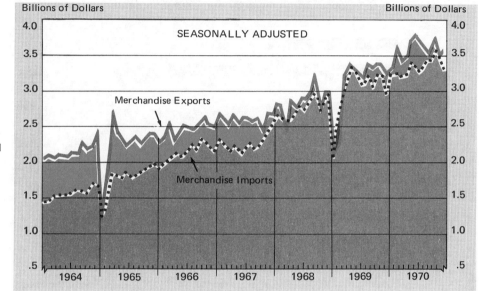

Merchandise Exports and Imports

Source: *Economic Indicators*, February, 1971. Prepared for the Joint Economic Committee by the Council of Economic Advisers.

The bar chart in Figure 12-2 on page 286 shows the United States trade with major world areas in dollar volume for the period 1964-1969.

The dollar volume of United States exports and imports in 1969, by major commodity groups, is shown in Table 12-1 on page 287.

The growth in volume of the international trade of the United States, together with the competition offered by firms in other countries, has focused the attention of marketing managers of exporting companies on certain aspects of their duties that have increased in importance along with the growth of their sales in other lands. The term *international marketing* has emerged as a group description of these enhanced responsibilities. This new concept requires the recognition of differences in

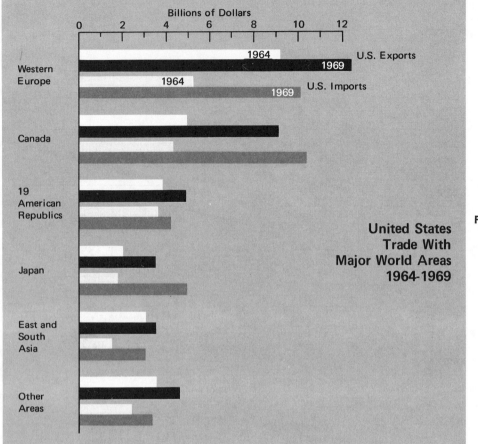

Billions of Dollars

Western Europe
1964 — U.S. Exports
1969
1964 — U.S. Imports
1969

Canada

19 American Republics

Japan

East and South Asia

Other Areas

Figure 12-2

**United States
Trade With
Major World Areas
1964-1969**

United States Trade with Major World Areas, 1964-1969

Source: Department of Commerce, *Overseas Business Reports.*

marketing procedures and in the legal, cultural, and economic factors in the different countries. All phases of planning and organizing for international marketing operations are covered, which include sales forecasts and market analyses; strategies of product, pricing, advertising, and selling; and the choice of channels of distribution. The *international marketing manager* must determine the characteristics of the products that can be sold in each country. He decides on whether to use salesmen from these countries or to train men from the States to handle the sales jobs. The determination of price policies, discounts, and terms of sale must be made with a full knowledge of the customs of the different nations involved.

U.S. EXPORTS AND IMPORTS BY SELECTED COMMODITY GROUPS, 1969

	Exports	Imports
	(Millions of Dollars)	
Machinery and Transport Equipment	$16,380	$ 9,768
Other Manufactured Goods	7,001	12,021
Food and Live Animals	3,733	4,531
Crude Materials, Inedible, Except Fuels	3,570	3,460
Chemicals	3,383	1,232
Mineral Fuels and Related Materials	1,131	2,794

Table 12-1

Source: United States Bureau of the Census, *Statistical Abstract of the United States: 1970.* (91st Edition.) Washington, D.C., 1970.

In many instances these matters require different procedures and practices from the marketing of goods in this country.

The International Business Concept

The rise of the international business concept may be attributed, with varying degrees of impact, to (a) the establishment of the European Common Market and the European Free Trade Association; (b) the increasing nationalism in many parts of the world; (c) the rising standards of living in many countries; (d) the gradual entry of some of the Eastern European Communist countries into the world economic scene; and (e) the decline of colonial empires, particularly in Africa, which holds out promise of enhanced economic activity as the governments of these emerging nations become more stable.

For firms that embrace the international business concept, there are several matters of considerable import. In many instances negotiations with the governments of foreign lands will be requisite to their operating in these countries. A pattern of ownership must be established—through licensing, joint control (where the ownership of stock is shared by a foreign company and a national company), or wholly owned subsidiaries. Control policies for subsidiaries or affiliates must be determined upon for such factors as the product mix, the budget, accounting procedures, and sources and uses of funds. Policies must be established determining the selection, training, transfer, and promotion of managerial personnel. In short, the foreign operations of a firm engaged in international business must be thoroughly integrated with the overall corporate direction of the company concerned.

There are several items of importance upon which successful international business is dependent. Among these are the following: (a) the development of a permanent market for the producers' goods; (b) the reinvestment of the earnings in additional plant facilities, research, and development; (c) the development of products which are fitted for the markets that are sought; (d) the establishment of business practices that conform to local customs; (e) the employment of local personnel above the semiskilled category; and (f) the providing of adequate, prompt service for technical products sold.

Piggyback export sales. An international business practice of some years standing, but which has grown rapidly recently, is that of *piggyback export sales.* This is a procedure in which one producer uses its international distribution facilities to sell the products of another company along with its own. Prominent American firms that engage in this practice are the General Electric, Merck, Borg-Warner, and General Tire and Rubber companies. The benefits ascribed to this practice include the giving of more things to sell to foreign distributors; the broadening of product lines of the carrier companies providing the base for piggyback sales; and the bolstering of faltering sales abroad. While there are a number of different practices in this field, in most instances the carrier company buys the product that it is going to sell from its domestic producer and sells it abroad either under its own name or that of the manufacturer.

Multinational business. The term *multinational business* is applied to a growing number of firms whose home bases are in the United States, but whose operations extend to many parts of the free world (see Figure 12-3). Among these companies are the Caterpillar Tractor Company, International Telegraph and Telephone Company, Standard Oil Company (New Jersey), National Cash Register Company, Colgate-Palmolive Company, H. J. Heinz Company, and F. W. Woolworth Company. Such firms do not regard their overseas operations as mere adjuncts to their business in this country. Instead, they conceive of their organizations as multinational corporations, companies that may be located and incorporated in many foreign lands, but which are managed from their home offices in this country. It should be noted, however, that the multinational company is not solely an American institution. A large number of firms based in other lands conduct similarly widespread but centrally directed operations.

The advantages that are derived from the multinational philosophy of management and organization include the availability of managerial know-how for the direction of overseas plants and offices; the interchangeability

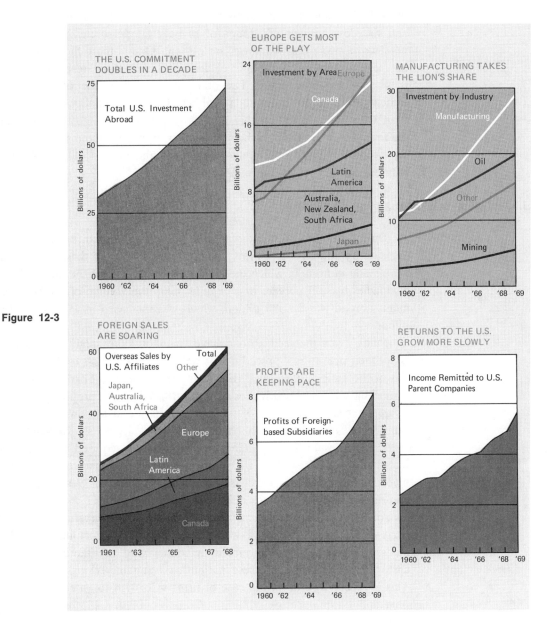

Figure 12-3

The Rise of the Multinationals

of both personnel and products between the different countries involved; and the development of groups of managerial personnel.

Two possible disadvantages are evident. One is the difficulty of securing personnel who are capable of assuming managerial responsibilities in these far-flung companies. The other is the rising tide of nationalism evident in many countries today, of which the potentiality of the European Common Market in this respect is perhaps the most serious. For the first problem, steps are being taken to arouse an interest in this field on the part of eligible personnel both here and abroad. The problem of nationalism is a much more difficult one.

U.S. Investments Abroad

During the 1960's, there was a notable growth of direct investments overseas by United States firms. About three fourths of these investments were made in firms in which the equity, or ownership, of the United States companies was 95 percent or more. In 1968 the volume of direct investments abroad was $3.025 billion, which was increased in 1969 to $3.060 billion.

Many firms that sell abroad have found it increasingly important to adapt their operational procedures as well as their products to the peculiarities of the nations concerned. For example, the Philco-Ford Corporation, a subsidiary of the Ford Motor Company, has found it profitable to adapt its appliances to the needs of the users in Italy and to construct production facilities in that country. It looks forward also to an expansion into other countries of Europe. General Electric has acquired a 49 percent interest in Machines Bull, the leading French manufacturer of business machines. Chrysler has purchased a majority interest in Simca of France and has substantial holdings in Britain's Rootes Motors.

American firms are coming to regard their foreign operations as integral parts of the companies as a whole, not merely as stepchildren in other lands. The need for management personnel who are familiar with the customs and practices of these nations is being increasingly recognized. This is especially true in the case of firms who wish to enter the fields of Asia and Latin America.

The Future of International Business

Assuming that there will not be a World War III, it would seem reasonable to anticipate that the concept of international business would continue to grow. As more and more United States firms become involved in international activity, it is expected that business will assume an ever greater international character. International operations will be handled on a vice-presidential level or higher, with more attention being given to this area by corporate executives. That there may be some deterring factors as the international economic situation develops is to be expected. Credit restrictions, exchange controls, rising tariff walls, and requirements that all or part of the goods offered for sale in some countries must be produced there, are circumstances to challenge the skill and resourcefulness of American businessmen.

FOREIGN AID PROGRAMS

For several years after the end of World War II, the United States undertook a broad program of foreign aid. By 1957 the European countries who benefited by this plan had recovered to the extent that the United States turned its attention along these lines to other lands. The Organization for European Economic Cooperation (OEEC), which had been formed by 18 European nations in 1948 to administer aid from the United States, was replaced by the Organization for Economic Cooperation and Development (OECD), of which the United States and Canada became members, along with the original 18 members of the OEEC. The purpose of this new group was not only to promote prosperity and economic growth among Western nations but also to assist underdeveloped nations to greater economic growth and stability.

At the same time the United States became active in aid to countries in the Near and Far East, in Africa, and particularly in Latin America. In the latter instance, the formation of the Alliance for Progress in 1960 signified the desire of the United States to aid the nations of Central and South America in their efforts to increase their per capita income, to achieve a more equitable distribution of their national income, and to diversify the economies of Latin American countries. The Inter-American Development Bank was established as an agency through which funds could be advanced to countries who qualified for aid under the Alliance for Progress.

INTERNATIONAL ARRANGEMENTS FOR TRADE AND PAYMENTS

After World War I, particularly during the depression years of the 1930's, and again since World War II, the intrusion of all governments into the international trade picture has been noteworthy. The balance of this chapter will be devoted to the principal arrangements that have been agreed upon between governments.

GENERAL AGREEMENT ON TARIFF AND TRADE

The General Agreement on Tariff and Trade, known commonly as GATT, contains a set of rules by which member governments agree to conduct their mutual international trade relations. It provides a means of reducing tariffs and other governmentally imposed barriers to international trade through negotiation. Established in 1947 at Geneva, Switzerland, 72 governments are associated with GATT. The United States participates under the authorization of the Trade Expansion Act.

TRADE EXPANSION ACT

The Trade Expansion Act of 1962 is a successor to a series of Reciprocal Trade Agreements Acts, which originated in 1934 and had been renewed periodically since then. This law permits the President of the United States to enter into international trade agreements for a period of five years. He is specifically empowered to cut any tariff up to 50 percent. Duties may be removed in part or entirely on goods in which 80 percent of world trade is accounted for by the United States and the European Economic Community.

The act includes provision for an *escape clause* whereby imports that are causing damage to domestic producers may be removed from the list of products upon which duties may be lowered. The President is also permitted to enter into marketing agreements with foreign countries, limiting the export of certain articles to the United States as a means of easing the impact of international competition on the producers of these goods in this country. There is also included a program of adjustment assistance to industries, firms, and worker groups who may be seriously injured or threatened with injury by increased imports resulting from concessions granted in trade agreements. This provision of the act has been invoked only rarely thus far.

The basic purpose of the act is to enable producers in this country to enter the European market by stimulating both exports and imports through reciprocal trade agreements.

As noted in Chapter 2, the United States took part under the authority of the Trade Expansion Act in the 53-nation Kennedy Round of tariff negotiations that took place from 1964 to 1967. At these negotiations the United States agreed to tariff concessions on a wide range of commodities including automobiles, steel, chemicals, apparel, appliances, and machinery. As a result of this series of negotiations, the reduction in tariffs on industrial goods averaged 35 percent.

EXPORT-IMPORT BANK

The Export-Import Bank is a federal lending agency created by an Act of Congress in 1934 and subsequently extended from time to time. Its purpose is to help promote trade between the United States and other countries through loans to importers and exporters in this country who are unable to secure adequate financing from private agencies. Aid may also be extended to foreign governments for the purpose of helping them in the development of their resources and in their international trade.

INTERNATIONAL BANK FOR RECONSTRUCTION AND DEVELOPMENT

This institution, commonly known as the World Bank, was organized in 1946 for the purpose of floating foreign loans in the private capital markets of members by giving an international guarantee. At present the subscription of member nations is around $22 billion of which the United States subscribed $6.4 billion. Over 100 countries are members, and the World Bank loans total nearly $10 billion.

The International Development Administration (IDA) was established in 1960 as an affiliate of the World Bank. Its purpose was to enable a number of developing countries to secure loans at no interest. As of the middle of 1968, some 100 countries had joined with total subscriptions of around $1 billion.

INTERNATIONAL MONETARY FUND

This institution began operations in 1947. Its aims are to provide the machinery for consultation and collaboration on international monetary problems; to facilitate the expansion and balanced growth of international trade; to promote stability of foreign exchange; to avoid competitive exchange depreciation; and to provide members with funds to meet temporary unfavorable trade balances.

FOREIGN TRADE ZONES

In 1934 the Foreign Trade Zones Act was passed by the Congress under which it has been possible for firms in the United States to bring in foreign materials to *foreign trade zones*, where they could be processed for reexport or for sale in this country. The advantageous aspect of the foreign trade zones is that the goods from other lands involved in this procedure are not subject to tariffs, quota restrictions, or other customs regulations, unless they are later destined for import into this country. The processing may take place in the established trade zones, or, more recently, the Foreign Trade Zones Board, which administers the law, has authorized the establishment of special purpose subzones which are set up at locations away from the regular zones for the purpose of manufacturing operations. This has resulted in substantial cost savings in manufacturing goods for export. As the volume of international business grows, it is expected that there will be a commensurate increase in the use of foreign trade zones by firms who are in a position to take advantage of these facilities. For some manufacturers where the duties on manufactured parts are less than on the materials from which they are made, there is a substantial saving through the use of the zones for goods intended for use in the United States. At present the seven foreign trade zones within the jurisdiction of the United States are in New York, New Orleans, San Francisco, Seattle, Toledo, Honolulu, and Mayaguez in Puerto Rico.

COMMON MARKETS

Two notable occurrences in Western Europe are bound to have far-reaching effects on international trade. In 1957, the Treaty of Rome established the European Economic Community (EEC) or the European Common Market. Signatories to the treaty were Belgium, France, Italy, Luxembourg, the Netherlands, and Western Germany. The broad purpose of this action was to lay the foundation for the gradual merging of the economies of these nations into a huge common market, to be accomplished by a progressive lowering of their tariffs and trade import quotas.

Following the organization of the European Common Market, Austria, Britain, Denmark, Norway, Portugal, Sweden, and Switzerland formed the European Free Trade Association (EFTA), sometimes called the Outer Seven, to promote trade among each other, but reserving the right to trade with other nations on terms of their own, which was a contrast with the nations of the EEC. Opinions have been expressed that eventually some or all of the EFTA nations would join the EEC.

The Central American Common Market, established in 1962, is made up of Costa Rica, El Salvador, Guatemala, Honduras, and Nicaragua. Its original objective was to enhance the economic growth of its members, but serious disagreement between El Salvador and Honduras has resulted in a significant lack of progress. Only the future will reveal its survival and possible growth of trade as originally envisioned.

The Latin American Free Trade Association was organized in 1961 with the hope of achieving essentially free trade by 1973 among its members which include Mexico, Venezuela, Colombia, Ecuador, Brazil, Peru, Chile, Bolivia, Paraguay, Argentina, and Uruguay. After some initial success, disagreements arose; so, the original goal date of 1973 may not be reached.

BUSINESS TERMS

QUESTIONS FOR DISCUSSION AND ANALYSIS

1. Should the government of the United States encourage domestic production of goods in which this country is at a cost disadvantage compared to other nations? Why or why not?

2. How important a factor in world peace is foreign trade?

3. The nations of the communist bloc are striving for a greater volume of trade with the noncommunist countries. Do you think this would be advantageous to this country if they should succeed? Explain.

4. What mutual advantages do you see in the resumption of United States trade with mainland China insofar as nonstrategic consumer goods are concerned?

5. Would there be any advantage to the adoption of a universal currency among the nations of the world? Why or why not?

6. Discuss the validity of each of the arguments in favor of a protective tariff.

7. Should all tariffs in the world be abolished? Why or why not?

8. Organized labor has generally taken a stand in favor of protective tariffs in order to keep out the products of lower-paid labor of other countries. What effect would the establishment of international unions have on this position?

9. Why does the United States contribute to the economic growth of countries that might eventually become competitors of ours?

10. Would you expect a resumption of trade with Cuba? Why or why not?

PROBLEMS AND SHORT CASES

1. A few of the nations of South America have taken over the plants owned by United States companies and have been very reluctant to recompense them for the loss of their investment caused by this action. Some of the other South American countries have threatened to take the same action. What should be the attitude of the United States companies to this expropriation and what action, if any, should be taken by the United States government? Prepare a short essay setting forth your views on this situation. Consult the files of *Business Week*, *Nation's Business*, *The Wall Street Journal*, and similar publications that you will find in your school library.

2. A number of American firms have established branch plants in Europe to manufacture products for both the European and the United States markets. Representatives of organized labor in this country have voiced disapproval of this practice, claiming that its main purpose is to secure the advantage of lower wage rates current in Europe. Prepare a statement in support of or in refutation to this charge, utilizing such arguments as you may secure from research among the various business publications in your school library.

3. The Sampson China Company is a manufacturer of vitrified dinnerware that is sold to hotels, restaurants, and private clubs. None of its products is designed for consumer purchase. It has two strong competitors in this field, but due to the excellence of its patterns and the sturdy character of the china, the company has long held a position of prominence in the industry. Since World War II, plastic dinnerware from Japan has been taking over an increasing share of the market for hotel dinnerware in this country, affecting the sales of the Sampson China Company quite unfavorably. To meet this competition, the members of the industry in this country are considering whether to try to secure higher tariffs on imported plastic dinnerware, to produce their own plastic products, or to engage in a strong sales promotional campaign designed to regain some of the market that has been lost to the Japanese products. The manufacturing processes involved in the production of plastic dinnerware are very different from those employed in making vitrified china dinnerware.

   What action should the Sampson China Company and the other members of this trade take? Justify your recommendations.

SUGGESTED READINGS

Kramer, Ronald L. *International Marketing*, Third Edition. Cincinnati: South-Western Publishing Co., 1970.

Leighton, Richard I. *Economics of International Trade*. New York: McGraw-Hill Book Company, 1970.

Powers, John J., Jr. "International Business: The Multinational Corporation," in *Preparing Tomorrow's Business Leaders Today* by Peter F. Drucker. Englewood Cliffs, New Jersey: Prentice-Hall, Inc., 1969.

Part 4

Personnel

Prologue to Part 4

Personnel

With due regard for the increasing mechanization of many aspects of the business world, the importance of the personnel phase must never be overlooked. The three chapters in Part 4 are designed to present the principal aspects of this vital segment of business.

Chapter 13 briefly refers to the problem of industrial human relations and then directs attention to the personnel department and its role in the finding and screening of potential employees for a wide range of jobs. Training methods for both new and current employees are described, as is the concept of the maintenance of employees' safety and health.

Chapter 14 is concerned with some of the economic theories of wages along with a recital of the major wage-determining factors. There is a discussion of the current methods of wage determination and their effectiveness in spurring workers to greater effort in their different job areas. This chapter also takes note of the roles of profit sharing, the guaranteed annual wage, and pensions.

Chapter 15 reviews certain aspects of the perennial subject of labor-management friction. The labor union movement is examined and its methods are discussed. The major labor laws of this country, which have been enacted in an attempt to alleviate labor-management friction, are set forth in some detail.

Chapter 13

Employee Selection and Training

With due regard for the great growth of automation, numerical control, and the many other advances that have been made in the productive processes of industry over the past few decades, it should never be overlooked that business is basically a phenomenon of people. Regardless of the size of the business, these essential people may be classified into two broad groups: employers and employees. Personnelwise, the major point of difference between small and large firms is the degree of detail involved in the selection and training of their employees. For the small business owner, whose contacts with his few employees may be constant and informal, the problem of finding, recruiting, and training workers is usually not too complex; whereas, the larger a company is, such as the General Motors Corporation or Sears, Roebuck and Company, the greater will be the question of personnel procurement and training and of maintaining a reasonably contented and productive work force. For the medium-size firms a continuous effort is required to find, select, and train the individuals whose skills, aptitudes, potentials, and personal preferences qualify them as employees.

The notable growth in the technological complexity in many of our industries, both in the office and in the factory, has placed increased emphasis on the problem of locating people who have the requisite skills or who are capable of acquiring them. The enhanced status of personnel departments, at least in the larger and more forward-looking firms in the country, gives evidence of the awareness by top management in these companies of the importance and complexity of the task of employee selection and training as well as that of human relations in industry.

NATURE AND BACKGROUND OF THE PROBLEM

A threefold problem is involved here: (a) the right people must be found and the proper choice made from those available; (b) those whose skill or experience is inadequate for the jobs in question must be trained to remedy this deficiency; and (c) it is very desirable that the conditions on the job be such that there will exist among the employees an attitude— a state of mind that will be favorable to the company—which is called "morale" or "esprit de corps."

In the period prior to the emergence of the medium-to-large-size companies, these problems were much simpler to handle. Then close contact was possible between employers and employees in all phases of personnel relationships.

The emergence of larger sized concerns, with employees numbering into the hundreds of thousands, brought about changes in all aspects of personnel dealings. This involved the development of different techniques for hiring new employees, for training them, and for the whole area of employer-employee relationships. While some of the old-time informality between bosses and workers still persists in small firms, in the larger companies today the applicant for a job meets a professional personnel manager or one of his assistants; the trainee goes through a routinized training procedure under the supervision of a professional training director; the worker, in many instances, feels little loyalty to the company; and, in some cases, the officers of the company apparently feel little sense of responsibility toward him.

The growing measure of labor unrest that has characterized the last 75 years or more is probably due, to a large degree, to the gap that has developed between employers and employees. Psychologists, sociologists, economists, and social anthropologists have been asked to study this problem and to suggest ways in which their disciplines could contribute toward the establishing of better relationships between employers and employees. From their efforts and researches has emerged the concept of industrial human relations described below.

INDUSTRIAL HUMAN RELATIONS

The basic objective of industrial human relations is to find newer and better methods of understanding man and his relationship to his work, and of motivating him to ever higher standards of workmanship. Management should so organize the work that it will provide the opportunity for self-realization on the part of the workers. Included in this objective is the need for management to provide the proper leadership and an organizational environment in which the workers may find satisfaction. Communication between workers and management should be improved so that necessary changes in policies and procedures may be understood and accepted affirmatively by the work force. Worker involvement in these matters should bring about a stronger and closer identification between workers, their work, and management.

The responsibility for the implementing of this concept of industrial human relations is not the province of the personnel department alone, although it should accept a major role in this endeavor. Rather, it should be the interest and duty of all managerial personnel to bring about the conditions just indicated. Furthermore, this must spring from a sincere belief in the desirability of achieving these objectives, for workers are quick to detect any artificiality on the part of management and will react unfavorably to it.

THE IMPORTANCE OF COMMUNICATION

A major contributing factor to the development of better personnel relations is found in the area of intracompany communication. The need for open channels of communication is coming to be recognized in a growing number of progressive firms. Communication is a three-way process—downward, upward, and horizontally. Workers should know more about managerial thinking, management should be aware of what is going on in the workers' minds, and there should be communication between those who occupy identical strata in the company's organization. There are several methods whereby this desirable communication can be achieved. Among these are: oral, face-to-face; employee newspapers and magazines; bulletin boards; handbooks; booklets; financial reports; letters from executives; and meetings.

A common practice in industry is the employee *suggestion box*, whereby workers are given the opportunity to present suggestions for improving efficiency or criticisms of company policies and practices. Many companies offer cash rewards to those workers whose contributions are of value to their employers. The establishing of open communication lines between employees and management has paid handsome dividends.

THE PERSONNEL DEPARTMENT—
STRUCTURE AND FUNCTIONS

Starting many years ago as an employment office, the personnel department has gradually expanded and added to its duties until now it embraces a rather wide range of personnel matters. The director of personnel is one of the key men in the firm, sometimes with vice-presidential rank. The other employees in the department are chosen for their demonstrated interest in and ability to meet the personnel problems of present-day industry.

The many duties of the personnel department are allocated naturally into the following divisions: employment, training, personnel services, safety and health, personnel research, wages and salaries, and labor relations (see Figure 13-1). The first five of these divisions will be discussed in this chapter; the subject of wages and salaries will be discussed in Chapter 14 and that of labor relations in Chapter 15.

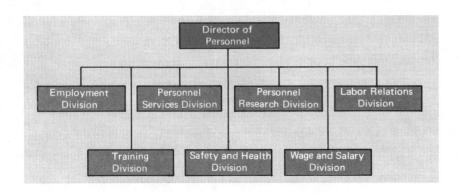

Figure 13-1

Organization Chart of the Personnel Department

EMPLOYMENT DIVISION

The principal purpose of modern hiring procedures is to fill all jobs that become vacant with the best equipped and trained workers that can be found. The so-called round pegs should be fitted into the round holes, and the square pegs into the square holes. This results in a more effective labor force and a lower labor turnover. The United States Department of Labor has defined *labor turnover* as "the replacements in a working force made necessary by employees leaving the service." It is generally regarded as an index of the stability of the employee group in a business concern. Where labor turnover is high, the presumption is that all is not well personnelwise within the plant. Conversely, where labor turnover is low, good personnel conditions are believed to exist. There may, of course, be external circumstances, such as a high rate of unemployment in an area, that might contribute to a low labor turnover rate without regard to whether or not good personnel conditions prevailed.

Job Analysis, Description, and Specification

The first step in an intelligent approach to the problem of securing the best people for a group of jobs is to discover all of the pertinent facts relative to each job. This procedure is known as *job analysis* and involves inquiry into all the details of each position in the company that the personnel department might be called upon to fill. Nothing that pertains to or affects a job is too small to be noted and set down on the record.

Among the topics that should be covered in a job analysis are the location of the job; its duties and responsibilities; the equipment, tools, or machines used; the working conditions; the pay; the opportunities for promotion; and whether or not any training for the job is offered. It is furthermore desirable that data be gathered concerning the qualifications that are required of the prospective employee. These data can be secured from department heads or the present workers, or both. Occasionally a firm of personnel management consultants is called in if the magnitude or complexity of this work warrants this action.

The information that is gathered during the job analysis which relates strictly to the job itself is then put in writing in the *job description*, a sample of which is shown in Figure 13-2. From the personnel data provided by the job analysis, the *job specification* is also prepared. This consists of a statement of the personal qualifications required of prospective employees for each type of job, such as skill, age, experience, and special aptitudes.

Armed with the job descriptions and job specifications for all positions, the employment division of the personnel department is equipped to proceed intelligently with the task of securing the best available workers for any jobs that must be filled.

Sources of Workers

The sources of supply for prospective employees are many and varied. The extent to which the more common ones can be utilized depends upon the nature of the business, the degree of skill required for the different jobs,

JOB TITLE: PERSONNEL CLERK

Department: Personnel

Employees in Department: 12

Employees on This Job: 3

Date: March 26, 1972

Name: James Thomas

General Description of the Job

Works under the supervision of the Personnel Manager; assists in clerical routine of induction which involves interviewing new workers; performs a variety of clerical and stenographic work.

Specific Duties of the Job

1. Interviews new workers after they have been given induction information such as hours, working conditions, services, etc., to verify personnel information and prepare records; checks information on application, statement of availability, draft, citizenship, and the like; obtains necessary information for income tax withholding, and determines classification; prepares forms for hospitalization, group insurance, and bond deductions; assigns clock number, makes up time card and badge card.

2. Calls previous employer to get reference information while applicant is being interviewed; may check references by mail after employee is hired, and occasionally records information from Dun & Bradstreet on personnel card.

3. Telephones employee's department or home after extended absence to determine when employee is expected to return, if at all; follows same procedure at end of leave of absence.

4. Handles stenographic work of Personnel Manager.

5. Does miscellaneous clerical work; assigns clock numbers and makes up time cards for employees transferred between departments; keeps record of equipment loaned to employees, such as micrometers, goggles, etc.; maintains current address file of employees in service; performs other clerical duties as assigned.

6. May substitute for Receptionist for short periods; give induction information to new employees in absence of Personnel Induction Clerk; escort new workers to departments; administer tests.

Figure 13-2

Job Description

and the character of the population in the area in which the plant is located. These sources include past and present employees, their friends and relatives, applications on file in the employment office, state employment agencies, private employment agencies, employment scouts, schools and colleges, trade and technical schools, classified advertising, and union headquarters and hiring halls. A recently developed source of workers is the *Opportunity Line*, a television placement show which originated in the Chicago area in 1967 and has since been copied by television stations in other major cities of the country. This show tells viewers of the jobs immediately available in the area as well as invites employers or personnel managers to phone special numbers to list their job openings. Although the original aim was to hit the emergency summer work force market, Opportunity Line now receives and disseminates information about jobs which range from low-skill, low-pay positions to professional and middle-management ones.[1]

Some concerns have a policy of looking first within their own organizations for workers to fill all jobs above the beginning or lowest grades. For example, the variety chains, such as the F. W. Woolworth Company and the S. S. Kresge Company, have long adhered strictly to this policy, which is presumed to enhance the morale among their employees. Other firms are more or less indifferent regarding the sources of their new workers, endeavoring always to obtain the best available candidates regardless of other factors.

A point of some consequence from the standpoint of human relations concerns the question of whether or not the employees should be informed of vacancies in departments other than their own and be given the opportunity to apply for them if they believe themselves qualified. In some instances workers have resented not being told of positions in other departments that were filled from outside the plant. That some managements are aware of this situation is evidenced by occasional "help wanted ads," particularly for positions of some responsibility, which contain a statement to the effect that the company's employees have been informed of the advertisement.

In many companies some executives hire relatives or personal friends when attractive positions are open. This frequently has a disquieting effect on the other employees, especially when more deserving applicants are turned away in favor of mediocre individuals. The hiring or promoting of relatives solely on the basis of family connections is known as *nepotism*.

---

[1] "How to Land a Job by Watching TV," *Business Week*, May 9, 1970, p. 24.

Within recent years a new element has been introduced in the form of a movement, sponsored in part by the National Alliance of Businessmen, whereby the so-called hard-core unemployed are encouraged to apply for jobs. The term *hard-core* has many definitions. It includes persons who are unemployed because they are illiterate, i.e., unable to read English at the sixth-grade level; who possess no employable skills; who have never applied for a job anywhere; and who come from disadvantaged backgrounds due to poverty, race, or national origins. The term *functional illiteracy* is used in referring to persons whose backgrounds have previously prevented them from being considered as eligible for employment. This new entrant into the area of sources of workers has brought with it many problems the solutions for which may require a long period of experimentation before they can be regarded as successful endeavors in the field of human relations.

The Employment Process

Several steps are involved in the employment process (see Figure 13-3). Any or all of them may be used in any given instance, depending upon the policies of the companies concerned. These include: (a) application blank, (b) preliminary interview, (c) tests, (d) investigation of applicant's background, (e) physical examination, and (f) main interview.

The order of the steps in employment procedures is frequently based on placing first the ones that may reveal the necessity of rejecting an applicant. Thus the physical examination might be placed ahead of the other steps in a company where some physical attributes were essential to the job, such as strength or unusual manual dexterity.

In recent years tests have been used as a means of determining the fitness of applicants for the jobs to which they aspire. These tests are used for the purpose of measuring (a) so-called general intelligence or mental alertness, (b) aptitude or basic talents along particular lines, and (c) ability or proficiency in given trades or skills. While there has been some criticism of the value and possible discriminatory effects of these tests, they are generally useful employment techniques.

The main interview is usually the occasion when the applicant is either definitely hired or rejected. If psychological tests are administered or a physical examination is required, these usually precede the main interview. During this conversation the employment official endeavors to make a final evaluation of the applicant and to determine whether or not he should be hired. It is a crucial point in the employment procedure, and one to which personnel experts have given considerable thought and

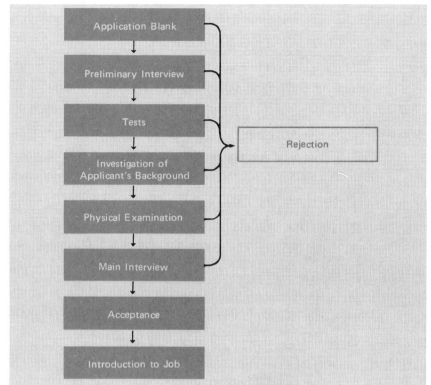

Figure 13-3

The Employment Process

study because of the wide variations in the conclusions that may result from several different people's interviewing the same applicant. In some companies the interviewer has a prescribed form to follow, with a fixed series of questions and remarks. Others allow their interviewers a free hand in conducting their conferences, merely holding them responsible for the selection of good workers and for the rejection of poor ones.

Legal Restrictions on Hiring Policies

Under the federal Civil Rights Act of 1964 it is illegal to hire or favor an applicant for a job over another solely on account of race. Employment cannot be denied to a woman solely for reasons of her sex. No worker can be discharged because of his color, religion, national origin, or sex. Preference in pay raises or promotions that discriminate against certain employees because of their sex or national origin is illegal. Aptitude tests can still be administered, but the employer must be sure that the tests administered are the same to all applicants. Unions and employment agencies are also forbidden to discriminate in membership or employment recommendations because of race, color, religion, national origin, or sex. The act applies to companies or unions with 25 or more employees or members.

The Equal Employment Opportunity Commission of five members has been established to administer the provisions of the act. There will probably be many points of law that must be determined by the EEOC, and eventually by the courts, before the full implications of the act become apparent. There are also 26 states that have Fair Employment Practices Codes, which have the same objectives as the federal act.

For government contractors and subcontractors the President's Commission on Equal Employment Opportunity has the power to cancel contracts held by companies that practice discrimination in employment.

Postemployment Procedures

The responsibility of the Employment Division for the new worker does not cease when his name is added to the payroll. It sees that he is properly launched on his new career and checks on his progress.

Introduction to the job. After the applicant has been hired, he must be properly introduced to all of the details and personnel connected with the job. He must be directed to the department where he will work and be presented to his superiors and, in some instances, to his co-workers.

The details of this introduction vary with different firms. A common procedure is for a representative of the personnel division to accompany the new employee to the locale of the job and arrange for the meeting with the foreman. The latter, in turn, shows the newcomer where he will work and explains the details of the job. Many foresighted companies have found it worthwhile to make this introduction as friendly and cordial as possible in order to put the new man in a good frame of mind and to enlist his best abilities right from the start.

Certain details concerning the company and the job must be imparted to new employees so that they may understand the policies and rules of the company and fit themselves into the picture with the least friction or delay. These matters include hours of work, lunchroom facilities, attendance rules, rest periods, safety rules, locker or coatroom facilities, methods and times of wage payment, employees' organizations, recreational facilities, and medical services available. This information is usually printed in booklet form and presented to the new employee with the request that he read it and familiarize himself with its contents.

Follow-ups. Some companies have a policy of periodic follow-up on new workers, the purpose of which is to discover the character of performance that they are putting forth, whether or not they are happy in their jobs, and so on. The first of these follow-ups may occur at any time within the first few days after employment and the others at more or less regular intervals thereafter, sometimes twice a year.

A few firms make an annual checkup on the performance of all of their employees. This is sometimes referred to as the *personnel audit.* The customary procedure is for a committee, consisting of representatives of top management as well as of the personnel division, to examine the records and achievements of all employees, including those in supervisory positions. As the result of their findings, the committee recommends promotions, pay changes, censure, demotion, or discharge, as the case may be. In some cases employee rating sheets are used as a means of standardizing the review procedures.

A number of companies hire firms of management engineers or of psychologists to check on the fitness of their employees for the jobs that they hold. This process is called *personal evaluation* and consists of setting up job descriptions for the various positions and then determining the competency of the incumbents for their jobs. It is only fair to state that there are rather sharp differences of opinion among businessmen concerning the value of this procedure.

Another evaluation method is used where each employee is rated by his superior on his performance on the job, personality, potentiality, attitude towards his work, promotion possibilities, and anything else that is important for management to determine his fitness for his job.

Both the personnel audit and the personal evaluation, or any other method which is used to appraise the work of employees, require careful preparation and execution in order to secure the maximum benefits both for the company and its workers. Failure to follow these procedures is apt to result in feelings of unrest and insecurity on the parts of those employees who are subjected to the evaluation process.

Transfer, Promotion, and Involuntary Termination

These three personnel functions are common to all companies. If not correctly handled, they may have very unfortunate results on employer-employee relations.

Transfer. *Transfer* is the shifting of a worker from one job to another that does not involve the employment of greater skills or the assumption of additional responsibilities. Transfers take place to offset a decrease in the work load in a department; to correct a faulty placement and to give an employee work more suited to his abilities; to take care of older workers who must be assigned to lighter tasks; to transfer promising employees from jobs without opportunity for promotion; to rotate workers in dangerous or unpleasant jobs; to afford employees training in several jobs; and frequently to alleviate unfortunate personal experiences or incompatibility with supervisors or fellow workers.

Policies and rules governing transfers must be established in order that the employees affected may feel certain that they are being given fair consideration and treatment, and not merely being pushed around at someone's whim.

Promotion. *Promotion* may be defined as the advancement of an employee to a job that requires greater skill and larger responsibilities with, customarily, a commensurate advance in compensation. There are many reasons for promotions, foremost among which is the need for a company to place its men in positions where their mental and physical capacities will be most useful for their employer. Other reasons include the rewarding of good performance; the retention of valuable employees; and the maintaining of the morale of the workers. It may be assumed that, whenever a promotion takes place, some of those not thus favored will be unhappy. If the advancement has come as a reward for demonstrated merit, however, and if it has been carefully considered before being announced, the effect on the other employees will be more favorable than when the opposite is the case.

A carefully thought-out promotion policy should be established. Apart from the ill effects of infrequent promotions, few circumstances will wreak more havoc with the esprit de corps of an organization than the practice of ill-advised or undeserved promotions.

Three factors should be considered when a promotion is being considered: (a) the personal and technical requirements of the job; (b) the ability of the worker under consideration to satisfy them, as compared to that of the other employees; and (c) the length of his service with the company. This latter point, which is called *seniority*, is of vital importance in its effect on other employees of the firm who regard themselves as eligible for the advancement. Where two or more individuals of approximately equal abilities are being considered for a promotion, it is usually the part of wisdom for management to select the one with the greatest seniority.

As mentioned earlier, nepotism sometimes also plays a part where promotions are concerned. If the favored persons have outstanding ability, the fact that they are related to the bosses will be a matter of passing moment, as their superiority will doubtless become quickly apparent and the wisdom of their being selected will be realized. The morale of the firm's personnel may be seriously impaired, however, if the persons concerned are less able than some of those who are passed over at times of promotions. These points must be borne in mind if the management wishes to avoid stirring up resentment among the other workers and crippling their morale. When a company establishes a policy of carefully scrutinizing every proposed promotion in these respects and then follows it consistently, the danger of unfavorable consequences is greatly diminished.

Involuntary termination. The involuntary termination of an employee's services may take either of two forms: a discharge or a layoff. A *discharge* involves the permanent separation of an employee from a company's service which is accompanied by a stigma against the employee. (The term "discharge" as used here should not be confused with that obtained from the Armed Forces after one has rendered his military duty.) Many of the reasons why an employee is discharged center on himself, such as incompetence, insubordination, laziness, and incompatibility. Some research into the reasons for the discharge of office personnel and junior executives has revealed that the inability of those discharged to get along with their fellow employees ranked at the top of the list.

To effect a discharge, policies range from the simplest, where the mere word of a superior is sufficient, to quite complex procedures that call for the referral of all proposed discharges to committees, formal statements of charges, hearings in which the prospective dischargee is given a chance to defend himself, and a final review by the personnel manager. In many companies it is the policy to endeavor to effect a transfer of the employee concerned to some other department, unless the charge is insubordination or something similar. Regardless of the length of the procedures specified, it is customary for the management to uphold the supervisor who initiated the move toward the discharge, at least as far as the department is concerned. And even when a foreman has made a mistake, management will generally consent to the worker's transfer from the department, rather than a discharge, if his foreman insists.

While a *layoff* may be either a permanent or a temporary separation, it casts no reflection upon the competence or character of the employee concerned. The reasons for a layoff are usually concerned with company policies, such as the elimination by automation of the activities in which the employee has been engaged or the presence of cyclical or competitive influences that necessitate a reduction in the work force. A layoff usually results from a diminution of work, either in a particular department or in the company as a whole, and it assumes reemployment as soon as conditions have become better. Within certain limits it is customary to effect layoffs in reverse order of seniority, i.e., those with the shortest period of service are the first to go.

In companies that are unionized, totally or in part, transfer, promotion, discharge, and layoff are customarily made the subjects of negotiation between the unions and the employers, with the result that the conditions affecting each action are set forth in considerable detail in the union-company contracts. Obviously where this is the case, the companies must abide by the contract provisions. In many of these contracts the matter of seniority is of first importance, at least in regard to transfer, layoff, and discharge. Frequently the union has the power to nullify the action of management if it sees fit. Whether this has contributed to better personnel relations in these companies is possibly open to some question.

TRAINING DIVISION

All new employees require a certain amount of training before they can give their best efforts to their jobs. This training is of two types: training for the job and training on the job.

Training for the Job

This type of training is given before the new worker starts on the job. It is used where the jobs are rather complex and where inexperienced operators cannot be permitted to function without seriously interfering with the production flow.

Many firms operate so-called *company schools* to which new employees are sent after they are hired but before they are assigned to their jobs. In these schools they are given the requisite instruction for handling their jobs and they are tested for the proficiency that they acquire. These schools are staffed by special instructors who frequently devote their entire time to teaching. Obviously this sort of school is useful only where many workers are to be trained and where the training period is of more than brief duration. The Ford Motor Company has long maintained a training school of this type. In some companies the term *vestibule school* is applied to this type of training setup.

The opening of employment opportunities by many companies to disadvantaged persons who would previously not have been considered, as mentioned earlier in this chapter, has brought with it many new training problems. In some instances the hard-core unemployed have had to be taught to read and write and to follow simple instructions before they could become eligible for consideration as prospective employees. Following this it has been necessary to attempt to instill a sufficient measure of self-confidence in the newly hired employees so that they can approach the training program with a reasonable hope of success. In addition, it has been necessary to convince supervisors of the need for and value of the hard-core training programs, not always an easy task. The automobile industry has been in the forefront of this movement with results that have been reported as better than acceptable. As the employment of the hard-core grows throughout industry, it is reasonable to assume that some of the racial tensions in the country may be relaxed, although it is perhaps too early to make a firm prediction along this line. It would appear that few activities offer as great a promise of hope among the hard-core unemployed as these which seek them out and give them training in the basic attitudes and skills requisite for them to become self-sustaining members of their communities.

Training on the Job

Certain types of work lend themselves to training on the job, whereby the employee learns while doing. These are usually fairly simple jobs, where the presence of unskilled workers does not seriously affect the smooth operation of the business.

The training may be given by foremen or supervisors, by experienced operators, or by special instructors employed for this purpose. In department stores the *sponsor system* is often used, whereby an older employee "sponsors" the new worker for the first few days and teaches her the details of the job. In some stores the sponsor receives the commission on the sales made by the new employee during the training period.

The *apprenticeship system* is one in which inexperienced workers are apprenticed to master craftsmen for a period of years, during which time they are supposed to become thoroughly grounded in their trades. This method of training is found in the building trades and, to some extent, in firms that manufacture machinery, but it is not common in other branches of industry. One of the reasons is that with the gradual change in the character of many factory jobs, whereby merely the ability to operate a specialized type of machine is required rather than the skill of an all-round machinist, the vestibule school is able to provide the requisite training in a matter of days, and the need for the prolonged period of apprenticeship no longer exists.

The building trades, which include carpenters, plumbers, and electrical workers, have presented a rather knotty problem in the area of training on the job. The apprenticeship system just noted has been blamed by civil rights officials for preventing the entry into these trades of minority group members, thus denying them the opportunity of gaining the necessary skills to become full-fledged journeymen in these fields. Only time will reveal the extent to which these complaints are justified.

Foremanship training. A considerable number of companies offer courses in foremanship. These are designed to enable foremen more adequately to discharge their duties as the representatives of management in closest contact with the workers. The old concept of the foreman as a rough, domineering boss, whose physique and language kept his workers in a state of constant awe, has long since been discarded. In its place has come the modern idea of the foreman as an executive whose main task is that of securing the greatest amount of production at the lowest cost. Instruction is now available in the many facets of the job, and as a result more intelligent and effective foremen are secured. In many industries the rapid pace of technological change has brought with it a need for the retraining of foremen in the new techniques and procedures that these developments require of supervision.

Increasing attention is now being given to the human relations and leadership aspects of foremanship. When a man is promoted to the job of foreman, he becomes a member of management, albeit at the lowest level, and he now finds himself more or less isolated from his former co-workers and must adjust his thinking to the possibility of role conflict with them. An intelligent foremanship training program will direct the trainee's attention to this situation and warn him of the difficulties that may confront him in his new role as a boss.

Executive training. Many firms maintain training courses for selected college graduates. These are frequently designed to provide broad schooling in all phases of the business, with the expectation that the trainees will find their own places in the organization as the plans unfold. The management training course of the Jones and Laughlin Steel Corporation is an example of such a program.

Executive training at rather high levels is offered by some firms which believe that the way to be assured of good executives is to select the individuals with great care and give them thorough training, not only in the essentials of their jobs, but also in the broader aspects of economics and business practices and policies. Increased emphasis is being placed on human relations and the development of leadership, skill in writing and speaking, creativity, and analytical skills. Sometimes these courses are given on the companies' premises with instructors drawn from the firms' executives; in other cases the facilities of local educational institutions are utilized, with the tuition paid by the company. The executive programs of the Harvard, Chicago, and Columbia Graduate Schools of Business are examples of the latter type of approach to executive training.

With the increasing importance of the personnel aspect of the managerial function has come the concept of personnel relations as an overall company activity. As a result, training in the techniques of good personnel relations is offered not merely to foremen and employees of the personnel division, but also to other supervisors and to company executives at all levels.

Among the methods used in executive training is the creation of staff assistant jobs as understudies to senior executives. Another procedure is *job rotation* which is designed to familiarize junior executives with the details of the many different positions that may be available to them and to reveal any natural abilities that they may possess. A recent development in this area is *sensitivity training* in which small groups of trainees hold sessions for several days for the purpose of helping them learn more about each other's personalities and about the ways in which others react to them, thereby improving their effectiveness in dealing with people. At present, however, this method of management training must be regarded as experimental.

Retraining

Retraining employees whose jobs have been discontinued has always been a problem in industry to some degree. However, the advent of automation, which in some instances has involved the replacement of relatively large numbers of workers by the automated machinery, has raised to a position of considerable importance the issue of the retraining of these unfortunate individuals. As stated previously, the fundamental reason for the adoption of automation is that of achieving cost savings, usually in labor costs. This can result in the permanent layoff of workers whose jobs are taken over by the machines, and many companies have been reluctant to take such a drastic step. On the other hand, there is the question of how these displaced workers can be absorbed in the organizations.

In many instances the introduction of automated equipment has eliminated the need for some unskilled or semiskilled workers at the same time that it has created a need for highly skilled operatives to set up, run, and repair the new complicated machinery. The question then arises as to whether the workers whose jobs have disappeared have sufficient native ability to qualify for retraining for the more skilled positions. Furthermore, unless there is a significant increase in the company's productivity or a decrease in the unit cost of the product, it would appear that only a fraction of the workers involved could be assimilated into the higher skills, leaving the remainder with the necessity of finding employment elsewhere.

Currently the Manpower Development and Training Act (MDTA) of 1962, administered by the Bureau of Apprenticeship and Training of the U. S. Department of Labor, provides occupational training and pay allowances to selected unemployed workers or those whose skills have become obsolete. In many instances this training is available "on the job" in the plants where the workers are employed.

PERSONNEL SERVICES DIVISION

The idea that the duty of an employer should include something other than paying good wages and providing a safe place to work has made notable headway in the past few decades. Progressive companies have come to recognize that *personnel services,* as this area of activity is known, if offered as a concomitant of acceptable wage rates and not as a substitute, are a potent force in bringing about a happier and more contented employee group, lessening labor turnover, and increasing the productive effectiveness of the personnel. It is through the many functions of this division that the attempt is made to bring about better human relations.

Types of Personnel Services

The list of personnel service activities is a long one. Eating facilities, rest rooms, and locker rooms are found in many plants and large stores. Recreational opportunities take the form of football, baseball, and bowling teams sponsored by the firms. Some plants provide handball, volley ball, and tennis courts, with the necessary equipment for the workers. Legal advice and assistance is sometimes made available to employees through the company's legal department. Many concerns encourage the establishment of credit unions. Employee savings plans help the workers put aside a part of their earnings. For all but the first three items of the foregoing group, the personnel services division customarily offers to assist the employees only if they wish to engage in these activities.

Group insurance and hospitalization plans have been common for several years. Retirement and disability plans, which are financed either by the employers alone or jointly by them and the employees, have become increasingly frequent. Since 1949, when certain unions in the automobile and steel industries won pensions financed entirely by the employers, public interest has been increasingly focused on this aspect of personnel relations. The advent of social security in 1935 has given added emphasis to the problem of taking care of superannuated workers.

Employee Counseling Service

A comparatively recent development in the field of personnel services is that of employee counseling. This usually involves the employment of professional psychologists whose services are made available without charge to those employees who wish assistance in the solution of their problems. In addition to their work along these lines, the psychologists devote a considerable part of their time to the devising and perfecting of tests to be used in screening applicants for employment. They may also assist in any other aspects of the hiring procedure where their professional training and experience are valuable.

A subject in which the managements of a growing number of firms have become interested in the past few years is the retirement plans of their older employees. Not only is provision made for pensions, but attempts are being made to prepare their workers for the forthcoming change in their status through counseling, suggesting hobbies, and otherwise trying to help them to effect the transition in as smooth a manner as possible. One company is experimenting with the idea of setting up a preretirement period of several months, during which the eligible employees gradually taper off their hours of work at the rate of one additional free day each month until finally they stop working altogether. As yet the results of this test are inconclusive, but it is indicative of some of the thinking that is taking place in this area of personnel relations.

SAFETY AND HEALTH DIVISION

The promotion of employee safety has made rapid strides, not merely as a humanitarian measure, but also because many firms have discovered that the prevention of industrial accidents is desirable as an aid to a continued high rate of production. This movement is manifested through the installation of safety devices of all kinds on dangerous machinery and through the dissemination of safety information to workers. In this latter activity, safety clubs, literature, posters, and contests are enlisted for the purpose of making employees safety-conscious. An added incentive for employers to stress the safety theme is the presence, in almost all states, of workmen's compensation acts which, while they vary somewhat from state to state, generally increase the cost to a company that has a bad accident record and, conversely, reward a concern that is able to reduce the number of its accidents by lowering its required contributions.

A few companies have quite adequate medical and dental facilities available to their employees; others have nurses on hand, with physicians available on call; but the majority of businesses, particularly small ones, have little or nothing along this line.

Where industrial medical attention is provided for the workers, it is intended to supplement rather than to supplant the outside medical care that they receive from their family physicians. First-aid treatment of injuries is of prime importance, and all other treatment is secondary. Many companies treat colds, headaches, and other ailments, and are thus able to provide a service that their employees might not otherwise enjoy, in addition to lowering the absentee rate in most instances. The dental services offered by a few concerns are supposed to be used solely for the treatment of emergency cases and probably follow this policy fairly closely.

Many companies offer periodic physical examinations to their employees as a means of helping to maintain their health. These are valuable to both employers and workers. In this way employers can detect physical defects of which the individuals are often unaware and suggest remedial measures before the trouble has progressed too far. A common requirement is that all persons who have been absent because of illness or injury report to the medical department for examination before returning to work.

In recent years the more far-seeing companies have recognized a condition among their employees that is known as *industrial fatigue*. It results from too long application to the job. It produces diminished perceptive faculties and a proneness to accidents. Long hours, overtime, and Sunday work, with insufficient rest, bring about industrial fatigue. Poor working conditions; faulty lighting, heating, or ventilation; and excessive monotony in the job are all contributing factors. Occasionally industrial fatigue appears as the result of the placement of individuals in jobs for which they are definitely unfitted.

The remedy for this condition is found in its causes. Shorter hours, rest periods, better working conditions, and, for the persons wrongly placed, transfer to more congenial work are the best methods of combating industrial fatigue. As a part of the growing interest in human relations in industry, some firms have been exploring the possibility of helping workers to gain a sense of accomplishment in their work as a further means of combating industrial fatigue.

To relieve the sense of boredom that is experienced by many workers in jobs which involve a considerable measure of repetition, some companies have introduced the concept of *job enlargement*. This involves the designing of an employee's job so that he performs several related operations in the production cycle, instead of just one, as previously. Another approach to this is to create a team which is responsible for the completion of several operations. How successful this procedure may be is dependent, to a considerable extent, on the personalities of the individuals involved.

PERSONNEL RESEARCH DIVISION

In those companies that maintain a personnel research division within the personnel department organization, it is customary for this group to be concerned with such matters as records and reports; statistical analyses of personnel records; the publication of manuals for the guidance of the department; the systems and procedures followed by or prescribed for the department; and the administration of personnel audits and evaluations. An activity which has been growing for some time is that of maintaining personnel records in computers. Prior to this development, all such facts were kept in personnel data folders, a practice that did not lend itself to a rapid retrieval of information regarding the employees of a company. With this new practice, such data as name, age, social security number, work experience, salary level, skills, and other pertinent characteristics can be recorded in the computer, permitting a speedy disclosure to personnel officers of a wide variety of specifications concerning the work force. This is especially valuable when management wishes to locate individuals in the company whose records, skills, and other characteristics would suggest their promotability to better jobs. A start has been made toward the recording of the results of researches in the behavioral sciences with the hope that further progress in this field will aid management in appraising the probability of success in their new jobs of the individuals whose other attributes appear favorable.

A few companies have developed a computerized file of prospective employees, which enables them to locate individuals not in the employ of the firms whose abilities have become needed. Among the companies that use computers for the storing of personnel information are Ford Motor Company, International Business Machines Corporation, Standard Oil Company (N. J.), and General Electric Company.

Another innovation in this field is that of research among employees in an attempt to discover worker attitudes toward the various aspects of their jobs, and particularly toward their employers. The General Motors Corporation has established its Employee Research to undertake this activity; this department endeavors to sound out employee thinking by questionnaires and by inviting the workers to submit written comments about their jobs. Other firms have employed outside research agencies to secure the same information, sometimes utilizing the group interview technique, in which a group of workers is invited to talk things over with representatives of the agency. One of the purposes of these researches is to provide better means of communication between workers and management, particularly in the upward flow of ideas, suggestions, and criticisms.

A phenomenon of the present is the changing points of view of the various age groups with whom management has to deal. Older workers tend to become more conservative in their thinking as the years pass while the younger ones exhibit impatience with what they conceive to be the slow progress which is available to them in the first years of their employment. This attitude makes for a varying degree of dissatisfaction with entering jobs and causes many young people to switch jobs in the hope of making more rapid progress. For management this is a disquieting phenomenon that prevents, to some extent, the development and maintenance of a stable, reliable work force. Viable solutions to this problem are not easy to find and must await the further evolving of young people's attitudes.

BUSINESS TERMS

QUESTIONS FOR DISCUSSION AND ANALYSIS

1. What steps can be taken to lower the labor turnover rate in a department where it is abnormally high?
2. Do you think that the Opportunity Line would be an effective method of bringing jobs and workers together? Why?
3. Do you agree with the policy of the limited-price variety stores of making promotions only from within their organizations? Why or why not?
4. Under what circumstances might a policy of nepotism be beneficial to a company?
5. What is your opinion of the value, to the companies and to the personnel involved, of the personal evaluation procedure? Explain your stand.
6. Evaluate the policy followed by some firms of transferring misfits from department to department in an endeavor to find suitable places for them.
7. How should a company which is about to introduce laborsaving machinery handle the problem of selecting the workers who will be adversely affected by this move?
8. Should a foreman have the final word with regard to the discharge of one of the workers in his department? Explain.
9. Do you approve of the apprenticeship system? Why or why not?
10. Do you believe that sensitivity training is an advantageous policy for improving the effectiveness of potential executives? Explain.

PROBLEMS AND SHORT CASES

1. A former prominent labor leader, noted during his lifetime for his outspoken views on the social aspects of labor relations, promulgated the concept of "inverted seniority" under which the so-called hard-core employees would be kept on the job during times of temporary layoffs and those with the greatest seniority would be asked to volunteer for layoff at 95% of their base pay for a year. Comment on the workability of such a scheme and give your opinion as to its justification.
2. Prepare a job description for a position with which you are familiar or for which you can secure the necessary information. Also prepare a job specification for this position.
3. The R. H. Platt Company manufactures highly specialized equipment that is rather widely used in the production of many different types of food products, particularly in the area of frozen fruits and vegetables. This company has been among the pioneers in the development and introduction of improvements in the food-processing industry and is very well regarded in the trade. Recently its

research and development division, quite by chance, invented some machinery that would be applicable to the petroleum refining industry. In the belief that there is a profitable market for this new product, the Platt Company is considering promoting it to oil refiners. Unfortunately there is no one in the organization who has had any experience in the oil business. Also, a long tradition of family ownership and management has tended to confine the managerial personnel to members of the Platt family, of whom there are a large number in the firm. The company is, therefore, faced with the problem of deciding whether to train some of the members of the family in the petroleum business or to hire, for managerial positions, personnel who know the oil business and can immediately assume the responsibility for marketing the new machinery. Prepare a written report advising the company with regard to its action in this situation. Give the reasons for your suggestions.

SUGGESTED READINGS

Chruden, Herbert J., and Arthur W. Sherman, Jr. *Personnel Management*, 4th Edition. Cincinnati: South-Western Publishing Co., 1972.

French, Wendell. *The Personnel Management Process: Human Resources Administration*, Second Edition. Boston: Houghton Mifflin Company, 1970. Parts V and VI.

Pigors, Paul, and Charles A. Myers. *Personnel Administration*, Sixth Edition. New York: McGraw-Hill Book Company, 1969. Part 4.

Reynolds, Lloyd G. *Labor Economics and Labor Relations*, 5th Ed. Englewood Cliffs, New Jersey: Prentice-Hall, Inc., 1970. Part One.

Siegel, Laurence. *Industrial Psychology*, Revised Edition. Homewood, Illinois: Richard D. Irwin, Inc., 1969. Part II.

Wasmuth, William J., *et al. Human Resources Administration: Problems of Growth and Change*. Boston: Houghton Mifflin Company, 1970.

Chapter 14

Employee Compensation

For most people the satisfaction of human needs is the driving force which impels them to engage in some form of economic endeavor in the hope of securing the wherewithal by which their requirements and aspirations may be realized. In a capitalistic economic system these efforts are broadly known as production, and the rewards that follow assume several different forms depending upon the status of the producers in the system. For the entrepreneur, this takes the form of profits; for the stockholder who invests his capital, dividends may be expected; for those who lend money to enterprise, the return is that of interest; for the property owners, there is rent; and for employees the combined reward and stimulus is that of employee compensation, customarily referred to as wages. The term "wages" is in more common usage than "employee compensation" and it will be used in most instances in this chapter in the interest of brevity. It is an all-inclusive term and embraces not only the remuneration received by workers in stores, factories, offices, banks, and all other forms of economic endeavor, but also the salaries of executives and managers, and the commissions paid to salesmen. As mentioned later in this chapter, certain patterns of wage payment are designed to serve as stimuli for workers to exert extra efforts on their jobs.

CONCEPTUAL BASES OF WAGES

In most cases the wages that employees receive constitute their sole income. There thus emerges the concept of wages as the source of

purchasing power—the means by which the goods and services produced by
our economic system are bought by those who need them. An additional
concept would equate the wages received by an individual to the value of
the productive effort that he exerts. Wages, then, play a dual role in our
economy. They comprise the prices that are paid by entrepreneurs for the
human effort that is put to use in the creation of goods and services and
at the same time provide the means by which these products are taken off
the market. The relationship and importance of employee compensation
to the total national income is graphically portrayed in Figure 2-1 on
page 47.

ECONOMIC THEORIES OF WAGES

Despite the fact that economists have theorized for many years on the
manner in which wages and wage levels are determined, none of these
theories is a complete and satisfactory explanation of the wage situation
today. Many economists are still searching for new theories that will explain the current wage situation more adequately than has been done thus
far. Because of this situation, only three currently recognized economic
wage theories are presented here: (1) marginal productivity theory,
(2) bargaining theory, and (3) standard-of-living theory. They do not
explain the entire wage picture, but they account for certain segments of it.

Marginal Productivity Theory

This rather complicated theory introduces two concepts: marginal
productivity and marginal revenue. *Marginal productivity* is the value
(selling price) of the goods produced by the last (or marginal) worker
hired by a firm. *Marginal revenue* is the amount of increase in the total
revenue (income) of a firm that results from the sale of one additional
unit of output. The marginal productivity theory says that, under conditions of pure competition, an entrepreneur, whose objective is *maximization of profit*, will continue to hire additional workers until the point is
reached where the value of the marginal product of the last worker hired
just equals the wages paid to the last (or marginal) worker. Furthermore,
the wages of all workers of the same ability in the firm will be determined
by that paid to the marginal worker and the number of workers employed
will be established at the point where their cost (wages) and marginal
revenue are equal. Presented in another way, the point at which the wage
of the marginal worker and the marginal revenue coincide will designate
both the wage level of the workers and the number to be employed.

The major drawbacks to this theory are the almost total absence of pure competition in our economy and the great difficulty in accurately determining the productivity of the marginal worker under conditions generally present in business today. It appears reasonable to assume, however, that an entrepreneur would not continue to hire workers beyond the point where the return from the output of the marginal worker is less than the wages paid him. A further difficulty is found in the suggestion of some writers in economics that entrepreneurs do not always maximize their profits but, instead, endeavor to increase their sales volumes or merely to maintain their competitive position in the industry.

Bargaining Theory

Many observers of the economic scene favor the bargaining theory of wages. The *bargaining theory* assumes that wages are set in more or less of a labor marketplace as the result of a bargaining process between labor, as sellers, and management, as buyers, and that the relative bargaining strengths of these two factors determine the wages to be paid. This theory has the virtue of describing an actual procedure in that it portrays the collective bargaining process with a fair degree of fidelity.[1] As this practice spreads in industry, as now seems quite probable, the pertinency of the theory will become even greater.

To assume, however, that an individual applicant seeking a job with an employer, particularly a large corporation, engages in a bargaining process, is to take an entirely unrealistic view. This statement is true, even though one aspect of the bargaining theory assumes that there are lower limits, below which the workers are unwilling to go, and upper limits to the employers' offerings. The fact of the matter is that most jobs carry price tags, so to speak, or at least have a range of wage rates that are set by the employers on a take-it-or-leave-it basis. When there is a range, the employing officials are usually allowed to use their judgment, but they are rarely permitted to go above the upper limits.

The bargaining theory is a satisfactory explanation of one segment of the wage-determining process, but it is inadequate as far as the rest of the picture is concerned. It fails to explain high wages in unorganized industries or fields. It overlooks the relative productive value of skilled and unskilled workers, and does not explain the variations in wages between workers of equal skills in identical jobs. In plants where unions exist but where all workers are not required to join the union (the open shop [2]), the

---

[1] A further discussion of collective bargaining will be found on pages 351-352.
[2] The open shop is further defined on page 354.

nonunion workers may receive the same benefits as the union members, frequently to keep them from joining the union. Also, in many plants senior workers receive automatic wage increases.

Standard-of-Living Theory

The *standard-of-living theory*, which is a comparatively recent development in wage theories, finds its roots in a rather pervasive belief that wages should be at least high enough to ensure workers a reasonable standard of living. The presumption upon which this theory is based is that all employers should pay wages high enough so that their employees may enjoy not only the necessities of life (food, clothing, and shelter) but also education for their children, adequate medical and dental care, and possibly savings.

This theory is obviously concerned only with the lower level of wages and seeks to establish a humanitarian, rather than an economic, basis for such minima. It is therefore not to be considered as an overall wage-fixing theory. The apparent assumption with regard to firms that cannot afford to pay such minimum rates is that they must either find ways of so doing or go out of business as socially undesirable. The concept of standard-of-living wages is at the root of minimum wage legislation.

MINIMUM WAGE LEGISLATION

The Fair Labor Standards Act, known as the Wage and Hours Act of 1938, was the first of a series of federal enactments designed to place a floor under the wages of labor and a ceiling on the number of hours of work per week for workers in private industry whose products enter interstate commerce. The philosophy behind the concept of minimum wages and maximum hours was that low wages constituted unfair competition and were detrimental to the health, efficiency, and general well-being of workers. Originally the minimum wage was 25 cents per hour and the maximum workweek, over which time and one-half rates had to be paid, was 44 hours, but this was soon reduced to 40 hours. Through several amendments, the minimum rate has been advanced to $1.60 an hour. Coverage has been extended to laundry and dry cleaning enterprises; construction enterprises; hospitals, nursing homes, and most schools. Hotels, motels, restaurants, retail and service enterprises, and gasoline service stations with sales above certain stated minima are included. Federal government hospitals are excluded. Under certain specified circumstances, the minimum wage law is applicable to farm labor. In addition to the federal legislation, 32 states have minimum wage laws applicable mainly to women and children in selected industries.

The argument in favor of these laws is that employers should be compelled to pay employees the minimum wage rates requisite for a fair standard of living. The labor unions have been particularly active in bringing pressure on the Congress and the state legislatures to enact such legislation and to raise the minimum standard. Opposed to this argument have been the claims of many economists that these laws do not benefit those whom they are ostensibly designed to help, namely, the unskilled. Rather than benefit by the establishing of legal wage minima, they maintain, the effect has been to place their wage rates above those that they were capable of earning, with the result that they have been forced into the ranks of the unemployed.

FACTORS ACTUALLY DETERMINING WAGES

The shortcomings of all wage theories, both old and new, arise from the attempt that each makes to explain the whole wage-determining process, which tends to oversimplify an exceedingly complex situation. A large number of different factors enter the wage-determining picture, and their relative weight in any situation varies with the peculiar conditions present in each instance. These wage-determining factors include the following:

1. Demand for the various classes of labor.
2. Wage philosophy of the employers.
3. Stage of the business cycle—prosperity or recession.
4. Profit situation in the various businesses.
5. Degree of skill required.
6. Prevailing wage rates in the community.
7. Wage rates paid by other communities.
8. Degree of organization among the workers.
9. Bargaining skill of the workers' organizations.
10. Cost of living in the community.
11. Supply of the various classes of labor.
12. Relative mobility of labor.
13. Relative disagreeableness or attractiveness of the work.
14. Social desirability of the jobs.

MONEY WAGES VERSUS REAL WAGES

An important distinction should be made between money wages and real wages. *Money wages* are, as the term implies, the actual dollars and cents that workers receive from their employers as payment for services rendered. *Real wages* are the goods and services that the money wages will buy at any given time. This means that real wages are dependent on the current price level as well as on the existing wage level. If money wages are high and the price level is relatively low, real wages are higher than if the price level were to be raised several points. In view of the fact that the value of money lies in the goods and services that it will buy, the test of the adequacy of any given wage level is in the real wage concept.

In order to portray correctly the real wage situation at any one time, the United States Department of Labor and other organizations publish wage data for various industries. In such data the wage rates are expressed in terms of some arbitrarily selected prior period rather than in terms of their current dollar values. By examining these data, it is possible to determine how the workers are faring as compared to their status in the reference period.

A great many workers and labor leaders appear to be entirely unaware of the importance of real wages. They struggle to secure higher money wages, quite without regard for the fact that, in many instances, their increased wages may result in higher prices for the things that they buy. Furthermore, they may do practically nothing to bring about a lowering of the price level, even though this might result in their being able to buy more goods and services on their present incomes than they could buy were they to secure the "raises" that they seek. Labor is "money wage" minded, whereas it needs to turn its attention more to the real wages aspect of its income problem.

The reasons for the failure of the "real wages" concept to be more widely adopted by workers and their leaders seem to be: (a) it is difficult to compute real wages on a basis that would be meaningful to individuals; (b) little, if any, instruction is offered in our schools that fosters a recognition of real wages; (c) labor leaders can bargain for visible money gains for their adherents, whereas a gain in real wages would be most difficult, if not impossible, to measure and report to their followers; and (d) the public, by and large, is money-minded rather than value-minded, a long-time attitude that shows no sign of changing.

WAGES AS A COST OF PRODUCTION

The wages paid to workers in a capitalistic system constitute one of the costs of production. Thus, if the degree of productivity of the workers remains the same, a wage increase becomes at once a cost increase and must result either in a narrowing of the profit margin or in a price increase. Among the sources of conflict between management and the representatives of organized labor in recent years has been the question of whether wage increases should be absorbed out of profits or be translated into price rises.

In many cases, however, wage increases accompanied by increased productivity on the workers' part do not result in cost increases but bring about unit cost decreases, which may permit prices to be lowered. In many, if not most, cases, however, this increased productivity has come about not because the employees are working any harder or longer hours, but through the introduction of more efficient machinery, thereby permitting the same number of workers to produce more units. When cost-cutting machines are introduced into industry, it is often possible to increase wages and to reduce unit costs at the same time. In a certain sense the workers are rewarded for the savings that are effected by the machines. As this process may bring about a more careful and effective operation of the machines by the workers, with continued lowered costs while maintaining a fair volume of profits, the consequent possible price reductions will complete the favorable cycle by benefiting the buyers also. The extent to which this actually occurs is, of course, unknown.

WAGES AND PRICES

Increasing the prices of many commodities reduces the demand for them. This is the effect if the demand is elastic, that is, if the demand drops significantly as the price goes up. If prices are increased too greatly, the demand will fall to the point where the goods are said to be "priced out of the market." This means that the prices are so high that the sale of these items is practically stopped.

This principle has two applications. The first application refers to the inescapable fact that wages are the prices paid for labor and that, if they are too high relative to the workers' productivity, management may be forced to switch to some other instrument of production, such as capital in the form of machinery that replaces labor. Labor, in this case, will have priced itself out of the market. Automation, in its present state of development, may be an example of this situation. A somewhat similar condition exists with regard to foreign-made products whose lower prices reflect the lower wage rates prevailing in other countries.

The second application of this principle is found in those situations in which increased wages have forced the management to raise its prices to the point where sales have experienced a significant decline. Although the product may not be forced off the market, a falling off in sales may result in actually lowered money wages for the workers whose demands for wage increases started the unfortunate chain of events. While many things, such as union contracts or adherence to federal or state wage laws, may prevent an employer from lowering his employees' wages, they may be subject to layoffs that will have the effect of reducing their take-home pay.

The operation of this same demand elasticity can be seen where, although wages may have been increased, the combined efforts of management and labor have brought about lowered unit costs and, hence, lower prices. In a case like this, the increase in demand results in greater sales and, not infrequently, in the creation of new jobs for workers to supply this augmented demand.

HIGHER WAGES, FEWER HOURS

The preceding statements apply with equal force to the matter of increasing wages and decreasing hours at the same time. When this takes place, (a) the productivity of the workers may be increased with unit production costs remaining constant; (b) under the same conditions, these costs may decline; (c) the workers' productivity may be lowered with a consequent increase in unit costs. Under the first two circumstances prices may remain constant or be reduced. In the third instance these higher unit costs must either be absorbed out of profits or be translated into higher prices, which may reduce sales. There are no other alternatives to these possibilities.

Many industries have been able to reduce hours and increase wages through the introduction of modern production methods that increased the workers' productivity. Sometimes the reduction of workers' fatigue through shortening the working hours has had a favorable effect on the rate of production. In other instances, motion and time study has resulted in increased worker efficiency so that production costs were not increased by curtailing the hours of daily or weekly labor and increasing wages. Figure 14-1 portrays the average weekly hours of work in four economic areas.

VARIATIONS IN WAGES

Wages paid for different types of jobs within a particular industry or business are subject to a wide degree of variation. The same wage phenomenon holds true for wages paid to workers in different industries.

VARIATIONS AMONG JOB LEVELS

An elevator operator receives a small fraction of the pay of a corporation president; a day laborer gets much less than a good salesman;

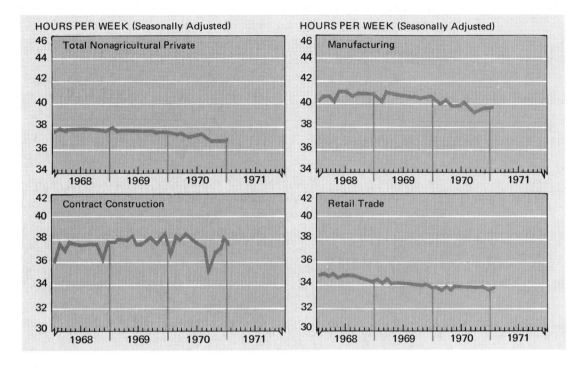

Figure 14-1

Weekly Hours of Work—Selected Industries

Source: *Economic Indicators*, February, 1971. Prepared for the Joint Economic Committee by the Council of Economic Advisers.

a filing clerk receives less than does an expert typist; and so on, through a long and diversified category of jobs. Why should this be so, and is there any justification for such wide variations?

Supply and Demand

Two basic reasons account for this divergent wage phenomenon. The first of these is a matter of supply and demand. Many people, whose capacities are limited or who find themselves in situations where the opportunity to develop their latent capacities is limited, are able to do work only approximating that of common laborers. The ratio of these workers to the number of jobs available is high; hence it is usually not necessary for management to pay high wages in order to secure as many workers of this type as it needs. As jobs become more complex and as the level of personal skills required to fill them rises, increasingly fewer individuals are qualified to fill them; therefore, they are paid higher and higher wages. This is especially true in the case of top executive positions, where the increasing need for competent managerial personnel has brought about not only very high salaries but also many additional rewards in the form of stock options,[3] bonuses, retirement compensation, vacation allowances, and other incentives.

Competition

The second reason for the variation in wages is a corollary of the first and is based on the fact that the instruments of production compete with each other on a cost basis for employment in the productive process. There is not only intergroup competition (labor competing with capital, man versus a machine) but also intragroup rivalry (laborers competing against laborers, executives against other executives).

Not only must a large number of laborers compete among themselves for the available jobs, but laborers, as a group, must compete against machines which can do the same things that they can do, and frequently can do them more cheaply. This situation tends to keep laborers' wages at a relatively low level. By the same token, not only are there comparatively few executives to compete among themselves, but also there is practically no competition offered by land or capital. Hence the remuneration of executives is relatively high. This same analysis can be made for all grades of jobs.

Other Factors

Among individuals performing the same types of work, wage differentials may be based on certain personal or geographic factors. One of these factors is seniority in the department, where the wage rates are based on length of service. Differences in the capabilities of the workers may also be reflected in varying rates of pay, the more skilled receiving the greater stipends. A situation of this sort serves a dual purpose—it acts as a reward for the better workers and as a stimulus to the poorer ones to improve their performance. Sometimes pay variations are due to the differing bargaining abilities of the employees when they were applying for their jobs; the better bargainers start out at higher levels than those who are less skilled at negotiating such matters. The warmer climate in the South, with a presumed lower cost of living, has often been advanced as a reason for wage differentials between the South and the North.

---

[3] See pages 480-481, Chapter 20.

The unions have generally tended to disapprove of different rates of pay by the same firm for the same work, except where this reflects seniority. Their philosophy of "equal pay for equal work" assumes that the quality of work done by all workers will be the same, which is not always so. Such thinking tends to deaden the ambition of the better workers without providing any stimulus to the poorer ones.

Historically, an unfair condition of wage differentials between men and women performing the same work has long existed. In 1963 the Equal Pay Act, an amendment to the Fair Labor Standards Act of 1938, was passed by Congress under which women must receive equal pay with men if their jobs are substantially the same and have the same working conditions. This act became effective in June, 1964, and affects industries whose products enter interstate commerce. Unfortunately, disparate wage rates between the sexes for performing the same work have continued to persist in many work areas, particularly in high-pay positions. In addition, the women in this country feel that they are prevented from expanding their employment opportunities. While it is not within the scope of this text to examine the pros and cons of the current agitation for women's equal rights, which means equality for women in much more than just wages, suffice it to say that a long bottled-up resolution calling for a constitutional amendment guaranteeing to women equality of rights under the law was finally passed by the U.S. House of Representatives in 1970. However, even after passage by the Senate, it would take three fourths of the states to ratify the amendment before it becomes law. Whether or not such a constitutional amendment will come to pass, it is hoped that discrimination in wages based solely on sex will soon become a thing of the past.

VARIATIONS AMONG INDUSTRIES

As shown in Figure 14-2, there are substantial differences in average hourly and weekly earnings between contract construction and retail trade. The explanation for this would appear to be found in the high degree of skill required in contract construction (for example, carpenters, structural steel workers, plumbers, electrical workers, painters, and others in this area) along with strong union pressure and relatively small-scale contractors. The retail trade, by contrast, includes a large number of relatively unskilled people who, while unionized to some extent, are unable to exert the upward pressure on their wage levels that is found in contract construction.

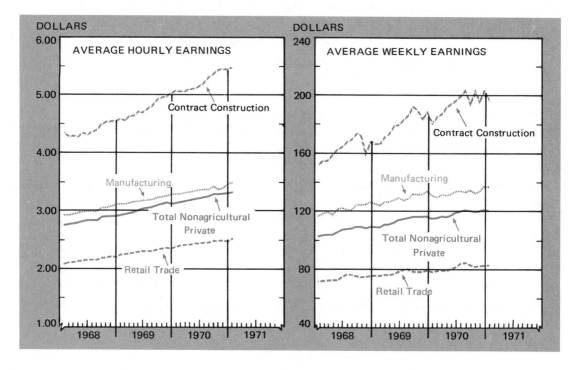

Figure 14-2

Average Hourly and Weekly Earnings—Selected Industries

Source: *Economic Indicators*, February, 1971. Prepared for the Joint Economic Committee by the Council of Economic Advisers.

WAGE INCENTIVES

The purpose of *wage incentives* is to induce workers at all levels to put forth greater productive efforts for which a cash reward is paid. The installation of a wage-incentive system in a company is a task that requires a high degree of skill, judgment, tact, and knowledge of the productive processes that are employed. Experience seems to indicate the desirability of "tailoring" each system to the plant in which it is to operate. The confidence of the workers must be gained, and they must understand thoroughly just how the system works. In unionized plants employees who are union representatives, known as *union stewards* or *shop stewards,* are brought into the operation and their approval secured.

Incentive plans can be used for office workers, salesmen, and even for executives. In each instance they must be fitted with care to the job to be done, and close attention should be paid to equalizing the extra reward to be paid with the additional effort required by the worker to secure it. The basic characteristics of a good incentive plan are: (a) it should provide a reward to the workers for the exercise of a reasonable measure of effort and attention, without creating a harmful physical or mental state on their part; (b) the production goals per worker should be reasonably attainable by the average employee affected; and (c) the added wage costs to the company should be at least balanced by the lowered production costs. A poor incentive plan would be lacking in one or more of these characteristics. A good incentive plan can do much to improve the productivity and morale of an organization, whereas a poor one can have a devastating effect on the personnel.

A rather common incentive plan for factory workers where extra effort on their part can result in additional production is known as the *full participation plan*. Where this plan is in operation, an employee becomes eligible for incentive payment when his efficiency, as measured by the ratio of his output to an established standard, becomes 100%. For each 1% increase in output beyond 100%, he receives 1% increase in earnings. This is also known as the *1 for 1 plan*. To illustrate, in an operation where the standard time per unit is 2 hours and the base pay rate is $4.00 per hour, if an employee requires only 1.6 hours to complete 1 unit of work, his efficiency is $2/1.6 = 125\%$. He has done 25% more work than is required; therefore, his earnings would be $4.00 plus $1.00 (25%) or $5.00 per hour.

In an attempt to overcome some disadvantages of individual incentive plans, several companies have instituted *group incentive plans*, which include all or most of their employees. In some of these plans, representatives of the workers meet with management to discuss wage rates, machine speeds, and other details of shop practice. In several instances reports of these group efforts indicate quite favorable results from the standpoint of increased productivity, lower unit labor costs, improvement in product quality, reduction in scrap, and enhanced employee morale. Some observers believe that the extension of automation will bring about the replacement of individual wage incentives with group incentive plans.

METHODS OF WAGE PAYMENT

The most common of the different methods of making wage payments to workers are: (1) straight salary, (2) time wages, (3) shift premium,

(4) bonus payments, (5) piece-rate payment, and (6) commission payment.

STRAIGHT SALARY

A straight salary, which is the simplest form of wage payment, may be expressed in terms of a stated amount per day, week, month, or year. Straight-salary plans may or may not provide for deductions for absence or tardiness according to the policies of the companies using them. There is little in this system other than the possibility of a salary increase to serve as an incentive to an employee to exert extra effort on the job.

TIME WAGES

In this system payment is made on the basis of stated rates per hour or per day worked, without regard to quantity or quality of output. If a worker's hourly rate is $2.25 and he works 8 hours, he receives a total wage of $18. Under the Fair Labor Standards Act employers must pay time and one half for overtime. Many contracts negotiated with management by labor unions also provide double time for work on Sundays and on holidays. It is customary for the regular working hours to be indicated either on a daily or a weekly basis. Except for the overtime feature and the possibility that markedly substandard work may involve discharge, there is nothing of the wage incentive in this system.

SHIFT PREMIUM

A variant of time wages occurs when a higher rate is paid to workers on the afternoon shift and also on the night shift, which is called the *graveyard shift*. This system is known as the *shift premium plan*. Appearing during World War II when additional rewards were required to induce employees to work on these two shifts, the system has continued in some industries.

BONUS PAYMENTS

A mild form of incentive wages is found in the bonus payments that many firms make to their employees. These bonuses, which are frequently paid on a yearly basis, are customarily related to length of service rather than to output. They are used in banks, offices, stores, and other establishments where a record of each individual's production would be difficult, if not pointless, to maintain. They are incentives to employees to stay with the company but have little other value. Executive bonuses, which are sometimes related to the profitableness of the company, may take on the nature of incentives.

A notable example of a bonus plan that does have an incentive effect on the employees is that of the Lincoln Electric Company of Cleveland, Ohio. Since 1934, all of the company's personnel have participated in year-end bonuses which, in many cases, have equaled or exceeded the annual wages of the individual workers. The base for the bonuses is the company's success for each year, and the distribution to the employees is in accordance with an evaluation procedure that measures the worker's worth to the company.

PIECE-RATE PAYMENT

The piece-rate payment plan involves payment at a stated rate per piece produced. Thus, if the piece rate for a given part is $.005 and a worker produces 2,500 pieces in a day, he receives $12.50 for his efforts. In many plants each worker has a day (or hour) rate that becomes effective whenever he is not working on piece work. This allows for time consumed in setting up the machine, sharpening tools, machine breakdown, power failure, waiting for stock, and so on. Usually these plants guarantee their workers their day rate of pay as minimum wages. This is customarily well below what they can earn on piece work.

It is through piece-rate systems that wage incentives are usually established. A large number of such systems have been in force during the past several years, all of them varying slightly from the others but all designed to induce additional effort on the worker's part and to reward him for it. Most of them establish a standard task that the worker must perform before he can begin to reap the additional remuneration that the system holds out. Another point of similarity has to do with the problem of whether the worker should receive all of the earnings from the incentive or whether part should go to the worker and part to his foreman.

COMMISSION PAYMENT

The *commission payment* type of wage payment is confined to salesmen and is, in effect, a piece-rate system. The salesman's remuneration is a commission that is paid for each unit of product that he sells. The commission may be either a certain sum of money per unit, or it may be a percentage of the value of the item sold.

Since some companies pay only on a commission basis, a salesman who fails to sell anything during any given period receives no pay for that time. Other companies pay a basic salary plus commissions. A number of firms give their salesmen drawing accounts, which are chargeable against commissions earned. For example, a salesman who has a drawing account of $100 a week might, during a 4-week period, earn $600 in commissions. A common method of handling this situation is to pay the salesman his $100 weekly for the first three weeks and then at the end of the fourth week to pay him $100 plus $200 ($600 commissions minus $400 drawings) or a total of $300. If, however, his commissions for the four weeks are less than $400, say $350, he would receive only $50 at the end of the fourth week.

A number of firms utilize a *guaranteed drawing account*. This operates in the same manner as the regular drawing account except that at the end of a stipulated period, such as four weeks, if a salesman's commissions are less than the total of his drawings, the debt is canceled and he starts with a clean slate. Thus a guaranteed drawing account is quite similar to a salary.

In department and specialty stores the practice of paying commissions to salespeople, in addition to their regular salaries, is quite common. A variant on this system is the payment of *PM's* (push money) for the selling of certain designated items. This form of commission may be paid by the store or, in some instances, by the manufacturer in order to promote the sale of his wares.

EMPLOYEE BENEFITS

During World War II and the years following, a group of so-called *fringe benefits* have come into being, as additions to workers' direct wage payments. Among these are health, accident, and life insurance, and hospital and surgical care with the cost paid wholly or in part by the employers; paid vacations and holidays; paid time off for voting; rest periods; *severance pay,* which is sometimes given an employee upon the termination of his employment over and above any unpaid wages due him; payments for work tools; and payment for work clothing.

In addition to these fringe benefits, which are now granted by most medium-to-large businesses, some companies have instituted plans which provide remuneration beyond their employees' basic pay schedules. The most common among these are the profit sharing plan, the guaranteed annual wage system, and the pension plan.

PROFIT SHARING

An employee benefit that has had some vogue in this country is the distribution of some fraction of a firm's profits to its employees without requiring them to purchase stock. This is called *profit sharing*. It may be accomplished either through cash payments or through distribution of company stock. The purposes of profit sharing include inducements for greater production, lower labor turnover, economy in worker use of materials and supplies, loyalty to the company, and resistance to pressure for unionization.

Profits are distributed according to some predetermined pattern. They frequently recognize length of service, both in the matter of the amounts paid to individuals and in the requirement of a certain minimum period of employment as a prerequisite to participation in the distribution. It should be recognized that profit sharing is an expense of doing business and is really a bonus based on the size of the profits.

Some firms feel that the effects of profit sharing have been most beneficial, while others have indicated their sentiments by discontinuing the plan. The critics say that the whole idea is unsound as it violates the fundamental purpose of profits, that is, to reward the stockholders for the risk that they are willing to take in investing their money in the company; and they point out that the employees have no financial stake in the company's success other than that of continued income if it succeeds or separation if it fails.

A profit-sharing scheme assumes the presence of profits available for distribution, which may not be realized in times of poor business or depression, or when it seems the part of wisdom to plow a large part of the earnings back into the business. The effect on the workers of the failure of the company to continue to distribute the profit bonuses is said to be distinctly unfavorable and to more than offset any benefits that previous distributions may have afforded.

The Merrill Manufacturing Corporation of Merrill, Wisconsin, has had a cash profit-sharing plan since 1949 that is reported to be quite successful. Through the operation of an arithmetical formula, a certain percentage of the company's yearly profits are distributed quarterly to all employees, except officers, who have been in the continuous employ of the company for three months or more. The workers are kept informed of the profit-sharing plan through their foremen and an annual meeting. A careful check is kept on quality control, and the employees responsible for spoiled material are informed about it. Suggestions for improvements in operations are invited by the management. A series of interviews with the employees by an outside agency indicated that the workers like the profit-sharing program, both because of the checks that they receive and because they understand how the plan operates.

GUARANTEED ANNUAL WAGE

The concept of the *guaranteed annual wage,* an idea that has been gaining considerable attention for several years, is that the employer agrees to pay eligible workers (usually with one or two years' service) a certain guaranteed wage every week of the year or for 48 weeks, regardless of sales volume or the stage of the business cycle. The best-known plans are probably those of the Procter and Gamble Company, which manufactures soap and detergents; George A. Hormel & Company, which produces meat products; and the Nunn-Bush Shoe Company. The plans of these concerns date back before World War II. Their products are consumer goods that have a considerable measure of stability in their sales volume. This means that there is a minimum of time when the plants are shut down or are working part time.

The big stumbling block to the widespread adoption of the guaranteed annual wage is the professed (and probably actual) inability of many employers to continue to pay wages when sales are low or nonexistent. Certain unions, however, have stated their intention to press for guaranteed annual wages from their employers, and in 1955 the United Auto Workers negotiated a contract with the Ford Motor Company that has been regarded as a step in this direction. The Ford contract, which has provided the pattern for similar agreements in more than 100 companies, is actually for *supplementary unemployment benefits*, commonly known as *SUB*. While there is considerable difference in detail among these agreements, the basic pattern is that the employer will make payments to laid-off eligible employees, which, when combined with unemployment compensation from the state, will not exceed 65 percent of the employees' take-home pay for the first 4 weeks of unemployment and up to 60 percent of such pay for the next 22 weeks. Eligibility is based on length of service. The total time during which payments are made varies from 26 to 52 weeks. The operation of these plans requires changes in state laws or rulings by state attorneys-general that will permit workers to receive both unemployment compensation and SUB in full amount at the same time. Several states have acted to permit this. The funds from which the employers make the SUB payments are built up by contributions made by the companies on the basis of from 3 cents to 5 cents per employee for each hour worked. If the funds go below certain specified levels, the payments may be reduced or even suspended.

It may be expected that the unions will continue to bring pressure toward a genuine guaranteed annual wage.

PENSIONS

The practice of employers' providing old-age pensions for their employees dates back into the 1800's; but since the passage of the federal Social Security Act in 1935, there has been a vast increase in the extent of such coverage. This has been particularly true in plants where the unions have contracts. Some pension plans are financed entirely by employers and others by joint contributions to the funds by both employers and employees. In either case a labor expense is involved for the companies concerned.

The details of these plans vary considerably. It seems probable, however, that either through the extension of federal social security, the growth of company financed projects, or perhaps both, pensions will become a fixed part of the employee remuneration picture in this country. The growth of pensions has been a potent instrument in the betterment of human relations in the companies that have adopted it, as it goes a long way toward satisfying workers' desire for economic security.

There has been some agitation, by union leaders, for what is called *portable pensions*. Under a plan of this sort, a worker with pension benefits accrued could take them with him to a new job. Workers in a plant that is closed down would receive the benefits due them at the time of its closing. At present the legal and financial problems involved appear quite formidable, but with the growing strength of many union groups, portable pensions may become a bargaining issue in future labor-management negotiations.

As a means of providing jobs for younger men, and also of enabling an employer to discontinue certain jobs, *early retirement* has become a provision of many retirement plans. This permits employees to retire at an earlier than normal age and still receive their pensions. The United Automobile Workers union has negotiated an early retirement agreement with many companies that permits workers with 10 years' service to retire at 60 and receive double the retirement benefit until they reach 65, after which they revert to their normal pension rates but become eligible for social security.

WAGE AND SALARY ADMINISTRATION

The overall control of all phases of employee compensation is a management function known as *wage and salary administration*. Its purpose is to provide adequate compensation for all employees, and as such it has an important influence on the existence of satisfactory employee human relations. The broad determination of wage and salary principles in any organization is a top management prerogative, but carrying out the details of wage and salary administration is entrusted to various divisions of different companies, among which are the industrial relations division, industrial engineering department, the treasurer or controller, and the personnel department.

In the setting of wage rates, a process known as *job evaluation* takes place, in which each job is rated on the basis of the necessary skill, experience, responsibility, and working conditions. From this procedure the wage rate for each job in a plant is computed. Commonly this is the function of the wage and salary administration.

BUSINESS TERMS

QUESTIONS FOR DISCUSSION AND ANALYSIS

1. Do you believe that the money value of the goods produced by the marginal worker in a firm can be accurately computed? Explain.
2. Does a small business that cannot afford to pay minimum wage rates have any economic reason for being in business? Why or why not?
3. Why has the concept of real wages not been more widely accepted by workers?

4. Labor leaders sometimes say that profits come out of wages, while managers maintain that wages come out of profits. Which of these, if either, is correct? Why?

5. Should two men in a factory who are doing identical work ever be paid different wages? Why?

6. If salesmen's commissions vary directly with the profits on the items which they sell, is this a form of profit sharing? Explain.

7. Why has profit sharing not been more widely accepted in business?

8. Should laid-off workers be permitted to receive supplementary employment benefits at the same time that they are receiving state unemployment compensation payments? Why or why not?

9. Do you believe that portable pensions might have the effect of creating a higher degree of employee turnover? Explain.

10. Do you think that workers should be paid $500 a month when they retire after thirty years' work for a company? Why or why not?

PROBLEMS AND SHORT CASES

1. There is a growing movement in this country that calls for complete economic equality between men and women. Prominent among the demands made by the women is that of equality of compensation for them with men for identical jobs. There has even been talk of a constitutional amendment to perpetuate their demands. Consult periodicals in your school library and prepare a report setting forth the arguments both for and against this movement, stating your own opinions and giving reasons for them.

2. The topic of minimum wage legislation, which has been so prominent in Congressional circles recently, has created a considerable controversy between those who favor the minimum wage and those who are opposed to it. The issues involved cover the question of whether the minimum wage increases the incomes of those whom it is ostensibly intended to benefit or merely prevents the unskilled from securing employment. There is also the question regarding the employer who is unable to pay the minimum wage to his workers, and, more recently, the point of whether farm workers should be covered by this legislation.

   Consult periodicals and newspaper articles in your school library and write a report covering this controversy, indicating your views on the subject and substantiating them.

3. One of the problems faced by companies that are engaged in the developing of new products for markets where their present products are not sold is that of recruiting and compensating the salesmen who will introduce their new products. The Rose Corporation, well-known for its hardware products, is now faced with this problem as it

recently purchased a small manufacturer of frozen food items whose market had been confined to the community where it was located.

Prior to its recent acquisition, the Rose Corporation's sales job was largely that of calling on their present wholesale and retail customers and taking replacement orders for the items they carried. The occasional introduction of new products presented no problem since their salesmen were well acquainted with their customers and had no difficulty in calling the latter's attention to the new products that appeared from time to time. Now the Rose Corporation's problem is to recruit salesmen who could introduce the frozen food products on a broad scale throughout the country. The company feels that once these frozen food products are accepted in the grocery trade, their distribution pattern would closely resemble that of their hardware line. Another problem the company faces is that of working out a compensation scheme for the new salesmen whom they propose to hire and whose job is initially that of introducing a product in a field where the Rose Corporation is virtually unknown. If these new salesmen should be successful, eventually their sales job would be that of routine supply, not dissimilar from the hardware salesmen's job.

Analyze the Rose Corporation's problems and devise a compensation scheme which will enable the company to get its frozen food products introduced, to do a good promotional job, and to retain its sales force even after the sales problem of the frozen food products becomes that of routine supply.

SUGGESTED READINGS

Chruden, Herbert J., and Arthur W. Sherman, Jr. *Personnel Management*, 4th Edition. Cincinnati: South-Western Publishing Co., 1972.

Dunn, J. D., and Frank M. Rachel. *Compensation Theory and Practices*. New York: McGraw-Hill Book Company, 1970.

French, Wendell. *The Personnel Management Process: Human Resources Administration*, Second Edition. Boston: Houghton Mifflin Company, 1970. Part VII.

Pigors, Paul, and Charles A. Myers. *Personnel Administration*, Sixth Edition. New York: McGraw-Hill Book Company, 1969. Part 5.

Reynolds, Lloyd G. *Labor Economics and Labor Relations*, 5th Ed. Englewood Cliffs, New Jersey: Prentice-Hall, Inc., 1970. Part One.

Zollitsch, Herbert G., and Adolph Langsner. *Wage and Salary Administration*, Second Edition. Cincinnati: South-Western Publishing Co., 1970.

Chapter 15

Labor Problems and Legislation

As the term "labor" has been commonly used, it refers to those individuals whose status in the companies where they are employed precludes them from being identified as members of management since they work in subordinate positions and normally do not have any authority over others. While in many cases it is probable that members of the labor group have little, if any, ambition to attain managerial status, they nevertheless have certain goals in life to which they aspire through the jobs they hold. Without indicating any order of precedence, the goals of individual workers are: (a) an increase in their standards of living, which usually means higher wages; (b) security, the removal of fear of the loss of jobs; (c) a feeling of creativity in their jobs, a sense of doing something worthwhile; (d) a feeling that they are important parts of the companies that employ them; and (e) a sense of dignity in their jobs, however lowly they may be in the economic scale.

The fact that in the past, and to some extent at present, many workers appear to believe that these goals are not being achieved, nor even recognized as such by management, has given rise to resentment and antagonism on the workers' part which, to a large extent, are the sources of the problems of labor-management relationships that have become more and more acute over the years. These problems in turn have led to legislation designed originally to strengthen the hands of labor in dealing with management and later to remedy some of the situations that have followed upon the enhanced power of labor.

GROWTH OF ORGANIZED LABOR

In many industries and companies, frictions of various kinds have led labor and management [1] into a state of mutual antagonism. To some observers, these irritations have been the result of the attitudes and actions of management, including its failure to recognize and to be sympathetic with the goals of the workers, rather than any behavior on labor's part. Labor's reaction to these stimuli, however, is what has aroused resentment on the part of management. Regardless of the real source of these animosities, there is no question about their existence.

SOURCES OF ANNOYANCE TO LABOR

Prominent among the causes of labor-management friction which management is accused of are: (1) management's preoccupation with profits, (2) management's concept of labor as a cost of production, (3) management impersonality and arbitrariness, (4) the incomprehensibility to labor of many common business methods, and (5) management's ignoring of workers' goals.

Management's Preoccupation with Profits

This, in the final analysis, is in line with management's main job, that of securing profits for the owners. A firm belief exists among many workers, however, that all business is extremely profitable and that most companies could easily pay higher wages without seriously impairing their profit positions. This belief, coupled with the conviction held by a large segment of labor that the purpose of business is to provide jobs rather than to make profits for the owners, accounts for labor's irritation at management's predominant profit consciousness. Workers do not appear to realize that one of the social responsibilities that business has to the community which it serves is to maintain a profit position that reasonably guarantees its continued existence.

Management's Concept of Labor as a Cost of Production

This concept is the result of the emphasis that many owners of businesses have placed on profits, which, in turn, has forced management to do its utmost to reduce costs. The development of modern cost accounting

---

[1] Management, in the sense that the term is used here, refers to the policy-making group in any company regardless of its identity with the owners.

methods has pointed up the cost phase of the labor picture. Thus some managers see labor, not as a group of human beings, but as a cost of production. The fact that the introduction of automated machinery has resulted, in some companies, in the displacement of workers has served to convince them of management's attitude in this respect. Competitively, management must subject its costs to the closest scrutiny as one of the prices of survival.

Management's Impersonality and Arbitrariness

In its dealings with labor, management has too often manifested an impersonality and arbitrariness that has antagonized workers, in many instances needlessly. Men have been hired, transferred, and discharged in a rigid manner that has given the impression that management had little regard for the workers' feelings. The growth of the concept of human relations in business, plus the strength of the unions in many areas, has served to blunt the force of this source of irritation to labor.

Incomprehensibility to Labor of Many Common Business Methods

Many of the everyday business procedures, particularly accounting and financial practices and those by which the payment of various jobs is computed, have long been a source of distrust on the part of the workers. The failure of management to educate the workers in the meaning and purpose of managerial procedures has served merely to aggravate labor's suspicion of these methods.

Management's Ignoring of Workers' Goals

Although some enlightened managers are aware of the goals of their workers, many are not—a circumstance that is both irritating and frustrating to labor. And even where management is sympathetic with its workers' aims, circumstances frequently prevent it from doing much to implement this understanding. Such factors as the pressure of competition that may set a ceiling on wages, the basic repetitive nature of many mass-production jobs that denies to the workers much sense of creativity, and the risks inherent in many enterprises that prevent management from guaranteeing security to its employees are hindrances to management's desires to assist its workers in the fulfillment of their objectives. In what is probably a declining number of instances, management feels that there exists an inherent conflict between the needs of production and the needs of people as workers. There are also some managers who are convinced that workers are basically lazy and have an innate dislike for work.

It is, perhaps, unfortunate that management has in many cases not undertaken to explain to the workers the economic facts of life as regards the relationship between costs, wages, and profits. The lack of communication along this line appears to confirm the workers' belief in the eternal profitability of all business, especially large companies.

REACTION OF LABOR

These management attitudes and actions have served to create resentment and distrust on the part of labor. This situation has made a large segment of labor receptive to the proposals of union organizers. Here they have found folks who talk their language and appear to have their interests at heart, who will listen to their troubles and try to do something about them. The workers have long since discovered the futility of trying to accomplish any betterment of their condition singlehandedly and now are confronted with the possibility of bringing this about through joint action. It is small wonder that labor organizations have grown in numbers and in strength, particularly during a period which has seen a phenomenal growth in the size and power of many industrial and commercial companies.

There is evidence to indicate that a sympathetic, more understanding attitude on the part of management would have retained the loyalty of the workers and made the task of the union organizers immeasurably more difficult. This statement is made because a great many workers feel an almost instinctive loyalty toward any organization of which they are a part. This is most noticeable in the case of new, young workers, who usually approach their first jobs with an enthusiasm and a desire to excel that would augur well for their employers if they would recognize and encourage it. Instead, management often appears more or less indifferent to this priceless offering and, as a result, this loyalty quickly subsides and is replaced by a sullen distrust and resentment. Workers in this frame of mind are quite favorably disposed toward the overtures of union organizers.

Until fairly recently, while the *white-collar workers* (those who work in offices and in engineering jobs) may have experienced some of the same reactions toward management as the *blue-collar* (or factory) *workers*, the former have been much less receptive toward union membership than the latter. The reason for this has appeared to lie in the attitudes of the white-collar groups who have traditionally regarded themselves as being more individualistic, aggressive, and closer to management in their

thinking. However, this attitude appears to be undergoing a rather significant change, and many types of white-collar employees have become more
interested in joining unions and bargaining collectively with their employers. Added to these have been such traditionally nonunionized groups
as teachers, insurance agents, and governmental employees at all levels.
It seems probable that this trend will continue.

SOURCES OF ANNOYANCE TO MANAGEMENT

Certain aspects of labor's reaction to management's attitudes and
actions have, in turn, caused considerable annoyance to management. The
following are the more common sources of this irritation: (1) loss of
workers' loyalty, (2) weakening of management's authority, (3) belliger-
ence of labor leaders, and (4) the generation gap.

Loss of Workers' Loyalty

When workers join unions, they are under considerable pressure from
the union leaders to transfer their loyalty from their employers to the
unions. This situation usually comes as a distressing discovery to
management.

Weakening of Management's Authority

A subject commonly covered by union-management contracts is the
transfer and discharge of workers. Before the advent of the union, management's authority in this regard was practically absolute; but when a
plant is unionized, the agreement of the union frequently must be secured
before a worker can be transferred, discharged, or made the object of
disciplinary action. This obviously dilutes management's authority, often
to the dismay of the executive personnel involved. Since this situation is
well known by the workers, some of them will assume a defiant attitude
when their work or conduct is questioned by their superiors. In many
such instances union representatives feel duty-bound to take the part of
the offenders even though they realize that the latter may be at fault.
No small part of the reason for this latter action lies in the political nature
of the union leaders' jobs. They are regarded by the union membership as
champions of the workers by whom they are elected, and their continued
occupancy of their jobs may well be jeopardized if the members come to
think that they are siding with management too frequently.

Belligerence of Labor Leaders

Although many leaders in organized labor are noted for their courtesy and reasonableness, some labor representatives assume a belligerent attitude when dealing with employers or when speaking to the public. Management's reaction to this stance is, in many instances, similarly aggressive, with the result that there is apt to be more heat than light generated when the representatives of labor and management meet.

The Generation Gap

A new circumstance that has been singularly irritating to managers of companies and unions alike is the result of the emergence of the so-called generation gap in many unions. This has manifested itself in many ways, particularly when the younger members of a union refuse to accept the terms of a settlement that have been agreed upon by management and the union bargaining unit. The dissenting groups have many times been able to force the union's bargainers to return to management and endeavor to secure better terms than those to which they had previously agreed. With the relative increase in the numbers of younger union members, it is feared that this condition will get worse.

OTHER REASONS FOR THE GROWTH OF LABOR ORGANIZATIONS

Several other factors have helped advance the growth of labor organizations. These factors are: (a) through organization, workers are placed in a much stronger position when dealing with management on matters of wages, hours of work, seniority, and working conditions than when they act as individuals; and (b) especially in large companies, the workers, through their organizations, are able to elect their own representatives to deal with management, whereas the very size of the firms is such that it would be virtually impossible for the individual worker to do this for himself.

EMERGENCE OF UNIONS AS PREFERRED LABOR ORGANIZATIONS

While some companies have had satisfactory experience with *shop committees* that meet with management to solve day-to-day problems, over the past 30 years or more unions have come increasingly to be preferred by workers who wish to be organized. Among the reasons for this preference are: (a) the recognition by many workers that only completely independent organizations can be certain of being free from possible domination by management; (b) the fact that the company-dominated union was outlawed by the National Labor Relations Act of 1935; (c) the availability in the unions of able and experienced negotiators whose skill in dealing with management assures the workers of a good chance that their requests will be granted; and (d) the aggressiveness and salesmanship of union organizers who have been successful in many fields in persuading the workers that their best interests would be served by joining the unions.

Teams of experienced organizers are continually being sent to try to convince the employees of unorganized companies of the benefits of union membership. Achieving the largest possible number of dues-paying members is obviously one of the major objectives of the unions. Table 15-1 shows total union membership in the United States from 1958 to 1968.

UNION MEMBERSHIP IN THE UNITED STATES, 1958-1968

Table 15-1

Year	Total Membership	Percent of Total Labor Force Belonging to Unions	Percent of Employees in Nonagricultural Establishments Belonging to Unions
1958	17,029,000	24.2	33.2
1959	17,117,000	24.1	32.1
1960	17,049,000	23.6	31.4
1961	16,303,000	22.3	30.2
1962	16,586,000	22.6	29.8
1963	16,524,000	22.2	29.2
1964	16,841,000	22.2	28.9
1965	17,299,000	22.4	28.4
1966	17,940,000	22.7	28.1
1967	18,367,000	22.7	28.0
1968	18,916,000	23.0	27.9

Source: United States Department of Labor, Bureau of Labor Statistics, 1970.

COLLECTIVE VERSUS INDIVIDUAL BARGAINING

When a company becomes unionized, collective bargaining is substituted for individual bargaining, and the union becomes the bargaining agent for its members, and, in some instances, for some or all of the non-union employees. (Although office workers were usually not included in the bargaining unit in the past because they were not union members, this situation is changing today due to the gradual unionization of office employees.) In *collective bargaining* the representatives of labor bargain with management over wages, hours, and other terms and conditions of employment, whereas in individual bargaining each individual bargains with the management on these matters. The power of collective bargaining lies in the saying "in union there is strength." When labor's representatives sit down around the conference table with management, they are in a much stronger position to secure their demands if they have all of the workers in the plant behind them than if each man represents only himself. The power behind the threat of a strike of all the workers is vastly greater than the possibility that a few individuals may quit if they are not given what they want.

For this reason collective bargaining is one of the major methods by which unions endeavor to achieve their objectives. It permits the unions to employ skilled negotiators in their bargaining activities, something that no individual could hope to do. It is through this process that labor is coming to have a voice in the operation of industry.

The collective bargaining agreement between a company and a union usually establishes procedures by which the union representatives in the shop can bring employee grievances to management's attention at any time. Likewise management may consult with the union on subjects that concern both parties. Also, the necessity for the interpretation of clauses in the agreement calls for more or less continuous contacts between union and management.

The main drawback to collective bargaining is that it tends to level out differences in income among workers doing the same tasks. It also acts as a deterrent to ambitious workers who might be able to advance through their own superior efforts or abilities. The lot of most workers under collective bargaining is probably better, however, than it would be without this process, and an exceptional worker can usually find ways of making his presence felt and of receiving a reward commensurate with his value.

In companies where a number of different unions have contracts, some unions have joined together in the bargaining process. This is known as *coalition bargaining* or *coordinated bargaining*. In one instance 26 unions bargained with and struck against the four largest companies in a single industry. The unions argue that, because of the growth of industrial conglomerates,[2] such tactics are necessary in order to balance union

[2] Conglomerates are discussed on page 489.

strength with that of their employers. The fear that this new maneuver may result in a superstrike, with its attendant disruption of production and possible large-scale violence, has raised the question whether Congress should take action to outlaw joint bargaining by unions that represent different trades although they may be in the same industrial areas. The Industrial Union Department of the AFL-CIO [3] has been promoting the idea of coalition or *conglomerate bargaining* while the National Association of Manufacturers and the U. S. Chamber of Commerce have been strongly opposed to this concept.

UNION OBJECTIVES

The aims of organized labor are both political and economic. The political aspects of union activity, which appeared with the passage of the National Labor Relations Act of 1935 and have expanded to a marked degree in the past decade, include lobbying activities designed to secure the passage of favorable legislation and the rejection of unfavorable proposed laws in Congress and the state legislatures. Efforts have been made to "bring out the labor vote" for the purpose of electing so-called friendly candidates for public office and defeating "unfriendly" ones.

The economic, and historically older, group of objectives, the purpose of which is to benefit the workers and to strengthen the unions, include the following: (1) higher wages and shorter hours, (2) seniority provisions, (3) union security or recognition, (4) checkoff, (5) restriction of output and job retention, and (6) fringe benefits.

Higher Wages and Shorter Hours

Foremost among the aims of unions are the raising of wages and the shortening of the number of hours of work. Any betterment in these factors is immediately recognized. In the long, slow movement toward higher wages and shorter hours since the early days of the Industrial Revolution, the unions have played a notable role.

Seniority Provisions

Many agreements contain seniority provisions that specify the rights and privileges of employees from the standpoint of length of service. These provisions are concerned mainly with layoffs, rehiring, transfers, and

---

[3] The largest formal union organization in this country which is discussed on pages 361-362.

promotions. Obviously this objective disregards individual ability, loyalty, and ambition.

Union Security or Recognition

With *union security* employers admit the right of employees to choose their own representatives and agree to recognize the chosen union as the sole bargaining agent for the workers, or at least that portion of the workers who want the union. The items that follow indicate the ways in which unions have sought security.

Under the *closed shop* the employer agrees to hire only persons who are union members, and all employees must remain members in good standing during their term of employment with the company. The Labor Management Relations Act of 1947, usually called the Taft-Hartley Act, outlawed the closed shop. It still exists in some industries, notably construction, printing, and maritime industries. The reason for this apparently illegal practice is that many workers in these industries get their jobs through *union hiring halls*. Employers who need qualified help contact the local union business agent, who sends out workers who are registered in the hiring halls as being available.

Criticism has frequently been directed against the construction unions for their rather rigid apprentice system, under which limited numbers of individuals are admitted to apprentice status to undergo a protracted period of instruction and performance before being certified as journeymen in their various crafts. It has been charged that through this procedure and their reluctance to admit large numbers of would-be apprentices, the construction unions virtually run an industry-wide closed shop. The unions involved have vigorously denied this accusation.

A *union shop* differs from a closed shop in that the employer may hire nonunion workers, but they must join the union after a prescribed period and remain in good standing as a requirement of continued employment. Most employers have been opposed to both the closed and the union shop. In their stead employers have preferred the *open shop* in which, at least theoretically, both union and nonunion workers may be employed. Labor leaders, on the other hand, have been most violently opposed to the open shop. Right-to-work laws place a ban on the union shop in several of the states.

In the *agency shop* all employees for whom the union, the *bargaining unit,* negotiates are required to pay dues to the union, but they do not have to join it. The agency shop is legal except where the states forbid it, which they have the right to do. Thus the agency shop is legal in Indiana but illegal in Florida. The agency shop was devised by the unions to circumvent state right-to-work laws.

Under a *maintenance-of-membership* arrangement, a worker need not belong to a union in order to obtain a job, nor must he join it in order to retain his job. If he is a member of the union at the time that the maintenance-of-membership shop becomes effective, however, or if he joins after that date, he must maintain his membership in good standing for the life of the existing contract as a requirement of continued employment.

In a *preferential shop* the employer agrees to give preference to union members in hiring and in layoffs. Thus union workers, if available, are hired before nonunion workers, and they are retained until the last when layoffs are necessary. The Taft-Hartley Act outlaws the preferential shop as well as the closed shop.

In some situations where not all employees are members of the union, the contract includes a provision by which the union is recognized as the sole or exclusive bargaining agent for all employees. Such a provision is characteristic of approximately one fifth of existing agreements. In some areas of public employment the union is recognized as representing only those employees who are members of the union. The employer deals with nonmembers on an individual basis.

Checkoff

The term *checkoff* is applied to the collection of union dues by the employer through payroll deductions. Provisions for this collection are contained in the agreement executed between the union and management.

Restriction of Output and Job Retention

One of the economic aims of unions, which may or may not be admitted by labor leaders, is some form of restriction on the amount of work that will be turned out daily. The union thinking back of this action is to preserve jobs, on the theory that there is only so much work to be done and that it should be so parceled out that all the present employees retain their jobs. The contract requirement stating that certain jobs be continued after management believes they are no longer needed is known as *featherbedding*, a practice that the employing companies have been trying for years to eliminate.

Fringe Benefits

In the past two decades or more, the unions have also sought and secured such fringe benefits as pensions, employee insurance, hospitalization, and many other items of advantage to their members.

EFFECTS OF THESE AIMS

The economic effect of higher wages and shorter hours was discussed in Chapter 14. The effect of the other objectives—particularly the union shop, and the closed shop if it should again be legalized by subsequent legislation—is to move toward a monopoly of labor, wherein it is conceivable that one would have to join and remain a member of a union as a prerequisite to holding and possibly to getting a job. The first of these conditions exists in many fields of industry and is spreading to others. It tightens the hold of labor leaders over the rank and file, and it probably forces into the unions many persons who would not join voluntarily.

Furthermore, the attainment of these objectives puts an exceedingly powerful club into the hands of the labor leaders, who have in some instances shown little reluctance to use it, without the slightest regard for the effects on the communities where the impact between labor and management takes place. It is doubtful that the best interests of the people of this country are to be served by permitting such a condition either to develop or to continue. It is interesting to note that abuses of monopoly power by business have been curbed through the Sherman Antitrust Act, the Clayton Act, and the vigilance of the antitrust division of the United States Department of Justice. Organized labor, on the other hand, was exempted from the antitrust laws by the Clayton Act of 1914.

BARGAINING TACTICS AND SETTLEMENT OF DISPUTES

In many instances unions have been able to achieve their objectives through the process of negotiating (or bargaining) with management. Unfortunately, however, there have been a large number of cases where labor and management have been unable to settle their differences on a peaceful basis and have had to resort to more strenuous practices.

LABOR'S METHODS

A *strike* is a temporary refusal by employees to continue their work until their demands have been granted by management. The term *walkout* is used as a synonym for strike.

Usually the workers on strike remain away from the plant, but there have been two types of strikes in which they remain in the plant. These are the *sitdown strike,* in which the workers appear at their posts but refuse to perform their appointed tasks or to leave the premises until their demands are met; and the *slowdown strike* where the workers continue to work but at a markedly reduced tempo so that production is curtailed but not completely halted. The sitdown strike has been declared illegal by the courts in some states and has almost disappeared.

In a *jurisdictional strike* the union tries to force the employer to recognize it instead of another union for certain stated types of work. Under the Taft-Hartley Act most jurisdictional strikes are unfair labor practices and, as such, are prohibited. A *wildcat* or *outlaw strike* occurs when a group of workers go on strike without the official consent of the officers of the union or in violation of the terms of the contract. The *sympathy strike* is found where a group of workers go on strike because of sympathy with another group who are also on strike. The sympathy strikers usually have no grievance against their own employers but strike as a part of the union strategy to help the original striking group.

It is probable that, in many cases, strikes are settled without all of labor's demands being granted by the employers. It is not at all uncommon for the labor leaders to be willing to compromise on some of their demands as a part of a strike settlement.

A fairly common practice is for unions to assess their members for the purpose of building up *strike funds* with which they can reimburse the members on the occasion of some subsequent strike and thus persuade them to hold out longer for a settlement than they might if the strike funds were not available.

Picketing consists of posting one or more persons at the entrance to the struck plant for the purpose of dissuading or preventing persons from entering the plant and of informing the public that a strike is in progress. *Mass picketing* occurs when a large number of pickets assemble at the entrances to a struck plant and forcibly prevent persons who may wish to go to work from crossing the picket lines. This is mob rule and has generally been frowned on by the courts.

Soldiering on the job occurs when one or more workers deliberately reduce the pace of their work, for the purpose of impeding production in the plants where they work. If this takes place on an organized basis, it is called a slowdown strike. The workers in this instance do not stop working, they merely slow down the tempo of their operations. *Sabotage* occurs when workers maliciously cripple or destroy the productive equipment of the plants where they work. This is illegal and is not often found at present.

A *boycott* takes place when union members refuse to purchase products from companies whose employees are on strike or where some condition prevails to which the union is opposed. This type of boycott is called a *primary boycott*. A *secondary boycott* exists when workers apply these tactics against a secondary handler, who offers for sale the goods of a struck or a nonunion plant. The Taft-Hartley Act prohibits certain types of secondary boycotts.

MANAGEMENT'S METHODS

These methods have consisted mainly of the lockout, the blacklist, and the injunction.

A *lockout* consists of an employer's refusal to permit workers to enter the plant to go to work. This usually takes place because the employer resents some action on the part of the workers. At other times lockouts have occurred for the purpose of denying union organizers access to the plants to prevent their holding organizing meetings.

A *blacklist* is a secret list of union organizers and members that is compiled by employers' associations and circulated among the members for the purpose of denying employment to the listed persons. Blacklisting is regarded as an unfair labor practice under a ruling of the National Labor Relations Board.

An *injunction* is a court order, secured by the employer, that aims to restrain the unions from interfering with the production of a plant in some manner, usually at the time of a strike. At one time, injunctions were issued against almost all forms of strike activity, but in recent years they have been restricted to mass picketing, acts of violence, or damage to the employer's property.

A *yellow-dog contract* is an agreement signed by workers, usually as a condition of securing jobs, whereby they promise not to join a union while working for their employers. The Norris-LaGuardia Act outlawed this type of contract.

Strike insurance funds have been established in the newspaper and air transport industries and in the railroads from which any member of these groups can receive payments during a strike. Contributions are made by all members on a self-insurance basis. The purpose of this action is to strengthen the managements of struck firms and to enable them to hold out for long periods of time in the event of strikes. The unions, naturally, are bitterly opposed to strike insurance, although, as previously noted, they have long had similar funds to aid strikers.

METHODS OF SETTLING LABOR DISPUTES

Inasmuch as labor disputes are regarded as such only if management and labor are completely unable to agree on the points in question, the methods for settling them must of necessity involve the intervention of some outside agency or person, who may or may not represent some phase of government. These methods are: (1) mediation, (2) arbitration, and (3) compulsory investigation.

Mediation

In *mediation* a third party attempts to bring both sides to a point of common agreement. This is done without coercion and purely on the basis of helpfulness and the disinterestedness of an impartial third party. The term conciliation is frequently used synonymously with mediation. In a strict sense *conciliation* means that the mediator reviews the proposals put forth by both parties, whereas mediation implies that the mediator also offers his own proposals.

The Federal Mediation and Conciliation Service, created in 1947, was established for the purpose of providing means whereby the good offices of a government agency could be made available to the parties of a labor dispute should they care to take advantage of them. Neither disputant is required to accept its offer of assistance or to abide by its suggestions for solution of a dispute. The National Board of Mediation, established under the provisions of the Railway Labor Act of 1926 (amended in 1934), exists to mediate disputes in the railroad business.

Arbitration

Arbitration involves the submission by labor and management of the issue at stake to an individual arbitrator or, more commonly, a board. Usually each side has one representative on an arbitration board and a third party, someone acceptable to both disputants, is chosen as chairman. He may be a public official or someone in the community who has a reputation for fairness and impartial judgment. Once both parties agree to submit the dispute, the decision becomes binding, morally if not legally. This method of settling labor problems is known as *voluntary arbitration*. It is included as a possible procedure in some contracts between companies and labor unions. *Compulsory arbitration*, whereby both labor and management are required to submit to arbitration upon failure to settle their differences by other means, has made very little headway in this country, except in a few states and cities where employees of nonprofit hospitals, public utilities, and police and fire departments are prohibited by the law from striking and must submit their grievances to binding arbitration.

In a few cases, mainly in public utilities, impartial umpires have been appointed to whom all unsolved disputes are submitted for settlement. Their decisions are usually binding on both parties.

Compulsory Investigation

Either through legislation or by contract agreement, threatened strikes that may imperil public health and safety are postponed for varying periods while impartial third parties investigate the disputes and make reports on their findings, which may or may not include recommendations for settlement. This is known as *compulsory investigation and delay*.

PROSPECTS FOR LABOR PEACE

Will the time come when strife will disappear from this area of economic activity and, in its stead, will come an era of peaceful relationships? In most companies, unionized or not, the relations between management and the workers present the appearance of harmony as far as strikes, lockouts, and the like are concerned. And it is probable that, aside from the inevitable frictions that are bound to develop when people work together, the employees and their bosses get along fairly well. Why, then, does trouble periodically break out in certain well-unionized industries year after year?

Is it because the conditions of employment are more onerous, or the pay scales lower, or the employer attitudes tougher in these fields than in most others?

Is there anything inherent in the character of the work in these industries that prompts the periodic eruptions that attract so much attention?

Is it possible that the personal ambitions of the labor leaders, in their attempts to gain prominence in the labor field, cause them to feel that they must continuously produce "rabbits out of a hat" —gain ever greater concessions from the employers regardless of dislocations that are often attendant upon the satisfying of these demands?

Is the answer to our labor problems to be found in an ever greater spread of unionism, the election of legislators "friendly" to labor, and the attempted subjugation of the public welfare to the demands of the unions?

Is the so-called generation gap in the union, with more and more younger men joining them and assuming a more militant attitude than the older ones, an important cause of labor unrest in the unions and companies affected?

These questions are difficult to answer. The present trend toward the extension of unionism is probably an inevitable consequence of prevailing conditions and has doubtless served to remedy some circumstances that could not have been altered by any other means. But, if there is ever to be any measure of industrial peace in this country, it will come about, not as the result of the mutual antagonisms of the representatives of both sides, but because labor and management can come to recognize the basic identity of their aims and aspirations. Each must bring to the bargaining table a respect for the other's opinions, viewpoints, and responsibilities. This condition is to be found now in many companies where management and labor meet to solve their various problems in an atmosphere of mutual confidence and trust and where each side realizes that the gaining of a temporary unfair advantage over the other can only lead to trouble. It is perhaps unfortunate, but probably inevitable, that the subject of labor-management relations has become so prominent in the political scene, thereby infusing an element of questionable relevance.

TYPES OF UNIONS

The two basic types of unions in this country are the craft union and the industrial union. *Craft unions* are organized according to crafts or trades, such as painters, plumbers, machinists, and teamsters. *Industrial unions* are organized according to industries, such as steel workers, clothing workers, and automobile workers.

Historically, unionism in this country developed on the trade or craft basis, and only since 1935 has industrial unionism made much headway. The years since then, however, have witnessed a profound trend toward the industrial union; and even the craft unions are now admitting to membership some of the unskilled and semiskilled workers in plants where formerly only the skilled workers could qualify.

At present there is one large formal union group in this country, the American Federation of Labor—Congress of Industrial Organizations, commonly known as the *AFL-CIO*. There are also a number of independent unions that are not affiliated with the AFL-CIO.

STRUCTURE OF THE AFL-CIO

The organizational structure of the AFL-CIO consists of an Executive Council that includes the president, the secretary-treasurer, and 27 vice presidents who are elected at the biennial convention and who govern the AFL-CIO between conventions. This group meets at least three times a year. The General Board consists of Executive Council members and one officer of each international union and affiliated department. This group meets at least once a year.

There are six trade and industrial departments—the Building and Construction Trades, Industrial Union, Maritime Union, Metal Trades, Railroad Employees, and Union Label and Service Trades—which work closely with the appropriate member unions.

The field organization of the AFL-CIO consists of the various state central bodies, 764 local central bodies, 122 national and international unions, and 192 local unions which are directly affiliated with the AFL-CIO.

The affiliated national and international unions are more or less autonomous, being subject only to suspension or expulsion from the AFL-CIO by vote of the biennial convention. The unaffiliated unions are directly attached to the AFL-CIO and are under its control.

The general structural organization of the American Federation of Labor—Congress of Industrial Organizations is shown in Figure 15-1.

INDEPENDENT UNIONS

The independent union picture is a somewhat confused one, due to the actions of the AFL and CIO, prior to their merger, in expelling the International Longshoreman's Organization by the AFL and the Office and Professional Workers; Public Workers; Food, Tobacco, and Agricultural Workers; United Electrical Workers; and Farm Equipment Workers, by the CIO. Since the merger, the AFL-CIO has expelled the International Brotherhood of Teamsters, the Laundry Workers International Union, and the International Chemical Workers Union. In 1968 the United Auto Workers withdrew from the AFL-CIO and with the Teamsters Union formed the *Alliance for Labor Action (ALA)*. In 1969 the Chemical Workers Union joined the ALA. According to ALA spokesmen, this organization does not represent a merger but rather that the groups will promote joint organizing drives, cooperate in collective bargaining, and work together on welfare and political action programs. Whether any or all of these unions will become affiliated with the AFL-CIO in the future is uncertain.

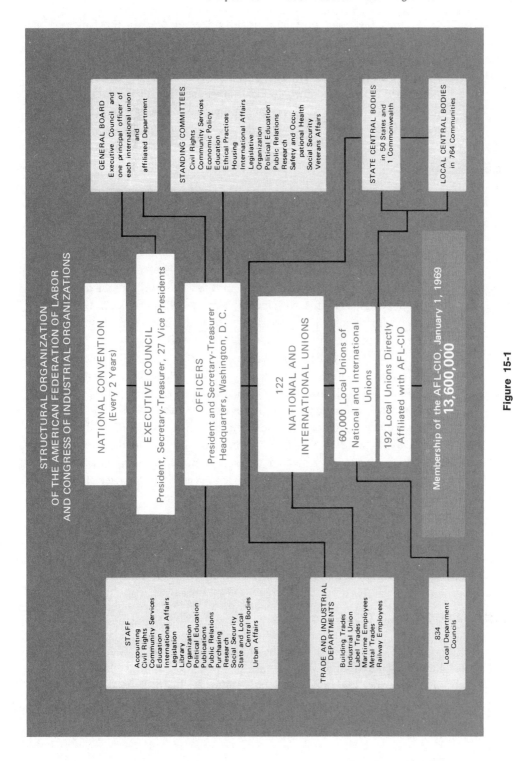

STRUCTURAL ORGANIZATION
OF THE AMERICAN FEDERATION OF LABOR
AND CONGRESS OF INDUSTRIAL ORGANIZATIONS

GENERAL BOARD
Executive Council and
one principal officer of
each international union
and
affiliated Department

STANDING COMMITTEES
Civil Rights
Community Services
Economic Policy
Education
Ethical Practices
Housing
International Affairs
Legislative
Organization
Political Education
Public Relations
Research
Safety and Occu-
pational Health
Social Security
Veterans Affairs

STATE CENTRAL BODIES
in 50 States and
1 Commonwealth

LOCAL CENTRAL BODIES
in 764 Communities

NATIONAL CONVENTION
(Every 2 Years)

EXECUTIVE COUNCIL
President, Secretary-Treasurer, 27 Vice Presidents

OFFICERS
President and Secretary-Treasurer
Headquarters, Washington, D. C.

122
NATIONAL AND
INTERNATIONAL UNIONS

60,000 Local Unions of
National and International
Unions

192 Local Unions Directly
Affiliated with AFL-CIO

Membership of the AFL-CIO, January 1, 1969
13,600,000

STAFF
Accounting
Civil Rights
Community Services
Education
International Affairs
Legislation
Library
Organization
Political Education
Publications
Public Relations
Purchasing
Research
Social Security
State and Local
Central Bodies
Urban Affairs

TRADE AND INDUSTRIAL
DEPARTMENTS
Building Trades
Industrial Union
Label Trades
Maritime Employees
Metal Trades
Railway Employees

834
Local Department
Councils

Figure 15-1

Structural Organization of the AFL-CIO

Among the other prominent independent unions are the United Mine Workers, the Order of Railway Conductors, and the Brotherhood of Locomotive Engineers. Of the other independent unions that are scattered over a wide variety of occupations, some are confined to a single plant; others are federations of many local units. Included in this latter classification are federal employees, postal employees, marine firemen, foundry and metal workers, and watch workers.

LABOR LEGISLATION

In the attempts that have been made by both labor and management to secure and retain advantages in their dealings with each other, legislation has come to play an increasingly important role. For some years the representatives of organized labor have striven to secure legislation favorable to their aims. At the same time employers have endeavored to retain the advantage that they had early in this century. The history of the more important labor laws since the early 1930's reflects the relative success with which these two parties have pursued their respective objectives at both the national and the state levels.

It is noteworthy that labor unions, over the years, have emerged from being purely economic organizations to ones which have strong political overtones. Many, if not most, national and international unions maintain lobbyists in Washington and in some of the state capitals whose function is to persuade legislators to vote favorably on measures that labor desires and against those to which it is opposed. The *Committee on Political Education*, commonly referred to as *COPE*, representing the AFL-CIO takes a very active part in the endeavor to secure prolabor legislation.

In the sections which follow, the laws that have had the most marked effect on management-labor relations are listed, and their more important provisions are set forth. In the main, the discussion will concern federal legislation, with the state laws occupying a secondary position, largely because of the variations in their provisions and their limited scope.

THE NATIONAL LABOR RELATIONS ACT

In 1935 Congress passed the National Labor Relations Act, commonly known as the Wagner Act because of the sponsorship of Senator Wagner of New York. The purpose of this law was to help workers organize into unions that were completely free from employer domination and to secure recognition for these unions from their employers. A National Labor

Relations Board, consisting of three members who were not to be affiliated with either labor or industry, was established to administer its provisions.

These provisions included a list of five so-called unfair labor practices in which employers were forbidden to engage. These were (a) to interfere with, restrain, or coerce employees in their collective bargaining or self-organizing activities; (b) to dominate or interfere with the formation or administration of any labor organization or to contribute financially to its support; (c) to discriminate in conditions of employment against employees for the purpose of encouraging or discouraging membership in any labor organization; (d) to discharge or otherwise discriminate against an employee because he has filed or given testimony under the act; and (e) to refuse to bargain collectively with the chosen representatives of his employees. The act did not recognize any unfair practices of unions.

Employees were given the right to self-organization; to form, join, or assist labor organizations; to bargain collectively through representatives of their own choosing; and to engage in concerted activities for the purpose of collective bargaining or other mutual aid or protection.

The Board was empowered to prevent employers from engaging in any of the listed unfair labor practices and also to conduct elections among employees in order to determine the representatives who should bargain collectively for them with the employers. The act also provided that representatives designated for collective bargaining by the majority of the employees in a plant should be the exclusive representatives of all the employees in the plant in matters of wages, hours of work, and other conditions of employment.

The Board was given the power to investigate instances where there appeared to be evidence of unfair labor practices by employers, together with the authorization to issue cease and desist orders where necessary.

After the validation of the act by the Supreme Court in 1937, the unionization of large segments of American industry proceeded rapidly. The so-called company union, insofar as it was company dominated and financed, underwent a change that resulted in divorcing it from the control of the company. Many completely independent unions exist, not affiliated with any outside labor groups, whose membership is confined to the employees of the companies where they are to be found. They are actually company unions but not under the influence of the employers.

From 1935 until 1947, except for the period of World War II when certain steps were taken in the area of labor relations to meet war conditions, the National Labor Relations Act remained in force without change, and organized labor never functioned under more favorable legal auspices than during those years.

THE LABOR MANAGEMENT RELATIONS ACT

As time went on, many observers felt that the Wagner Act had gone too far in trying to remedy a situation that had been more favorable to management than to labor. Accordingly, the Labor Management Relations (Taft-Hartley) Act was enacted in 1947. At first vetoed by the President, it was subsequently passed over his veto.

According to its preamble, this was "an act to amend the National Labor Relations Act, to provide additional facilities for the mediation of labor disputes affecting commerce, to equalize legal responsibilities of labor organizations and employers, and for other purposes." Under its terms all of the provisions of the National Labor Relations Act that were not amended or repealed remained in force. Some of its more important provisions concern: (1) the National Labor Relations Board (NLRB), (2) unfair labor practices, and (3) other provisions.

The National Labor Relations Board

The Board was increased from three to five members. The position of the General Counsel of the Board with rather wide powers was created. In addition to having general supervisory authority over the board's attorneys, he has charge of the investigation and prosecution of all unfair labor practices. At the same time the Board itself no longer prosecutes cases of this sort, but merely hands down decisions regarding them.

Unfair Labor Practices

The employer unfair labor practices listed in the National Labor Relations Act are continued in force except that it is no longer considered an unfair practice for the employer to express his opinion on the issues of a labor dispute provided "such expression contains no threat of reprisal or force or promise of benefit." This same clause applies to unions.

A notable feature of the new act is that it contains a list of unfair labor practices in which the unions are forbidden to engage. These are: (a) a union may not coerce employees into joining a union (except in the case of a union shop) nor employers in the selection of their representatives for collective bargaining or handling of employee grievances; (b) it may not try to force employers to discriminate against an employee (such as through discharge) except in the case of a union shop where the employee has not paid his union dues and initiation fee; (c) if a union has been certified as the bargaining agent for the employees, it cannot refuse to bargain collectively with the employer; (d) it is not permitted to engage in secondary boycotts or jurisdictional strikes, or to force assignment of certain work to certain unions; (e) the union may not charge excessive fees under union shop agreements; (f) it may not require an employer to pay for work that is not performed.

Other Provisions

The closed shop is outlawed and certain restrictions are established regarding the union shop. Unions may be sued for breach of contract and for damages resulting from strikes, jurisdictional disputes, or secondary boycotts. The NLRB may seek injunctions to prevent unions or employers from engaging in unfair labor practices. When, in the opinion of the President, an actual or threatened strike or lockout imperils the national health or safety, he may seek an injunction to postpone the action for 80 days, during which time attempts are to be made to effect a settlement of the dispute. Employers are not required to recognize or bargain with supervisors' or foremen's unions. Unions must file financial reports and copies of their rules and regulations annually with the Secretary of Labor, and the officers must certify that they are not connected with the Communist Party in any way, as prerequisites to the acquisition of any statutory rights under the act, such as petitioning the Board for an election and asking for an investigation of employer unfair practices. Unions, together with employers, are forbidden to make contributions to national political campaigns or candidates. Government employees are forbidden to strike. Of particular interest is that section of the Taft-Hartley Act (14b) which permits states to pass legislation forbidding the union shop. Further reference to this appears in the section under State Labor Legislation.

THE LABOR-MANAGEMENT REPORTING AND DISCLOSURE ACT OF 1959

This law, also known as the Landrum-Griffin Act, was enacted as a result of the revelations of the McClellan Committee in regard to racketeering and financial irresponsibility in certain unions and as a result of pressure from the public. Every union must file a detailed annual financial report with the Secretary of Labor and make the information in it available to members; disclosure of the financial and "conflict of interest" activities of union leaders is required; theft or embezzlement of union funds is made a crime; union officers must be bonded by American companies; new regulations are established for the election of union officers;

the NLRB is permitted to refuse jurisdiction over certain types of cases; *organizational picketing* (where a union places pickets outside a firm it is unsuccessfully trying to organize) is prohibited; certain aspects of secondary boycotts are eliminated; and the non-Communist affidavit clause of the Taft-Hartley Act is eliminated. Employers and labor-relations consultants must also report annually to the Secretary of Labor on all payments made or received to influence employees on labor matters.

OTHER FEDERAL LEGISLATION

Numerous other federal laws affect labor, some of which have been mentioned earlier in this chapter. Two interesting laws worthy of mention are the Byrnes Antistrikebreaker Act that prohibits the interstate shipment of strikebreakers and the Lea Act that lifted restrictions the musicians' union had placed on broadcasting school orchestras and bands. Because railroad workers have always been considered as employed in interstate commerce, much labor legislation concerning them has been separate but comparable to that applying to workers generally.

Also, the Walsh-Healey Act of 1936 requires all employers who sell goods to the federal government to an aggregate value of over $10,000 to compensate their employees at the prevailing wage rates and to observe certain standard conditions concerning hours of work, safety, and sanitary surroundings, etc.

STATE LABOR LEGISLATION

In addition to federal labor legislation, laws affecting many phases of the labor situation have been enacted by several states. Among these are laws outlawing the closed shop; banning strikes by public employees and employees of public utilities; forbidding jurisdictional, sitdown, and sympathy strikes; and prohibiting compulsory unionism. Incidentally, the Taft-Hartley Act permits states to outlaw the closed shop, the union shop, maintenance of membership, and preferential hiring; and it does not authorize any of these conditions in states where laws prohibiting them are in force. In the opinion of many students of the field of labor legislation, including many labor leaders, state laws are frequently harsher on labor in their provisions than are federal laws. This applies particularly to the so-called *right-to-work laws,* which stipulate that no one shall be required to join a union to secure or to retain a job.

The repeal of the right-to-work laws or the prevention of their being enacted by state legislatures has become a major objective of organized labor, as has also the repeal of section 14b of the Taft-Hartley Act.

BUSINESS TERMS

QUESTIONS FOR DISCUSSION AND ANALYSIS

1. Do you think that the relations between management and labor would be aided if management undertook to explain the role of profits in a capitalistic economy? Why or why not?

2. Is management justified in regarding labor as a production cost? Explain.

3. Should a worker's first loyalty be to his employer rather than to his union? Why or why not?

4. Do you think that the generation gap will tend to create disharmony between the rank and file of the unions and the union leaders? Explain.

5. Should a person ever be required to join a union in order to secure or hold a job? Why or why not?

6. Unions maintain that employers should not be permitted to establish strike insurance. Do you agree? Why or why not?

7. Do you believe that government workers should be forbidden to strike by law? Why or why not?

8. Should the membership of the National Labor Relations Board be increased to an even number with both political parties being equally represented? Explain.

9. Should strikes be permitted in public-utility industries where shut-downs would endanger the public welfare? Why or why not?

10. Do you believe that additional labor legislation is needed? If so, in what areas? If not, why?

PROBLEMS AND SHORT CASES

1. During recent years there has been a growth of union membership and militancy on the part of public and high school teachers, who are paid out of public funds raised through taxes. In several instances strikes have occurred which disrupted the education of the students in the schools which were affected. In a few cases, additional tax levies from which raises for teachers could be paid have repeatedly failed of passage by the taxpayers. There is some evidence that this situation will continue and possibly get worse. Analyze the rights and obligations of all concerned parties and prepare a short paper summarizing your conclusions as to what should be done to remedy this situation.

2. The Clayton Act of 1914 exempted labor unions and their members from the provisions of the antitrust laws. Recently this provision has been criticized and a demand for its repeal has come from several sources, principally business organizations such as the United States Chamber of Commerce and the National Association of Manufacturers. On what acts of labor have these criticisms been based? References to indexes of newspaper and magazine articles will be helpful in answering this question. In your opinion, should labor unions be subject to the antitrust laws as employers are? Why or why not?

SUGGESTED READINGS

Chruden, Herbert J., and Arthur W. Sherman, Jr. *Personnel Management,* 4th Edition. Cincinnati: South-Western Publishing Co., 1972.

French, Wendell. *The Personnel Management Process: Human Resources Administration,* Second Edition. Boston: Houghton Mifflin Company, 1970. Part VIII.

Reynolds, Lloyd G. *Labor Economics and Labor Relations,* 5th Ed. Englewood Cliffs, New Jersey: Prentice-Hall, Inc., 1970. Part Two.

Wortman, Max S., Jr. *Critical Issues in Labor, Text and Readings.* New York: The Macmillan Company, 1969.

Yoder, Dale. *Personnel Management and Industrial Relations,* 6th Ed. Englewood Cliffs, New Jersey: Prentice-Hall, Inc., 1970.

Part 5

Production

Prologue to Part 5

Production

The chapters that comprise this part deal with the acquisition and control of materials used in industry and the fabrication of these into the many different items which comprise the output of goods required by industry and consumers.

Chapter 16 describes the procedures and practices involved in the purchase of materials, including a discussion of buying practices at the producer, wholesaler, and retailer levels. The handling and control of materials is surveyed, as is inventory control at all levels. There is also a discussion of transportation problems, both within a plant and when goods have been shipped to customers.

Chapter 17 relates the more common production problems and processes that are found in the manufacture of goods. The most recent developments in production are presented, including automation and numerical control. The practices of motion and time study are examined, as are the organization and procedures of production control and the ways in which accuracy in manufacturing processes is accomplished.

Chapter 16

Materials Management

The materials employed by businesses may be divided into five broad classes. First, there are goods which are purchased infrequently and on a nonrepetitive basis such as machinery, office equipment, lighting fixtures, store counters, and cash registers. These materials have relatively long lives; they become part of the fixtures and equipment of the companies that buy them and are replaced only as they wear out or become obsolete. These goods are called capital goods or *durable goods*.

The second broad classification consists of goods that are purchased as required to facilitate the operations of a business. These do not directly become part of the goods manufactured or sold. These materials are called *supplies*, typical examples of which are office supplies and maintenance and janitorial products.

Raw materials, semifinished goods, and finished goods are the next three classes of materials, and these are directly involved in the operations of a business. *Raw materials* include ores, chemicals, paper pulp, castings, forgings, and similar products. *Semifinished goods* are also called *goods in process*. These materials have been subjected to certain manufacturing processes and are held in storage until they are needed for assembly into finished products. Among these are small motors, gears, lenses, carburetors, oil filters, and partially-machined castings. Both raw materials and semifinished goods must not only be purchased in the right quantities and qualities but they must also be controlled to make certain that they enter the production process at the right time and in the proper manner. As raw materials are worked upon, they become semifinished goods. When semifinished goods are completed, they become *finished goods* which are then placed in stock ready for shipment to customers. Control of this material is required to assure that proper quantities are on hand to satisfy customer demands.

How a particular material is classified depends upon the use to which it will be put. Iron ore is a finished good for a mining company, but it is a raw material to a steel producer. Cash register tape is a finished good for a paper manufacturer but a supply item for a retail store. A drill press is a finished good for a tool manufacturer but a piece of equipment to the maker of oil filters. An automotive supply manufacturer would consider a carburetor a finished good, but the manufacturer of automobiles would think of it as a semifinished good. Automobiles purchased by car dealers are finished goods, but those purchased by a manufacturing company for delivery purposes are equipment or capital goods.

Materials management encompasses all the activities relating to the acquisition, storage, and movement of the raw materials, semifinished goods, and finished goods used by a business. Its aim is to reduce the total cost involved in handling materials from the time an order is placed for their purchase until the finished goods are shipped to the customer. In different companies the meaning and scope of materials management vary. In general, however, it is concerned with the efficient execution of the following activities: (a) the purchase of raw materials, semifinished goods, and finished goods; (b) their handling and control after being received including the problems of storage; (c) the determination of the amounts that should be acquired; and (d) the transportation problems involved in receiving goods and in making shipments to customers.

Not only does the nature of materials management vary among companies but also the terms used to describe its various activities differ between manufacturers on one hand and wholesalers and retailers on the other. At the producers' level the procurement of goods is termed *purchasing*. At the wholesale and retail levels, the term *buying* predominates. *Inventory control* (or *stock control*) is the term used to describe the procedures and methods involved in taking care of the goods at all three levels. This chapter will discuss the problems of purchasing and inventory control as they affect producers of all goods, consumer and industrial, and the distributors of consumer goods. In the field of manufacturing, these goods are frequently called *materials*; in wholesaling and retailing, the term *merchandise* is in common usage. Following this discussion brief attention will be devoted to the incoming and outgoing transportation of these goods.

PURCHASE OF MATERIALS

Before the production of goods can proceed in a plant, the materials that make up the product must be purchased and brought into the factory. The requisite machinery, tools, transportation equipment, and other manufacturing facilities must also be present. For this discussion it is assumed that these facilities have been provided and that what is needed is to acquire the materials from which the finished products will be made. The function of the purchasing division is to assume the responsibility for seeing that this need is taken care of. Chronologically, purchasing might be regarded as the first step in production. Materials must be purchased before they can be processed.

PURCHASING DEPARTMENT

That part of the organization of a manufacturing firm that has the task of procuring the required materials for production is known as the *purchasing department*. The head of the purchasing department is usually called the *purchasing agent*. In small plants the purchasing agent and a clerk or two may comprise the purchasing department, while in larger establishments there may be a specialized group of buyers working under the supervision of a purchasing agent, who may bear the title of General Purchasing Agent or, occasionally, Vice President in Charge of Purchases.

Organization and Status of the Department

Figure 16-1 indicates the position of the purchasing department in a company of average size and shows the internal organization of the department. There is some variation in the status of purchasing departments. In many concerns the purchasing department has a separate status equivalent to sales, production, and finance. This situation is the result of a growing recognition of the importance of the purchasing function and of the need for according it appropriate organizational standing.

In companies in which purchasing is not a separate entity, it may be placed under the production manager or in the treasurer's department. In very small firms the job of purchasing agent may be a part-time activity handled by one of the executives of the firm in addition to his other duties.

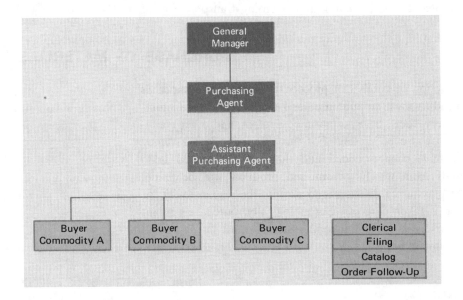

Figure 16-1

Organization Chart of a Purchasing Department

The division of the purchasing work is customarily on the basis of classes of materials rather than according to the use of the materials within the plant. Thus one man might be given authority for the buying of textiles only, rather than all the material needs of the shop. He would thus become an expert in textiles.

In some companies the receiving and material stores departments are placed under the purchasing agent as a part of the purchasing department, while in other companies these units are placed under the production manager. When they are part of the purchasing department, control routines can be established to effectuate the naturally close connection between purchasing, receiving, and storage. When they are under the production manager, interdepartmental liaison must be established so that the production division can work closely with purchasing.

Although Figure 16-1 portrays the basic organizational design of the purchasing function, such as might be found in a small-to-medium-size company, in many large firms a much greater number of buyers may be employed, depending upon the variety and breadth of the types of materials required.

The Prime Objectives of Purchasing

Every department in a business has certain prime objectives toward the attainment of which the departmental executives and personnel should constantly strive. In the case of a purchasing department four such goals can be stated quite succinctly. They are: (a) buying the proper products for the purpose required; (b) having the materials available at the time that they are needed; (c) securing the proper amount as required; and (d) paying the right price. To the extent that any purchasing department approaches the attainment of these objectives, it will be fulfilling its mission for its employer.

Centralization versus Decentralization of Purchasing Function

Many firms have widely separated plants, which brings up the question of whether the purchasing department should be centralized at the home office or decentralized and located in the field at the different branches. There is no single solution to this policy question, as there are arguments favoring both practices. For centralized buying, there is the fact of larger purchases, with frequently lower prices or larger discounts. For decentralized purchasing, the purchases would be smaller in quantity, but with possibly faster delivery, more favorable relations with local suppliers, and better inventory balance.

Extent of Purchasing Department's Authority

Although there is no question about the authority of the purchasing department to adopt procedures for the placing of orders, there are instances where the actual determination of the goods to be bought resides with the executives who will be responsible for their use in the plant or office. For example, the decision to purchase automated machine tools might well be that of the production manager, who would be accountable for the results obtained through their use. Or the selection of data processing equipment might be made by the controller or the chief statistician. These and other similar instances do not imply the downgrading of the purchasing department, but rather that those responsible for the use of certain items are given the right to choose the types or makes which they prefer. Situations of this sort have tended to increase in number with the growing complexity of the equipment used in business. Except for circumstances such as these, the purchasing department usually has the authority to buy most items bought on a repetitive basis.

Value Analysis and Purchasing

An activity that has attracted considerable attention in the past few years is known as *value analysis*. It involves a systematic appraisal and examination from time to time of products and parts for the purpose of discovering if any cost-saving changes in design, materials, or processes can be brought about. Among the participants in value analysis, along with representatives of engineering, production, and sometimes marketing, are members of the purchasing department, who can bring to bear on the problems their knowledge of suppliers' offerings and prices.

PURCHASING POLICIES

Some of the policies that govern the purchasing department may originate in that department and be decided by the purchasing agent, while others may arise in other parts of the plant and require that the executive heads of the company confer and establish the policies to be followed. Various purchasing policies deal with: (1) buying versus manufacturing, (2) hand-to-mouth buying versus forward buying, (3) speculative purchasing, (4) contract purchasing, (5) reciprocal buying, (6) sealed bids, and (7) buying ethics.

Buying Versus Manufacturing

The decision as to whether to purchase a certain part required in fabricating a firm's product or to manufacture it is obviously one that transcends the scope of the purchasing department and becomes a matter of company policy. For example, a manufacturer of washing machines must decide whether to purchase electric motors for his products or to make them. The part that the purchasing department plays in formulating such a rule is to furnish the company executives with sufficient information concerning the supply market for the item in question so that they may make a wise decision. The purchasing department should be constantly alert to any changes in the supply market that might influence the company heads to change their minds.

Hand-to-Mouth Buying Versus Forward Buying

The basic difference between hand-to-mouth and forward buying lies in the size and frequency of purchase. If a firm follows a policy of *hand-to-mouth buying*, it orders smaller amounts at more frequent intervals. On the other hand, *forward buying* involves orders for larger amounts issued less frequently. There is no sharp line of demarcation between the two; but purchasing departments tend to follow one or the other, depending upon the price aspect of the market. If prices tend to fluctuate rather unpredictably at frequent intervals, hand-to-mouth buying will probably govern the purchasing in order to minimize the risk of loss through inventory depreciation. On the other hand, if prices tend to be relatively stable over long periods of time, the company may be willing to commit itself to larger purchases at each ordering period, with longer intervals between orders.

Another factor that warrants consideration by many companies is the amount of capital tied up in their inventories of materials and parts. In recent years the concept of frequent turnover of inventories—with consequent savings in storage space required, a minimizing of risk of spoilage and damage, and the release of capital for other uses—has gained a number of adherents. Theirs is the philosophy of hand-to-mouth buying, the making of more frequent purchases of smaller amounts of materials. These firms have found, in many instances, that the savings that they are able to effect through this policy more than offset the additional purchasing, transportation, and receiving expenses, which are usually inescapable concomitants of hand-to-mouth buying. There is doubtless a point beyond which this policy cannot profitably be carried, when order sizes become so small and orders so frequent that the added costs more than offset the savings. Each company must determine this point for itself in the light of its own experience.

Speculative Purchasing

In contrast to the buying that arises directly from the current need for certain items, there is *speculative* or *market purchasing*. This means that the purchasing department, believing that prices of certain items are going to rise appreciably in the near future, places orders for them in quantities in excess of their usual amounts. This is done to take advantage of the anticipated price rise. If the amount ordered and the terms of buying bear little relationship to the current needs of the company, the speculative nature of the transaction is apparent. It is probable, in many if not most companies, that the purchasing agent would be required to secure authorization from top management before making a speculative purchase. Furthermore, the materials involved would, of necessity, have to be products that the company uses regularly in its manufacturing process.

The principal danger in speculative purchasing, apart from the amount of capital it ties up, lies in the possibility of an unforeseen price drop, which may not only wipe out the anticipated advantage that inspires this policy, but also entail a severe loss if the price decline is sufficiently far-reaching. Many businessmen believe that the proper function of a purchasing department is to buy materials to the best advantage at the time they are needed, and not to engage in extraordinary purchasing except where necessary to protect the company's supply against possible future shortages. An alert purchasing agent, however, constantly studies price trends and, if he thinks he discerns price increases in the immediate future, the temptation to try to take advantage of the situation may be overwhelming. If he guesses correctly, his company may benefit and his own prestige may be greatly enhanced.

Contract Purchasing

Contract purchasing is the policy of a company entering into contracts with its suppliers covering the purchase of certain materials, the delivery of which will be effected over long periods of time. There are two reasons for this practice—to protect the supply and to take advantage of low prices prevailing at the time the contracts are executed. Under some circumstances, where the vendor might have little control over his costs of raw material or labor, the price might not be guaranteed for a long period of time. However, the buyer would be assured of a source of supply and regular shipments.

Reciprocal Buying

Reciprocal buying means buying from customers or, stated somewhat more explicitly, favoring customers over prospective vendors who are not customers when purchase orders are placed. For example, a producer of motor trucks might buy coal only from a coal company that uses its trucks for delivery. Although this practice has been universally condemned as uneconomic and wasteful, it still persists in many lines of trade. The arguments against it are that it narrows the field of suppliers with the result that the buyer pays higher prices and possibly fails to procure the exact goods that he requires. The main argument in favor of reciprocal buying is that it helps to hold customers, a rather powerful persuasive factor.

Use of Sealed Bids

Sometimes the selection of a source of supply is made on the basis of sealed bids. When this method is used, the purchasing agent provides to prospective suppliers complete information in the way of specifications and quantities needed. The suppliers who are interested submit secret, written offers on or before a certain date, at which time the *sealed bids* are opened, the proposals are compared, and the order is given presumably to the lowest bidder. The sealed bid procedure is quite common in the procurement practices of governmental agencies—federal, state, and local—and is gaining adherents in private business and among schools and hospitals.

Buying Ethics

Unfortunately the field of purchasing has not been entirely free from some rather sharp practices on the part of the buyers. These practices have ranged from indiscriminate and pointless cancellations to the use of falsehoods in playing off one vendor against another. In some instances buyers favor salesmen who entertain them or give them valuable presents. Needless to say, these practices do not redound either to the credit or the long-time advantage of the perpetrators. Most firms recognize the value of ethical dealing with their suppliers as well as with their customers. The National Association of Purchasing Management has developed a set of rules known as the Principles and Standards of Purchasing Practice to which its members are pledged to adhere.

STEPS IN ORDERING AND RECEIVING MATERIALS

The steps leading to the purchase and receipt of certain materials are: (1) establishing specifications, (2) initiating the buying procedure, (3) investigating the supply market, (4) starting purchasing negotiations, (5) placing and following up the order, and (6) receiving the goods.

Establishing Specifications

Before the purchasing department can procure the needed goods, their descriptive details or *specifications* must be available. Industrial purchasing conforms almost entirely to specifications that are established by the purchasers. These specifications originate, usually not with the purchasing department, but customarily with the engineering staff. In setting up specifications, scientific accuracy is desirable in order that the purchasing department may purchase materials that will do the job required of them but that are not too good for the task at hand. It is uneconomical to buy a certain grade of material when a lower and cheaper grade will give satisfactory service.

Many industrial goods have industry-wide standards that are commonly recognized and accepted by all users. Nuts, bolts, screws, washers, steel bars, raw cotton, lumber, and many other finished or semifinished goods come into this category. In specifying these items, the engineering department merely indicates to the purchasing department the industry grades desired.

Initiating the Buying Procedure

In those plants where products do not vary greatly over long production runs and where the process involves repetitive manufacturing processes, the need for materials is revealed in the stock room. Records are established there that will call for the issuance of a purchase requisition when the stock of any item gets down to or below the predetermined minimum. The *purchase requisition* serves two purposes: (a) it sets forth the necessary details and specifications to guide the purchasing department in buying; and (b) it serves as a warning that the stock of the item in question has reached a point where a reorder is required at once to prevent a production delay.

Investigating the Supply Market

Before the purchasing agent is ready to place orders for requisitioned items, he must investigate the supply market for these commodities. He must know all the suppliers, whether producers or industrial distributors, their products, their prices, the quality of their wares, their terms and discounts, their reputations in the trade, their reliability to deliver goods when promised, and anything else that will enable him to perform his buying function more intelligently and to the advantage of his firm.

Starting Purchasing Negotiations

In the case of certain standardized products that are bought frequently, or in those instances in which the wanted items have been purchased before on a satisfactory basis, the order may be placed as soon as the requisition is received. This is particularly true if the price tends to remain stable over long periods of time.

In the case of goods for which the price is not stabilized, or when the company has never made a similar purchase before, or when industry standards are not available, the purchasing agent may send *letters of inquiry* to several suppliers, stating the company's needs and inviting the suppliers to submit bids or to call and demonstrate their products. Following this, there may be a series of conferences between the suppliers' representatives and the purchasing agent, who may call in the engineer or the plant superintendent to aid him in deciding on the best source of supply for the needed item.

Placing and Following up the Order

The practice of most companies is to execute a formal *purchase order*, specifying carefully all the facts pertaining to the transaction, such as an exact description of the goods wanted, the unit prices, the quantities desired, the delivery dates, the discount terms, shipping instructions, billing instructions, and an identifying order number.

In order to make certain that all orders will be delivered on time, many concerns install and operate an order follow-up system, which is designed to keep the purchasing agent informed regarding the status of all outstanding orders. Through frequent contacts with suppliers, the follow-up man endeavors to make certain that there are no delays in the receipt of goods for which orders have been placed.

Receiving the Goods

When the goods arrive, they are checked against the copy of the order by the receiving clerk to make certain that all of the provisions of the purchase order have been met. With certain types of goods it is desirable to institute an inspection routine to check on the quality of the shipment. If the shipment is correct in quantity, quality, and price, the goods are sent to stock, and the vendor's invoice is certified for payment. If there are any discrepancies between the order and the shipment, the purchasing department should be notified so that the shipper can be contacted and the error remedied. Pending rectification of the error, the goods may be held in the receiving room. Or, if the difference is one of quantity and the vendor is one of the firm's regular suppliers, the goods may be put in stock pending later adjustment.

HANDLING AND CONTROL OF MATERIALS

From the moment that industrial materials arrive at the receiving platform or yards until they emerge as the completed product and are loaded for shipment to customers, they must be handled and moved from place to place in accordance with the nature of the finished product and of the materials themselves. The movement from the receiving room is frequently to stock rooms, where the materials are stored until they are needed in production. Then they must be taken to the point of the first application of the production process and thence through the manufacturing routine until the finished product is ready to be shipped or sent to storage to await future shipment.

MATERIALS CONTROL

Industrial materials are placed under a system of strict control as soon as they reach the receiving department; and they remain under it, in one form or another, until the finished product is delivered to the shipping department for transportation to a customer. *Materials control*, which takes the form of records and procedures, is designed to keep the management constantly informed of what materials and how many units of each are in the plant, and in what departments they are located. It provides a written record of the transfer of materials from one department to another and of the manufacturing processes through which the materials pass, and it serves as the authority for such movement. It is likewise important as a source of cost data for the cost accounting department.

The details of materials control procedure vary considerably from industry to industry and from company to company. The basic philosophy of the operation, however, is much the same in all concerns. When the goods are first received and placed in stock, records are made of all pertinent data. All subsequent movements of the materials, however simple or complex, are accompanied by such paper work as is necessary to inform the management of their exact location at all times. Periodic counts are made to be certain that none of the items has been lost in the production process. Whenever materials move from one place to another within the plant, records are adjusted to reflect this transfer and to fix the responsibility for their custody. Identifying tags accompany all goods to facilitate accurate checking. As a means of providing information on the number of items of each kind in the stock room, perpetual inventory records are kept. As the stock minimums are reached, purchase requisitions are made out for the purchasing department. The use of computers is rising rapidly in this area of materials control, as through their memory capacities the location and quantity of each item can be stored and retrieved quickly.

METHODS OF HANDLING MATERIALS

The methods used in handling materials are determined by the nature of the materials, by the layout of the factory, and by the type of product made. No small part of the cost reduction in manufacturing that has taken place in recent years has been achieved through improvements in the handling and moving of materials. In the early days of manufacture most of the moving of materials was done by hand with trucks and skids, but recent years have seen a definite swing toward mechanical conveyors. Whenever possible, gravity has been harnessed for this purpose and in many industries it supplies almost the entire motive power for handling materials. Because of the multiplicity of devices in common usage and the specialized nature of the handling problems in each industry, the various conveying methods will be merely named here. No attempt will be made to describe them or to suggest the ways in which they might be employed. Chief among these devices are overhead cranes, conveyor belts, roller conveyors, pipe lines, trucks, overhead conveyors, and forklift trucks. A fast-growing device for handling materials is the driverless tractor, which, through a pattern of slots in the floor, enables a hidden towline to move them to any location desired in the warehouse. There materials may be either loaded on the tractors or removed from them by warehouse employees using various types of mechanical equipment.

STORAGE OF MATERIALS

To a large extent, the storage of materials is a problem the solution to which is dependent upon the nature of the goods and the manufacturing processes to which they are subjected. Coal and iron ore are usually stored on the ground; liquids, such as chemicals, paints, and oils, are kept in tanks; small metal parts are stored in bins in stock rooms; and so on.

Stock rooms may be centralized or decentralized, depending upon the area covered by the production division and the rapidity with which the stored materials are consumed in manufacture. The basic idea back of the stock room operating policy should be that of having the materials available for production at the times they are wanted, in such quantities as to ensure unbroken operation of the production facilities, and yet not to impede free movement of the operating personnel in performing their duties.

PURCHASE AND CONTROL OF MERCHANDISE

Problems of purchasing and control are also encountered by non-manufacturing enterprises, such as wholesalers and retailers, in connection with merchandise. The problem of purchasing in wholesale and retail businesses differs from that in manufacturing enterprises. Wholesalers and retailers buy only finished goods, and the major factor that determines which items shall be purchased is the probable salability of the goods.

WHOLESALERS' BUYING PERSONNEL

In wholesale establishments the persons who are responsible for the purchasing are known as *buyers*, except in small firms in which the buying function is assumed by one of the company heads. Larger concerns quite commonly employ a number of buyers, each concentrating on a group of related items. For example, in a grocery wholesale house there might be a buyer for canned and frozen goods; one for fancy groceries; one for cereals, flour, and other staples; and one for nonfood related items, such as soaps, cleansers, detergents, and paper goods. Concerns of this size frequently have a head buyer who is in charge of all buying personnel and is responsible to the top management for the operation of his department. In addition to his supervisory duties, he usually does some buying for his company. Frequently his position is of vice-presidential rank.

WHOLESALERS' BUYING PROCEDURES

Wholesale buying procedures are relatively simple and are divided into two kinds: original buying and repeat buying. In the case of original purchase, the buying of goods that have not been handled before, it is customary for the salesmen to contact the buyers and to demonstrate their wares, either in the manufacturers' showrooms or at the wholesalers' places of business. If the sale is consummated, a purchase order is made out, indicating the goods involved and such other data as prices, terms, delivery dates, and transportation methods. The purchase order forms are not essentially different from those used by industrial purchasing agents, except that the specifications cover finished goods rather than industrial materials. The initial stimulus to make the purchase may come from advertising put out by the producers, visits by salesmen, or requests from customers.

Repeat purchases (in many lines these comprise the bulk of such operations) are usually handled by mail on a routine basis. The incentive to make the purchase usually comes from the fact that the stock records indicate that the supply of the items to be purchased has fallen below the prescribed minimum requirements.

RETAILERS' BUYING PERSONNEL

Although retail buying follows the same general pattern in all stores, there is a notable difference between the carefully determined practices of the department stores, the chain stores, and the specialty stores on the one hand, and the unorganized buying procedures of small stores on the other. In the larger stores the purchasing personnel are called buyers and customarily are in complete charge of the departments for which they buy, including responsibility for sales, stocks, and personnel. Each buyer specializes in a relatively few closely related items and becomes quite expert in these fields. For example, in a typical department store there will be a furniture buyer, a toiletries buyer, a housefurnishings buyer, and others. Each buyer is responsible for the profitable operation of his department, and he endeavors constantly to buy the merchandise that will appeal to his customers.

Until the early 1920's, most department and specialty store buyers reported directly to the heads of their stores. Since then the position of *merchandise manager* has come into being for the purpose of securing for the store management a closer supervision over the activities of the buyers, which, of course, includes that of buying. For convenience, the various merchandise departments have customarily been separated into four groups, called divisions. They are the Main Floor, Apparel, Home Furnishings, and Basement divisions. Each division is headed by a merchandise manager whose authority extends over the buyers of the departments in his group.

In the chain stores, other than in department store chains, the personnel are likewise known as buyers, but they are usually situated at some central buying office, which may or may not be located at a merchandise warehouse. They customarily confine their activities to buying and have no other responsibilities. The buying organization is usually set up in the same manner as in the larger wholesale establishments, with a head buyer in charge of the others, each of whom buys only certain commodities. In most instances the member stores of department store chains do not follow the orthodox chain pattern in their buying practices, but instead each store maintains a complete corps of buyers who act in the same manner as the buyers of wholly independent stores.

In small stores the proprietors usually do the buying along with their other managerial and entrepreneurial duties.

RETAILERS' BUYING PROCEDURES

In the larger stores the buyers frequently take the initiative in seeking out new goods and make regular trips to the market centers for this purpose. They customarily buy the bulk of their merchandise direct from the manufacturers and employ wholesalers only rarely. Their buying practices for original purchases are simple and involve viewing available lines of merchandise, selecting the desired items, and making out the order. The order forms are much like those already described. Repeat buying is a routine procedure, usually handled by mail. The incentive to make original purchases arises from goods seen on previous market trips, magazine advertisements, competitors' offerings, and occasionally customers' requests. The incentive for repeat buying comes from the stock cards when the on-hand figures show that the stock is below the established minimum.

In the chain stores the opposite procedure is to be found, with the salesmen going to the buyers as a general rule.

Buying in small stores may take place in the stores with the wholesalers' salesmen in attendance or in some instances at the wholesalers' warehouses. Retailers' purchase order forms for these stores are practically unknown. The orders are taken on the wholesalers' blanks. Frequently the wholesalers' salesmen enter the stores, count the retailers' stocks of the goods concerned, and make out the orders for the quantities that they believe should be purchased. This procedure, of course, applies only to repeat purchases. For original purchases the salesmen display the goods and endeavor to persuade the retailers to buy them.

In the large stores careful preparations are made by the buyers in advance of their trips to the market. *Buying plans*, which set forth in detail the types, sizes, costs, and selling prices of goods to be bought, are prepared and followed quite closely during the time when the buyer is in the market. Limits to the amount of money to be spent, as well as the approximate retail prices at which the goods will be offered, are established. In the small stores buying is done more or less on the spur of the moment when the wholesalers' salesmen appear.

INVENTORY CONTROL IN MANUFACTURING

Most businesses cannot operate effectively without some stock of goods on hand. Generally companies must order goods ahead of customer demand. If a company does not maintain adequate inventories of merchandise or finished goods, customer relations are hurt, the reputation of the company as a dependable source of supply is damaged, and sales are lost. A manufacturer who does not avoid inventory shortages of raw materials and semifinished goods finds that the flow of production is interrupted, that machines and equipment are not fully utilized, and that costs are increased. On the other hand, if inventories are excessive in comparison to customer demand, funds are tied up which could be used for other company purposes, storage costs are increased, and the inventories are likely to suffer deterioration, obsolescence, or theft. Because companies cannot accurately predict the amount of inventory needed to fulfill customer orders and the times at which these amounts will be sold, management faces the twin dangers of either too much or too little stock on hand. It is the goal of inventory management to find the optimum level of stock on hand under conditions of changing market demand, production requirements, and financial resources.

INVENTORY CYCLE

The level of goods on hand within a company rises and falls in a cyclical manner. The *inventory cycle* consists of two phases: the period in which goods are ordered and received and the period in which they are put into production or sold.

Some of the problems of inventory control can be seen in a very simple, hypothetical situation. Suppose that Company X has annual sales of 20,800 units and that the sales are made uniformly throughout the year at the rate of 400 units a week. The units can be obtained from a dependable supplier in carload lots of 400 units. It takes one week to place and process an order and one week to deliver the order from the supplier to Company X. Lead time is, therefore, two weeks.[1] If an order is placed for 400 units on the first day of the first week of the inventory cycle, the goods will be available for use on the first day of the third week. By the beginning of the fourth week, the inventory will be depleted. Therefore, if an *out-of-stock* is to be prevented, a second order must be

---

[1] Lead time in this instance is the number of days, weeks, or months from the point when an order is placed to that when it may normally be received.

placed at the beginning of the second week. This cycle of ordering and using goods must be regularly repeated throughout the year. Figure 16-2 below illustrates the inventory cycle.

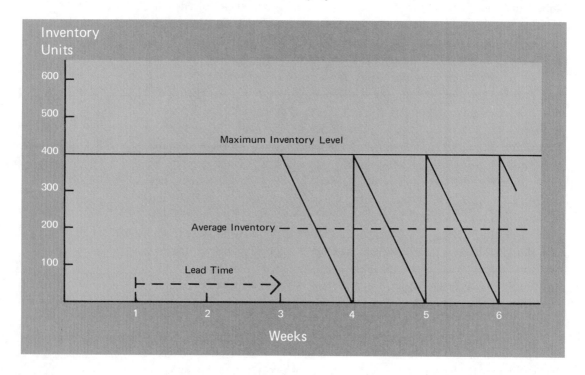

Figure 16-2

Inventory Cycle

The *average inventory* carried over the period of this regular cycle is equal to the minimum inventory plus one half of the order quantity. In this hypothetical situation there was no minimum inventory or *safety stock*. The average inventory was one half of the amount regularly ordered, or 200 units. If the minimum inventory were 200 units, the average inventory would be 400 units [200 + (400 ÷ 2)]. The size of the safety stock not only affects the average level of goods on hand but also has an important bearing on the cost of carrying the inventory.

Changes in lead time also affect the carrying cost of the inventory. If the lead time in this illustration could be reduced from two weeks to one week, the order quantity could be reduced and average inventory could be lowered.

MAXIMA AND MINIMA

The average inventory is obviously between the minimum and maximum levels of inventory. In the previous example when the average inventory was 200 units, the minimum inventory was zero, and the maximum inventory was 400 units. When the safety stock was set at 200 units, the maximum inventory was 600 units and the average inventory was 400 units. Thus, management may view the *minimum inventory* as the basic level necessary to provide uninterrupted production or good customer service and the *maximum inventory* as the level it can afford to carry in view of the costs involved. Maximum and minimum quantities of stock on hand are one set of guides for seeking the optimum level of inventories in view of cost, timing, and policy considerations.

In the same example presented, the demand for goods was accurately predictable, and the supply was regular and dependable. In actual practice, however, numerous factors influence management's decision concerning minimum and maximum inventory levels. Different policies are called for with respect to finished goods, goods in process, and raw materials.

In establishing the minimum and maximum levels of the raw materials inventory, management will consider such factors as:

1. The dependability of the supplier.
2. The distance between the supplier and the company.
3. The amount of storage space required.
4. The dollar value of the raw material and its susceptibility to price fluctuations.
5. The rate of flow of material from storage into productive operations.

The inventory level for goods in process is largely determined by the marketing characteristics of the product and the type of processes used in manufacturing the finished goods. Some of the major factors that influence the inventory level of semifinished goods are:

1. The relative proportions of raw material cost and labor and overhead costs in the finished product.
2. The seasonality of demand.
3. The number of customers.
4. The frequency of model changes.
5. The degree of standardization of the finished product.
6. The cost of storing semifinished goods.

In a similar manner there are factors which must be weighed in establishing the inventory level of finished goods. Some of the more important considerations are:

1. The customer's concept of "good service."
2. The ordering practices of customers.
3. The obsolescence rate or perishability of the product.
4. The relative value of the finished product.
5. The time required to convert raw materials into finished goods.
6. The cost of storing finished goods.

In recent years the use of the computer and the application of mathematics have helped many managers to achieve a better understanding of the relationships that exist between costs and risks involved in carrying inventories.

INVENTORY CONTROL IN WHOLESALING AND RETAILING

Department and specialty stores and the chains maintain fairly elaborate inventory control records as a guide to purchasing and to account for the merchandise that they handle. In the smaller stores such records are almost unknown and stock control is practically nonexistent.

A typical stock control record consists of a file of cards, one for each different type of goods, which provide for complete descriptions of the items and their sources, together with spaces to record the arrival of merchandise, its outward movement as the result of sales to customers, and the current balance of stock on hand. Minimums are computed for those items subject to repeat purchase for the purpose of notifying the buyers when the stock of these items is getting low. Maximums are also computed in order that the buyers may be advised of the items for which the stock on hand is running too high.

A new term has appeared in the area of control of retail inventories of style merchandise. This is known as *style life inventory management* (SLIM). With the aid of computers a procedure has been devised with the objective of preventing an accumulation of garments that are selling slowly, and also making certain that an adequate stock of fast selling items is always on hand.

Wholesalers customarily maintain these records for all of their merchandise, as do the chains. Department and specialty stores do likewise for goods for which repeat purchases are made and for some types of merchandise that move slowly and of which a reserve stock is kept in stock rooms. Many kinds of goods, such as women's apparel, toiletries, and accessories, sell so rapidly, however, that the entire stock is carried in the selling departments (*forward stock*); and only the most rudimentary stock records are kept, if indeed any are kept, on many fast-moving items.

TRANSPORTATION

Materials management is not only concerned with the purchase and storage of materials and with the control of costs relating to these two operations; it also attempts to minimize the cost associated with the shipment of goods to or from the company. The transportation factor in materials management involves decisions concerning costs, speed, and the selection of a particular carrier from among those that are available in a given locality. If the products concerned, such as lumber and cement, can be moved by water, the problem may take on quite a different aspect than if that form of transportation is not available. The expansion of the country's network of highways, which has greatly facilitated the development of truck transportation, has served to widen the markets for companies that are able to ship their products in this manner.

TRANSPORTATION MEDIA

The major methods of transportation are: (1) railroads, (2) motor trucks, (3) waterways, (4) pipelines, and (5) airplanes.

Railroads

The railroads handle the largest part of the transportation in this country, embracing a total trackage of some 390,000 miles, and carrying between 2 and 3 billion tons of freight each year. Railroad rates are generally expressed in rates per 100 pounds or per ton from the point of origin to the destination. A distinction is made in the rates applicable to goods shipped in carload lots (*CL*) and those shipped in less than carload lots (*LCL*). LCL rates are generally between 15 and 30 percent higher than those for carload shipments.

Motor Trucks

For relatively short hauls, up to 300 miles, motor trucks compete with railroads. They are of particular importance for communities with infrequent or no railroad service. Their rates vary from levels lower than those applied by the railroads to those measurably higher. In many parts of the country, a combination truck and rail service, known as *piggyback freight*, is available. In this instance, goods are loaded on trucks which, in turn, are driven up onto special railroad flat cars. These cars are then made a part of a train moving in the direction of the trucks' destinations, frequently overnight. Later at a predetermined point, the trucks are driven off the cars and proceed under their own power to the points to which the goods are consigned.

Waterways

The waterways of the country—rivers, the Great Lakes, and the coastwise routes—are of considerable importance in the movement of certain kinds of freight, such as goods of large bulk and low value, of which coal, grain, oil, lumber, sugar, and cotton are examples. Water transportation is the cheapest but also the slowest method of moving goods. The Great Lakes are important to the movement of iron ore, grain, and coal. The rivers are used to move cotton, coal, and building materials. Coastwise shipping is useful for oil, cotton, lumber, and coal. The St. Lawrence Seaway has increased the international trading facilities of Great Lakes ports. Water transportation also affords a type of service called *fishyback freight*, similar to the piggyback freight of the railroads, in which trucks can be driven onto ships and transported to points nearer their destinations.

Pipelines

A network of around 160,000 miles of pipelines is used to transport crude petroleum and natural gas. If the cost of building a pipeline is to be justified, there must be continuous processing of the material transported at each end of the line. For this reason, companies owning the pipelines consider them to be extensions of their productive facilities rather than as transportation devices. While pipelines have the disadvantages of governmental regulation and inflexible routes, they have a distinct cost advantage over transportation by railroad or motor carrier.

Airplanes

Air transportation is noteworthy for its speed, its advantage in long-distance hauling, its relatively high cost, and the fact that its cargoes must consist of items of relatively small bulk and high value, or quick perishability, although more recent developments would seem to indicate that quite large commodities can be flown to their destinations. Many of the major airlines of the country offer air-freight service to and from the bigger cities, utilizing large jet aircraft.

INTERNAL TRANSPORTATION

Intrafactory transportation of parts and materials is costly. A well-planned layout, having due regard for the materials-handling equipment on hand or available, will reduce this cost to a minimum. In recent years this factor has been receiving an increasing amount of attention from engineers and builders who have recognized the cost-saving aspects of layouts where crosshauling is reduced to a minimum and where a straight-line pattern of moving goods can be employed most fully.

THE TRAFFIC DEPARTMENT

Transportations costs generally range from 6 to 20 percent of the goods sold, and for some companies the costs may reach 50 percent. This significant expenditure must be controlled. In order to provide transportation service for the company at costs consistent with services rendered, traffic departments have been established in most companies. The traffic department is directed by a *traffic manager*.

The traffic department is principally concerned with the movement of incoming and outgoing freight. It commonly performs the following functions:

1. Packing, marking, and loading.
2. Freight rate negotiations.
3. Consolidation of shipments.
4. Preparation of bills of lading and other shipping papers.
5. Routing of shipments.
6. Handling of insurance coverage and claims against carriers.
7. Expediting and tracing shipments.
8. Warehousing.
9. Operating company-owned or leased transportation equipment.
10. Providing information on transportation aspects of new plant or warehouse locations.

The management of traffic affects many other departments of the company. The processing or manufacturing departments expect an adequate flow of materials scheduled at the right time. Careful scheduling of inbound and outbound shipments is required in controlling the size of inventories. The traffic department shows the purchasing department the most advantageous purchasing areas from the standpoint of transportation costs and services. Since the transportation rate for small quantities is relatively greater than that for large quantities, information from the traffic department can help the purchasing department determine the economical size of purchase. The traffic department can show, for example, how small shipments can be consolidated and shipped in carload or truckload lots at lower cost and better service.

PHYSICAL DISTRIBUTION

The use of the computer and the development of a more comprehensive management viewpoint have caused many companies to advocate *physical distribution management* or *business logistics*. The goal of this managerial concept is better customer service at lower costs. It emphasizes the control of total costs of transportation, warehousing, inventory control, protective packaging, and materials handling. It seeks to achieve its objective by a detailed analysis of the total cost of each stage in the flow of materials from the raw state to finished goods in the hands of customers. Within each stage of the physical distribution of goods there are alternative choices. Through this detailed study, the business logistician seeks to point out the decision which will lower total costs and improve service.

BUSINESS TERMS

QUESTIONS FOR DISCUSSION AND ANALYSIS

1. Why should the term purchasing be commonly used at the producers' level, while buying is the one found at the wholesale and retail levels?

2. In some companies materials management is the responsibility of the purchasing department, while in others a separate department exists for this purpose. Why should there be this difference in policies? Which is preferable?

3. Do you think that the purchasing agent for a factory should be a member of top management? Explain.

4. Why should purchasing agents be included in the group that works on value analysis?

5. Should a company have an inflexible rule prohibiting the purchasing agent from speculative purchasing? Why or why not?

6. Do you think that the arguments for reciprocal buying should carry greater weight than those against it? Why?

7. How can unethical buying practices be eliminated?

8. A common saying in retail stores is "think selling before buying." What does this mean to you?

9. In chain stores why is it customary for the suppliers' salesmen to go to the buyers rather than otherwise, as in department stores?

10. Are the transportation costs mentioned in this chapter higher or lower than you would have estimated? What was your reaction to the statement that these costs might run as high as 50 percent?

PROBLEMS AND SHORT CASES

1. For several years department store managements have been endeavoring to effect a separation of the buying and selling functions in an attempt to follow the practices of their chain store competitors, mainly specialty shop and variety store chains, where this procedure is the rule. Present arguments both for and against the department stores' effecting this change and also give reasons why the chain groups appear to be successful in their present practices.

2. The apparent rise of consumerism with the concomitant demand by consumers for better and more reliable merchandise has raised some rather crucial questions for sellers of consumer goods at all levels— production, wholesaling, and retailing. Consumer representatives have repeatedly complained of the shoddiness of many of the commodities that are to be found in the stores, including automobile and appliance dealers. Prepare an essay setting forth evidence of the validity of consumers' complaints and giving your opinion as to methods whereby these evidences of consumer dissatisfaction can be corrected. Current magazine and newspaper articles can provide you with abundant evidence of consumer dissatisfaction, with some suggestions as to what can be done to lessen their discontent.

3. Manufacturers, wholesalers, and retailers have long been faced with a common problem—either they do not have sufficient goods or materials on hand to satisfy the future demand, thereby losing potential sales, or they have stocks on hand in excess of the demand, thereby risking spoilage, obsolescence, necessary markdowns, and other losses. Formulate a method for all sellers that will alleviate this problem, if not entirely eliminate it.

SUGGESTED READINGS

Ammer, Dean S. *Materials Management*, Revised Edition. Homewood, Illinois: Richard D. Irwin, Inc., 1968.

England, Wilbur B. *Modern Procurement Management: Principles and Cases*, Fifth Edition. Homewood, Illinois: Richard D. Irwin, Inc., 1970.

Heinritz, Stuart F., and Paul Farrell, eds. *Purchasing Principles and Applications*, 4th Ed. Englewood Cliffs, New Jersey: Prentice-Hall, Inc., 1965.

McElhiney, Paul T., ed. *The Logistics of Materials Management: Readings in Modern Purchasing*. Boston: Houghton Mifflin Company, 1969.

Ullmann, John E., and Samuel E. Gluck. *Manufacturing Management: An Overview*. New York: Holt, Rinehart and Winston, 1968.

Chapter 17

Production Problems

The word "production" is often used in the sense of making things. This is, however, a narrow definition of the word. In a broader and more fundamental sense, *production* is the transformation of the inputs from human and physical resources into outputs desired by consumers. The outputs may be either goods or services. In this sense production is a wider concept than manufacturing, which is but a special form of production. In this sense, too, wholesalers, retailers, and service organizations are engaged in production. Any business firm is, therefore, an organization for converting skills, information, and materials into goods or services which satisfy customers and which, hopefully, will result in a profit to the owners.

The inputs into an enterprise are labor, materials, energy, information, and funds, as well as certain environmental factors. The contributors of these inputs are managers, employees, suppliers, customers, owners, creditors, and the general community. The inputs from the various contributors are combined and converted into goods and services to be sold to customers.

This very broad concept of production must be narrowed somewhat for practical purposes; otherwise it would encompass, and hence blur, the role of marketing in our economy. In narrower terms production is the business function concerned with the supply of goods or services, and marketing is directly concerned with the demand side of any business.

Production involves changing and blending a great variety of inputs into goods and services to be sold. Marketing revolves around the determination of consumer wants, the ability of consumers to buy, and the entire process of exchanging goods or services for income to the firm. Both production and marketing, as basic business functions, are aided by the functions of personnel (the acquiring and using of human skills and competence) and finance (the acquisition and utilization of funds). Clearly in each of these four basic functional areas—production, marketing, personnel, and finance—the management functions mentioned in Chapter 7 must be exercised with a high degree of skill if the company is to be successful.

KEY DECISIONS IN PRODUCTION

The problems of transforming inputs into salable outputs require two major types of decisions. One set of decisions relates to the design of the production system, which generally involves long-run strategic decisions. The other set pertains to the operation and control of the system in both the short- and long-run.

The long-run decisions affecting the design of the production system are:

1. Location of the production facility. Where will the factory or store be located in reference to nearness of markets, closeness to adequate supplies of labor and materials, environmental pollution controls, and other factors?
2. Layout of the facility. How shall the factory or store be arranged so that its operations are efficiently carried on?
3. Selection of equipment and processes. What equipment will be purchased so that goods or services may be produced at minimum cost?
4. Production design of items processed. In what form (pattern, style, quality) will goods and services be made?
5. Job design. How shall the human work of production be subdivided among people in view of skill, health, and costs involved?

The first four of these decisions are largely a matter of engineering and financial consideration. The fifth was alluded to in Chapters 6 and 7.

Decisions relating to the daily operations and control of the production system are those pertaining to: (a) the improvement of efficiency of operations, (b) the control of the quantity and quality of output, and (c) the maintenance of reliability of the system. To give some background for the making of these decisions is the purpose of this chapter. In order to make the discussion specific, the concept of production will now be confined to the process of manufacturing.

MANUFACTURING PROCESSES

The methods by which materials of industry are produced or made into the things that industry or consumers want are known as *manufacturing processes*. These methods of production may be classified in three different ways: according to the nature of the process, on the basis of the time of production, and in reference to the character of the product manufactured.

ACCORDING TO THE NATURE OF THE PROCESS

The classification of production processes according to their nature identifies types or forms of substances used in manufacturing a product. These processes are: (1) extractive, (2) analytic, (3) fabricating, and (4) synthetic.

Extractive Process

In some industries the basic production process is one of extracting substances from the earth or the sea, known as the *extractive process*. Examples of this process are the mining of coal, iron ore, lead, gold, and silver; drilling for petroleum; and the extraction of magnesium and other chemicals from the ocean. Farming and fishing may be called extractive industries, but they are on an ownership and operating basis different from the above industries.

Analytic Process

The *analytic process* is one in which a basic substance is broken down into a number of other materials, which may or may not bear any resemblance to the parent substance. In this category are petroleum refining, meat packing, and lumber milling.

Fabricating Process

The term *fabricating process*, although used principally in the structural steel business, refers to a process that is rather widespread in industry wherein a material has its form changed to some extent by being machined, woven, cut up, pressed, finished, or treated in some other manner. It is sometimes called the *converting process*, particularly in the textile field. Examples of the fabricating process are to be found in the manufacture of clothing, shoes, certain types of furniture, nuts, and bolts.

Synthetic Process

Synthetic process refers to those industries in which a number of different materials are combined to form a single product. In the manufacture of steel, glass, rayon, and dinnerware the final products are quite different from the original ingredients because of physical or chemical changes. In other industries, such as in the production of automobiles, electrical appliances, or radios and television sets, where the materials are merely assembled without undergoing physical or chemical change, this process is sometimes called the *assembly process*. This is particularly true in industries employing the assembly line as a part of their manufacturing process. The automobile industry is a good example of one that uses this method. In this case the frame of the car or truck is placed on a long, slowly moving conveyor; and as it passes the various stations on the line, the different component parts—such as the motor, the transmission, the drive shaft, the rear axle, the wheels, and the body—are attached; and at the end of the process the car is driven off the line under its own power and to the final inspection that it receives before shipment to some dealer.

It is quite common to find the fabricating and synthetic processes operating in a single company. The decision of some producers to make rather than to buy some or all of the components of their products results in the combining of these two processes in these firms. Continuing with the example of the automobile manufacturers, it is common practice for them to fabricate their motors, bodies, transmissions, and other metal parts, while buying tires, batteries, and fabrics for upholstery from the makers of these products. The comparative costs of buying or producing these parts are usually the determining factors in the decisions to make or to buy them.

ACCORDING TO THE TIME OF PRODUCTION

When production processes are characterized by the periods of time during which the productive facilities are kept in operation, they are identified as either (1) continuous processes or (2) intermittent processes.

Continuous Process

The term *continuous process* is used to describe a manufacturing situation where long periods of time may elapse before any radical changes are made in the set-up of the machinery and equipment involved, that is, most or all of the machines will perform the same operations indefinitely. The production of automobiles where model changes occur only once a year is an example of the continuous process. Another instance of continuous production is found in the steel industry where the productive facilities must be kept constantly in operation for relatively long periods of time, necessitating day and night shifts and Sunday work. In this business the furnaces must be kept hot, once they have been lit, until a shutdown is caused by a mechanical failure, lack of orders, or, occasionally, a labor dispute. If the furnaces are allowed to cool, they must usually be rebuilt before they can be used again. Thus it is evident that the term "continuous process" may include industries where production may be halted every night—a one-shift operation—and resumed the next morning, and also those where the characteristics of the production pattern require the operation to run without stopping for long periods of time—months or even years—depending on the demand for the products.

Intermittent Process

The term *intermittent process* involves manufacturing conditions in which the duration of each run is sufficiently short so that the machines are shut down rather frequently and retooled to produce some different product. Most so-called job shops come under this category. A *job shop* has certain manufacturing facilities, such as machine tools or foundry equipment, that are available to make almost anything that its customers want. What is being produced in a plant of this type at any given time is what the current customers have ordered; and it may differ radically from what will be made six months hence.

ACCORDING TO THE CHARACTER OF THE PRODUCT

Production processes which are characterized by the presence or absence of customers' specifications for a particular product are classified as (1) standard manufacture or (2) custom manufacture. Occasionally both of these types are found in the same company. The principal or standard product is one that bears the maker's brand name but, because it does not require the use of all of the producers' manufacturing facilities, the company keeps the factory fully employed by taking on a certain amount of custom business in addition to its own standard product.

Standard Manufacture

Standard manufacture is the production of articles which are frequently originated, developed, and branded by the manufacturers. Some common examples of standard articles are television receiving sets, refrigerators, men's hats, toothbrushes, and toiletries. Standard manufacture frequently involves producing for stock, as well as for immediate shipment to customers and to dealers. This may be occasioned by a seasonal selling period, even though production continues the year round, because of the need for a reserve stock from which deliveries can be made to customers who are unable or unwilling to wait for goods to be manufactured, and for the purpose of stabilizing production when the demand is irregular. This condition raises questions of securing sufficient capital to carry the inventories, of providing adequate storage space and custodial personnel, and of the risk of loss through market price declines, fire, or theft.

Custom Manufacture

To firms engaged in *custom manufacture*, the problems raised in standard manufacture are not usually present since the customers specify the quantities to be made and the firms limit their production to these amounts. Custom manufacture includes the production of such commodities as made-to-measure men's clothing, machine tools designed for special jobs, counters and fixtures for retail stores, and elevators and escalators.

The automobile industry provides something of a variation on both custom and standard manufacture. While there are certain fundamental features that are common to all models of a given make, such as the frame, wheels, motor, and basic body types, customers may specify such items as the color, character of upholstery, transmission type, power brakes and steering, and hi-fi equipment, which will be assembled at the factory in accordance with their individual choices. There thus emerges a combination of standard and custom manufacture for those buyers who wish to take advantage of this opportunity.

RECENT DEVELOPMENTS IN PRODUCTION

During World War II and the years following, the need for greater production of goods and more economical methods brought about a number of noteworthy developments in production that may conceivably rank in importance with the introduction of the assembly line shortly after the end of World War I. These include: (1) new materials, (2) new processes, (3) miniaturization, (4) numerical control, and (5) automation.

NEW MATERIALS

The first group of recent developments in production embraces those synthetic substances commonly called "plastics." It also includes the discovery of new alloys through the combining of various metals into compounds that possess greater strength than any of them alone and the finding of new uses for materials that have long been known to production engineers and metallurgists. The utilization of titanium alloys, cermets (metal-filled ceramic materials), beryllium, and chromium-based alloys, as well as the more recent applications of aluminum, are examples of this latter type.

NEW PROCESSES

A considerable number of new processes, or refinements of old ones, have appeared in recent years. Among these are: the use of liquid nitrogen to fast-freeze foods at —320 F, which permits of the freezing of tomatoes, avocados, and other foods that had previously resisted freezing for commercial purposes; the pelletizing of low-grade ore that allows the mining companies to use a grade of ore for steelmaking that had been previously considered worthless; continuous casting in the steel business that eliminates many time-consuming, costly steps in the making of steel; the basic oxygen furnace, also in steel, that is replacing the open-hearth method of many years' standing; and electrical discharge machining, whereby the metal is eaten away by an electric spark, which saves on expensive finishing operations.

MINIATURIZATION

Noteworthy progress has been made in the area of *miniaturization*, the development of products and production equipment on an ever-smaller scale. This has been particularly evident in the field of electronics, which has been characterized by frequent design changes in the interest of less material and less processing.

NUMERICAL CONTROL

Numerical control (N/C) is a procedure by which machine tools are actuated electronically by the use of coded tapes to perform a number of predetermined tasks. In the automobile industry a dramatic development is unfolding in the shortening of the lead time involved in the designing and developing of a new model. The lead time in the automobile field has traditionally been from 20 to 24 months. Through the use of N/C in the designing and producing of the dies for forming the various car body parts, this time has been cut dramatically. The procedure, somewhat simplified for explanation, calls for the stylist to construct a clay model of the proposed car, the contours of which are scanned by a device somewhat like a television camera, which translates these contours into computer language. The computer puts these data on a tape that can be fed into a N/C machine instructing it how to cut the body dies.

AUTOMATION

The term automation is applied to circumstances where computers control the operation of machine tools, with the assistance of a feedback by which information regarding the progress of the operation is relayed back to the computer to enable it to make any adjustments or corrections that may be necessary. If the computer is capable of making the requisite adjustments in the machine without human assistance, this is known as *closed-loop control*. In a circumstance where the computer is not connected with the instruments that can make machine adjustments, it will signal for the operator to reset the machine. This is known as *open-loop control*.

Of particular interest is the trend toward the automatic or "robot" factory—one in which machinery is substituted for manpower—a condition that has been closely approximated in the manufacture of petroleum and some chemicals. In some of the newer steel rolling mills, a computer governs the speed of the steel strips, makes continual adjustments in the roll openings to keep the gauge constant, takes X-ray pictures of the moving strips, and automatically corrects any errors in the process before the tolerances of the strip are exceeded. This is all done automatically by closed-loop control. In other factories metals are transported, machined, formed, perforated, or strengthened, in accord with the type of manufacturing processes involved. The devices that are employed for these purposes are called *servo-mechanisms*—the brains and muscles of completely automatic machine tools.

The fundamental purpose of automation, which has been called the "second industrial revolution" by some observers, is that of reducing the costs of production—and this usually means labor costs. In an era of advancing wages and a trend toward shorter working hours, managements have been forced to seek out new and effective methods of cutting costs in order to remain competitive. To the extent that automation, in the plants that have adopted it, results in lower production costs, it can be said to be an economical movement and it may be expected to increase in extent and importance as long as this objective is attained. From the standpoint of the workers who are displaced by automated processes and whose skills are no longer required, a personnel problem is involved the solution to which is presently unclear and which was discussed in Part 4.

RESEARCH AND PRODUCTION

The creation of new products and methods has come about as the result of unceasing research in these fields. Under the relentless pressure of competition, many far-sighted manufacturers have established research departments for the purpose of seeking out new products with which to invade the market and cheaper ways to produce those already in their lines. Very large sums of money are spent annually for these purposes. A few of the leaders in the field of product and production research are Procter and Gamble, General Motors, DuPont, General Electric, Dow Chemical, and Ford. The General Motors proving ground near Milford, Michigan, is the oldest, largest, and best equipped automotive testing ground in the world. Here and at two other locations, the corporation carries on extensive research and testing of its automotive products.

Governmental expenditures for defense and space exploration have also fostered new methods and products in manufacturing. The innovations pushed into use by World War II were digital computers, nuclear energy, jet propulsion, penicillin, DDT, and rocket engines. The application of mathematics to the study of defense against submarine attacks spurred the increasing use of quantitative methods for analyzing production management problems. From Project Apollo, which landed the first men on the moon, have come new technological advances in metal forming and in controlling the reliability of complex equipment.

PRODUCTION MANAGEMENT

Topics that are of particular interest to the manager of production in a manufacturing enterprise are: (1) the organization of production, (2) work improvement, (3) production control, (4) maintenance of equipment, and (5) quality control and inspection. How well he solves the problems arising in each of these areas greatly determines the cost of each unit of output produced.

ORGANIZATION OF PRODUCTION

In a manufacturing company the responsibility for producing the goods that the firm makes is placed with the production division, which is composed of groups of specialists, each of whom is expert in planning, supervising, or performing one or more of the various steps in the productive procedure. The extent and complexity of the organizations involved depend on both the size of the companies concerned and the relative intricacy of the manufacturing processes required. Figure 17-1 portrays the organizational aspects of a medium-sized firm that makes a fairly simple product. It should be noted that the production control and inspection divisions, while subordinate to the production manager, are completely independent of the actual manufacturing division, the pattern of whose work they control and whose products they inspect, respectively.

WORK IMPROVEMENT

The goal of *work improvement* is the reduction of effort, time, and cost in productive operations. Attaining this goal depends on understanding what each operation in a production system involves, studying details of each work step, and then trying to find a better way of performing the tasks. Work improvement seeks the answers to four questions: (a) Can some part of the work be eliminated? (b) Can some parts of the task be combined? (c) Can the sequence of work steps be changed? and (d) Can the operation be simplified? Answers to these questions depend on knowing in precise detail why the work is done and how it is done. One of the most widely used methods of work improvement in manufacturing is motion and time study.

Motion and Time Study

A common method of studying the motions of workers as they perform their tasks and of measuring the time that these motions require is known as *motion and time study*. In this manner management seeks to establish time standards for the performance of all productive work, which are of value in the exercise of production control. The principal purposes of motion and time study are as follows:

1. To determine the best methods of performing each task. Through breaking each job into its component elements and observing the time required to perform each element, management can determine the most efficient methods to be used.
2. To aid in planning production. When management is confronted with the task of planning production, the knowledge of the standard time required to perform each operation is of value in setting up the production schedule. This has an additional importance when the planned operations include some that have not yet been time studied. Through the study of the elements involved, for which time standards may have been previously recorded on other jobs, it is possible to arrive at approximate time standards for the new jobs that are useful in estimating the probable production time.
3. To control operating costs. Through the use of time standards established through time study, comparisons can be made between

Figure 17-1

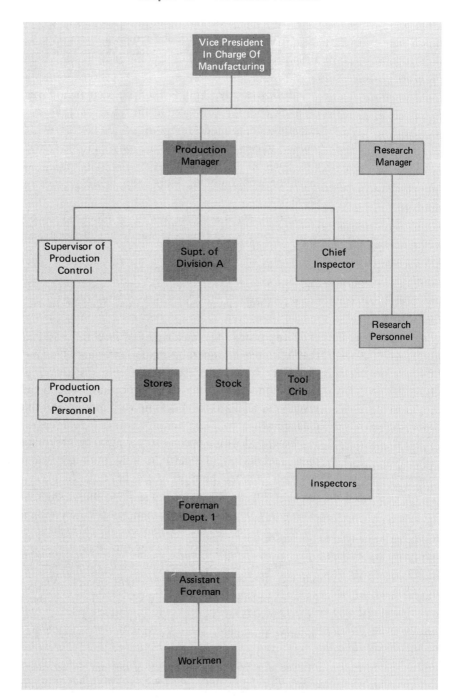

Organization Chart of a Production Department

the standards and the actual performances by the workers. Differences can be noted, and remedial measures can be applied to bring the actual performance into line with the standard performance. Thus, control of labor costs can be achieved.

Motion study. This is the first step in analyzing a job and consists of a careful scrutiny of all the motions that go to make up a task. Examination is made not only of the actual motions that the observed worker makes, but also of the physical conditions surrounding the job site, such as the distance from the machine to the boxes holding the incoming and outgoing work, the lighting, and anything else that may affect the job.

The principal purpose of *motion study* is to establish the most effective way of doing a job from the standpoint of the motions involved. A skilled observer can quickly detect waste movements that can be corrected in the interest of better performance. From this study will come a series of elemental motions that will produce the best method of doing the job. Each of these elemental motions can then be timed.

Time study. The mechanics of *time study* is a rather technical process that requires considerable experience and training on the part of the observer. It is not desirable in this discussion to go beyond a brief description of the time-study procedure. The details are more properly given in specialized texts dealing with motion and time study or production management.

Equipped with a special stop watch, an observation sheet for recording data, and a special board to hold both the watch and the sheet, the observer stations himself where he can see everything that the worker does during a *job cycle*.[1] He then times each elemental motion and records on the observation sheet the findings in each instance. This goes on until a considerable number of job cycles have been completed, sometimes as many as fifty. During this time the observer notes everything that happens, all delays—from whatever cause—and all of the worker's actions, whether cyclically recurrent or not. When the observations have been completed, a time-study clerk calculates the time allowance for a unit of work by adding the periods of time required for the elemental motions that make up that unit. The standard thus determined can be

---

[1] The term job cycle refers to all of the motions necessary to the complete processing of one unit of work, for example, the drilling of a certain number of holes in a piece of steel or iron. The job cycle includes everything the operator does from the moment he turns to pick up the undrilled iron piece until he lays down the finished piece.

used as a measure of efficiency in production as well as a base for determining the worker's compensation.

The extension of automation throughout industry would certainly
lessen the importance of motion and time study because of the progressive
elimination of the machine operators. The degree to which this situation
will affect skilled workers is uncertain at present.

Micromotion Study

A refinement of the time-study method is *micromotion study*, which
involves the use of a motion-picture camera. Instead of an observer who
watches the worker and records the times of the elemental motions, a
camera captures the actions as well as the times, which are taken from a
clock with a large dial that is placed in focus with the operator. The
analysis of the film is made later by trained engineers. This method is of
value when the operation involves a great many motions that are too rapid
or complicated for the human eye to follow. Micromotion study is probably used on a limited scale because of the cost involved, as compared
with the gains achieved, and the relative shortage of competent observers
and analysts.

PRODUCTION CONTROL

In its highest state of development, *production control* consists of a
well-defined set of procedures that has as its objective the coordination of
all of the elements of the productive process—men, machines, tools, and
materials—into a smoothly flowing whole, which results in the fabrication
of products with a minimum of interruption, in the fastest possible time,
and at the lowest obtainable cost. The details of the various systems of
production control differ according to the characteristics of the industries
in which they are used, but the basic principles are the same. The present
discussion will be limited to (1) types of production control, (2) steps
in production control, and (3) a new management tool known as Program
Evaluation and Review Technique.

Types of Production Control

There are two types of production control: order control and flow
control. *Order control* is used by manufacturing concerns that operate
their plants only when they have received orders from their customers.
Flow control is used in factories that produce for stock and are prepared
to make immediate deliveries from their finished goods inventories as soon

as customer orders are received. The procedures in both types are approximately the same, and it is their function either to make certain that the flow of materials through the factory is such that the promised delivery dates are met, or that the delivery to stock is so timed that a proper balance of stocks to sales may be maintained at all times.

Steps in Production Control

The basic steps in production control, in the order in which they occur, are described below.

Planning. When a customer's order or a company stock order is received by the production planning department, it is broken down into its component parts. This involves a *bill of material*, which lists the finished parts, subassemblies, and assemblies that are called for by the order. This list, in turn, is broken down into those parts that are purchased in finished form from other manufacturers and the materials that are bought for fabricating and processing in the company's own factory. After reference is made to the inventories, purchase requisitions for the parts and materials needed are issued to the purchasing department, which issues purchase orders to the proper vendors.

From the engineering and production departments information is secured that indicates the number and types of machines that are required, the processing time for each part, and the tools that will be needed. From this information the production control department can determine the starting dates for processing all parts and materials so that they will arrive at the assembly at the proper time. If any tools are not available, the purchasing department is notified so that it may place orders in time to assure their being on hand when needed.

Routing. *Routing* is the stage of production control which determines the route that the work will take through the shop and where and by whom the processing shall be done. It specifies the sequence of operations pertaining to a single part and also in regard to its relationship to other parts. Routing is sometimes regarded as part of the planning process.

Scheduling. *Scheduling* involves the setting up of the timetables that will govern the movement of the work as it is subjected to the various fabricating processes. A *master schedule*, which indicates the number of finished products that will come off the assembly each month or week until the order is completed, is created.

Weekly departmental schedules set forth the expected production of all parts in each department for each week of the production cycle. Care is taken not to schedule work for a department in excess of that department's capacity to deliver, taking into consideration the normal contingencies that must be met, such as machine breakdown, set-up time, length of shift, and number of shifts. By *set-up time* is meant the time required to prepare the machine for a particular job. This includes adjusting the cutting tools and the machine speeds.

Load ahead schedules are made up for each department. These indicate the amount of work that lies ahead of the department until the present run is completed. The load is altered from week to week as the actual production results are achieved. The load ahead schedule is very important from the standpoint of scheduling subsequent jobs as orders are received. It prevents scheduling more work for a department than it can handle.

Another part of this operation is that of scheduling purchase requisitions so that purchase orders may be placed with a view to achieving well-balanced inventories, and of scheduling tools so that the toolroom will have the proper tools on hand when needed.

Performance follow-up and control. After the preparatory steps have been completed, work orders are released and production starts. The putting into effect of the work orders and the transmission to the shop of the routing papers are called *dispatching*. Elaborate control boards are sometimes set up, utilizing various printed forms that show the progress of the work in the shop and serve as indicators of production irregularities which call for supervisory corrective action. The function of production control then becomes that of following up on all of its performance schedules to detect any significant variations from the plans, to discover and correct the causes of these variations, and to compensate for any irregularities.

Various follow-up routines are established, particularly for purchases, tools, and production. *Schedule performance reports* are issued by the production control department on the basis of parts and schedule follow-up reports received from the operating departments. These reports set forth the performance of all departments as compared to the schedules. In this way top management is kept informed of the flow of work through the shop, and it can note any deviations from the plans and fix accountability for them. *Scrap reports*, received from the inspection department, relate the number of pieces rejected and the reasons. These reports permit the production control department to notify the production department of an unusually large number of pieces scrapped so that arrangements can be made for additional production to take their places in order to prevent shortages from occurring at some later stage with a possible consequent delay in delivery of the products to customers.

As the flow of production progresses and the processed parts move to the subassemblies and to the final assembly and finally emerge as finished units, the paper work routine (see Figure 17-2) indicates this to the production control department and the records are marked accordingly. When the entire order is completed, the schedules are terminated, the whole project is wound up, and the records are filed for future use.

The foregoing description has been presented as if a single order were all that occupied the attention of the production control department at any one time. This is an oversimplification in many instances, as it is more likely that a large number of orders, in varying stages of completion, are running coincidentally. The principles of operation, however, are as outlined and, if followed through on each order, regardless of how many other orders the department may be processing at the same time, they will result in an intelligently controlled production situation, with a minimum of cost and a maximum utilization of productive facilities.

To an increasing degree the use of computers has been growing in the different areas of production control. In all of the steps involved in production control, it has been proven beneficial in some plants to employ these electronic devices as aids to the performance of the functions previously handled manually. The further extension of this trend will depend upon the relative costs of using computers or of continuing with the older methods.

In recent years certain statistical and mathematical techniques called operations research (see Chapter 26) have been adopted by many firms. One of these techniques, linear programming, is particularly useful in production control procedures. It has been helpful in problems involving the optimum, or lowest cost, allocation of all of the various instruments of production and production control. The development of high-speed computers has made large-scale linear programming possible.

Program Evaluation and Review Technique (PERT)

In 1959 the U.S. Navy and Booz, Allen & Hamilton, a management consulting firm, developed a new management tool for production control of the Polaris guided missile project. This new method of control is called *PERT* (Program Evaluation and Review Technique). It is a means of minimizing production delays and interruptions, of coordinating the various

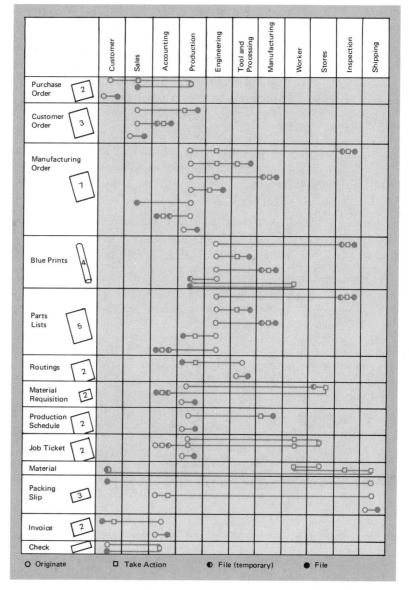

Figure 17-2

Courtesy John G. Carlson, Stanford University

Flow of Paperwork in a Production Control Procedure

parts of the overall project or job, and of expediting the completion of the work. It seeks to achieve the completion of projects on time.

No longer is PERT confined to military projects. Manufacturers, builders, and advertising agencies find PERT a useful tool in making the best use of time, money, and manpower.

One of the interesting and beneficial aspects of PERT has been the development of the *critical path method* (CPM). This is particularly helpful in the estimating of the length of time that will be required to complete an order for a customer. In brief, the procedure in establishing the critical path is to note the different times required for each separate productive operation and to add the times for operations that cannot be performed concurrently in order to arrive at the greatest amount of time that will be required to finish the order. In this way it becomes possible for a producer to quote reliable delivery dates with a greater probability of being able to meet these dates than might otherwise be the case.

Figure 17-3 is a simple example which may be used to illustrate the fundamental characteristics of PERT and CPM. Suppose that in a five-step process the first two steps, A and B, may be performed simultaneously. Steps C and D depend on the completion of Step A. Step E depends on the completion of A, B, and C. This type of sequence of steps or activities may arise in the making of parts in a machine shop, in arranging a meeting, in planning a trip, or in devising a promotion campaign. The pattern of events and activities may be represented graphically as a network.

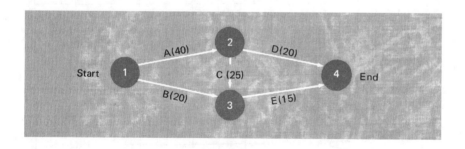

Figure 17-3

Simple PERT Network

The lines represent activities, or steps in the work; the circles indicate events, the point in time when an activity starts or is completed. At event 1, activity A begins and is scheduled to be completed in 40 hours; and at the time of completion of step A, event 2 occurs. Event 2 is the end of step A and also the beginning of both steps C and D, which are estimated to require 25 and 20 hours, respectively.

One of the first questions that should be asked of a network diagram is how long will the entire process take. What is the longest way through the network; in other words, what is the path with the least slack time? In the example shown in Figure 17-3, inspection indicates that the series of steps A, C, E, is the longest route, requiring 80 hours. The route of A-C-E is called the *critical path*. These three steps determine the completion time of the process. Activities B and D are slack steps: they allow leeway in the time of their completion and need not be strictly controlled. For example, step B could last as long as 65 hours without delaying the overall process. Activities B and D are noncritical in contrast to the path A-C-E which must be completed on time if the scheduled time of 80 hours is to be met. If the process is to be made more efficient in order to beat the scheduled completion time, activities A, C, and E are the steps which must be critically examined and streamlined.

In practice the PERT network consists of many hundreds of thousands of steps or activities, and the critical path cannot be found by inspection. The largest networks yet analyzed—those concerned with the production of new automobiles, rockets, or manned space vehicles—may be made up of from 20,000 to 30,000 different activities. The computer becomes a necessary instrument in finding the critical path in these situations.

MAINTENANCE OF EQUIPMENT

Modern factories are highly mechanized. Machine failure can have very serious effects and may result in the loss of thousands of man-hours of productive labor or even in the shutdown of the plant. Preventing breakdown of major equipment is a prime responsibility of any production manager. *Maintenance* embraces all the activities involved in keeping machinery and equipment working at a desired level of reliability. *Reliability* is the probability that a production system or individual piece of equipment will function properly for a specified time after it is installed.

Three direct methods of attaining a satisfactory level of equipment reliability are: establishing a repair facility, using preventive maintenance, and providing redundancy. The company that establishes and uses its own men and equipment to provide emergency repair service can usually shorten the *downtime* created by machine breakdowns. A repair facility is a necessary requirement for preventive maintenance. *Preventive maintenance* depends upon periodic inspection and systematic, routine care of machinery. Regular inspection often detects necessary repair or replacement in advance of breakdowns. *Routine maintenance* seeks to prevent excessive wear and deterioration by systematic oiling, cleaning, and overhauling of equipment. If the cost of downtime is very high and if preventive maintenance is both difficult and expensive, a company may turn to redundancy to avoid plant shutdowns. *Redundancy* is the use of a parallel path of production so that breakdowns will not paralyze the entire operation of the factory.

If a production manager seeks to minimize the costs of machine breakdown through any one of these three methods, a key element is the existence of satisfactory records that provide information about the frequency and cost of various types of maintenance and repair work. Without adequate records, management can only guess at the effectiveness and efficiency of a maintenance program. Without detailed records the cost of maintenance cannot be controlled nor can the newer mathematical analyses of maintenance and repair programs be used.

QUALITY CONTROL AND INSPECTION

In all manufacturing operations the work is produced to certain standards that must be met if the commodities in question are to meet the requirements of buyers in a satisfactory manner. These standards are usually set forth in writing for the guidance of production and inspection personnel. The function of *inspection* is to measure the extent to which these standards have been observed and to detect and reject any part of the product that is not up to the standard. The establishment of these standards and the subsequent inspection is called *quality control*.

Inspection is performed by a special department that is set up for that purpose and that is frequently under the supervision of the works manager; but only rarely are the inspectors under the control of production department foremen. The reason is that the duty of the inspectors is to "call them as they see them"; and as the rejection of material is somewhat of a reflection on the foreman in charge, a more objective determination of quality can be obtained if the foreman is not the inspector's immediate superior.

Time of Inspection

The problem of when inspection takes place is dependent upon the complexity of the manufacturing processes concerned and the wishes of the management. Most incoming parts and materials are inspected as they arrive from the vendors. After this point the minimum inspection requirement is one made of the finished article before it is shipped to the customer. The maximum conceivable number of inspections would include an inspection after each separate operation with a 100 percent final inspection. Originating during World War II and continuing since then, 100 percent inspection of all ordnance items has been generally required of their suppliers by the armed services.

In most cases the prevailing practice is somewhere in between these two extremes, depending upon the nature of the manufacturing processes, the tolerances permitted, and the past history of defective material and workmanship. The term *tolerance* refers to the practice of permitting a certain leeway in the measurements of manufactured parts.

Place of Inspection

The inspection operation may take place at one or more centralized locations to which the work is transported and where the inspection personnel are more or less specialized and completely removed from contact with the workers whose product is being examined; or it may be done at every work station. The latter method has the advantage of saving material transportation costs, but also the disadvantage of the proximity of the workers and the inspectors.

In certain complicated machining operations, the worker does his own preliminary inspection as the work progresses, but the work is checked by an inspector when the job is done. An inspection is quite common immediately after a machine has been set up for a new operation and before the production run has started.

Inspection Devices

A wide variety of tools and devices are used in inspection such as gauges, chemical processes, X-ray equipment and electrical apparatus. Some plug gauges are quite simple in their construction and application, while others are exceedingly complicated. Micrometer gauges are a part of the tool equipment of most machinists and are widely used in inspection work. Electrical devices are valuable in inspecting electrical apparatus, and the X-ray has recently been employed to detect flaws in castings and other materials where visual inspection methods are inadequate.

Inspection can aid in exposing weak points in the production process so that management can apply remedial measures. It can also help to build goodwill by preventing the shipment of finished products that vary from the prescribed standards.

Inspection must be conducted objectively according to a set of standards that should be sufficiently rigid to assure the satisfactory operation of the parts concerned, but flexible enough to allow for the permissible variations and tolerances within whose limits the materials are acceptable. Inspection standards should be as high as necessary, but should not be needlessly strict. The determination of these limits is the concern of the engineering department.

Quantity Inspected

There are three methods of meeting this problem—100 percent inspection, single-sample inspection, or multiple-sample inspection. The 100 percent method is required only in those instances where the products are of exceptionally high quality, where the accuracy of the manufacturing processes is dependent more on the skill of the operators than on that of machines, and when required by the Armed Services. The choice between the other two methods depends on how close the tolerances are and the extent to which the productive processes are mechanized.

Statistical Quality Control

An inspection procedure that has been growing in usage in American industry is known as *statistical quality control*. It involves the use of certain mathematical principles that are applied through statistics and has resulted in a reduction in the number of items that need to be inspected, with a consequent saving in the cost of inspection. This new system of inspection has been extended into a quality control of manufacturing processes so that variations from acceptable standards are detected before a large number of pieces have been spoiled.

BUSINESS TERMS

QUESTIONS FOR DISCUSSION AND ANALYSIS

1. Do you believe that there is any justification for the inclusion of wholesalers, retailers, and service organizations in a definition of production? Why or why not?

2. Do you think that the head of the manufacturing division in a plant should have the authority to decide what should be produced, or should this be the province of the sales manager? Explain.

3. In what ways would you expect the increasing emphasis on environment to affect manufacturing processes?

4. Give examples, other than those given in the text, of custom manufacture.

5. Would you anticipate that a completely automated plant would ever come into being? Explain.

6. One of the arguments advanced in favor of automation is that it removes the drudgery of repetitive work from human operators. Do you think that this would be a determining factor when a company is considering installing automated equipment? Explain.

7. Do you believe that workers, when subjected to a motion and time study observation, would always put forth their best efforts in the operation being studied? Explain.

8. Can you name any types of manufacturing businesses where modern methods of production control would not be necessary?

9. Would you expect to find both order control and flow control in the same plant? Explain.

10. Can you think of any circumstances where workers might be permitted to inspect their own work? Explain.

PROBLEMS AND SHORT CASES

1. Consult current and recent issues of such periodicals as *Business Week* and *Fortune* in your school library and collect a portfolio of at least five advertisements or articles that are illustrative of recent advances in production procedures. These could include such items as machine tools, automation, machinery, new inventions, electrical controls, etc. Write a brief report on your findings estimating the probable importance of each item to the field in which it is operative.

2. Make a motion and time study of some simple operation, such as shuffling and dealing cards for four hands of bridge, winding and resetting a clock that has been permitted to run down, or inserting a new lead in an automatic pencil. Prepare a report showing (a) the nature and purpose of the study; (b) the procedure that was followed; and (c) the findings including your recommendations regarding the best manner in which to perform the operation and a reasonable time standard. You should indicate the elemental motions into which the overall operation was divided.

3. Howlett and Houston, Inc., is a medium-sized firm producing a line of standardized pumps and compressors that are used in a large number of different industries. Its sales have averaged around $5 million yearly for the past decade or so. Basically this company is more of an assembling organization than a manufacturing one, since it has long been its policy to purchase most of the component parts of its pumps and compressors and to assemble them for delivery to its customers as orders are received. The firms supplying these parts number around 50, with most of whom Howlett and Houston has done business for many years.

The rapid advances made in the technology of production have created a number of problems for this firm. It is increasingly being requested to supply pumps and compressors that differ from those which have long comprised its line. This situation has required the firm to seek out new sources of supply, for many of its regular suppliers are unable to provide the parts needed for the types of pumps and compressors that are currently in demand. This circumstance has caused Howlett and Houston to lose occasional orders due to its inability to find suppliers who could provide it with parts in time to satisfy the delivery dates specified by its customers. Also, some of the items furnished by new resources do not come up to the standards of quality that are necessary for the more precise specifications of the present-day products, causing both delay in filling orders and an increased incidence of rejected parts. The executives of Howlett and Houston are giving a great deal of thought to adopting a policy of manufacturing all or most of the components that go to make up the company's products.

Write a report setting forth all of the factors that the company should take into consideration in arriving at a decision in this matter.

SUGGESTED READINGS

Abramowitz, Irving. *Production Management—Concepts and Analysis for Operation and Control.* New York: The Ronald Press Company, 1967.

Timms, Howard L., and Michael F. Pohlen. *The Production Function in Business*, Third Edition. Homewood, Illinois: Richard D. Irwin, Inc., 1970.

Part 6

Finance

Prologue to Part 6

Finance

Partly because of the daily stock market reports provided by television, radio, and newspapers, there is more interest on the part of the general public in financial matters than in such other business activities as production or sales. Furthermore, within a firm financial considerations are constantly affecting decisions made by management. It must know where to secure needed dollars and how to manage those in its possession.

Available sources of funds for business that are appropriate for short-term and long-term financing are discussed in Chapters 18 and 19. As a corollary to securing funds, the specialization of instruments and institutions that exist to assist businesses in solving their financial problems are also described.

The background provided by the above two chapters sets the stage for a meaningful discussion of financial problems and policies in Chapter 20. The emphasis in this chapter is on decision-making techniques that relate to the financial management of business enterprises.

The last chapters in this part cover two distinctly different financial areas. The relationship of security markets to all open corporations, with emphasis on their value plus that of selected financial information, is explained in Chapter 21. In Chapter 22 the types of risks that are a part of the environment surrounding business operations are reviewed with emphasis on those that can be transferred to insurance companies.

Chapter 18

Short-Term Financing

Every business unit, large or small, has financial needs and requirements. In most instances a business enterprise, without regard for its type of ownership, finds it necessary to own some combination of cash, inventories, equipment, and buildings. These items, as well as other properties, are called *assets*. When firms first begin business, they secure funds from their owners or creditors to purchase the necessary assets. Later, profits may be retained in the business or, if the firm is expanding, owners and creditors may make additional investments. These funds are considered as comprising the firm's *capital*, which is one common use of this term.

TYPES OF CAPITAL

There are two major types of assets: current and fixed. *Current assets* include cash, receivables (amounts due from customers, for example), and inventories. In general, current assets other than cash are those that in the normal course of business will be converted into cash within one year or, in some instances, will be consumed within this period of time. There tends to be a continuous flow of current assets to cash as inventories are sold and receivables are collected. Because of this constant movement, current assets are also called *circulating capital*. *Fixed assets* consist of real estate, machinery and equipment, and other tangible items that have a useful life of from one to many years. For many businesses funds that have been invested in these constitute the *fixed capital* of the firm, although this category may also include investments and intangible assets.

The distinction between the two types of capital is important because short-term financing is better suited to satisfying circulating capital needs, except for a minimum permanent supply that must be maintained year in and year out, whereas long-term financing is more appropriate for supplying fixed capital needs. It is usually satisfactory for a business to borrow money from a bank on a 60-day note to purchase merchandise that will be sold in less than 60 days because the receipts from the sale of these goods will provide the cash with which to repay the loan. On the other hand, the purchase of land and buildings, for example, should be financed with funds secured from the owners of the business or from lenders who do not expect to be repaid for a number of years.

This chapter will deal primarily with *short-term financing*, which consists of obligations, or debts as they are ordinarily called, that have a maturity date of less than one year. Typical debts include amounts owed to suppliers of goods purchased from them on credit terms, to banks and other financial institutions that have made short-term loans to the firm, and other types of payables. These are called *current liabilities*. The difference between the total current assets and the current liabilities is called *working capital*. This amount represents the total circulating capital that has been obtained from long-term financing sources.

Management of working capital is extremely important to the success of a firm. It is a task usually assigned to the treasurer or controller. It is inefficient to have too much cash on hand, but it is also hazardous not to have enough to pay wages, salaries, and outstanding bills when they are due. Too large an inventory is expensive, but not having enough can lose production time or sales. Money borrowed, except on trade credit terms, involves an interest cost. The job of financial management is to have the right amount and types of current assets on hand at all times and to provide these at the least possible cost, which generally involves the use of short-term debt.

ADVANTAGES OF SHORT-TERM FINANCING

The use of short-term financing is advantageous to a firm for several reasons: (1) seasonal needs can be met more efficiently, (2) acquiring a good credit reputation may prove helpful, (3) growth can be financed without constant resort to long-term sources, and (4) the total cost of financing may well be less.

SEASONAL NEEDS

The sales made by many businesses are uneven over the months of the year. Department stores, for example, have peak sales between Thanksgiving and Christmas. Merchandise to be sold during this period is purchased no later than September or October, and the suppliers expect to be paid long before the customers buy the goods. By borrowing for 60 or 90 days, the firm is able to pay promptly, often taking advantage of cash discounts offered. By the close of the year the receipts from sales have usually provided the cash necessary to repay the loan.

CREDIT RATING

Most business concerns buy the equipment, supplies, and goods needed by ordering from a supplier with the intent of paying after delivery has been made. If bills are met promptly, the firm acquires a good credit rating. Then, if an emergency arises in the future that precludes prompt payment, the supplier will usually be willing to carry the customer beyond a due date if past experience has been favorable.

GROWTH REQUIREMENTS

Although starting a business or acquiring an existing firm normally creates a demand for capital at a specific date, growth is usually gradual. Since resort to long-term financing is not done on a day-by-day basis, financing a steady increase in size is accomplished more efficiently by use of short-term financing. As loans mount in total, there will eventually come a time when management will decide to liquidate the short-term debt by resorting to long-term financing.

LOWER COST

To the extent that current assets in use are represented by amounts owed to suppliers, there is no cost to this portion of the total capital. If funds have been borrowed, the rate may well be higher than could be secured on a long-term commitment, but the time factor reduces the cost. If funds are needed for only 60 days in a year, it is less expensive to borrow for this length of time even at a higher rate than to pay a lower rate of interest for an entire year on a long-term obligation or to pay dividends on more shares of stock.

SHORT-TERM OBLIGATIONS

In order to meet short-term financing needs, business firms assume one or more of several types of obligations. These debts may be owed to trade creditors or to institutional and individual lenders. Practically all businesses, large and small, make regular use of at least one and, frequently, more than one of these sources of short-term funds. It would be unusual to find a firm that does not owe a supplier for goods bought on credit terms, and borrowing from a commercial bank on one or more occasions during a year is a common business practice.

TYPES OF SHORT-TERM OBLIGATIONS

Short-term obligations may take several forms with open-book accounts and notes payable in favor of a commercial bank being by far the most common. An examination of the following types of obligations will clarify the distinctions among them and indicate their appropriate uses: (1) open-book accounts, (2) notes payable, (3) commercial drafts, (4) bank acceptances, and (5) commercial paper.

Open-Book Accounts

When a manufacturer, wholesaler, or retailer buys materials, equipment, supplies, and merchandise from a supplier with the implied obligation to pay the invoice at a later date, an *open-book account* is entered on the books of both companies involved. Somewhere between 85 and 90 percent of all business transactions in the United States involving the sale and purchase of goods use an open-book account. Although not usually thought of as a loan, the net effect is that the seller is financing the buyer for the period of time between the receipt of the goods and the payment of the bill rendered. Between retailers and consumers the term *charge accounts* replaces open-book accounts.

The smooth flow of business transactions in this country could not be maintained without the use of open-book accounts. The manufacturer buys raw materials on credit terms, converts them into finished goods, and sells them to wholesalers on open account. The wholesaler sells the merchandise to retailers without requiring immediate payment, and the retailer may do likewise in his sale to the consumer. When consumers pay for their purchases, the cash received by the retailer permits him to pay the wholesaler who, in turn, can pay the manufacturer. Although the manufacturer, wholesaler, and retailer may have paid for the specific goods sold the ultimate consumer from their supplies of permanent work-ing capital, the receipt of cash all along the line permits payments for goods still in the distribution channels.

Length of credit terms. Because of the added amount of time needed by those farther back in the flow of goods from maker to user, credit terms granted to manufacturers are usually longer than those extended to the wholesaler, and so on to the retailer and consumer. For example, raw materials may be sold to the manufacturers on credit terms of 90 days, the manufacturer may extend 60 days credit to the wholesaler, the wholesaler may allow the retailer 30 days, and the retailer expects his regular charge accounts to be paid once a month, which means credit from 1 to 30 days. Actually, credit terms vary by industries and by differ-ent suppliers. Granting more liberal credit terms may be one of the ele-ments of competition.

Frequently the maximum length of the credit terms is not used because the seller allows the purchaser a cash discount. As described in Chapter 10, if an invoice carries the terms 2/10, net 30, the buyer can deduct 2 percent if he pays within 10 days after the date of the invoice. Although the payment of an open-book account within a cash-discount period shortens the duration of the use of this source of short-term financing, the saving is so substantial that many firms have a policy of taking advantage of every cash discount offered.

Actually, if the terms of an invoice dated, for example, June 15, are 2/10, net 30, the debtor firm has the option of paying the invoice price less 2 percent on or before June 25 or of waiting 20 more days to pay the full sum. This means that 2 percent is earned for the 20-day interval, and, since there are 18 such intervals in a 360-day interest year, the rate of interest on an annual basis is 36 percent.

Each different cash-discount allowance changes the interest-earned rate; but regardless of the rate of cash discount, money can usually be borrowed at a lower cost. Firms that receive the cash earlier may also be able to take advantage of cash discounts, which is one of the reasons they can afford to offer such generous terms.

Credit Information. Most established businesses have a proven repu-tation for prompt payment of their accounts, and sellers are willing to ship goods to them on an open-book account basis. New firms do not have this advantage and, in some instances, older firms are not acquainted with the credit reputations of new customers. In these circumstances the firms wishing to secure the credit usually furnish the names of their banks and invite correspondence to verify the financial responsibility of the organization. In order to facilitate this type of credit investigation, the name of the bank may appear on the letterhead of the newly organized or unknown firm.

There are also credit-rating agencies to whom a supplier can turn in order to check on the desirability of shipping goods on open account. Of these, Dun & Bradstreet, Inc. is outstanding. This is a nationwide mercantile credit-rating agency that lists thousands of large and small business organizations in its publications. Subscribers to its *Reference Book* can determine the credit standing of any one of approximately three million prospective customers on a moment's notice.

Another organization that operates on a national and international basis is the Retail Credit Company. It specializes on individuals rather than business firms. In many cities there are mercantile credit interchange bureaus and retail credit bureaus. Most of these belong to the National Credit Interchange System or the Associated Credit Bureaus of America so that information between bureaus is available on a nationwide basis.

Notes Payable

Next to the use of open-book accounts as a source of short-term debt capital is the use of notes that are payable to commercial banks or to individuals or firms. A *promissory note*, which is a note payable on the part of the issuing party, is a written instrument in which the maker promises to pay to the party named a definite sum of money at a determinable future date. The *maker* is the signer of the note and eventually becomes the one who pays the note. The bank or individual or company in whose favor the note is drawn is the *payee*. Most promissory notes bear interest at a rate that is stated on the face of the instrument. As used in short-term financing, most notes have a maturity date of from one to six months.

Most promissory notes carry the words "pay to the order of" before the name of the payee although sometimes the words "or order" or "or bearer" appear after the name. Any one of these three word combinations makes it possible for the payee to pass the note on to another party by signing on the reverse side of the instrument. This signature is known as an *endorsement*, and the ability to pass the note from hand to hand qualifies it as a *negotiable instrument*.[1] Most notes are designed to be negotiable although many are held by the named payee until they mature.

If a note is given by the buyer to a seller for merchandise or equipment purchased, the interest and the face value of the note are both due

---

[1] See pages 661-664 for a detailed discussion of negotiable instruments.

at maturity. In this case the note may be a substitute for an open-book account. The advantages to the payee of the note are that he has a written promise to pay on the part of the maker of the note, the amount involved and the time of payment are clearly stated, and he may receive interest in addition to the principal. Furthermore, if he so desires, he can raise cash on the note by discounting it at his bank. This procedure, however, merely changes the nature of his current assets; it does not increase total working capital.

Business loans from the bank. If a firm wishes to borrow $25,000 from a bank for 90 days or 3 months, it will sign a note payable to the bank for this amount and insert the rate of interest the bank agrees to charge. Assuming that this rate was 6 percent, the total cost of borrowing $25,000 for one fourth of a year would be $375. The bank may subtract this amount from the face of the note, in which case the proceeds would be $24,625 instead of $25,000. Interest deducted in advance by a bank is known as *bank discount*.

Discounting customers' notes. If a business has received a note from a customer and does not wish to wait until maturity to receive the cash, it can discount the note at its bank by endorsing it. The bank now has two sources of repayment as this *double-name paper* becomes an obligation of the endorser as well as of the maker. Discounting this kind of paper involves a more complicated calculation than the procedure outlined when a borrower signs his own note at a bank. It is necessary to (a) compute the interest on the note, (b) add this interest to the principal to arrive at the full maturity value, (c) find the maturity date, (d) determine the number of days in the discount period, (e) calculate the interest for this discount period on the maturity value at the discount rate, and (f) subtract this discount from the maturity value to arrive at the proceeds.

If the Reliable Furniture Company has given the Redwood Manufacturing Corporation a $900, 6 percent, 2-month note on August 1 and the Redwood Manufacturing Corporation discounts it at its bank on August 14 at 7 percent, the computation to determine the amount of the proceeds is as follows:

(a) $900 \times \frac{2}{12} \times \frac{6}{100} = \$9$.
(b) $\$900 + \$9 = \$909$.
(c) Two months after August 1 is October 1.
(d) August 14 to October 1 $= 48$ days.
(e) $\$909 \times \frac{48}{360} \times \frac{7}{100} = \$8.48$.
(f) $\$909 - \$8.48 = \$900.52$.

Installment purchases of equipment. Notes are also used in connection with purchases of machinery and equipment on an installment basis. Although the bulk of installment buying is done by consumers, businesses may purchase such items as delivery trucks, drill presses, and other forms of heavy machinery on an installment basis. This involves a down payment and the signing of a note specifying monthly payments, which may extend over a period as long as three years. The payee may hold the note or, as is more likely, sell it to a finance company interested in purchasing obligations of this type. To the extent that the repayment of a note is not completed within one year, the unpaid amount is neither a current liability nor does it qualify as short-term financing. Loans that have a maturity of from one to ten years fall into a time period to which the term *intermediate credit* is assigned. Because business needs for intermediate credit are relatively infrequent and because a portion of such debts normally are repayable within one year, such loans are usually handled as extensions of short-term financing.

Commercial Drafts

A *commercial draft* is a credit instrument not unlike a promissory note except that it comes into being upon the initiative of the person who is to receive the money. A *drawer*, usually the business firm that originates the draft, sends it to a *drawee*, the person who is obligated to the drawer, or to his bank. The drawee, if he accepts the draft, writes his name across the face of the instrument. Commercial drafts may be *time drafts*, in which case the drawer will indicate the length of time on the face of the draft, or they may be *sight drafts*. In the latter event the drawee pays upon presentation of the draft. A time draft that arises in connection with a shipment of merchandise is known as a *trade acceptance.*

Commercial drafts are sometimes used to attempt to collect an overdue open-book account. The firm to whom the money is owed draws on the delinquent debtor with the hope that the draft will be accepted. More frequently commercial drafts arise in connection with sales to businesses that do not have an established or satisfactory credit rating. When a manufacturer or wholesaler receives an order from an unknown firm, an attempt is made to determine the financial responsibility of the would-be customer. If the firm is not listed in Dun & Bradstreet, a request can be made for a special report from this organization or from any one of several other credit reporting services. If the investigation indicates a doubtful credit standing, a sale can be made by use of a commercial draft.

The procedure is to make a shipment by freight on a cash-on-delivery basis, which involves the use of a sight draft. The shipper secures a receipt called an *order bill of lading* from the railroad company when the goods are delivered for shipment. When this document is used, the railroad agent at the destination cannot release the goods until the order bill of lading is presented. The shipper attaches a sight draft to the order bill of lading and mails both papers to the bank of the purchaser of the goods. In order to secure delivery of the shipment, the purchaser must accept the sight draft by paying it. The order bill of lading is then given to him, and he can secure the goods from the railroad company.

Bank Acceptances

Bank acceptances provide a method of borrowing from a bank that has the advantage of securing only those funds actually needed and at the time of need. For example, the Foss Manufacturing Company wishes to purchase some raw materials and, before ordering, arranges with its bank to accept drafts drawn against the bank for the goods to be purchased. The bank issues statements to the effect that it will accept the drafts, which are known as *letters of credit*. The Foss Manufacturing Company then sends the letters of credit to the producers of the raw materials with instructions to send the bills of lading to the bank and to draw on the bank for the purchase price.

When the materials arrive, the bank accepts the drafts and, in return for the bills of lading, the purchasing company signs a note in favor of the bank and also a financing statement. A *financing statement*, as prescribed by the Uniform Commercial Code, describes the property that is pledged as security for a loan. By filing the financing statement with the secretary of state or at a county courthouse, or at both locations, other creditors are placed on notice that although a firm has title to and possession of certain assets, there is a lien against them in favor of the lending company.

In the case of the Foss Manufacturing Company, it is expected that the raw materials will be converted into finished goods but that, before they are sold, the company will pay the note owed to the bank. If it is unable to do so, other raw materials may be substituted for those originally pledged or, if the bank prefers, it has the right to sell the finished goods to satisfy its claims.

Although this procedure may appear very complicated, in actual operation the use of bank acceptances is relatively simple. They can be used when the credit standing of the buyer is unknown to the seller, which is especially true in international-trade transactions. By substituting the unquestioned ability of a bank to pay the draft for a company with only local credit standing, a business transaction is completed that otherwise might not have been consummated.

Commercial Paper

In the financial world *commercial paper* refers to unsecured promissory notes that well-known corporations sell on the open market. These notes are issued in such denominations as $5,000, $10,000, and $25,000. They amount in total to a substantial sum, run for from two to six months, and are sold to commercial paper houses who, in turn, sell them to such buyers as industrial corporations, pension funds, and financial institutions. Only large corporations with an unquestioned credit standing, such as the General Motors Acceptance Corporation, can use this source of short-term financing. To those who qualify, the advantages are that money can be borrowed at a lower rate of interest than would be charged by a bank and that the borrower can secure more funds than most banks would be willing or legally able to lend.

SECURITY FOR SHORT-TERM LOANS

The more widely used sources of short-term funds rarely involve providing any type of security for the loan. An open-book account, almost by definition, is an implied promise to pay in accordance with the credit terms. Bank loans for a month or two are normally unsecured. In both instances the ability of the firm to repay the amount borrowed and its reputation for prompt settlement are considered when credit is extended. The lender rightly assumes that the past performance of the borrower will be continued in the immediate future.

When a sole proprietorship, or any individual, is granted a bank loan solely on his own signature, it is known as a *character loan*. In some instances, because there may be some doubt about the ability of the individual to repay the loan either from business income or his personal assets, the bank may ask the would-be borrower to secure a third party, in whom it has confidence, to sign the note. If this individual signs on the face of the note along with the maker, he is known as a *comaker* or *cosigner*. If he endorses the note on the back, he is known as an *accommodation endorser*. The only difference between the two types of guarantee is that cosigners are equally liable along with the maker for the note whereas an accommodation endorser is not required to pay until after the maker has defaulted on his obligation.

In some instances firms engaged in short-term financing are either required to pledge assets as security for the loan or do so because they may then benefit from a lower interest cost. The common types of assets that are used in this manner are: (1) accounts receivable, (2) inventories, (3) movable property, and (4) other assets.

Accounts Receivable

Commercial banks and commercial finance companies will make a loan to a business on a short-term basis accepting as security the pledge of open-book accounts (called accounts receivable) owed to the firm by its customers. The usual procedure involves the allocation of a selected number of the accounts to the lending agency and receiving in return a loan of from 75 to 80 percent of their total value. The borrower promises to forward all cash received from these customers until such time as the loan plus interest has been repaid.

Under the circumstances outlined, the debtor of the borrowing firm is not aware that his account has been pledged as security for a loan. This is known as a *nonnotification plan* and is almost universally followed when such a loan is obtained from a commercial bank or commercial finance company. Because some business concerns borrow on their accounts receivable only as a last resort, there is an implied element of financial weakness in a firm that must secure short-term funds by this method. Such knowledge on the part of the customer could prove detrimental to future business relationships, although as such loans become more and more frequent, this objection may well disappear from the current business scene.

A variation on using accounts receivable as a basis for raising cash is to sell the accounts. A financing institution known as a factoring company takes over title and collects the amounts due for which it makes a service charge as well as charges interest on the money advanced. This procedure requires that the customer be informed of the sale of his account so that he will make his payments to the new owner of the receivable. This is known as a *notification plan*. Where trade custom has made it a common practice, the implication of financial weakness on the part of the seller is virtually eliminated. It has long been customary in the textile field to sell accounts receivable; and in recent years this method of raising short-term funds has been spreading to such industries as furniture, paper, furs, shoes, and men's clothing.

Inventories

There are two common methods of borrowing by using goods owned as security for a loan. One involves loss of physical possession and use of the raw materials or merchandise pledged while the other permits possession and processing of the security.

When goods are stored in a warehouse owned by an independent warehousing company, known as a *bonded public warehouse*, the owner of the goods receives a *warehouse receipt*. Usually such receipts specify that the goods will be released to the person who rented the space, or to his order or the bearer, upon payment of the storage charges. This wording makes warehouse receipts negotiable and allows firms to pledge the goods owned as collateral for a loan, which is usually secured from a commercial bank. For example, the Crescent Candy Company purchases one hundred tons of sugar, which is sold on terms of 2/10, net 30. The shipment arrives and is stored in a bonded public warehouse. The warehouse receipt is endorsed in favor of the firm's bank, thus serving as collateral for a promissory note. The cash received from the bank allows the candy company to pay the invoice within the discount period. When the note is due, the borrower will have to pay it or sacrifice the right to have the warehouse receipt returned. In the latter event the bank will sell the sugar to other users in order to avoid loss on the defaulted note.

In some instances the physical possession of and the ability to convert inventories into salable merchandise are essential to the firm's operations. This situation gives rise to the use of a financing statement as described in the discussion of bank acceptances.

Movable Property

The most widely used form of security for short-term loans is movable property such as automobiles and trucks, equipment, supplies, and even livestock, if ownership of animals is involved in the business. Actually, the most extensive use of this type of security for a loan results from financing consumer purchases of durable goods on an installment basis. Whereas businesses may also purchase cars and trucks, machinery, and other similar items with payments scheduled on a monthly basis, business loans made with movable property used as security are sometimes repayable at a single maturity date.

The procedure used for obtaining a loan secured by movable property involves signing a note, which specifies the terms of repayment, and also a financing statement of the type described on page 433. The seller of the goods pledged can repossess the article or articles if payments are not made in accordance with the terms of the loan. For example, the Acme Auto Sales Company sells a delivery truck to Chris Jensen, who operates a grocery store. Jensen makes a down payment of $600 on the $4,200 purchase price and signs a note and financing statement agreeing to pay $200 a month for the next 18 months. If payments are not made as scheduled, the Acme Auto Sales Company can repossess the truck.

An interesting exception to the need for filing a financing statement occurs in the case of automobiles, trucks, mobile homes, and other items for which a certificate of title is issued. Since the owner cannot sell the pledged property without delivering this certificate, the lending agency protects itself by retaining possession of it until the loan is paid.

Prior to the adoption of the Uniform Commercial Code, the credit sale of movable property frequently involved the use of a chattel mortgage or a conditional bill of sale. When a *chattel mortgage* was used, title passed to the purchaser immediately, but the seller retained a lien on the movable property until payment was made in full in a manner comparable to the use of a financing statement. If a *conditional bill of sale* was used, title remained with the seller until the buyer completed his payments. These methods of providing security for short-term loans are still legal if other conditions of a secured transaction as defined in the Code are satisfied.

Other Assets

Although receivables, inventories, and movable property are the common types of security used in connection with short-term financing, some other assets are also acceptable. For example, if the firm owns bonds and stocks, it may assign these to a bank as security for a loan. If the need for funds will only last a month or two, it may well be preferable to borrow against assets of this type rather than to sell the securities in order to raise the cash needed. Another asset sometimes available is the cash surrender value of life insurance policies carried on the lives of partners or executives of a company. The insurance company or companies involved will loan an amount equal to the cash surrender value of the policies, or a bank will accept an assignment of this asset as security for a loan of the same amount.

COST OF SHORT-TERM FINANCING

Sound financial management dictates that short-term funds should be secured at the lowest possible cost. The least expensive method of borrowing is the open-book account. Whereas some retailers add an interest charge of 1½ percent a month on unpaid monthly balances on customer charge accounts, interest on open-book accounts, even when overdue, is a rarity. The rate on interest-bearing obligations is affected by money rates generally and by the amount of risk assumed by the lender. A loan from an insurance company on the cash surrender value of a policy usually carries a rate of 5 percent per annum while the rate charged by a bank to a small business for an unsecured loan may well be in the range of from 7 to 9 percent.

In computing costs, business firms as well as consumers need to be aware of the difference between nominal and effective rates of interest. The *nominal rate of interest* is the one stated on the instrument used in connection with the loan, while the *effective rate of interest* is the true interest cost. Bank discount and the not uncommon requirement that a business obtaining a loan from a commercial bank must maintain a checking account balance equivalent to, for example, 20 percent of the loan, are examples of the higher cost of the effective rate since the interest is based on a larger total than usable funds. More commonly, the effective rate on loans repayable on an installment basis, e.g., most automobile financing, is almost double the nominal rate due to calculating interest on the full amount of the loan for the entire borrowing period despite the gradual reduction in the size of the loan.

FEDERAL CONSUMER CREDIT PROTECTION ACT

The lack of knowledge on the part of the public as to the cost of consumer credit has been a matter of concern to state and federal legislators, particularly the latter. In 1968 the Congress passed a law officially titled the Federal Consumer Credit Protection Act, more popularly known as the Truth-in-Lending Act of 1968, which went into effect on July 1, 1969. It requires retailers, banks, finance companies, and other creditors to make full disclosure of the cost of consumer credit.

The law is quite complex, but the following provisions affecting charge accounts are typical of the type of information that must be stated in writing to customers:

1. The conditions under which a finance charge may be imposed and the period within which payment may be made without incurring a finance charge. (The *finance charge* is the amount of money paid to obtain credit, which should include not only the interest charge but all other charges that may be levied by the creditor, such as a service charge or a carrying charge.)

2. The method of determining the balance on which a finance charge may be imposed.

3. The method of determining the finance charge.

4. The periodic (weekly or monthly) rate or rates used, the range of balances to which they apply, and the corresponding annual percentage rate or rates. (The annual percentage rate will usually be 12 times the monthly rate. It provides a way of comparing credit costs regardless of the dollar amount of those costs or the length of time over which payments are made.)

5. The conditions under which additional charges may be imposed, such as late payment charges and the method for determining them.

6. A description of any lien the creditor may acquire on the debtor's property.

7. The minimum periodic payment required.

In response to these regulations, retail stores have furnished the required data to their customers that, in most cases, allow a maximum of 30 days in which to pay without incurring a finance charge. After 30 days a rate of 1.5 percent a month, for example, or 18 percent a year is applied to the unpaid balance. In the case of bank loans and installment purchases, all finance charges and other deductions and restrictions must be itemized and used in computing a true annual interest cost. But it must be noted that the Truth-in-Lending Act does not fix interest rates or other credit charges. State laws that set limits on interest rates still apply.

The Truth-in-Lending Act also contains a provision that permits states to pass laws that could supersede the federal act. A Uniform Consumer Credit Code is being proposed in most state legislatures but, to date, has not been widely enacted. This uniform code is considered to be more favorable to lending agencies than the federal law, which is one reason it is opposed by consumer groups who prefer the protection of the Federal Consumer Credit Protection Act.

Any individual may sue a businessman who fails to make the required disclosures for twice the amount of the finance charge—for a minimum of $100 up to a maximum of $1,000—plus court costs and reasonable attorney's fees.

FINANCIAL INSTITUTIONS—SHORT-TERM CAPITAL

Several financial institutions assist businesses either directly or indirectly with their short-term capital problems. One of these, the commercial bank, is of direct value to practically every business unit while others, such as a sales finance company, are important to only certain types of firms. Still other institutions are of indirect value to businesses in that they provide loans to individuals who may then be able to pay their business debts. Since the commercial bank is the most important financial institution in the short-term capital field, its operations will be examined in some detail.

COMMERCIAL BANKS

A *commercial bank* is a financial institution that accepts deposits against which checks are drawn, loans money, and renders several other services. It is the best known of all financial institutions and the one with which businesses have the most frequent and recurring contacts. The relations between a banker and the owners and managers of businesses are usually close and also helpful and friendly. The services a commercial bank renders to businesses can be summarized as follows: (1) checking accounts, (2) bank drafts and checks, (3) short-term loans, (4) foreign exchange, and (5) other functions.

Checking Accounts

From the viewpoint of the business community, the chief function of a commercial bank is to accept money for deposit and to pay out these funds on order of the depositor by means of checks. A *check* is a negotiable instrument signed by the bank customer directing that the amount of money specified be paid by the bank to the payee or his order. With the exception of cash sales at the retail level, checks are used for the settlement of practically all business transactions.

After a check has been written but before it has been cleared by the bank on which it was drawn, it is possible to *stop payment* on the check by notifying the bank. This is not done unless a good reason for the procedure exists, such as discovering that a person obtained the payment under false pretenses. Payment cannot be stopped on certified checks, however, because they represent a liability of the bank. A *certified check* is one that a bank charges against the proper account at the same time that the check is stamped as "certified."

Many banks make a service charge for maintaining checking accounts if the business allows its daily balances to fall below a minimum figure adequate to compensate for the cost of handling its volume of deposits and checks. A charge is made for each deposit or check with an offsetting credit of interest on the lowest balance shown during a month. For personal accounts the same plan is followed, or the individual may purchase a book of 20 checks for $2 or more.

Bank Drafts, Cashier's Checks, and Traveler's Checks

If payment is to be made by check to a business located some distance away, this business might be reluctant about accepting a check from a small unknown firm. In order to avoid delays that might otherwise occur, the depositor can give his bank a check for the amount, and the bank will write a *bank draft*. This draft is really a check of the bank drawn on another larger bank. This is possible because the bank has on deposit certain amounts with the other bank. The big city bank is known as the *correspondent bank* in relation to the local institution.

For local transactions, usually confined to large cities, the bank may provide the depositor with a *cashier's check*, which differs from a bank draft in that it is drawn on the bank that issues it instead of a correspondent bank.

As a substitute for cashier's checks, some banks provide personal money orders. These are drawn on the bank issuing them; but, unlike cashier's checks, the user has a carbon copy indicating the date, amount, and the name of the debtor to whom he mails or delivers the money order.

When an officer or salesman takes a business trip and does not wish to carry large sums of money, *traveler's checks* may provide the most satisfactory solution to this problem. These are retailed to customers by most banks, who purchase them from The American Express Company or from a few other suppliers, notably the National City Bank of New York and the Bank of America in California. Traveler's checks are issued in convenient denominations, such as $10, $20, and larger figures. At the time of purchase, the user signs his name to each check and must sign again when the check is cashed. This identification through comparison of signatures permits traveler's checks to be cashed in most parts of the world.

Short-Term Loans

Commercial banks are a common source of short-term funds for businesses. Many firms negotiate loans one or more times each year. As noted previously in this chapter, the notes may be secured or unsecured, may or may not be discounted, and normally are repaid in one lump sum at their maturity. Outstanding commercial loans in excess of $60 billion provide some idea of the importance of commercial banks in the short-term capital field.

Some business firms, anticipating that they may need to borrow at some indefinite future time, submit detailed information to their banks covering such items as financial statements, names of officers and directors, and certain details about their operations. If an investigation of these facts seems to warrant making a loan, the firm will be notified that the bank has granted a *line of credit* for a specified amount such as $25,000 or $500,000. The obvious advantage in having established a line of credit is the advance knowledge of how much can be borrowed quickly at any time the need arises. Also, businesses that have established a line of credit are frequently eligible to borrow at the prime rate or at a fractional percentage higher. The *prime rate* is the best rate offered by banks on short-term loans to their most credit worthy customers. Any change in the rate made by large banks, particularly those located in New York City, is widely reported in newspapers and financial publications. This enables executives of a firm eligible to borrow at the prime rate or some variation thereof to know exactly what borrowed funds will cost, which can be an important decision-making factor.

Foreign Exchange

If a firm engages in foreign business, it faces the problem of making payments in foreign currencies or receiving payments involving, for example, francs or pesos in place of dollars. The bank is willing to handle the conversion of United States dollars into the proper amount of foreign currency, or of foreign currency into United States dollars.

Other Functions of Commercial Banks

In addition to the functions described above, commercial banks maintain savings departments; rent safe deposit boxes for the storing of valuable business papers; render business and investment advice; collect notes, drafts, and bond coupons; serve as a source of credit information; and may even assist in preparing payroll envelopes for employees. In recent years several banks have installed electronic data computing equipment that, for an hourly fee, is available for use by their customers.

REGULATION OF COMMERCIAL BANKS

Commercial banks are regulated by the federal government or by the state, depending, in part, on whether they are national or state banks. Actually, the federal government plays the more important part because many state banks as well as all national banks belong to the Federal Reserve System and to the Federal Deposit Insurance Corporation and must follow procedures prescribed by these agencies. Other regulations are administered by the comptroller of the currency for national banks and by state bank examiners for state banks.

Of primary importance to depositors is the fact that all banks are examined periodically by federal or state auditors who make a careful study of the financial condition of the bank and report any irregularities to the proper governmental officials. These examiners make unannounced visits so that the officers and employees do not have a chance to cover up any discrepancies or errors of poor judgment. Any irregularities that are discovered by the examiners must be corrected promptly or action will be taken against the bank by the proper governmental officials.

The Federal Reserve System is a powerful, independent, federal agency that has considerable influence on commercial banking. There are twelve federal reserve banks distributed geographically over the United States, and these banks have branches, such as the Pittsburgh and Cincinnati branches of the Cleveland Federal Reserve Bank. Member banks obtain from the federal reserve bank the currency that they pay out, and they are permitted to discount certain notes and drafts that they have accepted from their customers, in much the same manner as the original transactions. These notes and drafts, as well as bills of exchange and banker's acceptances, are known as *eligible paper*, and the rate of interest charged for discounting eligible paper is known as the *rediscount rate*.

One of the important functions of a federal reserve bank is clearing interdistrict and intradistrict checks for its members. If a check that is drawn on a bank in San Francisco is deposited in a Chicago bank, it must be sent to the bank in California for collection. This process is known as *clearing a check* and is handled by the two district federal reserve banks involved, the one in Chicago and the one in San Francisco. Or, if a check is received by a bank in San Antonio, Texas, drawn on a bank in Houston, Texas, it will be cleared by the Dallas Federal Reserve Bank as both of the other cities are located in the Dallas district.

Of numerous regulations emanating from the Federal Reserve System and other governmental agencies, two are of particular concern to businesses. One of these restricts the amount that may be loaned to any one firm to 10 percent of the total of the capital stock and undivided profits of the lending bank. The other prohibits paying interest on *demand deposits*, or checking accounts as they are usually known.

OTHER FINANCIAL INSTITUTIONS FOR SHORT-TERM CAPITAL

The following institutions also specialize in assisting businesses with their short-term financial problems: (1) commercial finance companies,

(2) factoring companies, (3) sales finance companies, (4) commercial paper houses, (5) consumer finance institutions, and (6) federal agencies. Some of these make loans to business units while others are active in the field of consumer finance.

Commercial Finance Companies

Although commercial banks make short-term loans to business with accounts receivable or inventories pledged as collateral, such loans are more commonly secured from commercial finance companies. This is particularly true when receivables are involved. A nonnotification arrangement, by which the borrower's customers are not notified of the plan, is customary. A *commercial finance company* is a financial institution operating on a local or national basis that makes loans to business by discounting accounts receivable or by taking chattel mortgages on inventories or machinery.

In addition to a large number of small commercial finance companies, two operate on a national basis. These well-known companies are the Commercial Credit Company division of Control Data Corporation and the CIT Financial Corporation. Interest charges on loans made are relatively high, usually between 10 and 15 percent. Because interest is computed on daily balances and there is no requirement to maintain a minimum bank balance, this seemingly high cost may actually be less expensive than regular bank credit obtained by borrowing with receivables used as security.

Factoring Companies

Factoring companies, or *factors* as they are more commonly called, specialize in accounts receivable financing for businesses but, in contrast with the commercial finance companies, they purchase the accounts and assume the credit risks. Since they own the accounts, a notification plan is universal. Factors make two types of charges for the financing they provide. They make an interest charge, usually 6 percent or slightly higher, and in addition assess a commission of approximately 1½ percent of the face value of the receivables factored.

Sales Finance Companies

Sales finance companies purchase installment sales contracts from the dealers who have sold the merchandise to the consumer. In this respect they differ from other types of loan companies that make loans directly to consumers repayable on an installment basis. Such companies are organized under the laws of a state, but several operate on a national scale.

The principle upon which sales finance companies operate is relatively simple. Aside from a small amount of cash received from the owners, funds are obtained by borrowing. Because the credit standing of the company is usually excellent, funds are secured at a low rate of interest. Installment contract paper is then purchased from businessmen who do not care to or cannot afford to handle their own sales financing. Gross earnings on these contracts should equal or exceed 12 percent in order to cover expenses, losses, and the cost of the money borrowed.

The largest number of sales finance companies operate in the automobile field, and the dollar volume of the business of all such organizations is greatest in installment contracts written to cover the sale of new and used cars. Over one half of all new cars and two thirds of all used cars sold are financed, and practically all of these contracts are sold to sales finance companies or other financial institutions. Three companies operate on a national scale: the General Motors Acceptance Corporation and two others that also engage in commercial financing, the Commercial Credit Company and the CIT Financial Corporation. In addition to these three giants numerous smaller companies are local in character or operate in one or more states.

Commercial Paper Houses

Firms that issue commercial paper, described on page 434, would have a problem of distribution were it not for the existence of *commercial paper houses*. These organizations specialize in handling such notes, either buying them outright or selling them on a commission basis. Commercial paper houses employ salesmen who retail commercial paper to commercial banks, investors, and other purchasers interested in this type of investment. They serve a useful purpose not only to the issuing firm but also to their customers in providing them with a diversified list of high-grade short-term paper.

Consumer Finance Institutions

The major types of institutions, other than commercial banks, that make loans to consumers are consumer finance companies, industrial banks, and credit unions. Other than the possibility that a sole proprietor or member of a partnership might seek a personal loan to increase his investment in his business, consumer finance institutions are valuable to business only by way of providing customers with funds to purchase goods, to settle accounts, or to maintain installment payments.

Consumer finance companies, also called *small loan companies* and *personal finance companies*, specialize in making cash loans of from $100 to $500 on single- or double-name paper although larger loans are also available, particularly if security is offered. Some companies are local and others, such as the Household Finance Corporation, operate in many cities. Loan repayments are almost universally on a weekly or monthly basis. In most states consumer finance companies are subject to regulation by a Uniform Small Loan Law that provides for licenses and a rate limit of from 2½ to 3 percent a month on the unpaid balance of the loan.

Industrial banks, also called *Morris Plan banks*, differ from consumer finance companies in that the money they loan has been received from depositors. Originally the idea had been to encourage industrial workers to save and to make loans to blue-collar employees. In recent years the activities of many industrial banks have expanded so that they have been granted a state charter as a commercial bank. The organization and operation of the third major type of consumer finance institution—credit unions—was described in Chapter 5 because they constitute a unique type of incorporated ownership.

Federal Agencies

The federal government has been active in the short-term financing area by creating corporations to guarantee loans made to consumers by commercial lending agencies, to loan funds to privately owned financial institutions, and to make direct loans. These activities have been most notable in the field of agriculture; for example, the Commodity Credit Corporation will loan farmers 100 percent of a predetermined support price on such commodities as corn and soybeans. Federal banks are also available from which rural cooperatives can secure funds.

In the business area commercial banks and savings and loan associations can make home repair and improvement loans that are 90 percent guaranteed by the Federal Housing Administration. Of more importance, however, is the Small Business Administration, which was created in 1953 to make short-term working capital loans to small businesses unable to secure funds elsewhere at reasonable rates of interest. The Small Business Administration will also make loans with maturity dates up to 10 years and will participate with private banks in loans they are willing to make to small businesses. Even though the maximum amount that can be loaned to one business is $350,000, over the years this agency has provided approximately $2 billion in short-term and intermediate credit.

BUSINESS TERMS

QUESTIONS FOR DISCUSSION AND ANALYSIS

1. Is it possible to increase a firm's circulating capital by resort to short-term financing? Explain.

2. For some firms might there be disadvantages as well as advantages to short-term financing? If so, state their nature and the steps a firm should take to minimize such risks.

3. Does the extensive use of open-book accounts and charge accounts in this country indicate that most firms and individuals are honest? Comment.

4. The credit terms of manufacturers and wholesalers customarily include a cash discount for prompt payment of the invoice. Why don't retailers extend a similar privilege to their customers?

5. What benefits, if any, accrue to an individual who becomes a cosigner or an accommodation endorser of a note? Why is he willing to sign the note?

6. Considering the widespread use of charge accounts and credit cards, why is security sometimes required for short-term loans?

7. What did the Congress hope to accomplish by passing the Consumer Credit Protection Act? Has this Truth-in-Lending legislation been successful?

8. Why don't commercial banks charge their business customers for the many services rendered?

9. Wouldn't an automobile dealer be better off if he would hold the installment paper he receives when he sells a car on time and borrow, when necessary, from a commercial bank or commercial finance company?

10. What financial institution should a recent college graduate patronize who accumulated $500 in debts before securing satisfactory employment?

PROBLEMS AND SHORT CASES

1. The Moorman Manufacturing Co. purchased semifinished parts at an invoice price of $36,000. The statement showed terms of 2/10, net 60, but the firm does not have the cash available to take advantage of the discount although it expects to be able to pay in full at the end of 60 days. The commercial bank with which the Moorman firm does business is willing to loan any amount up to $50,000 for 50 days at 8 percent, but it requires that the borrower maintain a balance of 20 percent of the loan in its checking account.

   Show calculations to indicate the net saving if the minimum necessary amount is borrowed for 50 days to take advantage of the cash discount.

2. The C. L. Green Company received a promissory note for $12,000 from the Walker Corporation. It was dated November 18, was to run for three months, and bore interest at the rate of 7 percent. On November 30 the Green Company discounted this note at its commercial bank at an 8 percent rate.

   Show calculations to determine the proceeds to the C. L. Green Company on the discount date.

3. The Wilcox Manufacturing Co. has been considering the desirability of upgrading practically all of its machinery by trading in the several items of equipment involved for new models. It has been determined that the cost of the new machines minus the trade-in allowance for the used equipment will amount to $800,000. It is estimated that the proposed modernization program will pay for itself in approximately two years.

The firm believes it can conserve about $200,000 in cash in the next 30 days that can be spared for the purchase of this equipment, leaving $600,000 that would need to be financed by one means or another. The manufacturer of the equipment will extend 30-day credit terms, which is about the length of time it will take to remove the old and install the new machines. At the end of the 30 days, the seller would be happy to receive all of the $800,000 but is willing to accept $200,000 in cash and a series of 7½ percent $25,000 notes, one due at the end of each month for 24 months. The commercial bank that has the Wilcox Manufacturing Co. account is willing to loan $600,000 for 6 months at 7 percent; and it has given every assurance that, if $150,000 is paid on the note at maturity, the balance can be extended for 6 months, and so on until the note is retired at the end of 24 months.

Assuming that the Wilcox Manufacturing Co. decides to purchase the new machines under the trade-in arrangement outlined above, which of the two sources of short-term financing would be preferable? Justify your decision by calculating the interest cost for each plan and give reasons for your conclusion. Would it be desirable for the Wilcox Manufacturing Co. to investigate still other sources of short-term funds?

SUGGESTED READINGS

Bradley, J. F. *Administrative Financial Management*, Second Edition. New York: Harcourt Brace Jovanovich, Inc., 1969. Chapters 9-12.

Brandt, L. K. *Business Finance: A Management Approach*. Englewood Cliffs, New Jersey: Prentice-Hall, Inc., 1965. Part IV.

Broom, H. N., and J. G. Longenecker. *Small Business Management*, Third Edition. Cincinnati: South-Western Publishing Co., 1971. Part C.

Cohen, J. B., and S. M. Robbins. *The Financial Manager: Basic Aspects of Financial Administration*. New York: Harper & Row, 1966. Part III.

Cooke, G. W., and E. C. Bomeli. *Business Financial Management*. Boston: Houghton Mifflin Company, 1967. Part IV.

Curran, W. S. *Principles of Financial Management*. New York: McGraw-Hill Book Co., 1970. Part Two.

Dauten, C. A., and M. Welshans. *Principles of Finance*, Third Edition. Cincinnati: South-Western Publishing Co., 1970. Part II.

Donaldson, E. F., and J. K. Pfahl. *Corporate Finance—Policy and Management*, Third Edition. New York: The Ronald Press Co., 1969. Part II.

Farwell, L. C., *et al. Financial Institutions*, Fourth Edition. Homewood, Illinois: Richard D. Irwin, Inc., 1966. Parts II and V.

Flink, S. J., and D. Gruenwald. *Managerial Finance*. New York: John Wiley & Sons, Inc., 1969. Part I.

Gruenwald, A. E., and E. E. Nemmers. *Basic Managerial Finance*. New York: Holt, Rinehart and Winston, Inc., 1970. Part Four.

Hastings, P. G. *The Management of Business Finance*. Princeton, New Jersey: Van Nostrand, 1966. Part III.

Polakoff, Murray E., *et al. Financial Institutions and Markets*. Boston: Houghton Mifflin Company, 1970.

Prather, C. K. *Financing Business Firms*, Third Edition. Homewood, Illinois: Richard D. Irwin, Inc., 1966. Part IV.

Van Horne, J. C. *Financial Management and Policy*. Englewood Cliffs, New Jersey: Prentice-Hall, Inc., 1968. Part VI.

Weston, J. F., and E. F. Brigham. *Managerial Finance*, Third Edition. New York: Holt, Rinehart and Winston, Inc., 1969. Part Five.

Chapter 19

Fixed assets, as defined in the previous chapter, consist of land, buildings, machinery, equipment, and other similar items of value. These normally have a useful life measured in years, usually ten or more. In addition to the tangible items that constitute fixed assets, a firm may also own other long-lasting assets such as bonds or stocks of another company or an unexpired patent. Thus, the fixed capital of a firm consists of the total value of its fixed assets, investments, and intangibles.

For fairly obvious reasons the dollars a firm has invested in fixed capital should be obtained on a long-term rather than a short-term basis. Borrowing money from a commercial bank on a 90-day note to buy a factory building would rarely be considered sound financial management. Rather, fixed capital requirements should be met by resorting to one or another or both of the two methods by which funds can be secured on a long-term basis. One method involves borrowing from lenders who do not expect to be repaid for several years. The other relies on the owners of the business to invest in their firm without any expectation of repayment of the principal. Funds that are secured from loans with a maturity date several years in the future or from the owners of the business comprise the area of *long-term financing*.

DEBT AND EQUITY CAPITAL

If firms borrow on a long-term basis, the debt or debts they owe are classified as *fixed liabilities*; and the total amount involved comprises the *debt capital* of the business. Funds contributed by the owners when the firm was started, plus subsequent additions either by way of additional investments or by allowing net income to remain in the business, are classified as the *net worth* of the firm and comprise the *equity capital*. The total amount of debt and equity capital equals the total amount of fixed and working capital of a business.

After making a distinction between noncorporate and corporate long-term financing, the remainder of this chapter will deal primarily with the types of instruments used to secure debt and equity capital. In addition, financial institutions that have been created to assist firms in solving their long-term financing problems will be discussed. In both instances emphasis will be placed on how financial managers arrive at decisions involving long-term financing when faced with a choice of securities and financial institutions.

NONCORPORATE AND CORPORATE LONG-TERM FINANCING

The ability of sole proprietorships and partnerships to raise funds either when starting a business or at a subsequent date is limited. The major source is, and should be, equity capital. This fact is chiefly responsible for the small size of most unincorporated businesses and explains why many growing proprietorships and partnerships are converted into corporations. Unless one or more owners are very wealthy and are willing to invest their fortunes into one business, funds available for long-term financing are likely to be limited in amount.

Equity capital is not, however, the sole source of long-term funds for unincorporated businesses since debt capital also offers some possibilities. If the fixed assets owned or to be acquired include land and buildings, the property can be mortgaged for approximately two thirds to three fourths of its value. Equipment can also provide collateral for a long-term loan. Although repayment of a real estate or chattel mortgage note is frequently on a monthly basis, payments usually extend over a number of years. A major disadvantage of this type of borrowing is the need to make periodic payments at a time when the firm may be struggling to make a profit. "Starting a business on a shoestring," which is an expression used to denote a high ratio of debt capital to equity capital, is extremely risky.

The sources of long-term funds mentioned above are also available to corporations. If the company is small, perhaps no larger than the average unincorporated business, its ability to engage in long-term financing is very comparable to the restrictions faced by sole proprietorships and partnerships. If, however, the corporation is large enough so that it can sell bonds and stocks to the general public, its ability to raise funds is greatly enhanced. The fact that many corporations can market both types of securities is basically the reason for the larger size of so many firms that embrace this type of business ownership.

Of the two types of securities, bonds, which will be examined first, are not a requirement of corporate financing; and many companies have no fixed liabilities. On the other hand, some corporations, particularly railroads and public utilities, secure over one half of their total capital from bond issues. By contrast, all corporations must issue stock as stock represents ownership, and there have to be stockholders who own the business. In other words, for corporations, debt capital is optional whereas equity capital is required.

BONDS

A *bond* is a type of security that is a debt of the issuing corporation that matures at a stated future date and on which interest is paid annually or semiannually. All bonds issued by private companies contain some common features. In addition, there are many special provisions, one or more of which may apply to a particular issue.

GENERAL FEATURES OF BONDS

Considerations applying to all bond issues sold by industries, railroads, public utilities, and financial enterprises are: (1) provision for trustee, (2) denomination of bonds, (3) maturity dates, and (4) registered versus coupon bonds.

Provision for Trustee

Bonds, which represent a debt of the issuing corporation, are usually held by a large number of investors. These investors may be widely scattered over the country and may not be acquainted with each other. They need someone to act in their behalf and to safeguard their interests. Such a person is known as a *trustee* and is chosen by the corporation at the time the bond issue is sold. Modern practice usually calls for a trust company or large bank to serve in the capacity of trustee.

The duties of the trustee are included in the agreement under which the bonds are issued. This legal document is called the *indenture*. Under it the trustee certifies that the bonds are genuine, holds any collateral that may be used as security for the issue, and collects money from the corporation to pay the interest and also the principal. In addition to these specific duties, the trustee undertakes, in behalf of the bondholders, to make sure that all provisions of the indenture are carefully followed during the lifetime of the issue.

Denomination of Bonds

Most industrial, railroad, financial, and public utility bonds are issued in units of $1,000. Sometimes the denominations of part of the issue will run higher, such as $5,000, $10,000, and $50,000 units, or may be printed in lower amounts, usually $500 or even down to the $100 level. If bonds have a face value of less than $500, they are frequently referred to as *baby bonds*. Despite these varying denominations, the price of a bond is quoted in terms of a ratio to 100, such as 101½. This quotation means that a $1,000 bond would cost $1,015.

Because of the promotional efforts of the federal government, including the possibility of purchase under a payroll deduction plan, many individuals are more familiar with United States savings bonds than they are with corporation bonds. Although the federal government issues many types of bonds, the average saver purchases Series E savings bonds, which are available in units as small as a $25 maturity value. A distinctive characteristic of this series is the method used to compensate the lender for the use of his money. Instead of paying interest semiannually, as is customary for practically all bond issues, these bonds are sold at a 25 percent discount; e.g., a $25 bond costs $18.75, a $50 bond costs $37.50, and the same ratio prevails for larger amounts. When these are bought on a regular basis, the individual is entitled to purchase so-called Freedom Shares that cost $20.25 and multiples thereof for a $25 bond or proportionally higher amounts. These United States savings notes mature in approximately 4½ years as opposed to 7 years for E bonds, and the holder earns interest at the rate of 5 percent instead of 4.25 percent. Securities that pay interest in this fashion are known as *accumulation bonds*.

Maturity Dates

Because bonds are a debt, they must be repaid at some future date. The length of time between the issue and repayment varies considerably, but practically all bonds will run for at least 10 years and may not mature for as long as 100 years. As an instrument of long-term financing, a period shorter than 10 years would hardly be satisfactory. Common lives of bond issues are 20, 30, and 40 years.

Registered Versus Coupon Bonds

A *fully registered bond* shows the name of the owner on the face of the security; a record of the owner is kept by the issuing corporation; and interest checks are mailed to the holder. A *coupon bond* shows no evidence of the owner; the corporation does not know who holds it; and interest is paid to the party who presents the dated coupons which are clipped from the bond.

The advantage of a registered bond is that the owner is protected against loss in case it is stolen. The coupon bond, which is a bearer instrument, is usually assumed to belong to the person who has it in his possession. The disadvantage of a registered bond is that title cannot pass unless the owner endorses the bond to a purchaser and this fact is recorded on the books of the issuing corporation. The coupon bond is easier to sell and is more satisfactory to deposit with a bank as security for a loan. Corporations floating a large issue may sell both types of bonds.

In some instances a coupon bond is registered as to principal only. Interest is collected by the coupon method as in the case of the ordinary bearer bond, but the owner is protected by registration against loss by theft as to the principal sum. This is known as *partial registration.*

SPECIAL FEATURES OF BONDS

Practically every bond issue is different in some respect from one issued by another company or from another series that is sold by the same organization. The names by which bond issues are advertised and sold frequently contain a descriptive phrase indicating the inclusion of one or more of the following special features: (1) security, (2) method of repayment, (3) callable or redeemable bonds, and (4) convertible bonds.

Security

Since bonds are a debt of the corporation, investors usually expect some type of security as protection in case the issuing party finds it impossible to live up to the terms of payment of interest or principal. Bonds usually run for a long period of time, and a corporation that is prosperous today may fall on evil times before the maturity date of the issue. Some of the common types of security offered to bondholders are described briefly in the following paragraphs.

Real estate mortgages as security. The most common type of security for a bond issue is a mortgage on real estate, which can be foreclosed by the trustee acting for the bondholders. Such bonds are called *real estate mortgage bonds*.

Mortgage bonds have an almost endless variety of special features such as first-mortgage bonds that rank ahead of second-mortgage bonds, and the inclusion of an *after-acquired clause* that has the effect of adding properties built or purchased subsequent to the sale of the issue to the real estate originally mortgaged. If the entire issue is sold at one time, it is known as a *closed-end issue* as opposed to an *open-end issue* that permits the sale of additional bonds at a later date under the original mortgage.

Chattel mortgages as security. If a mortgage on movable items, such as machinery and equipment, is used as security for bonds, the securities are known as *chattel mortgage bonds*. When used by railroads to purchase engines, freight cars, and passenger coaches, they are known as *equipment trust certificates*. Such bonds command a strong market because, in case of default, the trustee could easily sell the mortgaged equipment to another railroad.

Stocks and bonds as security. Stocks and bonds of various other companies that are owned by the corporation desiring to borrow funds from the investing public are frequently used as security for a bond issue. The securities are deposited with a trustee who, under the terms of the indenture, can sell them for the benefit of the bondholders in case of default on either interest or principal payments. Such bonds are called *collateral trust bonds*. If the pledged stocks and bonds are issues of good companies and have a value in excess of the amount of the bonds sold, collateral trust bonds are an attractive investment.

Excellent credit rating as security. Occasionally a firm is so strong that it does not feel the need for stating any security behind the issue except the general excellent credit standing of the corporation. In this case the bonds are called *debenture bonds*. All of the more than 20 outstanding bond issues sold by the American Telephone & Telegraph Company, some with maturity dates extending into the twenty-first century, are debenture bonds. Bonds issued directly by the United States Government are, without exception, of the debenture type.

Method of Repayment

Prospective investors would like to be sure that, when their bonds mature, the company will be financially able to pay back the money borrowed. Consequently, the plan by which this objective is to be attained is announced at the time the securities are sold. If the total issue runs into millions of dollars, the problem of repayment might be a very grave one.

There are two common methods of repayment, which result in liquidating the debt. One is to issue bonds that mature in different years so that the impact of the full amount will not be felt at a given date. Such bonds are known as *serial bonds*. For example, a 20-year $1 million issue might run for 10 years without any bonds maturing. At the end of the eleventh year and annually thereafter during the life of the bonds, $100,000 worth mature as specified when the bonds were first sold.

Another method of repayment is the establishment of a sinking fund. Under this plan, the issuing corporation deposits annually with the trustee an amount of money that, at the expiration of the bond issue, will equal the amount due. Using the same size of issue as that in the preceding illustration, the corporation might deposit $50,000 a year with a trustee. At the end of 20 years, assumed as the life of the bonds, the deposits would amount to the face value of the total issue. Actually, the size of the annual deposits could be smaller because of interest earnings on the funds in the hands of the trustee. Such bonds are known as *sinking-fund bonds*.

Some corporations, particularly railroads and public utilities that always have a large number of bonds outstanding, do not expect to liquidate the debt other than by retiring one issue with the proceeds received from another. Bonds sold for this purpose are called *refunding bonds*.

Callable or Redeemable Bonds

Although bonds must be retired when they mature, it may be desirable for the debtor corporation to liquidate the debt at an earlier date. To make this possible, a clause is frequently inserted in the indenture providing that the bonds can be called at the option of the issuer in accordance with announced terms that usually state a price higher than the face value. For example, a 40-year bond issue might not be callable

for 10 years; between 10 and 20 years it could be called at a premium of
$75; between 20 and 30 years, at a premium of $50; and thereafter at
its face value. The exact amount at which the bonds can be redeemed is
known as the *call price*. Bonds that have this feature are known as *callable*
or *redeemable bonds*.

In years of a declining interest rate, the privilege of repaying a bond
issue prior to maturity may be exercised. For example, assume that a
company sold $10 million worth of bonds in 1968 with a maturity date
40 years later and with an interest rate of 8½ percent. Later, this corporation believes it can sell a new issue at par with an interest rate of
6 percent. On the assumption that at this time the call price is $1,050 for
a $1,000 bond, the saving in interest for two years will, disregarding
the time element, offset the call premium. For the remaining life of the
bond issue, the corporation will make an annual saving of $250,000 in
interest expense.

Convertible Bonds

Bonds, as an investment, appeal to insurance companies, savings banks,
and individuals who desire a stated rate of return coupled with a high
degree of safety. In order to attract buyers who desire some speculative
possibilities as well, some bond indentures provide for the exchange of
bonds into common stock at the option of the holder during the life of the
bond issue. These are known as *convertible bonds*.

A typical convertible feature would allow the holder of a $1,000 bond
to exchange this security for 25 shares of common stock. If, at the time
the bond issue is sold, the shares are selling for $30 each, the conversion
privilege is of no value. If the stock advances to $50 per share, the bond
will rise in value to approximately $1,250; but the dividend on 25 shares
may well exceed the fixed yield on the bond. If a considerable portion of
the bond issue is converted, the corporation has solved a large part of its
redemption problem.

Because convertible bonds combine priority and stability of income
with the possibility of speculative profits, financial managers usually find
that these securities can be sold at par with a lower interest rate than that
required for other types of bond issues. This is attractive costwise; but when
bonds are converted, the result is a dilution of the equity position held by
the existing stockholders. For this reason the majority of corporations
would rather pay a slightly higher rate of interest and gain the advantages inherent in using a reasonable amount of debt capital.

BOND PREMIUM OR DISCOUNT

If the corporation selling a bond issue is highly regarded by investors, or if the bond market is favorable, or if the interest rate offered is higher than prevailing rates on comparable bonds, an issue may be sold for more than its face value. The amount by which the price exceeds the stated value is called a *bond premium*. If a bond with a face value of $1,000 is sold for $1,062.50, the $62.50 is the amount of the premium. If conditions are the reverse of those indicated above, a $1,000 bond may be sold for $987.50 and, in this case, the $12.50 reduction from the face value is known as the *bond discount*.

STOCKS

Equity capital in a corporation includes all funds contributed by the owners. The evidence of this ownership consists of stock certificates that, among other details, show the name of the owner, number of shares, and type of stock. There are two basic types of stock, preferred and common. Some firms have never sold any preferred stock; others have issued several separate series. All corporations, however, must have common stock outstanding as it represents ownership at the residual level.

PREFERRED STOCKS

Preferred stocks represent shares of ownership, the certificates show a stated rate of return that, when paid, is known as a dividend, and the stock does not have a maturity date. Because of the stated dividend rate and other possible features, such as convertibility, some investors feel that preferred stocks occupy a middle ground between bonds and common stocks. Legally there is no justification for this viewpoint as preferred stocks are a form of ownership rather than debt. Furthermore, although a preferred stock shows a rate of return, such as 6 percent, even this dividend is not owed until so declared by the board of directors. Also, unlike bonds, the authority to issue preferred stock must be obtained from the state in which it is incorporated. The number of shares to be authorized and a brief description of the type or types of preferred stock that may be issued are contained in the original application for a charter or might, at a later date, be the subject of a charter amendment.

As described below in some detail, preferred stock may have a number of different features. To the extent that they are incorporated in a particular issue, these features are printed on the face or reverse side of each preferred stock certificate. Other than the universal preference as to dividends, the owner would need to refer to his certificate to determine which of the following rights and privileges had been included in his shares: (1) preference as to dividends, (2) cumulative or noncumulative, (3) participating or nonparticipating, (4) voting or nonvoting, (5) callable or redeemable, (6) convertible, (7) preference as to assets, (8) par or no-par, and (9) series issues.

Preference as to Dividends

The very name "preferred stock" indicates that this type of stock must have a preference over another type. Without exception, preferred stockholders receive dividends before common stockholders. If a company has some earnings but not enough to warrant declaring dividends on both preferred and common stocks, the preferred stocks will be favored. The board of directors of a corporation has the right to *pass the dividend*, which means that the dividend that might be expected by the preferred stockholders is not declared. It would not be legal, then, to declare a dividend on the common stock.

Cumulative or Noncumulative

Dividends on preferred stock are usually declared on a quarterly basis although some companies pay on a semiannual or annual basis. If a dividend is passed by the board of directors, the question arises as to whether the amount is forever lost to the preferred stockholders. If the stock is *cumulative preferred stock*, the dividends omitted in previous periods must be declared before any action can be taken leading to a distribution of profits to the common stockholders. If the stock is *noncumulative preferred stock*, such omissions need not be taken into consideration at a later date.

For example, assume that a corporation has outstanding a 5 percent, preferred stock issue of $1,000,000. In 1971 the company just about breaks even financially, and the board of directors decides to pass the dividend on the preferred stock. In 1972 the corporation earns $100,000, and the board votes dividends equal to this amount of profit. If the preferred stock is noncumulative, $50,000 will be paid to these stockholders and the common stockholders will receive the same amount. If the preferred stock is cumulative, the entire $100,000 will be paid to the preferred stockholders because they are entitled to $50,000 for 1971 plus $50,000 for 1972.

Participating or Nonparticipating

Preferred stocks have an established dividend rate. For example, an issue may state that the return shall be $6 a year per share. When the firm is particularly successful, however, the preferred stockholders will be limited to an annual return of the amount stated unless the stock is participating. In other words, *participating preferred stock* allows the owners to share in excess earnings, whereas *nonparticipating preferred stock* limits the annual dividends to the amount stated at the time of issue.

If a company has outstanding 1,000 shares of preferred stock on which the established dividend rate is $5 and 1,000 shares of common stock, and has earnings of $25,000 available for dividends, the distribution of this amount will vary between the two stockholding groups depending on whether the preferred is participating or nonparticipating. If the latter, $5,000 will be paid to the preferred stockholders and $20,000 to the common stockholders. If the preferred stock is participating to the fullest extent possible, $5,000 will be paid to holders of preferred stock as a prior claim on earnings and the common stockholders will next benefit by a like sum. This leaves $15,000, which would be distributed equally on all shares outstanding. This would result in a total payment of $12.50 on each share of stock, whether it be preferred or common. Sometimes preferred stocks that are participating do not share in excess earnings until after the common stockholders have received a larger payment per share than the stated rate on the preferred stock.

Voting or Nonvoting

Common law holds that, since stock is ownership, all stock is entitled to vote. In the case of preferred stocks this privilege is frequently removed or restricted by the contract under which it is issued. It is a right that is sacrificed in return for securing other favored treatment.

If preferred stock does not have regular voting power, that is, one vote for each share, it may be given voting privileges on special matters, such as when a bond issue is proposed that might jeopardize the favored position of the preferred stockholders. An even more common provision is the extension of voting rights when a stated number of quarterly preferred dividends have been passed by the board of directors.

Callable or Redeemable

A feature of many preferred stocks, which is similar to a common provision in bond issues, is the inclusion of a call price at which preferred stocks may be redeemed at the option of the issuing corporation. If no such feature is included in the original agreement, there is no legal right by which a corporation can call in any outstanding preferred stock. The only possibility in this case is to buy the shares on the open market; but, if some owners refuse to sell, these shares will remain outstanding as long as the corporation is in existence.

Convertible

Preferred stocks, particularly if they are nonparticipating, may not be overly attractive to investors. The lack of assurance that the dividend will be declared more than offsets the slightly higher yield frequently available in comparison with bonds issued by the same corporation. In order to induce investors to purchase a preferred stock issue, the contract may include a clause providing for conversion into common stock at the option of the owner. If a preferred stock selling for $100 a share is convertible into four shares of common stock, and the common stock is quoted at $22 a share, there is no value to the conversion privilege. Should the selling price of the common stock rise beyond $25, the preferred stock will increase in value. At some point the holder might decide to convert if he did not object to owning common stock and if the yield on four shares of common was higher than the income from one share of preferred.

Preference as to Assets

Most preferred stocks have a prior claim on assets in case it is necessary to dissolve the corporation. This means that preferred stockholders will be paid the amount due them before any distribution is made to common stockholders.

In case a corporation is liquidated, the first task is to sell all of the assets. Cash received must be used to pay off all liabilities, including all bond issues, before giving any consideration to the ownership group represented by preferred and common stocks. At this stage the preferred stockholders are in an advantageous position if their stock is preferred as to assets for otherwise they would share equally with the common stockholders in any distribution that could be made.

Par or No-Par

All shares of stock, preferred or common, which are issued with a stated value printed on the face of the certificate known as its par, are classified as *par stock*. If a par is not indicated, it is classified as *no-par stock*. The difference between the two types is simply whether the stock certificate does or does not have a stated monetary value.

Historically, all stocks had a par value that the public, to its sorrow, frequently confused with market value. In order to combat this type of fraud, state legislatures authorized corporations to issue no-par stock. For accounting purposes the board of directors sometimes assigns an arbitrary stated value to each share of no-par stock, but such an action does not change its status. As far as owners are concerned, there is practically no choice between par and no-par stocks.

When the preferred stock has a par value, for example $100 a share, the dividend rate is given as a percent, such as 5 percent. Also, the stock may be sold at a premium or discount, above or below par, as in the case of bonds. If the stock has no face value, the dividend rate must be stated in terms of dollars, such as a $5 preferred stock.

Series Issues

Some corporations have more than one issue of preferred stock outstanding. Because each issue was originally sold on different dates involving varying market conditions, the stated rate of return is different for each series. Otherwise, the various issues are almost always on an equal footing. Series issues of preferred stocks are more widely used by public utility and railroad companies than by industrial corporations.

COMMON STOCKS

Common stocks represent ownership and are the least complicated of all securities used for long-term financing. No dividend rate is ever stated. They cannot be convertible, participating, cumulative, or callable. Voting rights are rarely restricted. Common stockholders take the greatest risks but stand to make the maximum gain if the corporation is successful.

The reason that common stocks cannot be convertible is that conversion features always provide for an exchange into a lower level security, and common stocks are at the bottom of the scale. They are automatically participating, and there would be no point in making a common stock cumulative. If it is possible to make up dividends not declared in previous years, the procedure is to pay a large dividend in the current year. Also, common stock cannot be callable since a corporation must have owners, and holders of preferred stock would no longer be preferred if there were no common stock outstanding.

As previously stated, common stocks can be of the par or no-par variety. There used to be more no-par common stock than par common stock, but recently many corporations have issued common stock with low par values, such as $1, $5, and $10. Under some circumstances low par value shares reduce incorporation costs, franchise fees, and taxes on the transfer of shares. As to voting rights, a few corporations have two types of common stock outstanding, Class A and Class B. One class votes, the other does not. The advantage to the owners of the voting class is that the investment necessary to control the corporation is reduced without sacrificing the advantages of using common stock for long-term financing needs.

The characteristics of common stocks, and of preferred stocks and bonds as well, are important factors that enter into the decision-making process about the type or types of securities a corporation should use. Figure 19-1 highlights the differences between the two major types of long-term financing instruments—bonds and stocks.

BONDS	STOCKS
1. Represent debt of issuing corporation.	1. Represent ownership in corporation.
2. Must be repaid at some future date.	2. No obligation to repay although sometimes stock is retired.
3. Definite rate of interest due at stated intervals.	3. Unless and until dividends are declared, no return is due stockholders even though preferred stock may state a specific rate of return.
4. Interest on bonds is an expense of doing business.	4. Dividends are a distribution of profits.

Figure 19-1

Major Differences Between Stocks and Bonds

FINANCIAL INSTITUTIONS—LONG-TERM CAPITAL

The high degree of specialization characteristic of our economic system, as observed in production and distribution and in the area of short-term financing, extends into the realm of long-term financing. No single financial institution attempts to perform all of the functions involved in solving the debt and equity capital requirements of large and small businesses. One of these institutions, investment banking companies, provides the greatest amount of direct assistance and is worthy of particular emphasis in the discussion that follows. As will be explained, the help provided by other institutions associated with long-term financing is usually indirect rather than direct, although not without considerable importance in specific instances.

INVESTMENT BANKING COMPANIES

The primary function of *investment banking companies* is to market securities for corporations that have long-term capital needs. Such banking companies are sometimes called "security houses" and this title describes, in part, their operations. The "merchandise" they purchase for subsequent sale to investors consists of bonds, preferred stocks, and common stocks of old and new companies.

If the Stoddard Manufacturing Co. decides to construct a new factory building and equip it with the necessary machinery, the company may need additional capital funds. If a decision is reached to obtain the funds needed, estimated at $50 million, from an issue of mortgage bonds, the problem of selling these securities to the public would loom as almost insurmountable to a company unfamiliar with this field of finance. An investment banking company can be contacted and, if it agrees to market the bonds, the entire problem is solved as far as the manufacturing company is concerned.

The investment banking company would make an investigation of the Stoddard Manufacturing Co. prior to making a commitment regarding the proposed bond issue. If reports received from engineers, accountants, and other experts were favorable, the investment banking company would then enter into negotiations to underwrite the bond issue. This means that an offer would be made to the Stoddard Manufacturing Co. to buy the bonds. An acceptance would result in immediate access to the cash needed. The price that the investment banking company would be willing to pay would depend on the amount that it anticipates can be realized from the sale of the bonds. If its experts conclude that the bonds can be sold at par, the company might pay $49,600,000 for the issue. The discount of $400,000, which would represent the gross profit to the investment banking company, is called the *spread*.

If the issue is not too large in relation to the size of the investment banking company, the institution may handle the entire transaction through its central office and branches. If the issue is too large for one firm, or if the risk is too great, several other investment banking companies may be invited to participate in the financing as a syndicate. Some investment banking companies specialize in organizing syndicates and in wholesaling blocks of securities to smaller dealers located in various cities.

Other investment banking companies operate many retail outlets and employ large numbers of salesmen. The well-known firm of Merrill Lynch, Pierce, Fenner & Smith, Inc. is in the latter class.

The preceding illustration assumed that a corporation was already in existence and that additional funds would be secured by floating a bond issue. Investment banking companies are also willing to sell securities of a company being organized as well as to market preferred and common stocks for old corporations. As will be explained in Chapter 20, additional common stock could not be sold to the public unless the existing stockholders had waived their rights to purchase these voting shares.

OTHER FINANCIAL INSTITUTIONS FOR LONG-TERM CAPITAL

The following financial institutions are essential elements in the overall long-term capital picture even though their assistance to corporations is, normally, more indirect than that provided by investment banking companies: (1) brokerage firms, (2) trust companies, (3) investment companies, (4) insurance companies, (5) savings and loan associations, and (6) savings banks.

Brokerage Firms

Brokers are persons who buy and sell for others, charging a commission for their services. They are found in many areas of business activity including finance where a number of brokers frequently join together to form a *brokerage firm*. This technique is so widely used and well known that, when an individual states that he is going to call his broker, it is generally understood that he is contacting a brokerage firm. A member of the firm is officially known as a *registered representative* since he has been required to pass examinations and to register with the National Association of Security Dealers.

Some brokerage firms function on occasion as investment banking companies, and many investment banking companies also provide a brokerage service. In the main, the chief activity of a brokerage firm is to serve its clients by buying and selling securities that have previously been issued and are currently outstanding. Some brokerage firms maintain an inventory of selected issues of bonds and stocks and sell these to its customers. In this event they hope to sell the securities they own at a profit, rather than to earn a commission, and are classified as *broker/dealers*.

Brokerage firms, by providing facilities for investors to buy and sell bonds and stocks, make long-term securities much more attractive than they would otherwise be; for a person is more likely to purchase a new issue from an investment banking company when he knows he can easily sell it should he wish to do so. Brokerage firms also provide investment advice without charge, thus making available to a customer extensive research materials including independent advisory services that would be expensive on an individual basis. In addition, brokerage firms will loan limited amounts to those who buy securities from them, thereby increasing the amount of money entering the long-term financing area.

Trust Companies

Trust companies are financial institutions that specialize in assuming the capacity of trustee for business firms and individuals. In today's financial world most trust companies also operate as commercial or savings banks, and the majority of large commercial banks maintain a trust department. Consequently, the functions of a trust company are frequently carried out by a department of a larger financial institution.

The major portion of a trust company's business consists of the management of estates and of serving as a trustee under the provisions of a will. In this connection funds turned over to the trust company are invested in such securities as bonds, preferred stocks, and common stocks. Under the *prudent-man rule*, which has been adopted by most states, the trustee can purchase securities that a careful investor would buy for his own account. In some instances specific securities are purchased for an estate, but a majority of the states now permit the use of a *common trust fund* by which the funds from several estates are combined for the purchase of securities.

As explained on page 453, a trust company function of particular interest to business is that of serving as trustee of a bond issue. The indenture under which bonds are issued always provides that there shall be a trustee to act for the bondholders in such a manner as to protect their best interests. Under the Trust Indenture Act of 1939, a federal law, the trustee for a bond issue must take an aggressive position in behalf of the bondholders.

Another financial service rendered many businesses by trust companies is that of acting as registrar and transfer agent for stock issues. In the role of *registrar*, the trust company guarantees to the investing public that the various issues of stock that may be outstanding are accurately stated and within the limits established by the charter. The duties of *transfer agent* involve recording changes in ownership following each sale of stock. For large businesses with thousands of outstanding shares of stock, which are traded daily on stock exchanges, the service of a transfer agent is necessary and important.

Still another function rendered business by a trust company is serving as a special depository for important papers that are not to be delivered until certain terms are met. For example, the Dodge Construction Company agrees to build a factory addition for the E-Z Tool Company provided this company will sell a bond issue in order to raise the necessary funds. The contract for building may be placed in the hands of the trust company to be delivered to the E-Z Tool Company when it completes the agreement to sell the necessary bonds. The legal term *in escrow* is used for such papers while they are in the hands of the trust company.

Other services of trust companies include writing and mailing dividend checks, serving as the trustee for employee profit-sharing funds, investing funds contributed for pensions, and exchanging corporation securities under a refinancing program.

Investment Companies

Investment companies sell shares to individual investors and use the capital raised in this manner to purchase securities in other companies. The holdings, called the *portfolio,* of some investment companies are diversified among bonds, preferred stocks, and common stocks; while others purchase and sell common stocks only. Still others restrict their activities to one industry, such as electronics or oil, or to one country, such as mining companies in Canada. In any event, investment companies provide an individual or business wishing to invest in corporate securities the opportunity to own, indirectly, an interest in many companies. Owners of investment company shares obtain the advantages of diversification and of professional management.

Investment companies can be organized as business trusts or as corporations. There are two main types—*the open-end investment company* and the *closed-end investment company.* Most of the largest companies are the open-end type and are the ones commonly called *mutual funds.* Shares can be purchased at any time and in any quantity by contacting a salesman and, in most instances, paying a commission. The company will redeem the shares by paying the liquidation price of each share computed on a daily basis. Since shares will be redeemed by the issuer at the request of the owner, they are not quoted on a stock exchange. Closed-end investment companies issue shares only when first organized. Afterwards, these shares can be purchased on a security exchange or on the over-the-counter market. The portfolio of most closed-end funds is subject to change by paid managers although a subsidiary type known as a *fixed-trust investment company* continues to hold the shares purchased at the time it was organized.

Investment companies have become an important factor in the long-term capital field. The shares they issue are purchased by trusts, pension funds, school and church endowments, and businesses as well as thousands of individuals. Although on occasion an investment trust may make a direct purchase of securities, particularly when it is eligible to purchase new shares because it owns old shares, its assistance is more commonly indirect rather than direct.

Shown in Table 19-1 is a list of 12 mutual funds, each with assets of over one billion dollars. According to the Investment Company Institute, the total assets of all mutual funds are in excess of $48 billion, and shares are owned by more than 10 million individuals and organizations.

Table 19-1

MUTUAL FUNDS WITH ASSETS OF MORE THAN ONE BILLION DOLLARS

Name of Fund	Total Assets (Millions of Dollars)
Investors Mutual	2,681.1
Dreyfus Fund	2,398.2
Investors Stock Fund	2,221.4
Massachusetts Investors Trust Fund	2,118.4
Affiliated Fund	1,595.0
Wellington Fund	1,421.8
United Accumulative Fund	1,256.0
Massachusetts Investors Growth Stock Fund	1,252.4
Fundamental Investors	1,166.9
Fidelity Trend Fund	1,096.1
Investment Company of America	1,065.1
Investors Variable Payment Stock Fund	1,050.7

Source: *Investment Companies, 1970.* Wiesenberger Services, Inc. Total Asset Values as of December 31, 1969.

Investment companies are regulated under the provisions of the Wagner-Lea Act, a law passed by Congress in 1940 and known officially as the Investment Company Act. Each company must register with the Securities and Exchange Commission, as must investment counselors and advisory services under the Investment Advisers Act, a companion piece of legislation. No investment trust can be organized with a capital of less than $100,000, the management must be selected by the stockholders, funds cannot be invested in other investment trusts or affiliated companies, and the types of securities that the investment trust can issue are subject to restrictions.

Insurance Companies

Organizations that insure individuals and businesses against many types of risks are known as *insurance companies*. The cash they receive from premiums paid by policyholders normally exceeds the payments on claims, policy loans, and other business expenditures, which leaves them a balance on hand. This excess is invested in mortgages on business and residential properties, in bonds issued by corporations and governments, and, to a lesser degree, in stocks. The amounts involved are so large that insurance companies are important sources of long-term capital for many corporations. In some instances an entire bond issue can be sold at a private sale, thus avoiding underwriting costs.

The types of securities that insurance companies can purchase are regulated by the several states. Companies must secure a license to sell in the state, and they are subject to an annual audit by the state commissioner or superintendent of insurance. Other regulatory features concern rates, policy forms, and methods of settling claims. Although most insurance is sold in interstate commerce, the McCarran Act, passed by Congress in 1945, allows the states to supervise the activities of companies that do business within their borders.

Savings and Loan Associations

Savings and loan associations, or *building and loan associations* as they are known in some areas, are formed for two major purposes: (a) to loan money for the purchase of home and business properties and (b) to enable individuals to invest funds with comparative safety at yields usually higher than available in savings accounts with banks. Their form of organization and ownership was described in Chapter 5. A first mortgage on property is almost universally required as security for a loan, and the interest rate charged on the unpaid balance is usually about 7½ to 7¾ percent. Although savings and loan associations specialize in making mortgage loans on residences, included in the more than $90 billion of credit extended are loans on office buildings, apartment houses, and other structures used for business purposes.

Membership in the Federal Savings and Loan Insurance Corporation is required for federally chartered associations and is available to those holding state charters. This federal agency, which was created in 1934, insures accounts in eligible savings and loan associations up to $20,000. Savings and loan associations may also join the Federal Home Loan Bank System, a federal agency organized for the purpose of extending credit to its member mortgage-lending institutions.

Savings Banks

Except in states that permit mutual savings banks, the common situation is to find a savings department in a commercial bank. *Savings banks* accept deposits from savers on which an announced rate of interest is paid. These funds are then invested in mortgages, bonds, and other securities permitted by law. Interest earned on these investments provides earnings that make possible the payment of interest on savings accounts. Many individuals find a savings account a convenient way of accumulating funds. Christmas savings clubs are featured by many savings banks and departments of commercial banks.

Membership in the Federal Deposit Insurance Corporation is available to savings banks as well as commercial banks. This organization, created in 1933 by the federal government, insures deposits up to $20,000 in any one bank in any one name. An individual can obtain insurance on all of his savings by patronizing more than one savings bank or department.

BUSINESS TERMS

QUESTIONS FOR DISCUSSION AND ANALYSIS

1. Why is debt capital restricted to fixed liabilities? May current liabilities also be a portion of total debt capital?

2. Most individuals feel more comfortable when they are out of debt. Should and does this attitude also apply to corporations?

3. Would it be satisfactory for a corporation, or any other entity for that matter, to issue bonds without a maturity date? Give reasons for either your yes or no answer.

4. Privately owned corporations do not issue accumulation bonds. Can they and, if so, why do they not issue this type of bond?

5. If first mortgage bonds run for 40 years, isn't there an excellent chance that the value of the security behind the issue will become practically worthless by the time the bonds mature?

6. Why would any investor be willing to buy a preferred stock if it was nonparticipating and noncumulative?

7. Common stocks are the most speculative of all corporate securities and yet there are approximately 30 million people who own them. Is this a clear indication that most individuals are gamblers at heart?

8. Is the general public confused by the inclusion of the word "banking" in the designation investment banking companies? Would it be preferable if these important financial institutions were uniformly called security houses?

9. Most mutual funds are of the open-end variety. Does this type have any advantages over a closed-end investment company?

10. Why shouldn't privately owned insurance companies insure deposits in savings banks and savings and loan associations rather than agencies of the federal government?

PROBLEMS AND SHORT CASES

1. The Argus Corporation has outstanding a $75,000,000 issue of 8 percent first mortgage bonds that were sold five years ago and which mature in 35 years from today. The bonds are callable at 110 ($1,100 for each $1,000 bond). At this time it appears that a refunding issue can be sold at par ($1,000 for each $1,000 bond) at an interest rate of 6 percent.

Compute the amount of saving over the remaining life of the bond issue if the Argus Corporation refinances its debt capital on the above basis. The interest payment due at the end of the fifth year has just been paid.

2. The capital structure of the Electron Company consists of the following:

Preferred stock—300,000 shares, par value $100 per share, 7%, cumulative, nonparticipating.
Common stock—1,000,000 shares, no-par.

Through 1971 dividends were paid on both classes of stock, but net profits after taxes were only $100,000 in 1972 and the board of directors passed the dividends. In 1973 the profits increased to $1,300,000 and the board declared a dividend of $4 a share on the preferred stock. In 1974 profits increased sharply to $5,700,000 and the board of directors wishes to resume dividend payments on the common stock.

Show calculations to determine the maximum per share dollar distribution available to the common stockholders in 1974, assuming distribution of all profits earned in 1972, 1973, and 1974.

3. A group of six businessmen have decided to form a corporation to be called Amusement Enterprises, Inc. Living in a community that has had very limited recreational facilities, these men came to the conclusion that the population of the area was more than adequate to support an amusement park. They have taken an option on 160 acres of land located a half mile from the city limits and only a quarter of a mile from an exit on an interstate highway.

Their plans for the area include a large swimming pool, a dance hall, a roller coaster and other rides, concession stands, and a midget car race track. The total cost of the entire project, including land, access roads, and parking lot, has been carefully estimated at $15,750,000. The promoters feel that they should raise $16,000,000 in order to proceed with construction.

Publicity about the project, which has been widespread due to an article in a financial paper, has aroused considerable interest on the part of various financial institutions and investors. It would appear that there would be no difficulty in marketing mortgage bonds, preferred stock, and common stock. Each of the six incorporators is in a position to invest $500,000 of his own money in the corporation.

On the basis of the information given, present a financial plan for Amusement Enterprises, Inc. and indicate the financial institution or institutions you would use. Justify the type, amount, and terms of each security selected and the institution or institutions selected to assist you in selling these securities.

SUGGESTED READINGS

Broom, H. N., and J. G. Longenecker. *Small Business Management,* Third Edition. Cincinnati: South-Western Publishing Co., 1971. Part C.

Cohen, J. B., and S. M. Robbins. *The Financial Manager: Basic Aspects of Financial Administration.* New York: Harper & Row, 1966. Part IV.

Cooke, G. W., and E. C. Bomeli. *Business Financial Management.* Boston: Houghton Mifflin Company, 1967. Part V.

Curran, W. S. *Principles of Financial Management.* New York: McGraw-Hill Book Company, 1970. Part Two.

Dauten, C. A., and M. Welshans. *Principles of Finance*, Third Edition. Cincinnati: South-Western Publishing Co., 1970. Part II.

Donaldson, E. F., and J. K. Pfahl. *Corporate Finance—Policy and Management,* Third Edition. New York: The Ronald Press Co., 1969. Part II.

Farwell, L. C., *et al. Financial Institutions*, Fourth Edition. Homewood, Illinois: Richard D. Irwin, Inc., 1966. Part III.

Flink, S. J., and D. Gruenwald. *Managerial Finance.* New York: John Wiley & Sons, Inc., 1969. Part III.

Gruenwald, A. E., and E. E. Nemmers. *Basic Managerial Finance.* New York: Holt, Rinehart and Winston, Inc., 1970. Parts Six and Seven.

Prather, C. K. *Financing Business Firms*, Third Edition. Homewood, Illinois: Richard D. Irwin, Inc., 1966. Part V.

Van Horne, J. C. *Financial Management and Policy.* Englewood Cliffs, New Jersey: Prentice-Hall, Inc., 1968. Part IV.

Weston, J. F., and E. F. Brigham. *Managerial Finance*, Third Edition. New York: Holt, Rinehart and Winston, Inc., 1969. Part Six.

Chapter 20

Financial Problems and Policies

Finance is one of the major functions of business. Efficient financial management is as important for profitability as production know-how or economical methods of distribution. Consequently, financial policies must be established and solutions to numerous financial problems reached at a high management level. In small firms the owner or owners usually assume responsibility for making financial decisions and policies. In larger corporations the officer in charge frequently carries the title of Vice President for Finance or Controller.

It is the purpose of this chapter to examine the major types of financial problems and policies encountered by business enterprises. These include the capital structure of the firm, policies on the distribution of earnings, and the background of decisions affecting the allocation of available funds. In addition, the various forms of combinations will be examined in light of the problem of financing these methods of growth. Finally, attention will be devoted to procedures available to salvage or liquidate firms that find themselves in critical financial trouble.

CAPITAL STRUCTURE

As noted in previous chapters, there are only two sources of funds at the time a firm is organized. One of these is the owner or owners of the business, and the other source is its creditors. Within this framework equity capital can come from different classes of investors, and borrowed funds can be secured on either a short-term or long-term basis.

Individuals who go into business as sole proprietors or as members of a partnership should invest a substantial proportion (preferably 70 to 80 percent) of the funds needed by the business. Rather than to borrow heavily, they should turn to some of the numerous methods available to reduce the funds needed to launch the enterprise. Land and buildings can be rented rather than purchased. Equipment can be secured on lease arrangements. Delivery or hauling services can be secured under contract arrangements. Manufactured parts can be purchased rather than produced. Subcontracting offers additional possibilities for conserving capital.

Corporations, particularly those classed as small businesses, can be placed in the same category as sole proprietorships and partnerships with regard to a desirable capital structure. Ability to borrow should be reserved for possible emergencies, and a generous ratio between equity and debt capital is most desirable. For larger firms with the ability to market various types of securities, more alternatives may be available; but a conservative capital structure is sound for large as well as small corporations.

In addition to starting a business with a sound capital structure, many of the same problems may arise if a decision is reached to expand the size of the firm. The owners may invest additional funds, or the existing debt structure may be expanded. Another possibility available to a going concern is to retain all or a substantial portion of the yearly profits. These earnings belong to the owners; but if they are not paid out, the net effect is to increase the investment of the owners in the firm. Unless all of the cash generated from profits is used to reduce debt, expansion will take place although, most likely, at a slower rate than if additional capital were secured.

When a firm decides to raise funds from external sources, several problems arise. One major problem is the selection of the proper type of security or securities. Once this decision is reached, the question arises as to how these can be sold. Finally, there may well come a time when refinancing the capital structure is more important than raising additional funds.

SECURITY SELECTION FACTORS

Assuming that capital is to be raised, either to start or to expand an enterprise, several factors must be considered in arriving at a choice as to the sources of these funds. These factors are (1) debt or equity capital, (2) taxes, (3) voting control, (4) market conditions, (5) stability of earnings, and (6) rate of earnings. Although the following discussion centers about corporations large enough to have access to alternate sources of capital, some of the items mentioned apply with equal force to small firms, both incorporated and unincorporated.

Debt or Equity Capital

As explained in Chapter 19, if bonds are issued, the amount involved becomes a debt of the corporation, which requires repayment at some future date. If stock is issued, there is no problem of repayment. For bonds, interest must be paid and, in the case of mortgage bonds, there is the danger of foreclosure if interest and principal payments are not maintained on schedule. On the other hand, more stock means sharing the expected profits with more owners.

Taxes

From the viewpoint of reducing taxes, raising funds by selling bonds is to be preferred over the sale of stock. Interest on bonds is a business expense and is allowable as a deduction in computing net earnings for purposes of income taxes. Dividends are not a business expense. They are a distribution of profits and, therefore, are taxable as part of earnings. Also, a tax on total stock outstanding is assessed by the state in which the corporation is organized.

Voting Control

In deciding whether to issue stocks or bonds, a corporation must consider the problem of voting power. Bondholders are not owners and rarely assume any voting rights. Although the voting rights of preferred stockholders are sometimes restricted, the general rule is that all stockholders are entitled to vote. Unless the existing stockholders buy new issues in proportion to their former holdings, voting control may pass to new investors in the firm.

Market Conditions

Market conditions may be an important factor when the sale of securities is to be made to existing stockholders or to the general public. As a general rule, when business conditions are prosperous, most investors prefer common stocks because these offer a potentially high return and provide a hedge against inflation. When business conditions are depressed, the surer return on preferred stocks and bonds is of greater interest.

In some instances in order to market the securities, special inducements are offered. For example, in 1970 the American Telephone & Telegraph Company allowed common stockholders to buy one $100, 8¾%, thirty-year bond for each thirty-five shares owned. Additionally, the buyer of a $100 bond received a warrant certificate permitting him to buy two shares of A. T. & T. stock for $52 a share between Nov. 15, 1970, and May 15, 1975. A more common inducement used by many corporations is to issue bonds convertible under stated conditions into common stock. Another incentive used when a corporation wishes to sell common stock instead of bonds is to offer one warrant with each share of stock purchased. This *warrant* allows the holder to buy a share of stock under stated terms as to time and price as described above for the American Telephone & Telegraph Company.

Stability of Earnings

The total amount of funds that can safely be secured from bonds varies directly with the stability of the earnings. A corporation that has stable earnings year in and year out can best afford to sell bonds. Such a concern can finance yearly interest payments and yearly deposits into a sinking fund for the retirement of the issue. A firm with highly fluctuating profits, on the other hand, can pay interest one year with ease and yet be seriously handicapped by this fixed charge in the next year.

This factor, together with a large investment in fixed assets available for mortgaging, explains why public utilities, such as gas and electric companies, frequently secure one half to two thirds of their total capital from bond issues. These firms are permitted by law to earn a fair return on their total investment, and consumers use about as much gas and electricity in one year as another. On the other hand, a firm that manufactures a luxury item is likely to have high profits one year and low profits another. Unless the amount of the bond issue outstanding is small in proportion to total capital, the financial burden imposed by fixed interest charges and sinking-fund payments might cause the firm to fail.

Rate of Earnings

If a firm expects that it can earn 15 percent on any amount of capital employed in the business and it can borrow money from bondholders at a rate somewhere between 5 and 8 percent, the difference between what it pays for money and what it earns on these funds is available for the stockholders. Rates of interest on bonds are fixed and have no relationship to the profits that may be earned on the capital contributed by bondholders. The principle of borrowing money at a lower rate than the rate of expected earnings on these funds, with a resulting excess available to the stockholders, is called *trading on the equity*.

For example, if a corporation has $100,000 in assets acquired from the sale of common stock and earns 15 percent on these assets, it has $15,000 in profits available for distribution to the owners assuming that the amount represents profits after taxes. The corporation now decides to double its size and secures an additional $100,000 by selling bonds with an 8 percent interest rate. If profits remain at 15 percent of assets, there will be $30,000 in earnings before bond interest is paid and $22,000 available to the owners after the interest payment. Without any additional investment on their part, the owners can share in an additional $7,000 profits.

Trading on the equity is a sound business principle, but it becomes increasingly risky as the percentage of borrowed capital increases in proportion to the total assets. A corporation can secure comparable advantages for its common stockholders by issuing nonparticipating preferred stock bearing a lower stated rate of return than the expected rate of earnings on its assets. Companies that have either bonds or nonparticipating preferred stock outstanding and that earn a higher rate on the assets acquired with the proceeds of these issues than the cost of the capital obtained have what is known as a *leverage factor*. The common stock of leverage companies is more speculative than that of companies with no senior securities outstanding.

METHODS OF SELLING SECURITIES

After a decision has been reached as to the securities to be sold, the next question involves the sales method to be used. If bonds are to be issued, there is not much question but that an investment banking company, or possibly an insurance company, will be contacted. If a new corporation is being formed and it is decided to sell stocks, unless the company is relatively small, once again an investment banking company would be the most logical choice to underwrite the securities. For local, relatively small companies, the promoters may have enough friends, relatives, and wealthy acquaintances to market the stock among these individuals.

If an investment banking company is used and if the issue is sizable, the chances are excellent that the investment banking company contacted by the corporation will organize an underwriting syndicate such as was described in Chapter 4. To make the securities attractive to the syndicate and hence to potential investors, inducements such as those described on page 478 may be offered.

If a corporation already in existence decides to expand by selling additional shares of stock, the law usually requires that the existing stockholders have the first opportunity to buy the issue unless these stockholders vote to waive this privilege. Only by this protection can a stockholder be sure that his percentage of ownership will not be diluted. This would be very important to an individual owning voting control of the corporation. The legal right of a stockholder to subscribe to new issues of stock in proportion to his holding of old stock is known as his *privileged subscription* or *preemptive right*.

If stockholders have not agreed to waive their preemptive right in a new stock issue, the corporation mails each one a certificate, called a *subscription warrant*, that indicates the number of rights to which he is entitled. One *right* is allotted to each share of old stock, and it customarily takes more than one right to purchase a share of the new stock. For example, a corporation with 500,000 shares of common stock outstanding may decide to sell an additional 100,000 shares. In this event it would take 5 rights to have the privilege of purchasing one share of the new stock. The holder of 100 shares of the old stock would receive a subscription warrant entitling him to use his 100 rights to purchase 20 shares of the new issue.

In order to make it desirable for the old stockholder to exercise his subscription warrant or to sell it to someone else, it is customary to offer him the opportunity to buy new shares for somewhat less than the current market price of the old shares. This differential makes it profitable for a nonstockholder to buy rights from those who do not wish to exercise them in their own behalf. If the stock referred to above is selling for $150 a share and the holder of 5 rights can purchase a share for $140, each right would sell for slightly less than $2. If a stockholder has only 4 rights, he will have to buy another or sell the ones he has, for fractional shares are not issued. If the stock involved is listed, rights are traded on national exchanges. In any event, the corporation or its agent will usually buy and sell rights for its stockholders.

Within recent years practically all large corporations have requested their stockholders to vote to waive their preemptive right on a stated number of shares in order to install a stock option plan. A *stock option* is a privilege granted to certain key executives to purchase stock of the company under certain specified conditions as to time and price. It has been heralded as an important device to attract and keep young executives of outstanding ability. If a vice president, for example, is given an option to purchase 10,000 shares of the company's stock at a time when it is selling for $8 a share, and the market price subsequently advances to $58 a share, the executive has a profit of a half million dollars. Although the granting and exercise of stock options do involve the sale of additional common stock, this result is not considered a primary purpose for using this device.

REFINANCING PROGRAMS

The financial structure of a business is subject to constant change, particularly as regards circulating capital. The amounts owed on open accounts and to banks may rise and fall month by month as changes take place in inventory accumulations, collections on accounts, the payment of dividends, and other similar receipts and expenditures. Fixed capital is more likely to change slowly unless new securities are sold. Retained earnings do increase the amount of equity capital, and payments on bond issues do reduce the amount of debt capital; but these shifts are usually relatively minor compared to the total value of all assets.

Occasionally a corporation may decide to make substantial changes in its capital structure even though no expansion is contemplated. The original plan may have proved to be faulty or market conditions may now be ripe for issuing some types of securities that were not previously in public favor. Some of the more common refinancing plans are as follows: (1) bonds for bonds, (2) stocks for bonds, (3) stock for stock, (4) long-term for short-term financing, and (5) spin-offs.

Bonds for Bonds

The indenture of a majority of bond issues includes a provision that the bonds may be called or redeemed prior to maturity at the option of the corporation. Usually a premium must be paid, which varies with the length of time the bonds have been outstanding. For example, a 40-year bond issue may not be callable for 10 years; then it may be redeemable at 110 percent of par for the next 10 years, and then at 105 for the remaining life of the issue.

Since issuing bonds for bonds does not change the financial structure of a firm, it might seem that there would be no point in refinancing on this basis. Actually there are two occasions when replacing old bonds with a new bond issue would be pertinent. The more common situation is the opportunity to replace a high-interest bond issue with one carrying a lower interest rate. The saving in the annual interest cost may well equal the bond premium in two or three years and, aside from the expense of exchanging or selling the new bonds, the reduced expense will prove to be a profitable move over the life of the issue. Another occasion when bonds might replace bonds arises when an old issue matures and no provision has been made for its retirement. The proceeds from a refunding issue are used to pay off the old bonds and the corporation's financial structure remains intact. The debt of the federal government is very largely managed in this manner; and some corporations, notably railroads, follow this practice.

Stocks for Bonds

A number of bond issues outstanding are convertible into common stock and, if the conversion feature is both worthwhile and has an expiration date, there is a possibility that this shift will take place almost automatically. Usually, however, when a shift from debt capital to equity capital is contemplated, the bonds outstanding are redeemed with the proceeds from a stock issue. The procedure is quite simple. The corporation sells preferred stock or common stock for cash by methods previously described. If necessary, the charter can be amended to provide for additional shares, or authority may have been granted originally for more stock than is presently outstanding. The money received is used to redeem the bonds either at maturity or earlier, if the bonds are callable and the company exercises its call privilege.

Stock for Stock

Corporations with preferred stock outstanding usually have a clause in the contract under which this class of stock was issued that allows for its redemption. This provision may be similar to those incorporated in a callable bond, or it may state a single premium at which the stock can be called at any time at the option of the corporation. For example, a $100 par preferred stock may have a redemption price of $110 that remains constant throughout the life of this stock.

The purposes of redeeming a preferred stock issue are to refinance with a new issue carrying a lower dividend rate or to eliminate this class of stock. If a corporation has outstanding a sizable issue of 7 percent preferred stock, the company may decide to replace this stock with an issue of 5 percent preferred. The change will increase common stock dividend possibilities, assuming that the preferred stock is nonparticipating. Or, the corporation may decide that the market is strong for common stocks and that now would be a good time to eliminate the preferred class. The advantage in this shift would be to remove a security senior to the common stock so that, if more capital is needed at a later date when the market is strong for preferred stocks, the way would be open for such an issue.

Long-Term for Short-Term Financing

Some refinancing plans are undertaken to convert, on a relatively permanent basis, all or a portion of the short-term debt into long-term securities. A corporation may find that its cash balance does not improve to a point where the short-term indebtedness can be liquidated out of current receipts at any time during the year either because the original financial plan was faulty or because the firm has expanded. As a result, the problem of paying these debts presents a constant source of financial difficulty, usually met by other short-term borrowing. A more satisfactory solution is to sell bonds or stock and to reduce the short-term debt to a manageable size.

Spin-Offs

Within recent years a different type of refinancing plan has been used by some corporations that wish to divest themselves of a segment of their businesses. In some instances the unwanted assets are transferred to a new corporation in exchange for shares of stock, which are then distributed to the stockholders of the original corporation. In other cases a division of the business is sold to another corporation for cash or other consideration. The divesture by a firm of a segment of its business is known as a *spin-off*. An advantage that may be gained, in addition to eliminating a business activity not compatible with the firm's main objective, is a reduction in federal corporate income taxes. If the spin-off results in a loss, the corporation can apply the amount against capital gains realized in three previous years and secure a tax refund.

As will be described later in this chapter, in the decade of the sixties a great many already large corporations bought up hundreds of smaller companies. Sometimes the firm that was absorbed had two or three divisions but only one of these was useful to the buyer. It is also true that a few of the purchasing corporations overextended themselves financially in making the acquisitions. Consequently, it appears that the seventies may be a decade of the un-merger as large corporations spin-off divisions either to raise badly needed cash or because the business activity does not produce desired profits.

DISTRIBUTION OF EARNINGS POLICIES

Another financial problem faced by all business enterprises requires a decision regarding the distribution of earnings. In the case of sole proprietorships and partnerships, the owners usually pay themselves a modest salary if they are actively engaged in the operation of the business. This amount probably covers their normal living costs. Any withdrawal beyond a salary allowance may or may not be prudent, depending upon the size of the profits and the extent to which borrowed capital is used. Some partnership agreements place restrictions on amounts a partner may withdraw without the written consent of all partners.

In some instances sole proprietors or partners have no personal need for withdrawing any of the profits. The question then arises as to whether better use of these funds would be in the business or in outside investments. If they are left in the business, the firm automatically will grow in size after debts have been liquidated. If they are withdrawn, the firm will not expand, which may be desirable in view of location, available volume of sales, or nature of the business. The chances are that the profits could be used either in or out of the business, and the policy of withdrawing all or a part calls for good judgment on the part of the owners.

The dividend policies of corporations are of more importance because thousands of stockholders may be affected. Dividends represent a distribution of earnings by a corporation to its stockholders. If a company has not earned a profit and has no retained earnings from former years to distribute, or if the board of directors feels that it is unwise to declare a dividend, the owners will receive no income from their investment. The majority of successful corporations, particularly those whose securities are listed on an exchange, do pay dividends regularly. These may be paid in (1) cash, (2) stock, or (3) securities or scrip, with cash dividends accounting for four fifths of all types.

CASH DIVIDENDS

Customarily dividend-paying corporations, or their agents, mail checks to their stockholders on a quarterly basis. In the case of preferred stocks, the amount paid per share is one fourth of the annual stated rate of return for these securities, assuming that the issue is nonparticipating. As for common stock, the distribution depends in part on the dividend policy of the corporation.

Regular Dividend Policy

Some corporations have a reputation for paying quarterly dividends of a fixed amount, year in and year out, without regard for their current profits. If preferred stocks are outstanding, they are probably nonparticipating, and the stated rate is paid. In a somewhat comparable manner a steady dividend rate is paid on common stocks. A variation of this type of dividend policy is used by the board of directors of many corporations in years of high profits. It consists of the declaration of the regular dividend plus a so-called extra, frequently added to the last quarterly payment of the year. Actually this means a higher yield to the stockholder, but from the psychological viewpoint the investor realizes that he should not expect a like sum the following year unless operations are again unusually profitable. If the extra dividend is sizable, the declaration may be termed *cutting a melon.*

Variable Dividend Policy

A variable dividend policy is the exact opposite of a steady yield in that in some years no dividends may be declared and in others the amount paid out may be a handsome return on the investment. If operations are not profitable, no distribution is made even though the corporation could do so legally and with no damage to its financial structure. On the other hand, if profits are large, dividend payments are generous. In some instances every dollar earned in a given year is distributed to the stockholders that year.

Conservative Dividend Policy

A modification of the variable dividend policy is the plan of declaring a certain percent of earnings in the form of dividends and retaining the rest as a reinvestment of earnings. The board of directors might decide that one half to two thirds of the earnings should be distributed each year but that the remainder should be retained in the business.

STOCK DIVIDENDS

Although over 80 percent of all dividend payments are made in cash, some companies either substitute stock dividends for cash distributions or supplement the cash dividend with shares of stock. The rate may be low, such as a 3 or 5 percent stock dividend, or as high as 50 or 100 percent. For example, if a firm declares a 10 percent stock dividend, each stockholder will receive one new share for each ten already owned. Unlike distributions in cash, stock dividends do not constitute taxable income to the stockholders unless these individuals sell the shares received. The main reason for stock dividends is that the corporation has urgent needs to retain the cash that would otherwise go to its owners but feels an obligation to distribute some tangible return to keep faith with those who have invested in it.

Although frequently confused with a stock dividend, a *stock split-up* is legally entirely different even though in both instances the investor receives additional shares of stock. A *stock dividend* is a distribution of profits earned in the current or prior years in the form of stock rather than cash. A stock split-up consists of dividing the common stock outstanding into additional units such as a two-for-one or three-for-one split. It merely increases the number of shares representing the amount of capital raised by selling common stock. For example, common stock may originally have been sold at $100 a share. Assuming no change in its market value, a two-for-one split would give each shareholder twice as many shares but the value of each would be $50.

The rationale behind a stock split-up is to bring the market price of a share of stock into a *trading range*, which is a price that is attractive to most investors and speculators. For example, if the stock of a corporation is quoted on the New York Stock Exchange at $240 a share, it is considered out of the trading range, which is usually thought of as falling between $20 and $80 a share. If a stock split-up of 4 for 1 is approved by the stockholders, the price will drop to somewhere in the neighborhood of $60 a share. Because stock split-ups are usually accompanied by a dividend rate that is not reduced in proportion to the split ratio, the market price would more likely fall to around $65 rather than $60. Consequently, stockholders favor stock split-ups because the demand for shares on the part of more buyers coupled with a higher yield generally increase the value of their holdings.

SECURITIES OR SCRIP DIVIDENDS

If a corporation owns stock in another company, it can distribute these securities as a dividend to its stockholders. In the early 60's, the E. I. duPont de Nemours & Company was ordered by a federal court to divest itself of the 63 million shares of General Motors Corporation stock that it owned, and it chose to distribute these to its owners as a securities dividend. Spin-offs and court orders are the major reasons for the use of this type of dividend.

On rare occasions when a corporation wishes to distribute a cash dividend but does not have an adequate balance in its checking account, it may issue a scrip dividend. A *scrip dividend* is a short-term paper somewhat similar to a note payable, which may or may not bear interest, and is usually due in a few months. Since a scrip dividend is clear evidence of a weak cash and credit position, its use is generally confined to close corporations.

ALLOCATION OF FUNDS

Decisions involving the capital structure and dividend policies are frequently long-lasting, subject only to occasional reexamination. The day-by-day activities of those who manage the financial affairs of a firm are more likely to be concerned with the allocation of funds among current assets although, on occasion, the acquisition of fixed assets may also be involved.

The management of cash, receivables, and inventory requires constant supervision; and appropriate actions must be taken in light of established policies. For example, a firm must decide on the length of the credit terms it will grant and, even more important, whether it should offer a cash discount. Terms of 3/10, net 60 will certainly increase cash and reduce receivables over what they would have been without a cash discount. Then the question arises as to whether the added amount of cash should be invested in short-term securities or should be retained in a checking account for later or emergency use. Other policies that affect cash and receivables would include such items as extension of credit, overdue accounts, lines of bank credit, and frequency of meeting payrolls, to name a few.

The finance division of a firm is interested in inventories because of the huge sums most firms have invested in this current asset. Although inventory management may be considered a production or sales function, sound financial management requires that the amount of capital used for this purpose should be carefully controlled. Every dollar that is needlessly tied up in inventory could be producing income for the firm if invested elsewhere.

A relatively new element in decision making that has attained stature in recent years is the cost-of-capital concept as related to a proposed fixed asset acquisition. The *cost of capital* is a complex and controversial topic but, basically, it is the cost to the firm of both debt and equity capital employed in the business. As applied to a proposed fixed asset purchase, or a choice of alternate assets, it means that the acquisition will be made if the interest rate used to discount future benefits to equal cost of the asset is greater than the firm's cost of capital.

An illustration may help to clarify how a financial manager would reach a decision on whether to recommend for or against a proposed purchase of a fixed asset. Assume that the item in question is an automatic folding machine that will replace a laborer. The cost is $12,500, and it is expected that the machine will last 10 years with no scrap value. Annual savings, net after taxes, are carefully computed to be $2,000. By reference to a table of present values of one dollar per year, a calculation shows that at 9 percent for 10 years (6.4176) the present value of the annual savings is $12,835.20; and at 10 percent for 10 years (6.1446) the savings amount to $12,289.20. It should be clear that the purchase of the asset will earn approximately 9½ percent, as $12,835.20 is not much greater than $12,500 as $12,289.20 is short of this amount. This 9½ percent rate is then compared to the firm's cost of capital; and, if higher, the decision should be to purchase the machine. If alternate machines are being considered, comparative rates could be obtained to aid in making the decision as to which machine to buy.

BUSINESS COMBINATIONS

The second half of the current century has witnessed a marked trend in the growth of many corporations that have achieved a larger size by buying up or joining forces with one or more formerly independent companies. The objectives behind these combinations are usually: to obtain the economies of large-scale production, distribution, and financing; to widen sales territories; to assure a continuous supply of some needed parts or materials; and, sometimes, to lessen the competitive stress in the company's particular field. The methods used to form combinations frequently create extensive financial problems.

Since financing may be related to the types of business activities brought under one management, the different kinds of combinations will be examined briefly. If different companies doing exactly the same business activity are combined, it is a *horizontal combination*. A chain of drugstores, restaurants, motels, hotels, supermarkets, lumber yards, or department stores, if under one ownership and management, provide an illustration of this common form of combination. By contrast, a *vertical combination* joins together types of companies doing different but related activities in the production and distribution of a product. For example, the United States Steel Co. owns coal and iron ore companies, shipping lines, railroads, blast furnaces, rolling mills, and fabricating plants.

Sometimes two businesses are combined because their activities are so closely interwoven that it seems preferable to have them under one management. Such a combination is called a *complementary combination*. Meat packers have joined forces with fertilizer factories; business machine companies have bought electronic data equipment manufacturers; and in some cases the need to dispose of by-products, such as gas from coke production, makes it advantageous for two formerly separate companies to join forces. In other instances the companies combined are in allied lines, which is a *circular combination*. For example, Standard Brands, Inc., when it was formed, combined coffee, baking powder, yeast, and other diverse food products into one organization.

More recently there has been a rash of companies joining forces that have little or no logic in their association together. These are called *conglomerate mergers*. Textron, Inc., for example, has bought up companies manufacturing helicopters, eyeglasses, wristwatch bands, golf carts, chain saws, ball bearings, home and industrial staplers, and a host of other consumer, industrial, and military products. The American Tobacco Company, plagued by extensive anti-cigarette publicity, changed its name to American Brands, Inc., and acquired Sunshine Biscuits, Inc., the James B. Beam Distilling Co., Duffy-Mott Co., Inc., the Andrew Jergens Co., Swingline Inc., Master Lock Co., and Acme Visible Records, Inc.

One of the reasons for the increase in conglomerates has been the activity of the Federal Trade Commission in opposing combinations that might result in a decrease in competition. For example, the Procter & Gamble Company was required to divest itself of the Clorox Company because it was already in the bleach business. No objections, however, were raised when this corporation acquired the Folger Coffee Company, the Duncan Hines Companies, and the Charmin Paper Products Company.

METHODS OF FINANCING COMBINATIONS

As might be expected, financing these various types of combinations can be extremely complex, particularly if the companies concerned are sizable in their own right. Occasionally when one large firm buys a relatively small company, it may do so for cash. In this case the financing may be no more of a problem to the buyer than would the purchase of a new piece of heavy equipment. More commonly, securities are involved as will be noted in the following examination of the three major methods used to form combinations: (1) mergers, (2) consolidations, and (3) holding companies.

Mergers

When a *merger* takes place between two or more companies, the dominant one absorbs the smaller units and they disappear as separate entities. If Company *A* makes an offer to Company *B* to purchase its assets and liabilities and the offer is accepted, Company *B* ceases to exist as a separate organization, and Company *A* is then a larger concern. If the payment to Company *B* is entirely in cash, as mentioned above, the only financial problem may be to arrive at a mutually agreed upon price. If, however, the payment is to be made in bonds, preferred stock, or common stock of Company *A*, or some combination that may even involve part cash, long hours may be spent by the financial managers of both firms in arriving at an equitable settlement.

Although there is no dominant single pattern, the most widely used technique is to make payment in common stock, partially because this method is tax free to the stockholders of Company *B*. If, for example, on the date of the sale, Company *A*'s stock is selling for $40 a share and Company *B*'s shares are quoted at $60, Company *A* will issue 1½ shares of its stock for each share of Company *B* stock outstanding. Company *B* will then be dissolved and, quite possibly, be operated as a division of Company *A*.

Of considerable interest to financial analysts is the accounting treatment used by Company *A* when it merges with Company *B*. Under a *pooling of interests* technique, the asset, liability, and capital accounts of the two companies are added together. In some circumstances this method is frowned on by the American Institute of Certified Public Accountants which takes the position that a merger represents a purchase by one company of another company. Since such a purchase frequently involves paying more for a firm than its books show it to be worth, good-will is created on the buyer's books that must subsequently be written off as an expense item.

Consolidations

The difference between a merger and a *consolidation*, also known as an *amalgamation*, is that consolidations result in the formation of a new company in order to combine two or more existing firms. If Company *A* and Company *B* decide to combine but neither one cares to merge with the other, a Company *C* can be organized to buy up the assets and liabilities of *A* and *B*. In this event, both of the old companies disappear and a new one is born. For example, the American Motors Corporation is a consolidation that combined the Hudson Motor Car Company and the Nash-Kelvinator Corporation.

Since a new company is formed in a consolidation, its financial structure can consist of any desirable combination of debt and equity capital. The size of the new firm will, obviously, be dictated by the amount paid for the companies forming the consolidation. The kinds of securities issued will, however, be influenced by what the stockholders of the old companies are willing to accept. If they wish a tax-free exchange, the new company will issue its common stock for the common stock of the original companies at some agreed upon exchange ratio.

Holding Companies

A popular device for combining a number of concerns is the *holding company*. In its pure form a holding company, known as the *parent company*, is organized for the sole purpose of acquiring enough of the voting stock in other companies, called *subsidiaries*, to insure control. Theoretically this should be more than 50 percent, but in actual practice some holding companies own all of the stock of their subsidiaries and in other cases much less than one half. When a corporation has a large number of stockholders, none of whom is a large stockholder, the current system of management-secured proxies is such that a 20 or 30 percent ownership is adequate for effective control. Also, in actual practice many holding companies conduct operations in their own names and function as holding companies as well.

Although practically every large corporation is a holding company to some extent, the best known is the American Telephone & Telegraph

Company. In addition to operating the long-distance lines in the United States and to other countries and engaging in research at the Bell Laboratories, it owns varying percentages of some 20 large telephone companies scattered across the country as well as 99.82 percent of the Western Electric Co., Inc., the manufacturing division of the Bell system.

If a holding company is organized to buy stock in the open market of companies it wishes to control, it can raise the necessary capital by selling bonds, preferred stock, or common stock, or some combination of these types of securities. The cash received from the sale of these securities is then used to buy voting shares in the company it wishes to control by purchase on a stock exchange or from individuals wishing to sell. Not infrequently, particularly if the corporation has resisted offers to merge or consolidate, the holding company will extend to each stockholder of the independent company an offer, called a *tender*, to buy his shares at a price that is usually in excess of the current market quotation. This price can be cash or a stated number of shares of the holding company's stock. If enough stockholders accept the tender offer, the directors and officers of the company involved may suddenly discover that they have a new boss.

FAILURES AND REORGANIZATIONS

Every year some businesses, including those both new and well established, meet with financial reverses. The fault may lie with the present management or may be caused by outside factors over which no control can be exercised. For example, a neighborhood grocery store that had been prosperous for many years found its profits changed to losses when a large supermarket was opened in the vicinity. Regardless of the reason or reasons, continued losses will usually weaken the financial structure of a firm to a point where some action must be taken by the owners or managers.

Under the National Bankruptcy Act, *insolvency* exists whenever the aggregate of a person's property is not, at a fair valuation, sufficient to pay his debts. Anyone who reads the financial pages of a local newspaper has probably noted that a corporation has been adjudged bankrupt, for example, with assets of $62,400 and liabilities of $3,295,000. An individual or a firm may also become insolvent under state laws merely because of inability to pay debts currently owing. A manufacturing firm may have assets valued at more than its liabilities but, because most of its capital is tied up in special machinery, the assets cannot be liquidated to pay accounts and notes payable that are due.

When a company becomes insolvent, there are two major avenues open for either salvaging or liquidating the business: (1) voluntary creditor agreements and (2) legal action.

VOLUNTARY CREDITOR AGREEMENTS

When the owner or owners of a business realize that the firm is in dire financial straits, the first step is to call a meeting of the creditors. At this time a decision can be reached as to whether to seek a solution with or without court assistance. The creditors know that if the company is adjudged bankrupt by a court, the legal costs will be high and it is most unlikely that they will receive full payment for their claims. Furthermore, a former customer who might otherwise be saved for future business is probably lost.

If the creditors believe that the business can operate at a profit in the future, despite past reverses, they may agree to postpone the due date of their claims. Such an *extension agreement* must be signed by all creditors in order to give the plan a fair chance to work out successfully. A variation of the extension agreement is a *composition settlement*, by which the creditors accept a reduction in the amounts due them. These amounts may be paid in cash immediately, or settlement may be postponed for a few months.

In these voluntary agreements the creditors usually elect a representative who assumes active management of the firm for a long enough period of time to guarantee that the plan will be followed. As soon as the organization is operating smoothly and successfully, the creditors' representative withdraws and allows the original managers to operate without supervision. If the creditors cannot agree on a voluntary solution or if there seems to be no hope of successful operation of the business, the only alternative is to turn to a court for help. Such a step can be taken by the insolvent firm, or the creditors may force the issue.

LEGAL ACTION

When the Constitution of the United States was written, it provided for a national and uniform bankruptcy law. Consequently, even though states have insolvency laws, legal actions involving bankruptcy are usually taken under the federal law and are brought in federal district courts. An individual or a corporation, with certain exceptions such as banks and insurance companies, may go into bankruptcy by declaring under oath that liabilities owed exceed the value of assets owned. Or, if an act of bankruptcy is committed such as assigning assets to a favored creditor, three other creditors (if there are more than 12) with claims of $500 or more can file a petition asking that the firm be declared a bankrupt. Unless the business can refute the charges, the court will approve the petition.

If creditors fear that assets might disappear, the judge may appoint a *receiver* who serves as a temporary custodian of the firm's assets until he can turn them over to a trustee. At this stage the court appoints a *referee in bankruptcy* who serves as his representative in subsequent proceedings. The referee calls a meeting of the creditors, and they elect a representative known as a *trustee in bankruptcy*. In most instances this trustee, with approval by the referee, liquidates the assets, pays preferred claims, and distributes the balance, if any, to the general creditors. The debtor is legally discharged from his obligations, and the creditors are given impartial treatment in accord with their legal status. The priority of claims by different classes of creditors is discussed in Chapter 27 on pages 669-670.

Under the Bankruptcy Act of 1898, as amended by the Chandler Act of 1938, liquidation of a bankrupt firm is not always mandatory. If a corporation is basically sound but has become bankrupt because of a capital structure that it cannot support, Chapters X and XI of the amended bankruptcy law provide for a possible financial reorganization. *Reorganization plans* usually involve the scaling down of amounts owed or the interest or dividend rates, with more sacrifices being taken by the common stockholders and other unsecured interests. For example, first-mortgage bondholders owning 6 percent securities might agree to accept 4 percent bonds in exchange. Second-mortgage bondholders might agree to a reduction in the interest rate and also in principal amount. Preferred stockholders might be given new preferred stock with a lower dividend rate or even common stock. Common stockholders are sometimes eliminated entirely or are given a small amount of new stock in exchange for their previous holdings. The net effect is to reduce the annual fixed charges for interest and debt retirement to the point where normal operations of the business will allow for these charges and still leave a profit margin.

Nationwide interest in bankruptcy was stimulated in 1970 when the huge Penn Central railroad became insolvent. Since railroads can neither become voluntary bankrupts nor be declared bankrupt on an involuntary basis, the only available recourse was for the railroad to reorganize under Chapter XI of the bankruptcy act. Eventually the railroad will petition a bankruptcy court for approval of a reorganization plan. In the meantime it will continue to operate and, hopefully, will again earn a profit.

BUSINESS TERMS

QUESTIONS FOR DISCUSSION AND ANALYSIS

1. Of three firms identical in size and in the same business, one is organized as a sole proprietorship, another as a partnership, and the third as a corporation. Would there by any difference among the three firms as to a desirable ratio between debt and equity capital? Discuss.

2. In the United States practically all open corporations pay out as dividends no more than approximately 70 percent of net income after taxes. Some do not pay any dividends even though the year's operations were profitable. Why should corporations not be required to pay each year all of its earnings after taxes to its stockholders?

3. The price paid for debt capital is interest, and dividends are the comparable cost for equity capital. Why does interest qualify as a business expense whereas dividends do not?

4. Doesn't the use of stock options give an unfair advantage to executives to whom they are granted over the firm's stockholders? If you were a stockholder, would you be opposed to the use of stock options by your company?

5. If a firm continually owes one or more commercial banks, should it engage in some type of long-term financing to liquidate all or a portion of its short-term debt? Discuss.

6. From the viewpoint of a stockholder, is a stock dividend of 100 percent preferable to a one-for-one stock split?

7. Would the Federal Trade Commission be more likely to take exception to a proposed horizontal combination than to à vertical combination?

8. What, if any, is the economic justification for a conglomerate merger? Why has this type of combination become so popular?

9. Sometimes a holding company that owns 100 percent of the voting shares of a subsidiary allows it to retain its corporate identity whereas in other similar situations it dissolves the corporation and operates the business as a division. Which procedure is preferable and why?

10. Would a common stockholder of an insolvent firm that has gone into bankruptcy prefer that the firm be liquidated rather than be reorganized? Justify your choice.

PROBLEMS AND SHORT CASES

1. The Richmond Furniture Company has consistently averaged a 16 percent operating profit, before interest, on its $34,000,000 in total assets. Debt and equity capital consist of $2,500,000 in open-book accounts, $4,000,000 borrowed from commercial banks at 6 percent interest, and $27,500,000 in common stock and retained earnings represented by 1,250,000 shares of common stock. The company decides to expand by selling $5,000,000 in 8 percent bonds and $5,000,000 in 7 percent nonparticipating preferred stock. The bank loans are to be liquidated but, with the increase in size of the company, it is estimated that the amount owed on open-book accounts will increase to $3,000,000.

   Assuming a continuation of the 16 percent return on operations and that all earnings are paid out either as interest or dividends, what dollar dividends per share were available to the common stockholders before and after the expansion? Show calculations.

2. The Cordovan Shoe Corporation's long-term capital came from $10,000,000 in 7 percent bonds and $15,000,000 in common stock represented by 1,250,000 no-par shares. For several years the corporation has been unable to show a net profit, although profits from operations before interest on bonds have averaged $600,000. All retained earnings from earlier years have now been exhausted and the firm is in default on its bond interest for the past two years. Currently relief is being sought under the National Bankruptcy Act.

   A reorganization plan is proposed and approved under which the bondholders accept $5,000,000 in 5 percent bonds, $5,000,000 in a $100 par 6 percent preferred stock, and 1,000,000 shares of common stock with the understanding that the $1,400,000 in interest owed will be cancelled. The common stockholders are required to turn in four shares for each one retained.

Assuming the continuation of operating earnings of $600,000, can the corporation meet its obligations on the bonds and preferred stock and still pay a dividend to the old stockholders? If so, how many dollars or cents per share will be available?

3. The capital structure of the Old Reliable Tobacco Company shows the following:

Commercial paper, 6%, maturing in one year ..... $ 5,000,000
First mortgage bonds, 7½%, callable at 105, due in
    1980 48,000,000
Preferred stock, 7%, $100 par, nonparticipating,
    convertible, redeemable at 110 20,000,000
Common stock, no-par, 10,000,000 shares autho-
    rized, 6,500,000 shares outstanding 40,000,000

The firm has been prosperous and has established a regular dividend policy of $3 a share on its common stock, which is listed on a national exchange. Recent trading in this stock has hovered around $60 a share, although the price range has fluctuated between $50 and $70 a share within the past year. The bonds and preferred stock are also listed and usually sell at or slightly above par.

The management of the Old Reliable Tobacco Company wishes to raise enough new capital to retire the commercial paper and to buy a large manufacturer of candy as a step toward diversification. The stockholders of the candy company are willing to accept $15,000,000 in cash for their business or to exchange their stock for 250,000 shares of the common stock of the Old Reliable Tobacco Company. The reputation of the company is such that it appears certain that the market will absorb any type of securities that it offers for sale, and more than one investment banking company has indicated an interest in forming a syndicate to sell appropriate securities.

Present a financial plan for the Old Reliable Tobacco Company that will accomplish the two stated objectives. Explain why your plan is preferable to alternate methods that could be used.

SUGGESTED READINGS

Archer, S. H., and C. A. D'Ambrosio. *Business Finance—Theory and Management*. New York: The Macmillan Company, 1966.

Bierman, H. Jr. *Financial Policy Decisions*. New York: The Macmillan Company, 1970.

Cooke, G. W., and E. C. Bomeli. *Business Financial Management*. Boston: Houghton Mifflin Company, 1967.

Curran, W. S. *Principles of Financial Management*. New York: McGraw-Hill Book Company, 1970.

Dauten, C. A., and M. Welshans. *Principles of Finance*, Third Edition. Cincinnati: South-Western Publishing Co., 1970.

Donaldson, E. F., and J. K. Pfahl. *Corporate Finance—Policy and Management*, Third Edition. New York: The Ronald Press Company, 1969.

Flink, S. J., and D. Grunewald. *Managerial Finance*. New York: John Wiley & Sons, Inc., 1969.

Grunewald, A. E., and E. E. Nemmers. *Basic Managerial Finance*. New York: Holt, Rinehart & Winston, Inc., 1970.

Hastings, P. G. *The Management of Business Finance*. Princeton, New Jersey: Van Nostrand, 1966.

Johnson, R. W. *Financial Management*, Third Edition. Boston: Allyn and Bacon, Inc., 1966.

Kent, R. P. *Corporate Financial Management*, Third Edition. Homewood, Illinois: Richard D. Irwin, Inc., 1969.

Van Horne, J. C. *Financial Management and Policy*. Englewood Cliffs, New Jersey: Prentice-Hall, Inc., 1968.

Weston, J. F., and E. F. Brigham. *Managerial Finance*, Third Edition. New York: Holt, Rinehart & Winston, Inc., 1969.

Chapter 21

Security Markets and Financial News

Today's businessman is knowledgeable about stocks and bonds, and it is very likely that he owns some securities. He is interested in current quotations on his holdings and in related news items, particularly those concerning companies in which he may have made an investment. He is joined in this interest by other businessmen, investors, speculators, and a sizable segment of the general public. Much of this attention is focused on security exchanges with the ups and downs of the stock market reflecting, in part, the optimism or pessimism felt by millions of stockholders about present and future business conditions.

The widespread interest in corporate and government securities is evident from the space devoted by almost all daily newspapers to reporting sales and prices and from the market reports carried on TV and radio news broadcasts. Metropolitan newspapers usually print full details concerning transactions on the New York Stock Exchange, Inc., and some carry news about stocks and bonds traded on other exchanges or in the over-the-counter market. In addition, other financial news on proposed mergers, new security sales, and changes in the prime interest rate are printed in the same section as that devoted to stock and bond transactions. Now and then some outstanding financial event, such as Congressional approval of a new federal debt ceiling, becomes front-page news.

This chapter will examine security markets in some detail with more attention devoted to stock exchanges than to the over-the-counter market. In addition to an explanation of how and where an individual can buy or sell stocks, the protection he receives because of the extensive state and federal regulation of security sales will be described. Attention will then be devoted to financial news reporting, including details about stock and bond quotations and averages as well as numerous other items valuable to financial managers and individual investors.

SECURITY EXCHANGES

A *security exchange*, commonly called a stock exchange, is an organization that provides facilities for its members to buy and sell securities. It is usually organized as an unincorporated association, a type of business ownership that was described in Chapter 4. Membership fees are charged, and dues or assessments cover the expenses of operation. The members elect a board of governors who, in turn, elect officers, including a president. The officers employ the necessary personnel to operate the exchange.

The most famous and largest of the security exchanges, the New York Stock Exchange, Inc., has a limited membership of 1,366. The members are individuals, many of them partners in brokerage firms. A membership is called a *seat*, and it can be sold if the prospective purchaser has been approved by the board of directors of the Exchange. The price on these seats has been as low as $17,000 and as high as $625,000 within the present century, although recently the range has been between $150,000 and $250,000. This Exchange was incorporated in 1971.

There are 13 other exchanges in the United States and, of these, 11 are large enough to be registered with the Securities and Exchange Commission. Even at that, most are relatively small and unimportant. The securities traded on these exchanges are usually some combination of a few local companies and a selection of the same stocks available on the *big board*, which is a nickname for the New York Stock Exchange, Inc. Exceptions to the foregoing generalizations include the American Stock Exchange in New York (also called Amex or *Curb Exchange*), the Midwest Stock Exchange in Chicago, and the Pacific Stock Exchange in San Francisco, although it should be noted that over 80 percent of the dollar volume of transactions on exchanges is concentrated on the New York Stock Exchange.

Stocks and bonds that have been approved for trading on a security exchange are known as *listed securities*. The New York Stock Exchange, Inc., lists approximately 1,500 stocks and 1,200 bond issues of nearly 1,300 corporations. Despite this small number in relation to the total number of corporations, almost every sizable industrial company is represented.

On a normal trading day transactions will take place in more than 1,250 different stocks.

The reasons that the stocks of many publicly held corporations are not listed on any exchange center around size, inability to qualify, and unwillingness to comply with requirements including a possible fee. The New York Stock Exchange, Inc., for example, will not grant an application for listing unless the corporation, in addition to securing approval from the Securities and Exchange Commission, meets the following standards: (a) the company must have 1,000,000 shares outstanding of which 700,000 must be publicly held; (b) there must be at least 2,000 stockholders of whom 1,700 must each own at least 100 shares; (c) annual earnings should exceed $2 million before taxes; and (d) the common stock publicly held must have a minimum market value of $12 million.

OPERATION OF SECURITY EXCHANGES

A description of the operation of security exchanges, insofar as the general public is concerned, will clarify the usefulness of this type of financial institution. The chief function is to provide a convenient means by which individuals and organizations can buy or sell stocks of well-known corporate enterprises. A security exchange is not a source of capital to the corporation that has its stocks and bonds listed. These securities have already been sold, usually through investment banking companies; and subsequent sales that take place on a stock exchange are between such diverse security holders as individuals, corporations, banks, insurance companies, pension funds, investment trusts, churches, hospitals, trust funds, and endowment funds.

For every buyer there must be a seller. The statement that "everybody is buying stocks" merely means that the demand is greater than the supply, with a resultant increase in prices. When an investor thinks a stock is going up in price, he would not be able to buy if a security holder did not believe it was a good time to sell or had to dispose of his holdings for other reasons. Conversely, even in a severely depressed market there is always a buyer if the seller is willing to accept his offering price.

Trading Procedures

An order to buy stocks on an exchange, regardless of the residence of the potential investor, is routed to the trading floor. Here it is given to a member of the exchange, usually a partner in the same brokerage firm patronized by the buyer, who is known as a *commission broker*.

On the floor of the exchange there are a number of *trading posts* at which a specified list of stocks are bought and sold. If the order placed by the investor is for 100 shares of common stock of United States Steel Corporation, the member locates the post and makes an offer to buy under terms specified by the customer. Assuming he is willing to pay the current, or even a somewhat higher, price per share, he would have placed a *market order*, which is usually filled immediately as someone is always ready to sell if his offering price is accepted. If, however, the purchaser had placed a *limited order*, such as $40 a share, and the stock is selling at $42 a share, the member leaves the order with another broker who spends most of his time at one post and is known as a *specialist* because he concentrates his attention on a limited number of securities. The specialist makes a memorandum of the order and, if at a later time in the day or at a later date an offer is made to sell U. S. Steel shares at $40, he executes the order.

Trading is conducted in *round-lots* that normally are 100-share units. If the order is for 25 shares, it is placed by the member with an *odd-lot broker* who makes a specialty of handling such orders, for which he receives a special commission. By grouping several odd-lot orders he may be able to buy one or more round lots, which are distributed to the several purchasers, or he may purchase the additional shares for his own account.

A sample transaction. Bob Jordan, who lives in a suburban area near St. Louis, has decided to buy 25 shares of International Harvester Company common stock. One of his neighbors is Ted Samuels, a stockbroker employed by a large brokerage firm with offices in many cities including downtown St. Louis. Jordan, after reaching Samuels by telephone, places an order to buy at $33, and this purchase request is immediately teletyped to the New York office of the brokerage firm. From there it is telephoned to the floor of the New York Stock Exchange (on which IHC is listed) and delivered to a partner on the trading floor.

This member goes to the post at which IHC is sold and, because the order is for only 25 shares and the trading unit is 100 shares, he turns the buy order over to an odd-lot specialist operating at that post. At this particular moment IHC has dipped to $32½, so the odd-lot specialist buys 100 shares and allocates 25 to the exchange member with whom we are concerned. This man reports back to his New York office that the stock has been bought, the teletype carries the news to St. Louis, and Samuels notifies Jordan that his order has been executed. A seller rather than a buyer of IHC stock will have gone through a similar process.

The machinery for buying or selling stocks is well established, and transactions are completed in a relatively short time. A buyer or a seller in a broker's office in a large city can expect to complete a transaction within one or two minutes if he is willing to do business at market quotations.

Stock quotations. How did Bob Jordan decide on a buying price of $33 a share? He may have been following the daily reports in his newspaper, or his stockbroker may have recommended the stock as a good buy at this price. If he had been in the St. Louis office of the brokerage firm that executed the order, he could have watched the *ticker tape* (see Figure 21-1). This is a transparent tape that is projected on a screen so that actual sales transactions on the large exchanges can be seen within a few seconds of the time of the sale. More recently, many large investment brokers have also installed the Ultronic Stockmaster, the Telequote, or the Quotron. These are electronic devices placed on the desks of account executives that will provide almost instantaneous information about stocks and their price quotations.

 Figure 21-1

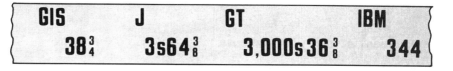

Ticker Tape Segment

This illustration shows a small segment of ticker tape. Each stock has an abbreviation, which may or may not be easily recognizable. Below the symbol is the sales price for 100 shares or, in the case of sales up to 1,000 shares, the number of hundreds is indicated. For large sales the exact quantity is shown. The letter "s" separates the size of the sale from the sales price when more than a single round-lot is involved. The reading of the tape shown is as follows:

    100 shares of General Mills, Inc. common at 38¾
    300 shares of Standard Oil Co. of New Jersey common at 64⅜
3,000 shares of Goodyear Tire & Rubber Co. common at 36⅜
    100 shares of International Business Machines Corp. common at 344

Cost of Trading

The customer of a brokerage firm pays a commission for the service rendered. Commissions charged by members of the New York Stock Exchange, which are shown in Table 21-1 for round-lot and odd-lot purchases and sales, are typical of charges made on other exchanges. As an example, if a customer buys or sells 100 shares of stock that has a market price of $30 a share, the commission will amount to $49 ($19 plus ½ percent of $3,000 plus $15).

NEW YORK STOCK EXCHANGE COMMISSION CHARGES ON STOCKS

Money Involved	Minimum Commission Per Transaction		
	Percent of Money Involved	Plus Stated Amount	
		For 100 Shares	Less Than 100 Shares
Basic Rates			
$ 100 to $ 399 *	2%	$ 3	$ 1
400 to 2,399	1%	7	5
2,400 to 4,999	1/2%	19	17
5,000 and above	1/10%	39	37
Surcharge			
One half of basic commission or $15, whichever is smaller.			
* Minimum commission $6.			

Table 21-1

Note: If money involved is under $100, the minimum commission is as mutually agreed. Top minimum is $75 per transaction, or $1.50 per share (subject to $6 minimum). For transactions in excess of 100 shares, each 100 shares or fraction thereof is considered separately as to basic rates but not as to surcharge. For transactions involving $500,000 or more, commission charges are negotiated.

Odd-lot brokers receive 12½ cents a share commission on stocks selling below $55 a share and 25 cents a share commission on stock selling for $55 and above per share. If a purchase order is entered at a fixed price, such as $35 a share, it will not be executed by the odd-lot broker until the market drops to 34⅞.

In addition to commissions, both the federal government and the state of New York levy a tax on the transfer of shares, which is paid by the seller. The federal tax is a Security and Exchange Commission fee of 1 cent for each $500 of the market price or fraction thereof. This fee is withheld by the broker from the proceeds that are due the seller of the stock. New York rates are (from July 1, 1970, to June 30, 1971, tax was reduced to 90 percent of the rates listed below):

Shares selling under $5	1¼ ¢ per share
Shares selling between $5 and $10	2½ ¢ per share
Shares selling between $10 and $20	3¾ ¢ per share
Shares selling for over $20	5¢ per share

Investors and Speculators

An *investor* is one who buys securities with the idea of holding them on a more or less permanent basis. In every market there are also *speculators* who hope to make a profit by buying and selling within a few weeks, days, or within the trading hours of a single day. Speculators who buy stocks in anticipation of a rise in price are known as *bulls*; and those who sell, expecting the market to go down in the days or weeks ahead, are known as *bears*.

As illogical as it may seem, a bear frequently sells stocks he does not own. This market operation is known as *selling short*. He sells today expecting to buy, or cover his short sale as the process is called, within a relatively short time after the market goes down to a point where he can make a profit. Of course, if the market does not go down, he suffers a loss. Because he must deliver stock to the purchaser, he borrows it from a broker who has it available. In return for the use of the cash proceeds from the sale, the broker usually loans the stock without charge. This stock may be shares owned by the brokerage firm or, more likely, shares that it is holding in its name for the benefit of one of its customers.

Another possibility for a speculator to enhance his profits is to buy stocks on a margin. If a buyer can *margin* his account with a broker up to 50 percent, it means that he needs to have only one half as much money as his purchase calls for. If a speculator has $1,000, he can buy either 100 shares of a stock selling at $10 or 200 shares at the same price by borrowing the extra $1,000 from his broker. In case the stock rises to $15, he can sell for a profit of $500 in one case and $1,000 in the other, minus commissions and taxes and, in the latter instance, interest on the money borrowed. On the other hand, if the stock declines in value, the broker will call for an additional deposit to protect himself against loss. If the margin trader cannot put up additional funds, his broker will sell the stock no later than when the price drops to $5 in order to protect the loan, and the speculator's original $1,000 deposit will be lost.

From the foregoing discussion of speculators, it might appear that they are using stock exchanges as a type of gambling casino. Although there is some truth in this accusation, speculators render a real service to investors and to the exchanges. They not only keep the market active but also hold price variations between sales of a particular stock to fractions of a point. Speculators are one important reason why an investor can always find a buyer or a seller for a stock or bond listed on an exchange.

Beginning in 1954, members of the New York Stock Exchange launched a venture designed to induce more investors to purchase stocks by offering a payment plan similar to that used for installment sales. Individuals select the stock or stocks they wish to own and pay for these by making regular monthly or quarterly deposits with their broker of an amount as low as $40 a quarter or as high as $999 a month. The Monthly Investors Plan, or *MIP* as it is sometimes called, allows an individual to channel regular savings into the ownership of corporation stocks. Over 125,000 persons have taken advantage of this opportunity, and the number seems to be growing each year.

VALUE OF SECURITY EXCHANGES

Security exchanges render an extremely valuable service in the field of finance. The maintenance of a free market, with prices established at all times by the forces of supply and demand, make listed securities more useful than unlisted stocks and bonds. They can be used as collateral at a bank for a loan or as the security for collateral trust bonds. Estates are easier to appraise to the extent that they contain listed securities.

For a corporation large enough to qualify, it is a matter of some prestige to have its stocks and bonds listed on an exchange. The chances are good that the number of stockholders will increase after listing, thus helping its sales and certainly making it easier for the "in group" to retain control. Of even greater importance is the added bargaining power a corporation has with an investment banking company when negotiating for the sale of additional securities. The market for new issues of bonds and stocks of well-known companies is much stronger than for unknown corporations.

From the viewpoint of an individual, security exchanges have provided a marketplace where he can invest some or all of his savings at a relatively low commission charge. The United States seems to be in a period of ever higher and higher prices resulting in a steady shrinking in the purchasing power of the dollar. Although there is no perfect hedge against inflation, common stocks do tend to increase in value when prices go up because corporations increase their prices to offset higher costs of labor and materials to such an extent that their profits also increase proportionally.

OVER-THE-COUNTER MARKETS

The number of different issues of stocks and bonds traded on all security exchanges is approximately 4,300. In addition to these listed securities, it has been estimated that there are in the neighborhood of 50,000 different bonds and stocks that are available to the general public for purchase and sale during every trading day. These bonds and stocks are known as *unlisted securities*, and they are traded in what is called the *over-the-counter market*. Actually, the over-the-counter market encompasses all transactions involving the purchase and sale of outstanding public and corporate securities that do not take place on an organized exchange.

BID AND ASKED PRICES

Unlike the technique used on security exchanges where brokers representing buyers and sellers meet face to face, the over-the-counter market is based on bid and asked prices. The *bid prices* are those that would-be buyers of over-the-counter securities are willing to pay, and the *asked prices* are those at which would-be sellers are willing to part with the bonds or stocks they own (see Figure 21-2). One or more of the approximately 4,000 security dealers who function in this market customarily establish the bid and asked prices. These dealers, who can also be classified as either investment banking companies or brokers or both, usually carry an inventory in several different unlisted bonds and stocks. They publicly announce that they "make a market" in these securities and will buy them at a bid price or sell them at an asked price. The difference represents their gross profit.

If an individual wishes to purchase a particular over-the-counter bond or stock and his broker's firm does not make a market in the security wanted, it is a simple matter for the brokerage firm to determine the dealer who does make a market, assuming that it subscribes to the services of the National Quotation Bureau, a subsidiary of Commerce Clearing House, Inc., which is a private enterprise specializing in publishing and selling topical law reports. Each day security dealers report bid and asked prices on stocks and bonds in which they make a market to the Bureau and this information is combined into a report made available to all subscribers. If the prospective purchaser is willing to pay the asked price plus, in this case, a commission since the broker is acting as an agent rather than a dealer, a telephone call will obtain the wanted bond or stock in a short space of time.

Bid and asked prices on a considerable number of securities in which there is a high degree of interest are reported regularly in financial newspapers, magazines, and on radio and TV. This information is available from the National Quotations Committee of the National Association of Security Dealers, a trade association to which a majority of security dealers belong.

There are also local committees that assemble bid and asked prices on bonds and stocks that have only a regional geographic interest. In 1971 the NASD began the distribution by computer of information on over-the-counter stock trading. Up-to-the-minute quotations are available on a selected group of stocks to security salesmen who have a desk-top device that is connected to the computer.

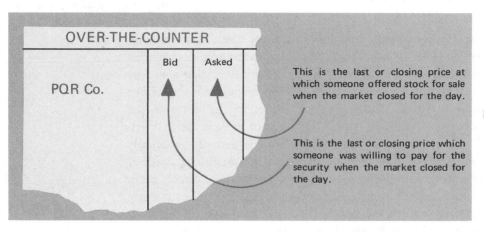

Figure 21-2

CBWL-Hayden, Stone Inc.

Over-the-Counter Bid and Asked Prices

SECURITIES TRADED OVER THE COUNTER

Securities traded on the over-the-counter market include United States government and other public bonds and notes, most corporate bonds, mutual funds, foreign securities, bank stocks, insurance stocks, and a large number of industrial and public utility stocks that, for the most part, do not qualify for listing on an exchange. Whereas there are no specific requirements for a security to be traded over the counter, the National Association of Security Dealers has established standards applicable to a bond or stock that is to be quoted on either the local or national lists. Sometimes a transaction in listed securities takes place off the organized exchange on which the bond or stock is listed and thus becomes a part of the over-the-counter market. In this specific instance the transaction is said to take place in the *third market*. Such transactions are, however, relatively unimportant although the third market poses a threat to commission earnings of members of security exchanges.

It has been estimated that the dollar volume of securities traded over the counter is substantially higher than the comparable figure for stocks and bonds traded on all security exchanges combined. It is difficult to obtain accurate figures because the transactions take place in thousands of locations in all 50 states and are not reported to a central agency. Furthermore, in addition to the thousands of corporations on which the National Quotation Bureau provides bid and asked prices, a broker is always willing to attempt to locate bonds or stocks of any publicly held corporation for a customer even though transactions in the securities of such companies occur only now and then rather than on a regular basis. In these situations the bid and asked prices are established by the potential buyers and sellers.

REGULATION OF SECURITY SALES

In the early part of the twentieth century less than a half million people owned corporate stocks and bonds, and no effective regulations covered security sales. The doctrine of caveat emptor—let the buyer beware—held full sway. Unscrupulous promoters sold shares of stock in ventures having scant, if any, hope of success, and the public was the victim of many security swindles. A group of men would organize a corporation and peddle stock to a so-called sucker list. Widows, preachers, physicians, dentists, school teachers, and other individuals who might be expected to having savings available for investment were considered the best prospects. Literature describing the golden opportunities of an oil company or a mining company with an invitation to subscribe to the stock would be mailed to these persons. Telephone calls and personal solicitations would follow. After the promoters had worked a territory for all of the cash possible, they would disappear from their impressive office quarters and, usually, the stockholders would not hear from them again. An aroused public finally demanded legislation to curb these swindles, and eventually both the states and the federal government enacted appropriate laws.

STATE REGULATION

Although in 1909 the United States Post Office had secured the passage of a law that made it a criminal offense to use the mails to defraud, this legislation did not prevent crooked security salesmen from operating in various cities and communities. In 1911 Kansas passed a law regulating security sales in that state. At the time it was under consideration, a member of the legislature remarked that some promoters would sell stock in the "blue sky" itself. Today, the laws regulating security sales that have been passed in most states are known as *blue-sky laws*.

These blue-sky laws frequently cover such items as (a) required registration of new security issues with an appropriate state official; (b) an annual license for dealers, brokers, and salesmen; and (c) a provision for prosecuting individuals charged with fraud in connection with the sale of stocks and bonds. Unfortunately, state regulation provides little or no control over interstate sales, a situation that the federal government had recognized as early as 1920 when it gave the Interstate Commerce Commission jurisdiction over the sale of railroad securities. Need for further controls was apparent, and since 1933 the federal government has played a dominant role in blue-sky legislation.

FEDERAL REGULATION

Although the federal government had taken some action, as indicated in the case of railroads, the fact is that state blue-sky laws provided about all the protection the public had against fraudulent security sales during the first third of the twentieth century. By 1933 the country was in a serious depression and people began to look to Congress to provide solutions to problems formerly considered to be of local rather than national concern. One of these problems was the lack of control over interstate sales of securities, which led to the passage of two regulatory laws within 12 months. Both of these are still very much in force today and have been supplemented by amendments and additional laws.

Federal Securities Act of 1933

The Securities Act of 1933 was predicated on the belief that potential investors had the right to know all pertinent facts about a company issuing new securities and that the officers, accountants, engineers, and lawyers providing such information should be held legally liable for supplying such facts. It has been called the "information law" because full disclosure of relevant financial facts is the major requirement of the act. This is accomplished by (a) requiring the filing of a *registration statement*, which contains extensive details about the company and the proposed issue of securities, and (b) the preparation of a condensed version of this statement, called a *prospectus*, that must be furnished to each prospective purchaser of the stocks or bonds offered for sale.

Since 1934 the enforcement of this law has been under the jurisdiction of the Securities and Exchange Commission. The Commission is given 20 days after the registration statement is on file to issue a *stop order* if it believes the proposed offering should not be made to the general public. Even though a stop order is not issued, the Commission does not guarantee the correctness of the information supplied and can request the Department of Justice to institute criminal proceedings if, at a later date, the law seems to have been violated.

Some security issues are exempt from registration. These include all forms of government securities, railroad issues subject to the ICC, and stocks and bonds of cooperatives and nonprofit institutions. Also, sales not involving the use of mails or interstate commerce are exempt, as well as those in which there has been no public offering. In recent years, many issues have been sold at private sale for the express purpose of avoiding registration under this law.

Federal Securities Exchange Act of 1934

Although the 1933 law was and is still effective, further legislation was passed less than a year later extending the regulatory jurisdiction of the federal government. The Securities Exchange Act of 1934, in addition to establishing the Securities and Exchange Commission, provided for three major reforms. These reforms were (a) registration of all corporations whose stocks were listed on exchanges, (b) regulation of national stock exchanges, and (c) credit restrictions through control of margin requirements for stock purchases.

Company registration. Every corporation whose stock was listed on one of the national exchanges was required to file a registration statement with the Securities and Exchange Commission. Furthermore, it was specified that this statement must be kept up to date by the filing of annual reports. Whether or not a company is in the process of selling new securities, an investor is able to find out the same type of information that formerly was available only when new securities were to be sold.

National stock exchanges. Practically all of the security exchanges, including the large ones previously mentioned, were classified as national and placed under the jurisdiction of the Commission. Although each had adopted certain trading rules, self-regulation had not prevented abuses by professional traders at the expense of the investing public. The "insiders" had been able to manipulate stock prices for their own profit with losses going to a gullible public who swallowed rumors and purchased shares at unjustified higher and higher prices. The legitimate functions of security exchanges were being abused and, due to the interstate nature of most transactions, regulation by a federal agency seemed to be the only available solution. Currently the Securities and Exchange Commission employs a competent staff to watch the sales on national exchanges and to investigate those that might either be illegal or give rise to unfair trading.

Margin requirements. A third purpose of the Securities Exchange Act of 1934 was to restrict the amount of credit that would be available for financing the purchase of stocks. Control over this feature was placed in the hands of the Federal Reserve Board, which governs the federal reserve banks. This Board determines the extent to which a purchaser can margin his account and also limits the amount of loans that can be made by a member bank or by a broker for the purpose of financing stock purchases. During the past 25 years the margin requirement has been placed as high as 100 percent, which means the equivalent of outright cash purchases, and as low as 50 percent.

Other provisions. Further provisions of the law required the registration of all securities brokers and dealers with the Securities and Exchange Commission, and members of security exchanges had to indicate whether they were operating for their own account or as brokers and also whether they were *floor traders* (members who buy and sell for their own accounts), odd-lot dealers, or specialists. Proxy statements are subject to scrutiny to make sure they are truthful and not misleading. A corporate officer who owns 10 percent or more of the stock of a company that is listed on a national exchange must list his holdings with the SEC, must not sell the company's securities on a "short" basis, and any profits made by him through the purchase and sale of securities of the corporation that are completed in a period of less than six months must be paid to the company.

Regulation of Over-the-Counter Markets

In 1938 Congress passed legislation known as the Maloney Amendment to the Securities Exchange Act. It authorized investment banking companies to form associations for the purpose of self-regulation. The only association ever formed under this authority was the National Association of Security Dealers, Inc. This is a nonprofit corporation composed of broker and dealer members each of whom has been required to pass a qualifying examination as a Registered Representative or Principal and to subscribe to extensive and detailed Rules of Fair Practice.

The Federal Securities Acts of 1933 and 1934 were both amended in 1964. One amendment gave the SEC and NASD disciplinary authority over brokers and security dealers, which means that the Rules of Fair Practice can now be enforced. Of even greater importance was the provision that publicly held companies whose shares are traded in the over-the-counter market must, unless specifically exempted, provide the same type of information formerly required only of corporations with shares listed on organized exchanges. All industrial corporations engaged in interstate commerce with total assets of $1,000,000 and 500 or more stockholders were included and came under the same requirements as to registration, proxy solicitation, and other trading provisions as those applicable to listed securities.

Although the security laws passed in 1933 and 1934 plus amendments may seem unduly strict to security dealers and brokers, the general public has benefited. Millions of investors now have reasonably adequate protection against losses due to outright misrepresentation or fraud on the part of persons or organizations offering securities for sale.

FINANCIAL NEWS

As mentioned earlier in this chapter, radio and TV stations include financial items in their news broadcasts and practically all daily newspapers have a financial section that is widely read by businessmen. In addition to the generous coverage of financial news in metropolitan newspapers, magazines including *Business Week, U. S. News and World Report, Time,* and *Newsweek* publish a number of articles on financial events. Even more slanted to news of interest to the financial community are such papers as the *Wall Street Journal* and such magazines as *Fortune, Barron's,* the *Commercial and Financial Chronicle, Forbes,* and *Dun's Review.*

The use of computers by financial analysts and reporters has made available information about corporations and industries that would have been impossible to compile a few years ago. So much information is printed in newspapers and magazines that reading and interpreting financial news requires selection and, above all, understanding. The remainder of this chapter will examine and comment on the more widely read items that provide useful information to businessmen. These will be divided into three classifications: stocks, bonds, and other financial news items.

STOCKS

Without much question, more people turn to the financial pages of newspapers (see Figure 21-3) to check the stock market than for any other reason. They may be interested in stocks they own or plan to purchase, or in the stock of the company for which they work. Corporate officials watch movements in the stocks of their competitors as well as their own company. Bankers, loan officers, statisticians, and many others including government officials are interested in the performance of individual stocks as well as the market generally. For example, a commercial bank may hold shares of stock as collateral for a loan, or the board of directors of a corporation may have to reach a decision on raising additional capital by selling additional shares of its stock.

Stock Quotations

A summary of transactions is prepared for publication after each day's trading on an exchange. Stocks are itemized alphabetically and for each the following facts are provided: high and low for the current year; abbreviated name of corporation; the kind of stock (if stock is a preferred issue, the letters "pf" are shown, otherwise the listing is common stock); the annual dividend rate or other information about the dividend; sales in round-lots for the day; the price per share at the opening of the market; the high and the low for the day; the closing price; and the net change between the closing price for the day and that of the previous day on which the stock was traded.

Prices per share are quoted in eighths, quarters, or one half. For convenience of printing, a few papers use decimals, but these are parts of eight rather than parts of ten. For example, a quotation of 23.7 is the same as 23⅞ or $23.875. As a footnote to the quotations, the meaning of the small letters shown in many cases after the corporate name and dividend is explained. These are frequently very important as, for example, if a stock is purchased "xd," the previous owner will receive the current dividend check.

Stock Averages

The general trend of stock quotations is shown in the daily movement of market averages for all stocks, which are further subdivided into industrials, railroads, and utilities. Two widely known *stock averages* are the Dow–Jones Averages and the Standard & Poor's Index. The Dow–Jones

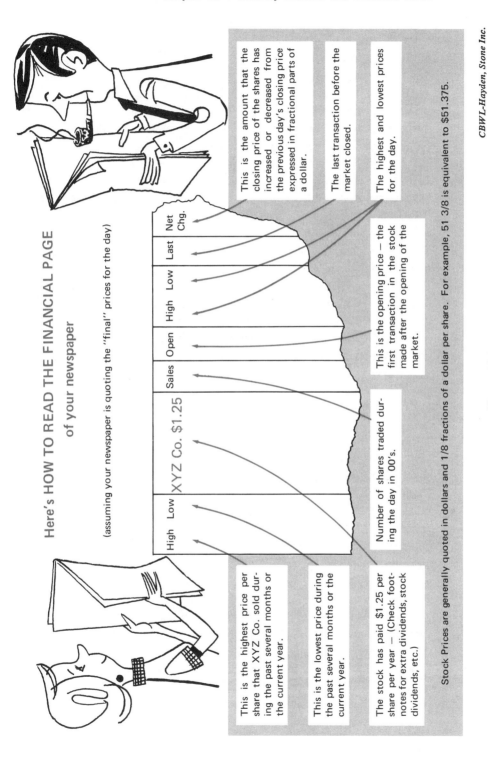

Here's HOW TO READ THE FINANCIAL PAGE
of your newspaper

(assuming your newspaper is quoting the "final" prices for the day)

High	Low		Sales	Open	High	Low	Last	Net Chg.
		XYZ Co. $1.25						

This is the highest price per share that XYZ Co. sold during the past several months or the current year.

This is the lowest price during the past several months or the current year.

The stock has paid $1.25 per share per year — (Check footnotes for extra dividends, stock dividends, etc.)

Number of shares traded during the day in 00's.

This is the opening price — the first transaction in the stock made after the opening of the market.

The highest and lowest prices for the day.

The last transaction before the market closed.

This is the amount that the closing price of the shares has increased or decreased from the previous day's closing price expressed in fractional parts of a dollar.

Stock Prices are generally quoted in dollars and 1/8 fractions of a dollar per share. For example, 51 3/8 is equivalent to $51.375.

CBWL-Hayden, Stone Inc.

Figure 21-3

How to Read the Financial Page

Averages are based on 30 industrial, 20 railroad, and 15 utility stocks whereas the Standard & Poor's Index uses 425 industrials, 25 rails, and 50 utilities. In each case the movement of the averages has been plotted day by day for many years.

Because the above averages, and others that have been compiled, are based on a limited number of stocks, many interested parties complained that they did not truly reflect market changes. In order to eliminate this criticism, the New York Stock Exchange since July, 1966, has issued an index of all of its more than 1,250 stocks (see Figure 21-4). These are also subdivided into four groups—industrial, transportation, utility, and finance. All five of these indexes were assigned a base of 50.00 as of December 31, 1965, which was an approximation of the dollar average of all stocks on that date.

Of considerable interest to many investors is a report made every half hour during the trading session and at the close of the day that shows the rise or fall in the average price of New York Stock Exchange common stocks expressed in dollars and cents. For example, the market report at the close of the day might state that stocks gained, on the average, 28 cents a share. The extensive calculations necessary to produce this average promptly became practical after the Exchange had installed its computer.

Over-the-Counter Stocks

As indicated earlier, bid and asked prices on over-the-counter stocks are available from two sources. The local committees and the national committee of the National Association of Security Dealers assemble and make available quotations on which there is a widespread interest. These are reported in whole or in part in the financial section of some newspapers, notably *The New York Times*, and those of local interest are also aired on radio and television stations. The *Wall Street Journal* provides a weekly list in the Monday issue in addition to its regular daily list, and *Barron's* gives extensive coverage to the over-the-counter markets.

At the wholesale level the National Quotation Bureau provides a service to its subscribers each trading day. Lists of stocks are divided into three sections—eastern, western, and Pacific Coast—which provide approximately 10,000 bid and asked quotations. Security dealers and brokers who subscribe to the three lists are also provided with a monthly summary giving information about inactive as well as active over-the-counter securities.

NEW YORK STOCK EXCHANGE INDEX

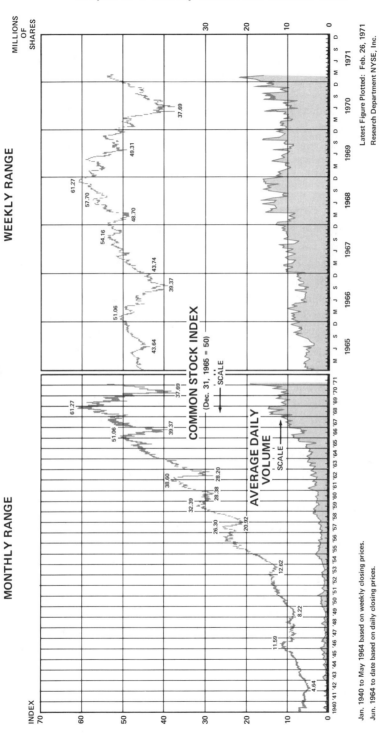

MONTHLY RANGE

WEEKLY RANGE

MILLIONS
OF
SHARES

COMMON STOCK INDEX

(Dec. 31, 1965 = 50)

SCALE

AVERAGE DAILY VOLUME

SCALE

Jan. 1940 to May 1964 based on weekly closing prices.

Jun. 1964 to date based on daily closing prices.

Latest Figure Plotted: Feb. 26, 1971
Research Department NYSE, Inc.

Figure 21-4

New York Stock Exchange Common Stock Index

BONDS

Bond issues are traded on national exchanges and in over-the-counter markets. Those that are listed are bought and sold daily, and reports of these transactions are printed in the financial pages of newspapers and in financial magazines. By following the ups and downs of the bond market, a businessman can determine the cost of borrowing long-term funds and can obtain an idea of the general availability of credit.

Bond Quotations

Although many similarities exist between stock and bond quotations, there are some important differences. For one, separate listings are provided for different types of bonds, such as domestic corporation bonds, foreign bonds, and United States Government bonds. Another difference is that bond prices are quoted in relationship to 100 regardless of the denomination of the bonds, which is usually $1,000. A bond selling for 91½ would cost $915 to purchase, and one selling for 134¼ would cost $1,342.50. The trading-unit variation in bonds is ⅛ except for government securities, which are quoted in 32nds. In order to simplify printing, a government bond is quoted at, for example, 95.24 ($95^{24}/_{32}$), which means that the price is $957.50.

The high and low for the year and for the day are shown as well as the last sale price and the net change from the previous day's trading. Opening prices are not shown. In place of information about the dividend, an abbreviated description of each issue shows the interest rate and maturity date and, when appropriate, reference is made to any special features such as, for example, "cv" meaning that the bond is convertible into common stock.

A corporation may have more bond issues outstanding than it has varieties of stock issues. Each separate bond issue demands a separate listing because the prices may vary for the different types and maturities. Another important fact is that the buyer of bonds pays accrued interest from the date of the last interest payment up to his purchase date in addition to the quoted price. He will, of course, recover this added amount when he receives his first interest payment which will cover six months since most bonds pay interest on a semiannual basis.

Bond Averages

In a manner somewhat similar to stocks, *bond averages* are computed daily. The best known, the Dow–Jones Bond Averages, show a composite average of 40 selected bonds and also averages of 10 Higher Grade Rails, 10 Second Grade Rails, 10 Public Utilities, and 10 Industrials. Other bond averages include those computed by *The New York Times*, which are grouped into railroad, public utility, industrial, and foreign classifications in addition to a composite average.

For the average businessman or investor, these averages present information that is more useful than individual quotations in that they reflect the general condition of the bond market. If a corporation is debating whether to sell more stock or to issue bonds in order to raise additional capital, the appropriate bond averages may well help in making an intelligent decision.

NEWS ITEMS

In addition to details on stocks and bonds, many other items of financial information are included in news stories. Some appear on the front pages of newspapers, such as indictments for violating the antitrust laws, but the majority are concentrated in financial magazines or the financial section of newspapers. They cover a wide range of topics, but it is possible to classify the majority of news items under the following headings: (1) corporate news, (2) money and credit, (3) commodity prices, (4) government news, and (5) international news.

Corporate News

Many of the actions of corporations, such as expansion plans, mergers proposed, promotions of key personnel, and actions taken by boards of directors, are newsworthy. The following list of stories taken from a single issue of a financial newspaper gives some idea of the scope and the variety of corporate news.

Reports of sales and earnings	Personnel changes
Dividend news	Court orders
Stock-split proposals	New products to be marketed
Sales of subsidiaries	New corporations organized
Backlogs of orders	Merger proposals
Tender offers	Unmerger sales

Money and Credit

Since a major proportion of business transactions involve credit and because most business firms borrow money for one purpose or another, the market for money and credit plays an important part in many business decisions. The cost of credit as reflected in interest rates for short-term and long-term borrowing, the rediscount rate of the federal reserve banks, and many other factors, including spending by the federal government, all play a part in determining the financial climate at any given time.

The reader of financial news can easily follow the cost of borrowing long-term funds by noting the effective interest rate of various types of securities offered to the public. This information is contained in news releases and advertisements of the syndicate handling the offering. Changes in short-term interest rates and in the rediscount rate of the Federal Reserve System are reported regularly.

Commodity Prices

The cost of raw materials is a vital element in the production of most manufactured goods and, in many instances, prices are established daily on a commodity exchange.[1] Firms that use agricultural products such as wheat, corn, and soybeans can determine not only the current cost of their materials but also the trend in prices by day-to-day reference to financial news. Livestock prices are also reported daily as are prices for feeds, eggs, dairy products, candy ingredients, fats and oils, hides, potatoes, onions, and several other commodities. Metals such as copper, tin, lead, and zinc are traded on exchanges centered chiefly in New York with the London Metal Exchange a world center for these raw materials.

Trading in grain, metals, and some other commodities on commodity exchanges can be on a cash (*spot market*) basis, or contracts can be purchased or sold for delivery in the future at a specified price. Both markets are of great interest to those manufacturers whose raw materials are bought and sold on commodity exchanges. The trend or the upward and downward movement of cash or futures prices can be followed by reference to the Dow-Jones Spot Commodity Price Index and the Dow-Jones Commodity Futures Index.

Government News

Because government has such a marked effect on business, many actions taken by federal, state, or local governments have financial implications. Foremost among these are changes in tax rates or decisions of tax courts that affect business. Other news items are concerned with issues of government securities, investigations by governmental agencies, and budget news, particularly of the federal government.

[1] See Chapter 22, page 529.

As an illustration, in recent years the Attorney General of the United States has taken action or threatened to take steps against business combinations including those of the conglomerate type. Although it is difficult to assess the full impact of this attitude, there seems to be little question but that merger proposals, stock tender offers, and outright purchase agreements have tended to slow down. The efforts of the federal government to promote competition by maintaining as many units as possible have thwarted the desires of some big businesses that wish to become even bigger.

International News

Now that the jet age has reduced the size of our globe, happenings in foreign countries have a greater effect on domestic conditions. The ability of foreign countries to purchase our goods, as reflected in overseas prosperity and currency exchange rates, is important financially to all firms that do an export business. News of trade agreements made between the United States and foreign governments, or among foreign countries such as those that comprise the Common Market, may have an effect on the prosperity of a company or an entire industry.

BUSINESS TERMS

QUESTIONS FOR DISCUSSION AND ANALYSIS

1. Each day the mood of thousands of adults who own shares of stock is influenced by the ups and downs of security prices. Are these periods of joy or gloom justified?

2. Is it possible that a large corporation that could qualify would prefer not to have its shares listed on the New York or any other stock exchange? If so, why?

3. A basic rule for brokers who deal in real estate, food, and other areas such as machinery or equipment, is that a broker can represent either a buyer or seller but not both in the same transaction, and can earn only one commission. This rule does not apply to stock brokerage firms. Why?

4. Do the commission charges for buying or selling shares of stock through a broker who uses the New York Stock Exchange seem low, reasonable, or high? Explain.

5. Why should an individual not be permitted to buy stocks on credit as he does his home, automobile, television, and other durable goods?

6. What advantages, if any, do listed securities have over unlisted securities on which daily bid and asked prices are available?

7. Have federal and state legislation removed most of the risks attached to ownership of bonds and stocks? Give reasons to support your yes or no answer.

8. Would speculation on security exchanges be reduced if individuals desiring to "play the market" were required to pay cash in full for securities purchased? Would such a rule be desirable?

9. Metropolitan newspapers seem to feel that, at a minimum, a daily report of transactions on the New York Stock Exchange is necessary to satisfy their readers. Is this a realistic assumption?

10. News out of Washington, D. C., frequently affects the prices of securities, particularly listed common stocks. Give several examples of actions by the Congress or by federal administrative agencies that affect the stock market and indicate for each whether, after the news was made public, stock prices would go up or down.

PROBLEMS AND SHORT CASES

1. Refer to a current issue of *The Wall Street Journal* or a metropolitan newspaper and itemize as much as you can about the following information:

   a. Dow–Jones common stock closing average.

   b. Closing price of a preferred stock listed on the New York Stock Exchange.

   c. Opening price of a common stock listed on the New York Stock Exchange.

d. Gain or loss in cents of closing average on the New York Stock Exchange from previous day.

e. Closing price of a bond listed on the New York Stock Exchange.

f. Closing price of a stock listed on the American Stock Exchange.

g. An asked price for an industrial or commercial over-the-counter stock.

h. A bid price for a bank or insurance stock listed on the over-the-counter market.

i. An asked price for a mutual fund.

j. A bid price for an United States government bond or note.

2. Trustees for the Bishop Foundation, a nonprofit enterprise, received a cash bequest that was promptly invested in the following list of common stocks. Compute the amount spent by the trustees, including commissions paid.

Shares	*Company*	*Price Paid*
100	American Telephone & Telegraph Co.	45
300	Bethlehem Steel Corporation	21⅜
50	E. I. duPont de Nemours & Co.	120½
100	General Foods Corporation	73¾
200	Texaco, Inc.	32⅞

3. Gordon Hall, an investment counselor, was contacted by Gerald Stevens who wanted advice on how to invest $500,000. Stevens, a long-time owner of a gravel pit, had just sold his company to a highway construction contractor, and the half million dollars represented the after-tax net on the sale.

Stevens, at 62, is in good health as are his wife and three married children. Prior to selling his business, Stevens had regularly allowed most of the operating profits to remain in the firm. He had withdrawn enough for the purchase of a home and the maintenance of a good standard of living but he had not made any outside investments. Consequently, since Stevens does not plan to seek employment, the investment of the $500,000 represents the only source of income available to him.

In discussing his problem with Hall, Stevens expressed a desire to keep the $500,000 intact for the ultimate benefit of his children. At the same time he indicated that he would have to receive a gross income annually of no less than $30,000 to be able to continue the standard of living to which he has become accustomed. Furthermore, it was obvious to Hall that his client was fearful that "time would hang heavy on his hands," so that checking on his investments day by day would be a welcome chore.

If you were Hall, what advice would you give Stevens? Be as specific as possible although if bonds, preferred stocks, or common stocks are included in your recommended investments, it is not necessary to name the exact company you selected.

SUGGESTED READINGS

Bellemore, D. H. *Investments: Principles, Practices, and Analysis*, Third Edition. Cincinnati: South-Western Publishing Co., 1969. Part 1.

Bowyer, J. W., Jr. *Investment Analysis and Management*, Third Edition. Homewood, Illinois: Richard D. Irwin, Inc., 1966. Chapter 9.

Clendenin, J. C., and G. A. Christy. *Investments*, Fifth Edition. New York: McGraw-Hill Book Company, 1969.

Donaldson, E. F., and J. K. Pfahl. *Personal Finance*, Fourth Edition. New York: The Ronald Press Company, 1966. Chapters 11-15.

Eiteman, W. J., C. A. Dice, and D. K. Eiteman. *The Stock Market*, Fourth Edition. McGraw-Hill Book Company, 1966.

Farwell, L. C., *et al. Financial Institutions*, Fourth Edition. Homewood, Illinois: Richard D. Irwin, Inc., 1966. Chapter 11.

Lefflar, G. L., and L. C. Farwell. *The Stock Market*, Third Edition. New York: The Ronald Press Company, 1963.

Phillips, E. B., and S. Lane. *Personal Finance: Text and Case Problems*, Second Edition. New York: John Wiley & Sons Inc., 1969. Part II.

Prime, J. H. *Investment Analysis*, Fourth Edition. Englewood Cliffs, New Jersey: Prentice-Hall, Inc., 1967.

Robbins, S. *The Securities Markets—Operations and Issues*. New York: The Free Press, 1966.

Chapter 22

Risks and Insurance

From birth to death every individual is continually faced with the possibility that an unexpected event will take place that will have unfortunate results. These frequent exposures to the dangers of incurring injuries or losses are risks inherent in living. The operation of a business also involves numerous possibilities that unforeseen or unanticipated happenings will occur with resulting financial losses. As has been stated in an earlier chapter, the assumption of risks by an entrepreneur is one of the justifications for an economic system that provides him with the opportunity to make profits.

Since risks are an unpleasant fact of life, businesses, and most individuals as well, prefer to avoid as many as they can, to reduce the impact of others, and to transfer, when possible, the burden of losses that may be incurred. Assume, for example, that a large business with plants and offices in 50 states has five key executives. If the corporation has a rule that none of the five can fly, it has avoided the risk of a fatal airplane accident. Since such a regulation would probably not be practicable, a policy that not more than one of the five can fly in any one airplane seems more realistic. This procedure reduces the risk even though it does not eliminate it entirely. Furthermore, if the company carries a $500,000 life insurance policy on each executive, should one be killed in an accident the payment may well equalize the loss of profits for which this individual would have been responsible.

Unfortunately not all business risks are subject to as satisfactory a solution as was suggested in the preceding hypothetical illustration. Because some risks must be absorbed in whole or in part, sound business management dictates transferring to someone else all those that are capable of being shifted. This is usually accomplished by carrying *insurance*, which can be defined as a social device by which many share the losses of a few. To carry out the mechanics involved, financial institutions known as insurance companies have been organized. By a process called *underwriting*, an insurance company will enter into an agreement with a business to reimburse it for certain stated losses that may be incurred. In return for a payment, known as a *premium*, which usually covers the cost for a limited period of time such as one year, the insured receives a printed document, called an *insurance policy*, that specifies the terms of the insurance contract.

This chapter examines briefly several of the various types of risks to which most businesses are exposed, indicating some that must be absorbed, others that can be reduced in one way or another, and those that can be transferred to an insurance company. Attention will be given to the various insurance coverages carried by large and small firms and the extent to which these companies are protected against certain types of losses. Since most of the policies that businessmen purchase are also available to individuals, an understanding of insurance will prove personally beneficial even though the emphasis in this chapter will be on business applications.

BUSINESS RISKS

Businessmen must recognize all of the different types of risks attached to the operation of their firms. They must make decisions as to a course of action which may or may not result in partial or full avoidance of possible losses. The following examination of certain specific types of risks indicates some that are uninsurable, some that can be avoided or reduced without buying insurance, and, when insurance is available, the characteristics that risks must have before an insurance company will issue a policy.

UNINSURABLE RISKS

The major uninsurable risk facing any business enterprise is the ever-present possibility that it cannot be operated at a profit. If the income from sales or services is inadequate to meet necessary expenses, losses result. If these continue for any length of time, sooner or later the business will have to discontinue operations. Thousands of businesses fail each year with resultant losses to the owners and, frequently, to creditors as well. The possibility that a business, old or new, may not be able to survive is a characteristic of our competitive economy.

In addition to management's inability to insure against operating losses, there are numerous other internal risks that are not insurable. For many retail stores shoplifting causes serious losses, but an insurance policy covering the pilfering of merchandise during store hours is not available. Most losses caused by employees who are careless or discourteous or who join together and strike are not insurable. Perfectly good merchandise can become obsolete and hence worthless. Former customers can boycott a business establishment because of real or fancied wrongs. The list may seem endless but, fortunately, businesses are usually able to keep losses of these types within manageable proportions.

The most serious types of risks that are not insurable are external rather than internal. A business unit frequently has little or no control over a course of events that may bring disaster to it. On the other hand, disaster may strike because a company refused to anticipate the future or adjust to change. Some of the different categories of risks that must be assumed are: (1) development of new products, (2) changes in distribution methods, (3) fluctuations in prices, and (4) changes in laws.

Development of New Products

A characteristic of the American economy is the rapid change brought about by technology and a more informed consumer. The development of automobiles, television, and the jet airplane has contributed to changing the American way of life. Companies that fail to anticipate the future or adjust to change tend to continue to make products that have become obsolete, and sooner or later they are compelled to go out of business. The classic example of the firm that continued to manufacture buggy whips after the advent of the automobile, or horseless carriage as it was called, points up the nature of this hazard to an established business. In recent years the demand for steam locomotives has all but disappeared, and airplane propellers seem doomed. If the automobile of the future is to be powered by electricity or steam, the continued existence of thousands of service stations selling gasoline could be in jeopardy.

Changes in Distribution Methods

The evolutionary development of chain stores, supermarkets, shopping centers, and discount houses has had an impact on the small, independently owned stores. Many have been forced to close their doors.

Fluctuations in Prices and Price Levels

If raw materials are an important element in the cost of a finished product, a sharp increase in their cost may cause losses to a firm that is committed to sell at a fixed price. Or, as happened in the thirties when prices dropped to depression levels, many businesses were operated at a loss as costs did not shrink in proportion to sales prices.

Changes in Laws

When changes are made in tariffs that permit increased imports of competitive goods, the local firm may find itself unable to price its products above its costs. Likewise, when a city, a town, a county, or a state votes to prohibit liquor sales, taverns, night clubs, and restaurants in that area may be forced out of business.

NONINSURANCE RISK PROTECTION

There are some steps a firm may take to protect itself against risks even if insurance is not available. It is fairly obvious that sound business management is one of the best antidotes against losses. Businesses compete with each other, and the efficient ones survive. A well-managed firm using modern equipment and methods has a much better chance of success than does a company with outmoded techniques of manufacturing and selling. It protects itself against the risks of obsolete products or methods of distribution by a generous allocation of funds for research and development. Capital may be conserved by leasing space and equipment or by subcontracting a portion of its manufacturing requirements until such time as equity capital is available. If the business is unincorporated, the owner or owners can safeguard their nonbusiness assets by forming a corporation.

For a limited number of firms, there are two devices worthy of mention that provide protection against certain types of risks without making use of an insurance company. One, self-insurance, is available only to large public or private units; the other, hedging, is valuable only to firms whose manufacturing operations use commodities traded on organized exchanges.

When a risk that could be transferred to an insurance company is deliberately retained and a method of paying losses is provided, the firm involved is engaged in *self-insurance*. For example, a large corporation might own hundreds of factories, warehouses, and office buildings valued at millions of dollars and scattered among the 50 states. An insurance policy covering these properties against loss by fire would demand a substantial premium payment year by year. By eliminating the costs and profit of an insurance company, the chances are excellent that a smaller amount set aside each year will prove adequate for the payment of such losses as do occur. Governmental bodies, such as a state, frequently do not carry insurance on buildings or vehicles owned.

Many firms buy and pay cash for commodities that must be delivered and processed before being offered for sale in a new form. If the cost of a raw material is a substantial proportion of the cost of the finished good, e.g., wheat flour, and if the price of the commodity goes down drastically during the time required for acquisition, manufacturing, and sale, the producer could suffer losses resulting from this price change. Fortunately many different types of raw materials, such as grain, foodstuffs, and metals, are bought and sold on *commodity exchanges*, which are similar in many respects to security exchanges. A major difference between the two types of exchanges is that on commodity exchanges—in addition to the spot or cash market—there is a *futures market* in which it is possible to buy or sell contracts for the future delivery of a specified quantity of the commodity involved. The sale and subsequent purchase of a futures contract on a commodity exchange by a business in order to protect a legitimate handling or manufacturing profit is called *hedging*.

Here is a simple illustration which involves handling grain, although the same procedure would be followed by a manufacturer who consumes the commodity in his manufacturing processes. When a Midwest farmer hauls 10,000 bushels of corn to a country elevator for sale, he expects to receive immediately the cash price being paid on a commodity exchange—probably the Chicago Board of Trade—minus transportation, other costs, and a profit for the elevator. Since, however, the corn cannot be shipped until a full carload is acquired and, in any event, will be delayed in transit, the elevator could suffer a loss if the price went down during the interval between the time the farmer is paid for his corn and the time it is sold. To protect against this risk, the elevator sells 10,000 bushels of corn in the futures market with a two months' maturity at the time the farmer is paid. When the grain is sold for cash in four to six weeks, a futures contract is purchased to offset the one previously sold. If the cash and the futures markets remain in proportion, which they have a tendency to do, a possible loss on the cash sale will be offset by a profit on the futures contracts, and vice versa.

In addition to the Chicago Board of Trade, other well-known commodity exchanges are the Chicago Mercantile Exchange, the Kansas City Board of Trade, the New Orleans and New York Cotton Exchanges, the New York Produce Exchange, and the London Metal Exchange.

CHARACTERISTICS OF INSURABLE RISKS

An understanding of business risks would not be complete without the realization that, before an insurance company is willing to underwrite possible losses, each risk must have some uniform characteristics. These are:

1. The annual loss must be predictable. The number of people who will die each year or the number of houses that will burn each year can be predicted with amazing accuracy. An exception to this statement could occur if a nuclear war killed millions of people and laid waste to miles and miles of buildings of all types. Insurance is written with the expectation that a catastrophe of this magnitude will not take place.

2. The risk must be spread over a wide geographical area. A fire insurance company could not afford to insure all the houses in one city only. A disastrous fire such as occurred in Chicago in 1871 would bankrupt the company.

3. Risks must be selected. No company can afford to insure only people who are seriously ill, have heart trouble, or make their living testing new airplanes.

4. The risks must be numerous enough to make the law of averages work. Insuring one life for a small annual premium could not be done on a scientific basis, but insuring the lives of 100,000 people can.

5. The premium cost must be low in relation to the insured's recovery possibilities. If the annual cost of a policy insuring a $5,000 truck against loss by theft was $1,000 instead of approximately $10, a business would try some method other than insurance to secure protection against this risk.

How does a policy insuring the hands of a piano player for $100,000 or the nose of a movie actor for a fabulous sum fit into the classification of insurable risks? The answer is that such policies are not written except by Lloyd's of London, an organization that is not an insurance company but rather an association through which members offer to underwrite hazards of all types. Marine insurance, which falls within the classification of insurable risks, forms the bulk, though not the spectacular portion, of the underwriting business of Lloyd's.

THE INSURANCE BUSINESS

Before detailing the different types of insurance policies available to businessmen and individuals, an understanding of these coverages will be aided by an examination of the insurance business. Although frequently taken for granted, the separation between public and private insurance underwriters is extremely important. Furthermore, within the private sector the specialization of insurance companies helps to explain why most firms and individuals purchase numerous insurance policies.

PUBLIC AND PRIVATE UNDERWRITERS

The extent to which government underwrites various risks, sometimes in competition with private industry, is startling for a capitalistic system. All states participate in a nationwide plan of unemployment insurance, which is required by federal law. Workmen's compensation insurance, now required by all states, is frequently a monopoly of state government. Although not universal, many states operate retirement plans for state employees including public school teachers.

The federal government has been in the insurance business for many years. It insures mail and deposits in banks, in savings and loan associations, and in credit unions. Through the Federal Housing Administration it insures private lending agencies against loss on FHA approved loans made to buy, build, or remodel homes. The U.S. Department of Agriculture owns and manages the Federal Crop Insurance Corporation that insures farmers against hail and other causes of crop failure. Low-cost life insurance has often been available to members of the Armed Services, and career military personnel can draw retirement pay after 20 or more years in uniform. Railway employees have separate retirement and unemployment insurance programs operated by the federal government as do federal civil service employees.

By far the most extensive entry of the federal government into the insurance business began in 1935 when the first Social Security Act was passed, and this activity was expanded in 1966 with the introduction of the related Medicare program. The Old-Age, Survivors, and Disability Insurance System, commonly called *Social Security*, provides a program of monthly payments to retired or disabled workers or their surviving dependents. *Medicare* covers hospital and medical insurance for those 65 years of age or older who are drawing retirement benefits. These programs require contributions on the part of the insured both before and after retirement, although the cost of the programs is shared by employers and the United States Treasury.

TYPES OF PRIVATE INSURANCE COMPANIES

Private insurance companies can be classified as to ownership. The two major types are mutual companies and stock companies, both of which were explained in Chapter 5. In the life insurance field mutual companies predominate, and the reverse situation is true for property and liability insurance companies. In one area, hospital costs and surgical fees, nonprofit Blue Cross and Blue Shield corporations play a dominant role.

Another classification of insurance companies can be made on the basis of the types of policies they write. Until a few years ago, partly because of state legal restrictions, companies tended to specialize in a limited area such as life, fire, or surety bonds. In recent years all states have liberalized their regulatory laws to permit a single insurance company to write many different coverages. This change has reduced specialization to two distinct types of insurance companies: (1) property and liability and (2) life. One coverage, health insurance, is written by both categories of insurance companies, but otherwise the areas are quite distinct. Another new related development is that protection against multiple perils of owning property can now be included in one policy. For example, a single home-owner's policy can provide protection against possible loss from fire, wind, hail, liability, theft, freezing, earthquake, vandalism, and many more risks.

The division of insurance companies into property and liability and life is in line with the sales outlets of insurance companies. Individuals or firms engaged in the business of selling insurance are customarily either general insurance agents or life insurance agents. A general insurance agency represents a number of different companies, including competing firms. The agency may represent a life insurance company, too, but it does not stress this area of its business. The life insurance agent normally sells policies on a commission basis for only one company.

Further evidence of these two classifications is found in the professional designations that are granted to individuals who qualify for and pass certain examinations. The *CLU* (Chartered Life Underwriter) certificate is granted by the American College of Life Underwriters. In a similar manner the American Institute for Property and Liability Underwriters grants the designation *CPCU* (Chartered Property and Casualty Underwriter).

The balance of this chapter will examine first some of the more common types of property and liability insurance, all of which are valuable to the businessman. Health insurance will then be discussed briefly, followed by a description of the different types and uses of life insurance policies with particular reference to their value to business.

PROPERTY AND LIABILITY INSURANCE

Approximately 3,000 insurance companies sell property and liability insurance and related lines. They own about $50 billion in assets and are responsible for employing nearly 600,000 people. The major classifications of property and liability insurance are: (1) fire, (2) automobile, (3) burglary and theft, (4) workmen's compensation, (5) marine, (6) fidelity and surety bonds, (7) liability, and (8) other coverages.

FIRE INSURANCE

One of the common risks against which insurance is carried is that of fire. Homes, apartment houses, store buildings, factories, and almost every type of building can be insured against loss resulting from fire. The same thing is true of the contents, whether it be furniture, merchandise, machinery, or supplies of any type and description. Policies are sold on a one-, three-, or five-year basis with a strong preference for the three-year maturity. The advantages of a three-year policy over a one-year policy are that the buyer is guaranteed against a rate increase in the second and third years and that he may be granted a discounted rate.

Premium rates are relatively low but vary considerably in different geographical areas and among types of construction (see Figure 22-1). For example, cities are graded on such items as water supply, fire alarms, building laws, and the efficiency of the fire department. Within the city the location of a building is important as it may stand between two old buildings or at some distance from other structures. If the construction is considered fireproof, the rate will be lower than on frame buildings. The lowest rates are in the neighborhood of 10 cents for each $100 of coverage, and more hazardous risks may cost $2 for each $100.

Coinsurance Clauses

Fire damage to industrial property resulting in complete destruction of the property insured is rare. If it were permissible to buy an insurance policy for one third or one half of the total value of the property owned, the annual saving in insurance premiums would probably offset a fire loss in excess of this coverage. Insurance companies protect themselves against this reduced premium income by inserting in the policy what is known as a *coinsurance clause*, which requires that the insured buy coverage up to a stipulated percent of the value of the property, usually 80 percent, or assume a proportion of each fire loss. In most states residence property is not subject to coinsurance clause restrictions.

If a factory is properly valued at $100,000 but is insured against fire for only $50,000, the risk is only partially covered because the minimum insurance for full protection against partial losses is 80 percent or $80,000. If a fire occurs with a total damage of $20,000, the insurance company will pay $50,000/$80,000 or ⅝ of the loss. This means a payment of $12,500 even though the loss was $20,000.

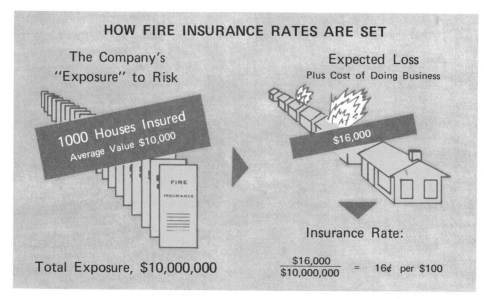

Figure 22-1

Institute of Life Insurance

How Fire Insurance Rates Are Set

Allied Coverages

By the addition to a fire insurance policy of a special agreement, known as a *rider* or endorsement, the insuring company will cover such losses as wind or water damage. Within recent years a fire and extended coverage policy has proved very popular. This type of policy, in addition to fire coverage, includes protection against windstorm, cyclone, tornado, hail, explosion, riot, aircraft, smoke, and vehicle damage. For individuals a comprehensive dwelling or so-called homeowners policy is available as has already been described. For businesses another desirable addition to a fire insurance policy is one covering what are known as consequential losses resulting from fire damage. For example, a retail store cannot earn profits while being repaired following a fire, so *business interruption insurance* is added which replaces earnings that are lost.

AUTOMOBILE INSURANCE

The usual types of automobile coverage include fire and theft, bodily injury liability, property damage, and collision insurance. If the policy covers fire and theft, the amount paid the insured in case of total loss is the value of the car at the date of the fire or theft. Within recent years automobile insurance companies have offered *comprehensive coverage*, which is a contract that covers practically all damage to the insured's automobile, including fire and theft, except that resulting from collision and upset. For example, claims have been paid for accidental damage to upholstery and for windshields broken by flying stones.

Bodily injury liability insurance will pay the policyholder's legal liability for injury to one person or to a group. If a driver hits a pedestrian or causes injury to persons in another car, the insurance company will pay damages up to the amount of coverage carried. A common policy fixes a maximum of $5,000 for liability resulting from the death or disability of one person, and $10,000 for similar reasons to more than one person. This type of policy is frequently identified by the fraction 5/10. Higher maximum coverages than 5/10 can be obtained in amounts such as 10/20 or 20/40 by paying a higher premium.

A *medical payments endorsement* can be purchased that will pay hospital and doctor bills up to a specified maximum for each occupant of the insured's car who is injured in an accident, including the policyholder. In many states legislation that relieves the driver of a car from liability for injury to his passengers arising from an accident has been enacted. Such "guest laws," as they are termed, were passed to prevent friendly suits against the car owner with the knowledge that the insurance company would finance the settlement.

Property damage liability insurance is stated at a single amount, such as $5,000. If the insured car damages another car, or runs into a house, or damages any property not belonging to the insured, the insurance company will settle the claim up to the amount of the policy. It will not pay anything for damages to the policyholder's car unless *collision* or *upset insurance* is carried. This type of coverage protects the car owner against any damage to his automobile resulting from an accident, but it is relatively expensive unless he purchases collision insurance with a deductible allowance, such as $50 or $100. In this event the insurance company pays for damages that are in excess of the stipulated deductible amount. Many drivers do not carry collision insurance because of the relatively high cost, although cars purchased on the installment plan are so covered in order to protect the finance company.

Many states have passed financial responsibility laws. These usually provide that the driver of a car at fault in an accident must show evidence that he has assumed his financial obligation in order to merit his continued right to operate his automobile. Ownership of an insurance policy covering bodily injury and property damage liability is the preferable method of demonstrating financial responsibility. This situation may change if states adopt a *no-fault rule* under which the injured party collects from his insurance company rather than the company patronized by the driver who caused an accident.

BURGLARY, ROBBERY, AND THEFT INSURANCE

Most businesses and many individuals carry insurance against the risk of having something of value taken illegally from their premises or person. *Burglary* involves the unlawful taking of property within premises closed for business, and evidence of forcible entry must be visible. *Robbery* is the forcible taking of property from another person. *Theft*, or its legal synonym *larceny*, covers any act of stealing without regard for forceful entry or violence and hence includes both burglary and robbery.

Although residence burglary insurance is the most common type written, the businessman is more interested in other forms. These include mercantile open stock, business safe, office burglary and robbery, and paymaster protection. Small retailers can obtain a comprehensive storekeepers' burglary and robbery policy that will cover safe and mercantile open stock burglary; damage to money, securities, merchandise, or equipment caused by burglary or robbery; theft of money or securities from a residence or night depository; kidnapping an employee to gain entrance; and robbery inside or outside the business premises. Pilferage of merchandise from a store during open hours is not covered by burglary insurance because the requirement of visible evidence of breaking or entering is lacking.

WORKMEN'S COMPENSATION INSURANCE

All 50 states have passed laws making it compulsory for employers to purchase workmen's compensation insurance. Certain classes of workers, notably farm and domestic laborers, are exempted, and a certain minimum number of employees is usually stated. In some states the workmen's compensation insurance is a monopoly of the state; in others, private insurance companies compete with state funds; and in still others, private insurance companies handle the business unless the employing company is large enough to warrant approval for self-insurance. The rates are assessed against the payroll, and they vary with the hazard of the industry.

The purpose of *workmen's compensation insurance* is to guarantee medical expenses and salary payments to workers who are injured on the job unless it can be shown that the employee's injury or death was willful or caused by intoxication. The usual practice is to specify weekly benefits. These are set at a fraction of the regular wage, such as one half or two thirds, in order to discourage those who might prefer to draw benefits rather than work. A waiting period of from a few days to two weeks is also a common provision of many laws. This means that no benefits can be drawn until the expiration of the waiting period, which eliminates claims for minor accidents. In case of death, weekly payments are made to the dependents of the deceased for a specified period, frequently eight years.

MARINE INSURANCE

Two general types of marine insurance are ocean marine and inland marine. Both are transportation insurance and, despite the connotation of the word "marine," inland marine insurance need not involve shipment by water.

Ocean Marine Insurance

The oldest form of insurance is that on ships of all types as well as their cargoes. An *ocean marine insurance* contract covers practically all perils of shipments on the high seas, including all degrees of loss from injury to the vessel and contents up to a complete loss of both as a result of sinking. Fire insurance is included as a part of the policy.

Inland Marine Insurance

A typical *inland marine insurance* policy provides protection against loss on movable goods while being transported by rail, truck, airplane, inland and coastwise steamers, and barges. Such a policy covers a variety of risks, such as hazards of water and land transport, fire, and theft. Of interest to many businessmen is a form of inland marine insurance designed to cover shipments of merchandise by parcel post. One method is to buy a coupon book that provides insurance tickets to be inserted in each parcel shipped; another is a blanket policy that covers all parcel post shipments. Either method is less expensive and less bothersome than insuring each package at the post office.

A type of inland marine insurance that has become quite popular in recent years is the *personal property floater*. This policy provides protection of personal property from all hazards wherever located—in the home, in transit, or abroad. It is a comprehensive type of coverage that includes fire and theft protection as well as other risks. Under such a policy the personal effects of a student attending college away from home can be covered in transit or while at his college residence.

FIDELITY AND SURETY BONDS

Fidelity and surety companies specialize in guaranteeing policyholders that other individuals, corporations, and agents with whom the insured may have business relations are reliable. In many cases losses might result from such connections, and the business firm is not in a position to investigate the character or financial responsibility of each of the persons or corporations involved. The only way that the company can protect itself against such losses is by carrying the proper insurance protection. In fact, members of a board of directors occupying a position of trust may find themselves personally liable for losses if employees are not properly bonded.

Fidelity bonds are usually written to cover an employee occupying a position of trust in which he has jurisdiction over funds. The employer is guaranteed against loss caused by the dishonesty of such employees, and the insurance company will reimburse the policyholder for losses up to the amount specified in the policy. Coverages may be individual, or group, or may name positions. For example, a business firm may secure a fidelity bond on specifically named employees for such varying amounts as the funds to which each has access. Or, the company may secure a policy covering a group of employees in a particular department. Still another possibility is to purchase a policy in which positions and the amounts of coverage are specified, such as treasurer—$50,000. Whoever is hired for a specified task is bonded for the stated amount.

Surety bonds are written to protect the insured against loss from the nonperformance of a contract or the nonperformance of any agreed-upon act or business transaction. A building contractor, for example, might be required to furnish a surety bond that he will erect a factory according to specifications and within the allowed time interval.

LIABILITY INSURANCE

Bodily injury liability and property damage liability resulting from the operation of a motor vehicle have been discussed as a part of automobile insurance. Manufacturers, contractors, retailers of goods and services, professional men and women, and even homeowners find it advantageous to protect themselves from other claims arising from injuries, real or fancied, to the property or person of others. To accomplish this objective they carry liability insurance that, particularly in the case of a homeowner, is sometimes incorporated as a part of a multiple peril policy.

Many liability policies are concerned with injuries that are received on the premises of the insured. Building operators are subject to elevator accident risks, people stumble and fall in darkened movie theaters, and visitors to an industrial plant may be hit by a moving crane. There is also the possibility that a faulty food or drug product, for example, may pass inspection and its use cause illness or death. Insurance against this risk is known as *products liability insurance*. Physicians and surgeons, dentists, lawyers, accountants, architects, pharmacists, and hospitals are constantly being sued for malpractice. Claims are frequently in six figures, so it is understandable that premium income for liability insurance is approximately $1½ billion annually.

OTHER COVERAGES

The different kinds of insurable risks inherent in operating a business are so extensive that it becomes difficult for management to determine proper coverage. One of the common types carried as a result of today's architecture is glass breakage. Another common type is boiler and machinery insurance, which features preventative engineering service provided by the company writing the insurance.

Other business coverages include false arrest, product warranties, rain insurance, forgery, power interruption, title insurance, and so on. A number of these risks can now be incorporated in a special multiperil policy that covers most of the property and liability insurance needed by a business.

HEALTH INSURANCE

Health insurance, sometimes identified as *accident and sickness insurance*, covers one or any combination of the following: (a) hospital, surgical, and other medical expenses; (b) loss of income during the period of disability; and (c) major medical expense. It is sold by life insurance companies, property and liability underwriters, and nonprofit associations such as Blue Cross and Blue Shield.

Assume that Jerome Green, married, with three children, is involved in a serious automobile accident while driving home after work. He is hospitalized for three weeks and another four weeks elapses before he can return to his job. While in the hospital, if he was properly insured, all or substantially all of his expenses including surgeon's fees would be covered. He would also receive a stated weekly income for the entire seven weeks, such as two thirds of his regular salary. If he owned a major medical policy and if his personal medical expenses exceeded an agreed upon deductible amount such as $300, he would receive reimbursement for the excess. Health insurance policies also may provide that, if the insured loses an eye or a hand or a foot, he will receive either a flat sum or weekly amounts for several weeks.

A substantial percentage of all types of health insurance is written on a group basis with employers providing the entire cost as a fringe benefit; in some instances, employees bear all or a share of the cost under a payroll deduction plan. The extent of the use of health insurance is far greater than most people realize. Approximately 80 percent of the entire population of the United States is covered by some type of health insurance, and premiums collected exceed $13 billion annually. So many adult men and women are insured that there are still unresolved conflicts with workmen's compensation insurance; with the disability provisions of Old-Age, Survivors, and Disability Insurance; and with Medicare. Also unresolved is the possibility that the Congress will enact a national health insurance law within a few years.

LIFE INSURANCE

Life insurance policies are written by more than 1,700 different companies that own assets of approximately $185 billion and employ 850,000 people. In the United States there are 130,000,000 policyholders whose lives are insured for $1,245 billion and who, in a recent year, paid some $31 billion in premiums. Truly, the life insurance industry is gigantic in all dimensions.

As in the case of other forms of insurance, life insurance is based on the law of averages. No one can predict whether a particular individual will die during any given year, but the number of persons living at the beginning of a year who will die within 12 months can be computed within narrow margins. The annual premium on a life insurance policy is related to statistics covering deaths as compiled by actuaries. An *actuary* is an individual employed by an insurance company who is an expert at computing risks and the size of insurance premiums necessary to the profitable operation of his company. Although insurance companies rely on more than one table, many states require the use of a mortality schedule compiled by the National Association of Insurance Commissioners, an organization of state insurance commissioners. In 1958 this body adopted the Commissioners Standard Ordinary Mortality Table, which is shown in Table 22-1.

Note that the *CSO 1958 Mortality Table* covers the life history of ten million people beginning at birth and continuing to the age of 99. For each year there is shown the number living at the beginning of the year, the number who will die during the year, and the death rate per 1,000 for that year. For example, at the age of 18 a total of 9,698,230 young men and women will be living out of the original group of 10 million. During the year 16,390 will die, which is a death rate of 1.69 per 1,000.

TYPES OF LIFE INSURANCE POLICIES

Life insurance policies can be classified in several different ways. One subdivision uses the categories of ordinary, industrial, group, and credit. *Ordinary insurance* consists of individual policies of $1,000 or more that require a physical examination and are written on a term, whole life,

COMMISSIONERS 1958 STANDARD ORDINARY MORTALITY TABLE

Age	Number Living	Deaths Each Year	Death Rate per 1,000	Age	Number Living	Deaths Each Year	Death Rate per 1,000
0	10,000,000	70,800	7.08	50	8,762,306	72,902	8.32
1	9,929,200	17,475	1.76	51	8,869,404	79,160	9.11
2	9,911,725	15,066	1.52	52	8,610,244	85,758	9.96
3	9,896,659	14,449	1.46	53	8,524,486	92,832	10.89
4	9,882,210	13,835	1.40	54	8,431,654	100,337	11.90
5	9,868,375	13,322	1.35	55	8,331,317	108,307	13.00
6	9,855,053	12,812	1.30	56	8,223,010	116,849	14.21
7	9,842,241	12,401	1.26	57	8,106,161	125,970	15.54
8	9,829,840	12,091	1.23	58	7,980,191	135,663	17.00
9	9,817,749	11,879	1.21	59	7,844,528	145,830	18.59
10	9,805,870	11,865	1.21	60	7,698,698	156,592	20.34
11	9,794,005	12,047	1.23	61	7,542,106	167,736	22.24
12	9,781,958	12,325	1.26	62	7,374,370	179,271	24.31
13	9,769,633	12,896	1.32	63	7,195,099	191,174	26.57
14	9,756,737	13,562	1.39	64	7,003,925	203,394	29.04
15	9,743,175	14,225	1.46	65	6,800,531	215,917	31.75
16	9,728,950	14,983	1.54	66	6,584,614	228,749	34.74
17	9,713,967	15,737	1.62	67	6,355,865	241,777	38.04
18	9,698,230	16,390	1.69	68	6,114,088	254,835	41.68
19	9,681,840	16,846	1.74	69	5,859,253	267,241	45.61
20	9,664,994	17,300	1.79	70	5,592,012	278,426	49.79
21	9,647,694	17,655	1.83	71	5,313,586	287,731	54.15
22	9,630,039	17,912	1.86	72	5,025,855	294,766	58.65
23	9,612,127	18,167	1.89	73	4,731,089	299,289	63.26
24	9,593,960	18,324	1.91	74	4,431,800	301,894	68.12
25	9,575,636	18,481	1.93	75	4,129,906	303,011	73.37
26	9,557,155	18,732	1.96	76	3,826,895	303,014	79.18
27	9,538,423	18,981	1.99	77	3,523,881	301,997	85.70
28	9,519,442	19,324	2.03	78	3,221,884	299,829	93.06
29	9,500,118	19,760	2.08	79	2,922,055	295,683	101.19
30	9,480,358	20,193	2.13	80	2,626,372	288,848	109.98
31	9,460,165	20,718	2.19	81	2,337,524	278,983	119.35
32	9,439,447	21,239	2.25	82	2,058,541	265,902	129.17
33	9,418,208	21,850	2.32	83	1,792,639	249,858	139.38
34	9,396,358	22,551	2.40	84	1,542,781	231,433	150.01
35	9,373,807	23,528	2.51	85	1,311,348	211,311	161.14
36	9,350,279	24,685	2.64	86	1,100,037	190,108	172.82
37	9,325,594	26,112	2.80	87	909,929	168,455	185.13
38	9,299,482	27,991	3.01	88	741,474	146,997	198.25
39	9,271,491	30,132	3.25	89	594,477	126,303	212.46
40	9,241,359	32,622	3.53	90	468,174	106,809	228.14
41	9,208,737	35,362	3.84	91	361,365	88,813	245.77
42	9,173,375	38,253	4.17	92	272,552	72,480	265.93
43	9,135,122	41,382	4.53	93	200,072	57,881	289.30
44	9,093,740	44,741	4.92	94	142,191	45,026	316.66
45	9,048,999	48,412	5.35	95	97,165	34,128	351.24
46	9,000,587	52,473	5.83	96	63,037	25,250	400.56
47	8,948,114	56,910	6.36	97	37,787	18,456	488.42
48	8,891,204	61,794	6.95	98	19,331	12,916	668.15
49	8,829,410	67,104	7.60	99	6,415	6,415	1,000.00

Table 22-1

or endowment basis or some combination of these types. *Industrial insurance* has the same subdivisions as ordinary insurance but differs in that policies are usually for less than $1,000, the agent collects the premium weekly or monthly, and no medical examination is required. The *whole life* segment of ordinary insurance covers policies that, without the time restrictions of term insurance, are payable to a beneficiary when the insured dies. This category can be further subdivided into straight life and limited payment life plus other forms of paid-up insurance.

For purposes of providing a background for understanding the business uses of life insurance, the following classifications of ordinary insurance will be examined in some detail prior to discussing group and credit insurance: (1) term life insurance, (2) straight life insurance, (3) limited payment life insurance, and (4) endowment life insurance.

Term Life Insurance

Term life insurance bears a similarity to fire insurance in that the insurance company is obligated to pay only if a loss (death in this case) occurs within the time limit covered by the policy. If the insured is living at the end of the specified term, all premiums paid are the property of the insurance company and the policy automatically expires. If term life insurance policies were written on an annual basis, the CSO 1958 Table can be used to compute a basic cost. Referring to the figures in the table, if all of the 9,698,230 eighteen-year-old men and women were insured for $1,000 for one year, the insurance company would pay out during the year $16,390,000 to the *beneficiaries* (the persons who receive the face value of a policy) of the 16,390 individuals who would die during the year. This means that, if a premium payment of $1.69 were made for each policy, the insurance company would have just enough money to meet the necessary outlay. The actual premium would, of course, need to be higher for several reasons, including meeting the expenses of doing business. Note that the costs of term insurance computed on this basis would increase year by year amounting to $3.53 per $1,000 at age 40 and increasing to $20.34 at age 60.

Individuals who buy term insurance usually prefer a *level-term contract*, that is, one that does not require a larger premium payment each year. Examples are 5-year, 10-year, and 20-year term insurance. These policies are usually renewable up to the age of 65 without the necessity of the policyholder providing evidence of his insurability. Group life insurance, which will be discussed later in this chapter, is written on a one-year term basis.

The chief advantage of term life insurance is its low cost. More protection can be purchased for a given premium payment than is available under any other type of life insurance policy. Since most term policies are convertible into more permanent forms of life insurance, they are especially attractive to young persons faced with family and home responsibilities.

Straight Life Insurance

The most popular form of life insurance is *straight life*. The premium, which remains constant throughout the life of the insured, varies with the age at which the coverage is purchased; and the policy combines a plan of protection and savings. The advantage of a straight life policy is that maximum protection can be attained for the lowest premium, with the single exception of term insurance. Disadvantages include the fact that the insured must die before full payment is made on the policy and also that premiums may be due in years after earning capacity has ceased. If a man retires at 65, he must still continue to pay premiums.

The reason that straight life premium rates are higher than those charged for term insurance is that each payment contains an element of savings as well as the amount necessary to buy protection. These savings remain with the life insurance company, unless the policy is canceled, and provide what is known as the *cash surrender value* of the insurance contract. If the policyholder lives a number of years, the cash value increases to a sizable amount in relationship to the face value.

Limited Payment Life Insurance

The differences between *limited payment life insurance* and straight life insurance are that premiums on limited-payment policies are due for only a stated number of years, the annual payments are larger, and the cash surrender values are higher. The most common period of time is 20 years, although any number of years can be selected. The advantage of this type of policy is that the individual is able to eliminate the drain of premium payments extending over a lifetime and can concentrate his expenditures for life insurance within the period of his maximum earning capacity. The chief disadvantage is that more protection could have been secured for the same annual outlay if straight life had been selected. As in the case of straight life, the insurance company pays the face value of the policy only upon the death of the insured.

Endowment Life Insurance

Endowment life insurance is similar to limited payment life insurance with the exception that it emphasizes the savings element in a contract over the protective features. The annual premium is larger than for straight or limited-payment life, and consequently the cash surrender value of the policy increases at a faster rate. At the expiration of a stated number of years, which may be an even figure such as 30 or the number of years before the insured reaches 65, the cash value of the policy equals its face. If, at the age of 30, a man takes out a $1,000 endowment policy running for 30 years, he has automatically created an estate of $1,000 by the time he is 60. If he dies within this period, the insurance company will pay the face of the policy. If, however, he lives to the age of 60, the company will pay him the face of the policy at that time, or he may elect to receive annual payments.

Table 22-2 shows the comparative annual premiums per $1,000 charged by one company for four different types of life insurance policies involving total coverages of from $10,000 to $25,000.

COMPARATIVE ANNUAL PREMIUM COSTS PER $1,000 INSURANCE

	Age	5-Year Renewable Term	Straight Life	20-Pay Life	20-Year Endowment
Table 22-2	20	$ 4.88	$15.21	$26.71	$47.96
	30	5.41	20.00	32.29	48.58
	40	7.90	27.85	40.12	50.86
	50	15.20	41.09	51.74	57.05

BUSINESS USES OF LIFE INSURANCE

Life insurance can be and is used by sole proprietorships, partnerships, and corporations. Some of the more common adaptations of policies to businesses uses are: (1) group life insurance, (2) credit life insurance, (3) insurance on owners or executives, and (4) retirement and pension plans.

Group Life Insurance

The most extensive use of life insurance by business in recent years has centered about *group life insurance*, which is simply a policy covering each employee of a single firm for a sum such as $5,000, or the amount may vary with different categories of employees. Such insurance is usually written on a one-year renewable term plan. It is distinctive in that no medical examination is required. This is possible because of the number, as well as the composition, of the group covered. Most employers do not hire workers who are not physically fit, and most workers are in a relatively healthy age bracket.

The employer usually pays at least a portion of the premium, which really constitutes a bonus to the employee. Rates are lower than for any form of an individual policy because the premiums are paid by the company in one check, which greatly reduces collection costs; there are no medical examination fees; and commission rates are lower than on other types. The $438 billion in group term insurance outstanding at the end of 1968 provides some idea of the extensive use business makes of this form of life insurance.

Credit Life Insurance

The extensive purchase of goods on the installment plan and the use of short-term borrowing by consumers has made credit life insurance the fastest-growing form of life insurance. *Credit life insurance* guarantees repayment of amounts due on installment contracts or personal loans in case the debtor dies. It has assumed one of the risks of consumer financing, both for the lender and the borrower.

Banks, finance companies, credit unions, retailers, and some mortgage lenders are the chief purchasers of credit life insurance. It is written on a one-year basis, and the amount applicable to a borrower decreases as he reduces his debt. Practically all credit life insurance is written on a group basis, although individual policies are available. The extensive use of credit life insurance has resulted in outstanding policies in excess of $75 billion.

Credit life insurance should not be confused with *credit insurance*, which is a type of policy available to a firm insuring it against unusually high losses resulting from the extension of credit on open-book accounts. An interesting feature of credit insurance policies is the requirement that the insured must bear part of each loss, which prevents him from being too generous in extending credit.

Insurance on Owners or Executives

If a sole proprietor dies, his business may have to be sold to pay funeral and administration expenses, and taxes. An adequate term life insurance policy payable to his estate can avoid the necessity for a sale, and his business can be continued by his widow, son, or other heirs. A straight, limited-payment, or endowment policy might be preferable, since any one of these types could be used during the lifetime of the owner as a support for his credit standing, as collateral for a bank loan, and as a basis for a retirement plan.

When a partner dies, the partnership must be dissolved; but the question remains as to who will buy the deceased's interest in the firm. A term life insurance contract payable to the surviving partner or partners can provide a fund with which to buy this interest and avoid the necessity of taking in a new partner. If it is assumed that the partner is to retire at a given age, an endowment policy maturing at the agreed retirement age guarantees that funds will be available to buy out his interest.

Some corporations have found that their profitability is closely connected to the abilities and contacts of one or two key executives. Carrying an insurance policy on their lives, payable to the corporation, can provide a cushion to absorb the reduction in earning power that might result from the death of one of these individuals. These funds could well carry the company through the months necessary to hire and train an adequate replacement.

Retirement and Pension Plans

Firms interested in providing a continuing income to retired employees above and beyond the benefits from the federal social security system can finance such a program through insurance companies. Currently some 9 million employees are covered by insured pension plans and the number is growing rapidly each year.

There are three commonly used methods of insuring pensions. The most widely favored by business is a so-called deposit administration plan in which a single fund is established with an insurance company that covers all employees. As each employee retires, money is withdrawn from the fund to purchase an annuity for him. Another method involves the purchase each year of a paid-up annuity benefit for each employee. Smaller firms frequently make use of a pension trust plan, which requires the purchase of a life insurance policy for each covered employee.

BUSINESS TERMS

QUESTIONS FOR DISCUSSION AND ANALYSIS

1. In addition to the text illustrations, give a specific example of an internal and of an external risk that businesses must absorb. In each case, what should management do to reduce the possible impact on the firm?

2. Do new products regularly make old ones obsolete or are most merely new models? Give specific examples.

3. Does the fact that the cruisers operated by the state highway patrol are probably not insured mean that if one is the cause of an automobile accident the injured party cannot collect damages?

4. Are there any common qualities to items that are traded on commodity exchanges? If so, explain the importance of these characteristics.

5. What explanations can be given to justify the extensive activities of government in the insurance business?

6. What coverages should a college senior carry on an automobile he owns? Give reasons for your selections.

7. Losses from shoplifting are reported to cause heavy burdens to retailers. Why is this risk not covered by insurance?

8. Do you favor a program of national health insurance financed by the federal government? Justify your yes or no answer.

9. Why should not all life insurance be sold on a term basis as is fire insurance? What is the logic in incorporating a savings feature into straight, limited payment, and endowment life insurance policies?

10. The most extensive use of life insurance by business involves group life policies. Why is this so?

PROBLEMS AND SHORT CASES

1. A factory building is appraised as being worth $6,000,000. Assuming that the corporation owning it takes out a fire insurance policy with an 80% coinsurance clause, how much insurance can be collected in each of the following situations?

	Fire Loss	Insurance Coverage
a.	$1,000,000	$2,400,000
b.	2,000,000	3,000,000
c.	3,000,000	3,600,000
d.	4,000,000	4,200,000
e.	6,000,000	4,800,000

2. A company wishes to purchase a $10,000 one-year term life insurance policy for each of its 5,000 employees. It is determined that the average age of the group is 35. If the insurance company needs a 20 percent margin on total premiums to cover its costs with a reasonable margin of safety, what would be a single premium cost for a group life insurance policy? Refer to the Commissioners 1958 Standard Ordinary Mortality Table on page 542 to compute your answer.

3. The Gardner Company was founded by Ralph Gardner in 1942 to manufacture pumps. Over the years it has grown and prospered with annual sales increasing to $21,000,000. As a result of stock splits, there are now 800,000 shares of common stock outstanding on which a dividend of $1.50 per share was paid to 823 stockholders out of last year's $1,800,000 after-tax profits.

Ralph Gardner is now Chairman of the Board of Directors and his son, Ralph, Jr., is President and Chief Executive Officer. Both of these men are disturbed by current persistent attempts to organize the 3,200 factory workers. Because the firm has always paid good wages and due to its location in a small nonunion town, the workers have been content with a company-sponsored committee organization that has settled the few labor disputes that have arisen from time to time.

Word has filtered through the grapevine that the union organizers have reluctantly accepted the fact that current wage rates coupled with a liberal policy of paid vacations leave little to be desired in this area. Consequently, they have decided to stress fringe benefits when making an appeal for membership to the rank-and-file employees. Major emphasis will be focused on various types of insurance, a complete void at the moment, with the entire cost to be paid by the company.

The Gardners, father and son, would prefer the status quo as far as labor relations are concerned. They believe that a voluntary offer of an insurance program will defeat the union as it has a $50 initiation fee and charges $10 a month dues. It has been determined that the annual cost per employee of various types of coverages would be as follows:

Pension Program (Deposit Administration Plan) $200
Blue Cross (Hospital Charges)
    Family Plan 250
    Single Coverage 115
Blue Shield (Surgeon's Fees)
    Family Plan 50
    Single Coverage 23
Major Medical (All costs in excess of $300) 28
Health and Accident Insurance
    Supplement to Workmen's Compensation 46
Group Life ($10,000 per employee) 32

On the basis of the above facts, what action should the Gardner Company take? If a company-financed insurance program is offered employees, what should it cover?

SUGGESTED READINGS

Athearn, J. L. *Risk and Insurance*, Second Edition. New York: Appleton-Century-Crofts, 1969.

Dickerson, O. D. *Health Insurance*, Third Edition. Homewood, Illinois: Richard D. Irwin, Inc., 1968.

Greene, M. R. *Risk and Insurance*, Second Edition. Cincinnati: South-Western Publishing Co., 1968.

Life Insurance Fact Book. New York: Institute of Life Insurance, 1970.

Michelbacher, G. F., and N. R. Ross. *Multiple Line Insurers: Their Nature and Operations*, Second Edition. New York: McGraw-Hill Book Company, 1970.

Mowbray, A. H., R. H. Blanchard, and C. A. Williams. *Insurance*, Sixth Edition. New York: McGraw-Hill Book Company, 1969.

Riegel, R., and S. J. Miller. *Insurance Principles and Practices*, Fifth Edition. Englewood Cliffs, New Jersey: Prentice-Hall, Inc., 1966.

Rodda, W. H. *Property and Liability Insurance*. Englewood Cliffs, New Jersey: Prentice-Hall, Inc., 1966.

Part 7

Quantitative Controls

Prologue to Part 7

Quantitative Controls

Control and planning are two important functions of management. In order to make intelligent decisions involving these responsibilities, all pertinent data are first assembled and evaluated. In most instances information that is quantitative in nature proves to be of maximum value.

Accounting provides figures that reflect an historical record of a firm's profit-seeking activities. Chapter 23 describes how the business transactions of a firm are assigned a dollar value and are subsequently summarized in periodic financial statements. Stress is placed on the managerial uses of such information for purposes of control and planning rather than on accounting techniques.

Electronic data processing has become commonplace in both large and small businesses. Consequently, students of business need to understand both the values and limitations of computers. Chapter 24 describes in relatively simple terms how these machines work. Their value to management is emphasized.

The last two chapters in this part deal with the past and the future as related to control and planning. Chapter 25 on business statistics and reports explains how facts and figures are collected, measured, and presented to management. It includes many of the more common types of statistical measurements useful to businesses. Both forecasting and budgeting, the topics covered in Chapter 26, look into the future with a view to controlling operations and reducing the risks management must take in making decisions affecting the firm.

Chapter 23

Accounting and Financial Statements

Even though accounting deals with figures rather than a product, it also involves an input and an output. The input consists of the dollar amounts of business transactions, and this encompasses almost all financial activities of the firm. The output consists of financial statements and other data useful to management in making decisions. *Business transactions* embrace such activities of a firm as making sales for credit or cash, meeting payrolls, paying for goods and services, and a wide variety of related events, some of which recur frequently while others are of a nonrecurring nature. Regardless of the volume of transactions—and in many businesses the number runs into the thousands daily—each one must be processed in order that its effect on operating results will be reflected in the financial statements.

Accounting may be defined as the recording, classifying, and summarizing of business transactions, and interpreting this compiled information. These four sequential steps require that a dollar-and-cents value must be assigned to each business transaction before it can be recorded. For example, the signing of a labor contract which grants a union a wage increase could be classified as a business transaction. The accounting effects, however, would not be reflected until covered employees were paid larger amounts for their services. Fortunately this limitation of accounting is relatively unimportant since a monetary value can immediately be assigned to most business transactions.

IMPORTANCE OF ACCOUNTING

A satisfactory accounting system is an absolute necessity for a successful business; otherwise management will not know where it stands financially and cannot make intelligent decisions that affect its profit-making activities. Some of the information that an accounting system provides is basic, such as cash and bank balances, accounts receivable and accounts payable, and the value of its inventory. Other figures show such details as interest paid for borrowed money, the cost of new equipment purchased, expenditures for advertising, and a variety of other dollar-and-cents facts about the business. Because of the relevance of such information, it is probably safe to say that not very many management decisions are reached without some reference to accounting data.

Outsiders, too, are interested in the information available when adequate accounting records are maintained. Commercial banks, investment banking companies, insurance companies writing fidelity and surety bonds, and credit rating firms are avid readers and interpreters of a firm's financial statements. Suppliers who have extended credit are interested in the financial strength of the companies that owe them on open account as are investors who own shares of stock in corporations. Governmental units at all levels are also concerned, partly because some taxes, such as the federal corporate income tax, are levied on the basis of accounting figures. It seems obvious that there is considerable substance to the claim that accounting is the language of business, which means it is the device used by firms to communicate with interested parties.

TYPES OF ACCOUNTANTS

In a very small firm the owner may keep such records as are maintained, he may employ a part-time accountant, or he may use an outside bookkeeping service. In large enterprises the accounting department is organized into numerous functions and each of these is headed by a specialist. As a result, *industrial accountants* may become known by such terms as cost accountant, tax accountant, systems accountant, internal auditor, or budget accountant. Figure 23-1 shows the organization of the accounting department of a large manufacturing concern.

In addition to the broad classification of industrial accountants, other categories are public accountants and governmental accountants. *Public accountants* are independent firms who offer their services to the public. If they have complied with the state rules governing certification, which includes passing a rigorous examination, they may designate themselves

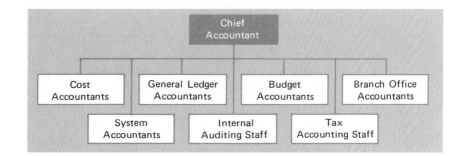

Figure 23-1

Organization Chart for an Accounting Department

as *certified public accountants*. CPA's, as they are generally known, audit the books and perform various services for the clients who employ them. Their work is professional in nature and requires ability and integrity of a very high order. *Governmental accountants* are those employed by local, state, and national governmental units including such federal agencies as the Federal Bureau of Investigation, the Bureau of Internal Revenue, and the General Accounting Office.

ACCOUNTING PROCEDURES

The first step in accounting procedures, as noted earlier, is the recording of business transactions. Many small firms rely on pen-and-ink records, but the use of adding machines, cash registers, and other types of business machines is widespread. More recently, electronic data processing has made rapid strides in assuming the burden of recording business transactions as well as classifying and summarizing these more rapidly than was formerly possible. Without regard for the specific techniques used, which are influenced by the types of mechanical aids employed, summarized or individual transactions are entered in some form of a *journal*, a book of original entry in which transactions are recorded in chronological order.

The next step is a procedure by which the transactions are classified. By a process known as *posting*, the entries in the journal are transferred to a *ledger*, which is a book of accounts. Each account brings together all transactions affecting one item, such as cash or sales. At stated periods— monthly, quarterly, semiannually, or annually—the ledger accounts are totaled or balanced; these provide the basic information for financial statements.

The third stage in accounting procedures, summarizing, is provided by constructing financial statements. The balance sheet and the income statement are the principal ones prepared at regular intervals. Since they are the result of, and the reason for, much of the work done by an accounting department, they will be examined in some detail in this chapter. In connection with the preparation of a balance sheet, a capital statement is usually prepared for firms operating as sole proprietorships or partnerships; and the comparable presentation for a corporation is a retained earnings statement. When preparing an income statement, a business engaged in manufacturing also makes use of a cost of goods manufactured schedule. Many progressive firms frequently compile a statement of source and application of funds. All of these supplementary statements will be defined and discussed briefly before the last step in accounting procedures—interpretation—is explained and illustrated.

THE BALANCE SHEET

A *balance sheet* lists the assets, the liabilities, and the capital of a firm as of the close of business on a specific date, which is frequently the end of a month, a quarter, or a year. As explained in Chapter 18, assets consist of the property owned and used in the operation of the firm, such as land, buildings, merchandise, office equipment, and cash. Some of these assets may have been acquired by buying on open account or by the use of borrowed funds secured from a bank or from the proceeds of a bond issue. Until such time as these debts are paid, creditors have a claim against the property owned by the business. The rights of these creditors in the assets of the business are known as *liabilities*, which may be either current or fixed. The remaining and secondary claim against the assets, which is the right of the owner or owners in the property, is the capital, an amount which was identified in Chapter 19 as equity capital. The word capital, when used in this sense, is also called net worth, *proprietorship*, or *owner's equity*. For corporations the term *stockholders'* or *shareholders' equity* is frequently used.

Because all of the assets of a business are subject to claims by creditors and owners, it follows that the total value of the property owned equals the total rights of creditors and owners. For example, Arnold Richardson buys a radio business for $25,000. Of this amount he is able to invest $20,000 of his own funds and borrows the remaining $5,000 at his bank. His balance sheet after purchase shows assets, $25,000; liabilities, $5,000; and capital, $20,000. This information can be expressed as an equation, as follows:

$$\text{Assets} = \text{Liabilities} + \text{Capital}$$
$$\$25,000 = \$5,000 + \$20,000$$

The truism that assets equal liabilities plus capital is known as the *balance sheet equation*. By transposing the liabilities, the equation can be made to read, assets minus liabilities equal capital. This equation stresses the fact that a business has an entity of its own in showing the amount of its obligation to its owner. Published balance sheets most frequently use the first formula and show equal totals for assets and for liabilities and capital combined.

Figure 23-2 shows a balance sheet for a sole proprietor, A. R. Morgan, who owns and operates a retail furniture store. Note that the balance sheet items not only have been grouped according to the three major classifications—assets, liabilities, and capital—but also have been divided into subclassifications. Assets have four classifications: (1) current assets, (2) plant assets, (3) investments, and (4) intangible assets. Liabilities are classified into: (1) current liabilities and (2) long-term liabilities.

Current Assets

Cash and other assets that will be converted into cash or consumed within a short time are current assets. The maximum length of time for conversion is usually one year, and it is expected that this process will take place in the normal operations of the business. If merchandise is sold on open book account or for notes, it is reasonable to assume that the accounts receivable or notes receivable will be collected in less than one year from the date of the sale. Such items as office supplies on hand will be used within a year and insurance currently prepaid will expire in the months ahead.

Plant Assets

Assets that possess a degree of permanence extending beyond one year and which are intended for use rather than for sale are known as *plant assets* or fixed assets. Some assets, such as automobiles or trucks, may not last more than three to five years, while land for a building site may last forever. Although such assets are sold when they are no longer useful to the firm, they are not purchased for this purpose.

With the exception of land, plant assets deteriorate in value with use and the passage of time. Because it is desirable to show the original cost of the asset as well as its reduced value year by year, two separate figures are required. The accumulated depreciation is increased each year until

MODERN FURNITURE MART
Balance Sheet
December 31, 1972

Assets

Current assets:
Cash		$ 7,200
Accounts receivable	$15,400	
Less allowance for doubtful accounts . .	2,800	12,600
Merchandise inventory		46,350
Store supplies		810
Office supplies		640
Prepaid insurance		480
Total current assets		$ 68,080

Plant assets:
Store equipment	$14,750	
Less accumulated depreciation	5,900	$ 8,850
Office equipment	$12,400	
Less accumulated depreciation	4,960	7,440
Building	$61,500	
Less accumulated depreciation	12,300	49,200
Land	5,000	
Total plant assets		70,490

Investments:
Stock in Toolcraft, Inc.		3,000

Intangible assets:
Goodwill		2,500

Total assets $144,070

Liabilities

Current liabilities:
Notes payable	$ 6,000	
Accounts payable	14,600	
Taxes payable	1,280	
Total current liabilities		$ 21,880

Long-term liabilities:
Mortgage payable		30,000

Total liabilities . . . . $ 51,880

Capital

A. R. Morgan, capital   92,190

Total liabilities and capital $144,070

Figure 23-2

Balance Sheet

it may equal the value of the asset from which it is subtracted. At that time, if the estimate of the useful life of the asset was accurate, the balance sheet value will be zero and the asset will be discarded. Scrap values are taken into account when warranted.

Investments

Stocks or bonds of other organizations that are purchased with the intent to hold them for income or for other reasons are known as *investments*. It is unusual for a sole proprietorship, such as that owned by A. R. Morgan, to have investments, although many corporations acquire assets of this character in order to cement trade relationships or to secure voting control of another corporation.

Intangible Assets

Assets in the nature of a legal right or some other value without physical substance that have been purchased are classified as *intangible assets*. The most common of these is *goodwill*, which is the price paid for a firm over and above the net fair value of its assets over its liabilities because of the good name, trade connections, or earning capacity of an operating business. Patents purchased by a firm may be valuable for the 17 years for which they are granted by the United States Patent Office. Copyrights are another example of an intangible asset with a somewhat longer life as they are granted for 28 years and can be renewed for a like period of time.

Current Liabilities

Debts that are owed and payable within a short time are classified as current liabilities. Amounts owed to trade creditors, banks, employees, and other debts of a similar nature are common current liabilities. For example, purchases of merchandise on open book account are due in 30, 60, or 90 days depending upon the terms of the transaction. As in the case of current assets, the usual rule is that liabilities that will come due and be payable within one year after the date of the balance sheet should be included under this heading.

Long-Term Liabilities

Long-term debts that will not be due for several years are called *long-term* or fixed *liabilities*. Money borrowed by selling bonds, long-term notes, or by assuming a mortgage payable results in liabilities classified in this section of the balance sheet. Adding the long-term liabilities to the current liabilities gives a total that represents that amount of the capital employed by a firm in its business that is secured from outsiders.

Capital

If a business is being operated as a sole proprietorship, a single line suffices to show the amount of capital at the date of the balance sheet. Supporting this figure is a *Capital Statement* that shows changes which have taken place since the date of the last balance sheet. Figure 23-3 presents this information for the Modern Furniture Mart.

MODERN FURNITURE MART
Capital Statement
For Year Ended December 31, 1972

Capital, January 1, 1972		$88,440
Net income for the year	$13,940	
Less withdrawals	10,190	
Net increase in capital		3,750
Capital, December 31, 1972		$92,190

Figure 23-3

Capital Statement

If a business firm is operating under a partnership agreement, the interests of the partners are shown in the capital section of the balance sheet. For example, if Carter, Nelson, and Prince own and operate a business under the name of the Carter Drug Company, the capital section of the balance sheet for this firm might appear as follows:

C. D. Carter, capital	$ 68,400
H. H. Nelson, capital	35,250
S. R. Prince, capital	19,800
Total capital	$123,450

The supporting capital statement for a partnership would be similar to the one shown for the Modern Furniture Mart in Figure 23-3 with the exception that it would show changes that had taken place during the year in each partner's capital account.

In the case of a business organized as a corporation, the individual interest of each stockholder is not shown on the balance sheet even though the company may have only three or four owners. Instead, dollar values for the different types of stock outstanding are shown as well as for paid-in surplus and the amount of retained earnings. Frequently only two items comprise the capital section: the original investment on the part of the stockholders in the common stock of the corporation and the sum of past earnings that have not been distributed to the owners. For a corporation with only two capital accounts, the stockholders' equity section of the balance sheet might appear as follows:

Capital stock	$25,000
Retained earnings	8,385
Total stockholders' equity	$33,385

In much the same manner that a capital statement supplements a balance sheet for a sole proprietorship or partnership, a *Retained Earnings Statement* presents details of changes that have taken place in this account during the year. Figure 23-4 on page 562 shows such a statement for a corporation that, as can be seen from dividend payments, has both preferred and common stock outstanding.

THE INCOME STATEMENT

The statement that summarizes the incomes and expenses of a business for a stated period of time is the *income statement*. It shows such information as the total merchandise purchased and sold, expenses incurred, and miscellaneous sources of income. Other names given to this statement are the *profit and loss statement, operating statement, income summary,* and *income account.*

The income statement is dynamic, whereas the balance sheet is static. This means that the income statement reflects summaries of operations over a period of time such as a year, six months, a quarter, or a month, while the balance sheet is a picture of the business at a given instant of time, usually the close of business on the date of the balance sheet. Both statements are prepared at the same time, and the net income or loss shown on the income statement is reflected in the capital section of the balance sheet.

```
                    INGERSOLL STEEL CORPORATION
                    Retained Earnings Statement
                  For Year Ended December 31, 1971


Balance, January 1, 1971 . . . . . . . . . . .  $12,486,750

Net income for the year  . . . . . . . . . .      3,190,486

    Total . . . . . . . . . . . . . . . . . .  $15,677,236        Figure 23-4

Less cash dividends:

    Preferred stock . . . . . .     $   300,000

    Common stock  . . . . . . .       1,200,000     1,500,000

Balance, December 31, 1971 . . . . . . . . . .  $14,177,236
```

Retained Earnings Statement

Figure 23-5 presents an income statement for the Modern Furniture Mart, whose balance sheet has already been illustrated. Note that the income statement is divided into sections for the grouping of like items, namely: (1) revenue from sales, (2) cost of merchandise sold, (3) gross profit on sales, (4) operating expenses, (5) net income from operations, (6) other income and other expense, and (7) net income.

Revenue from Sales

The major source of income for most firms is the sale of merchandise, and this is the first section on the income statement. The *sales* figure includes the amounts paid by customers and the amounts they have agreed to pay if sales have been made on account. It is a total for the year or for a shorter period of time if statements are prepared more often. From this total must be subtracted the value of the merchandise returned or reductions in price granted following complaints by the customer as to quality or quantity received. The resulting figure is called *net sales*.

```
                        MODERN FURNITURE MART
                          Income Statement
                   For Year Ended December 31, 1972


Revenue from sales:
  Sales . . . . . . . . . . . . . . . . . . . . .    $232,400
  Less sales returns and allowances . . . . . . . .     5,100
  Net sales . . . . . . . . . . . . . . . . . . . .                $227,300

Cost of merchandise sold:
  Merchandise inventory, January 1, 1972 . . . . . .  $ 51,200
  Purchases . . . . . . . . . . . . . . . . .   $152,210
  Less:  Purchases returns & allowances   $6,840
         Purchases discount . . . . . .    2,570     9,410
  Net purchases . . . . . . . . . . . . . . . . . .   142,800
  Cost of merchandise available for sale . . . . . .  $194,000
  Less merchandise inventory, December 31, 1972 . . .   46,350
    Cost of merchandise sold . . . . . . . . . . . .               147,650

Gross profit on sales . . . . . . . . . . . . . . .                $ 79,650

Operating expenses:
  Selling expenses:
    Salesmen's salaries . . . . . . . . . .   $ 23,900
    Advertising expense . . . . . . . . . .      8,100
    Store supplies expense . . . . . . . . .     1,240
    Depreciation expense--store equipment  . .    1,475
    Miscellaneous selling expenses . . . . . .    2,805
      Total selling expenses . . . . . . . . . . . .  $ 37,520

  General expenses:
    Office salaries . . . . . . . . . . .     $ 12,240
    Office supplies expense . . . . . . . . .       875
    Insurance expense . . . . . . . . . . . .     3,200
    Uncollectible accounts expense . . . . . .    1,230
    Taxes expense . . . . . . . . . . . . . .     3,455
    Depreciation expense--office equipment  . .    1,240
    Depreciation expense--building . . . . . .    2,460
    Miscellaneous general expense . . . . . .     1,980
      Total general expenses . . . . . . . . . . . .  $ 26,680
  Total operating expenses . . . . . . . . . . . . .                64,200

Net income from operations . . . . . . . . . . . . .               $ 15,450

Other income:
  Dividends on stock . . . . . . . . . . . . . . . .  $    300

Other expense:
  Interest expense . . . . . . . . . . . . . . . . .     1,810       1,510

Net income  . . . . . . . . . . . . . . . . . . . .                $ 13,940
```

Figure 23-5
Income Statement

Cost of Merchandise Sold

The *cost of merchandise sold* represents the purchase price of the merchandise that was sold by the firm during the year. The formula used for arriving at the cost figure is usually the one shown on the income statement. Merchandise on hand at the beginning of the year plus purchases, adjusted for returns and allowances and purchase discount, gives the total cost of all the merchandise that might have been sold. Subtracting the inventory figure at the end of the year from this total results in the cost of the merchandise sold.

The beginning and ending inventories are determined by a physical count of each item in stock and a valuation of these quantities. The purchases of merchandise made during the year can be secured from the ledger account in which have been posted all of the invoices covering the various shipments received. Returns and allowances follow the same pattern as indicated above for sales.

A. R. Morgan, as a retail furniture merchant, purchased all of the merchandise that he sold. Manufacturing firms, on the other hand, produce their goods from raw materials purchased. In this event the line titled "Purchases" in the income statement would be replaced with "Cost of Goods Manufactured, Schedule No. 1." An illustration of a *Schedule of Cost of Goods Manufactured* is shown in Figure 23-6. Note that inventories of raw materials and of goods in the process of manufacture are shown, and that the nature of the manufacturing expenses is somewhat different from operating expenses.

Gross Profit on Sales

The difference found by subtracting the cost of merchandise sold from the net sales is termed the *gross profit on sales*. If there were no expenses in connection with the sales, gross profit would be the amount of net income earned. For business firms that have substantial operating expenses, the gross profit on sales must be from one third to two thirds of the total sales figure. In retail circles the gross profit on sales is known as the *gross margin* and reflects the average overall markup percentage on goods sold.

Operating Expenses

Payrolls for salesclerks and office employees, supplies consumed, depreciation on plant or fixed assets, advertising costs, taxes, and expired

DONOVAN MANUFACTURING CORPORATION
Schedule No. 1 - Cost of Goods Manufactured
For Year Ended December 31, 1972

Work in process inventory, January 1, 1972			$ 29,000
Raw materials:			
Inventory, January 1, 1972		$ 61,000	
Purchases	$184,900		
Less purchases returns & allowances . . .	2,500		
Net purchases		182,400	
Total cost of materials available for use		$243,400	
Less inventory, December 31, 1972		70,000	
Cost of materials placed in production		$173,400	
Direct labor		152,000	
Factory overhead:			
Indirect labor	$ 14,800		
Repairs	12,000		
Heat, light, and power	19,600		
Depreciation--machinery & equipment . . .	25,350		
Factory supplies expense	10,400		
Patents expense	7,250		
Insurance expense	3,600		
Total factory overhead		$ 93,000	
Total manufacturing costs			418,400
Total work in process during year			$447,400
Less work in process inventory, December 31, 1972 . . .			34,800
Cost of goods manufactured			$412,600

Figure 23-6

Schedule of Cost of Goods Manufactured

insurance are examples of *operating expenses.* All of the costs that a business firm incurs in its normal operations are grouped under this classification. Individual items are shown so that the owner or owners can note the amount spent for each purpose. If certain expenses appear too large, as brought out by comparison with previous income statements, steps can be taken to correct this situation.

Operating expenses are usually subdivided into selling expenses and general or administrative expenses. *Selling expenses* are those that are incurred as a direct result of the sales activities of the firm. Such items as salaries of salesclerks, advertising, store supplies used, depreciation on store equipment, and delivery costs are examples of selling expenses. The advantage of segregating these from general expenses is that the total for one year compared with the total for another year may be significant. If selling expenses have increased in total, it is then possible to analyze the individual items to locate the cause or causes.

Office salaries, rent, taxes, insurance, office supplies used, depreciation on buildings and office equipment, and the cost of bad debts resulting from account sales that prove uncollectible are examples of *general expenses*. They are costs connected with the general operation of the business. If an expense is difficult to allocate between the selling and general classification, such as fire insurance on merchandise inventory, it is usually assigned to the general expense classification.

Net Income from Operations

The difference found by subtracting the total of the operating expenses from the gross profit on sales is known as the *net income from operations*. If there are no other items of income and expense, this figure is also the net income, but most businesses do have nonoperating incomes and costs. In some instances the total operating expenses may exceed the gross profit on sales. Should this occur, the difference between the two amounts would be known as the *net loss from operations*.

Other Income and Other Expense

Most firms secure some income and incur some expenses of a financial, rather than an operating, character. These are classified as *other income* and *other expense* and are added to or subtracted from the net income from operations. Other titles used for these sections are nonoperating income and expense and financial income and expense. The most common items are interest received and paid on notes, mortgages, and bonds.

Net Income

The final figure on an income statement and the one that represents the results of all operations of a business, both operating and nonoperating, is called the *net income* or *net loss*. It is, naturally, the most interesting single figure on an income statement. Although the amounts used in arriving at the final result are of interest to those connected with the management of the firm, others are more concerned with the amount of net income or net loss.

Income statements for unincorporated and incorporated businesses are identical with the single exception of the determination of the net income figure for corporations. As legal entities they must pay income taxes on the amount shown on the last line of an income statement for proprietorships and partnerships, assuming that operations have been profitable. Consequently, an income statement for a corporation ends as follows:

Net income before income taxes	$225,000
Income taxes	108,000
Net income	$117,000

THE STATEMENT OF SOURCE AND APPLICATION OF FUNDS

A recent development in statements prepared from accounting data and published in the annual report to stockholders is the *Statement of Source and Application of Funds*. It shows the major sources of the flow of funds (additions to current assets) into the business and the uses made of such funds. It is usually prepared on the same date as that of the balance sheet, and covers the same period of time as the income statement.

Current assets (circulating capital) are constantly subject to change, and the same can be said for current liabilities. The difference between the total current assets and total current liabilities is called working capital. A statement of source and application of funds does not detail the increases and decreases in each current asset and current liability account, although this information is frequently shown separately. Rather, the net difference between the working capital at the beginning and end of the period under review becomes the residual figure of the statement. If more funds have been received than used, the working capital will have increased; and if more funds have been used than received, the working capital will be a smaller figure.

As shown in Figure 23-7, the customary major source of funds is net income. Next in order is commonly the total of depreciation charges. These have reduced net income but did not require an outlay of cash during the current year. Other sources might include the sale of plant assets, such as unneeded land, or the receipt of cash from a bond issue. The application of funds of profitable corporations usually includes dividend payments, the purchase of plant assets, and, possibly, the reduction of long-term debt. All increases and decreases in noncurrent assets and liabilities, in the capital accounts, and the net change in working capital, are likely to reflect sources and applications of funds.

Closely allied to sources and applications of funds is a relatively recent concept known as cash flow analysis. *Cash flow* consists of the net income of a firm plus all expense charges that did not require an outlay of funds minus any income that did not generate cash. The figure that usually results—earnings plus depreciation and depletion allowances—is an approximation of the cash received during the period from internal operations. Funds received from external sources come from borrowing and equity financing.

```
                    CARPENTER CORPORATION
         Statement of Source and Application of Funds
               For Year Ended December 31, 1971


Source:

  Net income for year  . . . . . . . . . . . $2,189,000
  Depreciation charges on plant assets . . .    432,000
  Sale of warehouse  . . . . . . . . . . . .    120,000   $2,741,000

Application:

  Cash dividends paid  . . . . . . . . . . . $1,200,000
  Purchase of equipment  . . . . . . . . . .  1,108,000
  Retirement of serial bonds . . . . . . . .    250,000    2,558,000

Increase in working capital  . . . . . . . .             $   183,000
```

Figure 23-7

Statement of Source and Application of Funds

For financial managers cash flow is useful in determining the ability of the company to pay dividends, to purchase additional machinery and equipment, and to retire bonded debt without recourse to bank borrowing or the sale of additional securities. In some industries, moreover, various companies may use different accounting techniques which make their reported earnings noncomparable. Adjusting incomes to an approximate cash basis may aid in providing a better comparison in such a case. Cash flow is usually a considerably higher figure than net income and, when published on a per-share basis, may lead to stockholder dissatisfaction with the size of dividend checks.

INTERPRETATION OF FINANCIAL STATEMENTS

After the balance sheet, income statement, and any other desired statements are prepared, the fourth and last step in the work of an accountant, that of interpretation, can be performed. The fact that a business may or may not have been operated at a profit is of vital concern, but this one figure fails to tell the whole story. For example, a bank may be willing to extend a loan to a firm that has a strong financial structure despite recent operating losses. Judicious use of such borrowed funds might correct conditions so that future business operations would be profitable. On the other hand, a firm may be headed for financial trouble even though operating profitably.

By means of ratios, percentages, and other devices, it is possible to analyze the financial status of a company. The directions such an analysis may take are varied and extensive. The current balance sheet offers definite possibilities in itself, and comparisons can be made with previous balance sheets and also with the balance sheets of competing companies. For example, the balance sheet of the Modern Furniture Mart illustrated in Figure 23-2 on page 558 shows that the merchandise inventory comprises 68.1 percent of the current assets ($46,350 ÷ $68,080 = .681), and that 64.0 percent of the funds used in the business were contributed by the owner ($92,190 ÷ $144,070 = .64). A similar analysis of the income statement could be made with 100% being assigned to the net sales figure. There are also a number of important relationships between the two statements, and the other statements and schedules offer analytical possibilities in and of themselves or in conjunction with the balance sheet and the income statement.

Some of the most useful techniques for analyzing financial statements are described below. They are: (1) current ratio, (2) acid-test ratio, (3) working capital, (4) number of day's sales in receivables, (5) turnover of merchandise inventory, (6) ratio of ownership to debt, (7) rate of net income on capital, (8) rate of net income on sales, (9) rate of net income on total assets, and (10) earned per share of common stock. With the obvious exception of the last item, these have been restricted to the statements of the Modern Furniture Mart illustrated in Figure 23-2 on page 558 and Figure 23-5 on page 563. Consequently, no attempt has been made to show trends, to contrast the efficiency of Morgan's firm with any of his competitors, or to rely on any data not contained in a single balance sheet and income statement.

Current Ratio

The ratio of current assets to current liabilities is the *current ratio*. It is found by dividing the current assets by the current liabilities. This ratio is very important to the owners and to short-term creditors because the current assets constitute a source of funds to pay current liabilities. An acceptable minimum ratio is usually 2 to 1, which takes into consideration the fact that current assets sometimes shrink in value whereas current liabilities do not.

Reference to the balance sheet of A. R. Morgan shows that on December 31, 1972, his current assets totaled $68,080 and his current liabilities $21,880. The calculation for his current ratio is as follows:

$$\frac{68,080}{21,880} = 3.1 \text{ to } 1$$

Acid-Test Ratio

The *acid-test* or *quick ratio* is a refinement of the current ratio in that it determines the ability of a firm to meet its current debt on very short notice. It recognizes the fact that the conversion of merchandise inventory into cash takes more time than is true for other current assets. The formula is to divide the total cash and receivables by the current liabilities, and an acceptable minimum is 1 to 1. If the firm owns marketable securities purchased on a temporary basis, these may be added to the cash and receivables.

The balance sheet of A. R. Morgan shows that he owns cash and accounts receivable totaling $19,800 and that his current liabilities total $21,880. His acid-test ratio is computed as follows:

$$\frac{19,800}{21,880} = .9 \text{ to } 1$$

Whereas the current ratio was considerably in excess of the minimum, the above ratio falls short of the 1 to 1 requirement. This may indicate a situation that should be corrected by a more rapid turnover of the inventory; otherwise A. R. Morgan may not be able to meet maturities on his current debt.

Working Capital

As noted previously, the excess dollar value of the current assets over the current liabilities is the working capital of a firm. It should be large enough to absorb any possible shrinkages as inventories and receivables are converted into cash and still leave a comfortable margin to pay current liabilities as they mature. In the case of A. R. Morgan, the excess of $46,200 ($68,080–$21,880) should provide adequate protection.

Number of Days' Sales in Receivables

A measure of the efficiency of collecting amounts owed the business and of the firm's policies on extending credit can be computed by determining the number of days' sales in receivables resulting from charge sales. The Modern Furniture Mart shows net sales of $227,300 for the year that, when divided by 366, gives a daily average sales figure of $621.04. Dividing the total receivables of $15,400 by this figure shows that 24.8 days of sales were uncollected at the balance sheet date ($15,400 ÷ 621.04 = 24.8).

Assuming that the credit terms provide for payment by the tenth of the month following the charge and that the middle of a month is the average date for credit sales made during the month, it could be expected that a balance sheet would show a minimum of 15 days of sales in receivables. Since it can hardly be expected that all accounts will be paid when due, having no more than 24.8 days of sales represented by receivables probably indicates that Morgan is doing a good job in this area.

Turnover of Merchandise Inventory

A retail establishment must always be alert to "turn over" its stock of salable goods as rapidly as possible; in other words, to sell present stock before it loses its maximum value. The frequency with which this move is accomplished is called the *inventory turnover* and is a measure of efficiency.

The preferred method of determining the turnover of merchandise inventory is to divide the cost of merchandise sold by the average inventory. In the case of A. R. Morgan, only the beginning and ending inventories can be averaged because other inventory figures are not available.

The information available in Figure 23-5 on page 563 shows a merchandise inventory on January 1 of $51,200 and on December 31 of $46,350. These two amounts average $48,775, the cost of goods sold is shown as $147,650, and the turnover calculation is as follows:

$$\frac{147,650}{48,775} = 3.0 \text{ turns}$$

For a retail grocery store this would be a poor turnover, since from 5 to 10 turnovers each year are secured by efficient firms. A. R. Morgan, however, operates a furniture store, and the figure of 3.0 is very good. Most businesses of this type are not able to turn over their stock more than from 1 to 4 times a year.

Ratio of Ownership to Debt

Practically every business is financed by a combination of funds secured from the owners and by borrowed capital. The ratio of ownership to debt shows the relative proportion of capital secured from the two sources. A mark of conservative financing is substantial ownership on the part of the proprietors or stockholders. This means that the ownership equity is large enough to absorb even extensive and continued losses, and there is less danger of insolvency.

The balance sheet of A. R. Morgan shows total liabilities of $51,880 and total capital of $92,190. The ratio is found by dividing the ownership equity by the creditors' equity as follows:

$$\frac{92,190}{51,880} = 1.8 \text{ to } 1$$

This is a fairly conservative ratio, for A. R. Morgan has contributed almost two times as much capital as he has borrowed. (Percentagewise, as noted earlier, the figure is 64.0.) Many businesses use a larger amount of debt capital, with railroad and public utilities frequently showing a 1 to 1 ratio.

Rate of Net Income on Capital

The reason an owner invests his own funds in a business is to secure a return on his investment. Because of the risks involved, this rate should be higher than if a similar amount were invested in conservative securities. Furthermore, in the case of a sole proprietorship, the net income also includes the personal service factor. Despite the fact that an owner may devote full time to his business, he does not include a salary for himself as one of his operating expenses.

A. R. Morgan's investment in his business was $88,440 at the beginning of the year and $92,190 at the end of the year. An average of these two amounts is $90,315. (It would be preferable to compute a monthly average to determine the investment throughout the year.) The net income was $13,940. This return divided by the average investment shows a yield of 15.4 percent.

$$\frac{13,940}{90,315} = .154 = 15.4\%$$

Rate of Net Income on Sales

If a business is able to sell a large volume of goods on a small investment, the net return on each dollar's worth of goods sold can be very small, perhaps as low as one cent on the dollar. This is the principle under which chain stores and supermarkets operate. If the turnover of total assets (the number of times each dollar value of assets is converted into a sales dollar in one year) is low, however, the net return on each sales dollar must be substantial if a satisfactory return is to be secured.

The net sales made by the Modern Furniture Mart in 1972 totaled $227,300, as shown in Figure 23-5 on page 563, and the net income was $13,940. Since the furniture business does not lend itself to a high volume of sales on a low investment, the firm's return of 6.1 percent on its sales must be considered satisfactory.

$$\frac{13,940}{227,300} = .061 = 6.1\%$$

Rate of Net Income on Total Assets

In attempting to compare the cost of capital with the rate of earnings on assets purchased by borrowing or securing additional funds from owners, it is important to determine the percentage of net income on the assets employed in a business. The total assets of the Modern Furniture Mart, as shown in Figure 23-2 on page 558, were $144,070 on which the firm earned $13,940. The rate of net income of 9.7 percent must certainly have been in excess of the cost of any borrowed capital used as well as demonstrating a profitable use of the total capital employed in the business.

$$\frac{13,940}{144,070} = .097 = 9.7\%$$

Earned Per Share of Common Stock

A dollar-and-cents figure that is frequently shown in the printed annual reports of corporations and widely used by security analysts is the earnings per share of common stock. No such computation can be made for the Modern Furniture Mart, a sole proprietorship, and the same situation exists for all partnerships. Although a balance sheet and an income statement for a corporation were not illustrated, an example of calculating the earned per share of common stock may be illustrated for the Ingersoll Steel Corporation by (a) referring to Figure 23-4 on page 562 and (b) assuming that it has 800,000 shares of common stock outstanding.

The formula for computing the amount earned per share of common stock is simple. From the net income of a corporation for a year, the amount of the dividends paid on the preferred stock, if any, must be subtracted. The balance is divided by the number of shares of common stock outstanding, which may have to be averaged if there were several changes during the year. For the Ingersoll Steel Corporation, subtracting the $300,000 paid to the preferred stockholders from the $3,190,486 net income for the year leaves $2,890,486 available for the common stockholders. The calculation for the earned per share of common stock is shown below.

$$\frac{\$2,890,486}{800,000} = \$3.60 \text{ per share}$$

BUSINESS TERMS

QUESTIONS FOR DISCUSSION AND ANALYSIS

1. Management decisions are frequently reached after recourse to the facts available from accounting data. What types of problems would be involved? Give specific examples.

2. Certified public accountants comprise the only business group generally accepted as belonging to a profession. Why is this so?

3. For any business firm, is the total assets figure in the balance sheet an accurate dollar value of its gross worth? Why or why not?

4. If a firm has quadrupled in size exclusively by internal growth, could it have an account titled "goodwill" on its books? Explain.

5. Are the current and long-term liabilities as shown on a balance sheet accurate as to the amounts owed?

6. Items shown on an income statement are larger when the statement covers a year rather than a quarter, but this situation usually does not apply to a balance sheet. Why?

7. Are all business expenses as shown in an income statement accurately stated?

8. What is the difference, if any, between cash flow and the total dollar value shown under "source" in a statement of source and application of funds?

9. In attempting to evaluate the efficiency of management, what single ratio, percent, or turnover would be most useful? Why?

10. The exact amounts that are shown in accounting data are susceptible of precise measurement. Are the resulting ratios, percents, and turnovers reliable? Explain.

PROBLEMS AND SHORT CASES

1. a. The following account balances were taken from the books and records of the Gordon Hardware Company on December 31, 1973. Prepare a balance sheet using Figure 23-2 on page 558 for guidance as to form and arrangement.

Cash	$ 3,275	Accumulated depreciation-	
Accounts receivable	4,500	office equipment	$ 1,500
Allowance for doubtful		Building	28,000
accounts	250	Accumulated depreciation-	
Merchandise inventory ...	26,000	building	1,400
Store and office supplies ..	1,500	Land	4,750
Prepaid insurance	1,000	Goodwill	5,000
Store equipment	9,250	Notes payable	11,500
Accumulated depreciation-		Accounts payable	4,550
store equipment	1,850	Taxes payable	840
Office equipment	7,500	Mortgage payable	15,000
		William Gordon, capital ..	53,885

b. The following additional account balances were taken from the books and records of the Gordon Hardware Company on December 31, 1973. Prepare an income statement using Figure 23-5 on page 563 for guidance as to form and arrangement.

Sales	$193,150	Depreciation expense-store	
Sales returns & allowances	1,075	equipment	$ 925
Merchandise inventory,		Office salaries	11,200
January 1, 1973	19,750	Uncollectible accounts	
Purchases	137,500	expense	135
Purchases returns &		Depreciation expense-	
allowances	1,480	office equipment	750
Purchases discount	1,735	Depreciation expense-	
Merchandise inventory,		building	700
December 31, 1973 ...	26,000	Taxes expense	2,760
Sales salaries	17,500	Insurance expense	1,900
Advertising expense	6,590	Miscellaneous office expense	780
Store supplies expense ...	1,365	Interest expense	980

c. The following additional account balances were taken from the books and records of the Gordon Hardware Company on December 31, 1973. Prepare a capital statement using Figure 23-3 on page 560 for guidance as to form and arrangement.

William Gordon, capital,		William Gordon,	
January 1, 1973	$47,430	drawing	$12,000

2. The following figures were taken from the statements of the Bowman Clothing Store, Incorporated, for the year ended December 31, 1973. Compute the (a) current ratio, (b) acid-test ratio, (c) working capital, (d) number of days' sales in receivables, (e) turnover of merchandise inventory, (f) ratio of ownership to debt, (g) rate of net income on capital, (h) rate of net income on sales, (i) rate of net income on total assets, and (j) earned per share of common stock.

Current assets	$140,000	Current liabilities	$ 50,000
Cash	18,600	Total liabilities	80,000
Receivables	36,400	Capital, January 1, 1973	206,000
Merchandise inventory,		Capital, December 31,	
January 1, 1973	55,000	1973	220,000
Merchandise inventory,		Net sales	625,000
December 31, 1973 ...	87,500	Cost of merchandise sold	400,000
Total assets	300,000	Net income	34,000

Number of shares of common stock outstanding = 200,000

3. The Kiddy Korner, a shop carrying a wide range of merchandise for pre-school age children, has been operating with moderate success in a well-patronized shopping center. The owners, Bill and Karen Otis, were contacted by a competitor who has been operating a similar store in a downtown location. The competitor expressed a desire to close out his business and offered to sell his entire inventory at a distressed price of $30,000. The Otises accepted the offer with terms of cash in 30 days. They were sure that the merchandise could be sold for more than $60,000 although their merchandise turnover of 2.3 indicated that it would take several months to liquidate the new stock.

The balance sheet of Kiddy Korner, prior to making this purchase, showed the following current assets and liabilities:

Current assets:	
Cash	$ 6,800
Accounts receivable	17,300
Merchandise inventory	22,500
Total current assets	$46,600
Current liabilities:	
Accounts payable	$11,100
Notes payable	10,000
Total current liabilities	$21,100

The purchase of the competitor's merchandise increased the above inventory figure to $52,500 and the accounts payable to $41,100. When the Otises approached their bank for an additional loan of $30,000, they were told that the funds could not be loaned because their current ratio was now less than 2 to 1, and the acid-test ratio was less than 1 to 1. Their banker agreed that the purchase was a good move but that bank policy prevented him from making the requested loan until the ratios met minimum standards.

Assuming that no other source of credit is available, what steps must the owners of Kiddy Korner take in the next 30 days?

SUGGESTED READINGS

Almanac of Business and Industrial Financial Ratios: 1971 Edition. Englewood Cliffs, New Jersey: Prentice-Hall, Inc., 1971.

Black, H. A., J. E. Champion, and R. G. Brown. *Accounting in Business Decisions*, Second Edition. Englewood Cliffs, New Jersey: Prentice-Hall, Inc., 1967. Parts I and II.

Foulke, R. A. *Practical Financial Statement Analysis*, Sixth Edition. New York: McGraw-Hill Book Company, 1968.

Johnson, G. L., and J. A. Gentry, Jr. *Finney and Miller's Principles of Accounting, Introductory*, 7th Edition. Englewood Cliffs, New Jersey: Prentice-Hall, Inc., 1970. Chapters 1-3, 28.

Kennedy, R. D., and S. Y. McMullen. *Financial Statements. Form, Analysis, and Interpretation*, Fifth Edition. Homewood, Illinois: Richard D. Irwin, Inc., 1968. Chapters 1-17.

Meigs, W. B., and C. E. Johnson. *Accounting: The Basis for Business Decisions*, Second Edition. New York: McGraw-Hill Book Company, 1967. Parts One and Eight.

Moore, C. L., and R. J. Jaedicke. *Managerial Accounting*, Second Edition. Cincinnati: South-Western Publishing Co., 1967. Parts I and II.

Niswonger, C. R., and P. E. Fess. *Accounting Principles*, Tenth Edition. Cincinnati: South-Western Publishing Co., 1969. Parts One and Ten.

Pyle, W. W., and J. A. White. *Fundamental Accounting Principles*, Fifth Edition. Homewood, Illinois: Richard D. Irwin, Inc., 1969. Chapters 1-3, 22, and 25.

Schattke, R. W., H. G. Jensen, and V. L. Bean. *Accounting*. Boston: Allyn and Bacon, Inc., 1969. Chapters 1-19.

Shrader, W. J., R. E. Malcolm, and J. J. Allingham. *Financial Accounting*. Homewood, Illinois: Richard D. Irwin, Inc., 1970. Chapter 13.

Wixon, R., and R. G. Cox. *Principles of Accounting*, Second Edition. New York: The Ronald Press Company, 1969. Parts I and VI.

Chapter 24

Data Processing

Man does very little without facts. A housewife cannot shop without facts. The retail store cannot stock and sell merchandise without facts, and neither can the wholesaler or the manufacturer. The people within each business firm rely on facts for the performance of their daily duties. Every employee is affected by his employer's *data processing system*, which is an organized method of gathering, storing, and processing data.

NATURE OF DATA PROCESSING

Data processing begins with the origination or collection of data and ends with the communication of information to the people who will use it. Between the gathering and reporting steps, the processing of data may involve classifying, sorting, calculating, summarizing, recording, storing, retrieving, and reproducing them. All data processing, whether done manually, mechanically, or electronically, is an application of one or more of these operations. If both mechanical and electronic equipment are employed, the term *automated data processing* (*ADP*) is applicable; if all processing is done electronically, the term *electronic data processing* (*EDP*) is more descriptive.

Data are the "raw" facts that must be converted into information. There are many classes of data, but the common ones used in business are those which identify individuals, locations, objects, quantities, and monetary values. The word "data" might be defined as all the facts that have been gathered, and the term "information" may then denote the particular facts management wants to know. *Information* is the result of data processing and may be made available to company personnel as operating documents, reports, and analyses of problems. The procedure used to convert data into information is *data processing*. The goal of an efficient system of data processing is to produce the maximum amount of useful information for people within an organization in minimum time at reasonable cost.

HISTORY AND IMPORTANCE OF DATA PROCESSING

Man's first data processing tools were simple—his fingers, pebbles, notched sticks, and knotted ropes. A primitive nomad could classify his wealth into cattle, sheep, and chickens. By using different colored cords for each class of livestock and by tying knots in the cords, he could count and record the number of animals he owned.

The evolution of these simple counting and recording devices into high-speed electronic data processing systems took several thousand years. During this time many inventions helped to pave the way to the present level of development; notable among these were the following:

The abacus	1860—Babbage's differential analyzer
1642—Pascal's calculator	1889—Hollerith's punched card equipment

The first truly electronic computer was made at the University of Pennsylvania in 1946; it was called ENIAC (Electronic Numerical Integrator and Calculator) and was conceived to produce mathematical tables required for the accurate firing of projectiles.

Within the past 25 years the growth of computer utilization has been phenomenal. In 1970 approximately 90,000 computers were in use, processing a wide range of data from that used in routine business operations to the calculations upon which astronauts depend. Computers will increasingly touch upon all areas of life from household chores to the professions of law, medicine, and education.

Without the computer the problem of organizing data to uncover facts was dependent on the time and personnel available. For example, in a single sale on account of one hammer, a saw, and an assortment of nails in a large multiproduct hardware store, about all that could be done was to record the transaction as a sale and to see that the customer was charged properly for the merchandise. To secure additional information about this sale, such as the type of hammer purchased to determine which hammers were selling the fastest, the salesman to whom credit for the sale should be given, and the determination quantitatively as to when hammers needed to be reordered based on a perpetual inventory, required additional time, more clerks, and more detailed records.

With the computer, once the system is established, the basic transaction of recording the sale can be made on a punched card. Additional information can be punched into the card letting the machine do the storing, reorganizing, sorting, and collecting the various other bits of information that are needed.

TYPES OF COMPUTERS

There are two general classes of computers, analog and digital. There are also hybrid computers that combine the features of both.

An *analog computer* carries out its calculations by making measurements. It deals with continuous quantities; it translates such physical conditions as temperature, pressure, angular position, or voltage into related mechanical or electrical quantities.

The operating principle of an analog computer may be compared to the operating principle of an ordinary weather thermometer. As the weather becomes cooler or warmer, the mercury in the glass tube rises or falls. The graduated marks on the tube permit the interpretation of the climatic changes. The expansion and contraction of the mercury has a relationship to the conditions of the weather. The thermometer provides a continuous measurement that is analogous to the climatic temperature. Other examples of devices that make analogous measurements include the slide rule and automobile speedometer.

Commonly, analog computers are used in industry to make scientific computations, to solve equations, and to control manufacturing processes. An analog computer is used by the National Aeronautics and Space Administration to measure the speed, direction, and trajectory of manned space vehicles.

Digital computers deal solely with numbers. Whereas analog computers measure physical relationships, digital computers count numbers. A digital computer differs from the ordinary rotary calculator in four ways:

1. It is faster; it can perform arithmetic operations according to directions at speeds measured in billionths of a second.
2. It has the capability to make logical decisions, such as comparing one number with another and determining which is larger.
3. It has the capacity to store data and have them available for almost instantaneous recall.
4. It can follow a set of written instructions.

The remainder of this chapter will be devoted to digital computers because they are the type most commonly used in business.

THE BINARY CODE

Digital computers process data fundamentally by a system of counting, a form of arithmetic that is different from the decimal number system used in everyday calculations. In the decimal system ten numbers are used, zero through nine; and if a digit is moved one space to the left and a zero is placed after it, the resulting number is ten times the original number.

The arithmetic of computers is based on the binary code. The *binary code* is a system of arithmetic based on two digits, zero and one. A digit, either the zero or the one, in the binary code, is called a *bit,* which is a contraction of "binary digit." If a binary digit is moved one space to the left and a zero is placed after it, the resulting number is two times the original number.

In the binary code the value of 1 depends on the position of the 1 in a binary number, reading from right to left. A digit doubles its value each time it moves one place farther to the left. For example, 0001 means 1; 0010 means 2; 0100 means 4; 1000 means 8, as shown in Figure 24-1.

The following compares decimal numbers with binary numbers:

Decimal	0	1	2	3	4	5	6	7	8	9
Binary	0	1	10	11	100	101	110	111	1000	1001

Using six binary digit positions, a code may be developed, a portion of which is illustrated in Table 24-1.

Letters of the alphabet are indicated by a 1 appearing in the fifth or sixth positions. Symbols are indicated by a 1 appearing in the fifth and sixth positions.

In a computer only four digits (right to left) are used for the expression of numbers (0-9). Each digit in a decimal number is expressed by four binary digits. For example:

	(hundreds)	(tens)	(units)	
142 equals	0001	0100	0010	

	(thousands)	(hundreds)	(tens)	(units)
4,283 equals	0100	0010	1000	0011

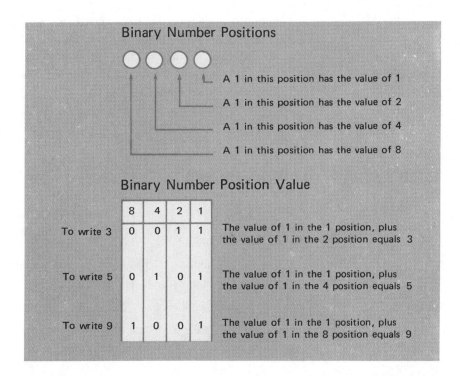

The Binary System

Figure 24-1

DEVELOPING A BINARY CODE

Decimal Number, Letter, or Symbol	Binary Code
1	000001
5	000101
9	001001
A	010001
B	010010
E	010101
I	011001
+	110000
$	111011
%	111100

Table 24-1

The binary code may seem awkward in comparison to the decimal system, but it fits the computer ideally. Each electronic circuit inside a computer can exist in only two possible states—the current is on or the current is off. Symbolically, the zero can indicate one state (off) and the 1 can indicate the other (on).

The binary code, thus, is the language into which data are translated. This language is then converted within the computer into electrical impulses.

COMPONENTS OF A COMPUTER

Basically a computer consists of the following five component sections or units: (1) input, (2) memory, (3) arithmetic, (4) control, and (5) output.

A schematic diagram of these five basic component units of a computer is shown in Figure 24-2.

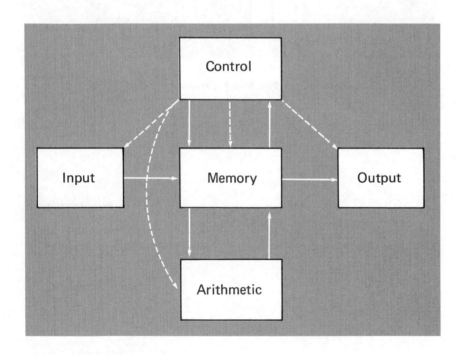

Figure 24-2

Schematic Diagram of Basic Digital Computer Components

Note: Solid lines indicate information flow; broken lines indicate control.

INPUT UNIT

The purpose of the *input unit* is to permit the computer operator to "communicate" with the computer. It carries out its function by translating codes from the external form in which the data are represented, such as holes in a punched card, to the internal form in which data are stored in the memory unit. The data thus translated and stored may be numbers used in calculations, instructions that tell the computer what to do, or numbers or letters to be used as names and addresses.

Input consists of data to be processed and the instructions required to process the data. The input unit of a computer involves devices that "read in" data and instructions from various media. The *input media* may be punched cards, punched paper tape, magnetic tape, magnetic disks or drums, optical characters, magnetic ink characters, or a console typewriter. Various types of input media are illustrated in Figure 24-3 on page 586.

MEMORY OR STORAGE UNIT

The *memory or storage unit* is the distinguishing component of a computer. It is the center of operations. All data being processed by the computer pass through the memory unit. By means of this unit immense quantities of data are immediately available to the commands of the computer. The memory holds the input data, the intermediate results of calculations, the final results to be "read out," and the program of instructions telling the computer what to do.

Several types of memory devices are used in computers, but *magnetic cores* are used in most of the high-speed computers. Magnetic cores are made of special magnetic material shaped into circles or "doughnuts" the size of pinheads. Each core can be magnetized at any time in one of two directions. One direction stands for the binary 0, and the other direction for a binary 1. Thousands of these cores are strung on crisscrossed wires, arranged like the strings of a tennis racket, inside a square frame. The frames are stacked one on top of another to make a basic memory unit.

The stacking arrangement places the cores in columns. Each of the columns is assigned an *address,* which is a specific location within the memory unit. Each column of cores can store either one fact or one instruction expressed in binary code. The stored data can be instantly "read out" from any address and used in working a problem. If desired, data can be erased from any address and be replaced with a new fact or instruction.

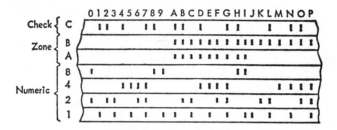

Magnetic tape is tape upon which data are recorded by the presence and absence of magnetized areas arranged according to code. Actual tape is one-half inch wide.

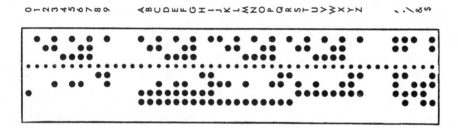

Punched paper tape is a special tape upon which data may be stored in the form of punched holes. Holes are located in columns across the width of the tape. Each column usually contains 5 to 8 positions, which are known as channels.

Figure 24-3

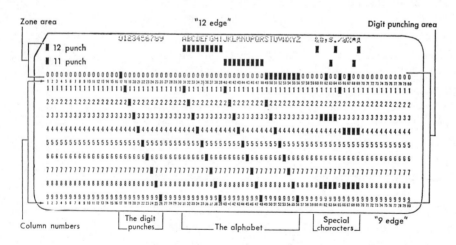

A *punched card* is made of heavy, stiff paper of constant size and shape. Data are stored in the form of punched holes arranged in 80 vertical columns. All holes in a single column are sensed simultaneously when a card is read by automated equipment. In each column there are 12 punching positions; (0-9) are identified as numeric punches and 11 and 12 are identified as zone punches.

Input Media Containing Data

There are other types of memory devices, such as disks, drums, and magnetic tapes, but in each case the computer performs the same basic operation. It converts data according to instructions into a series of magnetic charges and stores these charges.

The *capacity* of a memory device is measured in words. A *word,* which is a technical term, is defined as a group of binary digits that is treated as a unit and is stored in one location. A *location* is a unit-storage position in the main internal storage where one computer word may be stored or retrieved. Large-scale computers have memories with capacities of 32,768 words or more.

ARITHMETIC UNIT

The *arithmetic unit* of a computer performs the operations of addition, subtraction, multiplication, and division, as well as comparison operations.

CONTROL UNIT

The *control unit* has the function of interpreting the program or instructions stored in the memory. It directs the various processing operations, issues proper commands to computer circuits to execute instructions, and checks to see that the instructions are properly carried out.

Register is a term commonly used in discussing the arithmetic and control units. A register is a device for temporarily storing a unit of data— a word—while or until it is used for arithmetical, logical, or transferral operations.

OUTPUT UNIT

The *output unit* has the function of "reading out" or translating into convenient form the results of processing or the contents of the memory. The *output* is the end product of the computer. The output media used to "read out" may be punched cards, magnetic or paper tapes, or printed pages. Printed pages are the most important medium for obtaining information from a computer if the output is going to be used solely by human beings. High-speed printers are capable of printing 1,200 lines a minute. Some of the types of information that can be produced by a printer are accounts, journals, financial statements, bills and invoices, and checks.

In some kinds of research, it is desirable to have the results of computer processing graphically presented in the form of curves. In this case, the output can be flashed on a cathode ray tube (CRT) similar to a TV screen. If future reference to the graphic output will be made, its pattern on the cathode ray tube may be photographed.

COMPUTER HARDWARE

Each of the five components of a computer—input, arithmetic, control, memory, and output—may be an individual piece of physical equipment. One or more of the components may be located a few feet or many miles away from the central processing unit. The term *hardware* describes the central processing unit and its peripheral equipment. The *central processing unit* contains the circuits that control and perform the execution of instructions. *Peripheral equipment* is the collective term for input and output units, supplementary storage (memory) units, and printers that are linked to the main computer. For example, the typical system consists of seven pieces of hardware: the computer, console, card reader, card punch, high-speed printer, magnetic tape units, and disk storage units. The last five of these are classified as peripheral equipment.

It is convenient to speak of the developments in computer hardware in terms of three generations. In the first generation of computers beginning in 1955, the circuitry was based on vacuum tubes, such as were used in radio sets. The speed of operations was in the neighborhood of 500 additions a minute. By 1960, the vacuum tubes were replaced by transistors and speed had increased sevenfold. In the current generation of computers, the circuits are based on silicon chips much smaller than the eraser of a pencil and speed has reached the level of millions of instructions per second. Other recent improvements in computer hardware have been the development of larger memories; *optical scanning devices*, which can read printed matter or handwritten material and convert it into data for the computer; data transmission equipment, which links distant computers over standard communications facilities; and information retrieval instruments, which automatically store and recall filed data.

Scientists predict that within seven years there will be the commercial use of optical memories. In this device data are etched on a recording medium by laser beam. Optical memories will be able to place 100 million bits of data on a square inch in contrast to the present 100,000 bits on a square inch of magnetic tape. Retrieval of data from an optical memory will be 15 times faster than the methods in current use.

Another important hardware category, although perhaps less exciting and powerful than the large computer, is the modern desk-top scientific calculator which sells for around $5,000. This is a far cry from the noisy, clanking machine used to grind out relatively simple arithmetic calculations. Although today's third-generation calculator can be used to perform simple adding-machine types of calculations, many of them are capable of silently and swiftly performing complex operations encountered in educational, scientific, and engineering problems. The Hewlett-Packard calculator, for example, performs trigonometric, logarithmic, and mathematical functions in single key strokes.

The versatility of this type of hardware results from its ability to be programmed and to utilize two memory systems: a permanent "wired-in" memory containing many of the more popular subroutines, such as the mathematical functions mentioned above; and a magnetic-core memory which stores data and accepts programs from either magnetic cards inserted into the machine or directly from the keyboard as no special programming language is required. Exciting future generations of these calculators are expected along with the progress of the larger, more sophisticated computers.

COMPUTER SOFTWARE

Various programming aids that help make effective use of a computer are known collectively as computer *software*. A *program,* which is a software item, may be defined as a series of operating instructions to be performed in processing the data supplied to the computer, the results of which will give the required answer. The actual writing of a program is done by a person called a *programmer*. A program is prepared by listing in complete detail the logical steps which the computer must take in order to obtain the desired results. There are four basic considerations in the preparation of a program: (a) definition of the problem to be solved; (b) outlining each logical step required to reach the solution; (c) writing the program in machine or symbolic language; and (d) translation of the program into machine language when the program is written in symbolic language.

Each computer is wired to respond to basic combinations of characters or words. A *machine language* is a collection of words which a particular computer "understands." There is an IBM 360 machine language, an IBM 1620 machine language, and so on. For example, in IBM 1620 language, the word, 21 02005 11509, would be understood by the computer to add (the symbol 21 means add) the number stored at location 11509 to the number stored at location 02005, and to store the resulting sum in location 02005. This instruction, 21 02005 11509, would be key-punched on a card, and the card would be "read" by the input device. Then the computer would carry out the operation.

Symbolic languages enable the programmer to write instructions in English and algebraic symbols, rather than in machine language. Two of the most popular of the symbolic languages are COBOL and FORTRAN. *COBOL* is the abbreviation for Common Business Oriented Language, and *FORTRAN* is the contraction of Formula Translation.

In the foregoing example, using the IBM 1620 machine language, the number 21 was the symbol for "add." In FORTRAN a plus sign would be used, and in COBOL the word "ADD" would be used. The computer would translate these symbols into the correct binary code instructions. The computer can automatically do this translation because a special program, known as an assembler, has been written. Assemblers convert symbolic programs into fundamental machine language, the binary code. Once the symbolic program has been converted into binary code, it can move as electronic impulses into the computer's memory unit.

To write programs in machine language, the programmer must keep track of what is contained in the various memory addresses and does not have the benefit of many shorthand statements that are available in symbolic languages. In FORTRAN, the programmer is relieved of the task of keeping track of storage locations. Using FORTRAN, the programmer could give the computer the same instruction as that given above in the IBM 1620 machine language by writing: A = A + B.

FLOW CHARTS

The importance of outlining the logical steps required to arrive at the solution of a problem has been mentioned. One way to do this outlining is by means of flow charts. Not only in computer programming, but also in general logical thinking, flow charts are most useful.

A *flow chart* is a graphic representation of the logical steps to be used in solving a problem. It helps the programmer to do the following: (a) to break down a problem into workable segments; (b) to ensure that each step is accomplished in correct sequence; (c) to bring to light areas of the problem that need further clarification; (d) to prevent or to detect errors in a proposed solution; (e) to discover laborsaving and timesaving shortcuts to the solution.

Basically a flow chart is a drawing of boxes, lines, arrows, and comments, which indicate what is to be done. A well-designed flow chart will reveal all of the specific steps that are necessary for a completely logical solution to a problem.

For example, there may be as many as eleven distinct steps in solving the problem of crossing an intersection where there is a traffic light but no oncoming automobile traffic. The problem may be stated, how does one go from corner *A* to corner *B* without diagonal crossing? The diagram of the problem and its flow chart are shown in Figure 24-4.

Figure 24-4

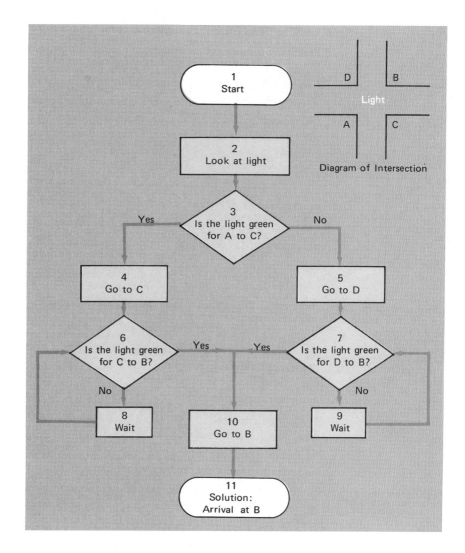

Flow Chart for Crossing Intersection from *A* to *B* with No Automobile Traffic

THE SYSTEMS CONCEPT

As the flow chart and its related program are developed for each data processing operation, computer specialists seek ways of combining, expanding, and coordinating them into larger units of operation. The systemization of data processing operations for the purpose of eliminating retranscriptions of data and of limiting the rehandling and resorting of data from one stage to the next is termed *integrated data processing* (*IDP*). The term is broadly used and may be applied to a particular group of operations of a company or to its entire operations. When the integrated data processing system is very comprehensive, it is called a *master systems plan* or *total systems concept*.

How subsystems may be coordinated into larger integrated data processing plans may be seen in the following illustrative steps.

SALES SUBSYSTEM

When a sales order is received from a customer, all pertinent information—name, address, items ordered, quantity of each, and delivery instructions—become input data and are recorded on magnetic tape. If the stock on hand is sufficient to fill the order, the output unit, acting upon instructions stored in the memory unit, will print the customer's name and address on the invoice, together with a description of the items, their quantities, sales prices, and total amount of the sale. Simultaneously a shipping order is prepared.

CREDIT CONTROL SUBSYSTEM

The current accounts receivable balance and credit limit for the customer, which are stored in the memory unit, are then automatically transmitted to the computer. The total of the sales invoice is added to the customer's previous account balance, and the new balance is compared with the credit limit. If the comparison indicates adequate credit, the invoice and shipping order are released. The calculation and comparisons are made during the time the output unit is printing the invoice and shipping order. If the customer's credit limitation has been reached, the sales invoice goes to the credit department for approval. If the credit department approves the sale, the invoice and shipping order are released. If the credit extension is not approved, sales cancellation data are entered into the system to cancel the data recorded for the order.

INVENTORY SUBSYSTEM

When the merchandise and quantity data from the sales order enter the system, comparisons are made with the perpetual inventory record contained in the memory unit. If the stock on hand is adequate to fill the order, the inventory balance, after providing for the order, is compared to the reorder quantity. If a reorder is indicated, a purchase order is printed. If the stock of the commodity is insufficient to fill the order, a lesser quantity and its sales price are recorded on the invoice and a "back order" is printed for the remaining quantity. Later, when the back-ordered goods are available, a sales invoice and shipping order for the quantity required to complete the original order are automatically prepared.

OTHER SUBSYSTEMS

Details of cash receipts, purchases, and cash disbursements may be processed in a similar manner. Payrolls are also handled in a like fashion with the output media being payroll checks. At the end of a day, week, or month, totals of the various accounts may be printed and financial statements prepared.

Commonly the installation of electronic data processing equipment has been the piecemeal application to routine subsystems. These subsystems are those which are best understood by the firm's employees. They are usually characterized by a high volume of transactions and a large amount of routine processing (sorting, calculating, etc.) that must be performed with each transaction. The potential cost savings from the application of electronic data processing is high. For these reasons it is typical to include billing accounts receivable, inventory control, the payroll, and similar subsystems in developing programs for a computer as first steps toward integrated data processing.

A growing number of companies are developing and experimenting with plans for a total systems concept. These comprehensive plans would give unity and coherence to the financial, production, marketing, and personnel functions of an enterprise. The total systems concept can properly subordinate departmental goals to the overall objectives of the company and give top management a broad, critical perspective of all the operations of the company.

REAL-TIME SYSTEMS

One term frequently occurring in discussions of the total systems concept is real time. *Real time* is a type of data processing that is performed concurrently with a physical process or business transaction. The purpose of this type of information for management is to produce results that are immediately useful in the control of the physical process or business transaction that is transpiring. A real-time computer system has three major characteristics. First, data are maintained *on-line*; that is, all data and instructions to be used in the processing are directly available to the computer by either being stored in the memory of the computer or being read in as required. Second, data are updated as events occur. Third, the computer can be "questioned" from remote terminals; that is, information stored in the computer can be obtained on request from a number of locations at a distance from the computer.

Semiautomatic Business Research Environment (SABRE)

One of the first commercial applications of real-time data processing is SABRE, a system built by IBM for American Airlines. This information system receives data pertaining to airplane passenger reservations from the company's agents throughout the country. It can immediately process the information and send a virtually instantaneous output message to the agent. SABRE is designed to handle tens of thousands of telephone inquiries every day together with requests for prices, passenger reservations, inquiries regarding seat availability to and from other airlines, and sales of tickets. On certain days American Airlines has nearly 600,000 passenger records in its electronic files. The processing of a reservation through SABRE takes approximately three seconds.

Westinghouse Tele-Computer System

An example of real-time data processing within the total systems concept is the Tele-Computer System of Westinghouse Electric Corporation. The center of the system is a Univac computer supplemented with 71 other computers placed in other localities. Among the numerous functions this system performs are the following:

1. Ninety percent of the industrial orders have their shipping instructions transmitted to the warehouse nearest to the customer in three seconds.
2. Orders for nonstock items are immediately sent to the proper manufacturing plants.
3. Inventory is maintained on a real-time basis, giving almost instantaneous answers to questions concerning stock levels.
4. A running cash balance on each of the corporation's 230 bank accounts is maintained.

5. Every sale is immediately recorded at the sales offices, transferred to regional sales headquarters and thence to the central sales office in Pittsburgh on a daily basis.
6. Checks are regularly prepared for 20,000 employees, 15,000 pensioners, and 200,000 stockholders for wages, pensions, and dividends.
7. Daily income statements and balance sheets are prepared for use by top management.

Top management of this corporation points out that the system is a management tool which processes information but that it does not make decisions. The system demands that a manager think about how he does things rather than just do them, and about how his actions mesh with those of other managers.

COMPUTER-BASED SERVICES

The computer software industry is evolving into a computer services industry, and over the past few years many firms have been created to sell computer services to other firms. These firms own the computer hardware and employ skilled personnel in data processing, programming, and systems design. Some banks have entered this new industry by providing payroll, accounts receivable, billing, and other accounting and clerical services to their clients.

Two differing and significant aspects of this computer service market are time-sharing and facilities management. *Time sharing* is a means of allowing many customers to share the capabilities of a large, central computer through the use of remote terminals hooked up to the computer. Although the computer actually services each user in sequence, the high speed of the computer makes it appear that the users are being serviced at the same time. This service benefits small businesses as well as large ones. For the smaller business the most powerful computers in the world are as accessible as the nearest telephone, which can be adapted for access to the distant computer. This multiple-access system allows large service corporations to provide these very sophisticated EDP resources to a small business which may neither be able to afford nor to utilize such resources fully on its own.

An executive may wish to start a computerized system of some type, but he may not feel financially nor technically capable of selecting the hardware, of training programmers to write the software for his particular needs, and generally of installing and overseeing the system. If he does not wish to use time-sharing, then he may turn to a computer service company specializing in *facilities management*. This company would set up and manage the complete function for him.

The financial burden to a company contemplating owning or leasing its computer hardware has frequently dictated the decision to make use of time sharing or facilities management. The cost of purchasing computer hardware adequate to serve the needs of a moderately large business will approximate $1,000,000 to $1,500,000. Alternately, if most of the units are leased, rentals will be in the neighborhood of from $18,000 to $25,000 a month. The cost of hiring competently trained programmers and operators can be expected to equal rental costs. Unless the firm is large enough to require 24-hour operation of its computer, it should be able to save money by using the computer service market.

Some managers may be hesitant to use time-sharing or facilities management, however, as these involve turning over important business information and functional responsibilities to outsiders. Nevertheless, it has been forecasted that time-sharing service sales alone will exceed $2 billion by 1975.

FUTURE ROLE OF COMPUTERS

Several trends sketch in broad outline the future role of computers in business. Computers are becoming increasingly faster, smaller, and less expensive. Within the last 15 years electronic data processing equipment has become approximately 100 times faster, 10 times smaller in size, and 1,000 times less expensive in handling a unit of information. Increasing simplification of programming has accompanied the improvement in hardware. Within the next few years new symbolic languages will be developed, each more closely geared to ordinary English and algebra. Moreover, computer services will become increasingly available in much the same way as electricity and telephone services have become widely available. These trends will change the concept of a computer from that of a lightning-fast electronic calculator to that of an information processing device which will handle data in any form—numbers, words, sounds, pictures, or symbols. The computer will provide new types of data that will give powerful new decision-making tools for management. New mathematical techniques are developing that will enable management to simulate through the use of the computer the operations of a company under varying conditions, and from the results of these simulations management will be able to make more timely and more accurate decisions concerning the future of the company. All of these trends indicate that the total impact of computers on the economy will be greater productivity from the resources of capital and labor.

BUSINESS TERMS

QUESTIONS FOR DISCUSSION AND ANALYSIS

1. If the binary numbers 0010 and 0001 are added together, what is the result in binary arithmetic? If the binary numbers 0010 and 0011 are multiplied, what is the result in binary arithmetic?

2. What parts of the diagram on page 584 would represent the central processing unit, and what parts would represent peripheral equipment? If the human element, people, were to be incorporated into the diagram, where would it fit?

3. Using a four-place binary code, what are the binary code numbers for the decimal numbers 17 and 117?

4. Explain the nature and the function of a program for a computer system.

5. Is the equals sign in the FORTRAN expression, $A=A+B$, used in its usual way or does it mean something different? Explain.

6. In most card games, the cards are shuffled to place them in random order before dealing. Explain how a skillful card player uses the

    basic operations of data processing after receiving the cards from the dealer.

7. Explain how the basic operations of data processing are used in preparing an income statement.

8. When we speak of the "solar system" and a "business procedures system," are we using the word "system" in the same sense? Explain.

9. Under a pen-and-ink data processing system, sales slips for charge-account customers are placed in batches and posted to the customer accounts once a week. Is this a real-time system? Explain.

10. What might cause inadequate or inaccurate information to be produced by a data processing system?

PROBLEMS AND SHORT CASES

1. In the discussion of flow charts, the problem of crossing an intersection of two streets was outlined. The problem assumed that there was no automobile traffic. Redo the problem assuming that there is automobile traffic and present a neatly organized flow chart.

2. You have six electric lamps arranged in a row, left to right. Each has a separate switch so that each lamp may be individually turned on or off. Starting at the right-hand side of the row, you designate the first four lamps with the numbers 1, 2, 4, and 8 respectively. When the last two lamps are off, the lights of the first four are used to signal numbers from zero to nine. When either of the last two lamps is on, the lamps will signal a letter.

    Thus, if all the lamps are off, the signal is that of zero; if the first lamp on the right is on, the signal is for one; if the fourth and the first lights are on, the signal is for nine (8+1); if the first and fifth lights are on, the signal is for the letter A.

    Write out a code for the numbers zero to nine inclusive and for all the letters of the alphabet. In writing out your code, use a zero to indicate that the light is off and a one to indicate that it is on.

3. The Polar Parts Company employs 1,500 people and has annual sales of approximately $40 million a year. It manufactures 150 different products that are sold throughout the world. It has been using a manual accounting system supplemented by the services of an electronic data processing center. The center prepares the weekly payroll and maintains inventory records. These services are purchased on an annual contract basis from the independent center.

    Two years ago, under the stimulus of the controller of the company, Polar Parts began to study the feasibility of installing a company-operated computer system. The task force that has been carrying out the study has gathered evidence that the company should gradually progress, after the computer is installed, toward a total systems concept. The controller believes that the task force's recommendation is "too far-reaching." The total system concept, he contends, is "day-dreaming," and that it calls for more hardware and software than the company presently needs. He favors the quick installation of a simple computer system for handling accounts receivable, accounts payable, payroll, and inventory. He believes that the computer is primarily a device to perform bookkeeping operations efficiently.

In recent discussions, questions have arisen concerning who should head the new computer department. The controller favors a man from his own staff, who is presently chairman of the task force. He says that the head of the data processing department should report directly to the general accountant, who is a subordinate of the controller. The chief engineer is opposed to this view. He believes that this arrangement will provide little or no time to use the computer for engineering studies; moreover, he is afraid that the task force chairman is not sufficiently acquainted with the engineering uses of a computer. The vice president in charge of sales is concerned that he and his staff will not receive detailed sales analysis reports promptly or that such reports might not be effectively presented. The chairman of the task force is privately recommending that the head of the proposed data processing system should be independent of all functional area executives and should be a vice president in charge of systems and procedures and report directly to the president.

You have been appointed chairman of a subcommittee of the task force to resolve this conflict. What factors would you consider in arriving at a recommendation?

SUGGESTED READINGS

Arnold, Robert R., Harold C. Hill, and Aylmer V. Nichols. *Modern Data Processing*. New York: John Wiley & Sons, Inc., 1969.

Brightman, Richard W., Bernard J. Luskin, and Theodore Tilton. *Data Processing for Decision Making, An Introduction to Third Generation Information Systems*. New York: The Macmillan Company, 1968.

Clark, Frank James. *Information Processing*. Pacific Palisades, California: Goodyear Publishing Co., Inc., 1970.

Davis, Gordon B. *Computer Data Processing*. New York: McGraw-Hill Book Company, 1969.

Dippel, Gene, and William C. House. *Information Systems, Data Processing and Evaluation*. Glenview, Illinois: Scott, Foresman and Company, 1969.

Emerick, Paul L., Jr., and Joseph W. Wilkinson. *Computer Programming for Business and Social Science*. Homewood, Illinois: Richard D. Irwin, Inc., 1970.

Greenberger, Martin, ed. *Computers, Communications, and the Public Interest*. Baltimore: The Johns Hopkins Press, 1971.

Gruenberger, Fred, ed. *Critical Factors in Data Management*. Englewood Cliffs, New Jersey: Prentice-Hall, Inc., 1969.

Gupta, Roger. *Electronic Information Processing*. New York: The Macmillan Company, 1971.

Heyel, Carl, and BEMA (Business Equipment Manufacturers Association). *Computers, Office Machines, and the New Information Technology*. New York: The Macmillan Company, 1969.

Kanter, Jerome. *Management Guide to Computer System Selection and Use*. Englewood Cliffs, New Jersey: Prentice-Hall, Inc., 1970.

Laurie, Edward J. *Modern Computer Concepts. The IBM 360 Series*. Cincinnati: South-Western Publishing Co., 1970.

Murach, Mike. *Principles of Business Data Processing*. Chicago: Science Research Associates, Inc., 1970.

Sanders, Donald H., ed. *Computers and Management*. New York: McGraw-Hill Book Company, 1969.

Saxon, James A., and Wesley W. Steyer. *Basic Principles of Data Processing,* Second Edition. Englewood Cliffs, New Jersey: Prentice-Hall, Inc., 1970.

Schmidt, Richard N., and William E. Meyers. *Introduction to Computer Science and Data Processing*. New York: Holt, Rinehart and Winston, 1970.

Tomeski, Edward A. *The Computer Revolution: The Executive and the New Information Technology*. New York: The Macmillan Company, 1970.

Weiss, Eric A., ed. *Computer Usage Applications*. New York: McGraw-Hill Book Company, 1970.

Withington, Frederic G. *The Real Computer: Its Influences, Uses, and Effects*. Reading, Massachusetts: Addison-Wesley Publishing Company, Inc., 1969.

Chapter 25

Business Statistics and Reports

Information is the lifeblood of management. In order to make sound decisions, every manager must know what has happened, what is going on, and what will likely occur in the future. When a company is small and its operations simple, information comes to the manager from sales reports, accounting statements, conversations with business associates, newspapers and magazines, and miscellaneous other sources. As a business grows and becomes more complex, the demand for information by management becomes more intense and the search for pertinent data becomes more formalized and more systematic.

The types of information available when adequate accounting records are maintained were explained in Chapter 23, and Chapter 24 stressed the role of computers in furnishing management with current data on a great variety of topics. In the next chapter the use of forecasts and budgets in providing information for purposes of decision making and control will be discussed. This chapter will focus its attention on the types and uses of facts and figures derived from the application of statistical measurements to business data and also on business reports.

BUSINESS STATISTICS

Modern business relies heavily on information obtained from quantitative data. *Quantitative data* are facts that are capable of being expressed in numbers or in symbols that facilitate mathematical manipulations. Management involves many complex relationships among numerous factors. These relationships can be expressed vaguely in words, but it is often more meaningful to state them in quantitative form. For example, a manager could say that costs increase with sales, but it is more helpful to state this fact in the following manner: Costs consist of two types— fixed and variable. *Fixed costs* are those that do not change with sales volume whereas *variable costs* vary proportionally with sales. If fixed costs are approximately $50,000 and variable costs increase by 60 cents for each dollar of sales and if the letter C represents total costs and the letter S total sales, then for the facts given:

$$C = \$50,000 + .60S$$

One of the most commonly used methods for handling quantitative data is statistics. *Business statistics* may be defined as (1) the collection, (2) analysis, summarization, and measurement, (3) presentation, and (4) interpretation of numerical data that are related to the problems of business. A most important function of business statistics is that of forcing the manager to explain situations or to state problems in explicit and specific form.

Since accounting is also based on quantitative data, it may be well to examine its relationship to the field of business statistics. One major difference is that business statistics is broader than accounting because it uses all units of measurement, whereas accounting is more or less restricted to dollars and cents. For example, if a firm sells 62,000 units for $100,000 to 3,500 customers located in 15 states, it is probable that the only fact of interest to the accountant is $100,000. To the statistician, the number of units involved, the average size of the orders from the 3,500 customers, and the dollar sales in each state may be just as important and significant as the total dollar sales.

Another difference between accounting and statistics is that accounting is restricted to internal data resulting from the profit-making transactions of the firm while statistics makes use of external data as well as internal data covering any and all measurable activities of a business. In estimating the sales potential of a consumer product in a new territory, for example, data released by the Bureau of the Census would be significant and helpful. Or, if the external data have not been made available by some governmental or private agency, the statistician may decide to collect his own information from outside sources.

COLLECTION OF DATA

Numerical data must be collected before they can be summarized and used. If the figures are concerned with operations of the company, without regard for outside influences, the source for these data lies within the records of the particular business. Financial statements, purchase invoices, sales reports, and payroll records can supply vital information that is subject to statistical analysis. As an illustration, a company may show an operating profit in the current year of $325,000 as contrasted with a corresponding figure of $300,000 for the preceding year. If these figures represent the output of a factory and no expansion took place during the current year, the conclusion might be reached that more efficient use was made of the production facilities or that the plant operated more hours. However, an analysis showed that 50,000 units were sold in the current year as contrasted with 60,000 in the preceding year and that the increased operating profit was due entirely to an increase in selling price. In this case, the sales manager rather than the plant superintendent may have deserved commendation.

Although internal data provide many useful figures, particularly for control at the executive level, external data are more helpful in arriving at sound solutions to many problems. If, by chance, the wanted information is available from outside agencies, its use will save time and money. More often, the statistical department of a business must secure the facts it needs by its own efforts. Three common methods are used to obtain needed original information: (a) mail surveys, involving questionnaires mailed to individuals or firms; (b) personal interviews, in which the interrogator fills out a questionnaire form; and (c) telephone calls, with answers noted on a suitable form. Each method has its advantages and disadvantages, some of which are fairly obvious. For example, for a given amount of money, more individuals can be contacted by a mail survey than by personal interviews, and unless telephone calls are restricted to one community, toll charges may prove to be prohibitive. In some instances a combination of two or all of the above methods may be preferable to relying on only one procedure.

When a questionnaire is used, it must be prepared carefully. It should not be too long, the questions must be clear and easy to answer, and, above all, questions must not be "loaded" in favor of a desired response. In a personal interview more answers can be obtained and the questions can be more complicated as the interviewer can clarify any misunderstandings. If questionnaires are mailed, only a 10 to 15 percent return can be expected if the mailing list is large or if the questionnaires are sent to individuals who do not have a vital interest in the subject. General Motors, through its Customers' Research Staff, has made extensive use of mail surveys in an attempt to find out what car owners want in the many details of their automobiles.

Sampling Techniques

Regardless of the method used to collect external data, most problems are of such a nature that a complete coverage is impracticable. For example, a department store in a community of 10,000 homes might want to know which evening or evenings customers and potential customers would prefer that it remain open. Obviously the task of contacting every family would be difficult and expensive. This leads to a process known as *sampling*. The theory of sampling is that the characteristics of an adequate sample are representative of those of the whole (called the *universe* by statisticians) of which it is a part. Applied to the problem stated, if interviews were held with 1,000 householders, it might be reasonable to assume that the answers would be consistent with those that would be obtained if all 10,000 were contacted.

Random sampling results when each individual in the group to be surveyed has an equal chance of being included. Again referring to the above situation, if 10,000 names were typed on identical cards and these were thoroughly shuffled, the top 1,000 names would constitute a random sample. If these names were taken from a telephone book, and calls replaced interviews, the fact that all homes do not have telephone service could invalidate the results of the survey.

Most sampling for business purposes is *controlled sampling* in that an effort is made to contact a small group that is representative of the larger number about whom some information is wanted. For example, a manufacturer of pipe tobacco might like to know whether an aromatic or nonaromatic product would sell better. It is obvious that contacts should be made with men of adult ages; but there might be differences between the tastes of rural and city dwellers, high and low income groups, indoor and outdoor workers, and among different age groups. The reliability of the results of the sampling would vary with the care used in determining the composition of the sample group so that the above-mentioned, and probably other, factors would be properly balanced.

Some business firms are not large enough to maintain a market research or other type of statistical department. In this event they may find it advantageous to hire an outside agency to make special studies for them. These agencies, operating in most cities, also collect information for more extensive distribution, such as newspaper releases. Polls of public opinion, particularly those that are concerned with election results, are well known to everyone. Although somewhat discredited because of incorrect forecasts in some elections, these polls have a very low percentage of error. At the same time, incorrect forecasts point up the truth that results obtained from questionnaires and interviews must always be interpreted with great care and that the validity of results from a sampling process are always open to some question.

Sources of Data for Business

Both internal and external data gathered by or for a firm for its use are known as *primary data*. If these facts are published or otherwise released, they are known as *secondary data* in the hands of subsequent users. Since additional handling of the figures allows more chances for errors, and time is likely to have elapsed since the data were first collected, secondary data should be used with caution. They are, nonetheless, widely used because of the enormous quantities of data available, frequently without cost, from government and private agencies.

U. S. government publications. The federal government is outstanding in providing secondary data of value to business. Various departments, bureaus, and agencies compile and publish statistical information covering a wide variety of activities related to the economic life of our country.

The Department of Commerce exists primarily to serve the needs of large and small businesses. Among its numerous publications are the monthly *Survey of Current Business* with its weekly supplement, the quarterly *Industry Reports*, and the *Small Business Management Series*.

The Bureau of the Census is another government department that makes available important statistical material. In addition to population figures, which are basic to many surveys, this Bureau issues many other publications, including the annual *Statistical Abstract of the United States*. The Bureau is responsible for the Census of Business, which classifies the channels of distribution on a geographical basis, and for the Census of Manufactures, which presents important information covering the various types of industries.

One of the most reliable indexes of industrial production is published monthly by the Board of Governors of the Federal Reserve System. The annual report of this body, as well as the bulletins issued by the individual federal reserve banks, are helpful in the field of banking and finance.

The Bureau of Labor Statistics of the Department of Labor issues the *Monthly Labor Review,* which gives information on price levels, unemployment, and wages. This Bureau is responsible for a number of indexes as well as other statistical measurements.

The Department of Agriculture, although primarily concerned with its own field, presents in its *Agricultural Yearbook* many facts that can be used by the businessman who is concerned with the use of raw materials grown on the farms. Soybean acreage or production, for example, would be of interest to a manufacturer of paints.

Nongovernment sources. Another valuable source of secondary data includes publications issued by newspapers and magazines, trade journals, trade associations, private agencies, and institutions.

In addition to newspapers and magazines, both general and specialized, that have been mentioned in previous chapters, many publications classified as trade journals deal with one segment of industry. *Modern Plastics* and *Air Transportation* are examples of such magazines. The publications of the American Iron and Steel Institute are examples of those issued by trade associations. Private agencies include such well-known organizations as Moody's Investors Service and Dun and Bradstreet, Inc. Publications issued by the Brookings Institution, the Twentieth Century Fund, the National Industrial Conference Board, and many universities are examples of institutional releases.

ANALYSIS, SUMMARIZATION, AND MEASUREMENT

Once the data are available, whether secured from a primary or a secondary source, or both, the figures must be processed. Sometimes they need to be broken down into segments, and at times they are summarized into usable totals. Various types of statistical measurement can then be applied to yield results ready for presentation and interpretation.

When thousands of individual items have been collected, the chore of summarizing the data can be simplified by various business machines. Calculators and adding machines are helpful, punched card equipment is invaluable for many situations, and, more recently, electronic computers have been added to process information at a much faster rate and with more variables. A punched card permits the coding of a great many items, which can then be tabulated by machines in a variety of ways.

An example may clarify the use of a punched card. Referring to the survey on aromatic and nonaromatic tobacco mentioned previously, each interview furnished the following information about the men: (a) age, (b) nationality, (c) married or single, (d) state of residence, (e) rural or city dweller, (f) occupation, (g) annual income, (h) indoor or outdoor worker, (i) pipe, cigar, or cigarette smoker, (j) occasional or habitual smoker, (k) brand of pipe tobacco used. The answers to these questions, punched on cards, permitted summaries and an analysis of each factor in relation to any other factor.

Assuming that the necessary data have been processed into usable details or summaries, the next procedure is to apply an appropriate type of measurement. Two possibilities, ratios and percentages, were illustrated in Chapter 23 in connection with the interpretation of financial statements. Both ratios and percentages are useful for data other than those secured from accounting information. For example, a firm had total sales of $1,000,000 of which $800,000 was derived in states east of the Mississippi River and $200,000 in states west of that dividing line. This fact could be expressed as a 4 to 1 ratio, or 80 percent.

In addition to ratios and percentages there are several other types of statistical measurement available and useful in specific situations. Some of the more common forms that are applied to numerical facts include averages, index numbers, correlation, and time series. Each of these will be explained with a view to indicating their unique and appropriate uses in connection with different types of raw data.

Averages

The vocabulary of most individuals includes the word "average," but different meanings are frequently involved. A parent tells his next door neighbor that his son is an "average" college student, which is his way of saying that he assumes his son's scholastic attainment is approximately equal to that of the majority of college students. On the other hand, a baseball player's batting average of .298 is based on a refined mathematical technique.

Three types of *averages*, which may be defined as measures of *central tendency*, are commonly calculated: the mode, the median, and the arithmetic average or mean. Each has its advantages, and one may give a much better picture of the "average" than the other in specific instances. For example, an instructor may grade an hour examination and wish to announce the average grade to his class. The size of the group is 17, and the papers, arranged numerically, show the following marks:

95	76
93	76
93	72
88	72
87	72
83	72
83	40
79	29
78	

This series of grades, or numbers, is known as an *array,* which is simply a list of all of the figures to be used in a statistical computation listed in order of size. The first step in computing an average might be to condense the array by noting the number of students who earned each different grade. This is known as a *frequency distribution.*

Grade	Number of Students
95	1
93	2
88	1
87	1
83	2
79	1
78	1
76	2
72	4
40	1
29	1

Mode. Without further handling of the data, the mode and median can be determined. The *mode* is the number that occurs most frequently in any distribution. In the example above, the mode is 72—the grade received by the largest number of students. Sometimes other grades might have been earned by an almost equal number of students in which case there would be subsidiary modes. In the event that no two students received the same grade, there would be no mode.

Median. The *median* is the number in an array that divides the group in half. Referring again to the previous example, since there were 17 students in this class, the ninth student in the list would have eight individuals above him and eight below him. Counting down from the top or up from the bottom, the ninth grade is 78 which is the median. If a class had an even number of students, it would be necessary to calculate an arithmetic average of the two middle grades if they were not identical.

Mean. The *arithmetic average* or *mean* is the most common type of average employed, so much so that it is implied in most requests to furnish an average. It is the result of dividing the total of a series of numbers by the number of units making up the series. To calculate the mean for the above problem would require less work if a frequency distribution were used as shown in Table 25-1.

CALCULATING AN ARITHMETIC MEAN

Grade	Number of Students	Total Grade Points
95	1	95
93	2	186
88	1	88
87	1	87
83	2	166
79	1	79
78	1	78
76	2	152
72	4	288
40	1	40
29	1	29
	17	1,288

Table 25-1

Divide the total grade points by the total number of students to obtain the mean: $1,288 \div 17 = 75.8$.

The arithmetic mean of 75.8 is less than the grades received by 11 of the 17 students as a result of two very low grades. This emphasizes a characteristic of the mean, which is that a few high or low figures have an undue influence on the result.

Comparison of the three averages. In the above example, the mode was the lowest average and the median the highest. Taking a different set of grades, the results might have been exactly opposite. Furthermore, if 300 or 400 grades are used, the averages normally approximate each other.

The question might well be asked, "Which method of averaging is the best to use?" In the problem given above, a substantial majority of the class received higher grades than either the mean or the mode. Consequently, the median is probably the best measure of central tendency to use in this case. On the other hand, if a manufacturer of men's hats wanted to specialize in one size, he would want to produce an average hat size that would fit the greatest number of people, which would be the mode.

For the majority of business problems, the arithmetic average or mean is used. If hourly wage rates in a factory are $1.75, $2.00, $2.20, $2.40, and $3.00, multiplying these wage rates by the number of employees at each level and dividing total payroll by total number of employees will give a significant average hourly wage rate. There are times, however, when the computation of an average is of little or no value. For example, two grandfathers, aged 78 and 82, decided to form a partnership with their mutual 23-year-old grandson. To say that the average age of the three partners is 61 is accurate but almost meaningless.

Index Numbers

An *index number* is a device for measuring the change that has taken place in a group of related items over a period of time. More use is probably made of index numbers by the business world than of any other kind of statistical measurement. Index numbers are constructed in order to determine (a) whether prices paid by consumers are rising or falling, (b) whether wholesale prices are up or down, or (c) the relative activity in the building industry, in stock price movements, and in many similar items. Some index numbers may have a direct effect on a firm as, for example, an agreement in a labor contract to adjust hourly rates of pay whenever the Consumer Price Index rises or falls an agreed-upon number of points.

Issued monthly by the Bureau of Labor Statistics of the Department of Labor, the *Consumer Price Index*, or *CPI* as it is called, measures changes in the retail prices of goods and services purchased by a typical family. It is expressed as a percentage of the average prices that prevailed in a base period, currently 1957-1959 (see Figure 25-1). Many other index numbers are issued by governmental and private agencies.

In order to clarify the meaning of index numbers and to illustrate their construction, a greatly simplified consumer price index computation is shown in Table 25-2 on page 612. Only three commodity items have been included instead of the 400 items used by the Bureau of Labor Statistics in preparing its Consumer Price Index. This brief illustration provides an opportunity to show the use of *relatives*, a device that permits the comparison of unlike figures. It also illustrates a *weighted index number* in that the quantities used of different items are taken into consideration. The calculation shown in Table 25-2 to measure the movement of prices assumes that the average family purchases only eggs, gasoline, and cloth.

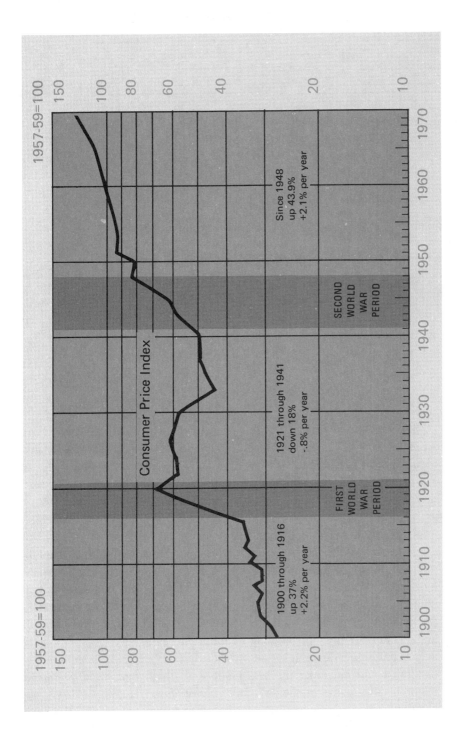

Figure 25-1

Inflation as Measured by the Consumer Price Index

Sources: U.S. Bureau of Census and the U.S. Bureau of Labor Statistics.

COMPUTING A SIMPLIFIED CONSUMER PRICE INDEX

	Base Year		Current Year	
	Price Per Unit	Total Amount	Price Per Unit	Total Amount
50 dozen eggs	$0.60	$ 30.00	$0.68	$ 34.00
200 gallons gasoline	.38	76.00	.40	80.00
25 yards cloth	.40	10.00	.42	10.50
		$116.00		$124.50
Index Number		$116.00 = 100		$124.50 = 107.3

Table 25-2

Divide the increase in total amount paid for the items in the current year by the total amount paid for the same items in the base year to obtain the increase in points of the index number for the current year over that of the base year: $8.50 ÷ $116 = 7.3%.

It should be obvious that the 7.3 increase over the base year would be different if more items were used and quantities were refined. These variation possibilities explain, in part, why two statistical organizations may produce different results even when attempting to measure the same change. Also, two different agencies may not agree on the base year.

Correlation

If it can be determined that there is a definite relationship between separate sets of figures, the measurement of the degree of relationship between the two variables is known as *correlation*. This statistical device can be used in forecasting when one variable can be measured earlier than the other, and it can also be used in estimating when one variable is known but the other is not.

Correlation as a forecasting device assumes a known time lag. For example, the probable total enrollment in the first grade of elementary schools should logically have a measurable degree of correlation with the birth rate. If the number of children born in any given year is higher than the number born the previous year, it is reasonable to forecast that the number of children entering the first grade six years later will be higher than the number entering in the fifth year. Several factors, such as an unforeseen high level of infant mortality or a law stating that children could not enter the first grade until they were seven years old, might invalidate the prediction. In the past, however, the two variables have shown a high degree of correlation, and the forecast is very likely to prove accurate.

Many statisticians concerned with business forecasting attempt to find series of figures that can be used to predict the level of business activity in the months or years ahead. The index of productivity in the machine tool industry is usually considered a fairly accurate forecast of business conditions in the year ahead as industry must "tool up" before it can produce. The Bureau of the Census has developed a monthly report in which it uses 30 series covering many facets including production, distribution, finance, labor, construction, and prices.

Sometimes one variable is available in accurate form but the other is not. Since every state keeps a record of all of the passenger cars it licenses, the number on the road each year is reasonably well known. If, in the past, there has been a high correlation between the gasoline sales of an oil company and the number of cars on the highways, the expected year's sales can be estimated not only by territories but even by months.

The preceding examples have assumed a functional relationship between two sets of variables, which is known as *simple correlation*. When three or more sets of data are used, the term applied is *multiple correlation*. The number of students who plan to enter college in 1978 can be predicted from the birthrate of 1960, but a more accurate estimate would result if the expected economic status of the family unit was also introduced as a factor. The number of parents who can afford to send their children to college might be more important than the number of high school graduates.

Time Series

Our economic system is in a constant state of change. At any given date it is possible to plot known data and to compute exactly where we are in reference to the past. Before action can be taken on the conclusions drawn from this calculation, however, conditions may have changed. Static analysis is valuable, but we live in a dynamic world. The various types of time series attempt to analyze changes that take place over a period of time. The most frequent movements that are measured are known as secular trends, cyclical fluctuations, and seasonal variations.

Secular trends. Over a long period of time a dominant characteristic of the United States has been growth. The population has increased, industries have grown, production has moved ahead, transportation facilities have been enlarged. Although the growth of population has been an important factor, it is not entirely responsible for other increases. This type of long-term movement is known as a *secular trend*. As this country or others become more mature, there is a tendency for the rate of growth to decrease, and it may be that a downward curve will eventually result.

In general, the secular trend in the United States has meant that business could expand in almost any direction. More people with more money means demands for food, housing, clothing, amusements, and other necessities, conveniences, and luxuries. To apply this logic to a particular industry, however, may prove to be a serious error. In the early days of the twentieth century there was a considerable expansion of the traction lines connecting various cities. With the advent of the large passenger bus and the automobile, the traction lines lost so much business, despite an increased population, that most were forced out of business.

Cyclical fluctuations. Although the secular trend in this country has been upward over many decades, there have been years of prosperity and years of depression. Ups and downs in the economy as a whole that tend to recur with some measure of regularity and that extend over a period of years rather than months are called *cyclical fluctuations*. A complete sequence from a stable economy to an expanding one followed by a period of contraction and then back to the starting point of stability is called a *business cycle*. A business cycle has a definite pattern of movement from one stage to another, but the duration and extent of any part of the complete cycle is unpredictable. The average duration of a business cycle in the past has been approximately seven years, but individual cycles have varied so extensively that this norm has little value.

Cyclical fluctuations have been accepted by economists as a natural result of our free-enterprise system. It is hoped that the severity of a downward swing, such as occurred in 1933, can be modified by government action on public works programs, subsidies, social security payments, and unemployment insurance payments. Only time will tell whether our economy can be kept at a point of equilibrium or whether the upward and downward swings of the past will continue. At the moment it appears that various controls have been successful only to the extent of smoothing the peaks and valleys of cyclical fluctuations.

Seasonal variations. Many businesses are subject to regular month-by-month changes during the calendar year. Department stores have an increase in trade before Easter and Christmas. Travel agencies are patronized heavily during the summer months and have a smaller boom in the mid-winter season. Such changes are known as *seasonal variations*.

Weather and holidays are reasons for many seasonal variations, but they are not the only factors responsible for month-by-month changes. If a manufacturer of automobiles brings out a new model each year, he can determine his own seasonal variation because of the large number of people who want to own the most up-to-date product and who place orders as soon as the new car is on display.

Underlying the various methods of statistically measuring and analyzing business data is the theory of probability. *Probability* is the likelihood that a particular form of an event will occur. It may be thought of as a scale of values ranging from one to zero. Thus, the probability of obtaining a head or a tail with a toss of a coin is one; the event is certain to happen. The probability of obtaining a head when a coin is tossed is one half.

Table 25-3 shows the probability of obtaining different numbers of heads when six coins are tossed simultaneously, which allows for 64 different combinations when each coin is considered separately.

THE THEORY OF PROBABILITY APPLIED TO A TOSS OF THE COIN

Table 25-3

Number of Heads	Number of Combinations Producing the Count of Heads	Probability
0	1	1/64
1	6	6/64
2	15	15/64
3	20	20/64
4	15	15/64
5	6	6/64
6	1	1/64
	64	64/64

Examining the table, it can be seen there is only one combination which will be all tails; there are 20 combinations in which 3 heads can appear, but there are only 6 chances out of 64 that 5 heads will appear. The chances that 1 or 2 heads will turn up is 21 out of 64.

A further examination of the frequency distribution shows that it is symmetrical. It also possesses central tendency, that is, there are more frequencies in the center of the distribution.

The theory of probability provides a framework by which a statistician can judge the range of accuracy of sampling, correlation, and other statistical techniques. It is the foundation of industrial quality control methods, of much market research, of various applications of game theory, and of PERT. It is the theory that changes the field of statistics from one of mere quantitative description into the basic method of making decisions in the face of uncertainty.

PRESENTATION OF STATISTICAL MATERIAL

In order to present statistical material in a manner that will be useful for purposes of analysis, two devices are commonly used. These are summary tables and graphic presentations. A statement that production in 1972 reached 10,000 tons, which was an increase of 25 percent over the 1971 output of 8,000 tons, might well be expressed in this narrative form. If the number of yearly production figures were increased, however, a summary table or graph would be more effective.

Summary Tables

A considerable amount of statistical material is presented in Table 25-4. Years, geographical areas, types of products, age groups, income groups, nationalities, and the like may be the bases for comparisons in summary tables.

Table 25-4

EMPLOYMENT AND UNEMPLOYMENT
(in thousands)

Employment Status	February 1971	January 1971	Annual Averages		
			1970	1969	1960
Civilian labor force	83,384	83,897	82,715	80,733	69,628
Employed	78,537	78,864	78,627	77,902	65,776
Agriculture	3,329	3,413	3,462	3,606	5,458
Nonagriculture	75,208	75,451	75,165	74,296	60,318
Unemployed	4,847	5,033	4,088	2,831	3,852
Unemployment rate	6.1%	6.0%	4.5%	3.1%	5.5%

Source: United States Department of Labor, Bureau of Labor Statistics, *Monthly Labor Review*, Vol. 94, No. 4 (April, 1971), p. 90.

Graphic Presentations

The pictorial presentation of statistical data has the great advantage of interest to the reader by presenting a visual analysis of the facts. Several forms are used.

One of the most common graphic statistical presentations is the *line* or *curve chart*, which uses a line or curve to indicate changes or a trend over a period of time (see Figure 25-2). Two or more lines may be used in the same chart to indicate changes in related items.

Figure 25-2

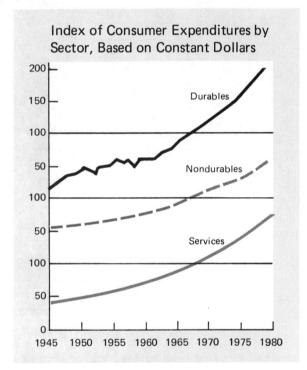

A Line Chart

Another common form of graphic presentation is the *bar chart*, which is used for the comparison of figures. The bars in the chart may be horizontal (see Figure 25-3 on page 618) or vertical.

The *pie diagram* or *circular chart* is particularly useful for explaining financial matters when the unit involved is 100 percent or $1. Many annual reports of corporations make use of the pie diagram in the manner illustrated in Figure 25-4 on page 619.

Statistical maps are commonly used when it is desired to present geographical information. By means of shading, coloring, pins, circles,

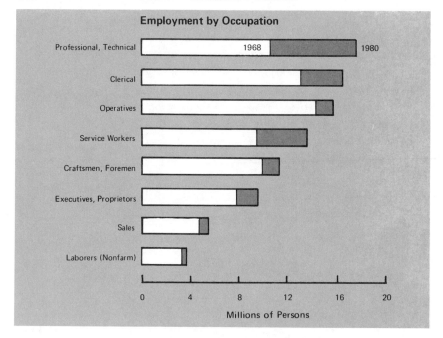

Figure 25-3

A Horizontal Bar Chart

and other devices, data can be presented for a city, state, the United States, or a larger geographical area.

Within recent years, bar charts particularly have been given added reader attention by the use of a series of small pictures or drawings of the data presented. These graphs are sometimes called *pictographs*. They are effective for comparisons of subject matter, which can be presented by a self-explanatory drawing.

INTERPRETATION OF BUSINESS STATISTICS

The final stage in the role that statistics may play in aiding management to make decisions and to control operations is that of interpretation. At this point two questions need to be resolved—"What conclusions can properly be drawn from the data?" and "Who should be responsible for this interpretation?"

As to the first question, considerable judgment needs to be used. In this country we have a great faith in figures, which, in most cases, is probably justified. If a controller reports to the board of directors of a company that its profits last year were $2.18 a share, this statistic is accepted as a fact. Caution, however, should be used in relying on

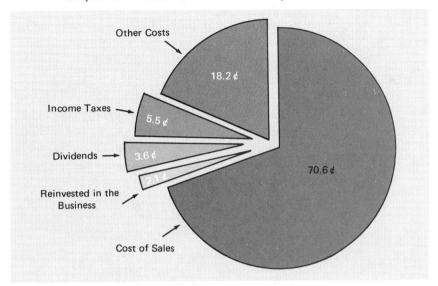

Figure 25-4

Other Costs

18.2 ¢

Income Taxes

5.5 ¢

Dividends

3.6 ¢

2.1 ¢

Reinvested in the Business

70.6 ¢

Cost of Sales

Corn Products Company

A Pie Diagram

statistical measurements to influence decisions, particularly those affecting the future operations of a firm. Despite the best of intentions, several types of errors can creep into a computation. Arithmetic errors are likely to occur, particularly when the quantity of data to be processed is extensive. In surveys, the sample selected may not be representative of the whole. If a computer is used, the programmed instructions may be faulty.

Even more inexcusable is a situation where the statistician is prejudiced in his views and uses only such information as supports his preconceived ideas, or where he manipulates accurate figures in such a manner as to arrive at a faulty conclusion. For example, it was reported to executives that the number of customers who were not paying their accounts within the normal credit period had increased 50 percent. This apparently alarming situation, when subjected to further investigation by the executive in charge, showed that previously only ten customers out of thousands had been delinquent and that the increase to fifteen involved only small accounts.

The location of responsibility for interpreting statistical measurements to top management or for using such measurements in routine operations varies with the size and complexity of a firm's organizational structure. Most large businesses maintain a statistical department. Smaller firms usually subdivide this responsibility among the various divisions of the company. For example, the sales manager interprets statistics based on market data while the controller restricts his activity to financial facts and figures.

BUSINESS REPORTS

A business report—accounting, statistical, narrative, or graphic—is built from the raw material of words and numbers. The words and numbers must be organized so that a maximum amount of useful information is available to management. A good business report generally satisfies the following guidelines:

1. It is clear and concise.
2. It aims at simplicity.
3. It is timely.
4. It pertains to the decision-making responsibilities of the reader.
5. It gives standards for comparison.
6. It is focused on future managerial actions.

Business reports help the manager answer four types of questions:

1. Questions of background or perspective: Does the present situation require me to change goals or objectives? Should I modify present plans?
2. Score-card questions: Am I doing well or badly?
3. Attention-directing questions: What problems should I look into?
4. Problem-solving questions: Of the several ways of doing the job, which is the best?

The purpose of the first three types of questions is to explain situations that will affect the soundness of a manager's decisions. These explanations may range from simple statements narrating the current state of affairs to well-researched descriptions of circumstances, inside or outside the company, which have in the past or will in the future influence managerial decisions. The fourth type of questions—problem solving—can be viewed as a process that involves three steps: problem analysis, prediction, and decision making. In the first step, problem analysis, the problem is formulated and alternative courses of action are outlined. The probable outcome of each of the alternative plans is estimated in the second step, prediction. In the final step, decision making, the most appropriate alternative or alternatives are selected in the light of the goals to be achieved.

Although there can be an infinite variety of business reports, two specific types will be illustrated that fulfill the criteria stated above and are of value to management. One is a break-even chart and the other a control chart.

BREAK-EVEN CHART

The *break-even chart* graphically represents the relationship among costs, sales volume, and profits at a given time. In its simplest form it uses straight lines to represent sales income, variable costs, and total costs. It assumes that variable costs, which were defined earlier in this chapter, are clearly distinguishable and that fixed costs will not vary regardless of sales volume.

Figure 25-5 shows the construction of a break-even chart. The sales price of the product is $100. Variable expenses are 60 percent of the sales price, or $60 a unit. The monthly fixed costs are $50,000. The plant, under normal operating conditions, has a maximum productive capacity of 2,000 units a month.

Figure 25-5

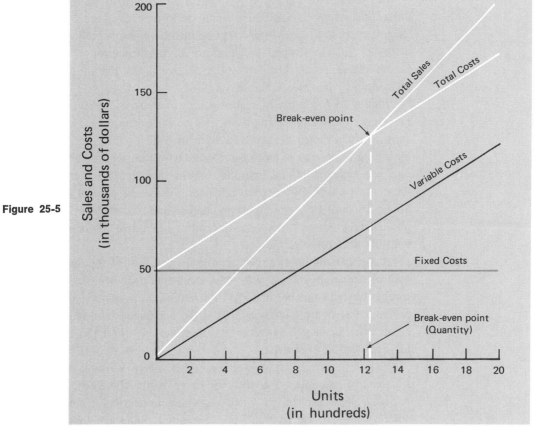

A Break-Even Chart

Figure 25-5 shows that total costs equal total sales income when 1,250 units are produced and sold. If less than this amount is produced and sold, the company suffers a loss. By producing and selling more than 1,250 units a month, the company makes a profit. For this reason, an output of 1,250 units a month is called the *break-even point*—neither profits nor losses are incurred.

CONTROL CHART

A *control chart* is a line chart which attempts to answer the question: Is the situation under control? While the statistics involved in constructing a control chart are a trifle complicated, the idea behind the chart is quite simple.

In its simplest dimensions, a control chart consists of three horizontal lines: one shows average or normal performance, another indicates the *lower control limit*, and a third represents the *upper control limit*. Statistical theory reveals that when the measure of performance goes beyond the acceptable range established by the control limits the situation is out of control and corrective action is required.

Figure 25-6 is fairly typical of a control chart. Here, by means of dots, the average breaking strength of 50 successive samples of cotton cloth is shown. The average breaking strength of each of the samples was found by testing four units of cloth each hour. It will be seen that these averages fluctuate across a central line and, for the most part, that they are within the control limits. Whenever a dot goes outside the control limit (samples 30 to 35 and 48), trouble is indicated; and the first-line supervisor is immediately alerted to look for the source of trouble. If found, the trouble will then be corrected.

Statistical computations determine the location of the upper and lower control limits in such a way that the supervisor will look for serious trouble but will not be distracted by random variations in the production process. The control limits should strike a balance between two types of errors: (a) looking for trouble that does not exist and (b) failing to look for trouble that does exist.

The control chart provides a graphic, early warning of trouble. In Figure 25-6, sample 30 is the first to go below the lower control limit. An alert supervisor might have suspected impending trouble earlier by noticing the downward trend in the plotted points. A long run of dots above or below the central line of normal performance should cause the

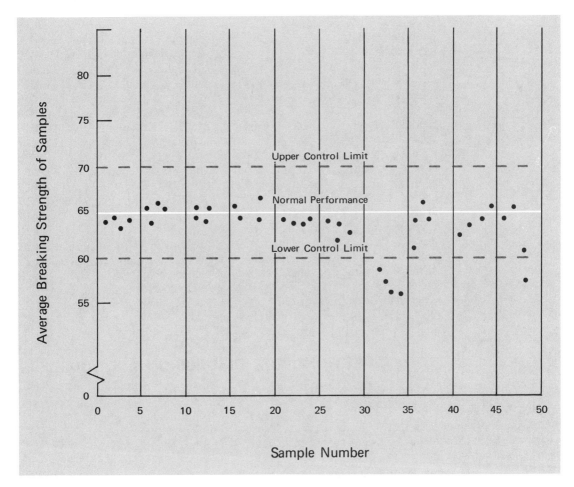

Figure 25-6

A Control Chart

supervisor to wonder whether there has been a significant change in normal operating conditions.

Control charts can be used not only for controlling the quality of production but may also be used in many other situations. For example, a marketing manager may construct a similar chart showing the ratio of the number of completed sales to the number of customers called upon. The manager of credit and collections may use a similar chart representing the average time required to receive payment on accounts receivable.

BUSINESS TERMS

QUESTIONS FOR DISCUSSION AND ANALYSIS

1. Are figures used by accountants apt to be more precise than data used by statisticians? Why or why not?

2. Are there any devices that might be used to secure a return of more than 10 to 15 percent for a mail survey on a general topic involving thousands of persons?

3. What method should a student governmental body use on a campus to sample student opinion on a topic such as library closing hours or campus parking meters? Justify your selection.

4. What is your opinion of the accuracy of the 1970 Census of Population? Are most figures released by the federal government reliable?

5. As a general proposition, do people who use the word "average" realize that, in a given situation, they might be referring to a mean, median, or mode? Illustrate your answer.

6. Is the statement that the Consumer Price Index advanced 1.6 points last month an accurate figure or an approximation? Give reasons for your decision.

7. In addition to the illustrations in the text, can you give a specific example of two sets of variables that have a high degree of correlation?

8. Do you prefer to examine statistical material presented in a bar or circular chart over a summary table? Why or why not?

9. In a break-even chart, will the lines for total costs and variable costs always parallel each other? Explain.

10. A control chart makes use of upper and lower control limits. How and by whom would these be established?

PROBLEMS AND SHORT CASES

1. The following grades were received on a final examination taken by students in a section of a first course in business: 77, 67, 91, 70, 42, 80, 98, 71, 63, 95, 82, 77, 65, 90, 35, 72, 59, 87, 77, 73, 96, 47, 85, 56, and 74.

   a. Compute the median, mode, and mean of these grades.
   b. The instructor, in posting these grades, wishes to indicate a single class average. Which one of the three computations do you think is preferable for this series? State reasons for your choice.

2. The following tabulation shows the distribution of the total income received in a fiscal year by the Geneva Office Equipment Corporation. Compute the percentage of each classification to the total and construct a chart to present this information in graphic form.

Materials and supplies	$1,500,000
Wages and salaries	2,400,000
Expenses	900,000
Taxes	600,000
Dividends	360,000
Retained earnings	240,000
Total income	$6,000,000

3. The Brown Manufacturing Company has already taken advantage of an opportunity to purchase a completely equipped factory that became available following the un-merger of a conglomerate. The management is considering the production of a motorized scooter, a product that the company can produce in the new facility and one that can be marketed with the present sales force.

   A careful estimate of expenses indicates that fixed costs will amount to $120,000 in the first year and that variable costs will run 80 percent of sales. The proposed selling price at the manufacturer's level is $300 per unit. The Vice President for Sales estimates that 1,500 units can be sold in the first year.

   You are requested to make a report to the management on the proposed course of action. What is your recommendation? Support this with a break-even chart.

SUGGESTED READINGS

Boot, J. C. G., and E. B. Cox. *Statistical Analysis for Managerial Decisions*. New York: McGraw-Hill Book Company, 1970.

Chance, W. A. *Statistical Methods for Decision Making*. Homewood, Illinois: Richard D. Irwin, Inc., 1969.

Chao, L. L. *Statistics: Methods and Analyses*. New York: McGraw-Hill Book Company, 1969.

Chou, Y. *Statistical Analysis with Business and Economic Applications*. New York: Holt, Rinehart and Winston, Inc., 1969.

Clark, C. T., and L. L. Schkade. *Statistical Methods for Business Decisions*. Cincinnati: South-Western Publishing Co., 1969.

Croxton, F. E., D. J. Cowden, and S. Klein. *Applied General Statistics*, Third Edition. Englewood Cliffs, New Jersey: Prentice-Hall, Inc., 1967.

Freund, J. E. *Statistics, A First Course*. Englewood Cliffs, New Jersey: Prentice-Hall, Inc., 1970.

Hamburg, M. *Statistical Analysis for Decision Making*. New York: Harcourt Brace Jovanovich, Inc., 1970.

Harnett, D. K. *Introduction to Statistical Methods*. Reading, Massachusetts: Addison-Wesley Publishing Company, Inc., 1970.

Leabo, D. A. *Basic Statistics*, Third Edition. Homewood, Illinois: Richard D. Irwin, Inc., 1968.

Mason, R. D. *Statistical Techniques in Business and Economics*. Homewood, Illinois: Richard D. Irwin, Inc., 1970.

Stockton, J. R., and Charles T. Clark. *Introduction to Business and Economic Statistics*, Fourth Edition. Cincinnati: South-Western Publishing Co., 1971.

Walpole, R. E. *Introduction to Statistics*. New York: The Macmillan Company, 1968.

Wonnacott, T. H., and R. J. Wonnacott. *Introductory Statistics*. New York: John Wiley & Sons, Inc., 1969.

Chapter 26

Forecasting and Budgeting

Change is a dominant characteristic of American business. For this reason businessmen are always concerned with the future and its implications for their operations. In order to anticipate some future state of affairs in society, in the economy, or in industry, they spend time analyzing reports on future business conditions. If the future were to be like the present, there would be no need to give thought preparing for it.

Businessmen prepare for the future through the use of forecasting and budgeting. These are tools necessary to the management functions of planning and control. Forecasting and budgeting have a common ground in that both involve predictions. Although forecasting does not involve a budget, a budget can be termed a forecast. Despite this seeming confusion, the commonly accepted meanings of the two terms are quite distinct. *Forecasting*, which usually involves a long period of time (frequently several years), is based almost entirely on external data and arrives at conclusions regarding the economy as a whole or some major segment of it. This knowledge is then analyzed in light of its probable effect on the individual firm. *Budgeting*, on the other hand, is the estimating by a firm of its anticipated incomes and expenditures over a definite future period (most frequently a year), and budget information is used not only for planning but also for purposes of control. The budget often appears as a projected income statement, and its construction is based very largely on past experience as measured by internal data.

Relying on these definitions, which are somewhat arbitrary, this chapter will first discuss forecasting as a vital element of long-range, strategic planning. Then the preparation and use of budgets, both as a tool of planning and as a control device, will be explained.

FORECASTING

Forecasting is an attempt to predict the future. It is an activity of business that is receiving increasing attention. Many reasons have been advanced in explaining why business managements are so deeply concerned about the future. A very common answer at this time is that people are aware that the coming turn of the century, the year 2,000, is within their lifetime. Some claim that predictions are needed because the rate of change in most aspects of life is accelerating. Others state that predictions are needed in order to correct the mistakes created in the past by the lack of foresight. This group points to the failure of both government and business to recognize in the 1950's the emerging problems of urban blight and poverty. A fourth group says that forecasting is needed in order that the benefits of scientific discovery may be realized and shared among the peoples of the world. In any event this era has become "future-oriented" in almost every dimension. A government has to anticipate changing demands on it; a business enterprise has to plan to meet future customer needs; and an individual is forced to think of long-range career choices, which may include rapidly changing and newly emerging occupations.

Forecasts may be classified in different ways. From the businessman's viewpoint, there are four major types of forecasts: (1) social, (2) technological, (3) economic, and (4) marketing. The last two types of forecasts are usually considered to be more pertinent to the immediate effort of business planning.

SOCIAL FORECASTS

Forecasting of social trends covers such topics as changing social structures, living patterns, customary values, and political relationships. Among these the businessman is interested in racial and ethnic problems; urban, suburban, and rural population shifts; attitudes toward work and leisure; the impact of affluence and poverty on buying habits; the shifting boundary between private and public sectors of the economy; and the prospects for international stability. There is no question but that this segment of the total business environment is frequently of prime importance to successful operations.

Social forecasting seeks to identify important long-term developments in social, political, and military affairs that seem likely to continue. One recent approach which attempts to discover future public-policy problems has been social forecasting by the use of scenarios. *Scenarios* are hypothetical sequences of events constructed for the purpose of focusing attention on causal processes and decision points. They attempt to answer two questions: How precisely could some hypothetical situation be created, step by step? What alternatives exist for preventing, diverting, or facilitating this turn of events? For example, scenarios have been written to explain, step by step, how the cities of Boston, New York, Philadelphia, and Washington could merge into one megapolis and how Japan could rise to be the third strongest industrial nation in the world.

TECHNOLOGICAL FORECASTS

In the attempt to answer the question as to what kinds of new products and new methods of production should be under development to get ready for the future, business executives have turned to *technological forecasting*. Very often the answer comes in the form of expert advice and opinion from scientists and engineers. Among experts, however, there may be varying degrees of disagreement. In an effort to reduce the range of disagreement over the feasibility of new processes and products and to predict more precisely the time of readiness for commercial development, some firms are now using the *Delphi technique*. The RAND Corporation devised Delphi forecasting which, in its simplest form, is a systematic procedure of arriving at a consensus of expert opinion concerning the potential and time of a technological advance. It depends upon an investigator acting as an intermediary and arbitrator among experts to prevent misunderstanding and to minimize the danger of submerging individual judgment in a vague majority view. The method has worked quite successfully in many situations, and its application to other types of forecasting seems promising at this time.

ECONOMIC FORECASTS

Businessmen turn to economic forecasting more often than to any other type. All business executives know that it is important to gain some idea of what general business conditions will be in a number of months or years ahead. *Economic forecasting* attempts to make such estimates, and, in so doing, places major reliance on external data.

Economic forecasting can be, and frequently is, a complicated process. In contrast to both social and technological forecasting, it is usually much more quantitative in nature. It is a basic factor in market forecasting and generally serves as a framework for the preparation of the budget of income and expense for a company. Because economic forecasting plays an important role in business decision making, particular attention will be given to who prepares economic forecasts and to three commonly used methods of preparing them.

Who Prepares Economic Forecasts?

There are three major groups who prepare and issue economic forecasts. Various agencies of the federal government play an important role in forecasting; there are several well-known private agencies, usually of the nonprofit variety, active in the field; and most large companies maintain their own staffs of economists. All three groups make use of any and all figures released by each other, and they also draw on other sources of information.

Agencies of the federal government. In 1946 Congress passed the so-called Full Employment Act. Among other provisions it created a Council of Economic Advisers who were instructed to report to the President of the United States. This Council makes reports that are published every six months and, on the basis of its work, the President issues an Economic Report each January. The basic idea of the act was to provide jobs for everyone by maintaining a healthy economy with the government providing employment on public works when necessary. Forecasts, obviously, become an important part of the duties of the Council. Some of these are made for the Council, at its request, by other federal agencies. Notable among these is the monthly *Business Cycle Developments* of the Bureau of the Census, which is available for business use.

The Federal Reserve Board is another governmental agency that releases a vast amount of statistical data including the Industrial Production Index published each month. In the forecasting area, its annual survey of the anticipated spending and saving habits of consumers provides information about this important but difficult-to-measure segment of future economic activity. Using a sampling technique, composite data are compiled on what people think their financial habits will be in the future.

Many other departments and divisions of the federal government are deserving of mention. As described on page 610, the Bureau of Labor Statistics publishes the Consumer Price Index. In connection with the budget the Treasury Department must make forecasts of general business conditions. The Department of Agriculture forecasts the crop situation as part of its concern with price supports. The Department of Commerce publishes some predictions in its monthly publication *Survey of Current Business*.

Private agencies. One group of private agencies that frequently make forecasts includes the trade associations. The American Iron & Steel Institute indicates the expected rate of steel production in the months ahead, and the National Association of Purchasing Management publishes figures in its weekly bulletin on the anticipated rate of placing orders.

Another group of private concerns includes such organizations as the National Bureau of Economic Research, the National Planning Association, the Chamber of Commerce of the United States, and the National Industrial Conference Board. In specific areas, the F. W. Dodge Corporation's figures on construction and the forecast of security prices by the Standard and Poor's Corporation are well known. Several universities also maintain research bureaus interested, in part, in forecasting; and some business magazines publish articles on anticipated future developments.

Corporation economists. One of the functions of a staff of economists on the payroll of a corporation is to make forecasts and to relate these to the company. For example, a manufacturer who is a heavy user of basic raw materials, such as coal, rubber, and copper, can either buy on a hand-to-mouth basis or practice forward buying. An accurate prediction of future price trends could easily produce savings amounting to hundreds of thousands of dollars.

How Are Economic Forecasts Made?

There are many different methods of making estimates of future business conditions. Three of the more commonly used methods will be mentioned here: (1) projections, (2) leads and lags, and (3) the use of gross national product data.

Projections. *Projections* as applied to business forecasting are the extensions of known trends of the past into the future. This is done by plotting data for past years on a chart and extending a line from the latest date that follows the pattern of prior years. This extension of a trend line is known as *extrapolation*. For example, between 1963 and 1968 per capita personal income in the United States increased from $2,458 to $3,409, or an annual average of about $190 a year. If past conditions prevail into the future, then the projected per capita personal income in the year 1978 would be $5,309. This extrapolated value was found by multiplying $190 by 10 and adding the product to the 1968 figure.

Despite the possibility that other factors may enter the picture and invalidate an extrapolation, projections are a very useful forecasting device. The influences that acted in the past to establish a specific trend can be assumed, with some degree of assurance, to continue to affect the future. So many indexes are available covering so many different economic indicators that projections of one or more of these may well provide a firm with a sound basis on which to base a business decision.

Leads and lags. Past figures are available on literally hundreds of different types of economic data. Quarterly reports can be obtained on such items as barrels of oil refined, business failures, government spending, man-hours worked, and many other series of data covering every conceivable type of economic activity. The *Survey of Current Business* and related publications of the Department of Commerce contain data on approximately 2,600 different series, which provide some idea of the vast extent of statistical data available. It has been the aim of forecasters to locate among the various series available some that have led the rest of the economy either into an upturn or a downturn, and others that lag behind general economic conditions. On the lead side, forecasters have favored common stock prices, machine tool orders, housing starts, business failures, hours worked per week, and approximately 25 other series. On the lag side a common indicator used is consumer debt.

It might appear that by combining several lead indicators and averaging the number of months by which they led an upturn in general business activity a foolproof forecast could be made. Actually, forecasters using this composite method have not been much more successful than others who have relied on a single series. It seems to be impossible to predict the future, but this statement does not mean that leads and lags do not constitute a valuable forecasting tool. The past has demonstrated enough consistency to warrant making an estimate of the future by this device that has a reasonable chance of being proved accurate.

Gross national product. A concept that has come into much favor with economists since World War II is that of *gross national product,* or GNP as it is commonly called. It is the nation's output of goods and services expressed as so many dollars per year or quarter. It may be defined as the total market value of all final goods and services produced during a stated period. There are four major components of the gross national product: (a) personal consumption expenditures, (b) gross private domestic investment, (c) government purchases of goods and services, and (d) net foreign investment.

Personal consumption expenditures include the amounts consumers spend for durable and nondurable goods and services. Gross private domestic investment represents expenditures for capital goods, chiefly by business concerns. The expenditures of local political subdivisions, the states, and the federal government are totaled to arrive at the item of government purchases of goods and services. In the case of foreign investment, only the net difference between goods and services exported and imported is used in this calculation.

Current GNP figures show the level of total business activity at that date. A forecaster can project each of the components to whatever period of time he wishes to measure and arrive at an estimate of the dollar value of the gross national product at that date. Since many decisions affecting the future of a firm are closely related to overall business conditions that will prevail in the years ahead, a projected GNP total may provide the best basis for judgment. In other cases one segment, such as personal consumption expenditures, can be more helpful than the overall figures.

MARKET FORECASTS

The bridge between economic forecasting and a company's estimate of next year's sales volume is *market forecasting.* It is a systematic study to discover not only how much a company can hope to sell but where, to whom, and how.

Market forecasting involves three basic steps: (a) a study of future business conditions based on economic forecasting; (b) an attempt to estimate the total demand for the industry of which the company is a part; and (c) a judgment concerning the share of the market to be captured by a particular company.

For a company manufacturing a product intended for ultimate consumer purchase, such as a household electrical appliance, the key factors to be considered in market forecasting are estimates concerning: (a) the number of consumers in the market; (b) the money income of the consumers; (c) the prices of competing goods and services; (d) consumer expectations with respect to future personal income and expenditures; and (e) changes in their brand preferences. This information may be supplemented with an analysis of past sales data of the company. The study of prior years' sales should provide information on the past share of the market—which products are selling best in what markets and to what type of customers.

A recent operational tool of economic and market planning which is spreading in use in government, business, and the academic world is input-output (I-O) analysis. Its advocates feel that the ultimate benefits will include more rational and better informed economic policy for government as well as more efficient and profitable planning for business. *Input-output analysis* is concerned with measuring the flow of materials and goods within a given economy—regional, national, or international. The method involves setting up tables showing who buys what from whom. Prior to I-O, economists traditionally looked at historical relationships between such factors as gross national product (GNP), employment, retail sales, or business spending for plant and equipment. If two segments of the economy moved up and down together in the past, it was considered likely that they would continue to do so in the future. I-O, on the other hand, attempts to trace actual production and consumption relationships between sectors of the national or regional economy.

For example, sales of paint as a percentage of GNP may not be of much help to a paintmaker planning a production schedule. But a breakdown that shows how much paint goes to the automobile industry would be valuable information, especially when coupled with a forecast of an increase or a drop in automobile production.

The concept of I-O dates back to the 1930's, but in recent years two factors have increased its usefulness. One is the computer with its ability to handle quickly huge masses of data which previously made I-O cumbersome. The second is a massive data-gathering effort by the Department of Commerce which recently produced a new set of I-O tables available for use by business in both printed and magnetic-tape form.

Recent success in the use of I-O by such companies as Dow Chemical, Bethlehem Steel, and Westinghouse Electric suggests that input-output analysis has great potential as a management tool for long-range economic and market planning and strategy.

RELIABILITY AND USES OF FORECASTS

No one has yet found a satisfactory way to look into the future, and this statement applies to forecasting. So far no method attempted seems to work consistently, but there is no doubt that predictions made on the basis of the techniques here described and many others are reasonably accurate in a majority of instances. Reliance placed on forecasts made by trained personnel is certainly to be preferred over any other known method of predicting the future.

The uses of forecasts are many and varied. Some of the more obvious managerial decisions based on the business outlook include plant expansion and location, inventory stockpiling, the sale of stocks or bonds, and the introduction of new products.

BUDGETING

Budgets were first adopted in this country by governmental units, and today their use by states, counties, townships, cities and villages, school districts, the federal government, and other political subdivisions is universal. Income, usually from taxes, can be predicted quite accurately; and expenditures, unless borrowing is authorized, must be kept within the bounds of the anticipated receipts. Personal budgets are also widely used by individuals and families who realize that their expenditures must be kept in line with their known incomes. In addition to these better known uses of budgets, all large companies and many smaller progressive concerns also use this tool as an aid in management planning and control.

When a business undertakes the preparation and use of a budget, three major steps are involved. First of all, it is necessary to establish a budget organization and to reach agreement on some basic policies. After this has been accomplished, it is then possible to proceed with the preparation of a budget. This task should be completed prior to the first day of the budget period. Finally, as operations move into the budgeted period, controls must be established so that corrective measures or revisions can be made promptly. Each of these steps will be explained in some detail with particular emphasis on the actual preparation of budget figures.

ORGANIZATION AND POLICIES

Assuming that a business has not previously used budgets, a number of preparatory steps must be taken in order to make certain that maximum managerial results will accrue. Some of the problems that need to be resolved are: (1) budget organization, (2) extent of budget adaptation, (3) length of budget period, and (4) control procedures.

Budget Organization

At the very outset someone should be named as the budget officer. Frequently he is the controller because of his contact and familiarity with the accounting system, although sometimes the president or general manager assumes this position. The direction of budgetary procedure is a task for top management; and, while the budget officer may function as a clearinghouse for the assembly of estimates and the transmission of performance data to and from the operating departments, the policy decisions that are required from time to time must emanate from the top. To carry out these policies and provide supervision at the operating level, a common practice is the appointment of an individual in each department to handle any budget matters that require attention during the budget period.

Many companies set up a budget committee, consisting of the president and the heads of the major departments, whose job is that of reviewing the figures that are collected and of counseling with the budget officer and the president as the program proceeds. This group may possess authority to pass on policy matters that arise, but in any case its decisions are subject to the approval of the president.

Extent of Budget Adaptation

Before installing a budget, management must determine the extent of its coverage. In most businesses it is possible and desirable to include every phase of its operations. Occasionally because of innate irregularities such as might be found in a research department, a few activities may not lend themselves to the limitations imposed by budgeting. Since a hoped-for goal of a budget is a projected income statement, it is more satisfactory if budgeting is adopted on a company-wide basis.

Length of Budget Period

It is inherent in a budget that it cover a specific period of time. The customary coverage for an operating budget is a year, which is then broken down into quarters or months. This subdivision is particularly important for firms that have seasonal variations although the major purpose is to make it possible to check the budget against actual operations at frequent intervals. A few budgets, such as one covering repair and replacement of machinery, may be for longer than a year although an annual breakdown would provide necessary information for an estimated income statement.

Control Procedures

A budget will not work unless it is carefully coordinated with the accounting procedures used by a firm. In addition to performing its usual functions, the accounting department must keep its accounts in such a manner that comparisons with the budget can be made quickly and easily. The installation of a budget may require revamping accounting procedures that were formerly considered satisfactory. Control procedures must also be established that will assure management that when any operating result is out of line with the budget estimate, this variance will be promptly called to the attention of the proper company official.

PREPARATION OF A BUDGET

The actual preparation of a budget should begin several weeks or even months before the beginning of the budget period. A typical procedure would involve preparing the following: (1) sales budget, (2) sales expense and advertising budgets, (3) production budget, (4) other departmental expense budgets, (5) cash budget, and (6) estimated statements.

Sales Budget

In view of the fact that all of the activities of a business depend primarily on the volume of sales, the first step in the preparation of a company budget is customarily to establish the *sales budget*. This involves the submission of the estimated sales volume by the sales manager, revision of this estimate by the budget committee in light of information furnished by the firm's statisticians, and the establishment of the revised figures as the goal for the sales budget. All of the other departmental budgets are then set up on the basis of their relation to the sales budget and involve only the single step of compiling and submitting the figures.

The most common method used by the sales manager to compile his estimate of total sales is to require each salesman to submit a detailed estimate of the sales, by items, that he believes he can make in his territory during the coming budget period. For example, salesmen of food lines, such as frozen fruits and vegetables, know how many grocery stores and supermarkets are in their territories, what new ones are to be opened, and what old ones may be closed. They also know conditions of employment and industrial activity that will affect the purchase of their products by consumers. Accordingly, they are in an excellent position to submit intelligent estimates of the sales of frozen foods in their areas. These estimates are then accumulated for each of the territories and finally for the company as a whole.

At the same time, the statisticians in the home office compute a tentative overall sales total, based on a consideration of past sales and a knowledge of general economic trends. The estimate submitted by the sales force is then compared with that developed by the head office, and any differences are composed by the budget committee unless they have been reconciled by the top sales executives. This final figure becomes the basis for determining the sales expense and advertising budgets that will be necessary to attain the agreed-upon sales goal and, as mentioned above, is the determining factor for all other budgets as well.

Sales Expense and Advertising Budgets

Two budgets are closely allied to the sales budget. These are the sales expense budget and the advertising budget. The *sales expense budget* consists of an estimate regarding the anticipated cost of securing the sales volume that is projected for the coming budgetary period. It includes sales office expense, traveling expense, salesmen's salaries or commissions, and sales supervision expense. It may also include storage costs for finished goods.

As a corollary of the sales expense budget, the *advertising budget* sets forth the expected cost of advertising the product as a means of helping to secure the planned sales. It is made out in great detail and usually embraces all advertisements and the dates of their scheduled appearances. Unusual advertising plans with a complete explanation of the reasons for them and the sales results that are expected because of the extraordinary expenditure are presented. For example, one company planned to spend $100,000 on a campaign to introduce its products on the West Coast. In making up his advertising budget, the advertising manager of the firm placed this item together with the required explanation in a section of his budget estimate separate from that in which his regular advertising expenditures were listed. Thus the budget committee was able to note quickly the increased advertising that was planned and to discern the reasons for it.

Production Budget

The drawing up of the *production budget* consists of determining the amounts of all products that will be made during the coming period and setting up the production schedules so that these goals can be attained. In most companies the production budget is dependent upon the development of the sales budget. In some firms the manufacturing division decides what and how much is to be made, and the sales budget is based on this estimate. This practice, however, is becoming less frequent.

Occasionally the manufacturing division takes issue with the sales department's budget figures, with the result that changes are made in the latter estimate. This situation may arise due to the production department's feeling that the sales department is asking it to do the impossible in agreeing to manufacture goods in the quantities asked. Perhaps a major alteration in the plant that will take a sizable part of the productive facilities out of action for a time is scheduled for the coming period. Or possibly a planned addition to the factory is behind schedule because of material or machine shortages. These or any number of other causes may force a revision of the sales budget to bring it in line with the productive capacity of the manufacturing division.

Materials budget. After the production budget has been established, it is necessary to plan for the materials that are required to make up the finished products. This involves the planning of purchases so that the needed materials will always be available to the production department on schedule. The *materials budget* thus serves as a guide to the activities of the purchasing department.

Labor budget. The personnel department is charged with the task of providing the workers needed to make the planned volume of production. It sets up its plans to procure and have on hand the number and types of operatives that will be required for the job.

Manufacturing expense budget. The *manufacturing expense budget* consists of an estimate of the expenses that will be incurred by the manufacturing division in producing the quantity and types of goods called for by the production budget. It is broken down into account classifications similar to those shown on page 565 under the heading "Factory overhead." Although the total of this as well as other expense classifications is of more interest to top management, within the department the details are necessary in order to pinpoint items that may become responsible for budget variations, such as "Heat, light, and power" or "Factory supplies expense."

Other Departmental Expense Budgets

In addition to the sales expense, advertising expense, and manufacturing expense budgets, it is a common practice to budget the expenses of operating the other major departments of a business. The department heads submit their estimates to the budget committee that approves or amends them.

Cash Budget

When a firm sets up a budget to control its selling and manufacturing operations, a cash budget (see Figure 26-1) should be established also. The purpose of the *cash budget* is to make certain that the company has sufficient cash on hand to meet its current needs as they arise. Bills of all kinds must be paid when due, and money must be available to meet the payrolls as they occur.

In order to accomplish this objective, estimates of all cash receipts and disbursements must be drawn up for each month (or even on a weekly basis) in the budget period and examined carefully to determine whether the amount that will be on hand from time to time will be adequate. If, at any time during the period under scrutiny, the supply of cash will not take care of the needs for it, it may be necessary for the company to negotiate a bank loan or to sell short-term notes. This condition frequently exists in those industries that have year-round production schedules but seasonal sales periods. The toy industry is an excellent example. Toy manufacturers produce throughout the year, but most of their orders, which constitute the source of their cash receipts, are secured during the late spring and summer months. Many firms in this business, therefore, must negotiate bank loans to carry them through the months when sales are not being made.

Related to the cash budget, but frequently prepared separately, are budgets that cover major repairs, replacements, and additions to plant and equipment. Although these budgets are likely to cover a period of time such as five or ten years, the applicable portion of the expenditures for any one year must be included in the cash budget for that year. Routine disbursements, such as paying interest on bonds outstanding or dividends on stock, plus nonroutine expenditures, such as retiring all or a portion of a long-term debt, must also be incorporated in the cash budget.

THE EDWARDS CORPORATION

Cash Budget

	JANUARY	FEBRUARY	DECEMBER
Cash on hand— beginning of month	40,173.00	85,038.40	24,535.86
Receipts:			
Cash sales	39,285.00	14,250.00	40,500.00
Collections	57,280.00	50,220.00	52,200.00
Total receipts	96,565.00	64,470.00	92,700.00
Total cash available	136,738.00	149,508.40	117,235.86
Disbursements:			
Purchases	33,460.00	48,052.00	20,500.00
Selling expenses	9,586.00	9,824.00	22,660.00
Administrative expenses	8,653.60	7,185.40	7,743.60
Other expenses	....	....	5,200.94
Total disbursements	51,699.60	65,061.40	56,104.54
Estimated cash at end of month.	85,038.40	84,447.00	61,131.32

Figure 26-1

Cash Budget

Estimated Statements

If all departments of a business are budgeted, it is possible to construct an estimated income statement that will show the anticipated income and expenses as well as net income for the budget period. It is also possible to construct a balance sheet that reflects these operating results, although this statement is less commonly prepared.

The 1971 income statement and the 1972 budget shown in Figure 26-2 for Loomis Rugs, Inc., indicate that this retail firm expects to increase its sales 20 percent in the budgeted year. The increased volume of purchases necessary to support the higher sales is expected to result in lower prices paid to manufacturers and to yield a higher gross margin of profit. Selling expenses are expected to rise proportionally to the increase in sales, but

LOOMIS RUGS, INC.

Income Statement for 1971 and Budget for 1972

	ACTUAL 1971		BUDGET 1972	
Sales		$220,000		$264,000
Cost of merchandise sold:				
Merchandise inventory,				
Jan. 1	$ 70,000		$ 66,700	
Purchases	159,250		190,000	
Merchandise available for				
sale	$229,250		$256,700	
Merchandise inventory,				
Dec. 31	66,700		75,000	
Cost of merchandise sold ..		162,550		181,700
Gross profit on sales		$ 57,450		$ 82,300
Operating expenses:				
Selling expenses:				
Sales salaries	$ 22,725		$ 26,000	
Advertising	6,250		9,000	
Delivery expense	2,790		3,200	
Misc. selling expenses ..	1,805		2,000	
Total selling expenses ..	$ 33,570		$ 40,200	
General expenses:				
Office salaries	$ 8,400		$ 9,000	
Rent	3,600		3,600	
Taxes	1,865		2,000	
Insurance	1,225		1,300	
Misc. general expenses ..	870		900	
Total general expenses ..	$ 15,960		$ 16,800	
Total operating expenses ..		49,530		57,000
Net income from operations .		$ 7,920		$ 25,300
Other expense:				
Interest expense		80		300
Net income		$ 7,840		$ 25,000

Figure 26-2

Estimated Income Statement

it is not anticipated that the increased volume will materially affect general expenses. Assuming the attainment of budgeted goals, Loomis Rugs, Inc., can anticipate a net income of $25,000 in 1972 as opposed to the low and unsatisfactory return of only $7,840 in 1971.

BUDGETARY CONTROL

The third and last step in installing and using budgeting as a management tool is that of control. When the budget committee has coordinated and reviewed the estimates received from divisions and departments, its final figures, assuming the approval of the firm's president or executive committee, become the goal toward which all activities are directed. The sales department subdivides its total into quotas for districts and individual salesmen, the production department sets up manufacturing schedules, and similar procedures are followed by other operating units. By the time all this has taken place, the chances are excellent that the beginning of the budgeted period is only a matter of days away.

Control is achieved by the use of forms that show the budget figures for a period of time, such as a month, with a space for inserting actual performance reports as soon as they are compiled. A comparison between the planned and actual results indicates how well each department is doing in measuring up to its budgeted figures. These performance reports are available to the budget committee and the chief executive officer of the company who may review them with the department managers concerned. Any variations will be noted and remedial steps, if required, can be instituted. For example, if sales in a certain territory are running below the budget, the sales manager can get in touch with the salesmen in that area to discover where the trouble lies.

The important point in this procedure is that the deviation from the budget is brought quickly to the attention of the responsible executive, who is enabled thereby to investigate the matter and do something about it while there is time for remedial action. This practice, which is also used for many other situations, is known as *management by exception*. It is a valuable means of conserving managerial energy, through the planning of a firm's records, so that only the exceptions to the company's plans are brought to the attention of the executives. As long as things are progressing according to plan, no special need exists for the management to exert other than the customary supervision over operations. It is when something that upsets these plans occurs, an exception to the plans, that management should be immediately notified. Intelligent administration calls for records that will provide this kind of information.

There is another facet to budgetary control and this occurs when evidence accumulates that the estimated figures are out of line with actual performance. The variance can be either over or under although plans are more likely to be optimistic than pessimistic. Assuming that five months of a budgeted year have gone by and sales are consistently running 10 percent below estimates, a revision of the budget for the remaining seven months may be in order. This will have far-reaching effects on almost every department and division of the firm, but there is no point in adhering slavishly to goals that seemingly cannot be attained.

Actually many firms prepare flexible budgets before the start of the budget period based on different sales estimates. In any event, the budget should be closely geared to actual conditions as they develop and necessary adjustments should be a part of the control process. A requirement of this element of control is that the accounting department be able to release operating figures promptly, a task that has been speeded up in recent years through the use of electronic data processing equipment. With both flexibility and prompt access to operating data, a budget becomes a managerial tool of great value.

OPERATIONS RESEARCH

One of the relatively recent developments in the area of managerial decision making that was originally used for military purposes in World War II is *operations research* or *OR* as it is popularly called. OR is characterized by the application of quantitative techniques to a wide variety of management problems, frequently by a team consisting of accountants, engineers, statisticians, economists, scientists, and mathematicians. The use of computers is almost a necessity; in fact, the ability to apply complicated mathematical formulas to business problems is interwoven with the programming of a computer to handle the data.

Although the majority of the various applications of OR are in operating areas, such as inventory management or production scheduling, there are two devices that can be of outstanding assistance in making forecasts and in preparing budgets. One of these is game theory and the other is simulation.

GAME THEORY

The purpose of *game theory* is to decide the strategy that is most likely to achieve maximum profits in a competitive situation. The businessman does not know what his competitors may do, but he must plan his moves to offset those of one or more of his opponents. For example, if his goal is to increase sales, he may be able to do so by lowering prices, by launching an advertising campaign, or by employing more salesmen. He does not know what his competitors will do to offset any one or a combination of his moves, but he can make any number of assumptions and by mathematical computations arrive at a plan that indicates maximum profit potential. This decision may well determine the sales budget and, as has been previously indicated, most of the other budgets as well.

SIMULATION

Simulation provides a technique for observing the interaction of a number of important elements in a business problem by using various mixes in an attempt to see what will happen if some elements remain constant and others change. If these decisions were actually made, one at a time, the possibility of expensive mistakes and the time required to note results would discourage making such experiments. By creating a model and by using a computer, the interaction of any number of variables can be observed promptly and without any danger of losing money.

For example, a business seeking more profits may wonder whether increased production would reduce manufacturing costs so that lower prices could be offered that would result in the needed sales. The extent of the cost saving per unit as well as the size of the reduction in sales price would be important as would labor costs, advertising expenses, general economic conditions, and the competitive situation. By trying numerous combinations, which the computer can process very rapidly, management may determine that one course of action seems to offer more promise than other alternatives. These figures can then be incorporated into appropriate budgets.

In recent years several large corporations have sought to combine economic forecasting and budgeting with simulation into a unified *corporate financial model*. For example, Sun Oil Company's corporate financial model combines 1,500 different types of data pertaining to product prices and volumes, raw material costs, economic conditions, investments, income from subsidiary companies, and discretionary expense items. In 14 seconds of computer time, a year's operations may be simulated. The model has shown itself to be very accurate in forecasting net income one year into the future. Because of speed and accuracy of the reports issued by the model, the Sun Oil Company believes it has a valuable tool for comparing and evaluating alternative courses of action that the company may take. It enables top management to react quickly to changing economic conditions and, at the same time, to make meaningful plans for the future.

BUSINESS TERMS

QUESTIONS FOR DISCUSSION AND ANALYSIS

1. Has forecasting become more essential in the second half of the twentieth century than it was in the first half as related to the successful operation of a business?

2. Why is business interested in social and technological forecasts? Give a specific example of each that could affect business profits.

3. Why does the federal government prepare economic forecasts? Is its motive primarily selfish?

4. Does extrapolation as a forecasting device recognize recent events or does it rely entirely on the expectation that trends established over several years will continue at the same rate in the future? Justify your position.

5. More facts are available today than ever before and computers can process these data rapidly in a multitude of combinations. As a result, are forecasts and budgets more accurate today than they were in pre-computer days?

6. Are budgets more likely to be more accurate than forecasts? Why or why not?

7. There is a strong tendency for each department head to submit inflated figures when asked to submit an expense budget. What can a budget committee do to eliminate or correct this situation?

8. What is the one most important advantage of a budget to a business firm? Does this advantage also rank first with governmental units?

9. Budgets establish goals. Isn't this advantage lost when flexible budgets are prepared in advance?

10. Operations research as applied to forecasting and budgets relies more or less on the use of models. Since a model is constructed by human beings, are not the results derived from its use likely to reflect the prejudices and biases of these individuals?

PROBLEMS AND SHORT CASES

1. The population of the United States including Alaska and Hawaii but excluding citizens living abroad was as follows for the ten-year periods of the twentieth century:

	Population (Thousands)
1900	76,212
1910	92,228
1920	106,022
1930	123,202
1940	132,165
1950	151,326
1960	179,323
1970	203,185

Plot the above statistics on graph paper allowing room for expansion to 300,000 (thousands) of people and for the years 1980, 1990, and 2000. Plot the known population figures and draw a trend line to the year 1970 that is the best possible fit to the data plotted. Then, starting with the year 1970, extrapolate this line to the year 2000.

On the basis of your completed graph, what are your estimates of the population of the United States in 1980, in 1990, and in 2000? Do you believe this projection is a satisfactory method of estimating the population of the United States?

2. Shown on page 648 is a condensed income statement for the Reliable Manufacturing Company for the year ending December 31, 1973. Top management is disturbed at a net income of less than 1 percent on $12,000,000 in sales and has asked the sales manager whether volume might be increased substantially in 1974. The chief executive believes that increased sales would have a favorable influence on net income, which he believes should be at least 8 percent on sales. After contacting the salesmen, the sales manager reports that he is convinced that a 50 percent gain in units sold could be achieved in the coming year if the price of each unit were reduced 10 percent.

RELIABLE MANUFACTURING COMPANY
Income Statement
For Year Ended December 31, 1973

Sales (500,000 units)		$12,000,000
Cost of goods manufactured and sold		7,500,000
Gross profit on sales		4,500,000
Selling expenses	$2,400,000	
General expenses	2,000,000	4,400,000
Net income		$ 100,000

Prepare an estimate of income, expense, and net income for 1974 taking into account the information given and also the following: (a) The cost of each unit will decrease 12 percent with increased volume of production; (b) Selling expenses will increase 20 percent due to the need for an advertising campaign plus increased sales commissions; and (c) General expenses will increase 5 percent due to the larger volume of orders to process.

On the basis of your budget, do you think that the management should reduce prices and expand production or will it have to look elsewhere for a solution to the problem of an unsatisfactory net income?

3. The Budget Committee of the Cunningham Corporation, a steel fabricating concern, consists of the following corporate officers: President, Executive Vice President, Vice President—Sales, Vice President—Manufacturing, Vice President—Finance, Vice President—Personnel, and a Budget Director. The President serves as chairman of the group, which has final authority for determining the budget for the following year.

Preliminary budget figures were assembled several weeks ago, and the Budget Committee has held three meetings. On the basis of these discussions the Budget Director has now presented a tentative budget that, in condensed form, appears as follows:

	Current Year	Budget
Sales	$10,000,000	$12,000,000
Cost of merchandise sold	6,500,000	8,200,000
Gross profit on sales	3,500,000	3,800,000
Selling expenses	1,600,000	1,700,000
General expenses	1,100,000	1,150,000
Total operating expenses	2,700,000	2,850,000
Net income from operations	$ 800,000	$ 950,000

The Vice President—Sales has agreed that the budgeted increase in sales is a realistic figure and one that is attainable but only if he is given a substantial increase in the amount allocated to advertising. During the current year selling expenses included $500,000 for advertising, and the budget prepared by the Budget Director shows an allocation of $550,000 for this item. The Vice President—Sales is adamant in insisting that he must have an increase of $100,000 over the $50,000 added by the Budget Director.

When it was pointed out to the Vice President—Sales that an added expense of $100,000 would reduce profits to a level only slightly better than the current year, he insisted that the increased number of units to be manufactured would provide savings in the cost of goods sold that could easily offset the increased advertising cost and not affect the budget net income from operations. The Vice President—Manufacturing took an opposite viewpoint and argued that any economies accruing from a more efficient use of plant facilities would be offset by higher costs of raw materials and of labor.

The matter finally came to a vote when it became apparent that both vice presidents were firm in their convictions. The Executive Vice President, a former sales manager, and the Vice President—Personnel supported the Vice President—Sales. The Vice President—Finance and the Budget Director voted with the Vice President—Manufacturing. This left the decision up to the President, who announced that he wanted a day or two to make some investigations on his own before rendering his decision. He immediately turned to a statistician in the market research department and requested projections of the wholesale price index and of wage rates. Both showed that an increase of 6 percent could be anticipated in the coming year, and the President determined that these items accounted for approximately one half of the cost of goods sold.

If you were the President of the Cunningham Corporation, how would you decide this issue? Support your conclusion by reference to the data available and make any assumptions you believe necessary consistent with the figures and facts supplied.

SUGGESTED READINGS

Butler, W. F., and R. A. Kavesh. *How Business Economists Forecast.* Englewood Cliffs, New Jersey: Prentice-Hall, Inc., 1966.

Dauten, C. A. *Business Cycles and Forecasting*, Third Edition. Cincinnati: South-Western Publishing Co., 1968.

Heckert, J. B., and J. D. Willson. *Business Budgeting and Control*, Third Edition. New York: The Ronald Press Company, 1967.

Knight, W. D., and E. H. Weinwurm. *Managerial Budgeting.* New York: The Macmillan Company, 1964.

McKinley, D. H., M. G. Lee, and H. Duffy. *Forecasting Business Conditions.* New York: The American Bankers Association, 1965.

Naylor, T. H., *et al. Computer Simulation Techniques.* New York: John Wiley & Sons, Inc., 1966.

Niswonger, C. R., and P. E. Fess. *Accounting Principles*, Tenth Edition. Cincinnati: South-Western Publishing Co., 1969. Chapter 22.

Pyle, W. W., and J. A. White. *Fundamental Accounting Principles*, Fifth Edition. Homewood, Illinois: Richard D. Irwin, Inc., 1969. Chapter 26.

Schattke, R. W., H. G. Jensen, and V. L. Bean. *Accounting.* Boston: Allyn and Bacon, Inc., 1969. Chapters 21-23.

Wolfe, H. D. *Business Forecasting Methods.* New York: Holt, Rinehart, and Winston, Inc., 1966.

Wagner, H. M. *Principles of Operations Research with Application to Managerial Decisions.* Englewood Cliffs, New Jersey: Prentice-Hall, Inc., 1969.

Part 8

Legal and Regulatory Environment of Business

Prologue to Part 8

Legal and Regulatory Environment of Business

Capitalism could not exist if business did not have a legal framework in which to conduct its operations. Some laws provide welcome protection to business; some are regulatory in nature; and still others require sizable outlays from profit-seeking enterprises. All of these enactments are a part of the legal environment that is necessary and appropriate to the functioning of a capitalistic economy.

How our legal system administers laws passed primarily by state and local governments serves as an introduction to Chapter 27. The specific sections of legislation that prescribe the rights and responsibilities of owners or managers of business enterprises are then explained.

Chapter 28 makes a sharp distinction between the regulation of competitive businesses and regulated industries. For the first category, which includes millions of firms, regulation takes the form of laws that restrain businesses from taking actions that would hinder the free play of competitive forces. On the other hand, regulated industries, such as public utilities and the railroads, are subject to price and service regulation by an appropriate governmental agency.

Chapter 29 describes the taxes levied against businesses by the federal, state, and local governments. The tax burden carried by small as well as large firms is so heavy that it is worthy of the detailed study accorded to it. Stress is placed on the necessary consideration given by management to the effect of taxes on a wide range of business decisions.

Chapter 27

Business Law

Businesses could not operate under a capitalistic system except in a legal environment. Both the rights and responsibilities of business firms are essentially prescribed by law. For example, owing property, collecting debts, overtime pay, paying taxes, and even prices charged are but a few of the many items that have strong legal overtones. Although both the permissions and restrictions of the law are generally taken for granted, they continually influence business management.

Law consists of constitutions, statutes, court decisions, rulings, and regulations that are administered by officials and enforced by various types of courts. *Business law* is concerned with the segment of the entire legal system that provides for an orderly conduct of business affairs and the just settlement of disputes that may arise in connection with business transactions. Although a case can be made that business law is merely attempting to enforce good business ethics, it goes much farther by providing fixed rules of conduct that have become standards applicable to all businessmen. These standards are the end result of what society, through the legislative process, has decided are right and just in the conduct of business affairs.

All business transactions have some legal overtones. Consequently, owners and managers of business enterprises need to have a general knowledge of business law as it relates to their day-by-day activities. A sole proprietor needs to know that, when he endorses checks received from customers in order to deposit them in his firm's bank account, he is liable for the amount if the maker defaults; and a partner should realize that when he signs a contract he is binding his partners as well as himself. Since ignorance of the law is no excuse, management cannot avoid the legal aspects of its overall responsibility.

In addition to a rudimentary and basic knowledge of business law, a businessman should also be aware that he should seek professional advice on many occasions. A lawyer should be consulted when, for example, real estate is purchased, when articles of partnership are drawn up, or when a court appearance is required. Large corporations have so much legal work that they customarily maintain a legal staff; medium-sized firms frequently have a continuing relationship with a law firm on a retaining-fee basis; and small businesses normally employ a lawyer only when a need for legal assistance arises.

This chapter will first examine briefly the existing legal systems, the classifications of law that apply to business, legal procedures, and the federal and state court systems. The remainder of the chapter will be devoted to an explanation of the various areas that comprise the scope of business law. Both state and federal legislation enacted primarily for regulatory purposes that has not been covered in previous chapters will be analyzed in Chapter 28.

LEGAL SYSTEMS

There are essentially two legal systems in operation throughout the world, common law and civil law. Common law began in England centuries ago and, considering the relationship of the thirteen colonies with that country, we logically inherited this system when we became an independent nation. The basic premise of *common law* is that each decision rendered by a court becomes a precedent for successive cases of a similar nature, which is known as the *doctrine of stare decisis*, a Latin phrase meaning "to stand by decided matters." These decisions, modified by changing times, regularly find their way into constitutions and statutes drawn up or enacted by the people or their duly elected representatives. Further interpretation then follows, creating more precedents for guidance in subsequent decisions or as a foundation for further legislation.

Civil law is based on codes, which consist of compilations of laws, rules, and regulations. Ancient Roman law was codified. The Code Napoleon of France was another example of a civil law code. In countries using civil laws, courts interpret the code. The legal system of many European countries is based on civil law; and in this country Louisiana, long under the domination of France, still uses some civil law. Common law, based on decisions, is frequently called unwritten law as opposed to the written law of the civil law system. As of today, however, so much common law has been written into laws passed by all levels of government that the differences between the two systems are inconsequential.

TORTS AND CRIMES

Laws that apply primarily to the general public are not usually recognized as separate segments of the area of business law. At the same time, such laws frequently affect the conduct of a businessman or provide him with protection and may be extremely important to his success or failure. Two such classifications are the law of torts and criminal law. It is essential that the business applications of these laws as well as the laws covering specific types of business transactions be understood.

BUSINESS TORTS

A *tort* is a private wrong resulting from a breach of duty created by law. Torts are primarily concerned with moral wrongs that one person may do to cause damage or loss to another. In business transactions torts arise from slander, libel, fraud, and the infringement of patents, copyrights, and trademarks. A businessman may not indulge in deceit, make libelous statements, induce someone to break a contract, make threats, try to intimidate those with whom he deals, or, in general, engage in unfair trade practices. For example, a restaurant owner in a small town repeatedly and untruthfully claimed that a rival establishment served horsemeat. It was proved that his intent was to destroy his competitor's business, and he was forced to pay damages.

A particularly vulnerable area for many businesses is the possibility of the infringement of patents, copyrights, and trademarks. If the federal government grants a patent, it gives the holder the exclusive right to its use for 17 years. Copyrights are good for 28 years and may be renewed for a like period. A registered trademark does not have an expiration date. Such well-known names as Kodak, Nabisco, and Frigidaire are the property of the corporations that registered these names, and others may not copy them or use any similar name that might mislead the public. Regardless of whether an infringement is deliberate or unintentional, the holder of a patent, a copyright, or a trademark can sue for damages, as it is the responsibility of each business to be sure that it does not commit torts of this nature.

BUSINESS CRIMES

A *crime* is a public wrong in that it violates a law that has been passed prohibiting certain conduct considered to be detrimental to the welfare of the state. As related to business, it includes forging checks or receipts, operating lotteries, selling goods on a short weight or measure basis, making fraudulent use of the post office, extortion, embezzlement, and bribery. For example, Congress has enacted legislation prohibiting the use of the mails to defraud. A promoter mailed literature to a "sucker" list describing a nonexistent company with an invitation to subscribe to shares of stock. Following a complaint from an individual who lost a sizable sum of money, the promoter was investigated by postal authorities, arrested, convicted, and imprisoned.

A crime can also be a tort and, obviously, some torts can also be crimes. Slander, for example, is a criminal offense in some states although generally it is thought of as a private rather than a public wrong. A distinction between the two types of offenses is that the state will bring an action to enforce a law when a crime has been committed, whereas torts require the injured party to bring an action against the offender. In some instances one action may follow the other if the wrong or injury is both a crime and a tort.

LEGAL PROCEDURES

If a businessman believes he has been wronged, either because another party has broken a law or has taken unfair advantage of him, he may initiate legal action. He is called the *plaintiff,* and the other party is known as the *defendant.* The plaintiff's attorney files a complaint with the proper court and a *summons* is issued, which requires the defendant to appear in court to answer the charges.

If the case involves a point of fact, it will be tried before a jury unless both parties waive this privilege. Assuming that a jury does hear the facts as presented by witnesses for both parties, it renders a decision in favor of the plaintiff or defendant. If a jury does not hear the case, the decision is rendered by the presiding judge.

The above procedures apply to all types of legal cases other than those involving a crime. If a businessman breaks a law, he can be arrested by a police officer and required to furnish bond or go to jail. For example, a dealer in radio and TV sets might be charged with receiving and selling stolen merchandise. If when he is brought to trial a conviction is obtained, the chances are that the judge will levy a fine and impose a jail sentence.

TYPES OF COURTS

In the United States there are systems of federal courts and of state courts. The lower courts in each system are known as *courts of original jurisdiction.* These are the courts in which the cases referred to above are heard. If the loser believes a principle of law has been violated, he may carry this issue into an *appellate court,* which is a higher court that has been established to hear appeals from the decisions of lower courts. If this court believes the case was improperly tried in the first instance, it may dismiss the decision or refer it to the original court for a retrial. The Supreme Court of the United States is the highest appellate court for matters under federal jurisdiction, and the supreme court of a state is the highest court for disputes having no federal implications.

If a case involves an alleged violation of a federal law or interstate commerce, it will be heard in a federal court. Most legal disputes, however, are of such a nature that they are tried in state courts. One of the resulting problems has been the lack of uniformity among the laws of the 50 states. To improve this situation, a National Conference of Commissioners on Uniform State Laws was formed several years ago with representatives from each state. This Conference promotes uniformity in state laws and over a period of years has been successful in securing the passage by many state legislatures of a number of uniform laws including the Uniform Negotiable Instruments Act, the Uniform Sales Act, and the Uniform Conditional Sales Act.

In 1957 the National Conference of Commissioners on Uniform State Laws in conjunction with the American Law Institute drafted a Uniform Commercial Code. One of the stated purposes of this Code was to simplify, clarify, and modernize the law governing commercial transactions. It has now been adopted by most states. In the ensuing discussion the provisions of this Code, where applicable, have been followed.

SCOPE OF BUSINESS LAW

The major topics that comprise the area of business law are contracts, agency, negotiable instruments, bailments, sales, suretyship and guaranty, partnerships, corporations, property, and bankruptcy. Partnerships and corporations have been covered adequately in previous chapters. An examination of the other topics will indicate the range and types of legal information that the average businessman should understand. It will also furnish some indication of the tremendous value of a system of law to the smooth functioning of our economic system.

CONTRACTS

A *contract* is a voluntary agreement between two or more competent persons by which, for a consideration, one party acquires the right to have the other party do or not do some lawful act. In a general sense, the entire field of business law is one of contracts because agreements between parties are essential to practically all business transactions. This subject therefore is not discussed as something apart from other applications of business law but rather as a fundamental background. The following features of contracts will explain the terms used in the above definition as well as discuss other aspects of this important area of business law: (1) voluntary agreement, (2) competent persons, (3) consideration, (4) lawful acts, (5) forms of contracts, and (6) performance, discharge, and remedies.

Voluntary Agreement

The essence of an agreement is an offer and an acceptance. The offer must be communicated in definite terms and with the intent to create a contract, and the acceptance must be indicated within a reasonable time or before the offer is withdrawn. Any means of communication may be used and, if the mail or telegraph is involved, the contract is in force just as soon as the acceptance is deposited with the post office or telegraph company. A reply that fails to conform to the exact terms of the offer, known as a *counteroffer*, does not constitute an acceptance because there is no mutual agreement or common understanding of the subject matter of the contract.

Contracts must also involve agreements in which both parties act in good faith and of their own free will. The term "voluntary" is used in the sense that there has been no fraud, duress, or undue influence brought to bear on one or the other party. Tricking someone into signing a written contract or threatening a person at the point of a gun to agree to a contract will provide grounds for relief. Even some mutual mistakes, such as agreeing to sell a building that, unknown to either party, burned down the night before will void the contract.

Competent Persons

Most people are legally competent to enter into a contract, but some groups, such as insane persons, are without the capacity to make a contract. In most states persons under 21 years of age are classed as *minors* and usually cannot make enforceable contracts. If a dealer sells an automobile on time to a minor who, after making a down payment and one or two installments, wrecks the car, the minor can return the vehicle and demand his money back.

An exception of particular interest to most college freshmen to the customary inability of minors to make enforceable contracts is contained in the Uniform Minor Student Capacity to Borrow Act. This law was written in 1969 by the National Conference of Commissioners on Uniform State Laws and is currently being considered by several state legislatures. This uniform law provides that a loan made to a minor for the purpose of furthering his education at an institution of higher learning is enforceable against the debtor with the same effect as if he were an adult at the time of the execution of the loan agreement, provided, however, that the lender had in his files at the time of making the loan a certificate stating that the borrower was enrolled or had been accepted for enrollment at a specific institution.

Consideration

Consideration, which is something of value received by one party or parted with by the other party, is essential to every contract. If Jones pays Smith $50 for an option to purchase property at a certain price within 30 days, the payment of the $50 is the consideration for this option contract. Smith gives up his right to sell the property for 30 days and Jones parts with $50. Also, any possible gain to one party or loss to another will serve as satisfactory consideration. For example, a wealthy uncle agrees to pay $1,000 to his nephew if he does not smoke until he is 21 years of age. The fact that the young man gives up a legal right provides adequate consideration. An offer to sell merchandise at a stated price, followed by an acceptance, includes adequate consideration.

Lawful Acts

The subject matter of a contract must involve lawful acts. A contract made with a person in which a promise is made to burn down a building illegally is not enforceable, nor is one with the intent to restrain trade unduly. Other contracts that are against public policy or that would violate specific laws are not enforceable. For example, most states have laws against gambling; and promises to pay gambling debts, whether written or oral, are not enforceable. Likewise, if a lender attempts to collect interest in excess of the legal rate permitted in the state, as a general rule he forfeits the right to collect any interest, although the debt is still owed.

Forms of Contracts

Most contracts do not need to be written, and oral agreements are fully enforceable although there may be difficulty in proving the facts. Under what is known as the *Statute of Frauds*, certain types of contracts must be in writing, including sales of real estate, of personal property in excess of a certain value (usually $500), and agreements that cannot be performed within one year. The reason for the unusual name for this rule of law dates back to England when persons wishing to prove the validity of an oral contract would induce friends and relatives to give false testimony in court.

Performance, Discharge, and Remedies

Most contracts are discharged by full performance on the part of both parties. Some contracts are not completed, however, and this condition may or may not give rise to a court action. In some instances the defendant may be excused under the operation of a law, such as bankruptcy; or if special conditions, such as illness, have arisen in a personal service contract, the courts may excuse performance.

When a contract has been broken, the remedy is to obtain from a court an order that requires the payment of damages or, in a few instances, compliance with the terms of the contract. If damages are in order, the court issues a *judgment* in favor of the plaintiff, which can be executed against the defendant. If necessary, a sheriff will sell enough property of the debtor to satisfy the judgment.

Of interest to many businessmen is the situation in which a person, against whom a judgment has been rendered, has no real or personal property that can be sold to satisfy the claim. If this person is a wage earner, it is possible in most states to force the employer to pay the amount owed by withholding a portion of the wage usually paid to the employee each payday. This is known as *garnishment*. Operators of business establishments not only may find it necessary to garnishee the wages of individuals who owe them money, but also may be served with an order to impose a garnishment on one or more of their own employees. Despite its effectiveness, garnishment should be regarded as a "last resort" effort to collect money. Most employers resent the added payroll bookwork it entails as well as the apparent point that one of their employees cannot manage his personal financial affairs. Often this results in an ultimatum from the employer to the employee that he clean up his financial problems within a specified period of time or lose his job.

Another drawback to garnishment is the length of time it may take to collect a debt. Under a federal law that became effective July 1, 1970, garnishment is limited to no more than 25 percent of a worker's monthly earnings. Although states were permitted to seek an exemption from this law, the vast majority have accepted the federal percentage limitation.

AGENCY

An *agent* is one who is authorized by another person, known as the *principal*, to deal with third persons on behalf of his principal. By contrast, an employee, sometimes identified as a *servant*, does not have authority to act for his employer in contract situations. It should also be understood that the word agency is sometimes used to denote a type of franchise relationship, such as an automobile agency. Agency, in its legal sense, is a vital necessity to the business world, particularly for large firms, as otherwise it would be virtually impossible to delegate authority.

A principal is liable for all acts of his agent within the actual or apparent scope of the authority vested in the agent. For example, the manager of a chain store held a contract that permitted him to operate the store at his discretion but with a limitation that all receipts were to be deposited in a specified bank to the credit of the principal. On several occasions he endorsed checks on hand and cashed them at the bank in order to obtain change for the store. The principal did not object. One day the manager endorsed several days' accumulation of checks and disappeared. In this case the bank had the right to assume that the manager was an agent with authority to cash the firm's checks.

Agents are bound to follow instructions, to serve loyally, to render proper accounts, and to use intelligence and due care in the acts that they perform. If they exceed their authority, they may become personally liable to their principals.

NEGOTIABLE INSTRUMENTS

A negotiable instrument is a form of business paper that can be transferred from one party to another as a substitute for money. Negotiable instruments can be classified as either drafts, which include checks, or promissory notes. In most states the law applicable to negotiable instruments is contained in Article 3 of the Uniform Commercial Code. Under the Code, negotiable instruments are also referred to as *commercial paper*.

The Code provides that an instrument to be negotiable must conform to all of the following requirements: (a) it must be in writing and signed by the maker or drawer; (b) it must contain an unconditional promise or order to pay a sum certain in money; (c) it must be payable on demand, or at a definite future date; (d) it must be payable "to order" or "to bearer"; and (e) where the instrument is addressed to a drawee or payee, he must be named or otherwise indicated with reasonable certainty. Some of the acceptable forms of negotiable instruments, such as checks, promissory notes, drafts, and trade acceptances, have been described in Chapter 18.

Some instruments are not negotiable because they lack one or more of the above stated requirements. An I.O.U., for example, cannot be transferred to a third party because it does not contain the words "to order" or "to bearer." A note payable to a prospective groom in the amount of $10,000 containing the words "after he marries my daughter" is not negotiable because there is not a definite future date. On the other hand, a note payable "after death" does fulfill the time requirement. These examples do not mean that nonnegotiable instruments are not enforceable as ordinary contracts, but they do mean that they cannot be transferred.

A person who receives a negotiable instrument is a *holder in due course* if the instrument is complete and regular on its face, if it is acquired before it is overdue, if it was taken in good faith and for value, and if there was available at the time of negotiation no knowledge of any infirmity in the instrument or defects in the title of the person from whom it was received. For example, when a merchant accepts a check from a student who has received it from his father, the merchant is a holder in due course if the check is presented for payment within a reasonable time. If the check was over 30 days old or bore signs of an erasure, the merchant might not be a holder in due course.

The individual named on the face of a negotiable instrument can transfer his rights in it by merely signing his name on the back of the draft or note, or he may add certain words above his signature. Four varieties of commonly used endorsements—blank, restrictive, special, and qualified—are illustrated in Figure 27-1.

Blank Endorsement

When the original payee signs his name on the back of a negotiable instrument without any qualifications, he provides what is known as a *blank endorsement*. Since it is the easiest to write, it is the most commonly used form although the endorser should be careful to duplicate the way his name appears on the face of the instrument. The use of a blank endorsement makes a draft or note into bearer paper, which poses problems if the instrument is lost before payment is received. Blank endorsements are satisfactory only at the time of actual transfer.

Restrictive Endorsement

A *restrictive endorsement* specifies the purpose for which the endorsement is made. Although there are several types, the most common is "For Deposit Only" or "For Deposit to the Account of." Individuals or firms making deposits into their bank accounts by mail or preparing a bank deposit at home or their places of business can protect themselves against possible losses by making use of a restrictive endorsement on each check. In order to reduce the work required for preparing a deposit to a firm's bank account, a rubber stamp is accepted in lieu of a pen and ink signature.

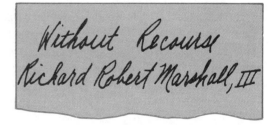

Blank Endorsement   Restrictive Endorsement

Special Endorsement   Qualified Endorsement

Figure 27-1

Various Types of Endorsements

Special Endorsement

When the endorser of a negotiable instrument wishes to specify the person to whom it is being transferred, he should use a *special endorsement*. For example, if William C. Bragg has a check drawn in his favor and he wishes to transfer it to Sheldon Jackson, Jr., he would endorse the instrument "Pay to the order of Sheldon Jackson, Jr., William C. Bragg." The advantages of a special endorsement are that it provides protection against loss while also allowing the original payee to specify the next holder in due course.

Qualified Endorsement

Sometimes the endorser of a negotiable instrument wishes to relieve himself of the contingent liability for payment in case the maker defaults on his obligation. He can do this by writing "Without Recourse" over his signature, which is known as a *qualified endorsement*. Although it might appear that no one would care to accept such a negotiable instrument, there are several situations where a qualified endorsement is useful and acceptable. For example, a check might be drawn in favor of a lawyer with instructions to endorse it to a third party when certain papers or goods are delivered. Since the lawyer is merely performing a service for a fee, he should not be liable if subsequent to delivery the check is returned to the third party marked *N.S.F.* (not sufficient funds).

Negotiable instruments, such as notes and time drafts, must be presented for payment at their maturities if the last holder wishes to hold endorsers as well as the maker or drawee. For demand paper, such as checks, unnecessary delay may relieve endorsers from liability. If a negotiable instrument is not paid when presented at the proper time, a *notice of dishonor* should be given to the maker or drawee and to each endorser. This notice can be either written or oral, although the safest procedure is to have a notary public complete a *notice of protest*. This is then mailed or delivered to all parties concerned. In order to avoid the expenses incurred by a formal protest, some businessmen stamp "No Protest" on checks and other negotiable instruments received, which means that they waive a notice of dishonor.

BAILMENTS

A *bailment* is a relationship in which one party, known as the *bailor,* leaves property with another, known as the *bailee,* for a certain purpose with the understanding that the goods will be returned to the bailor or delivered to someone else after the purpose is fulfilled. There is no passage of title, which means that a bailment is not a sale. Leaving a watch at a jeweler's for repairs or with a pawnbroker as security for a loan are examples of bailments.

As a general rule a bailee is required to exercise reasonable care of the personal property entrusted to his care. In return, at least in the case of business transactions, he receives a payment for his services. Use of a parking lot or a public warehouse involves a fee paid by the bailor to the bailee. In the dry cleaning business the firm is liable for damages resulting from negligence but not from defects in a garment.

Under common law more than reasonable care was enforced against an innkeeper for loss or injury to the personal property of his guests and to common carriers who transport merchandise. Today, most hotels avoid their liability by notifying guests to deposit valuables in their safes. Railroads and other forms of public transportation must pay for loss or damage to goods in transit unless excused for such reasons as a flood (act of God) or seizure (act of public authority or enemy). Poor packaging or crating or shipping perishable goods in nonrefrigerated cars may also relieve the carrier from responsibility.

SALES

A *sale* is an exchange of goods or personal property between two parties for money or other consideration paid immediately or to be paid in the future. It involves a contract and most of the comments already made about contracts are applicable to sales. In fact, sales are sometimes considered to be a specialized branch of the law of contracts. A *bill of sale*, which is a document signed by the seller giving evidence of the transfer of title to the buyer, may or may not be required. Sometimes it is a necessity for certain types of property, i.e., a bill of sale may be required to obtain a certificate of title for a motor vehicle.

A substantial number of the legal problems that the average businessman faces are concerned with sales. Manufacturers buy raw materials and then sell finished goods while retailers buy and sell the same merchandise. If retailers sell on the installment plan, they have the problem of repossession when payments are not made on schedule, a situation discussed in Chapter 18. Two other major problems that are created by sales are concerned with the (1) risk of loss and (2) warranties.

Risk of Loss

If merchandise is lost somewhere along the way from producer to consumer, there remains the question as to who bears this loss. For example, if a customer buys a gallon of vinegar in a retail grocery store that he drops and breaks after going through a checkout counter, who assumes this loss? Since title generally passes immediately in a cash transaction, the purchaser in this illustration must assume the loss. When goods are shipped f. o. b. factory, the risk of loss passes from the producer at the time they are delivered to a common carrier. If the terms are f. o. b. destination, the purchaser does not bear any risk until the goods are delivered to his place of business. Sometimes a buyer specifies a *c. i. f.* contract, which means that his invoice covers the cost of the goods, insurance on them, and the freight charges, thus shifting the risk of loss to an insurance company for the time the goods are in transit.

On occasion manufacturers and wholesalers wish to sell their products through dealers whose credit standing does not warrant the use of an open-book account. In this case, goods can be sent on *consignment*, which means that title remains in the hands of the shipper, known as the *consignor*, until such time as they are sold by the retailer, called the *consignee*. The fact that title does not pass until the merchandise is sold is important to the retailer because he need not insure the goods against fire and other hazards nor need he pay personal property taxes on such merchandise. For like reasons, the ownership is important to the wholesaler or manufacturer. Another advantage to a manufacturer or wholesaler of selling on consignment is the right to repossess unsold goods should the retailer become bankrupt while they are still in his possession.

Warranties

An *express warranty* is a statement on the part of the seller that the goods have certain characteristics, such as quality, which is made to induce the buyer to make the purchase. If an antique dealer states that a chest of drawers is over 100 years old and if it is subsequently discovered that 10 years is a more accurate estimate, the dealer can be sued for damages.

An *implied warranty* covers title and quality. The buyer has a right to assume that he receives a clear title to the goods and that the merchandise agrees with a sample or description and is usable for the purposes for which it was sold. A purchaser of stolen goods must return them to the original owner or pay for them, but he has a right of action against the seller because there was an implied warranty of clear title.

SURETYSHIP AND GUARANTY

Suretyship is a contract by which a third party, known as a *surety*, agrees to be answerable for the payment of a debt or performance of some act or duty in case another person fails to meet his obligation. *Guaranty* refers to a contract under which a third person, known as a *guarantor*, undertakes to perform a contract or to fulfill an obligation of another provided the individual who was responsible for discharging the contract is unable to do so. The main distinction between the two is that suretyship involves primary responsibility coextensive with that of the debtor, whereas guaranty is a secondary liability. The surety agrees to pay the debt or discharge the obligation if the principal does not, while the guarantor must discharge the obligation only if the principal cannot do so.

An example of the difference in responsibilities of a surety and a guarantor is afforded by the contrast between the comaker of a note and an accommodation endorser. An individual who signs a note on its face even though he has no personal interest in it is equally liable with the debtor who originated the instrument. On the other hand, if an individual merely endorses a note, the holder at the due date must first look to the maker for payment, and only after the maker has failed to pay can the holder collect from the endorser. A surety need not be notified if the debtor defaults because the obligation to pay at maturity is just as direct on him as it is on the maker, whereas a guarantor must be notified of a default if he is to be held for payment.

Sureties, and guarantors too, may be individuals or corporations. For example, a father wishing to assist his son start a retail business might agree to be responsible for the payment of invoices covering merchandise shipped to the new store. As noted in Chapter 22, there are surety companies in the insurance business who, in return for a premium, will contract to assume, if necessary, the obligations of the party purchasing the policy. The most common use of surety insurance companies is made by building contractors who are required to furnish a bond guaranteeing that they will complete a construction project according to plans and within the time allowed.

PROPERTY

Ownership of, or an interest in, anything subject to ownership is known as *property*. A businessman is vitally concerned with the laws on this subject because his daily transactions and the place in which they are carried on directly or indirectly involve rights and interests in property. When he buys merchandise, any subsequent loss that may occur falls on him even though payment has not yet been made for the goods. If he improves a building on which he has a lease, such improvements become the property of the owner when the lease expires.

The term property, when it refers to possessions or things owned, may be given several classifications, but the most important distinction from a business viewpoint is that of real property and personal property. *Real property* normally refers to land and buildings or, in a general way, to things immovable. *Personal property* refers to things owned that are movable. Personal property may be further subdivided into *tangibles* and *intangibles,* the former referring to merchandise in stock, fixtures, machinery and equipment, and the latter to stocks and bonds, notes and checks, bank accounts, and accounts receivable. The businessman is interested in these classifications because, if for no other reason, he may be required to pay taxes at different rates on each grouping.

Ownership

If a person has every possible right that can be attached to ownership, he has absolute ownership. In the case of real property, this common form is known as an *estate in fee simple*. Aside from the various types of restrictions that may be imposed by government, the owner may make such use of his property as he wishes. He can sell it, give it away, leave it to his heirs by drawing up a will to this effect, lease or rent it, or use it as security to borrow money. A customer who owns a fair amount of property usually has a satisfactory credit standing, but the businessman will do well to remember the rights of this individual concerning the property that has been used as a basis for granting credit. If it is given away or used as security for a loan, it is no longer available to satisfy claims of general creditors.

Ownership rights in real property that fall short of the extent of absolute ownership are usually for a fixed period of time. A common example is the relation of landlord to tenant. When a proprietor leases a store building for 10 years, the tenant has a right in the property for that period of time if he pays the stipulated rent. Repairs and improvements that he may make will usually revert to the owner at the conclusion of the 10 years.

Security for Loans

Property is frequently used as security for the extension of credit. If personal property is involved, the customary procedure is to execute an obligation known as a chattel mortgage. As described in Chapter 18, the use of chattel mortgages is an optional way of selling goods on an installment basis. The buyer has title to as well as physical possession of the goods and, if he completes the schedule of payments, the mortgage is canceled. If he fails to make the prescribed payments, the seller can, if necessary, take legal steps to regain possession of the goods. Such an action is known as a suit in *replevin.*

If real property is used as security, the obligation created is a real estate mortgage. This mortgage, as well as a chattel mortgage, should be recorded in a county courthouse. If the loan is not paid in accordance with the terms, the mortgage is usually foreclosed and title is transferred to the creditor. Intangible personal property, such as stocks and bonds, is also used as security for loans, but a mortgage is not necessary because the lender can take physical possession of the securities.

BANKRUPTCY

As noted in Chapter 20, an insolvent firm may go into bankruptcy on its own initiative, which is called *voluntary bankruptcy,* or it may be declared a bankrupt by a federal court, which is known as *involuntary bankruptcy.* In either case, the court-appointed referee calls the creditors together and they elect a trustee. As a general rule, the trustee then liquidates the assets and distributes the proceeds.

It would be very rare for the trustee to be able to pay all creditors in full, for a bankrupt owes more than he owns. The federal bankruptcy law has established a system of priority of claims that recognizes five classes of *preferred creditors,* as follows:

1. The actual and necessary costs of preserving the estate subsequent to the filing of the petition.
2. Wages due to workmen, clerks, traveling or city salesmen, or servants, that have been earned within three months prior to bankruptcy, not to exceed $600 to each claimant.
3. Reasonable expenses of creditors in opposing an arrangement or a plan for the discharge of a bankrupt.

4. Taxes due the United States or any state or subdivision.

5. Debts owed to any person who by law is entitled to priority.

Court costs are included in (1) above as are fees for the referee, trustee, and lawyers. Number (5) most frequently involves the holders of a first mortgage on the bankrupt's property. If this property is sold for more than the mortgage, the preferred creditors will be paid in full. If the property brings less than the amount of the mortgage, the lenders will receive the entire proceeds and join the general creditors for the balances due them.

Assuming that there is money available for distribution after preferred claims are settled, the *general creditors* will receive a percentage of their established claims. A final accounting is then filed with the court, and the debtor is legally discharged from further payments on the amounts owed. Although there are a few liabilities that cannot be discharged in a bankruptcy proceeding, in general the bankrupt can start a new business or take employment with a clean financial slate.

Banks, incorporated cities, insurance companies, railroads, and savings and loan associations may not become bankrupts. Wage earners whose annual income is less than $1,500, nonbusiness corporations, and farmers cannot be forced into bankruptcy. Other persons, partnerships, or corporations can become a bankrupt on either a voluntary or involuntary basis if debts of $1,000 or more are owed.

BUSINESS TERMS

QUESTIONS FOR DISCUSSION AND ANALYSIS

1. What is the relationship between business law and business ethics? Explain.

2. In this age of specialization, why shouldn't a businessman be able to refer all of his legal problems to a lawyer?

3. Are business customs more likely to be the subject of legislation in countries with a heritage of common law than in countries that rely on civil law?

4. Is the granting of patents, copyrights, and trademarks by the federal government consistent with a free enterprise system?

5. Does the existence of appellate courts tend to weaken the authority of courts of original jurisdiction? Justify your stand.

6. If young men and women 18 years of age are entitled to vote, why shouldn't they also be entitled to make valid contracts?

7. When a consignee sells goods that were shipped to him on consignment, he owes the consignor for the items sold. Is this debt likely to be paid more promptly than if the original shipment had been made on an open-account basis?

8. Is the ownership of property by individuals or corporations essentially a legal support for capitalism?

9. Why should an individual be permitted to gain a clean slate financially by going into voluntary bankruptcy?

10. Does business law help or hinder businesses from making a profit?

PROBLEMS AND SHORT CASES

1. a. A vacant lot in the business district attracted the attention of Jonas Quentin who thought it would be an ideal location for a parking lot.

An investigation of court records revealed that the owner was Adele Ferguson, who had moved away from the city several years earlier. Quentin was able to obtain her address and wrote inquiring as to whether the land was available for purchase. The owner replied indicating that she would sell for $50,000 cash. After Quentin received the letter, he wrote again calling her a highway robber but, nevertheless, he was enclosing a check for $10,000 and would pay the balance of $40,000 within 60 days. Adele Ferguson, incensed by the tone of Quentin's letter, immediately returned the $10,000 check and stated that she would not sell to him under any circumstances. Upon receipt of this letter, Quentin instituted a suit to compel Adele Ferguson to sell him the land for $50,000. What decision should the judge render?

b. A student delivered a dark dress to a dry cleaning outlet near her residence hall and explained that she had spilled some fingernail polish on the front of the dress. After the dress was cleaned the polish was gone, but in its place was a white area so noticeable that the garment could not be worn. The student felt that she was entitled to payment for the dress, but the dry cleaning firm insisted that the material was faulty as it had used only solvents regularly employed to remove fingernail polish. Is the student entitled to a fair price for the dress?

2. G. W. Spencer started a pizza parlor and carryout business that, for the first five years, was prosperous. Then three franchise operations specializing in hamburgers and chicken opened in his neighborhood with a resulting decline in the demand for pizzas. Now, after four years of losses, Spencer finds that he cannot pay his current debts, including payments on mortgages, and has decided to become a voluntary bankrupt. The trustee elected by the creditors found that Spencer's books showed the following assets and liabilities:

Assets		Liabilities	
Cash	$ 80	Wages payable ...	$ 500
Inventory	1,470	Taxes payable ...	1,450
Fixtures and equipment .	8,950	Accounts payable.	15,500
Land and buildings (net)	35,600	Mortgages payable	53,100
	$46,100		$70,550

The trustee sold the inventory for $700; the fixtures, on which there was a mortgage of $7,500, for $7,000; and the land and buildings, on which the mortgage amounted to $45,600, for $50,000. The cost of the sales, lawyer's fees, and court costs amounted to $2,750.

Compute the amount available for general creditors. How much did they receive on a cents-on-the-dollar basis?

3. The T. X. Electronics Co. maintains and generously supports a research laboratory. It has in its employ over 100 scientists, ably assisted by technicians, and the latest types of equipment. Each research worker, when accepting employment, signs an agreement that any discoveries he may make are to be the property of the T. X. Electronics Co. If the invention or process is patentable, the necessary papers are to be filed by company lawyers, and the patent rights are to be assigned to the employer.

Dr. Edmonds, a physicist, was in the employ of the T. X. Electronics Co. and diligently performed all research projects assigned to him. A man of considerable energy, he had equipped, at his own expense, a laboratory in the basement of his home. Working nights and weekends, he pursued an idea that he had held for some time that heat could be directly converted into electricity. Unknown to Dr. Edmonds, a similar project was under study at the research laboratory.

After two years of work, Dr. Edmonds devised a method of converting heat directly into electricity, and he was successful in securing a patent on his device. When this was issued, the T. X. Electronics Co. became aware of the outside activity of Dr. Edmonds and insisted he sign over the patent rights to the firm. Dr. Edmonds refused to do so unless he was paid $50,000.

At this point in the dispute, the T. X. Electronics Co. fired Dr. Edmonds and brought suit against him charging a breach of contract. Specifically, the company requested the court to compel Dr. Edmonds to assign his patent rights to T. X. Electronics Co. and to pay the court costs involved in this suit. If you were the lawyer for Dr. Edmonds, what defense could you offer? If you were the judge, what decision would you render?

SUGGESTED READINGS

Anderson, R. A., and W. A. Kumpf. *Business Law*, Eighth Edition. Cincinnati: South-Western Publishing Co., 1968.

Cataldo, B. F., *et al. Introductory Cases on Law and the Legal Process*. New York: John Wiley & Sons, Inc., 1967.

Corley, R. N., and R. L. Black, Jr. *The Legal Environment of Business*, Second Edition. New York: McGraw-Hill Book Company, 1968.

Fox, S. *Management and the Law*. New York: Appleton-Century-Crofts, 1966.

Litka, M. P. *Business Law*. New York: Harcourt Brace Jovanovich, Inc., 1970.

Lusk, H. F. *Business Law: Principles and Cases*, Uniform Commercial Code Edition. Homewood, Illinois: Richard D. Irwin, Inc., 1966.

Moore, C. C. *Business Law*. New York: The Macmillan Company, 1968.

Nelson, E. R., *et al*. *Business Law: Text and Cases*, Second Edition. Boston: Allyn and Bacon, Inc., 1968.

Robert, W. J., and R. N. Corley. *Dillavou and Howard's Principles of Business Law*, Eighth Edition. Englewood Cliffs, New Jersey: Prentice-Hall, Inc., 1967.

Votaw, D. *Legal Aspects of Business Administration*, Third Edition. Englewood Cliffs, New Jersey: Prentice-Hall, Inc., 1969.

Wyatt, J. W., and M. B. Wyatt. *Business Law*, Third Edition. New York: McGraw-Hill Book Company, 1966.

Chapter 28

Governmental Regulation of Business

The right of government to regulate business stems from the Constitution of the United States and from state constitutions, as interpreted by the courts. Each provides for a separation of powers into three branches—legislative, executive, and judicial—and all three are involved in the regulation of business. In addition, governmental administrative agencies, such as the Internal Revenue Service, have become important to business regulation.

The Constitution of the United States as ratified in 1788 contains Article I, Section 8, which gives the federal government the right to regulate commerce among the several states and the powers to tax, to coin money, to borrow, to establish the post office, and to declare war. Despite these delegated powers, for approximately 100 years the federal government showed little interest in regulation. This same remark could also be made of the states although a few had exercised a measure of control over such industries as banks, insurance companies, canals, and railroads. It was essentially a century of laissez-faire capitalism that functioned smoothly primarily because business in the United States was conducted by a large number of relatively small units in a highly individualistic social system. In this kind of a social and economic climate, and with only restricted use of such present-day necessities as electricity, gas, and the telephone, competition was an effective regulator of business and business practices.

Toward the close of the nineteenth century, the stockholders in several areas were induced to turn their shares over to a common group of trustees who then controlled and operated the several firms in such a manner as to minimize competition and maximize profits. Such organizations became known as *trusts* and were extremely successful in the oil, tobacco, sugar, and whiskey industries. The railroads were also assuming an important part in the development of the country, and the need for regulating the rates charged for rail transportation in areas served by only one line became apparent in the 1880's. These and other economic factors and social forces started a trend toward governmental regulation of business.

DISTINCTION BETWEEN COMPETITIVE BUSINESSES AND REGULATED INDUSTRIES

The problems of trusts and of railroad rates brought into focus an awareness that business enterprises fell into two categories as far as regulation was concerned. One of these areas encompassed enterprises that were expected to compete against each other with prices being determined by the forces of supply and demand operating in a free enterprise climate. The other included businesses such as gas, electricity, the telephone, rail transportation, and a few more like areas in which it was in the public interest to permit monopolies to exist. For example, two telephone companies serving one community with subscribers of one unable to make a direct call to patrons of the other company would not be satisfactory to the customers of either company.

It was obvious that a single common pattern would not solve the problems of regulating both competitive and noncompetitive businesses. Hence, governments made a sharp distinction between the two categories and began to apply different methods of supervision and control to each. In the case of competitive type businesses, which constitute the much larger group, efforts were and still are directed toward enacting and enforcing laws designed to create an economic climate in which business units can and must compete with each other in a fair and equitable manner. In this area the federal government plays a dominant role, although in specific instances laws passed at the state or local level may have an even greater impact on a particular firm.

In certain industries it has been recognized that one company should have the exclusive right to provide a particular service in a specified geographical area. For these industries, which are classified as regulated industries, specially created governmental agencies—usually called commissions—substitute for the marketplace in determining allowable prices and levels of service. Since the major share of the business done by these monopolies, with the exception of the railroads, is intrastate in character, states originally assumed more regulatory functions than the federal government. Today both levels of government are kept busy with either the intrastate or the interstate activities of companies in regulated industries.

This chapter will first describe the regulation of competitive businesses at the federal level and then by states and local governments. Following this discussion the methods and procedures used by commissions to supervise regulated industries will be explained. A description of the specific agencies involved will clarify this area of governmental activity as will an enumeration of the types of companies that today comprise this important segment of business.

REGULATION OF COMPETITIVE BUSINESS

Numerous laws that have been enacted by the Congress of the United States and by state legislatures, the administration of these laws by governmental agencies, and their interpretation by the courts have had far-reaching effects on competitive business throughout our nation. Some of these laws have been directed to functional areas of business such as marketing, labor, or finance. The impact of much of the legislation of this type has been adequately described in previous chapters. For example, Chapter 10 explained the requirement in some states that a retailer cannot sell a branded product at a lower price than that specified by the manufacturer; and Chapter 14 pointed out that firms engaged in interstate commerce must pay a minimum hourly wage of $1.60.

Federal laws promoting competition apply more generally than any other legislation designed to regulate competitive businesses. More recently, the federal government has seen fit to pass regulatory laws applying to companies producing such consumer goods as automobiles and drugs. Both of these categories will be examined in some detail before touching on the regulation of competitive businesses by states.

FEDERAL LAWS TO PROMOTE COMPETITION

Laws against trusts were the first of a series of acts and amendments passed by the Congress of the United States designed to benefit the public by assuring a healthy competitive business climate. Over the years the emphasis in legislation shifted from monopolies to illegal or unfair trade practices, although even today many businesses find their efforts to merge with competitors or companies in allied lines opposed by the

Department of Justice or the Federal Trade Commission. The following laws are the ones most effective today in restraining businesses that would, if unchecked, limit competition or otherwise create unhealthy competitive conditions: (1) Sherman Antitrust Act, (2) Clayton Act, (3) Federal Trade Commission Act, (4) Robinson-Patman Act, (5) Wheeler-Lea Act, and (6) Celler-Kefauver Act.

Sherman Antitrust Act

In 1890 the federal government moved against the trusts that had been formed by enacting the Sherman Antitrust Act. The extent of opinion favorable to such a measure can be judged by the fact that this law was passed by both houses of Congress with only one dissenting vote. It provided that "every contract, combination . . . or conspiracy in restraint of trade or commerce among the several states . . . is hereby declared to be illegal," and that "every person who shall monopolize or . . . combine or conspire to monopolize . . . shall be deemed guilty of a misdemeanor." Persons convicted of violating the act were subject to a fine not to exceed $50,000 and/or imprisonment for one year. Triple damages were to be awarded to those injured by the actions of trusts.

The Sherman Act was predicated on the fear, not without foundation in 1890, that large organizations were automatically detrimental to the best interests of the public. Bigness and badness were considered synonyms. The act gave the Attorney General of the United States the authority to take action against the trusts and, after extensive legal delays, most of them were broken up. The act was, however, weakened when the federal Supreme Court adopted the *rule of reason*. Under this rule a combination, contract, or conspiracy was judged as to whether or not it constituted an undue or unreasonable restraint on interstate commerce.

Furthermore, as time went on, the fear of large corporations subsided as more than one giant company appeared in several industries. In rubber products, for example, Goodyear, Firestone, Goodrich, and Uniroyal, Incorporated are all large corporations; but several somewhat smaller companies do not hesitate to compete with these giants. Today the Sherman Act is more likely to be applied to a group of companies in the same type of business conspiring among themselves rather than to a single large company. One illegal device a group sometimes uses is *collusive bidding* in which supposedly competing firms either agree to submit identical prices or agree that one of them is to be the low bidder on a contract. In the latter case, geographical areas might be assigned for the exclusive benefit of each firm, resulting in a *territorial pool*. Another possibility for a conspiracy, *patent licensing*, which is an arrangement under which the owner of a patent allows others to use it upon payment of a royalty, can be illegal when used to restrain trade. Likewise, if several competing firms agree that it would be desirable to raise prices in a group consensus known as a *gentlemen's agreement*, a resulting increase in prices could be illegal if the government can prove a conspiracy in restraint of competition.

Clayton Act

By 1914 it was apparent that the legislation of 1890 was not a complete answer to the trust problem. The Clayton Act was the second attempt by Congress to deal with monopolies. The new law, which was more specific than the Sherman Act, recognized that the trust problem was no longer one of size but rather one of business practices.

The act stated that it was unlawful for persons engaged in interstate commerce to "discriminate in price between different purchasers of commodities . . . where the effect of such discrimination may be substantially to lessen competition or tend to create a monopoly in any line of commerce." Exceptions could be made where such discrimination took into account differences in grade, quality, quantity, or cost, or where such discrimination was made in good faith to meet bona fide competition. The law also prohibited exclusive agreements "for the sale of goods, wares, merchandise, machinery, supplies, or other commodities . . . for use, consumption, or resale within the United States," if the result of such an agreement "may be substantially to lessen competition or tend to create a monopoly in any line of commerce." Further, the act specifically prohibited *tying contracts* under which a buyer, in order to obtain wanted merchandise, had to agree to buy other goods from the same vendor.

The *interlocking directorate*, a situation that exists when the majority of the members of two or more boards of directors are the same individuals, was declared unlawful if either corporation had assets in excess of $1 million and if the corporations were in competition with each other. The purchase by one corporation of another corporation's stock, if the effect was substantially to lessen competition or to tend to create a monopoly, was prohibited. Approximately a half century later this provision of the law was invoked against the Du Pont company which was required in 1962 to divest itself of the 63,000,000 shares of General Motors common stock that it owned. Somewhat similar to an interlocking directorate is a *community of interests*, a situation in which a few stockholders are in a position to dictate the composition of the boards of directors of two or more competing corporations.

Federal Trade Commission Act

The Federal Trade Commission Act passed in September, 1914, a month earlier than the Clayton Act, provided that unfair methods of competition in commerce were illegal. To enforce this law, as well as many of the provisions of the Clayton Act, it also created the Federal Trade Commission. This is a federal agency that consists of five commissioners aided by a large staff of accountants, economists, and lawyers. It investigates alleged unfair methods of competition, issues complaints against offending firms, conducts hearings, and, where necessary, issues cease and desist orders against those found guilty of engaging in forbidden practices.

Over the years the powers of the FTC have been expanded and its current activities include making surveys into various business practices, which sometimes result in "trade practice conferences" designed to secure voluntary agreement among firms in a particular industry as to what constitutes unfair competitive methods. Out of these may come a set of Trade Practice Rules that are mutually agreeable to the Commission and to the members of the trades affected. The mere fact that the FTC is in existence is a deterrent to the actions of firms that might be tempted to violate either laws or ethical principles, which is one of the reasons that the Commission is sometimes called "the policeman of the business world."

Robinson-Patman Act

Price discrimination, which was covered in Section 2 of the Clayton Act, was clarified with the passage of the Robinson-Patman Act in 1936. This act was designed to eliminate the lower prices that had been available to large purchasers, such as the chain grocery stores. Even though price differentials might be justified on the basis of quantity, if the results gave the buyer a monopolistic advantage, they would be illegal. The act also provided for penalties if larger discounts were given or received, and a seller could be fined if goods were sold at low prices with the intent of eliminating competition or a competitor. Other details of this act were described in Chapter 10.

Wheeler-Lea Act

The Wheeler-Lea Act was passed by the Congress in 1938 as an amendment to the Federal Trade Commission Act. Whereas the earlier law had stated that unfair methods of competition were illegal, this act provided that any unfair or deceptive practice that may be harmful to the public is illegal. Formerly it had been necessary to prove that competitors, rather than the general public, had been injured by the unfair methods used by the offender.

Celler-Kefauver Act

Although the Clayton Act stated that it was illegal for a corporation to buy stock in another corporation when the effect was to create a monopoly or to lessen competition, it did not prohibit the elimination of competition by the merger of different companies. In 1950 the Celler-Kefauver Act was passed as an amendment to the Clayton Act. It prohibited mergers when the result would be to lessen competition or tend to create a monopoly.

FEDERAL CONSUMER PROTECTION LAWS

In addition to the regulation of business through legislation designed to promote competition, in recent years the federal government has passed numerous laws for the specific purpose of protecting consumers. Two major categories of this type of legislation are concerned with (1) foods, drugs, and cosmetics, and (2) proper labels. The following applicable laws illustrate how the Congress has attempted to protect the best interests of consumers.

Food, Drug, and Cosmetic Act

Although the Food and Drug Administration, now a part of the Department of Health, Education, and Welfare, was established in 1906, its authority was increased with the enactment of the Food, Drug, and Cosmetic Act in 1938. Powers of the Administration include insistence on sanitary methods of manufacture, purity of content, and proper labeling. The package must show the accurate weight, ingredients in proportion, and whether coloratives or preservatives have been used. Drugs must be labeled as to use and, if the drug is habit-forming, a statement to this effect must be included. New drugs cannot be distributed until they have been proved safe to use. Heavy penalties are provided with a limit of a fine of $1,000 and/or imprisonment for one year for a mere infraction of the law, and maximums of $10,000 and imprisonment for three years for deliberate intent to defraud or mislead.

Other legislation has given the Food and Drug Administration the power to control adulteration of insecticides, labeling of caustic poisons for household use, and maintenance of standards. The Administration has authority to make semiannual inspections of drug factories, to make checks on the quality of products, and to withhold approval of new drugs until it has been demonstrated that these are safe and effective. Also, drugs already on the market can be removed from an approved list as was done in the elimination of cyclamates from many diet-type soft drinks.

Labeling Acts

In order to protect consumers against unfair or deceptive trade practices as applied to clothing, the Congress has enacted several laws requiring that labels attached to garments must show the types of materials used. The Wool Products Labeling Act of 1939 requires that each product be labeled to show the total fiber weight of the wool; whether it is new, processed, or reused; the percentage of nonwool filling; and the name of the manufacturer. The Fur Products Labeling Act of 1951 requires that the correct name of the animal that produced the fur, as well as manufacturing details, appear on the label of each such item offered for sale. Protection from burning fabrics was provided by the Federal Flammable Fabrics Act of 1953, and the Textile Fiber Products Identification Act of 1958 requires the use of labels that show the percentage of natural and synthetic fibers used in the manufacture of cloth and other materials. The protection of the public through proper labeling is further extended by the Fair Packaging and Labeling Act of 1966.

The above laws are enforced by the Federal Trade Commission. In 1960 Congress passed the Hazardous Substances Labeling Act, and jurisdiction over this law was given to the Food and Drug Administration, which also enforces the Toy Safety Act.

Another labeling act of interest that is concerned with price rather than raw materials is the Automobile Information Disclosure Act of 1958. Under this act the manufacturer is required to show the suggested retail price of each new car itemized as to base cost, extras, and freight.

Further efforts by the Congress to protect consumers are evidenced by the truth-in-lending law described in Chapter 18, the law requiring cigarette packages to carry a health warning, and laws on safety devices for automobiles. Attention has also been given to special controls over depressant, stimulant, and counterfeit drugs; food and color additives; and insecticides, fungicides, and rodenticides.

ENVIRONMENTAL CONTROL LAWS

A new direction in the federal regulation of business that seems destined for increased attention in the seventies is antipollution legislation.

Although states and groups of states as well as municipalities have attempted to cope with the problem, it is generally agreed that federal standards will have to be established and, in many instances, enforced. Unfortunately for many businesses, they are substantial contributors to the pollution of both water and air and are the target for much of the legislation contemplated or already on the books. For example, the automobile industry has been directed to produce pollution-free engines within a few years.

The federal government has already taken some steps to reduce and eliminate the causes of the pollution of our waters and air. In 1965 the Congress enacted the Water Quality Act; the Clean Water Restoration Act was passed in 1966; and an Air Quality Act became law in 1967. Federal agencies, such as the Federal Water Quality Administration and the National Air Pollution Control Administration, were established and subsequently placed under a well-financed Environmental Protection Agency. A Council on Environmental Quality has been established as a policy-making group. Additional laws or executive actions may create more administrative agencies or increase the authority of those now in existence but, in any event, it seems certain that business firms will incur substantial additional costs as they submit to a new type of regulation.

STATE LAWS AND REGULATIONS

Cities, villages, townships, counties, parishes, and other governing units within a state are created and exist under the constitution of that state. Consequently, state regulation of business encompasses all legislation passed by the state legislature and any of its political subdivisions that have legislative authority. As long as these laws do not conflict with the state constitution, the federal constitution, or federal legislation, they are legal and enforceable.

Under what is known as the *police power*, it is not only the right but also the duty of a state to protect the health, safety, and morals of its citizens and to promote the general welfare. This power is not dependent upon state constitutions or enabling legislation but is inherent in the power to govern. For example, a state can establish a weighing station and stop overloaded trucks, even those moving in interstate commerce. There may or may not be a law covering this activity although, in general, most business regulation is covered by specific legislation.

Considering that there are 50 states and thousands of political subdivisions, it is obvious that the regulation of competitive businesses varies considerably among these governmental units. There are, however, some areas that are quite commonly considered by governing bodies as proper restraints on business activities. These are: (1) labor legislation, (2) health and sanitation laws, (3) prices, (4) usury laws, (5) zoning ordinances and building codes, and (6) licenses.

Labor Legislation

State laws dealing with labor have long been recognized as a valid field for legislation. At the outset, the chief concern was with necessary minimum standards for working conditions. Most states provide that factory buildings shall be fireproof or have adequate protection against fire hazards to workers. Each employee is entitled to a certain amount of space. Adequate washrooms and other sanitary facilities must be available. Safety devices must be installed where the occupational hazard is excessive; for example, mines must be equipped with ventilating devices, emergency exits, and proper shafts.

The Federal Fair Labor Standards Act states maximum hours, minimum wages, and overtime pay for those working in interstate commerce, and the state laws commonly do the same for businesses that are not deemed in interstate commerce. The actual hours in a day that women and children may work have frequently been specified; for example, children cannot be employed before a specified hour in the morning or later than a specified hour in the evening. In some occupations a woman may not work more than eight hours a day, and she must be given a certain amount of rest time including a lunch hour.

The Labor-Management Relations Act of 1947 granted permission to the states to pass laws designed to protect the right of workers to continue their employment without having to join a union. Over the past 25 years a number of states enacted so-called right-to-work laws although a few of these were subsequently repealed. The Congress of the United States has been under constant pressure from labor unions to repeal Section 14b of the Taft-Hartley Act, which is the applicable portion of the 1947 law. If and when the Congress takes such an action, state right-to-work laws would be illegal as applied to firms engaged in interstate commerce.

Health and Sanitation Laws

In addition to the application of health and sanitation rules to factories, laws to protect customers of retail establishments have been passed. For example, a restaurant is usually subject to a periodic inspection and, if certain minimum standards of cleanliness are not maintained, the owner's license to operate can be withdrawn. His employees who handle food may also be subject to annual health examinations.

The price at which a retailer is permitted to sell a certain product may be affected by state legislation. As described in Chapter 10, fair trade laws and unfair trade laws have been passed by a considerable number of the states.

Sellers of commodities in intrastate commerce are very likely to find that the state has copied many of the federal laws against monopolies, trade practices, and pricing policies. Goods of like grade and quality must be sold at the same price to all purchasers unless the difference can be justified on the grounds of manufacturing, selling, or delivery costs. Any other price practices that might tend to create a monopoly or in any other manner restrain trade would also be illegal.

Usury Laws

Laws passed by states stipulating the maximum rates of interest that can be charged on different types of loans are known as *usury laws*. Many people find it necessary to borrow money, and those with little or no credit standing cannot expect lending agencies to compete for their business. If they do locate a source of funds, however, the interest and other charges that the financial institution can charge will be limited by the state usury law. These charges vary with the type of loan and terms of repayment.

Zoning Ordinances and Building Codes

Most people who build a home do not want their residential area invaded by hot dog stands, pool halls, and other similar types of business enterprises. Laws establishing areas that are available for business sites and others that are restricted to homes are known as *zoning ordinances*. Such laws are passed by village, town, or city councils, and recently townships and counties have established zoning boards to control the use of suburban and rural land areas. Zoning ordinances interfere with the right of a property owner to use his land in any manner that he may desire, but this interference is considered a necessary protection for his neighbors and others who own land in the same geographical area.

Assuming that the requirements of a zoning ordinance have been met, there may still remain the restriction of a building code. *Building codes,* both state and local, are regulations that provide minimum specifications for construction details. For example, a code may provide that only fireproof buildings can be constructed in a certain area, or that electric wires must be laid within a pipe or cable. After work is completed, a building inspector checks it and, if the specifications provided by law have not been followed, necessary corrections must be made.

Licenses

A *license* is a formal document issued by a governmental body to a business or a person authorizing the holder to engage in an activity. It is illegal to engage in such activities without the necessary license. Licenses are issued by states, counties, cities, and towns. Most licenses are on an annual basis although some are for an event only, such as a parade or carnival permit. Several states list over 100 different types of businesses that must secure a license, such as restaurants, barbershops, dry cleaning establishments, hotels, ice plants, laundries, motion-picture houses, soda fountains, and dealers in tobacco, fireworks, office machines, and automobiles. In some areas local licenses are more numerous than state licenses. Local licenses affect most commonly pool halls, bowling alleys, and other places of amusement.

The use of licenses as regulatory devices plays an important part for businesses that sell liquor, for the professions, and for some types of occupations. Stores that sell liquor in bottles, other than those that may be operated by a state, are required to secure a special license. Also, hotels, inns, taverns, and other places where liquor is sold for consumption on the premises are licensed. By refusing to issue a license or to renew one, the state can control the number and types of outlets. The practice of medicine, law, accounting, dentistry, and other professions is usually regulated in that the individual concerned must secure a license from the state before he can offer his services to the public. Brokers, real estate salesmen, barbers, insurance salesmen, and many other workers in occupations not classed as professions must also secure a license from the state. The ability of the individuals concerned to continue in business is based on keeping their licenses in force.

REGULATED INDUSTRIES

The types of businesses currently considered to be desirable monopolies and hence qualifying as regulated industries can, in one sense, all be classified as public utilities. A *public utility* may be defined as a privately owned industrial firm that renders a service so essential to its customers that it is allowed to operate legally as a monopoly under governmental regulation of rates and standards of service. Under this broad definition electric, gas, water, telephone, and telegraph companies qualify as do railroads, street railways and buses, subways, oil and gas pipelines, and air, water, and motor transport companies. Sometimes steam heating, cold storage, irrigation, and sewage disposal companies are also included.

In modern usage the term "public utility" refers to all of the preceding categories with a few exceptions that include the railroads and some other forms of transportation. The remainder of this chapter will be devoted, in part, to describing the characteristics and the regulation of public utilities, sometimes called public-service companies, including an explanation of the general principles that apply to all types of regulated industries. Following an examination of the criteria used by commissions to make decisions affecting the various types of companies under their jurisdiction, the regulation of several specific industries will be discussed.

CHARACTERISTICS OF PUBLIC UTILITIES

The major classifications of public-utility companies have certain characteristics that are lacking in other forms of private business such as: (1) public necessity, (2) natural monopoly, (3) large investment, and (4) special privileges. An examination of these differences will explain, in part, why government regulation has replaced competition as the means by which the public secures reasonable prices and satisfactory services.

Public Necessity

Most public utilities provide a service to the general public that it could not do without under present-day living conditions. For this reason millions of individuals are vitally concerned with the problems of services and rates. If a water-softening service company charges high prices and renders poor service, the user can discontinue his contract. He cannot, however, do the same with the water service itself. If he lives in a city, he is dependent upon the water company to furnish a continuous flow of clean water at rates he can afford to pay. This specific example points up the fact that there is no acceptable substitute for many of the services rendered by a public utility, the need for them cannot be postponed, and the consumer has no choice but to pay whatever he is charged.

Because the services rendered by a public utility are necessary, some municipalities have established departments or created governmental corporations to own and operate the water system, street buses, and, less frequently, an electric plant. Despite these encroachments into areas in which private enterprise would be happy to operate, the fact is that public-utility companies, as previously defined, render most of the services that the public needs and demands.

Natural Monopoly

A second characteristic of public utilities is that they function in business areas where the existence of competing units would be inefficient and undesirable. It is in the public interest to permit one firm to have all the business of its type available in a given community. As previously mentioned, two competing telephone companies in one city would be completely unsatisfactory. In a similar manner, there is a disadvantage in having two gas companies, two electric light companies, or two water companies serving the same community.

Large Investment

Most public utilities require a large investment in plant and equipment before they can begin operations. The cost of building a dam to generate hydroelectric power or providing a water supply for a city is tremendous. It would not be economical to duplicate such facilities in any one geographic area. One of the reasons why competition between public utilities is not desirable is the high cost of plant and equipment ordinarily required by most companies. As a direct result of a large investment in plant and equipment, public-utility operations are characterized by sizable annual expenses in the form of depreciation on the fixed assets owned, plus repairs and upkeep. Labor costs and other out-of-pocket expenditures are frequently low, as it takes, for example, only a few employees to handle the controls of an electric generating plant. This means that utility operating costs are predominantly fixed rather than variable and, if consumers are to enjoy low rates, a large volume of business is necessary. The rates charged by a public utility can be much lower if annual fixed charges of, for example, $1 million are passed on to 100,000 customers rather than 10,000.

Special Privileges

Another characteristic of many public utilities is the right to secure special privileges from governmental units. These include the *right of eminent domain*, which is the power of a government to take private property for a public purpose by the payment of a fair price that, if necessary, will be determined by a court. This privilege may be and is commonly granted to telephone, telegraph, gas, electric-services companies, and other public utilities. For example, many long-distance electric transmission lines run overland on a straight line between two terminals, making use of private property for the erection of support towers regardless of whether or not such use of the land is agreeable to the owner.

PUBLIC-UTILITY REGULATORY AGENCIES

As previously pointed out, part of the burden that a public utility must carry for its special privileges, such as monopoly status and the right of eminent domain, is to be subject to much more extensive regulation than is imposed on any and all types of competitive businesses. Such additional regulation is largely centered on rates and service. The determination and enforcement of what constitutes fair rates and satisfactory service falls under one or more of three levels of government depending on the territory served by the utility.

If the public utility is a street railway or a bus line, a local water or electric company, or any other privately owned organization selling its services exclusively within the confines of a municipality, it will be regulated by the city council or a comparable counterpart. At the time a *franchise*, which is an exclusive right to serve the community for a specified number of years, is granted, regulatory conditions are imposed. Customarily a committee of the council is charged with the responsibility for overseeing that the rates charged and the services rendered are in accord with the terms of the franchise.

More commonly, a utility serves more than one community within a state. In this event its regulation will fall under the jurisdiction of a state public-utility commission, which is a branch of the state government. Although the utility must still obtain a franchise to operate in each city, this commission can overrule the terms of a franchise if these would obstruct the overall regulation of the utility company. For example, if a city insisted on a very low rate structure before granting a franchise to a natural gas company, it might mean that the company would have to charge high rates in other areas it serves in order to earn a fair profit. Under these conditions the state commission could overrule the municipality, although it is more likely that it would have entered into the negotiations before the local franchise in question was granted. Although the competence of the commissions varies widely among the 50 states, the appointment of intelligent commissioners, who employ a staff of experts, has frequently resulted in efficient and capable state regulation.

From 1907, when the first state utility commissions were established in New York and Wisconsin, until 1935, when the first of several laws affecting utilities was enacted, the federal government did not regulate public utilities. During this time it became increasingly clear that the interstate operations of some utilities, notably electric and natural gas companies, were so extensive that state commissions could not regulate these companies effectively. The federal government, as will be discussed later, has now established several agencies that either regulate a phase of public-utility company operations or the interstate rates and services of a particular industry. These agencies cooperate with the state commissions whenever a problem is of both an interstate and an intrastate nature and, in general, have filled a previous void in a competent manner.

The actions of regulatory bodies, at all levels, are subject to court actions whenever a ruling is not acceptable either to the public-utility company or to the consumers of the service. So many decisions have been rendered that it seems fair to say that the courts have also played an important part in the regulation of utilities. This role will become apparent in the examination of the techniques of public-utility regulation that follows. Since state commissions play a dominant role in the determination of rates and service, the methods they use will be described in some detail although the basic concepts apply with equal force to all regulation by administrative agencies.

STATE REGULATION OF PUBLIC-UTILITY RATES

Of prime importance to the public utility and to its customers are the rates charged for its services. Although many business firms have found that a low profit on a high volume of sales produces maximum profits for the owners, there is a justifiable fear that a monopoly would not follow this price policy. Consequently, all of the states regulate the rates that public utilities may charge for their services.

As a general working principle, commissions have tried to establish rate structures that permit each public-utility company to earn a fair return on a fair value of its property. This principle follows a line of argument adopted by the Supreme Court of the United States in a decision that read, in part, as follows: "A public utility is entitled to such rates as will permit it to earn a return on the value of the property which it employs for the convenience of the public equal to that generally being made at the same time and in the same general part of the country on investments in other business undertakings which are attended by corresponding risks and uncertainties."

Fair Rate of Return

A rate of return that is fair to the utility and to the public is extremely difficult to establish. In most instances the rates allowed have varied from

5 to 8 percent on the fair value of its property, with 6 and 7 percent favored over the extremes. Of course, once a rate of return is established, there is no guarantee that the return will equal the rate. If operations produce a loss or a very low rate of return, the company can apply for an adjustment in rates. If the commission should refuse to grant such a request, the courts on an appeal would probably decide that the allowed rates were too low. On the other hand, if operations result in a high rate of return, the public will soon bring pressure to bear on the commission to reduce the charges made by the utility.

Fair Value of Property

Assuming that a fair rate of return has been determined, it must also be decided what is a fair value of the property owned by the public utility that is used for the purpose of rendering services to the public. This involves placing a price tag on every item of such property, which is extremely difficult to do. Even if there is mutual agreement on the properties to be included, there is likely to be a lack of agreement as to a method to be used in arriving at a true value.

Two widely used measures are (a) *original cost* less depreciation and (b) *reproduction cost new* less depreciation. The first of these is known as *historical cost* and corresponds to values shown on the balance sheet. The reproduction cost method prices properties at current costs rather than at prices actually paid. Both methods have been sanctioned by the United States Supreme Court.

Rate Differentials

One of the special problems that arise in determining fair rates is that all customers of a particular public utility cannot be charged the same rates. In a given locality, like users of the street railways, water service, electric service, and telephone service do pay the same amount. Rates may vary between two communities located some distance apart, however, even though they are served by the same company. This condition may result from negotiating franchises in different years or under other diverse circumstances. Of even more importance is the difference between rates charged to classes of consumers, such as the homeowner and a manufacturing company. The kilowatt-hour rate charged for electricity in the case of the individual is much higher than that charged to the manufacturer.

STATE REGULATION OF PUBLIC-UTILITY SERVICES

Several features of the problem of service might not be apparent to a casual observer. The public takes most of these for granted without recognizing that its best interests are being protected by the commission.

Entry into Public-Utility Field

A public-utility company cannot enter the field in any locality without first of all securing permission from the commission. This usually takes the form of a *certificate of convenience and necessity*. If a group of men want to form an electric company to serve a geographic area, they need to secure a certificate from the state regulatory body. If the area includes a municipality, it will also be necessary to secure a franchise from the local authorities.

Standards of Service

Most public-utility commissions have the right to insist on certain minimum standards of service. A bus route must maintain regular schedules, which means that equipment and drivers must be available to meet published timetables. The heating value of gas furnished to homes must not fall below established minimums. Water must be pure, and the pressure must be maintained in order to insure protection against fire losses.

Service Without Discrimination

A public-utility company cannot choose its customers or render different classes of service to like users. Every person whose residence is on a street that carries gas, telephone, and electrical connections has a right to demand the use of these services. Furthermore, he is entitled to the same service and rates as exist for other like users of the services. There are, of course, reasonable limitations on these duties, such as the right to discontinue a service for nonpayment of a monthly bill.

Extension and Abandonment

A public utility usually may not extend, reduce, or abandon the service it renders in any territory without first securing approval from the state commission. In the case of extension, the entry problem has already been discussed; but it should be added that a commission may require an extension where such a move would be economically sound and of benefit to the public served. Partial or complete abandonment of service is also restricted by the commission. Even though a public utility is losing money on a particular segment of its operation, it may not abandon the service without prior commission approval.

FEDERAL REGULATION OF PUBLIC UTILITIES

Although the operations of public utilities are primarily intrastate, electricity and natural gas move across state lines and are thus in interstate commerce. Furthermore, between 1920 and 1935 there was a tremendous increase in public utility holding companies that created interstate transactions among its operating companies which formerly had been independent and domiciled in one state. Public recognition that state commissions lacked constitutional authority to cope with interstate utility problems led to a demand for remedial action by the federal government. In 1935 the Congress of the United States responded by passing the first of several laws that brought the interstate activities of public utilities under federal supervision.

Public Utility Holding Company Act of 1935

As the title of this law indicates, one of its purposes was to exert a measure of control over public utility holding companies. Too many of those organized in the previous 15 years were so far removed from operating companies that they were uneconomic and strictly speculative in nature. The act required all holding companies to register with the Securities and Exchange Commission and specified that a holding company could control two or more holding companies that, in turn, owned operating companies, but it could not be owned by another holding company. Holding companies that violated these limitations were required to dissolve and go out of business, which explains why this provision was commonly called the *death sentence clause* of the act.

As a means of forcing the holding companies to register, the law provided that unregistered companies were forbidden to use the mails and other instrumentalities of interstate commerce. Registered companies were not allowed to borrow from subsidiaries, to pay excessive dividends, or to make political contributions. Sales, service, and construction contracts between the holding company and the subsidiaries were subject to review by the Commission.

The act also gave the Federal Power Commission, an existing federal agency, the right to regulate interstate electric rates. This eliminated one of the problems that had vexed state utility commissions. The law further provided control over charges for electric service through the creation of joint boards of federal and state commissions. The act also gave the Federal Power Commission direction to coordinate and interconnect transmission lines in the United States and to control sales and purchases of companies transmitting electricity in interstate commerce.

Natural Gas Act of 1938

As in the case of electric service, the Natural Gas Act of 1938 gave the Federal Power Commission jurisdiction over the rates charged by companies engaged in the interstate transmission of natural gas. The reason that manufactured gas was not included was that almost all gas so produced is consumed in the city in which it is manufactured or in nearby areas and does not, normally, enter into interstate commerce. This act added to the jurisdiction of the Federal Power Commission another important interstate public-utility operation.

RAILROAD REGULATION

As early as 1870 the farmers in the midwestern grain-growing states became so incensed concerning the high rates charged by the railroads that they insisted in their state legislatures that commissions be created to control these monopoly prices. State commissions, however, could regulate only intrastate transportation, and practically all railroads operated in interstate commerce. Since the federal government is the only legislative body authorized to control interstate commerce, pressure was exerted on the Congress to take appropriate action. As a result, the Interstate Commerce Act was passed in 1887. This legislation, designed to regulate the transportation of goods across state lines, represents a milestone in the history of the federal regulation of business.

The 1887 law created the Interstate Commerce Commission and gave it the right to end rate discriminations, stated that rates were to be just and reasonable, and required schedules of rates and fares to be published. It also included a *long-and-short-haul clause,* which made it illegal for a railroad to charge a higher rate for a short haul than for a long haul under substantially similar conditions. Some railroads had been charging a low competitive rate between two points served by another line, but between cities not served by another carrier they charged a high monopoly rate. Although the Commission was not given the necessary authority to enforce the provisions of the 1887 Act and several adverse court decisions further weakened the law, subsequent acts and amendments have corrected these deficiencies.

The early recognition of the public-utility characteristics of the railroads and of the need for extensive regulation of common carriers in interstate commerce has, over the years, resulted in more and more legislation expanding the scope and extent of Commission control. Currently, the Interstate Commerce Commission has extensive jurisdiction over practically all facets of railroad operations. Rates, service, valuation, security issues, consolidations, safety appliances, accounting, and many other phases of this industry are controlled by the seven commissioners, aided by a large staff of experts. Problems involving both intrastate and interstate commerce are handled cooperatively with the state commissions.

MOTOR CARRIER REGULATION

Motor carriers engaged in interstate hauling are under the jurisdiction of the Interstate Commerce Commission, although those engaged strictly in intrastate traffic are subject only to regulation by state commissions. All of the states exercise a certain amount of control over trucks using the roads within their boundaries; that is, they regulate the length, width, height, and the gross weight of the vehicle and its contents. Safety regulations covering the operation of motor vehicles have been prescribed by the Interstate Commerce Commission, and the states generally follow such regulations.

Motor trucks and buses engaging in interstate traffic were first regulated by the federal government under the authority of the Motor Carrier Act of 1935. Under this act the Interstate Commerce Commission was given power over interstate motor transport carriers very similar to the extensive supervision that existed for railroads. The extent of control varies for common, contract, and private carriers. *Common carriers* operate on regular schedules and offer service to the general public. *Contract carriers* hire their services for special hauls, such as moving household goods. Trucks and buses used by the firm owning them are known as *private carriers*. Common carriers are subject to rate and service regulations and cannot do business without obtaining from the commission a certificate of convenience and necessity. Carriers holding such certificates have a franchised monopoly similar to that discussed earlier in this chapter. Permits and minimum rates are prescribed for contract carriers, while private carriers are subject merely to safety regulations.

REGULATION OF AIR TRANSPORT, WATER TRANSPORTATION, AND PIPELINES

In addition to interstate traffic by rail and truck, raw materials and other types of merchandise move by air, water, and pipelines. In each of these areas an appropriate agency of the federal government regulates rates, services, and other details in a manner more or less comparable to that described for railroads. In each instance a different regulatory body is involved insofar as the controls are on an interstate level.

Air transport is subject to control by local or municipal, state, and federal agencies. The first two deal with the construction and operation of airports and regulations concerning their use. The federal regulation of air transport is primarily under the jurisdiction of the Civil Aeronautics Board. This five-member agency has the authority to prescribe rates for passengers and air mail, to approve domestic and overseas routes for airline companies, and to establish standards of service. The certification of aircraft and personnel as well as the development of airports are supervised by the Federal Aviation Administration, a division of the Department of Transportation.

Water transportation between the states was placed under the control of the Interstate Commerce Commission in 1940, although from its beginnings this Commission had the authority to fix rates involving joint water-rail interstate transportation. Regulation of water transportation is similar to that for motor trucks, but several types of contract and common carriers are exempt from supervision over rates. Where rates are controlled, they are usually established at a 10 to 20 percent reduction from the charges allowed the railroads for similar classes of goods.

The interstate shipment of oil by pipelines has been under the jurisdiction of the Interstate Commerce Commission since 1906. As noted earlier, however, when natural gas shipment by pipelines was placed under regulation in 1938, the authority to regulate these common carriers was given to the Federal Power Commission. Actually, most oil pipelines are owned by the companies using them even though they become common carriers on occasion by transporting oil of independents. Gas pipelines are generally owned by companies that buy natural gas at the fields and sell to companies engaged in the business of retailing to consumers. The rates charged for this transportation service are an important element in the cost of natural gas delivered to those who consume it.

REGULATION OF COMMUNICATIONS INDUSTRIES

In the areas of telegraph, interstate telephone, radio, and television, the federal government has seen fit to establish a regulatory agency with varying degrees of authority over companies engaged in these businesses. This is the Federal Communications Commission, which received most of its authority under the Communications Act of 1934. The FCC, as it is known, has the authority to regulate rates and services for interstate communications by wire, which includes telegraph messages and long-distance telephone calls. It also supervises charges for cable and radio overseas messages, satellite communications, and community antenna television.

In the fields of commercial television and radio, since stations do not charge the public for their programs, there is no rate regulation. Rather, the Federal Communications Commission has concentrated its attention on allocating television channels and radio frequencies. Each station is licensed for three years, and must follow prescribed rules or endanger its chances of having the permit renewed. One of the problems faced by the Commission was that only 12 channels were available in the VHF (very high frequency) band, which led to station interference in some areas of the country. To solve this problem, 70 new channels were allocated space in the UHF (ultra high frequency) band. In order to make effective use of these new channels, since many TV sets could not receive UHF programs, Congress amended the Federal Communication Act specifying that, after April, 1964, all television sets manufactured had to be able to receive programs broadcast by stations using channels 2 to 83. This requirement is an interesting example of the effect regulation may have on the freedom an industry usually has regarding the products it manufactures.

BUSINESS TERMS

QUESTIONS FOR DISCUSSION AND ANALYSIS

1. Is competition today more effective in business areas that include a large number of small firms as opposed to the types of business activity dominated by a few large companies?

2. Assuming that large corporations do compete vigorously with each other, e. g., Procter & Gamble and Colgate-Palmolive, would the public be better off if such industrial giants were broken up into smaller units as is frequently proposed for the General Motors Corporation?

3. Should consumers be provided with even more protection than is presently available by the passage of additional legislation and by more vigorous enforcement of the consumer-protection laws already enacted?

4. Are federal laws on environmental control necessary and desirable? Isn't this problem one that should be settled at the local level?

5. Does the present level of the regulation of competitive businesses by states and their political subdivisions seem reasonable and in the best interests of its citizens? Would you feel differently if you were a businessman?

6. Wouldn't one regulated supermarket and one regulated drugstore in a community serve the best interests of consumers in the same manner as having one telephone company?

7. Isn't the right of eminent domain repugnant to the capitalistic concept of property rights? In any event, shouldn't this right be restricted to governmental units?

8. Doesn't the rate-making principle of a fair return on a fair value encourage wasteful spending and inefficient operation for public-utility companies?

9. The partial abandonment of passenger train service by the railroads has been cited as an example of management's failure to sell the public on this mode of transportation. Do you agree? Will the National Railroad Passenger Corp. (Amtrak) succeed?

10. Businessmen have been known to yearn for the "good old days" when they were free to pursue their profits without governmental interference. Would a return to laissez-faire capitalism work in today's economic climate?

PROBLEMS AND SHORT CASES

1. a. A local personal loan office located in a state with a usury law that specified a maximum rate of 3 percent a month made a loan to T. N. Strong on the following terms:

Note signed $375
Cash received $300
Length of loan .... 1 year
Interest at a discounted annual rate of 20%
Monthly payments on loan $31.25

Was this loan made at usurious rates? Show your calculations to justify your answer.

b. An electric public-utility company has had the following rates approved for residential customers:

First 100 kilowatt hours . . . . 5.0⊄ per kilowatt hour
Next 100 kilowatt hours . . . . 4.0⊄ per kilowatt hour
Next 900 kilowatt hours . . . . 3.5¢ per kilowatt hour
Additional kilowatt hours . . . . 2.5¢ per kilowatt hour
Minimum monthly rate $2.00

Compute the monthly bill if the consumer uses the following number of kilowatt hours: (1) 30, (2) 75, (3) 180, (4) 500, (5) 2,000.

2. A group of entrepreneurs formed the SCD Corporation for the purpose of establishing a chain of quick service restaurants known as Street Car Diners. Originally the outlets were company owned, but the immediate success of the chain encouraged the owners to expand by granting franchises. There are now 78 units operating in 10 states of which only 15 are owned. Every item from napkins to buildings is standardized and both food and nonfood supplies are furnished from central warehouses.

G. R. Fox secured a franchise for a Street Car Diner and signed an agreement that he would purchase all items used from the parent company at prices stated in the contract. He soon discovered, however, that his meat deliveries were irregular and on several occasions he patronized a local meat packer in order to serve his customers. To his surprise Fox found that he could do better pricewise by purchasing his meat from this nearby wholesaler, so he gradually ordered less and less from the SCD Corporation and more and more from his local source.

When the SCD Corporation became aware of what Fox was doing, it ordered him to cease making any local purchases. Despite repeated warnings, Fox refused to comply and the SCD Corporation sued him for breach of contract. A lower court held for Fox on the grounds that the contract with the SCD Corporation was in violation of both the Sherman and Clayton Antitrust Acts. The SCD Corporation is now considering what action it should take. It can appeal the case and hope for a reversal by a higher court, or it can make changes in the contractual relationships with franchise holders. Its future expansion program is at stake and the management is faced with a difficult decision. What should it do?

3. The Central Arizona Electric Co. has filed a rate increase application with the Arizona Utility Commission. The company has been valued for rate-making purposes at $120,000,000 based on original costs less depreciation, and its earnings for the past year were $6,000,000. It is the contention of the company that it should have been allowed to earn at least $10,000,000, and it also disputes the method used for valuing its facilities. It has produced detailed figures to show that its present value based on reproduction cost new less depreciation is $160,000,000.

An examination of the company's financial statements shows that it secured 60 percent of its capital by selling bonds that carry an interest rate of 4 percent and that do not mature for another 20 years. Another 20 percent was obtained from an issue of 5 percent non-participating preferred stock. The company admits that, because it sold bonds and preferred stock at a most favorable time, the common stockholders have been receiving generous dividends.

Lawyers for the company appearing before the Arizona Utility Commission contend that the decision of the United States Supreme Court, quoted on page 690, is not being followed. They contend that because of the optional use of natural gas and of industry-owned generating plants, the Central Arizona Electric Co. is in competition for much of its business and that its risks and uncertainties are comparable to those of manufacturing firms. Evidence presented indicated that such firms, on the average, earn 9.5 percent on their total assets.

If you were a member of the Arizona Utility Commission, how would you form your opinion on this request for a rate increase? How would you vote?

SUGGESTED READINGS

Anderson, R. A. *Government and Business*, Third Edition. Cincinnati: South-Western Publishing Co., 1966.

Garfield, P. J., and W. F. Lovejoy. *Public Utility Economics*. Englewood Cliffs, New Jersey: Prentice-Hall, Inc., 1964.

Glaeser, M. G. *Public Utilities in American Capitalism*. New York: The Macmillan Company, 1957.

Kintner, E. W. *A Robinson-Patman Primer*. New York: The Macmillan Company, 1970.

Liebhafsky, H. H., Jr. *American Government and Business*. New York: John Wiley & Sons, Inc., 1970.

Locklin, D. P. *Economics of Transportation*, Sixth Edition. Homewood, Illinois: Richard D. Irwin, Inc., 1966.

Pegrum, D. F. *Public Regulation of Business*, Revised Edition. Homewood, Illinois: Richard D. Irwin, Inc., 1965.

Phillips, C. F., Jr. *The Economics of Regulation: Theory and Practice in the Transportation and Public Utility Industries*. Homewood, Illinois: Richard D. Irwin, Inc., 1965.

Sampson, R., Jr., and M. T. Fariss. *Domestic Transportation: Practice, Theory and Policy*. Boston: Houghton Mifflin Company, 1966.

Slesinger, R. E., and A. Isaacs. *Business, Government, and Public Policy*, Second Edition. Princeton, New Jersey: Van Nostrand, 1968.

Stelzer, I. M. *Selected Antitrust Cases: Landmark Decisions*, Third Edition. Homewood, Illinois: Richard D. Irwin, Inc., 1966.

Wilcox, C. *Public Policies Toward Business*, Third Edition. Homewood, Illinois: Richard D. Irwin, Inc., 1965.

Chapter 29

Business and Taxes

The taxation of business units and activities is an important element of the environment in which large and small firms currently operate. As governmental units at all levels of authority spend more and more, lawmakers seeking additional sources of revenue have frequently focused their attention on business. To the credit of practically all of the firms that function in the United States, they have learned to live with and to assume responsibility for the resulting heavy tax burden. This acceptance, however, does not mean that taxes are not avoided by all legal means. Consequently, the environmental situation that results is one in which tax consequences enter into many business decisions.

As an aid to understanding the exact nature of the tax burden carried by businesses, this chapter will examine some principles of taxation and explain the types of taxes levied by local, state, and federal governments. It should be understood that local governments include cities, towns and villages, townships, parishes, counties, school districts, drainage districts, and other subdivisions of our 50 states. After the several types of taxes have been explained, specific examples will illustrate various ways in which the impact of tax burdens does enter into, and on occasion dictate, the most advantageous solutions to certain business problems.

Also, as a further aid to understanding business taxes, specific rates have been extensively used in the discussion that follows. It should be understood, however, that these are constantly being changed as legislative bodies meet and pass new laws. Furthermore, it should also be kept in mind that new sources of revenue may be found. For example, a *value added tax*, which is a sales tax levied on each sale of a good to the extent of its increased value as it moves through successive manufacturing and distributive channels, may well be adopted by the federal government. Such a tax is already in use by several European countries.

PRINCIPLES OF TAXATION

The problem of enacting a suitable program of taxation for any governmental unit is most difficult. The total revenue secured should be adequate to meet necessary current expenditures. The burden should be distributed on an equitable basis. The tax law must be reasonably simple and the funds easy to collect. In some instances it may be desirable to use the tax as a means of regulation as well as revenue.

At the federal level taxation is also used as a means of attempting to exercise some measure of control over the economy. For example, during the sixties business was encouraged to spend money for new plant and equipment by receiving a 7 percent credit against income taxes. The enactment in 1968 of a 10 percent income tax surcharge, reduced to 5 percent in 1970 and then abandoned, was designed to reduce business and consumer spending and hence aid in combating inflation. In other years, in order to maintain purchasing power, income tax rates on individuals have remained constant despite the knowledge that failure to increase them would result in a budget deficit.

Some tax rates remain constant regardless of the size of the tax base. Any tax fulfilling this specification is known as a *proportional tax*. For example, in a taxing district the same tax rate on the appraised value of property is used regardless of the amount of property owned by one person. Rates of a *regressive tax* become lower as the tax base increases in size. The cost of securing a corporation charter, when based on the number of shares authorized, involves lower rates on the shares in excess of a stated minimum. The opposite of a regressive tax is a *progressive tax*, which applies higher and higher rates as the tax base grows in size. Income taxes are usually designed so that higher rates apply to the upper brackets of income. Likewise, inheritance and estate tax rates are higher for large bequests or estates.

From the businessman's point of view, the impact and incidence of taxes are important. *Impact* refers to the person who is liable for the tax and who keeps the necessary records and mails out a check in payment of the amount due. In many instances it is possible, through a process known as shifting, to pass the tax on to others, usually the final consumer.

The place at which the ultimate burden falls is known as the *incidence* of the tax. A gasoline tax may be paid by the man who owns the service station but, if he is able to add this tax to the purchase price paid by the customer, he is merely serving as a collection agency for a governmental unit. If the tax cannot be shifted, the businessman must absorb the amount. If the incidence can be made to fall elsewhere, the tax, aside from the burden of record keeping, does not affect his operations except to the extent that his prices are necessarily higher.

The reasons for selecting certain bases for purposes of taxation are not always apparent. Obviously, broad bases, such as sales, income, or property, offer an opportunity to raise sizable sums without using excessively high rates. Taxes on gasoline have the advantage of raising funds from those who use the highways that are maintained and improved with these revenues. Taxes on liquor and tobacco are types of *sumptuary taxes*, which are taxes designed to discourage consumption of the items taxed by increasing their retail prices.

TYPES OF STATE AND LOCAL TAXES

The following partial list of the taxes that are most frequently levied by the several states and their various political units will indicate the nature and extent of this relationship between business and government: (1) general sales taxes, (2) selective sales or excise taxes, (3) income taxes, (4) property taxes, (5) payroll taxes, (6) corporation taxes, (7) special business taxes, (8) inheritance and estate taxes, (9) severance taxes, and (10) assessments. Some of these are duplicated by the federal government while others are not. Although there have been some efforts to allocate different types of taxes to the various taxing units, the need for revenue is so great that a good source, such as income, is used by cities, states, and the federal government.

GENERAL SALES TAXES

A tax to be paid by consumers which is levied on all, or nearly all, retail sales of goods or services or both is a *general sales tax*. It provides the largest single source of revenue for government at the state level, and several cities and counties also make use of this source of income. The District of Columbia and 45 states have enacted some form of a general sales tax. Rates vary between 2 and 6 percent of retail prices, with 3 percent used by approximately half of the states. City and county sales taxes vary between 1 and 3 percent. Some states allow certain exemptions, such as food purchases not consumed on the premises or sales under a minimum amount.

To supplement the general sales tax, most states have enacted a *use tax,* which is a sales tax on goods entering the state from another state. Out-of-state firms that are licensed to do business in a state must collect the use tax on sales to customers living in a state that has a general sales tax despite the fact that a particular transaction is interstate in character. Other out-of-state merchants do not collect use taxes but, when a title is necessary, such as for an automobile, the purchaser who went out of his state to buy the car is required to pay the tax.

SELECTIVE SALES OR EXCISE TAXES

A *selective sales* or *excise tax* is one levied on the producer or seller of a particular commodity or group of commodities manufactured and sold within the country. States usually levy such taxes at the retail level on liquor, tobacco, motor fuel, and a few miscellaneous items such as hotel accommodations or tickets for entertainment. Rates can be specific; for example, 7 cents a gallon. Or rates can be ad valorem, such as 10 percent of the price of an admission to an athletic event.

Common examples of this type of taxation are levies made by states on the sale of alcoholic beverages and cigarettes. All states tax beer, wine, and whiskey, even when the liquor business is a state monopoly and the stores are expected to show a profit. All states also tax cigarettes with rates ranging from 2 cents to 18.5 cents per package.

The taxation of gasoline sold for consumption on the public highways is another widely used tax as all states and the District of Columbia secure revenue from this source. Rates vary from a low of 5 cents per gallon to a high of 9 cents with more than one half of all states using a 7-cent levy. Substantial revenues are derived from this tax and, in general, these funds are used for building and improving highways, roads, and streets. Payments are made to the state, but a common practice is to return a proportion of the amount collected to the county, township, city, or village on the basis of the collections originating in the various political subdivisions.

INCOME TAXES

The District of Columbia and 38 states have enacted some type of a personal income tax, and 43 states tax the incomes of corporations. In several of these states income taxes are the major source of revenue although 45 states also levy sales taxes (see Figure 29-1). An *income tax*

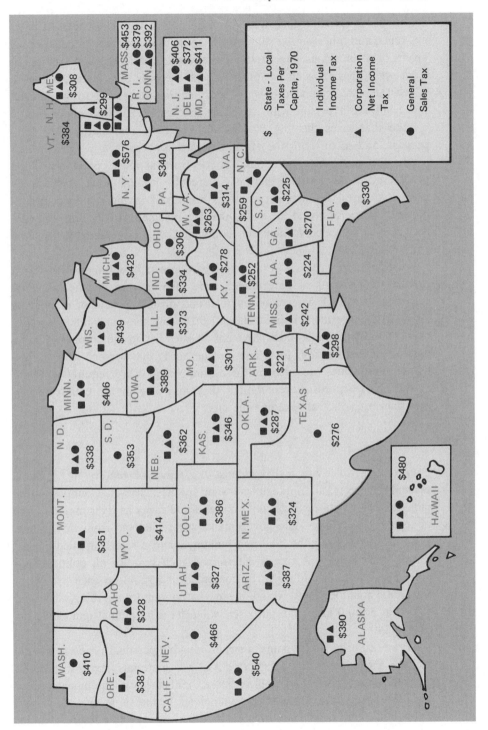

Figure 29-1

Where the Money Comes From—Major Tax Sources

Source: Tax Foundation, Inc.

is one that is levied against wages, salaries, commissions, dividends, interest, rents, and other similar sources of income to individuals and against net profits of corporations. Most states allow certain deductions and exemptions from gross income, such as $600 for each member of a family, following which rates are graduated upwards with a range of from 1 to 14 percent. For example, a person with a taxable income of $50,000 might live in a state that taxes the first $2,000 at 1 percent, the next $2,000 at 2 percent, and so on until the maximum rate applies.

In the case of corporations, the tax rate is most commonly a flat percent of all net income, such as 5 percent, although some states apply graduated rates. Foreign corporations are taxed in the same manner as domestic corporations to the extent that the income of the foreign corporation can be allocated to activities conducted within the state levying the tax.

Within recent years several cities, hard pressed for funds with which to meet rising costs of government, have also enacted income tax laws. Rates are usually 1 percent on payrolls and profits of resident individuals and firms; nonresident individuals and firms pay the same rate on wages or incomes attributable to employment or sales within the corporate limits. One of the justifications for a city income tax is that persons who use the numerous facilities provided by these municipalities are required to share in the necessary costs even though they may live in the country or in suburban areas not annexed to the city.

PROPERTY TAXES

Property taxes are levied against the value of real estate, tangible personal property, and intangibles owned by the taxpayer. Counties, cities, villages, and school districts rely on real estate taxes as their major source of revenue, and some state governments secure income from this source. Local assessors value the land and buildings, and a rate is applied against this appraised value. A rate is determined each year for all political subdivisions. The total rate might be computed at $32.48 on each $1,000 of assessed valuation. This would mean that a factory building and land valued at $500,000 for tax purposes would have an annual real estate tax of $16,240.

From a business viewpoint, a tax on tangible personal property usually includes the value of machinery, stocks of raw materials, goods in process, finished merchandise, and office, store, and factory equipment. Some localities assess the values of these tangibles in the same manner as real estate, and the same rates apply. In other taxing districts cost minus depreciation is used as a basis for valuation, and special rates that have no relationship to real estate tax rates apply against the value of tangible personal property.

An intangible personal property tax is the weakest form of the general property tax in that it is easy to conceal assets of this type. Intangibles subject to taxation include stocks, bonds, mortgages, and notes. Some states have laws that apply special rates to such values; others include intangibles in the total value of all property owned. An interesting development in recent years particularly applicable to intangibles has been the trading of tax information between state governments and the federal government. Individuals and businesses who report dividends and interest on their federal income tax returns soon discover that their local and state tax returns are being checked against this information.

PAYROLL TAXES

Two types of payroll taxes may be paid by employers into the state treasury. The federal Social Security Act of 1935 provided for a nationwide plan of *unemployment insurance*, which is a program designed to pay partial wages to workers while they are involuntarily unemployed. Unemployment insurance is a federal-state program and each state has its own rates, schedules of benefits, and rules and regulations. A 1970 amendment to the Federal Unemployment Tax Act provided for a levy of 3.2 percent on the first $4,200 of wages earned by each person covered by the act. A credit of 2.7 percent of this amount is allowed for payments made to state funds that are used to finance payments to unemployed individuals. Approximately 64 million workers are protected by this law.

Another payroll tax for workmen's compensation, which is a form of accident insurance for employees who are injured on the job, is compulsory in most states. Although some states permit employers to purchase a policy from a private insurance company, several states operate the fund from which such benefits are paid. The cost is assessed against the employer as a percent of his payroll, with rates that vary according to the hazard of the industry. A contractor who builds bridges and skyscrapers pays a higher rate than does a retail merchant. The subject of workmen's compensation insurance was discussed in greater detail on page 537.

CORPORATION TAXES

Various types of taxes are levied on domestic and foreign corporations as a prerequisite to organizing and conducting a business in the state under this form of business ownership. At the time a corporation secures a charter from a state, it is charged an organization tax, termed an incorporation fee, as was explained in Chapter 5. An *entrance tax* is similar except that it refers to a foreign corporation that wishes to conduct business in states other than the one from which it received its charter. Incorporation fees are usually based on the amount of stock authorized, and some states assess their entrance taxes on the same base. More commonly, entrance taxes are a fixed amount such as, for example, $100.

In addition to incorporation fees and entrance taxes, states levy an annual tax on both domestic and foreign corporations. The amount of the tax for domestic corporations is normally based on the amount of stock either outstanding or authorized. For foreign corporations the base may be the amount of stock owned by residents of the state, the value of the assets located within the state, or a flat fee. The annual fee levied on domestic corporations is known as a franchise tax, whereas for foreign corporations the term *privilege tax* is commonly used.

SPECIAL BUSINESS TAXES

Many of the states have enacted *special business taxes* that are levied against the incomes of businesses in selected industries. The most common ones chosen for these special taxes are insurance companies, railroads, public utilities, and banks. Less frequently, taxes in this classification are levied against railroad terminals, express companies, mining companies, lumber producers, and grain elevators.

The customary method of taxing insurance companies is to levy a gross premium assessment of 2 percent. All premiums collected within the state are subject to this rate regardless of whether the company is organized under the laws of the state or of another state, although some laws favor domestic corporations. Before a company can sell policies within the state, it must be licensed and agree to pay the tax applicable. Sometimes the amount is payable to the county, village, or city, although most states provide for central collection.

All types of banks generally pay, in addition to real estate taxes, a tax on the basis of total deposits on hand at a specific date during a year. This type of tax may also apply to other financial institutions accepting deposits from customers, such as savings and loan associations.

Railroads, whether interstate or intrastate, are frequently taxed on the regular real estate basis. This means that the value of the property in each state must be determined, which is a difficult problem. In order to lessen these complications, some states tax the railroads on the basis of the gross earnings. Even this method is cumbersome because it becomes necessary to apportion the earnings among the several states in which the railroad may operate.

Public utilities are usually taxed on the basis of gross earnings. Many utilities confine their operations within the borders of a particular state, which eliminates the interstate problems faced in the taxation of most railroads. For those that cross state lines, the problems of allocation are involved. The taxes are determined on the basis of volume of business in the state or by calculating the pro rata share of assets owned in the state.

Another type of a special business tax is based on the occupation in which the business is engaged rather than on its income. These taxes are more prevalent in the southern states and are usually restricted to such industries as the manufacture and wholesale distribution of malted drinks, bottling companies, and the manufacture and wholesale distribution of tobacco products. Chain-store taxes, when based on the number of stores in the chain, are also an example of a special business tax based on occupation.

One additional special business tax worthy of mention is that levied on pari-mutuel betting at race tracks where this type of gambling is permitted. Over one half of the states collect a share, which is usually 5 percent of the total amount wagered on each race.

INHERITANCE AND ESTATE TAXES

Both estate and inheritance taxes are levies against the wealth passed on to heirs by a deceased person. They are frequently called *death duties*. The difference between the two is that *estate taxes* are assessed against the entire net value of the holdings formerly belonging to the deceased, while *inheritance taxes* are based upon the separate bequests made to individual heirs. Inheritance tax rates usually vary depending upon the directness of descent; for example, widows and children pay a lower rate than do nephews and grandchildren.

All states except one levy inheritance and/or estate taxes. Because the rates vary in the several states, businessmen have sometimes found it advantageous to transfer their holdings and legal residences to a more favorable state prior to the time at which they expect to die.

SEVERANCE TAXES

A *severance tax* is a fee levied upon the owner of timberland or mineral deposits whenever the timber is cut or the minerals are removed from the ground. The advantage of a severance tax is that it encourages conservation. For example, if a real estate tax is assessed against timberlands on which trees are being allowed to mature, the owner might find it necessary to conduct logging operations in order to raise enough money to pay the taxes. If a severance tax is substituted, the owner pays it only during the years when revenue is being received from the property.

ASSESSMENTS

Although assessments are purely a local problem and should not be classed as a tax, the general effect is the same as a tax. An *assessment* is for government services presumed to be of direct benefit to the property owner involved. Ordinary real estate taxes usually support the fire department, police, schools, parks, and other municipal functions, whereas a special assessment is made for building a sidewalk, highway, or sewer system available to a particular property owner. This type of improvement is supposed to add to the value of the property, which is the justification for taxing, or more properly, assessing those who benefit from the improvement. A $1,000 unimproved lot might easily be worth $2,000 after the street on which it faces is paved, sidewalks are laid, and a sewer connection is available.

TYPES OF FEDERAL TAXES

The current expenditures of the federal government are in the neighborhood of $200 billion annually. In years when the budget is balanced, all of this huge sum has come from tax receipts. An examination of the following types of taxes levied by the federal government will indicate the sources from which billions of dollars are collected each year as well as the relative importance of the various bases used: (1) income taxes, (2) manufacturers' excise taxes, (3) retailers' excise taxes, (4) employment taxes, (5) estate and gift taxes, (6) communications and transportation taxes, (7) miscellaneous taxes, and (8) customs duties.

INCOME TAXES

Income taxes are levied on the net profits of businesses organized as proprietorships, partnerships, or corporations and on the gross receipts of individuals not engaged in business. They comprise the largest single source of revenue for the federal government. In recent years income taxes have produced receipts in excess of $100 billion annually. Of this huge sum, individuals pay close to 70 percent and corporations the remaining

30 percent. The rates and methods of computation vary considerably between taxes for individuals and for corporations, and these will be discussed separately.

Personal Income Tax

Every citizen or resident of the United States, whether an adult or a minor, who had annual income in excess of a prescribed amount must file a tax return and may be liable for taxes on his income. For many years this prescribed amount was $600. Under the Tax Reform Act of 1969, filing requirements have been correlated with the new low-income allowance that was primarily designed to remove poverty-level taxpayers from the tax rolls. Thus, for taxable years beginning after December 31, 1969, the income level at which an individual must file an income tax return has been as follows:

Single individual $1,700
Single individual 65 or over 2,300
Married couple (filing jointly) 2,300
Married couple, one spouse 65 or over 2,900
Married couple, both 65 or over 3,500

The income level for filing a return remains at $600 for married persons filing separate returns and for those living apart. If any other taxpayer is entitled to claim a dependency exemption for the spouse, the $600 income filing requirement still applies. Also, individuals with self-employment income of more than $400 must file a return.

For taxable years beginning after December 31, 1972, the income levels at which a return must be filed will be increased to $1,750 for a single individual and to $2,500 for a married couple filing jointly. For the married person filing separately, the income level at which a return is required will be raised to $750 for taxable years beginning after 1972.

Income subject to tax includes money received from such sources as wages, dividends, interest, sale of property, and the net profit from a business or profession. Sole proprietors or partners who are engaged in any form of business have their net incomes taxed on the basis of such profits forming all or a part of the income of the individuals concerned. Also, the owners of close corporations having 10 or fewer stockholders may elect to be taxed in the same manner as if the firm were organized as a partnership.

All individuals are entitled to a personal exemption and are also allowed to deduct certain nonbusiness expenses such as interest paid, charitable contributions, most state and local taxes, and certain types and amounts of medical expenses. If a joint return is filed, a taxpayer is also allowed an exemption for his wife and for each child who is under 19 years of age or is a full-time student. Exemptions may also be claimed for relatives and for persons living in the taxpayer's home if more than one half of their support was furnished by the taxpayer and they did not have income of their own in excess of the amount of the exemption. The value for personal as well as dependency exemptions, which used to be $600, has been increased under the Tax Reform Act over a four-year period as follows:

For calendar year 1970 .... $625
For calendar year 1971 .... $650
For calendar year 1972 .... $700
For calendar year 1973 and thereafter $750

As mentioned earlier in this chapter, the personal income tax is an example of a progressive tax. For married taxpayers filing joint returns, the tax rate schedules divide taxable income into 25 brackets with progressively higher rates applying to each bracket of income greater than the preceding one. For example, the rate for taxable income of less than $1,000 is 14 percent; for taxable income of from $1,000 to $2,000, the tax is $140 plus 15 percent of the excess over $1,000; and for taxable income of from $2,000 to $3,000 the tax is $290 plus 16 percent. At higher levels the brackets are wider than one thousand dollars, and income in excess of $200,000 is taxed at a rate of 70 percent. The maximum tax on earned taxable income received after December 31, 1971, however, cannot exceed 50 percent, which represents a reduction from the 60 percent that prevailed for the year 1971.

In addition to the rate schedule described above, there are three other classifications of taxpayers to which distinctive brackets and percentages have been assigned. The total of four categories are as follows:

1. Unmarried individuals (other than surviving spouses and heads of households).
2. Heads of households.
3. Married individuals filing joint returns and surviving spouses.
4. Married individuals filing separate returns; estates and trusts.

Individuals who are married are permitted to allocate one half of the taxable income to the wife and one half to the husband regardless of which one produced the revenue. Since the rates increase with each tax bracket, the tax liability is usually less for married couples who have over $500 in taxable income if the so-called "split-income" feature is used, which is reflected in the rates applicable to married individuals filing a joint return. The reason for this is that each is allowed up to $500 in the first bracket, which means that the second bracket of 15 percent does not apply until income is in excess of $1,000. Unmarried individuals pay 14 percent on the first $500 of taxable income and 15 percent on the second $500. Separate returns for married persons are permissible, however, and in a few instances will provide a lower total tax.

An illustration of the actual tax calculation of a businessman and his wife will show the application of 1972 rates on 1971 income. Albert Dunham operates a hardware store and also owns a one-third interest in a garage that was purchased by a partnership. The income statement for the store showed a net income of $31,840 and the partnership return allocated $9,375 to Dunham as his share of the profits earned by the garage. In addition, Dunham's wife received interest income from accounts in savings banks and savings and loan associations and from investments in United States bonds totaling, in all, $7,335. These items constituted their entire income. The Dunhams have one son enrolled in college and a daughter attending high school. The calculation of their income, exemptions and deductions, and tax is as follows:

Income from hardware store		$31,840.00
Share of profits from partnership		9,375.00
Interest income		7,335.00
Total income		$48,550.00
Exemptions, 4 at $650 each	$2,600.00	
Deductions for contributions, etc.	1,750,00	
Total exemptions and deductions		4,350.00
Taxable income		$44,200.00
Computation of tax: (Married Taxpayer's Table)		
Tax on $44,000.00		$14,060.00
Excess over $44,000.00 ($200 at 50%)		100.00
Total tax on $44,200.00		$14,160.00

Personal income taxes are on a pay-as-you-go plan that requires employers to withhold a portion of each salary or wage payment. If the employee has no other source of income, the amounts withheld over a year will approximate his total tax liability. Individuals, such as the Dunhams mentioned above, who receive taxable income from sources other than salaries and wages are required to estimate their total tax a year in advance and make quarterly payments that, in combination with withholdings, will approximate their tax liability. These payments are due on April 15, June 15, and September 15 of the taxable year, and January 15 of the following year. If income prospects change during the year, an amended declaration can be filed on any of the above dates.

The individual income tax is far more involved than this discussion might indicate. The computation of net profits from businesses, the taxation of capital gains and losses, a tax credit against dividends received, and allowable deductions for persons not using the standard deduction are just a few of the complications that face many taxpayers. Penalties for failure to report the correct amount of income and to pay the tax thereon may result in severe monetary penalties as well as imprisonment.

Corporation Income Taxes

Corporations engaged in industry or trade are subject to two rates known as normal taxes and surtaxes. These rates on profits earned in 1971 were 22 percent and 26 percent, respectively. The 26 percent surtax rate did not apply to the first $25,000 of taxable net income, which supplied some relief for the small corporation. Larger corporations do not benefit to any great extent from the lower normal tax as, for example, the tax on $1,000,000 of net income amounts to $473,500.

Corporations also prepay their income taxes. One fourth of the estimated total in excess of a statutory exemption for estimated tax purposes is payable on the 15th of April, June, September, and December of the taxable year. Until 1968 the statutory exemption for corporations was $100,000, but this amount is being rapidly reduced and all but $5,500 was eliminated by the end of 1971. Even this small amount will be phased out in 1977.

Some types of corporations do not pay income taxes. Examples of exempt organizations include those operated exclusively for religious, charitable, scientific, literary, or educational purposes or for the prevention of cruelty to children or to animals. Labor unions, fraternal societies, some mutual companies and cooperatives, and civic organizations and clubs are also exempt. In all cases no part of the net earnings of these organizations can benefit any private stockholder or individual, nor can the organization engage in political activities. Furthermore, if any of these corporations has income from the operation of a business enterprise which is not related to the purpose on which its exempt status is based, such income is taxable. Tax-exempt corporations are required to file an annual information return which is examined to make sure that they are entitled to retain their favored status.

MANUFACTURERS' EXCISE TAXES

Federal excise taxes that apply to prices charged by manufacturers on selected items are known as *manufacturers' excise taxes*. These excise taxes constitute an important source of federal revenue with annual collections exceeding $12 billion. Because of the importance of alcohol and tobacco manufacturers' excise taxes, these two have been segregated from other commodities selected for taxation in the discussion that follows.

Alcohol and Tobacco Taxes

Taxes on the production of alcoholic beverages total over $3½ billion each year, and the taxation of tobacco products yields more than $2 billion annually. Rates are high in relation to selling prices, e.g., the federal tax on a package of cigarettes is 8 cents. The taxes on alcoholic beverages include all forms of distilled spirits, wines, and beer. Tobacco products taxed are cigarettes and cigars.

Other Manufacturers' Excise Taxes

Other items subject to manufacturers' excise taxes are all types of motor vehicles that use the highways, tires, gasoline and other fuels, firearms, and fishing equipment. Rates vary from 5 to 11 percent of the manufacturer's sales price or from 1½ to 9 cents a pound or gallon. The tax of 9 cents per pound on highway type tires, which is scheduled to be reduced to 5 cents after October 1, 1972, is an example of a manufacturers' excise tax.

RETAILERS' EXCISE TAXES

Many consumers remember the federal taxes on such items as furs, luggage, cosmetics, and jewelry, which were examples of *retailers' excise taxes*. Currently the only items on which an excise tax is levied at the retail level are diesel and special motor fuels and noncommercial aviation fuels and gasoline. The tax of 4 cents a gallon on diesel fuels is scheduled to be reduced to 1½ cents on October 1, 1972, and the taxes on noncommercial aviation fuel and gasoline are scheduled to expire July 1, 1980.

EMPLOYMENT TAXES

Every employer and each employee subject to the provisions of the Federal Insurance Contributions Act (FICA) must pay a tax on wages paid or received in order to finance old-age, survivors', and disability insurance benefits and for hospital insurance (Part A of Medicare). The current law provides a schedule of rates to be applied to the first $7,800 of earnings as shown in Table 29-1:

PROJECTED SCHEDULE OF FICA TAX RATES

Years	Social Security	Hospital	Combined
1971-1972	4.6%	.6%	5.2%
1973-1975	5.0	.65	5.65
1976-1979	5.0	.7	5.7
1980-1986	5.0	.8	5.8
1987—	5.0	.9	5.9

Table 29-1

Self-employed persons pay on the first $7,800 of earnings a special rate of 7.5 percent, which is scheduled to grow to 7.9 percent by 1986. Judging from past history, the maximum amount subject to tax is likely to be increased, and there is no guarantee that the Congress will hold to the present projected rate schedule. In addition, as explained earlier in this chapter under state unemployment insurance taxes, .5 percent of the first $4,200 paid to covered employees goes to the federal government. Employment taxes provide over $34 billion in revenues annually to the federal treasury, but even this huge sum appears inadequate to finance the outlays required for old-age, survivors', and disability insurance benefits and for hospital insurance.

ESTATE AND GIFT TAXES

The federal government did not enter the field of estate taxation until 1926, and the first gift tax law was enacted in 1934. These laws complement each other in that it is no longer possible to avoid estate taxes by gifts made prior to death. Despite the fact that there is an exemption of $30,000 for gift tax purposes, plus $3,000 each year to any number of donees, and an exemption of $60,000 for estates, these two taxes produce a sizable amount of revenue each year.

Gift tax rates start at 2¼ percent and increase, by brackets, to a high of 57¾ percent on taxable amounts in excess of $10 million. The estate tax rate is 3 percent for the first bracket and reaches a high of 77 percent at the $10 million level. The effect of these taxes is to make it almost impossible for large concentrations of wealth to remain in one family for many generations. This leveling factor provides a contrast between the distribution of wealth in the United States and many South American and European countries. In the latter countries it has long been the right of the eldest son, under the doctrine of primogeniture, to inherit the whole of his father's estate without regard for the fact that there may be a number of younger children in the family.

COMMUNICATIONS AND TRANSPORTATION TAXES

Prior to January 1, 1971, local and toll telephone service and teletypewriter service were taxed at a rate of 10 percent. In 1971 the rate was reduced to 5 percent, in 1972 to 3 percent, and by 1973 the rate is scheduled to be cut to 1 percent. The transportation of persons by air is currently subject to an 8 percent tax on the cost of the ticket purchased, there is a fee of $3 for international travel, and airfreight carries a 5 percent charge. There is also a tax on airway users. As of June 30, 1980, the tax on air travel is to be reduced to 5 percent—the same rate that was in effect during the 1960's—and the $3 fee is scheduled to expire.

MISCELLANEOUS TAXES

In searching for suitable sources of revenue, the federal government has singled out a number of miscellaneous sources on which taxes are levied. Motor vehicles are charged $3 for each 1,000 pounds of weight in excess of 26,000 pounds. Wagers placed with bookmakers and lottery operators are subject to a 10 percent tax, and persons accepting wagers must pay a fee of $50 each year. Occupational taxes are assessed against brewers and rectifiers of distilled spirits as well as retail and wholesale dealers in liquor and beer; and fairs, outings, etc., selling beer or wine must pay a fee of $2.20 a month.

In some instances a tax seems to have been levied primarily for purposes of regulation rather than income, in which case it is known as a *regulatory tax*. An example of such a tax is an annual tax of $250 for all slot machines. If states and the federal government did not derive such substantial amounts of revenue from liquor and tobacco taxes, these levies would also provide examples of regulatory taxes. Although in our affluent society the regulatory features of high taxes on liquor and tobacco products seem ineffective, it is probable that retail prices that are approximately double what they would otherwise be do have an effect on the consumption of these items.

CUSTOMS DUTIES

Customs duties, commonly called tariffs, are taxes levied on the importation of foreign goods. Unlike all of the federal taxes described above, they do not constitute a part of the internal revenue system of the United

States and are not supervised by the Internal Revenue Service. Congress enacts separate legislation on customs duties, and the collection of these taxes is under the jurisdiction of the Bureau of Customs of the Treasury Department.

All importations of merchandise from sources outside the United States are either on the free list or subject to duties. Goods of the types that are not grown, mined, or made in this country are frequently permitted to enter the country tax free. Coffee is a good example of a commodity on the free list. Other goods that compete with goods produced in this country are charged a tax, which discourages imports or at least affords protection to local producers against lower prices for the foreign goods. The import rate of 7 cents a pound on butter is obviously protective in nature, as is the tax of 15 cents a pound on imported oleomargarine.

During the early history of the United States, the receipts from customs duties were considered a major source of income to the federal government. More recently, newer forms of tax legislation have overshadowed the receipts from this source, even though the amount collected has grown in total. At present the receipts from customs duties approximate $2 billion annually. The subject of tariffs, including levies for protection and for revenue, was discussed in Chapter 12.

TAXATION AND BUSINESS DECISIONS

The tax burdens carried by businesses enter into many business decisions. Ideally, according to fiscal experts, taxes should not affect courses of action; but the fact is that they do. When a business has to absorb all or a part of a tax levy, its profits are reduced, thus restricting its ability to expand without resorting to outside financing or decreasing its earnings available for distribution to its owners. If the tax can be shifted to consumers, the resulting higher prices usually reduce sales; so, if a business can control its prices, it has to decide whether to absorb all or part of the tax in order not to lose sales volume.

Although each different type of tax may have its effect on business operations, a few illustrations of specific situations will serve to emphasize the importance of taxation to decision making. The examples provided will be divided between state and local tax levies and those assessed by the federal government.

STATE TAXES AND BUSINESS DECISIONS

Local and state taxes frequently enter into the problem of plant location. A firm that plans to build a new factory is interested in a state that, preferably, does not have an income tax and in a county or township where property taxes are relatively low. Other location factors are also important; but, assuming equality on many other factors, types of taxes and rates may well determine the final decision.

The location of certain types of retail stores, particularly in cities close to a state line, will be affected if tax rates vary between the two states. For example, if the gasoline tax in one state is 6 cents a gallon as opposed to 8 cents a gallon in a neighboring state, it might not be wise to open a service station in the high tax state. Taxes on liquor and cigarettes have similar effects on retail store locations.

States that have a sales tax usually supplement this levy with a use tax. If an enterprise needs to be licensed to do business in these states because of the location of a branch or sales office, it must collect the use tax on sales to consumers resident in such states even though the goods are shipped in interstate commerce. Firms that are not registered generally do not pay use taxes, and states cannot prohibit shipments that cross state lines. A business may well find it costly to open a sales or branch office in a state that has and enforces a use tax.

Property taxes on tangible personal property are affected by not only rates but also the method used to arrive at the taxable value. If the burden is heavy, a firm may find it advantageous to lease rather than to own certain items of equipment.

FEDERAL TAXES AND BUSINESS DECISIONS

When a business needs new capital, it may well have the option of borrowing the required funds or securing the same amount from the owner or owners. In the case of corporations, this choice usually involves issuing either bonds or stocks. Interest on bonds, or any type of debt capital, is a legitimate business expense; whereas dividends on stocks are considered a distribution of profits after taxes. If the corporation is in the 48 percent bracket, that is, it has income in excess of $25,000, the advantage of securing this interest deduction is obvious.

In some instances the double taxation of corporate income distributed to stockholders works a hardship on the owners. Where this situation exists, if the corporation is not eligible to be taxed as a partnership, it might well consider the tax-saving advantage of changing to this form of ownership. Likewise, partnerships owned by wealthy individuals might find it advantageous to incorporate.

Most businesses have some flexibility in allocating income to one year or another. Depreciation charges, the write-off of worthless accounts, selling machinery or investments, and even sales can be routed to the year that seems better taxwise. Contributions to charitable and educational organizations, bonuses to employees, and payments to pension plans must be examined in light of their reduced cost when taxes are considered.

In recent years many corporations have given key employees stock options in order to induce them to remain with the company. If members of top management are receiving a salary that places them in the high brackets of the income tax on individuals, further increases are of little value since most of the added salary will be taxed away. There is no question but that tax consequences influence and sometimes dictate decisions on executive remuneration.

Customs duties have a tremendous impact on firms whose products are in competition with goods imported into this country. A change in rates could lead to a decision to start or to abandon production of a part or a product. Customs duties also have a marked effect on some industries because of the different rates that customarily apply to certain goods imported in either a finished or semifinished state. The decision as to whether to build a factory in this country may hinge on whether it is cheaper to import parts than finished goods.

There is little hope that the tax burden will become any lighter in the years ahead. Year by year governments spend more and more for such items as schools, roads, recreational facilities, welfare programs, national defense, and space exploration, to name a few categories. More people, higher prices for necessary materials and supplies, ever-increasing wage rates for employees, and public demand that governments render more services to their citizens—all these increase costs that must be paid by taxation or borrowing. Since revenues from taxes provide the major source from which public funds are derived, it appears that tax consequences will, in the future, have an expanding influence on business decisions.

BUSINESS TERMS

QUESTIONS FOR DISCUSSION AND ANALYSIS

1. Does business rightfully carry a heavy tax burden or is it closely related to the fact that business units do not vote?

2. Of the three types of taxes labeled proportional, regressive, and progressive, which one is the most equitable?

3. Doesn't business pass on all of its tax burden so that, although it may feel the impact, the incidence falls elsewhere?

4. Although they are levied on a proportional basis, general sales taxes are frequently called regressive. Why?

5. The property tax, particularly on real estate, is the major source of revenue for cities, towns and villages, and school districts. Why do these local units place so much reliance on this type of tax?

6. If federal personal income taxes were not on a pay-as-you-go basis, would individuals fail to pay the full amounts owed at the time of filing their tax returns?

7. Corporations have to pay almost one half of their net income to the federal government. Is this tax passed on to their customers?

8. If alcohol and tobacco taxes are good sources of revenue for the federal government, why shouldn't luxuries such as TV sets, radios, and diamonds also be taxed?

9. Is the required withholding on wages for social security and hospital insurance a bargain for the college student who enters employment after graduation?

10. Would it be possible to devise a tax system that would practically eliminate the tax problem from business decision making? If so, would such a system be desirable?

PROBLEMS AND SHORT CASES

1. The Reliance Arms Company manufactures a line of revolvers, pistols, and ammunition. It has a factory located in Missouri but its products are sold throughout the world by manufacturers' representatives, company salesmen, franchised dealers and through company-owned retail outlets in several states. It imports parts and exports finished products.

    a. Voters in the school district in which the factory is located recently approved a 6.8 mill levy to upgrade the school system. The factory is on the tax assessment role at $972,000. How much additional tax will the Reliance Arms Company have to pay?

    b. Itemize the different types of state and federal taxes this company will pay during a year.

2. In 1973 Jerome Rutledge earned a net profit of $21,200 from his furniture store. In addition, he received $1,000 for serving on the board of directors of a local savings and loan association and $600 for his services on the village council. The savings and loan association with which he is associated credited him with $1,250 in interest on his deposits.

Rutledge is married and has three small children. His allowable deductions for charitable contributions, taxes paid, and other items amount to $1,500. He has already paid $3,600 to the federal government on a quarterly basis.

Using the appropriate rate from the ones listed below and following the form shown on page 713, how much tax will Rutledge owe on April 15, 1974?

Over—	but not over—		of excess over—
$12,000	$16,000	$2,260 + 25%	$12,000
$16,000	$20,000	$3,260 + 28%	$16,000
$20,000	$24,000	$4,380 + 32%	$20,000

3. At a session that lasted most of one night, the legislature of a state, in a rebellious mood against the governor, took action to repeal all taxes that produced revenue for the state. The next day responsible legislators realized that this situation was intolerable, but they also recognized an opportunity to enact a tax law that would be an improvement over the former patchwork series of laws. It was decided by leaders of the legislature that, while adequate income for the state was a necessity, the new law should take into account the federal tax system and also the taxes currently levied by local governmental units to support their functions.

You are called in as a tax consultant to a legislative committee appointed for the purpose of recommending a new law to the state legislature. What would be your recommendations, and what reasons would you advance for each type of tax selected?

SUGGESTED READINGS

Bower, J. B., and H. Q. Langenderfer. *Income Tax Procedure.* Cincinnati: South-Western Publishing Co., 1971.

Due, J. F. *Government Finance: Economics of the Public Sector,* Fourth Edition. Homewood, Illinois: Richard D. Irwin, Inc., 1968.

McCarthy, C. F., *et al. The Federal Income Tax: Its Sources and Applications.* Englewood Cliffs, New Jersey: Prentice-Hall, Inc., 1968.

Netzer, D. *Economics of the Property Tax.* Washington, D. C.: The Brookings Institution, 1966.

Newman, H. E. *An Introduction to Public Finance.* New York: John Wiley & Sons, Inc., 1968.

Niswonger, C. R., and P. E. Fess. *Accounting Principles,* 10th Edition. Cincinnati: South-Western Publishing Co., 1969. Chapter 23.

Pechman, J. A. *Federal Tax Policy.* Washington, D. C.: The Brookings Institution, 1966.

Williams, J. E. *Preparing Federal Estate and Gift Tax Returns,* Second Edition. New York: The Ronald Press Company, 1968.

Appendix A

A perplexing problem facing the college student today is how to derive personal, relevant meaning from the advice given by parents, teachers, counselors, and friends regarding the choice of a career. In his readings, the student comes across numerous articles and pamphlets urging that he make a specific choice of occupation. The span of career opportunities, however, is very wide. The continuing growth of population, upward trend in business activity, growth of governmental functions, and technological advances have all combined to create more than 40,000 different occupations.

The choice of a vocation, particularly in the area of business, is made even more difficult by shifting trends in employment, by the projected influence of automation, by the role of working women, and by increasing opportunities for blacks. Some experts predict that people entering the labor market within the next few years can anticipate an average of four or five major job changes in the course of their working life. Occupational mobility is expected; and employment in a different city, state, or even foreign country is not uncommon. Within these numerous changes it should be recognized that competition extends into career planning and profoundly affects those who are looking forward to careers in business. This preemployment competition is a two-way operation—business firms compete for the best qualified students, and students compete among themselves to secure jobs that appear to offer them the best career opportunities.

To obtain the most benefit from college years, the student must choose his career carefully and plan toward it as early as possible. Through foresight and intelligent, flexible planning the student will be able not only to survive future occupational changes but also to build upon them toward a satisfying, rewarding career.

One way of thinking about a future career is to consider it to be the resultant of opportunities, effort, and resistances. Opportunities exist whenever the time is right and it appears likely that a proposed venture will succeed. The dictionary defines opportunity as "a favorable juncture of circumstances; a good chance." A career opportunity is a challenge to purposeful, personal action. An opportunity is only a challenge. There is no guarantee of success. Success depends on how well the opportunity is seized. Grasping the opportunity depends on the extent of effort expended. It will also depend on the resistances encountered and overcome. A career opportunity calls for a knowledge of one's own personal goals, objectives, and life style; it is a purposeful challenge. It calls for action. It is a chance to put forth effort to engage in a satisfying occupation and to meet one's personal goals. It demands that one does not just sit back and wait for the "right" job to come along.

OCCUPATIONAL SELECTION AIDS

To scan the wide spectrum of career opportunities in business and, for that matter, any area of human endeavor, requires time and diligence. A student's college years should be the time to learn the relative merits of various careers. During this period a student can discover his own qualifications and the characteristics of a wide variety of occupations from: (1) personal evaluation, (2) college courses, (3) work experience, (4) vocational literature, (5) industry contacts, (6) biographies, business histories, and magazine articles, and (7) placement bureaus.

PERSONAL EVALUATION

Some of the following appraisals of your qualifications for a vocation can be measured objectively; other evaluations require a subjective treatment.

Mental Ability

Intelligence tests are available that can measure accurately your mental capacities in relationship to other college students. If you have not already taken such tests, they are available at most schools or in private counseling agencies in larger cities. Scores, and their meanings, should be obtained from persons competent to interpret them properly.

There are different types of mental ability, too. If you find mathematics enjoyable and easy, perhaps you should find employment in market research. If English is your forte, you might be a good copywriter for an advertising agency.

Aptitudes and Interests

The extent of the ability of a person to learn how to perform certain jobs can be measured by aptitude tests. These tests measure such items as finger and manual dexterity, numerical aptitude, and eye-hand coordination. A very bright young lady who thought she wanted to be a secretary found that her eye-hand coordination was so poor that she could not learn to type rapidly without making mistakes.

Two tests that measure these aptitudes are the Differential Aptitude Tests of the Psychological Corporation and the General Aptitude Test Battery of the United States Training and Employment Service. The latter test is available to job applicants who register with the State Employment Service.

Interest tests are also available that provide an index of similarity between one's interests and those of successful men and women in a wide range of occupations. The best-known interest tests are the Kuder Preference Record and the Strong Vocational Interest Blank. These tests are usually available wherever general intelligence tests are given.

In vocational guidance centers, which are to be found in most cities, in state employment service offices, and at most colleges and universities, there are individuals with graduate degrees in psychology or guidance counseling who are trained to diagnose mental ability, aptitudes, and potential for achievement in a job. They are equipped to administer tests designed to measure intelligence, reasoning power, reading comprehension, and interests. They are also informed regarding the areas of opportunities and the job requirements of applicants for these positions. You may wish to compare results obtained from two sources. Fees incurred for professional service of this type may well pay dividends in later life.

Personality

Personality traits are important in the selection of a vocation. The ability to make friends easily and to get along well with other people and a good character are a few personality elements that are necessary for success in all types of work. Other traits, such as initiative, judgment, emotional stability, and physical size and fitness, are frequently more important in one type of work than in another. Although tests and self-rating scales are available, it is doubtful if personality traits can be measured with as much accuracy as can intelligence, aptitudes, and interests.

Avocations

It is not at all unusual for students to gain a useful clue to their future choice of vocations through an introspective analysis of their avocations or hobbies. Many individuals have certain likes and dislikes that are frequently manifested in the activities in which they engage. Students who enjoy art, writing, mathematics, working with tools, or constructing things may well find that these interests offer useful suggestions in the choice of their college majors and eventual vocational selections.

COLLEGE COURSES

When you complete this course and others in business subjects, you will have learned a great deal about the various areas of business activity and the functions performed in each. In most instances these activities can be translated into job opportunities. There may be some particular kind of work that, prior to your contact with it during your course of instruction, was unknown to you. It may prove to be the right answer to your problem of a vocation. A young man studied motion and time study in a course in industrial management. Although this type of work had never occurred to him as a career opportunity, he became so interested in this technique that it became his vocational choice.

WORK EXPERIENCE

Some work experience either during the school year or in vacations is desirable. To the extent possible, consistent with financial necessity, a variety of jobs is most satisfactory. Working in a factory, an office, and a retail store, for example, will give you a firsthand contact with various jobs. This procedure should help you to make some positive choices as well as to eliminate others.

VOCATIONAL LITERATURE

A wealth of vocational literature is available in your college library as well as in the public libraries of your home communities. At the end of this appendix, some general references about the selection of a vocation, as well as pamphlets and books that cover specific vocations, are given.

A useful reference in investigating specific jobs is the *Dictionary of Occupational Titles* (1965) prepared by the United States Training and Employment Service. It lists almost 22,000 occupations with more than 35,000 occupational titles and classifies them under the following nine headings: (a) professional, technical, and managerial occupations; (b) clerical and sales occupations; (c) service occupations; (d) farming, fishery, forestry, and related occupations; (e) processing occupations; (f) machine trades occupations; (g) bench work occupations; (h) structural work occupations; and (i) miscellaneous occupations.

Three samples from this dictionary give some idea of the type of information provided about the jobs listed.

Employment Interviewer. Interviews applicants to determine their suitability for employment with company: Records information and impressions gained from applicants and evaluates information to determine suitability for employment. Administers tests and interprets results. Prepares rating on applicants and makes recommendations for future consideration of those not immediately employed. Supplies such information to applicants as company and union policies, duties, responsibilities, working conditions, hours and pay, and promotional opportunities. Prepares and maintains records of those interviewed, accepted or rejected, and those declining appointment. Discusses hiring activity with supervisors to determine adequacy of selection techniques or recruitment program. Observes jobs to obtain firsthand information of job requirements and needs.

Market-Research Analyst. Researches market conditions in local, regional, or national area to determine potential sales of a product or service: Examines and analyzes statistical data on past sales and wholesale or retail trade trends to forecast future sales trends. Gathers data on competitors and analyzes their prices, sales, and methods of operation. Collects data on buying habits and preferences of prospective customers. May specialize in advertising analysis and be designated Advertising Analyst.

Programmer, Business. Converts symbolic statement of business problems to detailed logical flow charts for coding into computer language and solution by means of automatic data-processing equipment: Analyzes all or part of workflow chart or diagram representing business problem by applying knowledge of computer capabilities, subject matter, algebra, and symbolic logic to develop sequence of program steps. Confers with supervisor and representatives of departments affected by program to resolve questions of program intent, output requirements, input data acquisition, extent of automatic programming and coding use and modification, and inclusion of internal checks and controls. Writes detailed logical flow chart in symbolic form to represent work order of data to be processed by computer system, and to describe input, output, and arithmetic and logical operations involved. May convert detailed logical flow chart to language processable by computer. Devises sample input data to provide test of program adequacy. Prepares block diagrams to specify equipment configuration. Observes or runs tests of coded program on computer, using actual or sample input data. Corrects program errors by such methods as altering program steps and sequence. Prepares written instructions (run book) to guide operating personnel during production runs. Analyzes, reviews, and rewrites programs to increase operating efficiency or adapt to new requirements. Compiles documentation of program development and subsequent revisions. May specialize in writing programs for one make and type of computer.

INDUSTRY CONTACTS

Whenever the opportunity presents itself, preferably through class trips planned by the instructor, visit a factory, or a store, or a bank, and see business in action. Try to imagine yourself in some of the jobs you see others filling. Also talk with employees at all levels of management about their jobs. Try to find out what they believe is important for success in their particular line of endeavor. Friends of your family and acquaintances may give you some worthwhile ideas.

BIOGRAPHIES, BUSINESS HISTORIES, AND MAGAZINE ARTICLES

A great many books have been written about businessmen and outstanding business firms. Many of these not only make fascinating reading but also provide a description of an industry or an individual who achieved success. Articles such as those that appear in *Fortune*, *Business Week*, *Time*, and other magazines also provide information about companies and jobs.

PLACEMENT BUREAUS

Many colleges and universities maintain placement bureaus whose primary purpose is to provide the facilities through which prospective graduates and the recruiting officers from business may meet and discuss job availabilities. These bureaus frequently post on bulletin boards notices of employment opportunities offered by firms whose personnel officers visit the campus or request help in filling vacancies. Knowledge of the types of openings that will become available to you when you approach graduation will be helpful in stimulating your thinking along vocational lines. Also, many of the firms who recruit college graduates have compiled brochures describing their opportunities and positions, and these are usually available in the placement bureau office.

AREAS OF EMPLOYMENT OPPORTUNITIES

All businesses have some common activities, such as selling products or services and record keeping, but their major functions vary considerably. Retailers do not manufacture goods; transportation companies do not accept deposits from their customers. Various classifications of these diverse types of business activity can be made. The following division of areas of business employment parallels, in general, the several parts of the text: (1) going into business for yourself, (2) marketing, (3) personnel, (4) production, (5) finance, (6) accounting, computer operation, and statistics, (7) regulated industries, and (8) government service.

GOING INTO BUSINESS FOR YOURSELF

Some of the vocational opportunities suggested by Part 2, Ownership, Organization, and Management, center around going into business for yourself. If you believe that you want to make your career in your own organization, several factors should be given consideration. Some of these are strictly personal, and others are related to the type of business activity chosen. Personal factors include willingness to work hard, perseverance in the face of discouragements, and the ability to make friends of customers and employees. Factors related to the business include the amount of capital needed, the experience necessary for a reasonable expectation of success, and the mental and physical qualities demanded by the type of business selected.

Most young men and women who go into business for themselves find that the better opportunities are in their local communities and in a business that sells goods or services to the public. The operation of a motel, a tearoom, a television and radio repair shop, and a ladies' accessories shop are a few examples of such enterprises. Occasionally new manufacturing operations are established to produce a good, but such enterprises are less common than the retailing of goods and services. The growth of franchising has provided a new field of self-employment for persons who have the requisite capital and abilities.

Many individuals who hope to go into business for themselves realize that they must have certain resources, both personal and financial, but they fail to consider that they should have some experience in the proposed line of endeavor or one related to it. Unless such experience has been acquired by the time the person completes college training, it may well be the wisest course of action to work for someone else who is established in the same or a related business. Going into business for yourself offers opportunities for great rewards, but the risks are much higher than when working for someone else. Before deciding to operate your own business, be sure that you have the necessary personal qualities, have access to adequate capital funds, and possess the requisite experience for the type of business selected.

MARKETING

The field of marketing offers numerous as well as widely varied vocational opportunities for both men and women. Salesmen are needed by manufacturers, wholesalers, retailers, and all others who produce and sell goods and services. With the exception of a very few goods that require technical training as a background for their sale, college-trained personnel with a business background are sought by many types of firms. Men predominate in the selling of industrial goods, but both sexes are well represented at the retail level.

Because of the large number of salesmen employed, advancement possibilities are excellent. In the industrial field, openings such as sales supervisor, district sales manager, divisional sales manager, and sales manager are available to those who have achieved outstanding sales records and possess supervisory abilities. Department stores usually promote salesmen first to the rank of assistant buyer and then to buyer for a particular department of a store. Recognizing the need for a larger number of competent and trainable personnel than is to be found in their employee ranks, many department stores are instituting executive training programs to fill their future requirements at the managerial level. In this they are following the lead of Macy's and a few other stores that established such programs many years ago.

Advertising is another area of marketing that offers a number of possibilities. Openings are available in the advertising departments of large firms and also in advertising agencies. Duties may involve copy writing and layout, or they may deal with such problems as buying or selling space. In the advertising department of a firm, one can advance to the position of an assistant advertising manager and then to advertising manager. In agencies, the first step might be to an account executive or to the managership of one of the departments or branches of the business.

There is an increasing demand for competent personnel in marketing research. College graduates with a background in marketing and statistics are sought after both by marketing research firms and by the marketing research departments of many companies. The initial positions might be as interviewers or in questionnaire construction, with possible eventual promotion to supervisor or editor. A knowledge of statistics can lead to positions in the area of sample construction and validation.

With the expansion of international trade that has taken place during the last two decades, particularly the growth of firms with branch offices and factories in other countries, there have appeared opportunities for those who can qualify for positions in international marketing management. The duties involved in these positions were described in Chapter 12. It is coming to be recognized by the firms involved that careful selection and training of these individuals will be required and that considerable pioneering in both of these areas will be necessary. Aside from this, export and import houses located in coast cities have openings that may lead to overseas assignments after some experience has been acquired.

PERSONNEL

Although the openings in the field of personnel and labor relations are limited, this area has been one of great interest to business students in recent years. Most of the larger factories maintain personnel departments; and employment possibilities in this field are greater in industry than they are in mercantile, financial, and other nonmanufacturing enterprises. Personnel departments usually prefer to select new people from other departments of the firm. Once a connection has been made, advancement possibilities include heading a division, such as training, recruitment, welfare, employment, or safety. From one of these posts an outstanding individual should be able to secure a position as personnel manager, and many firms now have a vice president in charge of labor relations.

Women are more likely to find opportunities in this field in department stores, offices, and government service. A student who decides to choose personnel as a vocation should recognize the fact that entry into the field usually follows some years of experience with the company in the area of its major activity.

PRODUCTION

Industries engaged in manufacturing employ approximately one fourth of all workers in the United States. Within these organizations, both large and small, there are numerous opportunities for college-trained students of business. Some graduates begin as machine operators and advance to such supervisory positions as foreman, production supervisor, and plant manager. Others work in motion and time study, inspection, and planning departments. Production control, inventory control, shipping, warehousing, and plant maintenance offer career possibilities.

Purchasing for a factory offers an excellent opportunity for students of business. The opening wedge may be a clerical position in the purchasing department or work in some other phase of factory operations. Promotions to assistant purchasing agent, purchasing agent, and even to a rank such as vice president in charge of purchasing are advancement possibilities.

FINANCE

The field of finance offers a wealth and variety of vocational opportunities for men and women with collegiate training in business. The majority of such openings involve indoor work. They require an individual who has some liking for and ability to handle figures, but at the same time many positions involve meeting the public. Integrity, accuracy, and reliability are some personal traits especially necessary for success.

Both manufacturing and retailing firms employ men and women for positions in their credit and collection departments, and similar jobs can be secured in finance companies and credit-investigating agencies. Most openings are clerical in nature at the outset, but they lead to such positions as credit manager, collection manager, or manager of a branch office.

Commercial banking offers many opportunities to both sexes. Advancement possibilities include cashier, branch manager, and loan officer. All of these positions involve meeting the public, and a good personality is essential for success. Positions are also available in governmental banking agencies, including that of a bank examiner.

One of the largest fields of endeavor for college-trained people is insurance. Life and property and liability insurance companies are continually looking for salesmen, and other types of work are also available in the home and branch offices of these financial institutions. Those who sell frequently prefer to retain this status because earnings are based on commissions received and, if a good clientele has been developed, such individuals do not care to give up a lucrative business. Others move on to positions as supervisors and agency managers. Nonselling jobs include adjusters, agency supervisors, actuaries, and all types of office management.

The broad area of finance also includes many other types of openings. Investment banking companies and brokerage firms employ college graduates to sell stocks and bonds, to handle accounts, and to perform tasks involving the analyses of securities. If an industrial concern operates employee insurance programs and handles its own security transfers and registration, job opportunities exist in these areas as well as the financial department of the firm.

The field of real estate properly falls in the financial category, and both selling and property management are involved. Several types of financial institutions, such as savings and loan associations, sales finance companies, and trust companies, have openings for those who possess the necessary experience.

ACCOUNTING, COMPUTER OPERATION, AND STATISTICS

Accounting is a large field with three major subdivisions—public, private, and governmental. Public accounting is a profession, and the usual goal is to qualify as a Certified Public Accountant. This designation is given by all states to those who pass an examination and have gained the required experience. The method of acquiring experience is to secure employment as a junior accountant with a public accounting firm with the expectation that, over the years, progress will lead to a partnership in the firm, or the individual may open his own office.

In addition to C.P.A.'s there are a number of accountants who perform services of a somewhat comparable nature except that their clients are usually smaller organizations and they may do more detailed work for them.

Private accounting embraces the accounting activities of all types of firms. A major subdivision of this classification is industrial accounting, including cost accounting for manufacturing firms. Many companies also employ internal auditors whose duties are somewhat similar to those performed by public accountants. Although many starting positions are clerical, such as handling receivables or payrolls, opportunities for advancement are excellent. Many corporation treasurers and controllers have risen to their positions from routine jobs.

Governmental accounting positions are open in numerous branches of state and federal activities. Positions in the Federal Bureau of Investigation and in the Internal Revenue Service are available to graduates of collegiate schools of business who have majored in accounting. Other agencies, such as the armed services, Atomic Energy Commission, and Department of Agriculture, employ accountants, who then attain a civil-service status.

The recent widespread introduction of computers and related data processing equipment has provided a growing field for college graduates with a solid background of business courses. The growth of computerization in the office has created such opportunities as director of data processing, management operations analyst, computer programmer, business-systems coordinator, program manager, and other similar managerial positions. Some of these opportunities require mathematical ability and aptitude in addition to a basic knowledge of business operations.

Persons qualified as statisticians are needed by industry, research organizations, and the government. Many large firms maintain their own statistical department and recruit college graduates into this field. All types of research organizations have trained statisticians on their staffs. Numerous civil-service appointments as statisticians are available to qualified men and women. A number of beginning jobs require the services of tabulating equipment operators, investigators and interviewers, and statistical clerks. Advancement to more responsible positions may lead to such managerial posts as chief statistician or director of research.

REGULATED INDUSTRIES

Public service companies have a wide variety of openings for college men and women with business training. Gas and electric companies maintain large offices with all types of related problems and opportunities for positions in office-type work. The telephone companies make use of college graduates as adjusters, complaint specialists, new business salesmen, and branch managers. Opportunities for advancement are not spectacular but, on the other hand, progress can be steady and reasonably sure.

Only recently has the railroad industry begun to recruit college men. Many problems in the management area remain to be solved, not the least of which is the deeply entrenched seniority system. Other forms of transportation, particularly air and highway, offer more positions oriented toward business-trained college people. Highway bus and truck companies maintain numerous offices in which both clerical and supervisory positions are available. The airlines hire college men and women as reservation clerks, ticket sellers, dispatchers, and the like. Many young women who start out as airline hostesses find that supervisory positions are available to them after some years of experience.

GOVERNMENT SERVICE

With the increased emphasis on governmental activities in recent years, new bureaus, administrations, departments, and commissions have come into being and old ones have increased in size. Many types of employment opportunities exist in these organizations at both state and national levels. Jobs usually carry a state or federal civil-service classification. Increases in salary and grade can be earned by those whose performance on the job merits recognition.

College men and women who expect to make their careers with the federal government should take the special examinations that are given periodically. Individuals who score the required grade are employed as management trainees in a manner somewhat comparable to the training programs available in many industries. Starting salaries approximate those offered by business and, whereas promotion will probably be slower than that in private firms, job security is very high.

VOCATIONAL DECISION MAKING

After making use of some or all of the suggested aids to occupational selection and after acquiring some knowledge about the areas of employment opportunities, the concerned individual should be ready to consider specific vocations. Having acquired a reasonable background, the student should be able to formulate answers to such questions as:

1. What are the duties and responsibilities of this occupation?
2. What is the future of this occupation?
3. What are the opportunities for promotion?
4. Would the work be interesting and stimulating?
5. Where does one start or enter this occupation?
6. What qualifications and training are required?
7. What are the working conditions and remuneration?

To find suitable answers to these questions calls for effort. An effort is the exertion of strength or the commitment of capacity directed toward a particular goal. As applied to vocational decision making, effort can be viewed as a person's commitment of his time, talent, and energy to develop a particular career opportunity. Each student has a unique set of talents and the questions before him are:

1. How fully will I commit my talents and interests in the pursuit of this career?
2. Are my talents, interests, and attitudes equal to the occupational demands of this career?
3. Will I find personal satisfaction by devoting time and energy in preparing for this career?
4. Will the demands of this occupation match the life-style I wish to follow?

In every aspect of life where effort is applied to opportunity there are barriers, obstacles, or resistance to success. Few opportunities are unalloyed successes; most have some negative factors or detracting elements. Resistance can result in the failure to find a satisfying career.

Some of the major resistances to be overcome in seeking a fitting occupation are:

1. Pressure from parents or peers that limit one's freedom of choice.
2. Lack of ability.
3. Temptation to go directly into the first available job.
4. Poor health.
5. Personality limitations.
6. Lack of funds for education.
7. Obligations, both marital and martial.
8. Lack of information concerning job opportunities.
9. Lack of work experience.

Every student must assess the magnitudes of each of these resistances which restrain his effort from being directly applied to a career opportunity.

A successful career results from vocational planning. A vocational choice results from a weighing of the relative merits of opportunities, efforts, and resistances. This weighing process starts when the student begins asking questions of himself and others. In career planning the student is expected to consult with counselors, teachers, parents, peers, and specialists in various occupations. He should not hesitate to seek assistance, whatever the source, but he must personally weigh the significance of the answers. Advice, assistance, and an occasional push in the right direction may come from others. The final decision on a vocation, however, should be made by the student.

SUGGESTED READINGS

General

Careers in Business/71. New York: Careers, Incorporated, 1970.

College Occupational Exploration Kit. Chicago: Science Research Associates, 1967.

Dunphy, Philip W. (ed.). *Career Development for the College Student.* Cranston, Rhode Island: Carroll Press, 1969.

Fanning, Odom. *Opportunities in Environmental Careers.* New York: Vocational Guidance Manuals, 1971.

Hopke, Wm. E. (ed.). *The Encyclopedia of Careers and Vocational Guidance,* Vols. 1 and 2. Garden City, New York: Doubleday & Company, Inc., 1967.

Guide to Careers Through College Majors. San Diego, California: Robert R. Knapp, Publisher.

Kauffman, Warren E. (ed.). *College Placement Annual, 1971.* Bethlehem: Pennsylvania: The College Placement Council, Inc., 1970.

King, Alice G. *Help Wanted: Female: The Young Woman's Guide to Job-Hunting.* New York: Charles Scribner's Sons, 1968.

Peterson, Clarence E. *Careers for College Graduates.* New York: Barnes & Noble, Inc., 1968.

Schill, W. J., and H. E. Nichols. *Career Choice and Career Preparation.* Danville, Illinois: The Interstate Printers & Publishers, Inc., 1970.

United States Department of Labor. *Dictionary of Occupational Titles,* Third Edition, Vols. I and II. Washington, D.C.: United States Government Printing Office, 1965.

————————. *Occupational Outlook Handbook,* 1970-71 Edition. Washington, D.C.: United States Government Printing Office.

Part 2. Ownership, Organization, and Management

Administrative Assistant—Officer, Fourth Edition. New York: Arco Publishing Co., Inc., 1966.

Grow with an Exciting Business. New York: American Paper Institute.

Kleiner, Sanford. *Careers in Corporate Management.* Washington, D.C.: B'nai B'rith Vocational Service.

Management Trainee. Sacramento, California: California Department of Employment, 1968.

Place, Irene, and Leonard Robertson. *Opportunities in Management Careers.* New York: Universal Publishing and Distributing Corporation, 1969.

Starting a Travel Agency Business. New York: American Society of Travel Agents, 1969.

Part 3. Marketing

Advertising: A Career of Action and Variety for Exceptional Men and Women. New York: American Association of Advertising Agencies, Inc., 1969.

Advertising Account Executives. Chicago: Science Research Associates, Inc., 1966.

Buyer. Largo, Florida: Careers, 1968.

Career Opportunities in Advertising for Men and Women. Chicago: The Institute for Research, 1968.

Careers for Women—Management Retailing. Chicago: The Institute for Research, 1969.

Careers in Foreign Commerce. Chicago: The Institute for Research, 1970.

Careers in Retailing. Columbus, Ohio: Ohio State Council of Retail Merchants, 1969.

Comparison Shopper. Moravia, New York: Chronicle Guidance Publications, Inc., 1968.

How Does the Food Broker Serve You? Washington, D.C.: National Food Brokers Association.

Merchandising as a Career. Chicago: The Institute for Research, 1968.

Supermarket Manager. Largo, Florida: Careers, 1968.

The Salesman—Ambassador of Progress. New York: Sales and Marketing Executives International, 1968.

United States Department of Commerce. *Career Opportunities in Domestic and International Business*. Washington, D.C.: United States Government Printing Office, 1969.

Wiggs, G. D. (ed.). *Career Opportunities—Marketing, Business and Office Specialists*. New York: Doubleday & Company, Inc.

Wilinsky, Harriet. *Careers and Opportunities in Retailing*. New York: E. P. Dutton & Co., Inc., 1970.

Part 4. Personnel

Arco Editorial Board. *Personnel Assistant*. New York: Arco Publishing Co., Inc.

Guidance Handbook for Counselors. United States Army Recruiting Command, Army Opportunities, Hampton, Virginia.

Personnel Worker. Toronto, Canada: Guidance Centre, 1968.

Pond, John. *Your Future in Personnel Work*. New York: Richards Rosen Press, Inc., 1969.

Turner, David R. *Employment Interviewer*. New York: Arco Publishing Co., Inc., 1968.

——————. *Personnel Examiner: All Grades—All Merit Administration,* Second Edition. New York: Arco Publishing Co., Inc., 1970.

Your Career in Public Personnel Administration. Chicago: Public Personnel Association.

Part 5. Production

Arco Editorial Board. *Foreman,* Revised Edition. New York: Arco Publishing Co., Inc., 1968.

Manager, Traffic. Moravia, New York: Chronicle Guidance Publications, Inc., 1968.

Purchasing Agent. Chicago: Science Research Associates, 1964.

Purchasing Agent. Sacramento, California: California Department of Employment, 1968.

Purchasing Agent. Toronto, Canada: Guidance Centre, 1968.

Quality Control Manager. Sacramento, California: California Department of Employment, 1968.

Part 6. Finance

Arco Editorial Board. *Bank Examiner: Trainee and Assistant*. New York: Arco Publishing Co., Inc., 1968.

—————————. *Real Estate Salesman and Broker,* Third Edition. New York: Arco Publishing Co., Inc., 1968.

Bank Officers. Chicago: Science Research Associates, Inc., 1966.

Banking—An Opportunity for You. Washington, D.C.: The American Bankers Association.

Careers in Credit Departments—Retail, Banks, Finance, Business. Chicago: The Institute for Research, 1968.

Credit Manager. Moravia, New York: Chronicle Guidance Publications, Inc., 1968.

Credit Workers. Chicago: Science Research Associates, Inc., 1968.

It's Up to You. New York: Institute of Life Insurance, 1969.

Real Estate: A Career with a Bright Future. Chicago: National Association of Real Estate Boards, 1968.

Sarnoff, Paul. *Wall Street Careers.* New York: Julian Messner, 1969.

Securities Salesmen. Chicago: Science Research Associates, Inc., 1966.

The Challenge of Real Estate. Washington, D. C.: National Association of Real Estate Boards.

Your Future—Careers in Consumer Finance. Washington, D.C.: National Consumer Finance Association.

Part 7. Quantitative Controls

A Job with a Future in Computers. New York: Grosset & Dunlop, Inc., 1969.

Ankers, Raymond. *Opportunities in an Accounting Career.* New York: Universal Publishing and Distributing Corporation, 1967.

Arco Editorial Board. *Internal Revenue Agent,* Third Edition. New York: Arco Publishing Co., Inc., 1968.

—————————. *Statistician and Statistical Clerk,* Sixth Edition. New York: Arco Publishing Co., Inc., 1968.

Aulick, J., and W. Cross. *Careers in the Age of Automation.* New York: Hawthorn Books, Inc., 1969.

Barnett, L., and L. E. Davis. *Careers in Computer Programming.* New York: Henry Z. Walck, Inc., 1967.

Career as a Certified Public Accountant. Chicago: The Institute for Research, 1968.

Carroll, J. M. *Careers and Opportunities in Computer Science.* New York: E. P. Dutton & Co., Inc., 1967.

Cashiers. Chicago: Science Research Associates, 1968.

Certified Public Accountants. Chicago: Science Research Associates, 1966.

Data-Processing Machine Operators. Chicago: Science Research Associates, 1968.

Englebardt, S. L. *Careers in Data Processing.* New York: Lothrop, Lee & Shepard Co., Inc., 1969.

Jobs in Electronic Data Processing. Chicago: Science Research Associates, 1968.

Locklear, Edmond, Jr. *Your Future in Accounting.* New York: Arco Publishing Co., Inc., 1970.

Turner, David R. *Assistant Accountant.* New York: Arco Publishing Co., Inc., 1970.

What's It Like to be An Accountant? New York: American Institute of Certified Public Accountants.

Part 8. Legal and Regulatory Environment of Business

Arco Editorial Board. *Junior Federal Assistant.* New York: Arco Publishing Co., Inc., 1968.

——————. *Treasury Enforcement Agent,* Third Edition. New York: Arco Publishing Co., Inc., 1968.

Arnold, W. M. (ed.). *Career Opportunities: Community Service and Related Specialists.* New York: Doubleday & Company, Inc.

Cohn, A. *Careers in Public Planning and Administration.* New York: Henry Z. Walck, Inc., 1967.

Sarnoff, P. *Careers in the Legal Profession.* New York: Julian Messner, 1970.

Turner, David R. *U.S. Professional Mid-Level Positions Grades GS-9 Through GS-12.* New York: Arco Publishing Co., Inc., 1969.

United States Department of Justice. *FBI Career Opportunities.* Washington, D.C.: Federal Bureau of Investigation.

United States Department of Labor. *Clerical Careers in the Federal Service.* Washington, D. C.: United States Government Printing Office, 1968.

Your Career with the Airlines. Washington, D.C.: Air Transport Association of America.

Appendix B—Case 1

Kiley Coffee Maker Company, Inc.

In 1957 Howard Kiley, age 33, was a skilled machine operator at the Oak Creek plant of ARV Industries. His annual earnings were consistently in the $12,000 range and he was considered an exceptional and talented worker by his superiors. Kiley was an avid coffee drinker and, in his home workshop, had experimented with various types of coffee makers. One of his contrivances made use of steam under pressure. Several friends suggested that he ought to patent his device. So, Kiley consulted a patent attorney, an application was filed, and in 1958 a patent was granted.

Following receipt of his patent Kiley attempted to interest several companies in producing his coffee maker either by buying his patent outright or by granting him a royalty on each one manufactured and sold. Although each company he contacted expressed some interest in his machine, all felt that there wouldn't be a home market for the coffee maker because of its price and also because housewives would be afraid to use steam under pressure. These firms did not believe the institutional market was large enough to warrant going into production on an unknown and unproved coffee maker.

Although somewhat discouraged, Kiley decided to produce his coffee maker himself, hoping that hotels and restaurants would provide the necessary market. He quit his lucrative job despite the fact that he was married and had two sons—6 and 10—and a daughter 12. By using all of his savings, leasing machinery, buying materials on credit, and subcontracting some parts, he began production. Space was not a problem as he and his family lived with his wife's father on a small farm located on the outskirts of Oak Creek that had several unused out-buildings which were in good shape.

With his father-in-law as a helper, Kiley was soon able to turn out five units a day. He had been able to locate a specialty wholesaler of restaurant equipment who was willing to take his entire output at $25 each. Although Kiley had originally been interested only in taste, it so happened that an important advantage of his coffee maker was its ability to turn out more cups per pound without any diminution in flavor. This factor was used as an important selling aid by the specialty wholesaler, who was the sole distributor of the coffee maker.

Over a period of approximately 13 years the business prospered. Kiley built a factory building on the farm property and now employed twenty workmen, one salesman, and three office people. Output averaged slightly better than 60 units each working day and, despite increases in the cost of raw materials, the added volume plus the economy of fabricating parts originally purchased made it possible to hold the selling price at $25. The patent had effectively discouraged competition and, due to the activities of the one salesman plus advertising and other dealer aids, additional specialty wholesalers had been secured to market the larger output.

Kiley had always believed that there was a tremendous home market just waiting to be tapped. Housewives used steam irons and, furthermore, his coffee maker had proved entirely safe. Although the business had produced a living for Kiley and his family, he had personal ambitions and goals that were not being realized. Consequently, when ARV Industries decided to close its Oak Creek plant, Kiley saw an opportunity to make a major expansion move. The factory was for sale at a very reasonable price as was the machinery, most of which was easily adaptable to producing coffee makers. Another important factor was that skilled workers were available, for many of his former co-workers preferred to retain their homes in Oak Creek even though ARV Industries had several other plants spread around the country and had promised continuing employment to those willing to move.

When the local Chamber of Commerce learned of Kiley's interest in the soon-to-be-vacant plant, it volunteered to provide advice and assistance. Following a series of conferences, it was decided to form a corporation and to sell shares to local investors. A charter was secured from the state for the Kiley Coffee Maker Company, Inc., that authorized 100,000 shares of no-par common stock. These shares were offered for sale at $10 each with the understanding that 30,000 shares would be paid to

Kiley for his established business, including all tangible and intangible assets and the assumption of all liabilities.

Due to local enthusiasm and a hope on the part of some ARV employees that owning stock would improve their chances for employment, all of the shares were sold. The factory building and the equipment vacated by ARV Industries were purchased and 50 additional craftsmen were employed. Kiley selected these individuals from a number of applicants and was confident that he had an excellent work force. At an organizational meeting of the 190 stockholders, he was elected to the Board of Directors along with his wife and seven Oak Creek businessmen. Following the stockholders' meeting Kiley was selected by the board as President and General Manager and was voted an annual salary of $36,000.

Since it was late in the calendar year before all details could be completed, it was decided that the corporation would purchase the sole proprietorship as of January 1, 1972. When Kiley closed his books on December 31, 1971, his balance sheet, income statement, and schedule of cost of goods manufactured were as shown on pages 744-746.

On January 1, 1972, the books of Kiley Coffee Maker Company, Inc. were opened. All of the assets and liabilities of the sole proprietorship were taken over and additional assets were as follows: Cash—$50,000; Machinery—$150,000; Building—$400,000; and Land—$100,000. The old building was to be used for the office and for storage, and the land on which it was built was to be rented from Mrs. Kiley for $600 a year. The difference between the $175,900 equity of Kiley shown on the balance sheet and the $300,000 paid to him in stock was capitalized as Goodwill—$124,100. It was planned to write this asset off over ten years and the patent over the three remaining years of its life.

During 1972 a number of problems arose. Kiley brought in his older son with the title of Sales Manager. As a result the former salesman quit and his replacement lacked the contacts his predecessor had established with specialty wholesalers. The new sales manager concentrated his attention on retail sales and was able to sign up one large hardware wholesaler after agreeing to provide point-of-purchase displays for hardware stores and to pay for newspaper advertising in the hometowns of the wholesaler's customers. Negotiations were currently under way with other hardware wholesalers and also with a retail chain discount organization but, at the close of the year, these were only prospects.

In the factory some personnel problems had arisen although, other than reduced per capita production, they were not serious. Kiley had always supervised the factory employees, and directing 20 had been relatively simple. When the number grew to 70, even though Kiley worked

KILEY'S COFFEE MAKER
Balance Sheet
December 31, 1971

Assets

Current assets:

Cash		$ 4,780	
Accounts receivable		2,890	
Inventories			
Raw materials	$ 7,150		
Work in process	8,500		
Finished goods	15,750	31,400	
Supplies		2,600	
Prepaid insurance		420	
Total current assets			$ 42,090

Plant assets:

Office equipment	$ 3,460		
Less accumulated depreciation	1,140	$ 2,320	
Machinery	$ 82,500		
Less accumulated depreciation	31,700	50,800	
Building	$115,000		
Less accumulated depreciation	16,400	98,600	
Total plant assets			151,720

Intangible assets:

Patent			540
Total assets			$194,350

Liabilities

Current liabilities:

Notes payable		$ 10,000	
Accounts payable		8,450	
Total current liabilities			$ 18,450

Proprietorship

Howard Kiley, Capital, January 1, 1971		$160,400	
Net income for 1971	$ 35,500		
Less withdrawals in 1971	20,000	15,500	
Howard Kiley, Capital, December 31, 1971			175,900
Total liabilities and proprietorship			$194,350

longer hours, the men took advantage of the lack of close supervision. Problems also arose in the office, which was now physically separated from the plant.

By the close of the first year, it was well known in the community that the company was not the resounding success that had been predicted for it a year earlier. Consequently, the annual meeting of the corporation was well attended. At this meeting financial statements were distributed as shown on pages 747-749.

KILEY'S COFFEE MAKER
Income Statement
For Year Ended December 31, 1971

Revenue from sales:		
Sales		$377,200
Cost of goods sold:		
Finished goods inventory, January 1, 1971	$ 12,920	
Cost of goods manufactured	300,660	
Cost of finished goods available for sale	313,580	
Less finished goods inventory, December 31, 1971	15,750	
Cost of goods sold		297,830
Gross profit on sales		$ 79,370
Operating expenses:		
Selling expenses:		
Salesmen's salaries .... $ 9,600		
Advertising 5,000		
Miscellaneous selling expenses 1,300		
Total selling expenses	$ 15,900	
General expenses:		
Office salaries .... $ 21,000		
Taxes expense 1,175		
Office supplies expense 280		
Insurance expense 590		
Miscellaneous general expenses 4,275		
Total general expenses	27,320	
Total operating expenses		43,220
Net income from operations		$ 36,150
Other expense:		
Interest expense		650
Net income		$ 35,500

After distributing the financial statements, the President made a candid report to the stockholders in attendance. His main points were as follows: (a) the first year of any business is difficult and a second year should be better, (b) even a very small profit is better than a loss, (c) it was proving more difficult than he had anticipated to enter the consumer market but progress was being made, (d) the factory payroll had been good for the community, (e) a good product would certainly find a market, and (f) he faced the future with confidence. Some of the questions asked and answered were as follows:

Question: What would happen to the company if the President became ill?

Answer: I'm in good health and plan to continue that way.

KILEY'S COFFEE MAKER
Schedule of Cost of Goods Manufactured
For Year Ended December 31, 1971

Work in process inventory, January 1, 1971		$ 7,800
Raw materials:		
Inventory, January 1, 1971	$ 9,600	
Purchases	118,300	
Cost of materials available for use	127,900	
Less inventory, December 31, 1971	7,150	
Cost of materials placed in production	120,750	
Direct labor	152,475	
Factory overhead:		
Depreciation—machinery $8,250		
Heat, light, and power 8,800		
Property taxes 1,250		
Depreciation—building 3,125		
Insurance expired 1,140		
Factory supplies used 920		
Miscellaneous factory expenses 4,650		
Total factory overhead	28,135	
Total manufacturing costs		301,360
Total work in process during year		309,160
Less work in process inventory, December 31, 1971		8,500
Cost of goods manufactured		$300,660

Question: Those of us who drew out our savings to invest in the company are not receiving the income we need for living expenses. When will dividends be paid?

Answer: Just as soon as justified by adequate earnings.

Question: Isn't this corporation being run as a sole proprietorship? How many meetings did the board of directors hold this past year?

Answer: No meetings were held but we don't pay our board members either.

After the question-and-answer session the stockholders voted either in person or by proxy for members of the board of directors. A stockholder representing Kiley nominated the existing board members for reelection. A nomination was then made from the floor for a well-liked local lawyer who had been deliberately by-passed at the time the corporation was formed. Partly because there wasn't a lawyer on the board and partly because the state permitted cumulative voting, the lawyer was elected in place of Mrs. Kiley. Other nominees were reelected.

The board met the following day and Kiley was reelected to his position as President and General Manager but without any increase in salary.

KILEY COFFEE MAKER COMPANY, INC.
Balance Sheet
December 31, 1972

Assets

Current assets:

Cash		$ 18,400	
Accounts receivable		22,280	
Inventories:			
Raw materials	$ 21,700		
Work in process	29,400		
Finished goods	60,580	111,680	
Supplies		7,700	
Prepaid insurance		1,505	
Total current assets			$ 161,565

Plant assets:

Office equipment	$ 11,700		
Less accumulated depreciation	2,310	$ 9,390	
Machinery	$232,500		
Less accumulated depreciation	54,950	177,550	
Buildings	$515,000		
Less accumulated depreciaiton	29,275	485,725	
Land		100,000	
Total plant assets			772,665

Intangible assets:

Patent		$ 360	
Goodwill		111,690	
Total intangible assets			112,050
Total assets			$1,046,280

Liabilities

Current liabilities:

Notes payable		$ 25,000	
Accounts payable		17,940	
Total current liabilities			$ 42,940

Capital

Capital stock		$1,000,000	
Retained earnings		3,340	
Total capital			1,003,340
Total liabilities and capital			$1,046,280

The new member of the board proposed that there be monthly meetings that would include a report from the President on progress toward operating a more profitable company. This suggestion was moved, seconded, and adopted by a majority of the board despite Kiley's objections.

KILEY COFFEE MAKER COMPANY, INC.
Income Statement
For Year Ended December 31, 1972

Revenue from sales:		
Sales		$995,950
Cost of goods sold:		
Finished goods inventory, January 1, 1972	$ 15,750	
Cost of goods manufactured	905,000	
Cost of finished goods available for sale	920,750	
Less finished goods inventory, December 31, 1972	60,580	
Cost of goods sold		860,170
Gross profit on sales		$135,780
Operating expenses:		
Selling expenses:		
Salesmen's salaries $29,300		
Advertising 25,000		
Miscellaneous selling expenses 3,400		
Total selling expenses	$ 57,700	
General expenses:		
Office salaries $52,400		
Taxes expense 1,850		
Office supplies expense 340		
Insurance expense 610		
Amortization of intangible assets 12,590		
Miscellaneous general expenses 5,750		
Total general expenses	73,540	
Total operating expenses		131,240
Net income from operations		$ 4,540
Other expense:		
Interest expense		1,200
Net income *		$ 3,340

* Due to a tax adjustment for accelerated depreciation no provision was necessary for federal income tax.

A few days after the meeting Kiley was visited at his office by Jed Huston, who had recently retired from ARV Industries where he had made a brilliant record as Executive Vice President. Huston had lived in Oak Creek for five years while managing the local factory, and his daughter had married the town's leading merchant. Kiley confided to Huston his fears that his position as President and General Manager was in jeopardy and requested advice as to what he should do. Huston indicated that he was at loose ends and, for a modest fee, would be willing to spend two or three weeks in Oak Creek applying his expertise to any problems that Kiley might wish to refer to him for study. He did indicate that his report would be objective and might not be pleasant reading.

KILEY COFFEE MAKER COMPANY, INC.
Schedule of Cost of Goods Manufactured
For Year Ended December 31, 1972

Work in process inventory, January 1, 1972			$ 8,500
Raw materials:			
Inventory, January 1, 1972		$ 7,150	
Purchases		381,550	
Cost of materials available for use		388,700	
Less inventory, December 31, 1972		21,700	
Cost of materials placed in production		367,000	
Direct labor		480,270	
Factory overhead:			
Depreciation—machinery	$23,250		
Heat, light, and power	16,700		
Property taxes	4,800		
Depreciation—buildings	12,875		
Insurance expired	2,845		
Factory supplies used	3,100		
Land rent	600		
Miscellaneous factory expenses	14,460		
Total factory overhead		78,630	
Total manufacturing costs			925,900
Total work in process during year			934,400
Less work in process inventory, December 31, 1972			29,400
Cost of goods manufactured			$905,000

Kiley immediately engaged Huston and agreed to prepare a list of questions which would be presented to Huston when he returned to Oak Creek a week later. During this week Kiley gave more thought to the problems of the corporation than he had all year and prepared the following list of questions that he hoped would focus attention on his predicament as well as on needed corporate decisions:

1. Was it a mistake to incorporate or to incorporate without retaining a majority of the voting stock? At this date are there any steps available that would guarantee him continuity in his present position?

2. Is a formal organization structure needed? If so, what form should it take? Do the manufacturing subdivisions of casting the boilers, the subassembly of the boilers and the built-in heating units, and the final assembly of the coffee maker offer a useful possibility for organizing the production staff?

3. What should the firm do about marketing its product? Should the consumer market be abandoned? If this market isn't abandoned, should wholesalers be used or should sales be made direct? What steps should be taken to create a demand for the coffee maker?

4. Should efforts be made to market the coffee maker overseas?

5. Although most of the employees formerly belonged to a union, a new local had not been formed since ARV Industries moved away. There have been, however, persistent rumors that organizers would shortly appear in Oak Creek. Should management encourage the unionization of its workers or should it resist organization efforts, when and if made?

6. Does the use of the old factory building create a problem in materials management? How else could the current large inventory of finished goods be stored? Should steps be taken to concentrate all activity, including the office, at one location?

7. Was the corporate financial plan sound? Is the current debt too large in relation to the equity of the owners? Was it wise to issue only one class of stock? If 1973 operations are not profitable, is the corporation likely to find itself in serious financial difficulties?

8. Should the company have a budget for 1973? Should it lease a computer? What strengths or weaknesses are revealed by the financial statements? Are some costs out-of-line?

9. If the company is able to interest a large retail chain outfit in handling the coffee maker, would there be any legal problems if this customer was granted a better price than the $25 quotations to the specialty and hardware wholesalers? Does the patent expiration date present problems?

10. Why have profits decreased despite an appreciable increase in the sales volume? What can be done to restore local confidence in the company? What goals should be established for the company? What steps should be taken to make a start toward the achievement of these stated objectives? What decisions should management make or what actions should management take immediately?

In addition to the financial reports of the proprietorship and the corporation, Huston did have available 1972 figures of a division of ARV Industries that manufactured and sold a consumer product. Although the exact figures were confidential, Huston had secured permission to make a percentage analysis that showed the following:

Sales		100.0%
Cost of goods sold		72.4
Gross profit on sales		27.6
Operating expenses:		
Selling expenses	13.7	
General expenses	6.1	19.8
Net income from operations		7.8
Other expenses		.3
Net income before income taxes		7.5
Income taxes		3.6
Net income after income taxes		3.9

On the basis of the facts available, plus any reasonable assumptions that are consistent with known data, if you were Huston what answers would you give Kiley?

Appendix B—Case 2

Bozart Metal Company

On May 8, 1972, at a rather informal meeting of the board of directors, John Petersen had been appointed President of the Bozart Metal Company. Two weeks earlier, his father-in-law, Albert Zarzar, who had served as President since 1950, had died while on a sales trip.

John Petersen had worked for Bozart Metal for ten years. He joined the company in 1962, three years after he was graduated from college during which time he had been employed by a firm of certified public accountants. A major consideration in his taking the position of Assistant Controller at that time had been the fact that James Boscam, Controller-Treasurer, was 64 years of age. In 1965 he married Joan Zarzar, Albert Zarzar's only daughter. A year later, James Boscam retired and John Petersen was elected Vice President for Finance.

The Bozart Metal Company had been founded in Fort Wayne, Indiana, as a partnership for the cutting, bending, and plating of steel tubing. It operated as a job shop for furniture and toy manufacturers. The original capital investment was $21,000 divided equally among James Boscam, Albert Zarzar, and Paul Thomas.

In 1950 Albert Zarzar obtained two major sales contracts. The first was from the Southern Furniture Company for production of chrome-plated chair frames and dinette table legs. The second was from the Chicago Restaurant Supply Corporation for barstool parts. The partnership was converted to a corporation. Three thousand shares of $10 par value common stock were issued. The original stockholders were:

James Boscam	700 shares	Roger Johnson	400 shares
Albert Zarzar	700 shares	Pietro Cellini	300 shares
Paul Thomas	700 shares	Josiah Collins	100 shares
		Lila Baker	100 shares

Roger Johnson was President of the Southern Furniture Company; Pietro Cellini was President of the Chicago Restaurant Supply Company; and Josiah Collins and Lila Baker were long-time employees, having joined the company shortly after it was founded. These individuals were permitted to purchase their shares at $25 each ($10 of this amount was credited to the capital stock account and $15 to paid-in surplus). The partners accepted 700 shares each, reflecting their original investments, even though their partnership accounts had grown to $37,000 each.

In 1959 the company agreed to buy back the stock of Paul Thomas at book value. In return for the stock, the company agreed to give Thomas half of the value of the stock in cash and the balance in a 10-year note bearing 8 percent annual interest. In 1969 the last installment on the note was paid. The treasury stock is shown on the balance sheet as a subtraction from the value of the original 3,000 shares issued.

The first board of directors consisted of the original stockholders. When Pietro Cellini died in 1957 and when Paul Thomas sold his stock to the corporation, no one was elected to replace these men on the board. Under the terms of his will, the shares purchased by Pietro Cellini were transferred on the books of the company to his widow, who is still living.

At the board meeting that appointed John Petersen as President, the following were present: James Boscam, Mrs. Albert Zarzar, and Lila Baker. Zarzar's will, which had been read but not probated, provided that 100 of his shares were to be distributed to his widow and 200 shares each to his daughter Joan, his son-in-law John Petersen, and his son George.

Marketing

The Bozart Metal Company had enjoyed steadily increasing sales since 1950. In the next 20 years, sales had grown from $701,000 to $1,930,000 in 1970. Sales for 1971 were $2,001,000 and the expected sales for 1972 were $2,100,000.

For the past three years the distribution of sales, by customer, had been approximately as shown on the top of page 753.

Typically, sales to the Southern Furniture Company constituted 43 to 48 percent of sales. Sales to the Chicago Restaurant Supply Corporation were almost constant in amount each year, averaging $165,000 for five years. Other categories of sales were subject to large annual variations.

Southern Furniture Company	45%
Chicago Restaurant Supply Corp.	8%
Toy manufacturers	20%
Kitchen appliances distributors	12%
Hospital supply houses	5%
Job shop orders and subcontracts to defense companies	10%

One of Albert Zarzar's skills was his ability to find new customers to counterbalance declines in orders from other customers. For example, the trip during which he had died was for the purpose of exploring a new market in the event the Cellini estate decided to liquidate the Chicago Restaurant Supply Corporation.

While Albert Zarzar was the chief salesman for the company, he was assisted by three manufacturer's representatives; by his only son George; and by William Collins, the son of Josiah Collins. George Zarzar is 32 years of age and holds the position of Purchasing Agent for the company; he, however, spends a portion of his time in making sales contacts. William Collins works in the factory under his father. He is 26 years of age and is a sports car enthusiast. As a result of his hobby, he has regularly brought to the company job shop orders for the chrome-plating of automotive parts.

Production

The production process of the company is simple: (a) raw strip steel is processed into tubes; (b) the tubes are buffed to remove welded spots; (c) the buffed tube is cut to desired lengths; (d) the cut tube is bent into the desired shape; (e) the bent tube is pierced at specified locations; (f) surface irregularities are removed; (g) the pieces are then nickel- or chrome-plated; and (h) the pieces are wrapped and shipped.

The equipment of the company varies from the most modern to that which is 20 or more years old. A substantial amount of new machinery was purchased six years ago to handle the need for more production. The cost of this equipment was financed by signing a mortgage note that was repaid in 1971. Four full-time skilled repairmen maintain and rebuild the equipment.

The company employs 103 workers, most of whom are unskilled or semiskilled. Of the factory employees, 22 are women engaged chiefly in wrapping and packaging operations. Four employees are black. Eighty-two employees have been with the company for more than five years.

There is no formal program of inspection or quality control. Each foreman is responsible for the quality of output of his department.

Personnel Policies

The factory employees are not unionized. Albert Zarzar believed there was no need for a union in any company that provided continuous employment at the going community wage rate supplemented by a profit-sharing plan.

When the company was started in 1945, Albert Zarzar told the employees: "We are all in this together. If we make a go of this company, no one should be out of work. Unless you're a drunkard or a thief, you've got a job for life." Since no one was laid off during the first five years of operations, he later told the employees at a dinner celebrating the formation of the corporation: "We've all had our probation. Our new employees will do the same. During the first five years they will be on probation. When times get rough, they'll be laid off. But you, who have passed the probation, and the others that follow, after their probation, will not be laid off."

Every year in March, James Boscam used to make a survey of wage rates in Fort Wayne and then post it on the bulletin board. The posted rates became the rates for the jobs in the company for the next year. When John Petersen succeeded Boscam, he continued this practice.

Each year in January the company posted its financial statements on the bulletin board. Albert Zarzar attached to it his letter explaining that 15 percent of net operating income would be divided among the employees in proportion to their annual earnings. The profit share for each employee was then computed and a check for the proper amount mailed to his home, together with an explanatory letter.

Organization

The company had never prepared an organization chart. Albert Zarzar and James Boscam had both agreed that it seemed unnecessary. A chart would "freeze" people to jobs and duties. The need for a growing, competitive firm was flexibility. "A man should pitch in and do anything he can. Teamwork, not a fixed job, is the key to flexibility."

The Board of Directors

Albert Zarzar had been quite blunt about the role of the board of directors. After Paul Thomas had been bought out, he stated: "Boscam and I are the major stockholders and, inasmuch as we operate the company, the board can be nothing but a rubber stamp."

John Petersen knew he could not operate in the manner of Albert Zarzar with respect to the board. It was his opinion that any board of directors should be an active one. Moreover, unless the board fully understood the plans and operations of the business, there would be pressure for dividend payments. The company had not declared a dividend since 1965, primarily because it seemed necessary to conserve cash. Prior to 1965, a regular rate of $3 a share per annum had been maintained.

BOZART METAL COMPANY
Balance Sheets
December 31, 1970, and December 31, 1971

Assets	1970	1971
Current assets		
Cash	$ 66,000	$ 32,000
Accounts receivable (net)	152,000	135,000
Inventories	292,000	333,000
Prepaid expenses	9,000	9,900
Total current assets	$ 519,000	$ 509,900
Plant assets		
Machinery and equipment (net)	$ 527,000	$ 531,000
Building (net)	136,000	129,400
Land	8,400	8,400
Total plant assets	$ 671,400	$ 668,800
Total assets	$1,190,400	$1,178,700
Liabilities		
Current liabilities		
Notes payable	$ 108,000	$ 38,000
Accounts payable	120,000	132,000
Total current liabilities	$ 228,000	$ 170,000
Long-term liabilities		
Mortgage payable	$ 130,000	$........
Total liabilities	$ 358,000	$ 170,000
Capital		
Capital stock—3,000 shares issued	$ 30,000	$ 30,000
Less: Treasury stock	7,000	7,000
Issued and outstanding	$ 23,000	$ 23,000
Paid-in surplus	73,500	73,500
Retained earnings	735,900	912,200
Total capital	$ 832,400	$1,008,700
Total liabilities and capital	$1,190,400	$1,178,700

BOZART METAL COMPANY
Income Statements
For Years Ended December 13, 1970, and December 31, 1971

	1970	1971
Sales (net)	$1,930,000	$2,001,000
Cost of goods manufactured and sold	1,448,000	1,498,000
Gross profit on sales	$ 482,000	$ 503,000
Operating expenses	96,000	119,000
Net income from operations	$ 386,000	$ 384,000
Profit sharing	57,900	57,600
Net income before income tax	$ 328,100	$ 326,400
Federal tax on income	151,000	150,100
Net income after income tax	$ 177,100	$ 176,300

Finance

The books and other financial records of the company are, in Petersen's view, in excellent order. The last certified financial statements are the balance sheets shown on page 755 and the income statements shown above.

On the basis of the foregoing information and any reasonable assumptions consistent with the known facts, what problems does John Petersen face and what should he do about them? Your solution to this case should provide answers to the following questions as well as any others that may seem relevant.

1. What should Petersen do about the board of directors? Should he take steps to be elected rather than appointed as president? Considering the fact that there will be only nine stockholders, is the corporation the best form of ownership for this business?
2. Is an organization structure needed? If so, what type should be recommended? Construct a chart to show a specific proposal that might be adopted.
3. Should new sales policies be adopted? If so, how should they be carried out?
4. Should new products be developed? What particular new product lines should be investigated?
5. Should the company modify the current personnel policies?
6. What are the financial strengths and weaknesses of the company? How can the weaknesses be overcome? Considering the fact that over half of the stockholders are not on the company payroll, should dividend payments be resumed?

Index